The Hardball Times Baseball Annual 2006

Featuring contributions by THT's staff writers:
Brian Borawski • John Brattain • Craig Burley
Joe Dimino • Dan Fox • David Gassko
Aaron Gleeman • Brian Gunn • Ben Jacobs
Dave Studenmund • Greg Tamer • Steve Treder

With additional contributions by guest writers:
Bill James • Rob Neyer • John Dewan
Jon Weisman • Matt Welch • David Cameron
Maury Brown • Alex Belth • J.C. Bradbury

Edited by Aaron Gleeman and Dave Studenmund

ACTA SPORTS

The Hardball Times Baseball Annual 2006
New articles daily at www.hardballtimes.com

Edited by Aaron Gleeman, Carolina Bolado, Bryan Tsao and Greg Tamer
Stats developed by Dave Studenmund and Bryan Donovan
Cover design by Tom Wright
Typesetting by Dave Studenmund

Published by: ACTA Sports
                5559 W. Howard Street
                Skokie, IL 60077
                1-800-397-2282
                acta@actapublications.com
                www.actasports.com

ISBN: 0-87946-308-2
Printed in the United States of America
Year: 12 11 10 09 08 07 06 05
Printing: 10 9 8 7 6 5 4 3 2 1

What's Inside

What's Inside (cont.)

Welcome to Our Book

by Aaron Gleeman

Welcome to *The Hardball Times Baseball Annual 2006*. If you love baseball, you have your hands on the right book.

The 2005 season was both exciting and surprising, with a World Series that pitted a team few picked to make the playoffs against a team that was 19-32 at the end of May. And for the second year in a row the World Series winners broke a nearly century-long drought, as the White Sox became champions for the first time since 1917.

In the pages that follow you'll find the season covered from every angle, with division reviews and a unique look at the postseason, articles examining the steroids scandal and the business of baseball, and analysis of the year in the minor leagues and Japan. And stats … lots of stats.

You'll also find articles dealing with topics that stretch beyond 2005, like the very brief and controversial Paul DePodesta Era in Los Angeles, the very successful Mike Scioscia Era in Anaheim, the underrated Walt Jocketty Era in St. Louis, and the always interesting New York Yankees.

We'll preview both the upcoming World Baseball Classic and Collective Bargaining Agreement, tackle issues like pitch counts and the Hall of Fame, and dig into the impact of base running, ballparks, defense, and luck.

Oh, and did I mention the stats? There are over 150 pages of stats and graphs in this book, including full leaderboards, league stats, team stats, and individual player stats. We have the standard stuff you're used to seeing, like batting averages, RBIs, stolen bases, and ERAs, and a whole lot more: Win Shares, Win Probability Added, Fielding Range, Runs Created, Gross Production Average, Fielding-Independent Pitching, Pitching Runs, and Defensive Efficiency Ratio.

In addition to all of that, we also have plate appearances broken down by outcomes and batted-ball types. What does that mean, exactly? Well, not only can we tell you that David Ortiz hit .300 with 47 homers and 148 RBIs in 2005, we can tell you how often his 713 plate appearances resulted in a ground ball (21%), fly ball (28%), line drive (15%), infield fly (3%), strikeout (17%), and walk (14%).

We hope that *The Hardball Times Baseball Annual 2006* will be a great read and can find a home on your bookshelf as both an interesting look back at the 2005 season and a valuable reference guide.

Tons of work went into the making of this book, and there are a lot of people to thank. First, thanks to John Dewan, Greg Pierce, and Andrew Yankech at ACTA Publications, as well as Baseball Info Solutions for providing the stats we love so much and Bryan Donovan for helping us organize them.

Thanks to THT's writing staff, who worked so hard on this book and also provide daily content at www. HardballTimes.com all year long. A special thanks goes to our many outstanding guest contributors: Bill James, Rob Neyer, Jon Weisman, Matt Welch, David Cameron, J.C. Bradbury, Maury Brown, and Alex Belth.

And last but certainly not least I would like to personally thank Dave Studenmund for the incredible amount of work he put into this book, and THT editors Carolina Bolado, Bryan Tsao, and Greg Tamer for the tireless work they did on this book and do each day on THT's website.

Happy Baseball,

Aaron Gleeman
Editor-in-Chief, The Hardball Times
www.HardballTimes.com

The 2005 Season

Ten Things I Learned This Year

by Dave Studenmund

Baseball never fails to delight. If you don't feel the same way, well, you probably picked up the wrong book by mistake. Unbelievers complain about the length of baseball games or their lack of action, but true baseball fans understand the importance of pitch sequences and the terrible consequences of the mundane, such as overthrowing the cutoff man. The game is deep and nuanced. As you learn more about it, you realize how much more there is to learn.

On The Hardball Times website (www.hardball-times.com), I write a weekly column called "Ten Things I Didn't Know Last Week." Each week I recount the new and unusual in the baseball world. Sometimes I discuss things statistical, or newsworthy, or I just revel in the game's quirks. And sometimes I wonder about the silly things people repeatedly say and do.

Following is a list of the top 10 things I learned this past year. It's a list of major baseball developments and some baseball insights. You could call it a list of things we learned together in 2005, a very good year for baseball and its fans.

It's curse-bustin' time.

Are you cursed? Well, now might be a really good time to do something about it because baseball curses are dropping like flies.

Last year, the Boston Red Sox captivated the sporting world by winning their first World Series since 1918, which was a year before they traded Babe Ruth to the Yankees. That trade begat the Curse of the Bambino, by which the baseball gods cursed the Sox for trading the greatest player in history and made their fans suffer through tragic near-misses (think Bucky Dent and Bill Buckner) and incidents (Tony Conigliaro).

At the end of last year, and again at the beginning of this season, there was also talk of a curse in Chicago, the supposed "Curse of the Billy Goat," which had been frustrating Cubs fans since 1945. Since the Red Sox had broken their curse, the Cubs were due, too. Or so said the mainstream media.

Right city, wrong curse.

The more compelling curse was the one located in the south side of town, the Curse of the Black Sox. You know, the Black Sox of 1919, who conspired to throw the World Series to make some real money. This was the greatest scandal in the history of the game, and it created a black cloud that shadowed the White Sox for nearly a century. Although their curse wasn't as dramatic or tragic as the Red Sox's, they suffered years of mediocrity and only made it back to the Series once, in 1959, when they lost to the Dodgers.

The two curses were inextricably linked. The game only truly recovered from the Black Sox scandal in the public's eye when Babe Ruth, with his colorful personality and presence, became an American icon in New York. Perhaps the baseball gods would only allow the White Sox redemption after the Red Sox had earned theirs. Perhaps, in fact, they required it. Perhaps it was karma, as Earl in *My Name is Earl* would say.

White Sox GM Ken Williams didn't care about any silly curse. He just wanted to change and improve a White Sox club that had finished second to the Twins for three straight years. In retrospect, his key moves for 2005 were picking up good solid regular players in the free-agent market, such as Jermaine Dye, A.J. Pierzynski and Tadahito Iguchi, and improving his starting staff by trading for Jose Contreras and signing Orlando Hernandez and Dustin Hermanson. The White Sox sprang out of the gate behind their pitching staff and didn't look back until the Cleveland Indians posted a remarkable late-season surge, almost overtaking the Chicago club.

But like all championship teams, this one would not be denied. After fending off the youthful Indians, the Sox went 11-1 through the postseason against the Red Sox (of course they would have to play the Red Sox), Angels and Astros. When all was said and done, another curse had been reversed and the White Sox were World Champs, the sixth different team to win the World Series over the past six years.

> **We're Champions Too**
>
> In the spring, the La Cueva Bears of Albuquerque, New Mexico broke the record for most consecutive victories by a high school team by beating Highland 15-1 and 11-0 in a doubleheader for their 70th consecutive win.
>
> The previous record of 68 was set by Archbishop Malloy High of Briarwood, New York in 1963-1966.

Maybe all this curse-breaking is the result of a new curse in the air. Call it the Curse of the Strong Baseball Players. But I'm getting ahead of myself ...

The Houston Astros are the champions of the National League.

You could never have said that before. Although they've only existed half as long as the White Sox were cursed, the Astros certainly broke their fans' hearts in the postseason many times. In fact, no team had stayed in one city as long as the Astros without making it to the Series. Most notably, they had finished in first place four times from 1997 to 2001, only to lose in the first round of the playoffs each time. Last year, the Astros actually made it to the League Championship Series and led after five games but still lost to the Cardinals. After Carlos Beltran deserted town and the Astros got off to a slow start this year, it looked as though they were going to sink into a curse of their own, the Curse of the Killer Bees.

I'm talking about Craig Biggio and Jeff Bagwell, Hall of Fame-worthy teammates for 14 years, plus Derek Bell or Lance Berkman, depending on the year. Biggio and Bagwell have been two of the finest, most consistent players in the game, yet postseason success had constantly eluded them. Things got so bad, in fact, that Rob Neyer referred to them as "the biggest flop in postseason history" in his *Big Book of Baseball Lineups*. Rob duly noted that this was probably caused by nothing other than luck.

> **That Hurts**
>
> A weblog called Plunk Biggio (plunkbiggio.blogspot.com) tracked Craig Biggio's pursuit of the all-time record for being hit by pitches. According to the site, Biggio ended the year 14 short of Hughie Jennings' record with 273.
>
> Among other things, the site noted that Bobby Jenks was the largest pitcher to ever hit a batter in the World Series (plunking Willy Tavares in the third game), five Astros were hit in the Series but none of them scored (a record) and when the Chicago Cubs last won the World Series in 1908, they beat the Detroit Tigers, who were managed by one Hughie Jennings.

Luck seemed to turn the B's way in this postseason, thanks primarily to a truly remarkable pitching staff led by the ageless Roger Clemens. At the age of 42, Clemens led the league with a 1.87 ERA and produced the greatest pitching year ever by someone over 40. Joined by Andy Pettitte and Roy Oswalt (both healthy for the entire year), the Astros were unstoppable until reaching the World Series. Despite being swept by the Sox in the Series, this was as close as any sweep ever, with no game decided by more than two runs. I think it is fair to say that the Curse of the Killer Bees was crushed before it ever really got started.

The divisions are crazy!

There may have never been a more entertaining year to follow division races. This season featured the best and the worst of divisions, as well as some of the better midseason and second-half surges in recent memory.

The National League East was arguably the best, most competitive division ever. For the first time in major league history, every single team in the division finished .500 or better. The last-place team was only nine games behind the first-place team, the closest full-season first-to-last difference ever.

What's more, in little more than two weeks from May 24 to June 15, four of the five teams completely switched positions. The Nationals and Phillies rose from fourth and fifth to first and second, and the Marlins and Braves went from first and second to third and fourth. I don't believe any division has ever experienced such a dramatic crossover so late in the season.

On the other hand, the National League West was arguably the worst full-season division ever, with every team playing below .500 ball until a surge by the Padres in the last week of the season gave them an 82-80 record. No division had ever gone so late in the season without a single team over .500.

The NL West played .368 ball against the American League, .422 against the National League East and .453 against the National League Central. They were even 5-7 against the hapless Kansas City Royals. Thank goodness they were able to win half the time against each other.

Then we had the Oakland Athletics in the American League West, who were 15 games under .500 on May 29, the third-worst record in the majors, yet were tied for first place a little more than two months later. Not the biggest surge in major league history, but one of the biggest. That they finished second was due less to their talent and character than it was to the fine year turned in by the gentlemen in Los Angeles of Anaheim.

The Orioles led the American League East for much of the first

> **So Close and Yet So Far**
>
> Cleveland had the most tough losses of the year. Here are the top five teams ranked by percent of losses by one or two runs:
>
> | | |
> |---|---|
> | CLE | 67% |
> | STL | 58% |
> | LAA | 55% |
> | CHA | 54% |
> | TOR | 54% |

half of the season, but The Order eventually asserted itself. Yes, the Red Sox and Yankees both made the playoffs thanks to strong second-half play, though I'm still not sure which one won the division and which one was the Wild Card team. It actually didn't seem to matter.

The two Centrals, American and National, were home to the two best teams of the regular season, the White Sox and Cardinals, respectively. But even those divisions had their drama. For the second year in a row, the Houston Astros put together a second-half drive to take the Wild Card slot in the National League. But the fiercest second-half drive was that of the Cleveland Indians, a young team that suddenly seemed to find itself, going 44-23 after July 22 and nearly overtaking the eventual World Champions.

For an entirely different view of the division races, read Steve Treder's "Night Sky: the 2005 Season in Historical Perspective."

There's a hot new trend in baseball: Starting Pitching.

I've mentioned this a couple of times, so I might as well get it over with. Starting pitching is big. Alert the media.

Making Himself Useful

On September 22, pitcher Dontrelle Willis batted seventh for the Marlins. The last time a pitcher batted that high in the order was 1973, when Steve Renko batted seventh for the Expos. Thanks to friends from the Society for American Baseball Research (SABR) for the factoid, as well as several other factoids mentioned here.

It began last winter, during the free-agent season. Some say it began with the Kris Benson contract, a $22.5 million deal for a pitcher whose ERA has been below 4.00 only once. Others point to the Yankees' signing of Jaret Wright for $22.5 million, the Diamondbacks' deal with Russ Ortiz for $33 million, and the Reds' $25.5 million deal with Eric Milton. Your perception is correct; the deals just got crazier.

Very few of these contracts turned out well, as you can read in our "Net Win Shares Value" article. But everyone is still talking about starting pitching, thanks primarily to the two World Series participants.

For a while there, it looked like everybody was going to be talking about Ozzie Ball, the supposed new way of scoring runs in Chicago. Eventually people figured out that the White Sox weren't really scoring all that many runs and, even when they did, they were doing it the "old fashioned way:" with home runs.

No, the keys to the White Sox's success were their five starting pitchers, all of whom had remarkably good seasons and all of whom stayed healthy. Manager Ozzie Guillen contributed to the trend by allowing his starters to pitch complete games in four consecutive postseason games against the Angels, the first time this has happened in the postseason since 1956 (when Don Larsen threw a perfect game). Gasps were heard across the baseball ether.

But the starting pitching trend was cemented by Houston's Big Three: Clemens, Pettitte and Oswalt. Despite a mediocre offense, Houston was able to ride their three strong shoulders all the way to the World Series, seemingly cementing the observation that nothing matters more in the postseason than dominant starting pitching.

With very few top-notch free-agent starting pitchers on the "market" this year, it will be very interesting to see what happens.

Evidently, some baseball players used to take steroids.

Including some who swore they hadn't. This was the year the steroids scandal finally, publicly, reared its ugly head. The first shot across the bow was Jose Canseco's book, *Juiced: Wild Times, Rampant 'Roids, Smash Hits, and How Baseball Got Big.* Sorry, but I didn't read it. I was actually more tempted to read *Juicy: Confessions of a Former Baseball Wife*, by Jose's former wife Jessica. Seriously. But I didn't read that either.

Apparently, Canseco (Jose, that is) wrote that he introduced Mark McGwire to steroids and that several other players had taken steroids as well, including Rafael Palmeiro. What's more, he used the book to promote the idea of better living through steroids and predicted that within 10 years all professional athletes will be taking steroids under medical supervision and living better because of it. (Well I did browse through it in the bookstore). Evidently, it was the wrong thing to say.

Congress got involved, McGwire took the fifth, and

Title Goes Here

I didn't read Canseco's book, but some of the baseball books we did read and recommend are:

- *Juicing the Game* by Howard Bryant
- *Baseball's All-Time Greatest Sluggers* by Michael Schell
- *Wrong Side of the Wall* by Eric Stone
- *Scout's Honor* by Bill Shanks

Palmeiro told Congress that he had never, ever taken steroids. Major League Baseball and the player's union agreed to tougher testing standards, and Alex Sanchez, Ryan Franklin and Juan Rincon, among others, were suspended for testing positive. In the biggest shock of all, Palmeiro himself tested positive and was suspended toward the end of the year.

The parts played by two of the leading actors in this tragedy, Jason Giambi and Barry Bonds, were also dramatic. Giambi, who had admittedly taken steroids in the past and then struggled with severe health problems last year, had a tremendous season in 2005. Apparently drug-free, Giambi batted .271/.440/.535 with 32 home runs. For the Yankees first baseman, it was a year of redemption.

Bonds had been establishing himself as arguably the greatest player ever when the scandal broke, undermining that claim, and he spent most of 2005 on the sidelines with a bum knee. His status for 2006 is unclear. He is entering his final act, and only when the play is well over will we know what history says of the man and his craft.

Some argue that the steroids scandal is the biggest black mark on the game since the Black Sox. While I don't get quite so worked up about it, MLB obviously has to continue to address the issue head-on. I'm quite sure you'll be hearing more about it for a long, long time.

Young phenoms grow old and vulnerable.

There's steroid use, and then there's real drug abuse. The spectacle of Dwight Gooden appearing in court for charges of resisting arrest and subsequently fleeing the scene was dismaying. Gooden's drug abuse was obviously out of control; he had lost 58 pounds in the previous six months and looked haggard and lost. Gooden was once the toast of New York, a 19-year-old phenom whose season at the age of 20 was one of the best ever. For me, the spectacle of a wasted Dwight Gooden put the steroid scandal in true perspective.

Dwight Gooden's picture reflected both the dark side of drug use and the other side of the young-phenom looking glass. So it was no small irony that Gooden's brush with the law occurred just 18 days after the major league debut of the hottest young phenom since Gooden: Felix Hernandez.

Hernandez made his debut with Seattle in early August and posted a 2.67 ERA in 12 starts. Not bad for a 19-year-old and, truth be told, he looked even better than that. Hernandez is a strikeout/groundball pitcher,

Canes and Cribs	
Teams ranked by Win Shares Age	
Oldest	
NYA	32.8
BOS	32.5
SF	31.8
SD	31.3
HOU	31.1
Youngest	
TB	26.9
OAK	27.3
CLE	27.4
MIN	27.4
PIT	27.6

a lethal combination. If he stays healthy, he will have a great career.

Hernandez wasn't the only youngster making waves, however. The Atlanta Braves seemed to resemble a Little League team at times, pushing 21-year-olds like Jeff Francoeur, Brian McCann and Kyle Davies into action. The youngsters produced and Atlanta won the National League East (thanks in no small part to Andruw Jones' 51 home runs, too). Francoeur was particularly impressive, batting .300/.336/.549 and evoking comparisons to Bob "Hurricane" Hazle, who helped lead the Braves to the World Championship in 1957 by batting .403/.477/.649 in 41 games as a rookie. Hazle was barely heard from again; let's hope Francoeur does better.

Still, the Braves' average Win Shares Age (the age of each player multiplied by his Win Shares contribution) was only slightly below the major league average of 29.3 years. That was partly due to Julio Franco, the best 46-year-old batter to ever play the game. Franco batted .275/.348/.451 as a first baseman for the Braves, which are very good figures for guys 10-15 years younger.

With three 70-year-old managers (the Nationals' Frank Robinson, the Marlins' Jack McKeon and the Giants' Felipe Alou), the best 46-year-old batter ever and the most remarkable season for a pitcher over 40 (Clemens, by the way, broke into the majors the same year as Gooden), 2005 belonged to young and old alike.

Baseball belongs in Washington, D.C.

Steroids weren't the only baseball topic in Washington, D.C. There was a new ball club in town, the first in our nation's capital since the Senators moved to Texas over 30 years ago.

The Nationals had a fine first year in Washington, leading the National League East for several giddy weeks, finishing .500 and drawing 2.7 million fans. Led by Chad Cordero, Nick Johnson, Brad Wilkerson and John Patterson, the Nationals put a competitive team in RFK Stadium and became the hottest ticket in town.

You could tell Washington had become obsessed with baseball when Supreme Court nominee John Roberts compared the role of a judge to an umpire:

> *Judges are like umpires. Umpires don't make the rules; they apply them. The role of an umpire and a judge is critical. They make sure everybody plays by the rules. But it is a limited role. Nobody ever went to a ballgame to see the umpire.*

Obviously, the umpires in the postseason forgot about Roberts' remarks. Anyway, it even turns out that the President's nominee for chairman of the Federal Reserve, Ben S. Bernanke, is a Bill James nut who supposedly wrote a dissertation while at MIT on the Boston Red Sox, using advanced sabermetric stats.

At Least There Were No Filibusters

According to the Baseball Esoterica weblog (baseballesoterica.blogspot.com), the Nationals had four eerily similar, crazy games in the span of a month.

- 8/20: They were losing against the Mets, 8-0, came back to tie it but lost in extra innings.
- 9/1: Losing 7-1 to the Braves, they came back to tie but lost in extra innings.
- 9/11: Fell behind 6-0 to the Braves, caught up to pass them 7-6, but lost on two homers in the ninth.
- 9/17: For a change of pace, they took a 5-0 lead against the Padres, who scored five in the ninth to tie it up. The Nationals then lost in 12 innings, 8-5.

I briefly visited D.C. in the late spring. While walking along the Mall, I looked to my right to glance at the White House and saw a man playing ball with his son in the foreground. It was a powerful sight, and I thought, "Well, this is just right." Major league baseball has returned to a town it never should have left.

Having said that, there really is no excuse for the way MLB's leadership handled the ownership mess in Montreal. The last years of the Expos, playing without a real owner and under threat of contraction, will be a blight on baseball's history forever.

It's better to be lucky than it's lucky to be good

Luck was one of the themes of the year, and we've devoted an entire article to the subject in the *Annual*. But I'd like to tell you my favorite luck-related story from earlier in the year.

In April, a Japanese CEO decided he wanted to sell some of his company's art through an auction house. He couldn't decide between the two major auction houses, Christie's and Sotheby's, so he asked them to play a game of "rock, paper, scissors" to determine who would get to auction the art.

According to *The New York Times*, the head of the Christie's division spent the weekend researching strategy for "rock, paper, scissors," asking various experts for the best approach. The best expert turned out to be an associate's 11-year-old daughter, who gave this advice: "Everyone knows you always start with scissors. Rock is way too obvious, and scissors beats paper."

Monday morning, the representatives for the two auction houses (and their accountants) entered a conference room with a long table, sat at opposite ends, and filled in a form with their opening move. The head of Christie's chose scissors. As predicted by an 11-year-old, Sotheby's opened with paper and Christie's won the award.

What I want to know is, why did this guy do this? If he couldn't choose between the two, why didn't he just flip a coin himself? Did he believe there was some inherent worth in having them play the game? Was it better to let fate intervene through rock, paper, scissors instead of eenie, meenie, miney, mo?

At the beginning of each season, baseball analysts like to run computer simulations to predict which team is most likely to win. The best known of these is by Diamond Mind Baseball, who gave the White Sox an 11% chance of qualifying for postseason play this year. I know some people who have scoffed at the White Sox's pennant, because it wasn't predicted, because it must have been lucky, because it seemed like the baseball gods were just playing eenie, meenie, miney, mo.

Results count. That's why they're called results. I love stats as much as anyone (if you don't believe me, check out some of my other articles in the *Annual*), but I love the game more. In fact, I only love stats because they help me better appreciate the game. Without the games, there would be no drama, no play, no curses. And yes, there would be no luck. In this season alone, we saw a fair share of luck ...

Two for One Sale

On September 6, Cardinals' right fielder Hector Luna made two errors on two separate plays on the same batter in the same at-bat. Neifi Perez hit a foul fly ball that Luna dropped for an error, and then Perez hit a fair ball that Luna misplayed for another error.

- The Washington Nationals won 12 consecutive one-run games, then lost 13 consecutive one-run games, the longest such double streak in baseball history, according to my friends at SABR.
- The Dodgers were so decimated by injuries that at one point they only had one regular player (Jeff Kent) still playing from their lineup at the beginning of the season.
- On the other hand, the Cardinals' top five starting pitchers started 160 of their 162 games. I'm not sure if that's a record, but it's certainly notable.
- The Diamondbacks won 12 games more than their run differential (Runs Scored minus Runs Allowed) predicted them to. This tied for the second-highest difference ever.

When it comes to baseball, it's better to be lucky than it's lucky to be good. Analysts may gnash their teeth, but that's why they play the games.

Baseball statistics are growing up.

As they have been for years. As baseball data becomes more accessible, thanks to websites like Retrosheet (www.Retrosheet.org) and BaseballReference (www.baseballreference.com), as well as companies like Baseball Info Solutions, baseball statistics and analysis are becoming more insightful and useful. Baseball clubs are hopping on board, purchasing new data and hiring analysts to produce complex base running and fielding analyses.

Bill James began this trend over 20 years ago when he started using baseball statistics to actually answer common baseball questions. It's safe to say that you wouldn't be reading this book today if James hadn't written his *Baseball Abstract* series in the 1980s. So when James printed an article in SABR's *Baseball Research Journal*, it got some attention.

The article was called "Underestimating the Fog." The "fog" to which James referred is the fog of data analysis and sample size, when baseball analysts sometimes conclude something doesn't exist when they really just can't find it. James listed nine findings that

Mr. Consistency
Albert Pujols' seasonal at-bat totals:
2001: 590
2002: 590
2003: 591
2004: 592
2005: 591

he felt were victims of the fog, including "clutch hitters don't exist" and "winning or losing close games is luck."

As a result, statisticians started openly talking about these issues again, particularly the issue of clutch hitting. I don't know if many of them changed their minds, but it's always good to question your assumptions, and the baseball stats community is richer for it.

Baseball statisticians are learning how to better assess fielding and base running skills all the time. James Click, of Baseball Prospectus, and our own Dan Fox have published in-depth studies of how often runners advance around the bases on base hits. They've looked at how often this differs by ballpark, and Click even published an article examining whether runners advance more often on hits by certain batters at BaseballAnalysts (www.baseballanalysts.com.

He Works Hard For His Money

On September 14, Gabe Kapler ruptured his Achilles tendon running the bases on Tony Graffanino's home run and had to be removed for a pinch runner in the middle of the play. Graffanino waited on the basepaths for nearly 20 minutes while Kapler was tended to. Eventually, Alejandro Machado was inserted as a pinch runner and the home run trot resumed.

It was Machado's first appearance in a major league game. Two days later, Machado was inserted as a pinch runner for Graffanino and subsequently scored the winning run when Manny Ramirez was plunked by a game-ending HBP.

Fielding analyses such as Mitchel Lichtman's Ultimate Zone Rating have also added to our understanding of who the best fielders are, and how much impact they have on a game. And commentators continue to make subtle modifications to Voros McCracken's findings a few years ago that pitchers have virtually no impact on balls that are batted off of them. In this very *Annual*, David Gassko and J.C. Bradbury add more insight in "Do Players Control Batted Balls?"

The last interesting area of current baseball analysis is the idea of "win assignment." On The Hardball Times' site, we track Bill James's Win Shares for the year, and we've also published articles and books that focus on a system called "Win Probability Added." The two systems differ substantially, but the basic idea is the same: to give the right amount of credit to each player for his contribution to each win. It's a fascinating subject to me, and you'll find examples of both systems in this *Annual*.

The business of baseball has probably never been better.

Baseball set attendance records in both the major and minor leagues this year. Major league attendance reached 75 million thanks to the Nationals' move to Washington. The Yankees became only the third franchise to attract more than 4 million folks to its games. Minor league attendance topped 41 million.

Toward the end of the season, MLB signed a new deal with ESPN worth $337 million a year, in addition to MLB's current deals with media outlets such as Fox and XM Radio. Major League Baseball Advanced Media (MLBAM), which manages the awesome video capabilities of MLB.com is generating profits of $130 million a year and would reportedly be worth $3 billion on the public markets. All of these developments are covered by Brian Borawski and Maury Brown in the book you're holding, so I won't go into details here.

But in a nutshell, baseball is swimming in cash, just like Scrooge McDuck used to do.

You have to give MLB credit for this. MLBAM, in particular, is an impressive operation that shows what is possible when businesses embrace the Internet. Remember, however, that too much money can cause its own problems, as people fight over the spoils.

Of course, not everything is perfect in baseball land. To name just a few of my pet peeves, they really should cut back on the interleague games. One round is enough. The umpiring was awful in the postseason and needs to be addressed. Why do we keep that silly dropped third strike rule, anyway?

And there is that steroids thing.

But overall, 2005 was a great year. Especially if you live in Chicago.

I would be remiss if I didn't mention some of the real-life lessons of this past year. For instance, we've learned once again the terrible devastation that nature can inflict. We witnessed 225,000 deaths by tsunami, a hurricane that ravaged the south and turned a beautiful city into a toxic swamp, and an earthquake in Kashmir that has killed as many as 100,000. I don't mean to finish this article on a downer, but it's always worth remembering that baseball is not life and death. Life and death are.

For many of us, baseball provides solace in the ruin of the routine, protection in the tumult of the everyday world. It is both comforting and surprising, this intense game played in parks. It allows us to glide on its whims, renew our sense of wonder at the subtle and obvious, and return to the real world with a new sense of what's possible. That is, anything.

American League East Review

by Ben Jacobs

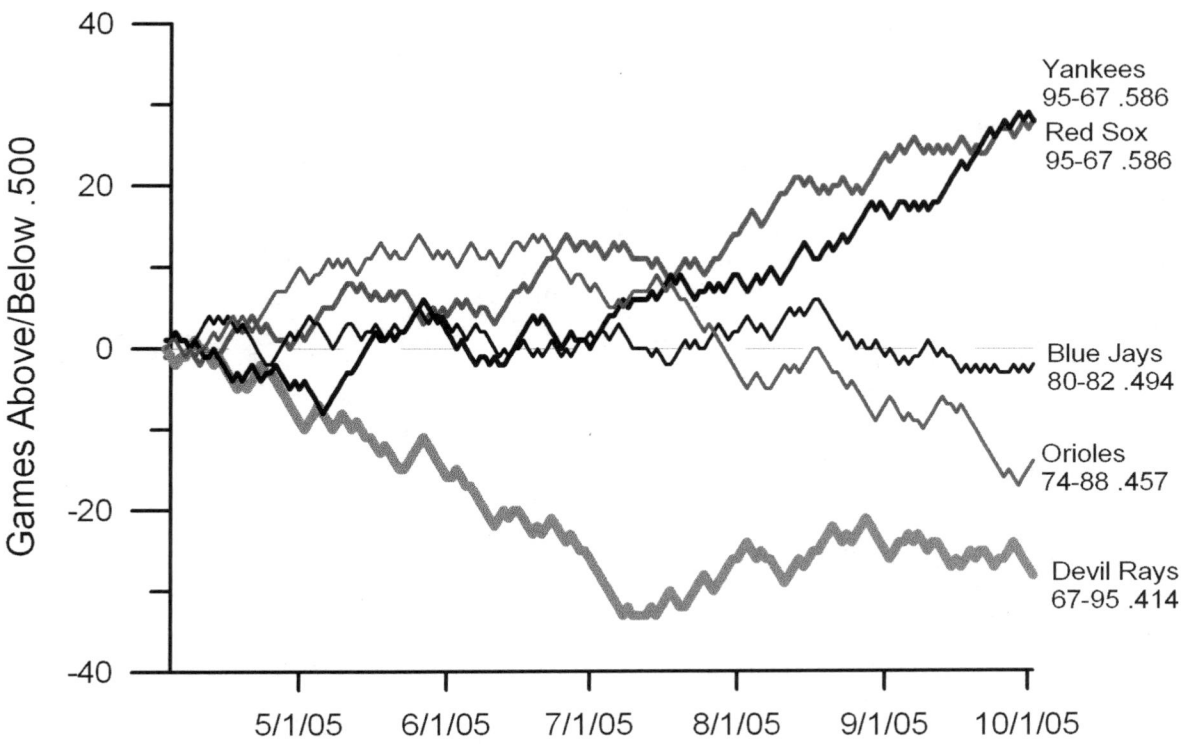

For such a strange season, the final result was surprisingly familiar in the American League East. After a shakeup at the bottom of the division in 2004, the 2005 season saw a return to the order of the previous seven years: Yankees, Red Sox, Blue Jays, Orioles and Devil Rays. Since the division added Tampa Bay in 1998, that's been the order, with Toronto's fall into last place in 2004 the only hiccup.

Of course, it wasn't so simple this year. The Yankees and Red Sox actually tied for the best record in the division at 95-67. But since both teams qualified for the playoffs, the division title was determined by their season series, which New York took 10-9. Nor was it a straight path back to the order of the seven-year streak. The Yankees started the season 11-19, and the team that spent almost the entire first half of the season in first place finished in fourth.

Ultimately, it all came down to the final weekend of the season. But instead of being decided in Boston, where the Red Sox hosted the Yankees, the important action unfolded in Ohio. While Boston took two out of three games from New York at Fenway Park to forge a first-place tie, the Cleveland Indians were busy getting swept by the Chicago White Sox to finish two games behind both the Yankees and Red Sox.

Had Cleveland won two of those games, the Red Sox and Yankees would have played for the division title the Monday after the season, with the loser taking on the Indians for the Wild Card. Had the Indians swept instead of getting swept, it would have been a winner-move-on, loser-go-home playoff game for Boston and New York, just as it was in 1978, but in Yankee Stadium this time instead of Fenway. Instead, the Yankees celebrated a division title on the first day of October despite only holding a one-game lead with one game to play. The next day, Boston's players, coaches and owners were able to congratulate each other mid-game on a third straight trip to the playoffs.

The division story began the same way it finished in 2005, with the Yankees facing the Red Sox. The Yankees took two out of three in that first matchup, but you wouldn't have known from the reactions to the series. After new Yankees ace Randy Johnson outpitched old Yankees ace David Wells in the season-opener, Mariano Rivera blew saves in the next two games, giving him four consecutive blown saves against the Red Sox.

Then both Boston and New York started to struggle, leaving the top of the division to Toronto and Baltimore for most of the month. The Blue Jays, who had followed seven consecutive third-place finishes with a plummet into the basement in 2004, won their first game and then just stayed in first place for a while.

After winning their first two games, they dropped their next two, and the entire division finished April 8 at 2-2. Toronto then ran off four straight wins before their 13-day stay in first place ended with an 8-5 loss to Texas. They couldn't have believed it at the time, but that was the last the Blue Jays would see of first place, as the other birds in the division took over and actually started to run away a little.

Baltimore had a dream April, going 16-7 to take an early four-game lead over both Toronto and Boston, with the Yankees struggling another 2.5 games back. What contributed to the hot start for the Orioles? Well, they basically battered opponents into submission. Miguel Tejada did what the Orioles signed him to do, hitting .347 with eight homers in 95 at-bats. Brian Roberts shocked everybody and did even better, hitting .379 with eight homers in the same 95 at-bats. As a team, Baltimore hit an astounding .302 with 35 homers in 23 games in the month. The pitching wasn't nearly as good, posting a 4.61 ERA in April. The bright spot in the rotation was Erik Bedard, who had a 2.84 ERA in his first five starts, while the bullpen trio of B.J. Ryan, Jorge Julio and Todd Williams allowed just five earned runs in their first 35.1 innings.

Boston spent a few days in first place in April, but finished the month at 12-11. The Red Sox won five of their next six games to get within 2 ½ games of the first-place Orioles, but nobody was looking at the top of the division at that point. Everybody was watching the bottom, where Tampa Bay had already taken up residence at 11-19 but had to settle for a tie for last with the Yankees, nine games out of first.

The Yankees' offense was scoring five runs a game despite only fielding half a lineup. Hideki Matsui, Bernie Williams, Jorge Posada and Jason Giambi were hitting a combined .237 with just eight home runs in 384 at-bats. Tony Womack was hitting .287 in 101 at-bats but with no power (just four doubles) and only five walks. Alex Rodriguez (.290 with 10 homers in 124 at-bats) and Gary Sheffield (.336 with 10 doubles and four homers in 119 at-bats) were the only reasons the Bronx would-be-Bombers weren't completely punchless.

And the pitching was a complete mess. Jaret Wright was already on the disabled list with a bum shoulder and a 6.75 ERA, while Kevin Brown was off the disabled list but had lost all four of his starts and had an 8.25 ERA.

Mike Mussina had a 4.50 ERA, and the Yankees were 2-4 in his starts. Carl Pavano was completely inconsistent, with four good starts (10 runs in 28 1/3 innings) and three terrible outings (16 runs in 13 2/3 innings). And although Randy Johnson's 3.74 ERA wasn't terrible (the best on the team, in fact), he had given up at least five runs in three of his six starts. So, people wondered, was this the year the New York Yankees turned into the New York Rangers of baseball, spending gobs of money with nothing to show for it?

Before that debate had even heated up, the Yankees reeled off 10 straight wins, improving to 21-19 and pulling within five games of first place. After two losses in three games, they won five more in a row to move up to second place at 27-21. The key was the temporarily rejuvenated Tino Martinez, who hit eight of his 17 home runs and had 19 of his 49 RBIs during that 10-game winning streak.

But this season was destined to be a rollercoaster ride for the Yankees and their fans all the way through, and New York followed up its stretch of 16 wins in 18 games by losing nine of their next 10 to fall back below .500 (28-30) and into fourth place (seven games out). Through all the early ups and downs for the Yankees, the Orioles kept plugging along. Baltimore had kept its hold on first place since April 23, and they led by at least three games from May 21 until June 17.

But the Orioles were starting to struggle, and they wouldn't be able to hold off the charging Red Sox. Boston won 12 of 13 games from June 12 to June 26, taking over first place with an 8-0 win over Philadelphia on June 24. The two wins to complete the sweep of the Phillies put the Red Sox at 44-30, 2.5 games ahead of Baltimore. It was a remarkable place for Boston, considering how badly the two most important pitchers from the 2004 team were performing. Curt Schilling had only made three starts in the season, losing two of them, and Keith Foulke had a 5.05 ERA, although he had somehow managed to convert 14 of his 17 save opportunities.

Fortunately for the Red Sox, other players were picking up the slack. Matt Clement was 9-1 with a 3.33 ERA to lead the rotation, Mike Timlin had a miniscule 1.21 ERA in 37.1 innings out of the bullpen, and David Ortiz (hitting .306 with 19 homers in 288 at-bats) was the headliner on an offense scoring 5.7 runs per game.

The Red Sox were up-and-down over the next month, letting the Yankees move into first place for the first time since April for one day on July 17. But on July 26, with their lead over the Yankees just a game, the Red Sox got hot again, and it started with one of the craziest games they played all year.

With Clement on the mound against the Devil Rays, the Red Sox jumped out to a 5-0 lead. But Clement let runners reach first and third with one out in the bottom of the inning, and then things fell apart. Carl Crawford lined a single off Clement's head, knocking in a run and knocking out, almost literally, Clement. He never lost consciousness, but he had to leave the game. Chad Bradford came in and loaded the bases before Aubrey Huff tied the game with a grand slam. The Devil Rays took a 6-5 lead in the bottom of the sixth, but the Red Sox tied it in the top of the seventh. Then Tampa took an 8-6 lead in the bottom of the seventh. On the verge of a devastating loss, the Red Sox scored twice—on a Jason Varitek homer and a Bill Mueller RBI double—to tie the game in the ninth. Johnny Damon made a running catch in deep center in the bottom of the ninth to prevent the winning run from scoring, and then hit a go-ahead homer in the top of the 10th as the Red Sox went on to win 10-9.

That win sparked an eight-game winning streak. After a couple of losses, the Red Sox then spun off six more wins in a row to move to 68-47, five games ahead of the Yankees with only 47 games remaining.

In 2005, Boston's only real moves were to trade for Tony Graffanino and Bradford and release Alan Embree and Mark Bellhorn, while the Yankees tried to shake things up. They picked up Embree and Bellhorn, to no avail, but they did find surprisingly good replacements for the rotation, which had lost Pavano, Wright, Brown and impressive rookie Chien-Ming Wang to the disabled list. Journeyman Aaron Small was 4-0 with a 2.57 ERA in 29 innings, although he wouldn't have a regular spot in the rotation until September. And Colorado reject Shawn Chacon had allowed just three earned runs in his first 20 innings with the team. Even Al Leiter timed his best start with the Yankees perfectly. He allowed one run in 6 1/3 innings in a Sunday win over the Red Sox that allowed the Yankees to take three of four at Fenway and move into first place for that one day in July.

And on offense, things were really clicking for New York, thanks to an unexpected resurgence. Giambi, who was hovering around a .200 batting average and a .700 OPS in mid-May, got on track and had his OPS above 1.000 by early August. After a couple more slumps and hot streaks, he was amazingly able to finish with 32 homers and a .975 OPS.

Boston's lead grew to as many as five games in August, but it was back down to 2.5 by the end of the month. While the Red Sox and Yankees were gearing up for a fight to the finish, the Blue Jays and Orioles were coming to the realization that the high hopes they entered the season with were not going to be fulfilled.

Baltimore's season fell apart quickly after falling out of first place in late June. After a 12-15 June left the Orioles 2.5 games out of first at the end of the month, they proceeded to go 8-18 in July. Roberts (.705 OPS in 106 at-bats) and Melvin Mora (.729 in 99 at-bats) struggled on offense, and the pitching staff posted an ugly 4.88 ERA. Sidney Ponson, Bruce Chen and Rodrigo Lopez went 3-8 with a 6.80 ERA in 17 starts. After the All-Star break, Baltimore had two five-game losing streaks, as well as losing streaks of six, eight and nine games. Following the horrible showing in July, August started with a disaster off the field.

Rafael Palmeiro, who had recently celebrated joining the 3,000-hit, 500-homer club, was suspended for 10 days for testing positive for steroids. After vehemently denying using steroids before Congress, every story that came out after the suspension made Palmeiro look more guilty. His season fell apart as he only played seven games the rest of the year while dealing with injuries as well as abuse from fans across the country. Palmeiro went home to rehabilitate an injury away from the team in September and then pointed to Tejada as the player who gave him a legal B12 vitamin that may have produced the positive test. At that point, he was told not to show up again, and most of his teammates didn't show up much either. After beginning the season 41-27 (a .603 winning percentage), the Orioles went 33-61 (.351) the rest of the way.

The Blue Jays didn't fall quite so far, but they did fall pretty quickly. After winning on July 28, Toronto stood three games out of the Wild Card and four games behind Boston for first place in the division. After losing nine of their next 13 games, the Blue Jays were already eight games out in both the division and Wild Card races. The biggest problem for Toronto was losing its ace. Roy Halladay was 12-4 with a 2.41 ERA when he fractured his leg in early July. The Blue Jays went from allowing 4.2 runs per game while Halladay was active to allowing 4.5 runs per game while he was on the disabled list. After falling eight games out, Toronto did win seven of its next nine games to pull back within four games of Oakland in the Wild Card race. But the five-game losing streak that followed knocked the Blue Jays 6.5 games out with 37 games remaining and four teams ahead of them, effectively ending any hope for a playoff spot.

While both Baltimore and Toronto ultimately had disappointing seasons, at least both teams got a taste of contention. Tampa Bay fell into last place almost immediately and never rose out of the cellar. But that's not to say the Devil Rays weren't a factor in the division. Tampa Bay was a big contributor to New York's slow start, winning four of six games from the Yankees in April and May. Even when the Yankees had begun to right themselves in late June, they still had trouble with Tampa Bay, losing three of four in a series at Yankee Stadium. Then, in mid-August and early-September, the Yankees lost two of three to the Devil Rays in series in New York and Tampa. With one series remaining between the two teams, Tampa Bay had already ensured its first winning season against the Yankees by taking 11 of the first 16 games.

Then, after harassing the Yankees all season long, the Devil Rays returned to their losing ways against New York at the most critical time of the year. After coming off a weekend series with the Red Sox in which they won two of three games to move within three games of first place, the Yankees swept the Devil Rays to cut that deficit in half. The following week, Tampa Bay completed the transformation from a nemesis of New York to an ally, taking two of three from the Red Sox to drop Boston half a game behind the Yankees. The Yankees beat Baltimore while Boston had an off day to take a full one-game lead, but Boston rebounded with a sweep of the Orioles while the Yankees lost one of three to Toronto, knotting the division once again.

In the penultimate series of the season, the Red Sox nearly fell apart. The Yankees won three of four games from Baltimore, but Boston lost two of the first three games against Toronto and appeared to be on the way to a loss in the fourth game as well. Instead, Ortiz homered to tie the game in the bottom of the eighth inning and singled in the winning run in the bottom of the ninth, sending Boston into the final series against the Yankees trailing by just a game. It should have been an awesome three-game set for all the marbles, filled with amazing drama. Instead, thanks to the Cleveland Indians, it was a take-your-turn celebration weekend.

American League Central Review

by Aaron Gleeman

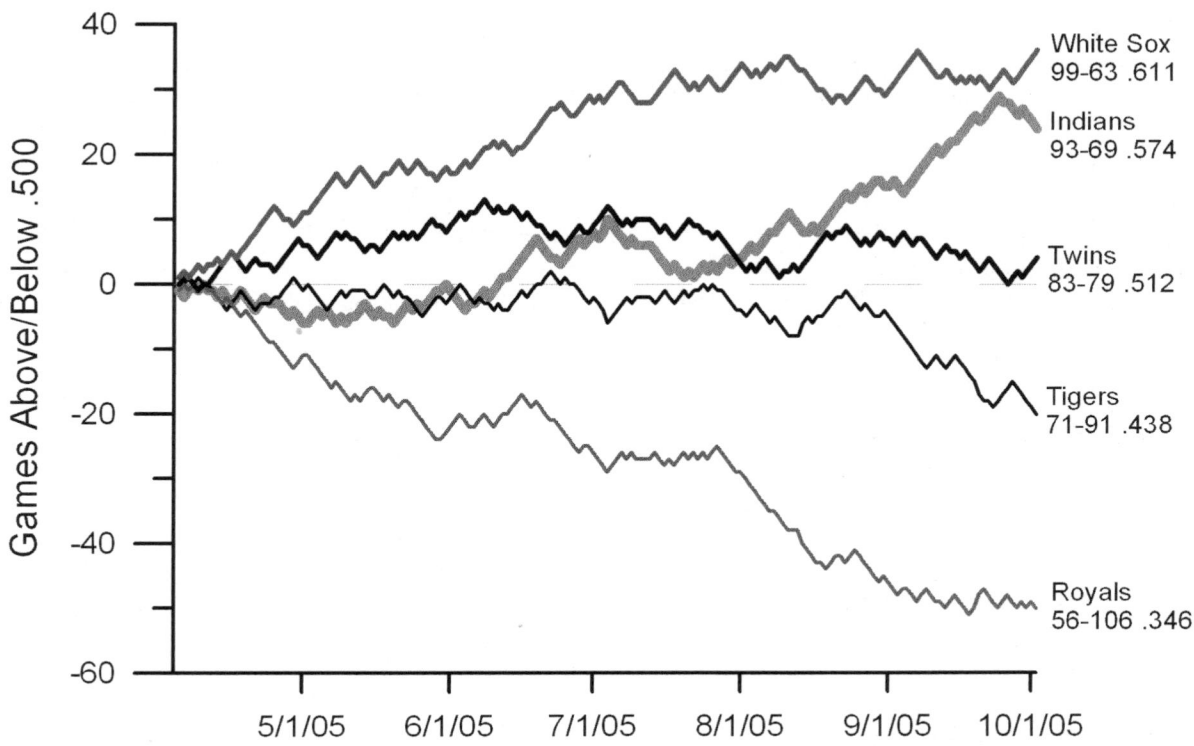

One of my favorite "Seinfeld" episodes, "The Race," centers around a race that Jerry won back in high school. I'll let him explain:

When we were in the ninth grade they had us all line up at one end of the schoolyard for this big race to see who was going to represent the school in this track meet .... [Mr. Bevilacqua the gym teacher] was down at the other end. So he yells out, "Ready ... on your mark ... get set ..." and I was so keyed up I just took off. By the time he said "go" I was 10 yards ahead of everybody. ... By the time the race was over I had won. I was shocked nobody had noticed the head start. ... And I had won by so much a myth began to grow about my speed.

Then, in order to maintain the myth of his incredible speed, Jerry decided never to run again:

In four years of high school I would never race anyone again. Not even to the end of the block to catch a bus. And so the legend grew. Everyone wanted me to race. They begged me. The track coach called my parents. Pleading. Telling them it was a sin to waste my God-given talent. But I answered him in the same way I answered everyone: I choose not to run.

I have seen "The Race" numerous times and have often wondered what would have happened that day in ninth grade if the race had been a marathon instead of a sprint. How long would Jerry's lead have held up if he had to actually run? Fortunately, the teams in the

American League Central were kind enough to reenact the race for our enjoyment this season.

Picked to finish third in the division by many (including me), the White Sox stormed out of the gates on fire. They began the year by winning 16 of their first 20 games, suffered through a three-game losing streak, and then reeled off another eight wins in a row. At the end of May Chicago was 35-17, and they stretched that to 53-24 by the end of June.

Much like Jerry's head start that fateful day in ninth grade, it looked like the White Sox were off to such a great start that there wouldn't be a race in the AL Central at all.

The Indians and the three-time defending division champion Twins played relatively well, sitting at 42-35 and 42-34 on July 1, respectively. That put both teams on pace for 90 wins and also put them 10.5 and 11 games behind the White Sox after less than half the season.

Chicago stretched this seemingly insurmountable division lead even further after the All-Star break by winning 12 of their first 18 games in the second half. When newspapers hit front steps on the morning of August 1, the White Sox were 68-35, on pace for 107 wins and leading the division by 14.5 games over both the Indians (55-51) and Twins (54-50). It looked like Chicago could simply jog to the finish line.

Minnesota basically folded up shop and coasted down the stretch as their offense went completely in the tank and their key players (Torii Hunter, Shannon Stewart, Carlos Silva, Brad Radke) started dropping like flies to injuries. In the meantime, Cleveland began to catch fire.

Everyone was trying to figure out how the White Sox would align their postseason roster with two months left to play, while the Indians quietly went 19-8 in August to slash the White Sox's lead to seven games. Cleveland then began September by dropping two out of three games to Minnesota and then winning 17 of their next 19 games.

Chicago's lead was very suddenly down to just 1.5 games on September 25. In less than two months, the Indians had closed the gap from 14.5 games to 1.5 games, and the amazing thing is that they did so while the White Sox played .500 baseball.

Because while the September headlines in Chicago were filled with talk of "choking" and "collapsing," the fact is that the White Sox simply came back down to earth a bit. After playing nearly .700 baseball for the first four months of the season, Chicago went 25-26 (.490) from August 1 to September 24. Playing .500 baseball after jumping out to such a massive lead would normally be enough to stroll to a division title, but the Indians went 37-12 (.755) over that same span.

Then a funny thing happened on the way to one of the greatest comebacks in baseball history. Having closed the gap to a measly 1.5 games with a little over a week remaining on the schedule by winning 76% of their last 50 games, the Indians were no doubt looking ahead to the season-ending three-game series they had coming up against the White Sox at Jacobs Field in Cleveland.

The Indians were in a perfect position to overtake the White Sox in the season's final days, but they couldn't. On Sunday, September 25, while the White Sox beat the Twins 4-1, the Indians lost 5-4 to the last-place Royals. Then, after an off day September 26, the Indians lost 5-4 to the last-place Devil Rays. And then they lost again to Tampa Bay, 1-0 on September 28 as one of the hottest lineups in baseball was shut out for eight innings by Seth "Cy Young" McClung.

After playing extraordinary baseball for two months, the Indians had the division title in their sights. With games against two cellar-dwelling teams while Chicago battled within the division against Minnesota and Detroit, the 2005 AL Central title was teed up for

Cleveland. All they had to do was swing away. Instead, they lost three in a row to two of baseball's worst teams, and what looked like an exciting final weekend ended up meaning nothing to the White Sox.

Chicago clinched the AL Central championship and their first trip to the postseason since 2000 on the final Thursday of the season. In the first game of their season-ending series with the Indians, the White Sox—after no doubt celebrating the night before—trotted out the following lineup:

1) Scott Podsednik, LF
2) Brian Anderson, CF
3) Ross Gload, 1B
4) Joe Borchard, DH
5) Joe Crede, 3B
6) Timo Perez, RF
7) Chris Widger, C
8) Geoff Blum, SS
9) Willie Harris, 2B

The Indians' opponents that day were more Charlotte Knights (Chicago's Triple-A team) than Chicago White Sox, but Cleveland couldn't take advantage. They lost 3-2 in 13 innings and then dropped each of the final two games of the series to fall out of the Wild Card picture.

When the dust settled, the damage was severe: At 92-63 with seven games left to play, Cleveland finished the season by going 1-6 against the Royals, Devil Rays and post-clinch White Sox. The Indians' finish was like a boxer knocking his opponent out, failing to go to his corner so the referee could count to 10, and then being floored by an uppercut after the should-be-knocked-out fighter got back up and dusted himself off. Rarely has momentum so strong come to such a screeching halt and then turned around 180 degrees.

In the end, the 2005 AL Central was a perfect example of the baseball season being a marathon and not a sprint. The White Sox came flying out of the blocks as fast as just about any team in baseball history, but by mid-September their fast start hardly guaranteed them anything—they still had to run. The Indians did their sprinting in the middle of the season, all but catching the White Sox as the two teams entered the home stretch, but that didn't guarantee anything either.

Early on, the White Sox were the hottest team in baseball and the Indians were an afterthought. Later, the Indians were the hottest team in baseball and the White Sox were being accused of choking away a massive lead. And as it always does, the division came down to a 162-game schedule that cared little about whether the wins came in April or September. The White Sox finished 99-63 for the best record in the league, claiming homefield advantage throughout the postseason and winning the division by six games.

For all the talk about choking down the stretch, they went charging into the postseason winners of five straight and eight of their last 10, racking up the franchise's most wins since the Carlton Fisk-led 1983 team also went 99-63 to win the AL West title by 20 games. While the 1983 team was a juggernaut that ranked first in the league in both runs scored and runs allowed, the 2005 version succeeded primarily through outstanding pitching and good defense all over the diamond.

Chicago general manager Kenny Williams rebuilt the roster during the offseason, saying he wanted to get away from relying on home runs as much as the White Sox had while finishing second to the Twins for three straight years. But while Williams brought in speedy players like Scott Podsednik and Tadahito Iguchi, the White Sox still relied on the long ball a lot more than the average team.

In fact, Chicago blasted 200 homers in 2005, ranking fourth in the AL. Their home run ranks from 2002-2004? Third, fourth, first. If anything, the White Sox became *more* reliant on homers than they had been in the past, in large part because they stopped doing other things well offensively. They no longer had a strong offensive core that featured the likes of Magglio Ordoñez, Carlos Lee and a healthy Frank Thomas; instead they had a club that was basically limited to hitting homers, stealing bases and bunting.

The 2005 White Sox finished 11th in the league in batting average, 11th in walks, and dead last in doubles. The end result was an offense that scored just 741 runs to rank ninth in the league after averaging 837 runs per year from 2002-2004. So how did they finally find the formula for winning despite losing so much offense? Well their pitching improved even more than the offense declined.

After ranking 10th in the AL with 831 runs allowed in 2004, Chicago sliced nearly 200 runs off that number to rank third in the league with 645 runs allowed. Think about that for a moment—an improvement of 186 runs in one season. Considering how offense-friendly their home ballpark is, the argument could easily be made that the White Sox had the best pitching staff in the AL.

Chicago's 3.42 team ERA away from U.S. Cellular Field led all of baseball, showing how good they could be when the ballpark wasn't playing heavily in the hitter's favor. The White Sox had four starters—Mark Buehrle, Freddy Garcia, Jon Garland and Jose Contreras—toss at least 200 innings with a sub-4.00 ERA and got a combined 397.2 innings of 3.26 ERA pitching out of the bullpen.

Chicago's deep, balanced, and dominant relief corps of Dustin Hermanson (2.04 ERA, 57.1 innings), Bobby Jenks (2.75, 39.1), Neal Cotts (1.94, 60.1), Cliff Politte (2.00, 67.1), Damaso Marte (3.77, 45.1) and Luis Vizcaino (3.73, 70.0) was a huge part of how they went an incredible 35-19 in one-run games. Another big factor was manager Ozzie Guillen's handling of the bullpen and willingness to mix and match those quality relievers in the late innings rather than rely upon strict bullpen roles.

When Chicago's 2004 closer, Shingo Takatsu, struggled early, Guillen cut bait and turned to Hermanson in the ninth inning. When Hermanson had some back problems in the second half, Guillen turned to the 24-year-old Jenks, who was fresh up from the minors. Even Marte got into the act with four saves, being called upon to close out games when the opponents had a lefty-heavy portion of the lineup due up in the ninth.

And last but not least is an overlooked aspect of Chicago's success: defense. Their outfield defense featured two center fielders, with Podsednik in left field and Aaron Rowand in center, and the infield had Juan Uribe at shortstop and a former shortstop, Iguchi, at second base. Toss in solid glove work from Joe Crede and Paul Konerko on the infield corners, and the White Sox converted balls in play into outs at an outstanding rate.

On the year, 71.3% of the balls put in play (not homers, walks or strikeouts) against the White Sox were turned into outs, which ranked second in the AL behind only the A's (71.7%). Not only did they have excellent range defensively, but when they got to balls they were very sure-handed. The White Sox committed just 94 errors all season to rank tied for third in the AL with a .985 fielding percentage.

The 2005 AL Central champs may not look like they fit the mold of an Earl Weaver ball club, but just as teams led by the Earl of Baltimore tended to do, the White Sox relied on pitching, defense, and homers. Small-ball and Podsednik's running got the headlines, but pitching and Konerko's power got the wins.

American League West Review

by John Brattain

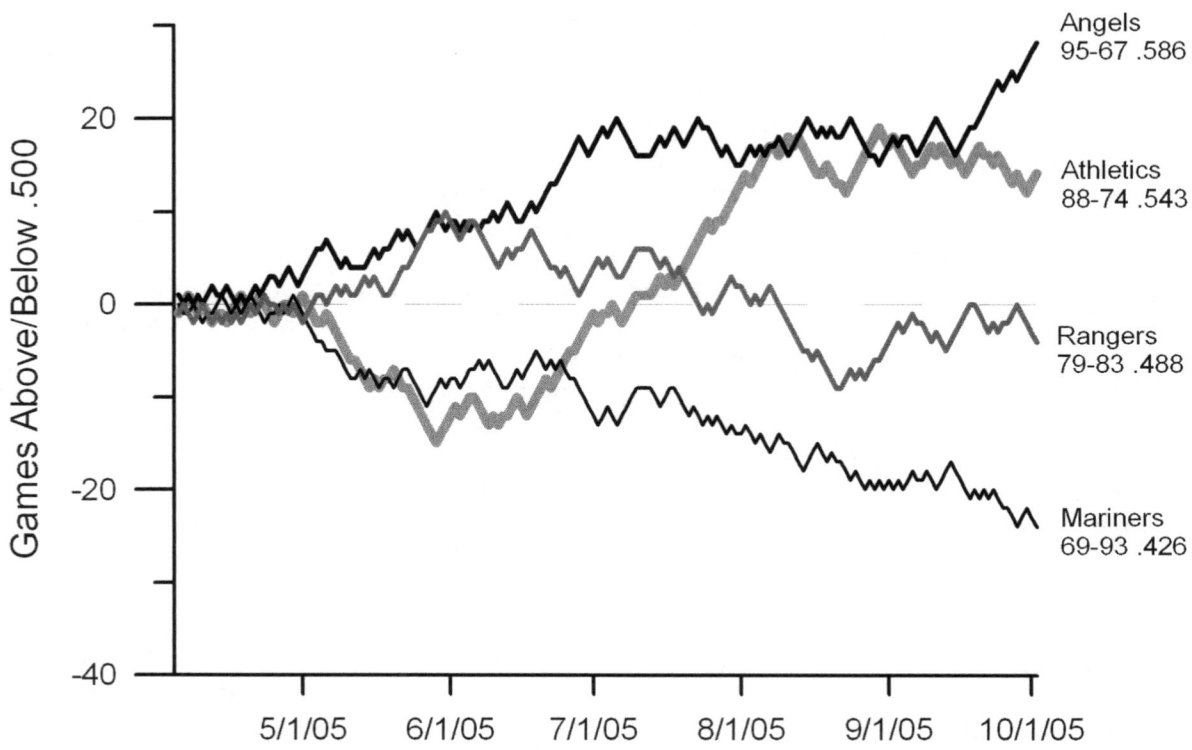

One team loaded up and went into the tank. Another team bid sayonara to 2005 before Opening Day and almost said hello to the postseason. The kids were all right for a while, but it was a heavenly 14-2 finish that put the Los Angeles Angels of Anaheim into the postseason.

The biggest news of the offseason was the A's dealing two-thirds of their fantastic triumvirate of ace starters. Mark Mulder went to the St. Louis Cardinals for pitchers Danny Haren and Kiko Calero and intriguing young catching prospect Daric Barton. Tim Hudson was sent to the Braves for pitchers Dan Meyer and Juan Cruz along with outfielder Charles Thomas. Facing the loss of catcher Damian Miller to free agency, the A's jettisoned 2004 busts Arthur Rhodes and Mark Redman to the Pirates for Jason Kendall. They bolstered the bench by adding Keith Ginter from the Brewers for Justin Lehr and minor leaguer Nelson Cruz.

Meanwhile, big changes were happening in the Pacific Northwest. Manager Doug Melvin was bid adieu and the "Human Rain Delay" Mike Hargrove was brought in. Aaron Sele was welcomed back into the fold. The Mariners opened their wallets in a big

way, hoping to bolster an offense that was the worst in the AL—and looked worse on paper with the retirement of iconic designated hitter Edgar Martinez—in 2004 by signing first baseman Richie Sexson to a four-year $50 million contract and third baseman Adrian Beltre to a five-year $64 million deal. After enjoying four straight seasons of contention and 90+ wins, the Mariners crashed to the bottom of the AL West and failed to win 70 games (in a non-strike year) for the first time since 1992.

The newly named Los Angeles Angels of Anaheim expelled problem child Jose Guillen, sending him to the also newly named Washington Nationals for infielder Maicer Izturis and outfielder Juan Rivera. Also gone was fan favorite David Eckstein, and Orlando Cabrera was brought in to fill in at shortstop. The Halos also said goodbye to Aaron Sele and Ramon Ortiz and said hello to Steve Finley. The Texas Rangers had a relatively quiet offseason (Scott Boras had a new pigeon in Detroit) and took a flyer on Richard Hidalgo, signing him to a one-year contract. The kids had looked good in 2004, as the Rangers finished 83-79, just three games out in the AL West.

At the end of April, an epic dogfight looked to be in the works, as only 1.5 games separated the first place Angels from the last place Mariners. The Rangers, however, went 18-7 in May to vault into first place. The Angels kept pace just a game back, while the early season losses of shortstop Bobby Crosby, outfielder Nick Swisher, pitcher Rich Harden and closer Octavio Dotel hurt the A's. They stumbled badly, going 7-19 and dropping to the division cellar. The Mariners fared no better as prized acquisition Beltre struggled mightily at the plate and Ichiro Suzuki had an off month. Sexson's seven home runs were the team's lone offensive bright spots. The rotation was hit hard as Jamie Moyer, Ryan Franklin, Gil Meche and Joel Pineiro combined to go 4-10 with a 6.36 ERA; the lone bright spot was the return of Sele, who posted a 2-2 record and a 3.77 ERA in May. The Mariners went 8-18, and only the dismal play of the A's kept them out of last place.

As May wound down, the A's lost eight straight, but in the final two games of the month they beat the Tampa Bay Devil Rays to begin a hot streak that would take them literally from worst to first. The A's won 58 of 75 games over this stretch. In May's final game, Danny Haren threw a complete game win and stayed hot through June, when he went (including his final start in May) 6-0 with a 2.73 ERA. Joe Blanton was 5-1, 2.06 ERA for the month of June, and Kirk Saarloos chipped in a perfect 3-0, 2.08 ERA for the month. Although the trio cooled a bit in the coming months, the slack was picked up by Barry Zito, who went 10-2, 2.74 ERA over that stretch, and Rich Harden, who returned from the disabled list on June 21 and was a stellar 7-2, 2.97 through mid-August. The bullpen became stingy; Huston Street replaced Dotel as closer, and it was the final piece of what shaped up to be the end of an excellent bullpen that included setup men Justin Duchscherer and Kiko Calero.

The Angels, however, were hanging tough. While the A's were going 58-17, the Angels' 12.5-game lead evaporated, but they still played at a solid .569 clip during the A's hot streak despite losing four of six to Oakland. Los Angeles got solid pitching from their starting four of Bartolo Colon, Jarrod Washburn, John Lackey and Paul Byrd and had the best ERA for a starting staff in the AL in 2005.

The Rangers couldn't hold on to first. Their lineup, which included Michael Young, Mark Teixeira, Alfonso Soriano and the surprising David Dellucci, was the best offense in the AL West and the third-best in the AL, but as usual their pitching was lacking. On June 29—with the Rangers sitting at 39-37—erstwhile staff ace and All-Star Kenny Rogers assaulted KDFW cameraman Larry Rodriguez and was suspended for 20 games. (The decision was later overturned.) The Rangers surged briefly and were 46-40 two weeks later, but that was as far as they could go. The Rangers' pitchers posted an ERA of 5.50 from June until August and lost 26 of their next 37, placing the team 13 games out. The Rangers officially punted on the season at the trade deadline and sent the final remnant of the Scott Boras years in Texas, lame-winged albatross Chan Ho Park, to the San Diego Padres for first baseman Phil Nevin.

While the A's were hot, the Mariners, most assuredly, were not; they went 29-37 during the same time and took over last place, where they remained. Pitcher Ryan Franklin and rookie Michael Morse's 10-day suspensions for steroid use in early August capped the Mariners' summer of discontent.

But it wasn't all doom and gloom in the Pacific Northwest. On August 4 at Comerica Park in Detroit, the Mariners sent 19-year-old phenom Felix Hernandez (also known as "King Felix") to the hill against the Tigers' Sean Douglass. Despite taking the loss, Hernandez scattered three hits, one earned run and four strikeouts with 81 pitches in five innings. Five days later in his Safeco debut against the Minnesota Twins, he threw just 94 pitches in eight shutout innings in which he gave up five hits, no walks and struck out six. But the Mariners raised the white flag at the trade deadline by sending catcher Miguel Olivo to the Padres for catcher Miguel Ojeda and pitcher Nathanael Mateo. They also jettisoned outfielder Randy Winn to the San Francisco Giants for pitcher Jesse Foppert and catcher Yorvit Torrealba.

On August 13 the Angels and A's were tied atop the AL West and were primed for a run at the division title; the Wild Card was also a possibility for whichever team finished second. The dates August 30-September 1 and September 26-29 loomed large on the schedule. They were the last seven head-to-head games that would decide the division and possibly spell the difference between being invited to the postseason prom and being left at home to brood about next year.

When August 30 rolled around on the calendar the Angels had relinquished their lead. Five days previous they enjoyed a 3.5 game lead which had evaporated courtesy of an A's six game winning streak coupled by the Angels being swept by the lowly Tampa Bay Devil Rays which left them one game in arrears of the lead. The first game in the series shaped up to be an excellent pitching duel. The Angels sent Bartolo Colon (17-6, 3.34 ERA) to the mound and the A's countered with Barry Zito (12-10, 3.49 ERA). They did not disappoint; after nine innings the game was knotted 1-1 as both starters went nine. In the top of the inning Colon answered the bell and was lifted with one out, man on third in the tenth for closer Francisco Rodriguez who bailed out Colon. Zito was replaced by Kiko Calero who pitched a scoreless tenth. Rodriguez came out to start the 11th and the A's led off with Bobby Kielty who promptly homered making it 2-1. Huston Street came out to close the game and two walks made it interesting when Vladimir Guerrero came up to bat. Street induced a weak grounder to end the threat and the game.

The A's had a two-game cushion.

For game two, the Angels sent John Lackey (10-5, 3.59 ERA) to the hill to face Joe Blanton (8-9 3.61 ERA). Like game one, the starters both pitched superlatively. In the fourth inning Vladimir Guerrero led off with a single and Darin Erstad doubled on Blanton's next pitch. Three batters later, Maicer Izturis blooped a single scoring Erstad as Anaheim grabbed a 2-0 lead. Meanwhile Lackey kept the A's off-balance allowing just three hits, four walks and striking out seven over seven innings and gave way to Scot Shields who worked in and out of a jam in the eighth as Eric Chavez ripped a single with one out for his 1,000th career hit. Two batters later, Jay Payton singled to put runners at first and second with two outs. Scott Hatteberg cut Oakland's deficit in half to 2-1 with an RBI single into left field. Shields then loaded the bases after plunking Bobby Kielty but retired rookie Nick Swisher to end the inning. Francisco Rodriguez bounced back from his loss the previous night by converting his 31st save of the year.

The Angels had cut the lead in half.

For the final game of the set the Angels sent 22 year old Dominican rookie Ervin Santana (7-6, 4.94 ERA) to face off against A's swingman Joe Kennedy (7-8, 6.18 ERA). The Angels scored runs in the third, fourth and eighth innings while Santana had a shutout going into the ninth.

After Eric Chavez singled with one out, Francisco Rodriguez was brought in to get the final two outs to finish the 3-0 whitewash.

The Angels and A's were now deadlocked—September would decide things. Anaheim continued to win and the A's started to stumble. The Angels led the West by four games by the time they had to go to Oakland on September 26 for a four game series that could either put the division away or allow the A's once again to get back into things.

Meanwhile the Rangers were enjoying a resurgent September that saw them resurface at .500 on September 28 (79-79), but a .500 season was not to be as they lost their final four games of the season. Mariners fans, despite having to endure a last place finish, could take solace in the spectacular rookie debut of Felix Hernandez who, although he finished just 4-4, sported a tidy ERA of 2.67 while averaging seven innings per start and one base runner per inning.

September 26 at McAfee Coliseum saw a rematch of the August 31 tilt: John Lackey (12-5, 3.55 ERA) vs. Joe Blanton (11-11, 3.60 ERA). A Bobby Crosby throwing error, a double by Darin Erstad and a single by Juan Rivera in the second inning put the Angels up 2-0. Steve Finley connected for a two-run home run in the fourth making it 4-0. Lackey didn't cough up a hit until the fifth, when Jay Payton led off with a base hit. With two outs Mark Ellis singled and Jason Kendall doubled to slice the deficit in half to 4-2. Lackey left after six and was replaced by Kelvim Escobar, who coughed up a solo home run to Eric Chavez in the eighth, pulling the A's to within a run. Francisco Rodriguez, however, earned his 42nd save by retiring the side in order striking out two, increasing the Angels lead to five games with six to play.

The A's were now fighting for their playoff lives. They needed a win to preserve their remote chance at the division after being eliminated from the Wild Card hunt. It would be a rematch of September 1. The Angels sent Ervin Santana (10-8, 4.69 ERA) to the hill against Joe Kennedy (7-12, 6.08 ERA). The A's drew first blood, scoring a run in the bottom of the first on consecutive doubles by Mark Kotsay and Eric Chavez. The Angels quickly struck back with two in the top of the second as Bengie Molina stroked a one-out double and scored on a double by Juan Rivera. Molina connected for a home run in the fourth making it 3-1, and the A's added another marker in the frame and Kennedy was gone. The Athletics' Dan Johnson doubled in a run in the bottom of the inning. Santana didn't surrender another run and took the game into the seventh, when he was replaced by Scot Shields, who didn't give up a base runner through the end of eight.

Rodriguez was summoned from the bullpen to close out the division title. Marco Scutaro led off the inning with a home run, making it 4-3. Then Rodriguez stiffened, retiring Johnson, Jay Payton and pinch hitter Bobby Kielty (who had homered off Rodriguez in the previous series) in order and the Angels were AL West champions. The A's and Angels would split the final two games with Bartolo Colon, notching his league-leading 21st win in the finale. The Angels then swept the Rangers in the final three games to finish the year 95-67.

National League East Review
by Brian Borawski

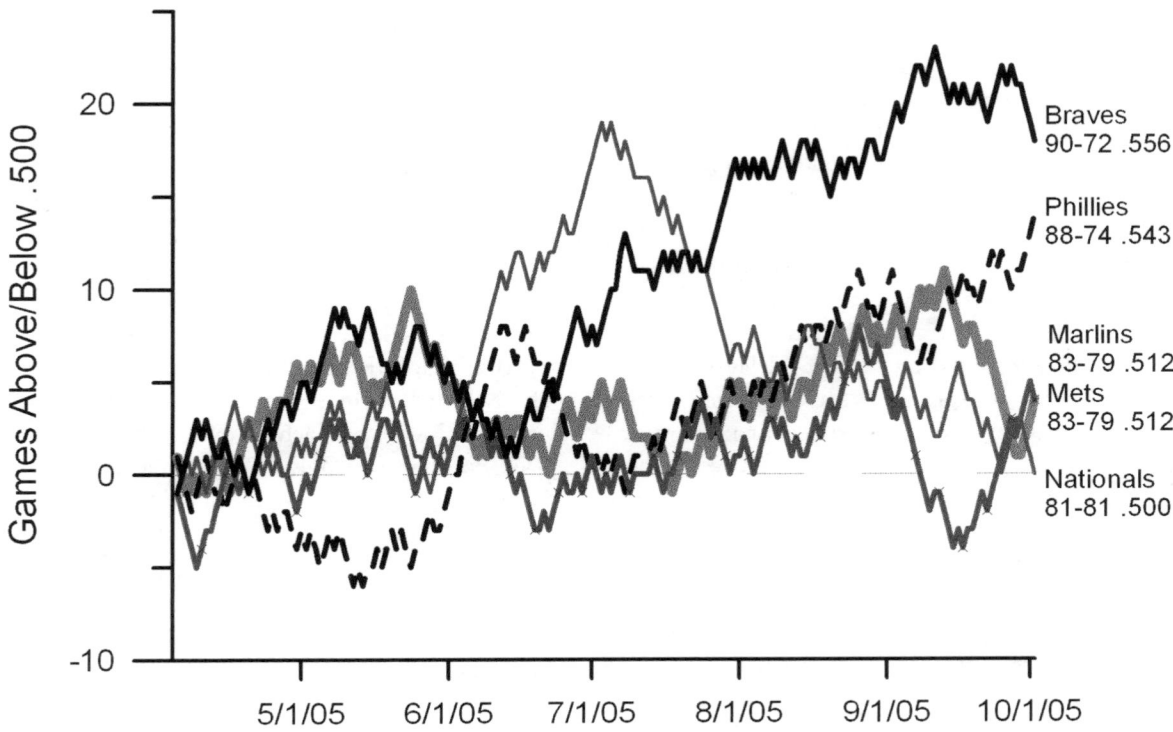

The more things change, the more they stay the same.

Since 2003, the Atlanta Braves have lost Javy Lopez, Vinny Castilla, Gary Sheffield, Greg Maddux, Russ Ortiz, J.D Drew, Jaret Wright and Paul Byrd. Add in the fact that they lost Tom Glavine and Kevin Millwood after the 2002 season and you have the makings of an All-Star team's worth of lost players. By my count, three of them are future Hall of Famers.

Somehow, despite the losses, the Braves continue to win. In 2004, they won their 13th consecutive National League East division title and were gunning for their 14th. The last time the Braves didn't win the NL East was 1990. George Bush, the father, was President. We've fought two different wars in Iraq since then. At the end of the 1990 season, the Dow Jones Industrial Average was around 2,500; it now stands at 10,000. We've also gone through two recessions since the Braves found themselves anywhere except first place in their division. Fay Vincent was the commissioner of baseball, Bud Selig was just an influential owner, baseball hadn't yet cancelled a World Series and the Cincinnati Reds were the World Series Champions. All four of the last-place teams in 1990 are some of the strongest teams in the current decade. The New York Yankees, St. Louis Cardinals, Minnesota Twins and the Atlanta Braves all finished dead last in their respective divisions 15 years ago.

Like 2003, the Braves lost more then they added. Their biggest free agent signing was keeping Julio Franco, who was set to turn 47 during the 2005 season. The only other player who garnered a seven-figure salary was Raul Mondesi. Mondesi was signed to help fill the hole left by J.D. Drew's departure, but by the end of May, he was hitting barely over the Mendoza line and would be designated for assignment and eventually lost. The most significant move the Braves made was moving John Smoltz from the bullpen to the starting rotation. Smoltz hadn't started a game since 2001 after coming back from an injured elbow.

The Mets appeared to be trying to accomplish what their cross-town rivals have attempted and in some instances succeeded. They were trying to buy their way to their first World Series win in almost 20 years. The Mets re-signed Kris Benson, and while they lost veteran starter Al Leiter, they replaced him with Pedro Martinez, one of the best arms in the league. They also got the big prize: Carlos Beltran. Beltran set career highs in walks, runs, home runs and OPS in 2004 and has 192 career stolen bases in 215 attempts. Throw in the fact that he's an above-average fielder, and you have a player that you can build your team around.

25

The Phillies let the long ball-prone Eric Milton go and signed Jon Lieber to take his place. They also let Kevin Millwood go to the Cleveland Indians after an injury-plagued year. The Marlins lost Carl Pavano to the Yankees after a career year and replaced him in the rotation with Al Leiter. They also lost their closer, Armando Benitez, but they signed free agent slugger Carlos Delgado to fill the hole at first base that they never quite filled after trading Derrek Lee in late 2003.

While the Braves had to contend with losing stars and the Mets had to contend with picking up two superstars, none of it compared to what the former Montreal Expos had to go through. With the team still owned by the other 29 baseball teams' owners, Bud Selig finally made a decision, and after essentially a two-year delay, he moved the team to Washington, D.C. With a new stadium set to be built for the team and the prospects of an increased revenue stream, the Washington Nationals were given some leeway in their budget, at least compared to years past. The Nationals let Tony Batista go and replaced him with Vinny Castilla, who had put up some nice Coors Field-inflated numbers the year before. They also traded for the volatile Jose Guillen to help out in right field. The Nationals' biggest signing, at least dollar-wise, was their pickup of the light-hitting Cristian Guzman to fill the hole at shortstop left by the previous year's trade deadline deal that sent Orlando Cabrera to the Boston Red Sox.

The defending division champions began their season by getting trounced by the Florida Marlins. John Smoltz was hit hard in his first Opening Day start since 1997. Josh Beckett, the hero of the 2003 World Series, held the Braves to two hits through six innings of work as he and three other relievers combined for the shutout. Atlanta's Pete Orr made his major league debut as a pinch hitter. He'd be the first of 11 different Braves who'd make their major league debuts during the season. Another rookie, albeit one with cups of coffee in both 2002 and 2003, that played in the game as a pinch hitter was Ryan Langerhans. Langerhans went on to log 326 at-bats and switched between right and left fields, giving manager Bobby Cox some flexibility with how he used his outfield.

The second week of the season saw baseball return to Washington, D.C. for the first time since 1971. After starting the season with a 5-4 record, the Nationals swept the Arizona Diamondbacks in their first home series. Combined with the two straight wins against the Braves in the series before, the Nationals finished the series with a five-game winning streak, a mark they wouldn't reach again for nearly two months.

At the end of April, the Marlins stood atop the division. Dontrelle Willis won all five of his starts that month, and people were already whispering "Cy Young"

whenever he was mentioned. The Braves stood one game behind the Marlins (two losses) and close on the Braves' heels just one game behind were the Nationals. The Phillies ended the month by losing seven of eight and stood in the cellar five games behind the Marlins.

Both the Mets and the Braves opened up the month of May with hot streaks. The Mets won six of seven, with two of those wins coming from the rotation's anchor, Pedro Martinez. Martinez finished 2-1 in April, with two no-decisions in which he gave up only three and two runs respectively. The Braves also started May by winning six of seven, and once again moved into first place. As was typical in the first half of the season within the NL East, no team led for very long. By the end of the month, it was the Braves and the Marlins who were tied for first place. The Nationals were a game back, and the last-place Phillies were slowly approaching .500. They were still in last place, but they were only 3.5 games back.

The Phillies, Nationals and Mets all started the month of June on hot streaks. The Phillies won all four of their games while both the Nationals and the Mets opened the month by winning four of five. The Marlins and the Braves both opened June in a slump. The Marlins lost four of their first five games, and the Braves lost three of five. The end result was that an already tight division got even tighter. The Nationals moved into first place, and the Marlins, just a week ago the division leaders, now found themselves in the cellar. The interesting thing was that the difference between first place and last place was a mere game and a half. There would eventually be some separation, but things were shaping up to be a close, competitive race with all five teams in the mix.

The rest of June was dominated by the Nationals and the Phillies. Just a year away from having the second worst record in the National League, the Nationals went on a 10-game winning streak. During that same time, the Phillies won nine of 10. The difference between the two was that the Nationals kept winning. They finished the month of June with a record of 20-6 and a 4.5-game lead over the second-place Braves.

The Nationals carried this cushion into the All-Star break. In the meantime, despite their big spending in the offseason, the Mets were in last place with a 44-44 record. Interestingly enough, each team in the NL East had at least a .500 record. Their big money center fielder, Carlos Beltran, was struggling along at a .266/.321/.434 clip with only 10 home runs. Pedro Martinez was at least earning his keep and he stood at 10-3 with a 0.84 WHIP.

The Phillies were just a half game ahead of the last-place Mets. To make things worse, star first baseman

Jim Thome was placed on the disabled list on July 1; he was out for the season. His replacement, blue chip prospect Ryan Howard, did an admirable job in his absence. He had a ton of help from the underrated star outfielder Bobby Abreu. Consistently good for several years, Abreu was doing what he did best, and that's get on base. He was one of only eight players to finish the season with an OBP above .400. The Phillies also got a nice contribution from Pat Burrell. After two disappointing seasons, Burrell broke out and led the team in home runs with 32.

The Nationals appeared to be in over their heads despite their breakout in June. At one point heading into the All-Star break, the Nationals won 12 straight one-run games. Even when they were as many as 18 games above .500, they usually projected to be right around .500 based on how many runs they scored and how many they allowed. Not too soon after winning that 12th straight one-run game, the Nationals proceeded to lose 13 straight one-run games through most of July and into early August. Talk about regressing to the mean.

Jose Guillen, while vilified for his outbursts in Anaheim, led the team on offense. His 24 homers were nine better then Nick Johnson, who was second on the team with 15. In the end, the Nationals finished with the worst offense in the major leagues with 3.94 runs per game. They were the only team to finish below four runs per game, and they were also dead last with a .386 slugging percentage. It was their pitching that carried them through most games. Chad Cordero was one of the most effective relievers in the first half of the season. His ERA was right around 1.00 for most of the season, but he had a couple of bad outings in September that bloated his statistics. Livan Hernandez was also effective, and while he ran out of gas in the second half, he ended the season with 15 wins.

Dontrelle Willis fell victim to the sophomore slump in 2004. After winning the Rookie of the Year award in 2003, Willis fell to 10-11 in 2004. In 2005, he was nothing short of spectacular. He won his first seven starts, and he was instrumental in the Marlins' early lead in the division. On offense it was another third-year player, Miguel Cabrera, who also broke out. He finished the season hitting .323/.385/.561 and tied slugger Carlos Delgado for the team lead with 33 homers. Delgado hit an equally impressive .301/.399/.582.

The Braves were never far behind the division leader. Just prior to the All Star Break, the Braves brought up Jeff Francoeur to help fill the corner outfield spot left by Raul Mondesi's departure. In 70 games and 246 at-bats, Francoeur homered 16 times and put up an admirable

.300/.336/.549 line. No player was more instrumental to the Braves, however, than Andruw Jones. At the break he had 27 home runs. He'd go on to hit 24 more in the second half to become the first Brave to ever hit 50 home runs. The Braves' primary liability was their bullpen, and they made an attempt to shore this up by trading for Detroit Tigers closer Kyle Farnsworth.

The second half of the season wasn't very kind to the Nationals. They lost 14 of their next 18 games after the All-Star break, and on July 26 they surrendered first place to the Braves, who remained in first for the rest of the season.

Despite this, the remaining four teams in the division were never quite out of the playoff picture. Since losing their first five games of the season and then winning their next six, the Mets were always either four games above or four games below .500 until August 11. On that day, they saw their playoff chances crumble before their eyes as Carlos Beltran and Mike Cameron had a vicious collision attempting to field a fly ball. Cameron's season was finished, and while Beltran returned, he never broke out from what turned into a disappointing season. To add insult to injury (no pun intended), two weeks later Mike Piazza broke his hand and was subsequently place on the disabled list. The Mets ended up finishing August on a hot streak by winning eight of their last 12 games, but their playoff hopes were put to rest when they opened September by losing 12 of 14 games.

Heading into the final full month of the season, the Nationals continued their slide, and the Phillies inched their way into a tight Wild Card race with the Marlins and the Houston Astros. The Marlins went on a horrific slump, losing 12 of their final 15 games in September and slipping out of the Wild Card race. The Phillies, in the meantime, hung tight with the Astros until the very end, but despite finishing the season with four straight wins, they fell a single game short of a postseason berth.

So we come to a familiar ending. Led by their star center fielder Andruw Jones, and despite nagging injuries to their other star, Chipper Jones, the Braves won their 14th consecutive division title. The Braves also got productive seasons from Marcus Giles (.291/.365/.461) and leadoff hitter Rafael Furcal (.284/.348/.429). Smoltz finished the season just how he started it, in the rotation. He never hit the disabled list and he logged 229.2 innings, the most for him since 1997. Farnsworth went from a closer with the Tigers to a middle reliever when he initially got traded to the Braves. He'd end the season as the Braves' closer, holding hitters to a .161 batting average in 27.1 innings of work.

National League Central Review

by Greg Tamer

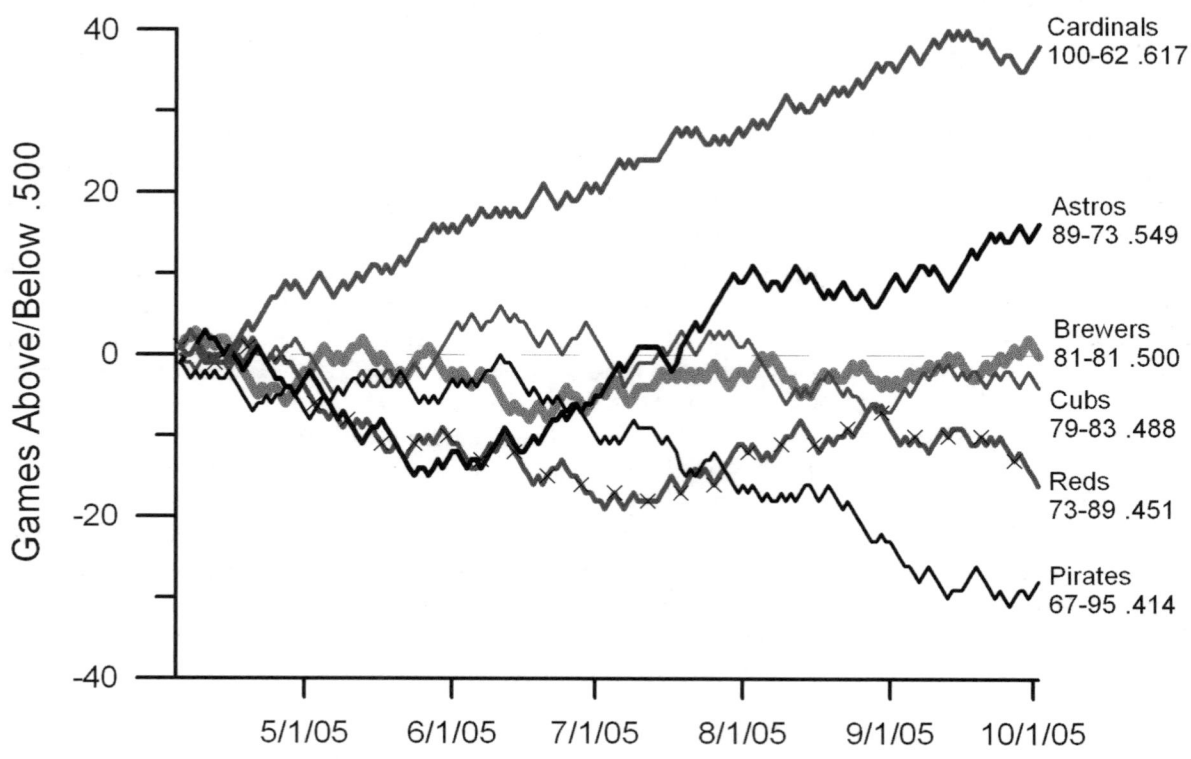

On April 16, 2005, the St. Louis Cardinals moved into first place in the National League Central division with a 5-4 record. As illustrated in the accompanying "Games Above/Below .500" figure, the Cardinals henceforth were not threatened for the NL Central title. What's also illustrated in the figure was the Cardinals' consistency until the middle of September, as they suffered only two three-game losing streaks in the first five months—minor blips in an otherwise linear climb to 100 wins in what was the 40th and final season played at Busch Stadium.

Various metrics arguably place the Cardinals' pitching and fielding (run prevention) in the top three in the NL (with the Houston Astros and New York Mets) and place the offense (hitting and running) only slightly above average. But the combination of the two resulted in the Cardinals winning the most games and most likely being the best team overall in the NL.

Every pitcher who threw at least eight innings finished with an above-average ERA+. The "worst" were starters Jason Marquis and Matt Morris, who threw 207 and 192.2 innings and still managed to finish above average in ERA+, with 103 and 104, respectively. Joining them in the formidable rotation were Chris Carpenter

(241.2 innings, 151 ERA+), Mark Mulder (205 innings, 117 ERA+) and Jeff Suppan (194.1 innings, 120 ERA+). Combined, these five gentlemen would start all but two games for the Cardinals.

The relief pitching for the Cardinals was even better. Jason Isringhausen (59 innings, 200 ERA+), Al Reyes (62.2 innings, 198 ERA+) and Cal Eldred (37 innings, 195 ERA+) were nearly unhittable, while Ray King, Julian Tavarez, Randy Flores and Brad Thompson also contributed significantly out of the bullpen.

But the fielding also contributed to those excellent ERA+ numbers, and the Redbird hurlers should thank catcher Yadier Molina, shortstop David Eckstein, second baseman Mark Grudzielanek and center fielder Jim Edmonds for collectively providing excellent fielding in the middle of the field. The corner positions weren't too shabby either, resulting in arguably above average fielding at every position.

Meanwhile, the offense for the Cardinals was led once again by first baseman Albert Pujols (700 PA, 167 OPS+), but significant injuries limited the overall run production. Third baseman Scott Rolen only played in 56 games (injured shoulder in collision on May 10) and was well below average at the plate (83

OPS+). Left fielder Reggie Sanders was productive (126 OPS+) but only appeared in 93 games due to a broken leg suffered in a collision with Edmonds (136 OPS+, by the way) on July 15. Right fielder Larry Walker also was a threat at the plate (129 OPS+), but various injuries and injury-prevention bench warming limited him to just 100 games. The replacements (third baseman Abraham Nuñez, outfielder So Taguchi, outfielder John Mabry), however, along with Molina, weren't nearly as good—thus the slightly above average team offense.

While the Cardinals were mechanically building their lead in the division, the entertainment in the standings had to come from elsewhere, and the Houston Astros obliged. They decided to not join the race until May 25, at which point their record was 15-30. They won 63% of their games thereafter but weren't able to catch the Cardinals. But thanks to the Wild Card, they clinched a trip to the postseason on the final day of the season, edging out the Philadelphia Phillies by a single game.

The Astros climbed out of the NL Central cellar with a performance increase across the board. This is clearly shown in the Astros' Team Batting and Pitching/Fielding Stats by Month table in our statistics section. Note the significant increase from May to June and July for OBP (.290 to .329 and .340) and SLG (.365 to .421 and .549) as well as a significant decrease in FIP (4.59 to 3.62 and 3.32) and an increase in DER (.697 to .706 and .733). They weren't as great in August and September, but at that point, they were simply good enough to fend off the other Wild Card hopefuls.

Well, someone needs credit for this turnaround. Let's start with first baseman Lance Berkman, who didn't return to action until May 6 due to offseason knee surgery. He was terrible the remainder of May—.234/.337/.325—but would crush the ball in June (.308/.427/.538) and July (.362/.455/.638). Outfielders Willy Taveras and Jason Lane also significantly increased their run production from their putrid May performances, while second baseman Craig Biggio, third baseman Morgan Ensberg and company were more consistent.

But what about Houston's pitching? It appears the May culprits were Andy Pettitte (3.98 ERA in 31.2 innings in May), Brad Lidge (4.72 ERA in 13.1 innings), Ezequiel Astacio (10.98 ERA in 19.2 innings), and essentially all the other relievers except for Dan Wheeler. But Pettitte and Lidge rebounded to post great numbers the rest of the season, and Roy Oswalt also improved from a 3.20 ERA in 39.1 innings in May to 1.71 ERA in 99.1 innings in June and July.

It should be noted that a flurry of various illnesses besieged the Astros in the early part of the season, and it wouldn't be surprising if this was the cause of their May performance.

And, of course, their postseason odds were greatly increased by the overall outstanding pitching from not only Pettitte (222.1 innings, 174 ERA+), Oswalt (241.2, 141 ERA+), Lidge (70.2 innings, 181 ERA+), Wheeler (73.1 innings, 188 ERA+) and Chad Qualls (79.2 innings, 127 ERA+), but also a Texas native who allowed only 44 earned runs in 211.1 innings (that's a 1.87 RA, 221 ERA+, folks) in a shocking performance. Why shocking? Because future Hall of Famer Roger Clemens is 42 years old!

To dominate the NL as Clemens did in 2005 is simply amazing, especially considering he's the only pitcher to date on the single-season ERA+ leaderboard (minimum 1 inning per team game and 1 decision for every 10 team games) who posted a 200 ERA+ or better and was at least 40 years old. The only season by a pitcher in his 40s that was arguably better (and only because of more innings) was Cy Young's 41-year-old season in 1908 when he pitched 299 innings (87.2 innings more than Clemens) with an ERA+ of 194. Not one other pitcher in his 40s is found on the ERA+ list that contains 100 individual seasons (list found at www.baseball-reference.com).

Clemens only won 13 games, however, due to lack of run support (only 3.56 runs per nine innings with league average at 4.45), as Houston's offense ranked in the bottom fourth of the league in run production. While Berkman, Ensberg, Biggio and Lane positively contributed at the plate, catcher Brad Ausmus, shortstop Adam Everett, left fielder Chris Burke, center fielder Taveras and utility man Mike Lamb couldn't even muster OPS+ numbers greater than 90. And only fourth outfielder Orlando Palmeiro contributed off of the bench.

Though not contending for even the Wild Card spot, the Milwaukee Brewers nonetheless were impressive for two reasons. They didn't suffer a losing season, the first time they've accomplished that since 1992 when they finished second to the Blue Jays (the World Series champs that year) in the AL East. They also played well without any significant above-average contribution from their promising rookies (shortstop J.J. Hardy, second baseman Rickie Weeks, first baseman Prince Fielder and starting pitcher Jose Capellan), which indicates they just might be able to compete in the immediate future should these rookies develop and their current veterans remain productive.

I should note that in September of 1992, Bud Selig, the owner in control of the Brewers, was chosen as the chairman of MLB's executive council and appointed acting commissioner. I should also point out that Selig and company sold the Brewers to Mark Attanasio before the 2005 season. So during the duration of Selig's tenure as an owner and commissioner, the Brewers were lousy. But immediately prior to his appointment, they were good, and the very first season with a new owner, they reached .500 and most likely will have a bright future.

Leading the Brewers' average offense were first baseman Lyle Overbay, outfielders Carlos Lee, Brady Clark and Geoff Jenkins, and utility infielder Bill Hall (who improved from a 70 OPS+ in 2004 in 415 PA to a 117 OPS+ in 2005 in 546 PA; the other four essentially produced as expected based on career statistics).

The only area perhaps better than average in Milwaukee was the pitching, as a waiver claim from the Los Angeles Angels of Anaheim at the end of last season turned into their dominant closer (a position that was open thanks to a shrewd trade of veteran Danny Kolb to Atlanta for Capellan). Derrick Turnbow, with only 59.2 innings over the past four years in Anaheim, recorded his first save on April 24 and stayed in the closer role for the remainder of the season. He finished with 67.1 innings and a 243 ERA+.

Doug Davis, signed in 2003 after clearing waivers, continued to impress in Milwaukee (222.2 innings, 110 ERA+), joining Ben Sheets (who suffered a few injuries and only threw 156.2 innings, but 127 ERA+) and Chris Capuano (219 innings, 106 ERA+) to form a solid front end of the rotation for the Brewers.

Meanwhile, 88 miles south in Chicago, the Cubs were flirting with Wild Card status through June but then went 13-15 in July and 10-18 in August, eliminating them from contention. With just average offense and defense, the bright spots on the disappointing season were first baseman Derrek Lee (for his production) and starting pitcher Greg Maddux (for his career achievement).

Lee started the season strong and actually led the league in all three Triple Crown categories (batting average, home runs, RBI) as late as July 22. He would finish the season (691 PA, 177 OPS+) as arguably the best hitter in the National League.

Maddux, on the season, was average as a pitcher (225 innings, 101 ERA+), but he made history on July 26 when he struck out Omar Vizquel, becoming only the 13th player in the history of MLB to strike out 3,000 batters in a career. Maddux would unfortunately only

win 13 games, ending a 17-year run of winning at least 15 games in a season.

Lack of playing time from shortstop Nomar Garciaparra (only 247 PA, 99 OPS+) and a dismal season out in center field by Corey Patterson (481 PA, 56 OPS+) hurt the Cubs. It also didn't help, offensively, to have Neifi Perez (609 PA, 77 OPS+) filling in for Garciaparra.

Notable contributions also came from third baseman Aramis Ramirez (506 PA, 137 OPS+) and starting pitcher Carlos Zambrano (223.1 innings, 131 ERA+). Zambrano has actually been the best and most consistent pitcher for the Cubs, as pitchers Mark Prior and Kerry Wood have struggled with injuries, despite high expectations for the two (and rightfully so after their excellent 2003 season, when they led the Cubs to the NL Central title).

Cincinnati would be so lucky to even sniff Wild Card status. Instead the Reds tumbled early (30-47 and in the cellar on June 30) and even a second half surge (17-11 in July, 15-12 in August) couldn't save their season (11-19 after August). And this occurred in spite of having the best park-adjusted offense in the National League. How is this possible? Well, they also had the worst park-adjusted run prevention. So it wasn't surprising when manager Dave Miley and pitching coach Don Gullett were dismissed on June 21 and replaced by Jerry Narron and Vern Ruhle.

Center fielder Ken Griffey Jr. and left fielder Adam Dunn led a Cincinnati offense in which almost every hitter contributed positively. Griffey actually managed to play in 128 games (555 PA, 138 OPS+) after playing in just 70, 53 and 83 games the last three seasons due to various injuries. As a result of his ability to stay in the starting lineup until September 4, and maintain his career value (at least at the plate), Griffey was voted by the fans as the NL's Comeback Player of the Year.

The Reds' pitching should not even be discussed, but Eric Milton's season cannot be dismissed. Signed before the season to a three-year deal, Milton produced one of the worst seasons of all time, throwing 186.1 innings with an ERA+ of 69. He set the single-season team record for home runs allowed, letting 40 balls leave the park.

Actually, Aaron Harang and Brandon Claussen, both young pitchers, pitched well (211.2 innings, 116 ERA+ and 166.2 innings, 105 ERA+, respectively) in the starting rotation, and Dave Weathers (77.2 innings, 113 ERA+), Kent Mercker (61.2 innings, 122 ERA+) and Matt Belisle (85.2 innings, 101 ERA+) contributed from the pen.

In Pittsburgh, the Pirates were a hopeful 30-30 on June 11, but then went 37-65 afterwards to clinch the cellar spot in the NL Central. This performance cost manager Lloyd McClendon his job, as he was fired on September 6 and replaced by bench coach Pete Mackanin for the remainder of the season.

Not all hope is lost in Pittsburgh, however, as their future offense can be built around 26-year-old Jason Bay (599 PA, 148 OPS+ in 2005) while their pitching can be led by 22-year-old Zach Duke (84.2 innings, 236 ERA+) and 23-year-old Pat Maholm (41.1 innings, 196 ERA+). If Oliver Perez can rebound from his terrible 2005 season (103 innings, 73 ERA+) and return to his 2004 form (196 innings, 139 ERA+), the Pirates could have three exceptional arms fronting their rotation.

So in the end, the Cardinals and Astros once again return to the postseason, while the Cubs declined from their 2003 and 2004 success. The Brewers are hoping to improve upon their 2005 performance, especially with their top prospects now playing with the parent club. Meanwhile, the Reds need to find average pitching to join Harang and Claussen, while the Pirates have to surround Bay with some good hitters and hope Oliver Perez can rebound. Thanks to the Wild Card position and a well-balanced league in terms of parity and economics (sort of), all of these teams realistically have a shot at the postseason next year. It just depends on their offseason additions and subtractions, as well as a little bit of luck with regards to injuries and the ball bouncing in their favor.

National League West Review

by Steve Treder

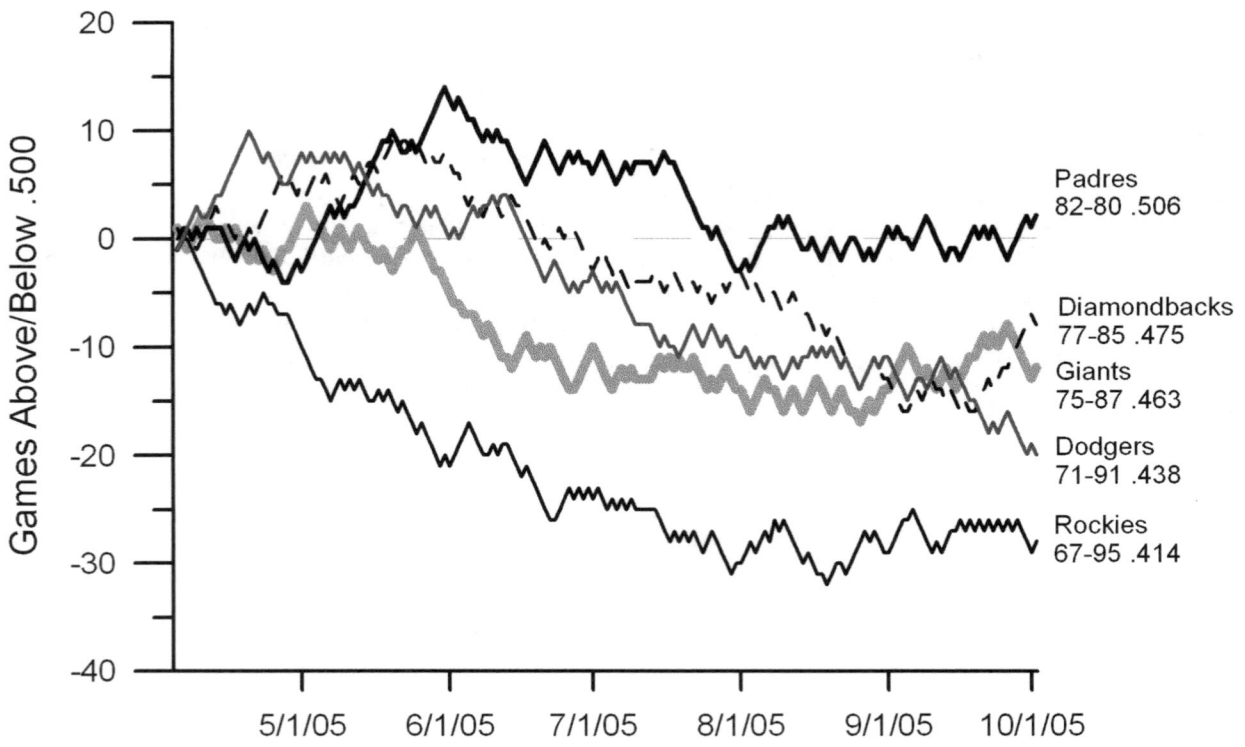

Padres
82-80 .506

Diamondbacks
77-85 .475

Giants
75-87 .463

Dodgers
71-91 .438

Rockies
67-95 .414

Say what you will about this division, it stimulated the mastery of vocabulary. I mean, watching this slow-motion train wreck unfold all season long, week after wincing week, whose powers of description weren't challenged? How best to sum up this darkly farcical production? Which acid-tongued adjective captures it most suitably?

The division-champion team in the 2005 National League West had a winning percentage of .506, which is the lowest of any full-season division winner in history. The aggregate winning (?) percentage of the division was .459, also the lowest of any full-season division in history. The only division that has ever outdone (?) this year's NL West was the 1994 American League West Division, which was wheezing along at a cumulative .437 in early-mid-August when work stoppage aborted the season, with the Texas Rangers leading (?) at 52-62, .456. While a strike-shortened season can only tentatively be compared with a completed one, it might be that this year's National League West was not the worst division in the history of divisions. But it also remains entirely conceivable, all things considered, that it *was*. At any rate, this was a division that was unquestionably … well, what is the word, exactly, that describes it?

Here at THT, we spare no effort in providing you with the very best. So, we went straight to the source

of all matters descriptive and inquired of none other than the English alphabet itself to offer its fullest observations.

The alphabet's Front End—breezy, stylish, nicely tanned—confidently provided us with some worthy candidates. Right away it offered a description of this division with which no one can disagree: "ailing." Nor could we argue with the other suggestions the Front End presented, in its laid-back surfer drawl: "anemic, appalling, atrocious, and awful," and, of course, the Front End's evergreen "bad." The Front End went on to offer the more-than-apt "bleak," as well as the well-put "cheerless." But it was with its letter "d" that the Front End demonstrated its best stuff, describing our '05 NL West as "decayed, decrepit, defective, deficient, depressing, deprived, despicable, desolate, destitute, detestable, dilapidated, dire, disgraceful, disfavored, dismal, distressing, downtrodden, drab, drained, dreadful, dreary, and dull." Dude!

Then the alphabet's solid, hearty Middle Range cheerfully asked to be heard, and in its modest, efficient manner, offered up gems. One can only agree with the depiction, presented in a chirpy Minnesota brogue (think Frances McDormand in *Fargo*) as, "enervated, exhausted, faint, faulty, feeble, flaccid, forlorn, fragile, frail, ghastly, gloomy, grim, hideous, hopeless, horrendous, horrific, indigent, ineffective, inert, inferior, lackluster, lame, lifeless, limp, loathsome, lousy, malodorous, meager, miserable, moldy, moribund, nasty, and needy." Oh, you betcha.

But for my money, the most spot-on descriptors were those provided by the black-leather-jacketed Back End of the alphabet. The most heavy-duty conjurers of images unattractive lurk on the alphabet's mean streets, far from the serene, sun-dappled Front End. In the dim recesses and dark alleys of workaday language, words are hardier, tougher; they don't waste energy on nuance or subtlety. These words don't mess around, they just get it done. Ah, yes. This is where we encountered the truest and finest linguistic portrayal of the 2005 National League West Division, spat out in a Joe Pesci Back End snarl: "pathetic, pitiful, poor, puny, putrid, reeking, repulsive, revolting, rotten, sad, sagging, scanty, scrawny, shabby, shameful, shocking, shoddy, shriveled, sickly, smelly, sorry, stinking, stupid, terrible, tired, torpid, trashy, ugly, useless, vile, wanting, weak, weedy, and wretched."

I think I like "weedy" the best of all. This was unquestionably your *weediest* of divisions.

The San Diego Padres were the 2005 NL West Champions, which is a bit like declaring someone the best singer in Milli Vanilli. Taking place in any other divisional context, the '05 Padres' season would be considered a letdown, a step backward from their very encouraging 87-75, third-place performance of 2004. San Diego's 2005 record was an uninspiring 82-80 (including a 34-39 post-All-Star sag), and they were lucky to achieve that, allowing 42 more runs than they scored for a 77-85 Pythagorean mark. Truly, more things went wrong than right for the Padres in 2005:

- They were bedeviled by significant injuries to shortstop Khalil Greene, second baseman Mark Loretta, catcher Ramon Hernandez and starting pitcher Adam Eaton.
- Sean Burroughs, the 24-year-old third baseman who a couple of years ago looked like a can't-miss star, regressed so badly he spent most of the second half in the minors.
- Longtime cleanup hitter Phil Nevin struggled and was dumped off to the Texas Rangers at the trade deadline in exchange for starting pitcher Chan Ho Park, who wasn't any good either.
- Starter Brian Lawrence, a 15-game winner in 2004, skidded to 7-15, 4.83.
- Veteran starter Woody Williams, at age 38, suffered his first losing season since 1998, slogging through a 9-12, 4.85 campaign.

The Padres were able to achieve the modest success they did thanks primarily to outstanding years from right fielder Brian Giles (.301/.423/.483, fourth in the NL with 35 Win Shares) and ace starter Jake Peavy (13-7, 2.88, with a league-leading 216 strikeouts). They enjoyed outstanding bullpen work, in support of eversteady closer Trevor Hoffman, from erstwhile journeymen Scott Linebrink (8-1, 1.83 in 73 games, 74 innings) and Rudy Seanez (7-1, 2.69, including 84 strikeouts in 60 innings). And the Padres got a pleasant surprise in 35-year-old warhorse Pedro Astacio, salvaged off the scrap heap in July, who turned in a 4-2, 3.17 performance as a starter.

Two veterans were solid in semi-regular platoon roles: 33-year-old center fielder Dave Roberts (.275/.356/.428), and 34-year-old left fielder Ryan Klesko (.248/.358/.418). San Diego also received excellent bench contributions from two veteran utility men, first baseman/outfielder Mark Sweeney (.294/.395/.466) and infielder/outfielder Damian Jackson (.255/.335/.342, plus 15-for-17 base stealing and outstanding defensive versatility).

The Arizona Diamondbacks had a season that was simply weird. To begin with, they finished in second place despite a record of 77-85, but that mark was a tremendous leap forward from their 51-111 fiasco of 2004. Yet the 77-85 mark was also misleading, given that the '05 Diamondbacks were outscored by a margin of 160 runs; they outperformed their Pythagorean record by a whopping 12 wins, by far the most in the major leagues in 2005 and among the widest margins in history.

The D-backs were wildly inconsistent. They started strong, and in late May were sparring with the Padres for first place. Then the pitching collapsed, and through June and early July, Arizona went into a 12-25 free fall. They then stabilized for a while, only to suffer yet another staff meltdown: in the course of a 9-19 August, the Diamondbacks were hammered by such scores as 10-5, 11-3, 13-8, 13-6, 14-7, 14-1, 17-3, and 18-4. By early September they had fallen to fourth place, and it appeared their Houdini act of defying Pythagorean norms had been exposed as Snake oil, but then the wily rattlers rebounded with a strong final month and reclaimed second place.

The season might be seen as a mixed blessing for Arizona fans. On the one hand, the 26-game improvement over 2004 had to be considered a rousing success, but on the other, the Diamondbacks' capacity to build upon it is clouded by two factors. First, as we've observed, is its Pythag-suggested flukiness. Second is the fact that many of the 2005 team's key contributors were veterans on the far side of 30: first baseman Tony Clark (coming out of nowhere at 33 with a .304,

30-homer contribution in 349 at-bats), left fielder Luis Gonzalez (37 doubles and 90 runs scored at age 37), second baseman Craig Counsell (having pretty much a career year—such as it was—at 34) and right fielder Shawn Green (not worth his $8.5 million salary, but a solid performance at age 32). The Diamondbacks also got a 37-homer season from 28-year-old third baseman Troy Glaus, but it was his first time avoiding serious injury in three years, and he was limping at the end.

Three of Arizona's best young talents clearly did step forward: 25-year-old first baseman/outfielder Chad Tracy (308/359/553), 26-year-old ace starter Brandon Webb (14-12, 3.54, reducing his walks from 119 to 59) and 25-year-old relief ace Jose Valverde (2.44 ERA and 75 strikeouts in 66 innings). But they got a poor return on extravagant investments in two big-name starters. Eleven-million-dollar man Javier Vazquez, acquired in trade for Randy Johnson, was up-and-down: 192 strikeouts but 35 homers allowed and an 11-15, 4.42 result. Russ Ortiz, signed to a 4-year, $33 million free-agent deal, was nothing but down, a spectacular flop at 5-11, 6.89.

For the first time since 1992, the San Francisco Giants experienced a season essentially without Barry Bonds, and the results were predictably negative, as the Giants fell from 91-71 to 75-87. To make matters worse, many of the team's problems were clearly the result of issues other than their superduperstar's near-season-long absence:

- Ace Jason Schmidt battled chronic arm trouble and fell from Cy Young-candidate status to just another starter at 12-7, 4.40.

- Projected closer Armando Benitez, signed to a three-year deal in the offseason, missed most of the year with a serious hamstring injury, and was able to contribute only a 4.50 ERA in 30 innings.

- Jerome Williams, the 23-year-old third-year starter widely considered a potential star, fell out of favor with management and was farmed out and then traded to the Cubs for veteran reliever LaTroy Hawkins, who was so-so at best.

- Edgardo Alfonzo, the 31-year-old third baseman making $7.5 million in the third year of a four-year contract, spent more than a month on the DL and hit a punchless .277/.327/.345.

- Several others on the team's ultraveteran roster fought chronic injuries, including 39-year-old slugging outfielder Moises Alou, 33-year-old second baseman Ray Durham and 37-year-old first baseman J.T. Snow.

The result was a ball club without any particular strength, patching together makeshift lineups, struggling to score runs, thin in both starting and relief pitching.

Nonetheless, the Giants were able to forestall complete collapse, and in the season's closing weeks, they even mildly threatened to catch the Padres for the division's joke of a first place. Several things did go well in San Francisco. Twenty-four-year-old sophomore left-hander Noah Lowry came on very strong in the second half, finishing 13-13, 3.78 with 172 strikeouts. Trade-deadline acquisition center fielder Randy Winn unleashed an incredibly torrid September (in 114 at-bats, an astonishing .447 batting average and .877 slugging percentage) to set career highs, at age 31, in hits, doubles, homers, average, and slugging. And 20-year-old rookie right-hander Matt Cain came up in late August and mowed down major league hitters in seven starts, allowing just 24 hits in 46 innings while compiling a 2.33 ERA.

Bonds did return, of course, though only in mid-September and obviously still significantly bothered by his right knee. But he showed that even at age 41, hobbling, in far-from-peak shape, badgered by the steroid-scandal-focused media, a magnet for hostile opposing fans (though treated to thunderous standing ovations at home), the big fellow could still really hit: 5 homers in his very brief 42-at-bat season, bringing his career total to a tantalizing 708.

For the Los Angeles Dodgers, 2005 was the quintessential Murphy's Law season—and then some, as even a few things that *couldn't* go wrong seemed to find a way to do so. Things didn't start out that way, as the defending division champs, despite having peerless closer Eric Gagne on the shelf, bolted out of the gate at 12-2. They hit a rough patch in mid-May and fell out of first place, but at that point Gagne returned and recorded his first save on May 26. The burly Quebecois then began racking them up with his accustomed alacrity, and on June 12, Gagne picked up his eighth save (and had 22 strikeouts in 13 innings), and the Dodgers were at 33-29, breathing down the Padres' necks.

It was at precisely this point that things began to go to hell in a hand basket. That Gagne appearance proved to be his last of the year, and his replacement at closer, Yhency Brazoban, utterly unraveled in July and August. Worse yet, Gagne's elbow injury was only one on a staggeringly long list of Los Angeles medical calamities. Most significantly, in early July right fielder J.D. Drew, hitting .286/.412/.520, broke his wrist and was lost for the season; center fielder Milton Bradley (who hit .290/.350/.484) was limited by multiple ailments to just 75 games; and defensive whiz shortstop Cesar Izturis, hitting .345 on June 1, struggled mightily with back trouble the rest of the way, watching his average caree to .257 before being forced, most alarmingly, to shut it down for the season in early September and undergo Tommy John surgery on his throwing arm.

Following June 12, the Dodgers lost 23 of 31 and were never close to .500 again. Yet another bad slump in September sentenced them to a 71-91 finish, their worst since 1992. The lone key Dodger who might have been considered to be doing splendidly—37-year-old free agent acquisition second baseman Jeff Kent, healthy all year long, and punishing pitchers at the rate of .289/.377/.512—was reported to be feuding with the mercurial Bradley, as even clubhouse harmony was apparently a casualty. On top of everything else, manager Jim Tracy was evidently at odds with sophomore GM Paul DePodesta over how best to deploy 26-year-old power-hitting first baseman Hee-Seop Choi. Tracy gave Choi, who hit .253/.336/.453, just 78 starts, and given all the turmoil, it wasn't surprising that Tracy was fired at season's end. Then Depodesta himself was sacked, completing the sense of meltdown.

A few things went okay for the Dodgers. Derek Lowe (12-15, 3.61 in 222 innings), Jeff Weaver (14-11, 4.22 in 224 innings) and Brad Penny (7-9, 3.90 in 175 innings) provided solid, if unspectacular, starting pitching. And two highly touted rookies, 21-year-old catcher Dioner Navarro and 22-year-old third baseman Willy Aybar, performed well in late-season opportunities.

It's a measure of the chronic futility of the Colorado Rockies franchise that their 67-95, last-place season might have been, all things considered, a positive step forward. Obviously it wasn't in terms of on-field results (it was their worst showing since their first-year expansion performance in 1993), but at least in 2005, for once, *at last*, the Rockies made a priority of granting space for young players to develop. For the first time in a very long while, Colorado's lineup wasn't fully stocked with "proven veteran" mediocrities.

This isn't to say that the youthful talent to which the Rockies committed in 2005 will necessarily blossom, and clearly they struggled plenty this year. But there is at least the *possibility* that the experience gained by several of the '05 Rockies will pay off in improvement down the road, and this couldn't be said of many recent Colorado teams.

Two Rockie youngsters were particularly interesting. Twenty-five-year-old left fielder Matt Holliday missed five weeks with a broken finger, and his .307/.361/.505 stat line wasn't overly impressive given the mile-high context, but he showed a breadth of skill, including genuine power and good speed. Twenty-four-year-old starter Jeff Francis went 14-12, though with a typically Rockie-ish 5.68 ERA in 183 innings—but the interesting thing about Francis is that his ERA was significantly better *at home* (4.88) than at lower altitudes (6.40); this very atypical pattern alone is reason enough to keep an eye on him.

Other young Rockies who got a lot of playing time included 25-year-old third baseman Garrett Atkins (.339/.395/.508 at home, .238/.301/.347 away), 26-year-old shortstop Clint Barmes (.332/.369/.508 at home, .239/.286/.350 away), 26-year-old second baseman Luis Gonzalez (whose .292/.333/.421 overall line was about the same home and away), and 25-year-old center fielder Cory Sullivan (.348/.406/.438 at home, .245/.286/.340 away).

Two older Rockies stood out. Longtime star first baseman Todd Helton turned 32 in August, was bothered by injuries and generally had his least impressive showing since 1998, but his .381 average following late June demonstrated that he remains a formidable hitter. Twenty-nine-year-old journeyman reliever Brian Fuentes won the closer role and was extremely good, with 91 strikeouts in 74 innings and virtually identical ERAs at home and on the road; his 2.91 overall ERA was in fact the best ever posted by a Colorado closer.

But they wouldn't be the Rockies if they didn't pull off at least a couple of head-scratchers. Twenty-seven-year-old Shawn Chacon, back in the starting rotation after a disastrous turn at closer in 2004, had a 1-7 record in late July but otherwise decent stats (4.09 ERA). He then was pointlessly dumped off to the Yankees, for whom he went 7-3, 2.85 the rest of the way. And in mid-July, the Rockies shipped two serviceable pitchers (Joe Kennedy and Jay Witasick) to Oakland for nothing-special outfielder Eric Byrnes, and then two weeks later swapped Byrnes to Baltimore for another nothing-special outfielder, Larry Bigbie, who generally rode the bench.

So think of the 2005 National League West Division as a crossword puzzle. It's a big one, a Sunday *New York Times* humdinger. And its every entry—across and down, from top to bottom—is another synonym for "weak." It turns out there are many, many different ways to express the concept, and this division demonstrated that there are also many, many different ways to animate it.

Perhaps "2005 NL West" will someday itself be a term employed as a symbol of profound futility ...

"How was your golf game yesterday, Steve?"

"Um, well, let me put it this way: I really '05 NL Wested it out there."

"Ouch."

"Tell me about it."

Postseason Review

by Aaron Gleeman and Dave Studenmund

On The Hardball Times website (www.hardball-times.com), we track something called "Win Probability Added." It's not so much a new statistic as a new way of watching a game, and we wrote several columns during the year reviewing the WPA of regular-season games. To give a sense of what WPA is, here's an excerpt from Dave Studenmund's initial article on the subject:

> *Here's the basic idea. An average team, at any point in a game, has a certain likelihood of winning the game. For instance, if you're leading by two runs in the ninth inning, your chances of winning the game are much greater than if you're leading by three runs in the first inning. With each change in the score, inning, number of outs, base situation or even pitch, there is a change in the average team's probability of winning the game.*

The trick is to develop the correct math for calculating Win Probability. Thanks to the efforts of baseball analysts like Keith Woolner and Doug Drinen, and the Tangotiger website (www.tangotiger.net), you can now build your own spreadsheet to calculate Win Probability and track it during games. So we did. In fact, we tracked Win Probability throughout the postseason, including every play of the World Series.

The impact of each play and its impact on the game's Win Probability was logged as "Win Probability Added" (WPA) and assigned to specific players. In the WPA system, each team begins with a 50% chance of winning the game. During the game, the probabilities move up and down, depending on the score and the plays, until one team is at 100% and the other is at 0%. In other words, when the game is over.

When you sum up everything at the end, the winning team has added 50 WPA points (going from 50% at the beginning to 100% at the end) and the losing team has lost 50 WPA points. That's the system in a nutshell. You should be able to pick it up as we review the postseason and then use it to analyze each World Series game.

ALDS: Boston Red Sox vs. Chicago White Sox

In a series that was supposed to pit what was arguably baseball's best offense against what was arguably baseball's best pitching, the White Sox inexplicably opened up their blitz through the postseason by turning into the Red Sox. Amidst talk of "small-ball" and "doing the little things," the White Sox smacked five home runs in Game 1, including two from A.J. Pierzynski, and destroyed the Red Sox 14-2.

Tabbed by manager Ozzie Guillen to start Game 1 over Mark Buehrle, Jose Contreras pitched very well, limiting the powerful Boston lineup to two runs over 7.2 innings. Of course, it helped that Contreras was pitching with a huge lead all game, as Chicago jumped out to a 5-0 lead in the first inning thanks to Pierzynski's three-run shot off Matt Clement. Chicago added another run in the third, two more in the fourth, four more in the sixth, and put the finishing touches on the blowout with two runs in the eighth.

In all, 10 of the White Sox's 14 runs came by way of the long ball and a graph of Chicago's WP from the beginning of the game until the end shows just how dominant Chicago was:

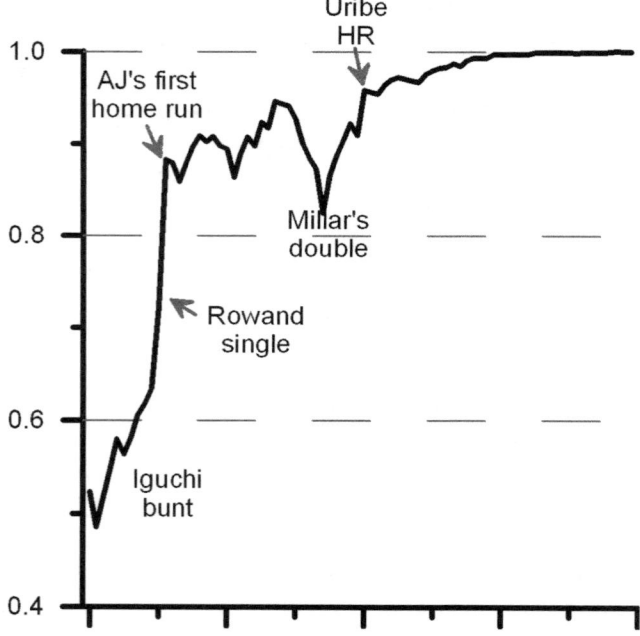

When Pierzynski's homer put Chicago up 5-0 in the first, their Win Probability was already at 88%, and it never fell below 80%. Interestingly, the White Sox laid down one sacrifice bunt in the game, as Guillen had Tadahito Iguchi move Scott Podsednik over with the game still tied at zero in the first. The move actually *lowered* Chicago's WP from 58.0% to 56.4%, and mattered little once the fireworks started.

Chicago won Game 2 in more typical fashion; keeping the game close, taking the lead with a home run, and turning the ball over to Bobby Jenks to slam the door in the ninth. Down 4-0 in the fifth, Chicago mounted a comeback with two singles and a double to cut Boston's lead to 4-2. With Joe Crede on first base and one out, Juan Uribe hit a grounder to Red Sox second baseman Tony Graffanino that could only be described as tailor-made for an inning-ending double play.

In a Buckner-esque moment, Graffanino got into position to field the ball and flip it to second base, and instead watched as it rolled under his glove. Uribe was safe at first, Crede advanced to third, and two batters later Iguchi gave the White Sox a 5-4 lead with a three-run homer off David Wells. As was the case all season, Chicago's bullpen held tight to the lead, as Jenks relieved Buehrle in the eighth and pitched two scoreless frames to close out the 5-4 win.

Chicago finished off the sweep in Game 3 by again using their season-long recipe for success. With the score tied at two in the sixth, Paul Konerko launched a two-run homer off Tim Wakefield over the Green Monster and then the bullpen—which this time included an amazing performance from Orlando Hernandez before the game was put into Jenks' hands—went to work.

El Duque's outing was one the highlights of the postseason. He came out of the bullpen in the sixth inning, relieving Damaso Marte with the White Sox clinging to a one-run lead. Boston had the bases loaded, no outs, and Jason Varitek at the plate—Boston's WP for the game was 66.2% despite the fact that they were still trailing.

Hernandez coaxed a harmless pop up out of Varitek, raising Chicago's WP from 33.8% to 44.0%. He induced another pop up from Graffanino, as Chicago's WP suddenly jumped over 50% to 55.8%. And then Hernandez finished his masterpiece by striking out Johnny Damon in an eight-pitch at-bat that had El Duque throwing everything in his expansive arsenal up to the plate, including several kitchen sinks.

The White Sox were out of the jam, their WP was back up to 68.2%, and they were once again in control of the game. Hernandez retired six of the next seven batters he faced, turned things over to Jenks in the ninth, and the White Sox were headed to the ALCS. When handing out WPA credit for Game 3 to individual players, El Duque comes out looking like the hero. And to think, he was nearly left off the postseason roster!

NLDS: San Diego Padres vs. St. Louis Cardinals

What looked like the most lopsided postseason match up turned out to be just that, as the Cardinals swept the Padres in three games to advance to the NLCS. The Game 1 match up of aces, with Chris Carpenter going up against Jake Peavy, never materialized, as St. Louis got to Peavy early and often. Peavy's final line (4.1 innings, 8 H, 8 R, 8 ER, 3 BB, 3 SO, 2 HR, 16.62 ERA) was ugly, and it was revealed shortly after the game that he had a broken rib thanks to celebrating the Padres' NL West championship.

Remarkably, the Padres made things interesting once Peavy left, climbing out of an 8-0 hole and knocking the Cardinals' bullpen around once Carpenter exited after six shutout innings. San Diego scored five runs in the final three innings to make the score 8-5, and with two outs in the top of the ninth loaded up the bases and brought the go-ahead run to the plate in Ramon Hernandez. After giving up four hits to put San Diego back in the game, Jason Isringhausen ended the Padres' comeback by striking Hernandez out on three pitches.

Much was made of whether or not Peavy could come back to start Game 4 or 5 if the Padres extended the series, but it never became an issue. The Cardinals jumped out to an early 4-0 lead in Game 2, as Mark Mulder tossed shutout ball into the seventh despite being hit in the left arm with a second-inning line drive. St. Louis' bullpen once again gave the Padres some hope, as San Diego loaded the bases with two outs and the score 6-2 in the eighth, but Randy Flores relieved Julian Tavarez and came up with a big strikeout of Mark Sweeney.

At home for Game 3 and their backs against the wall, the Padres once again fell behind big early. Woody Williams was knocked out after recording just four outs, as a David Eckstein homer and a slew of singles and doubles put the Cardinals up 5-0 after two innings. St. Louis added two more runs in the fifth to make it 7-0 and held off yet another late charge by San Diego's offense to take the game 7-4 and complete the first-round sweep.

NLDS: Houston Astros vs. Atlanta Braves

After dropping two of the first three games, the Braves appeared set to even up the series in Game 4 and send the NLDS to an all-or-nothing Game 5. Atlanta took a 5-0 lead thanks to Adam LaRoche's third-inning grand slam, and when Brian McCann led off the eighth with a solo homer the Braves were leading 6-1 with six outs left to get. Atlanta's WP was at 98.1%, and that's when things got interesting.

Tim Hudson, who had held the Astros to a lone run through seven innings, began to struggle, walking Brad Ausmus leading off the inning and allowing an infield single to Eric Bruntlett. With two men on and none out, manager Bobby Cox brought Kyle Farnsworth in from the bullpen despite the fact that Farnsworth had just one appearance all season that lasted two innings or more.

He got Craig Biggio to hit into a fielder's choice, with the Braves throwing Ausmus out at third base for the first out of the inning. And then it all fell apart. The Astros pulled off a double steal, Farnsworth walked Luke Scott, and Lance Berkman hit a grand slam into the Crawford Boxes in left field. Even with the implosion, the Braves still held a slim 6-5 lead, and Farnsworth escaped the inning by striking Morgan Ensberg out and getting Mike Lamb on a fly out.

Chad Qualls held the Braves scoreless in the top of the ninth and Farnsworth came out for the bottom of the inning to hold the one-run lead. He quickly recorded the first two outs and Ausmus came up again, this time as the potential tying run. With two outs, the Braves' WP was a healthy 95.2%. Ausmus got ahead in the count 2-0 and then tied the game with a home run off the column in left-center. Farnsworth got Bruntlett to strike out, ending the inning, but the damage had already been done.

The Braves had blown a 6-1 lead and were now headed to extra innings on the brink of elimination. Well, maybe "on the brink" is a bad choice of words, because the game was far from over. In fact, the Braves and Astros stayed tied at six for the next eight-and-a-half innings—nearly two complete-game shutouts—as pitchers shuffled in and out of the game while looking like Hall of Famers. And there was an actual Hall of Famer too, with Roger Clemens coming in from the bullpen to pitch three shutout innings of his own on two days' rest when the Astros ran out of other options.

Then, with the longest game in postseason history still knotted at six in the bottom of the 18th inning, Chris Burke stepped to the plate against fellow rookie Joey Devine, and delivered the series-winning homer into the seats in left field. It wasn't so much a classic, back-and-forth battle as it was a war of attrition, with both teams blowing several chances in extra frames. Burke's homer not only ended the series, it kept the game from lasting all night.

ALDS: New York Yankees vs. Los Angeles Angels

After splitting the first two games, the Angels took charge of Game 3 by knocking Randy Johnson around for five runs in three innings. The Yankees stormed back with four runs in the fourth to cut Los Angeles' lead to 5-4 and then actually took the lead with two more runs in the sixth, but the Angels kept pounding out hits—a team postseason record 19 to be exact—on their way to an 11-7 win.

After rain pushed Game 4 back a day, the Yankees turned to Shawn Chacon on the brink of elimination. He held the Angels scoreless through five innings before allowing two runs in the sixth, as Los Angeles took a 2-0 lead. Al Leiter and Mariano Rivera combined for 2.2 innings of scoreless relief, allowing the Yankees' offense to stage a comeback with three runs off the Angels' bullpen in the sixth and seventh innings. New York took the lead for good when Jorge Posada scampered home on a Derek Jeter grounder to third base, beating a poor throw from Chone Figgins.

The series-deciding fifth game was an odd one. The pitching match up of Bartolo Colon versus Mike Mussina was promising, but Colon left in the second inning with a shoulder injury and Mussina was yanked in the third after squandering a 2-0 lead by allowing five runs. Much like Clemens in the NLDS, Randy Johnson came out of New York's bullpen and pitched brilliantly with 4.1 shutout innings, but the Yankees' lineup couldn't put anything together against Colon's replacement, rookie Ervin Santana.

Santana looked shaky immediately after relieving Colon, which was to be expected considering he was on in an emergency spot. Miraculously, he settled down enough to hold the Yankees off the board for four straight innings, before allowing a solo homer from Jeter leading off the seventh. Manager Mike Scioscia gave Santana a quick hook, bringing Kelvim Escobar in to bridge the gap to closer Francisco Rodriguez. Holding a 5-3 lead in the ninth, Rodriguez made things interesting by giving up a leadoff single to Jeter.

With Jeter on first, the tying run came to the plate in the form of Alex Rodriguez, who hit .321 with 48 homers and 130 RBIs during the regular season. But whether the reputation is deserved or not, Rodriguez lived up to his "choker" label, grounding into a rally-killing double play. Jason Giambi started up another rally with a two-out single and the Yankees once again had the Angels on the ropes when Gary Sheffield reached on a squibber to third base. Like Rodriguez, Hideki Matsui couldn't come through when it mattered most, grounding out to first base to end the series.

As you can see from the WP graph below, the Angels were in serious trouble early on, especially considering Colon's quick exit. The Yankees had several opportunities to get back into the game, but simply couldn't come through with the big hits the team is so accustomed to getting in the postseason.

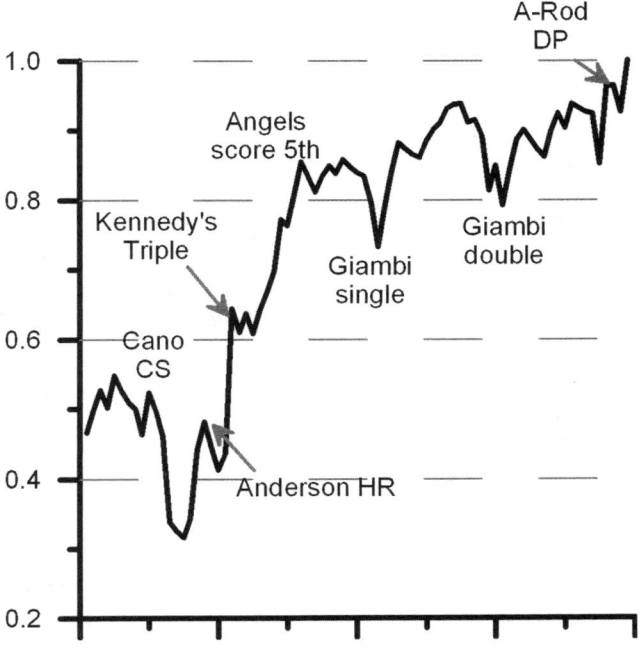

Rodriguez was labeled the goat, but New York's WP prior to his double play was just 11.2%—it dropped to 3.5% when the Angels turned two. The biggest play of the game? Adam Kennedy's triple with the Angels down 2-1 in the second inning. Kennedy hit a deep fly ball to right-center that scored two runs when Sheffield and Bubba Crosby collided trying to make the catch. The play put the Angels up 3-2—a lead they kept for the rest of the game—and bumped their WP from 43.6% to 64.4%.

ALCS: Los Angeles Angels vs. Chicago White Sox

Thanks to their five-game, rain-delayed ALDS win over the Yankees, the Angels entered the ALCS beat up and worn out. Game 1 began just a dozen hours after they arrived in Chicago, and Bartolo Colon's shoulder injury kept him out for the series. In addition to that, Jarrod Washburn was sick (he had his Game 4 start skipped in the division series), Ervin Santana had been used in relief of Colon a day earlier, and John Lackey had already pitched on short rest in place of Washburn. Their rotation was a mess.

The White Sox, meanwhile, were ready and rested, having finished off their sweep of the Red Sox four days earlier. Despite all of that, the Angels struck first, taking Game 1 3-2 after jumping out to an early 3-0 lead, and were in a great position to take Game 2 as well. And then A.J. Pierzynski came to the plate.

With Game 2 tied at 1-1 in the bottom of the ninth, Pierzynski appeared to strike out swinging to send the game to extra innings. But home-plate umpire Doug Eddings ruled that the ball hit the dirt before landing in catcher Josh Paul's glove. After initially taking a step back toward Chicago's dugout, Pierzynski sprinted to first base as chaos ensued. Paul had rolled the ball back to the mound and made his way to the dugout, and the Angels were unable to make a play on Pierzynski.

Eddings conferred with his fellow umpires, Mike Scioscia came storming out of the Angels' dugout to argue, and Fox showed the replay of Paul catching the third strike approximately 1,000 times. The call was upheld and, in a moment that was about as inevitable as it gets, the White Sox took advantage of the extra out when Pablo Ozuna pinch-ran for Pierzynski and stole second base, and Joe Crede laced a game-winning double down the left-field line.

Eddings's call certainly did not hand the White Sox the game. Rather than going to extra innings tied, they simply had a runner on first base with two outs in the ninth. What it did was give them some life, and when Kelvim Escobar threw a two-strike meatball over the plate to Crede, the White Sox took advantage. One good pitch from Escobar and Eddings's call would have mattered little. One good pitch from Escobar and the game goes to extra frames and everyone gets to see if Mark Buehrle would have come out to pitch a 10th inning after shutting the Angels down while using only 99 pitches through nine.

It would be easy to say that the Angels never recovered from Eddings's call and Crede's hit, and it would be hard to blame them. However, while they lost the next three games to lose the series 4-1, they did anything but give up. Instead, they simply couldn't do any damage against Chicago's outstanding pitching staff and the White Sox were able to score runs in bunches against the Angels' makeshift rotation.

After Buehrle's complete game in Game 2, Jon Garland followed with a complete game in Game 3, allowing just four hits and two runs. Game 4 was the same story, as the White Sox jumped out to a 3-0 lead on Paul Konerko's first-inning homer and the Angels managed just two runs against Freddy Garcia, who tossed Chicago's third straight complete game. And just for good measure, Jose Contreras went the distance in the series-clinching Game 5, holding the Angels to three runs while the White Sox came back from a 3-2 deficit to score four unanswered runs off Los Angeles' bullpen.

For the series, the Angels hit .179, scoring 11 runs in five games, and Chicago's starters put up the following lines:

Starter	IP	H	R	ER	BB	SO	HR	PIT
Contreras	8.1	7	3	3	0	4	1	102
Buehrle	9.0	5	1	1	0	4	1	99
Garland	9.0	4	2	2	1	7	1	118
Garcia	9.0	6	2	2	1	5	0	116
Contreras	9.0	5	3	3	2	2	0	114
TOTAL	44.1	27	11	11	4	22	3	549

The White Sox used their bullpen exactly one time in the five-game series, calling on Neal Cotts to record two outs in Game 1. After that it was all starting pitching, as Ozzie Guillen showed remarkable confidence in his rotation. Considering several of the crucial moments in the series came when the White Sox did damage against the Angels' bullpen, Guillen's trust in Contreras, Buehrle, Garland, and Garcia made a huge difference.

NLCS: Houston Astros vs. St. Louis Cardinals

Andy Pettitte went 11-2 with a 1.69 ERA in the second half and beat Atlanta in the NLDS, but the Cardinals had his number in Game 1. Reggie Sanders blasted a two-run homer in the first inning and St. Louis tacked on three more runs to make it 5-0 before the Astros put their first run on the board against Chris Carpenter in the seventh. Houston made things interesting in ninth, loading the bases with one out and the score 5-2, but Jason Isringhausen coaxed a sacrifice fly out of Brad Ausmus to make it 5-3 and then got Jose Vizcaino on a grounder to end the game.

Momentum quickly shifted and the Astros took the next three games behind outstanding starting pitching, as Roy Oswalt (7.0 IP, 1 ER), Roger Clemens (6.0 IP, 2 ER), and Brandon Backe (5.2 IP, 1 ER) combined to allow four runs in 18.2 innings. Brad Lidge came on for the save in all three wins, and Houston took a commanding 3-1 lead into Game 5.

With a 4-2 lead in the ninth, the Astros once again brought in Lidge from the bullpen. Lidge overpowered both John Rodriguez and John Mabry, getting two swinging strikeouts to put the Astros one out away from their first World Series. He then got ahead of David Eckstein 1-2, but Eckstein squeezed a single into left field to keep St. Louis' season alive. Jim Edmonds followed with a walk and suddenly Albert Pujols stepped to the plate as the go-ahead run while the champagne sat on ice in the Astros' clubhouse.

After taking strike one, Pujols unleashed a monstrous cut on Lidge's second offering, a hanging slider, sending it into orbit and over the train tracks in left field for

a no-doubt-about-it three-run homer. As THT's resident Cardinals fan, Brian Gunn, wrote in his euphoric write-up of the game: "Albert Pujols's home run may well stand as the most shocking turn of events I've ever seen in a game."

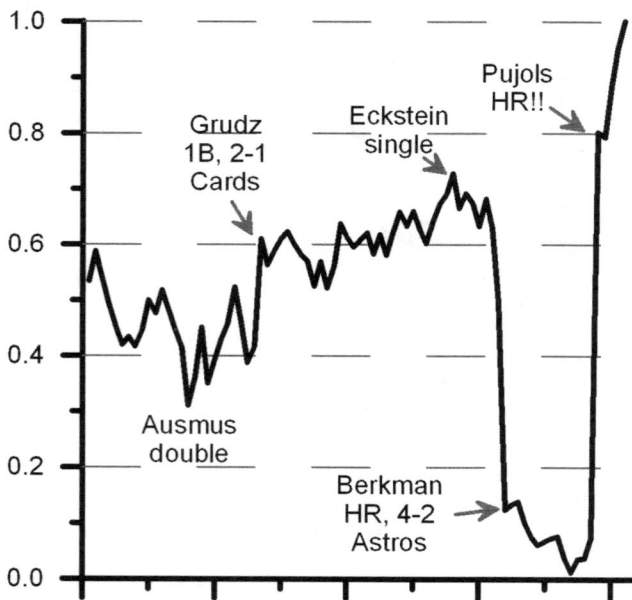

In the off day before Game 6, sports pages across the country were filled with columnists wondering how the Astros could possibly come back from such a painful, emotionally jarring loss. According to WP, the Cardinals were at 1.2% to win when Eckstein stepped to the plate and just 7.6% when Pujols came up. The answer was simple and turned out to be the same thing that carried Houston all season: Pitching.

Handed an early 3-0 lead in Game 6, Roy Oswalt held the powerful St. Louis lineup to one run over seven innings. As Brian Gunn wrote in eulogizing the Cardinals' season, "Roy Oswalt pitched like he was pissed off he had to fly to St. Louis." Armed with a 5-1 lead when he exited after seven strong innings, Oswalt turned things over to the bullpen. Chad Qualls and Dan Wheeler closed things out, sending the Astros to Chicago for Game 1 of the World Series while Lidge looked on from the bullpen.

World Series Game 1

Game 1 of the World Series featured a pitching matchup between the Astros' legendary Roger Clemens and the White Sox's second-half ace, Jose Contreras. But it didn't play like a pitching matchup. The White Sox struck quickly in the first inning when Jermaine Dye homered to up the Sox's WP to 60%, but Mike Lamb responded with a solo shot in the top of the second to knot the score and reduce the Sox's WP to 52%. Even though the score was tied, the Sox had a higher WP because the Astros had already made an out in the top of the second.

The action picked up in the bottom of the second. Carl Everett and Aaron Rowand hit back-to-back singles with no one out. While no runs had scored yet, the probability of scoring runs with two runners on and no one out is pretty high, so the Sox's WP jumped to 66%. Sure enough, A.J. Pierzynski's force out plated one run and then Juan Uribe hit a two-out double to score another. The score was 3-1 and the Sox's WP was 74% at the end of the inning.

The biggest hit of the inning was Uribe's, which added 9 WPA points for the Sox. But the second most important hit was Rowand's (8 WPA) even though he didn't score a run or gain an RBI, because it put runners on first and third with no outs. This is an example of how WPA can help you appreciate the ins and outs of a game in a way ordinary stats can't.

The Astros bounced right back in the third inning. Brad Ausmus and Craig Biggio singled and, after a sacrifice bunt, the Astros had runners on second and third with two outs and Lance Berkman at the plate. This was good for the Astros, but the Sox still had a 70% WP because there were two outs.

Berkman doubled to knot the score at three and the Sox's WP fell to 52%, giving Berkman a WPA of 18. This would turn out to be the biggest play of the game, one of many for Berkman throughout the series.

Joe Crede hit a home run in the bottom of the fourth to put the Sox back up 4-3 and raise their WP to 66% (Crede's HR had a WPA of 12). In the bottom of the fifth, the Sox threatened again, loading the bases with one out. In that situation their WP was 78%, but the Astros turned a nifty double play to lower it back to 65%, ending the inning, for a WPA of 13. In other words, that double play was just as important as Crede's home run. Double plays can do that.

The game had a few dramatic ups and downs the next two innings. Crede probably saved a couple of runs with his glove at third base; each play had a WPA of 9, so he gained 18 WPA points with his glove. Assigning WPA credit to pitchers and fielders is a judgment call, but there's no doubt that Crede made a huge impact defensively.

In general, the real WP action happens in the late innings of close games. Willy Taveras led off the eighth with a double and Berkman followed with a single. By putting runners on first and third with no outs, the Astros lowered the Sox's WP to 53%. But Neal Cotts struck out the next two batters to raise their WP to 74% (meaning Cotts picked up 21 WPA points in two plate appearances) and after Chris Burke stole second, Bobby Jenks finished the inning by striking out Jeff Bagwell. On that play alone,

the Sox's WP rose from 72% to 86%. There is no doubt that relief pitchers get their due in Win Probability.

In the top of the ninth, Podsednik hit a two-out RBI triple (WPA of 8, WP up to 93%) and Jenks closed out the bottom of the ninth to add the last seven WPA points. With so many ups and downs, it's useful to see how WP changed throughout a game. Here's a graph of Game 1 Win Probability:

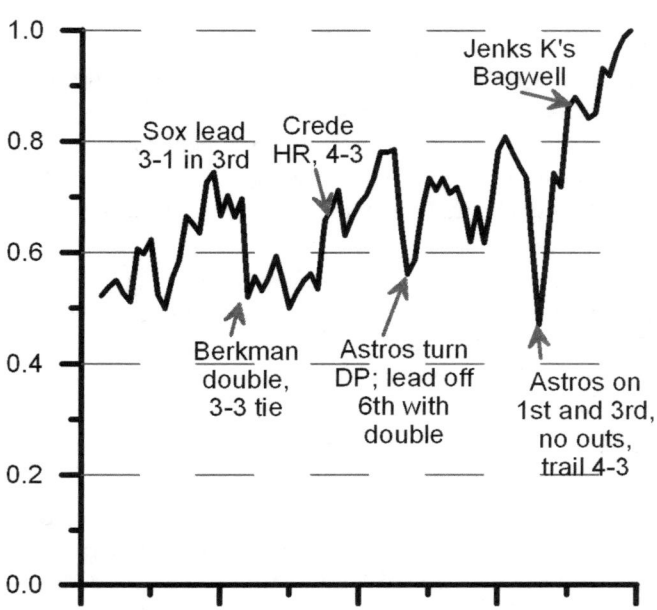

Adding up each play, Berkman actually led the game in WPA points with 27. The Sox's leaders were Crede (solo home run and two great plays in the field) and Jenks, with 27 and 21 WPA points, respectively. The lowest WPA totals went to Morgan Ensberg, who failed to come through in several critical situations (-27 points), and Roger Clemens, who allowed three runs before leaving with a hamstring injury (-26).

World Series Game 2

It was a miserable night for a ballgame; one of those October contests played in the cold rain against all common sense. The game would have been postponed during the regular season, but it had to be played in October because who wants to extend the baseball season into November?

But this second game of the World Series was a surprisingly entertaining affair filled with the familiar twists and turns of baseball. It included heroic efforts against the elements, great and bad plays in the field, clutch hits, and a bum umpiring call. In the end, the White Sox won 7-6 on a ninth-inning home run by the unlikeliest home run hitter of all.

This was perhaps the key game of the series. Both Andy Pettitte and Roy Oswalt were pitching extremely well for the Astros leading up to the World Series, and a

Chicago win required the Pale Hose to win at least one game against those two. With Pettitte on the mound opposing Mark Buehrle in Game 2, this was their first chance. Also, if the Astros managed to split the first two games in Chicago, they would be in a good position heading back to Houston.

In the top of the second inning Morgan Ensberg hit a solo homer to make the Astros' WP 60%. The Astros gave the momentum back in the bottom of the second, however, when Chris Burke misplayed a catchable fly ball at the wall in left and Craig Biggio just outright dropped a pop fly. In both cases, negative WPA credit went to the fielder, and the White Sox held a 2-1 lead at the end of the second inning, with a WP of 61%. The key play was a single by Crede, which tied the score at one and notched a WPA of 13.

The Astros came right back the next inning with a triple by Taveras (WPA of 8) and a sacrifice fly to tie the score. That's how things remained until the fifth inning, when the Astros took a 4-2 lead. The big hit was again supplied by Berkman: a double into the left-field corner to score two runs. The WPA of his hit was 25 (half a win's worth), the biggest play of the series up to that point.

Then came the bottom half of the seventh, the biggest inning of the series. Still trailing 4-2, the Sox managed to load the bases with two outs, thanks to a double, a walk, and a hit batter. Well, sort of a hit batter. Actually replays showed that Dan Wheeler's pitch didn't hit Jermaine Dye, it glanced off his bat, but the call stood. Even with the bases loaded, the Sox's WP was only 26%, so the call didn't cost the Astros the game.

Paul Konerko did. Konerko smashed a high fastball from Chad Qualls into the wet, cold joyful fans in left field to give the Sox a 6-4 lead and raise their WP to 87%, a gain of 61 points. This was the single most important hit and play of the entire World Series.

The Astros entered the top of the ninth behind 6-4, their WP only 7%. But the game is magnified in the late innings, as each play has a much bigger impact on each team's probability of winning. Jenks came on once again to pitch the ninth for the Sox, but the Astros managed a single and walk to put runners on second and third with two out, and pinch hitter Jose Vizcaino strode to the plate. Even so, the Astros' WP was only 11%. But Vizcaino beat those odds by stroking a two-run single to left for WPA of 36, the fourth-biggest hit of the series.

It was the bottom of the ninth, scored tied at six, Astros closer Brad Lidge on the mound. One out. Scott Podsednik, who hadn't hit a home run the entire regular season, was at the plate. So, naturally, Podsednik smacked a fly ball into the right-field stands to end this

most dramatic of games. His hit registered a WPA of 42. In fact, this game featured three of the four most important hits of the series. Despite, or perhaps because of, the elements.

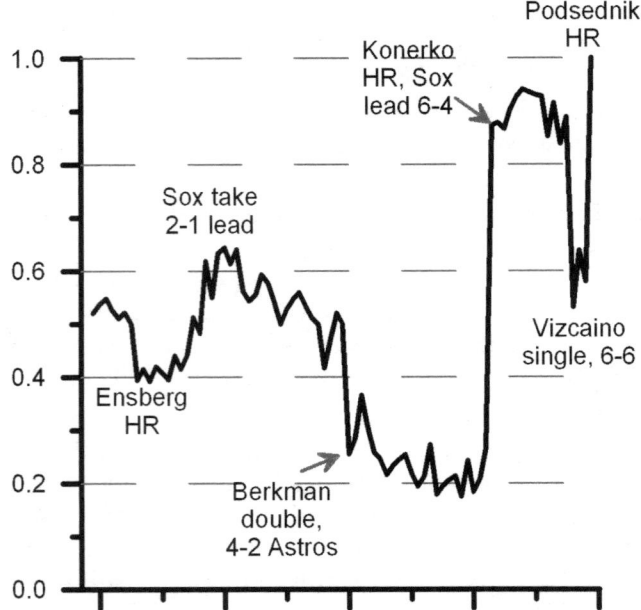

The WPA leaders for the game were Konerko, Podsednik, and Vizcaino, of course. The biggest negative WPAs belonged to the pitchers who gave up the big hits: Qualls (-60), Jenks (-40) and Lidge (-37). Clearly, Win Probability has a love/hate relationship with relievers.

World Series Game 3

The series moved to Houston, where the Astros hoped to gain ground with the phenomenal Roy Oswalt on the mound. The White Sox countered with Jon Garland. The weather was much nicer, but the game was another nail biter. In fact, it was 14 innings of tension, heroic efforts, and unlikely heroes.

The Astros battered Garland early. They took a 1-0 lead in the first on a run-scoring single by—who else?—Lance Berkman. WP of 60% at the end of the first, WPA of 8 for Berkman. The two teams then swapped a few scoreless half-innings and the Astros' WP slowly but surely rose to 67%.

The Astros scored two more runs in the bottom of the third without a single play worth more than 8 WPA. Actually, the most interesting play of the game occurred when the Sox caught Adam Everett off first, but Juan Uribe threw the ball smack dab into Everett's chest, the ball caromed and Everett scampered back to first. Uribe's error cost the Sox 5 WPA points, but singles by Biggio (8 WPA) and Ensberg (7 WPA) did more damage. With the score Astros 3, White Sox 0, the Astros' WP was 82%.

Jason Lane actually raised their WP further to 91% with a solo homer in the fourth (WPA of 5). But things fell apart for Roy Oswalt and the Astros in the fifth. Truth be told, Oswalt wasn't his typical dominant self in this game. His stuff seemed a bit off for much of the night, and the White Sox finally took advantage in the fifth.

The first cut was Crede's leadoff homer, though it didn't make too much of a dent (WPA of 6). But four singles narrowed the lead to 4-3 (the biggest hit being Dye's at 12 WPA), and then A.J. Pierzynski delivered the biggest hit of the inning, a two-run double deep in the right-field gap. The Sox suddenly had a 5-4 lead and a 59% WP at the end of the inning. Pierzynski's blow was good for 28 WPA, the sixth-biggest hit of the series. But the Sox would not score for eight more innings.

The score still stood at 5-4 in the bottom of the eighth, and the Sox's WP at 81%, when their bullpen walked a couple of guys. Still, with two out, their WP was 71%. But Jason Lane turned things around with a double down the left-field line off Dustin Hermanson (WPA of 33), tying the game.

The Astros had a great chance to win the game against Orlando Hernandez in the bottom of the ninth. Hernandez was wild and hittable (and later left the game due to injury) and the Astros had a runner on third with only one out. Even though the game was tied, their WP was 83% because a runner on third with less than two out usually scores. In fact, Chris Burke's steal of third had a WPA of 13, making it one of the 10 most important plays in this long, crazy game.

But Hernandez managed to get out of the jam by striking out Taveras and Ensberg in between two walks, and the game entered extra innings. WP for both teams was 50%, just like the beginning of the game.

It hovered around 50% for the next four innings, hitting 67% when Podsednik led off the 11th with a single and stole second, but the Sox stranded him there. Finally, an unlikely hero stepped forward. Bench player and former Astro Geoff Blum, who had entered the game in the 13th, hit a drive down the right-field line off rookie Ezequiel Astacio and into the stands to give the Sox a 6-5 14th-inning lead. Blum's blast carried a WPA of 41. The Sox added another run on a bases-loaded walk, and led 8-6.

Things were a little dicey in the bottom of the 14th due to a walk and an error, and Adam Everett represented the tying run at the plate. But even so, the Sox's WP didn't drop below 90% and Mark Buehrle entered the game as a reliever to retire Everett. After 14 grueling innings (tying the World Series record), the Sox had a commanding 3-0 series lead.

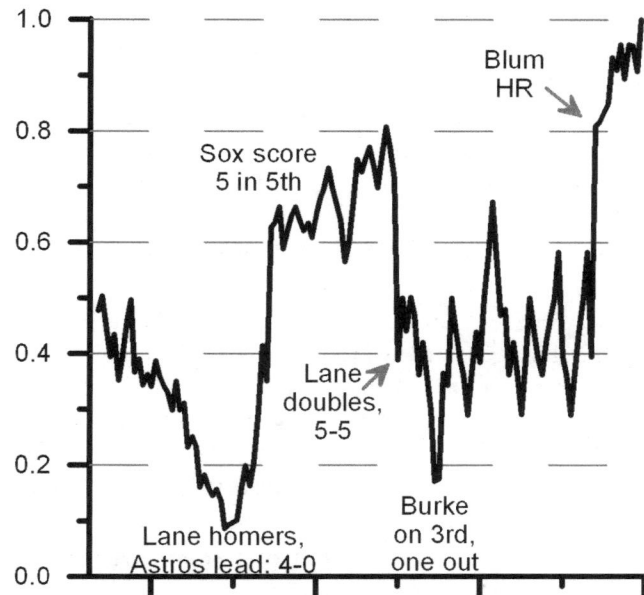

Blum and Pierzynski were the WPA leaders, followed by several White Sox relievers (Jenks, Vizcaino and Marte). Every extra inning is just like the ninth inning in importance, and Win Probability reflects this. Along the same lines, Qualls (30) and Lidge (23) were the Astros WPA leaders (Lane had 20), but the biggest negative total was Astacio's. At -62, his WPA represented an entire loss, all by itself.

World Series Game 4

Both teams put their #4 starters on the mound for Game 4, with Brandon Backe facing Freddy Garcia, so it's only natural that this would be the lowest-scoring game of this mixed-up series. A 1-0 game, in fact. Now, I love pitcher's duels, but from a WPA perspective there's not much to say.

Each team's WP hovered around 50% for the first seven innings. The biggest WP threat came in the bottom of the sixth, when a single and a walk raised the Astros' WP to 63%. Garcia responded with a couple strikeouts to end that threat. The White Sox did put runners on second and third in the seventh, but with two out. Their WP only reached 51%, though if Aaron Rowand hadn't had a bit of base running brain lock on a Crede double, he might have scored.

Both Garcia and Backe looked tremendous. Their curves were breaking, their fastballs were jumping, and their location was spotless. There were a few good defensive plays behind them, but neither pitcher relied too much on his defense. They were just pitching great ball. At the end of the game, both pitchers would lead their teams in WPA. Backe's total was 36 and Garcia's was 32. But both were out of the game when someone finally scored.

Willie Harris led off the top of the eighth with a pinch-hit single off Brad Lidge, upping the Sox's WP to 57%. Podsednik sacrificed him to second, which actually lowered Chicago's probability of winning to 55% (WP hates giving up outs). But Jermaine Dye hit a single up the middle to score Harris, for a WPA of 24, the eighth biggest hit of the series. At the end of their half inning, the Sox's WP stood at 70%. They had the lead, but they weren't out of the woods.

Sox reliever Cliff Politte was wild in the bottom of the eighth, hitting a batter, throwing a wild pitch, and almost throwing away the ball on an intentional walk. The Astros had runners on first and second with one out, and the Sox WP was down to 60%. But Politte got Ensberg to fly out and Neal Cotts managed to retire the pesky Jose Vizcaino, jumping their WP 24 points to 84%.

Jason Lane led off the bottom of the ninth with a single off Bobby Jenks to give the Astros a 33% WP, but Juan Uribe made two great plays to end the game: the first a diving catch into the foul seats to retire Chris Burke, and the second a nice pickup of a slow ground ball to just nip Orlando Palmeiro at first. I gave Uribe full credit for the foul catch and half credit for the grounder, meaning that he added 20 WPA with his glove in the bottom of the ninth. That's what you call a closer.

Those two plays landed Uribe third on the White Sox's WPA leaderboard, with Garcia and Dye ahead of him. Morgan Ensberg once again was last on the Astro WPA leaderboard with -23 WPA, due to his failure to deliver with men on base.

Graphically speaking ...

It had been 88 years, but the White Sox finally won the World Championship once again. Dye won the World Series MVP, which is logical if the award must go to a player on the winning team. However, Berkman was the WPA leader overall. Here is the full World Series WPA leaderboard:

Houston Astros		Chicago White Sox	
Player	WPA	Player	WPA
Berkman	0.70	Dye	0.44
Backe	0.36	Blum	0.41
Jose Vizcaino	0.29	Crede	0.41
Pettitte	0.21	Konerko	0.34
Springer	0.03	Garcia	0.32
Gallo	0.03	Cotts	0.27
Taveras	0.01	Podsednik	0.24
Rodriguez	0.01	Luis Vizcaino	0.21
Bruntlett	0.00	Marte	0.18
Lane	-0.01	Widger	0.13
Wheeler	-0.02	Politte	0.09
Backe	-0.02	Harris	0.09
Burke	-0.09	Hernandez	0.08
Palmeiro	-0.12	Uribe	0.07
Ausmus	-0.14	Pierzynski	0.02
Bagwell	-0.16	Jenks	0.02
Qualls	-0.18	Garland	-0.02
Lamb	-0.22	Timo	-0.12
Clemens	-0.25	Carl Everett	-0.13
Lidge	-0.30	Contreras	-0.13
Oswalt	-0.33	Buehrle	-0.13
Biggio	-0.46	Hermanson	-0.21
Adam Everett	-0.51	Rowand	-0.27
Ensberg	-0.53	Iguchi	-0.29
Astacio	-0.61		

For more on the 2005 postseason and the White Sox's championship, go to http://www.hardballtimes.com/main/catlist/category/Postseason%20Play/

To read more about Win Probability, you can start with the Hardball Times article "The One About Win Probability" at the following URL: http://www.hardballtimes.com/main/article/the-one-about-win-probability/

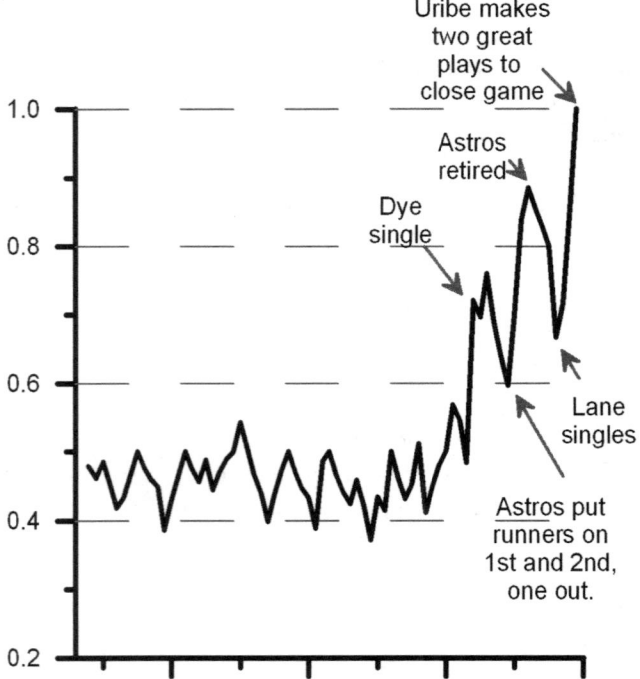

Uribe makes two great plays to close game

Astros retired

Dye single

Lane singles

Astros put runners on 1st and 2nd, one out.

2005 Commentary

For Want of a Nail...

by Rob Neyer

I'm working on a book about mistakes. Sometimes they're big mistakes that wind up costing very little, and sometimes they're small mistakes that wind up costing quite a lot. In a way, this is incredibly unfair of me, because of course nobody's perfect, and if we expect perfection, if we *demand* perfection, we'll be disappointed every time. Let's say a general manager makes all the right moves, except one, and his team winds up losing the pennant by one game. Let's say a manager makes all the right moves, except one, and his team winds up losing the pennant, or the World Series, by one game. Is it really fair to focus on that one mistake—and this assumes that we have enough information to know whether it was really a mistake or not—while ignoring all the good moves that put the team in a position to win in the first place?

No, of course it's not fair. But hey, that's sportswriting. If you want fair, watch NewsHour with Jim Lehrer. For the moment you're stuck with me, and my mission for the moment is to identify CIMMs—Clearly Identifiable Management Mistakes—that probably made a big difference in the top of the standings.

Here are the key 2005 statistics for two Red Sox first basemen:

	Games	At-Bats	OBP	SLG
Millar	134	449	.355	.399
Petagine	92	298	.444	.614

The great majority of Roberto Petagine's action came with Pawtucket in the International League. I understand that, given a full season in the American League, he probably would not bat .322 (not pictured), probably would not get on base nearly 45% of the time, and probably would not post a .600-plus slugging percentage.

I also understand that a 1.058 OPS in the International League is equivalent to something better than .754 in the American League. Significantly better.

Nevertheless, Petagine didn't debut with the Red Sox until August 4, and—this is the part that really, really gets me—he batted exactly six times in September. Four of those times were in blowouts. In September, the Red Sox lost five games by three runs or fewer; Petagine batted in one of them. In August, the Red Sox lost six games by three runs or fewer; Petagine batted in two of them. By that point, the Red Sox had John Olerud and he was doing well, and David Ortiz's burly presence was always a given, and of course there's room for only so many 1B/DHs in the lineup. But Petagine should have played more than he did.

But it's not just Petagine that gets me. It's the utter lack of imagination, or perhaps courage, shown by Red Sox management in 2005.

Against right-handed pitchers, the Red Sox could have fielded this fantastic lineup for much of the season:

CF Damon
3B Mueller
DH Ortiz
LF Ramirez
RF Nixon
C Varitek
1B Petagine/Olerud
2B Graffanino
SS Renteria

And against lefties, this one:
CF Damon
3B Youkilis
DH Ortiz
LF Ramirez
C Varitek
1B Mueller/Millar
2B Graffanino
RF Nixon
SS Renteria

Renteria's actually pretty good against left-handed pitching, and his place at the bottom of this lineup is both indicative of its strength and an example of my reluctance to tinker *too* much. Damon probably shouldn't bat leadoff against lefties, and Nixon probably shouldn't be in the lineup up at all. Ideally, there would be a right-handed hitter to play right field against lefties, but once the Red Sox traded Jay Payton they never had a right-handed-hitting outfielder worth using.

People will tell you, "The Red Sox scored plenty of runs. Their problem was their pitching." Well, yes. And there is a diminishing return when you're talking about increasing the number of runs you score. But scoring more runs certainly isn't a *bad* thing, and the Sox could have scored more with just a few tweaks to the lineup, using players already in the organization. It's simple, really; if you're not going to out-pitch your opponents, then you might as well out-slug them to the extent that you can.

Frankly, the Red Sox didn't drop Renteria in the order, or play Youkilis more often, or give more at-bats to Petagine, because they were afraid. They were afraid to upset the team's delicate *chemistry*, as defined by—among others—Manny Ramirez.

After Gabe Kapler lost his job in Japan, the Red Sox signed him. Why? Because they knew him. When the Sox were looking for a fifth outfielder in July, they picked up Adam Hyzdu. Why? Because they knew him. When they realized they needed a lefty-hitting first baseman, they signed and then promoted John Olerud. Why? Because they knew him.

Our friends at Baseball Prospectus wrote a book titled *Mind Game: How the Boston Red Sox Got Smart, Won a World Series, and Created a New Blueprint for Winning*. But there was nothing smart about the Red Sox in 2005. They were either cowardly or unimaginative. Were Kapler and Hyzdu really the best they could do? Did they really think Manny Ramirez would stop hitting if his pal Kevin Millar was released?

The Red Sox made some big moves that just didn't work. Matt Clement didn't pitch as well as Kevin Millwood. Edgar Renteria didn't play well enough to justify his salary (let alone his long-term contract). Most of the name relievers were awful. But most and perhaps all of the big moves were defensible when they were made, so it's the little moves with which I'll quibble. Most of the time, the little moves don't make a difference. But when you lose home field advantage in the first round of the playoffs by the razor-thin margin of one measly win? Everything made a difference. And if Terry Francona hadn't forgotten about Roberto Petagine in September, if management had acquired a *good* platoon partner for Trot Nixon, if everybody hadn't been afraid to offend Manny Ramirez by sitting Kevin Millar against right-handed pitching, if any one of those things had happened, the Red Sox's season might have lasted at least a few days more than it did.

The Yankees, like the Red Sox, spent a huge amount of money, won 95 games, were the visiting team in their Division Series, and got their butts kicked. Like the Red Sox, the Yankees suffered from poor pitching but were able to power their way to the second-best record in the American League. It's easy to see what the Yankees did wrong: They counted on Jaret Wright and Kevin Brown, both of whom were (predictably) useless for most of the season. Throw in the non-predictable injury that felled Carl Pavano, and it's not a surprise they were forced to rely on Aaron Small and Shawn Chacon. The surprise was that Small and Chacon won 17 games.

What nobody seemed to notice was that if the Yankees were blessed with a decent bench—any sort of bench at all, really—they would easily have beat out the Red Sox, and they would have hosted the Division Series against the Angels instead of vice versa.

Eight Yankees played enough (i.e. 502 plate appearances) to qualify for the batting title (and yes, they were exceptionally lucky in this regard). Seven of them—the exception being Bernie Williams—were either good or great. That's why the Yankees finished behind only the Red Sox in scoring.

On the other hand, six Yankees batted at least 50 times without qualifying for the batting crown, and five of them—the exception being Tino Martinez—were absolutely horrible. Mind you, Martinez wasn't *good*; despite an incredible surge in the spring, he finished at .241/.328/.439, poor numbers for a first baseman. But compared to his bench-mates he was Don Mattingly.

Tony Womack (351 plate appearances), Ruben Sierra (181), John Flaherty (138), Bubba Crosby (103) and Matt Lawton (57) combined for 830 plate appearances, a not inconsiderable number. They also combined for a .226 batting average, a .265 on-base percentage and a .299 slugging percentage—certainly *not* considerable numbers.

Of course, this wasn't completely anybody's fault. But did nobody in New York or Tampa realize that Ruben Sierra, for example, was done? From 2000 through 2004, his season on-base percentages were .281, .322, .319, .327 and .296.

Okay, so the Yankees couldn't reasonably have guessed that Sierra—even though he'd be 39—would post a .265 on-base percentage in 2005. But they should have known Sierra wouldn't be *good*, shouldn't they?

Similarly, while they couldn't have known that back-up catcher John Flaherty would bat .165 (.165?) in 47 games, they certainly did know that Flaherty hadn't put up a .300-plus OBP since 1999 when he was 31. And then there's Tony Womack ... but don't get me—or any analytical Yankees fan—going on that subject.

Look around the American League. The Angels had Casey Kotchman, Juan Rivera and Robb Quinlan. The Royals had Matt Stairs. The Devil Rays—chrissakes, the *Devil Rays*—had Joey Gathright and Josh Phelps. Granted, there's something to be said for putting as much of your payroll as possible on the field at one time. But the Yankees couldn't have found an extra million dollars and a roster spot for an outstanding defensive center fielder? Couldn't have figured out a way to acquire a couple of decent middle relievers to complement Gordon and Rivera?

The 2005 Yankees were, in many ways, unlucky. Their great players all played about as well as expected, but their less-than-great players all played worse than expected. But there was apparently a sense in the organization that this team simply couldn't lose, because its lineup and rotation were so incredibly impressive. The Yankees could lose, though. And they did.

Last season the Phillies finished two games behind the first-place Braves and one game behind the Wild Card-winning Astros. And their failure to qualify for the World Championship Derby for an 11th straight season can be directly traced to three questionable decisions.

- On November 24, 2002, the Phillies signed free-agent third baseman David Bell to a four-year contract for $17 million.
- Twelve days later, the Phillies signed Jim Thome to a six-year contract for $82 million.
- On June 8, 2005, the Phillies traded Placido Polanco to the Tigers for Ugueth Urbina.

If they hadn't signed Thome, in 2005 they would have enjoyed the valuable services of Ryan Howard for 140 games rather than 88. If they hadn't signed Bell, they wouldn't have suffered the services of David Bell for 150 games. And if they hadn't traded Polanco, they would have enjoyed his services for 120 games rather than 43.

Given any *one* of these eventualities, the Phillies would almost certainly have won two or three more games, and two or three more wins put them in the playoffs.

Of course, two of them are inextricably linked. If the Phillies hadn't signed Bell in 2002, it's highly unlikely they'd have traded Polanco in 2005. The first of those moves probably cost Phillies general manager Ed Wade

his job—he was fired after last season—and the second probably cost the Phillies a shot at the World Series.

As the authors of *Baseball Prospectus* wrote shortly after the Phillies signed David Bell, "No one—except maybe a guy who works in the Phillies payroll department—would consider Bell an elite player ... He'll be a valuable, if overpaid, piece of the Phillies' puzzle next year."

BP was right and wrong. Right: Nobody except the Phillies considered Bell an elite player. Wrong: Due to back and hip injuries, he was far from valuable to the Phillies in 2003. Bell did bounce back with good numbers in 2004, but that's almost beside the point. You shouldn't spend big money on decent players, because eventually you'll feel compelled to keep playing the guy—because of his salary—even when there might be somebody else who's more deserving.

Somebody like Placido Polanco.

Polanco reached the majors in 1998 with the Cardinals. Polanco was born to play for Tony La Russa; he could play every infield position, and he did. Before the Cardinals traded Polanco in late July 2002, he played in 121 games at shortstop, 152 at second base, and 226 at third, thus establishing himself as perhaps the game's No. 1 utility infielder. Why would the Cardinals give him up? Because they really, really, *really* wanted Scott Rolen from the Phillies.

In Philadelphia, Polanco was immediately installed as the everyday third baseman and played well ... so the Phillies went out and signed David Bell. Now, the Phillies still had a place for Polanco, at second base, except if Polanco played second base, there wouldn't be a place for Chase Utley, who'd already proved his mettle in the International League after completely skipping Double-A.

The Phillies then committed a classic mistake: they overpaid a Proven Veteran™ *and* blocked the path of a much younger, much cheaper player of similar (and perhaps superior) abilities. So Utley spent most of 2003 languishing in the minors and much of 2004 languishing on the Phillies' bench. Finally, in 2005 the Phillies finally realized that maybe this kid—actually, *ex*-kid, since by then he was 26 years old—should actually be in the lineup just about every day.

But where? It would have to be second base. Which meant David Bell or Placido Polanco would have to go. Ed Wade essentially had four options:

a) Bench David Bell and his $4.5 million salary.
b) Trade Bell for a Lickskillet League pitcher and a bucket of scuffed baseballs, in which case he would also have been obliged to pick up a

hefty chunk of Bell's salary (including the $4.5 million he's owed in 2006).

c) Trade Polanco.

d) None of the above (i.e. curl up into a little ball and hope somebody gets hurt—hey, it worked with Jim Thome!).

To Wade's credit, he didn't curl up into a little ball. Unfortunately for the fortunes of the 2005 Philadelphia Phillies, Wade did the next-worst thing. On June 8, he traded Polanco, a solid everyday player, for Ugueth Urbina, a one-inning reliever. Sure, Urbina's a *good* one-inning reliever. But his skills have limited utility, particularly on a roster that already includes Billy Wagner.

After joining the Tigers, Polanco batted .338 with 28 long hits in 86 games. After Polanco joined the Tigers, Bell batted .239 with 29 long hits in 94 games. Bell walked seven more times than Polanco; Polanco singled 32 more times than Bell. The difference between them, then, was something like 25 bases.

Urbina did pitch well for the Phillies—4-3 with a 4.13 ERA in 52 innings—but it's not likely that his

contributions balance what Polanco would have done. It seems to me not only *possible*, but *likely* that if Polanco would have been in the lineup all season, the Phillies would have won at least two more games and earned a slot in the playoffs. And if they had, Ed Wade wouldn't have been fired on October 10.

There's one other team that came up short, by just a smidgen. But try as I might, I can't find anything the Cleveland Indians should have done differently. In the rotation, even Scott Elarton was decent. Their bullpen posted the lowest ERA in the league. And while Aaron Boone delivered sub-par numbers, he was the best third baseman in the organization, and it wouldn't have made sense for the Indians to trade prospects for somebody better. The people who run the Indians—unlike those who run the Red Sox, Yankees, and Phillies—should have absolutely no regrets about what happened in 2005. Standings be damned.

GM in a Box: Walt Jocketty

by Brian Gunn

Here's a game: pick out any general manager in baseball, punch his name into Google, and see what you come up with. Not much, huh? Maybe a newspaper article from last year, perhaps a stray reference in a blog entry, but unless your favorite GM's name is Beane or Epstein, I doubt you dredge up anything useful.

It's odd that in this age of fantasy sports—when even casual fans recognize that a general manager is the single most important figure in any organization—there's so little info about who these men are and what they do. (And yes, until Dodgers' assistant GM Kim Ng gets a promotion, I'm going to have to use masculine pronouns for the rest of this article.) In the last few years, analysts have devised ways to measure general managers. Doug Pappas's "marginal dollars spent per marginal win" was a nice start, and there have been other attempts over the years (THT's contribution came in the form of David Gassko's article "Ranking the General Managers").

But I'd like to talk about GMs in more qualitative terms, the same way Bill James did with his "Manager in a Box" series. Like James, I'll ask a series of questions that get at a GM's tendencies, preferences, likes and dislikes. My goal is not to judge but to describe. As a test case, I'll explore the general manager I know best, Walt Jocketty of the St. Louis Cardinals.

Record and Background

Age: 54

Previous organizations:

1975-1980: White Sox—various minor league positions under GM Roland Hemond

1980-1993: Athletics—farm director mostly under GM Sandy Alderson

1993: Rockies—assistant GM to Bob Gebhard

Jocketty has said that he learned people skills from the genial Hemond and technical/contractual skills from the lawyerly Alderson.

Years of service with current organization: 11 (Third longest in the majors, after the Braves' John Schuerholz and the Twins' Terry Ryan.)

Cumulative record: 956-806, .543 winning percentage

Did he play professional ball and if so, what type of player was he?

No. He played college ball as a pitcher, but that's it.

Personnel and Philosophy

Any notable changes from the previous regime?

The Cardinals' previous GM, Dal Maxvill, oversaw the club in the waning days of the Anheuser-Busch ownership. By most accounts he was guarded and risk averse, resigned to treat the Cardinals like the well-heeled public face of the brewery.

Jocketty, on the other hand, immediately took chances. He dumped the avuncular Joe Torre as manager, hauled in the fiery Tony La Russa, unloaded aloof players like Todd Zeile and pounced on high-priced free agents like Tom Henke and Danny Jackson. (Believe it or not, Jackson landed the most lucrative contract of any pitcher in the 1994-95 offseason.) From the get-go Jocketty operated like a big-time player in a mid-sized market.

What characterizes his relationship with ownership? What types of people does he hire to work under him? Is he more collaborative or authoritative?

While Maxvill was intensely private, Jocketty is much chummier—a clubhouse schmoozer with a very collaborative managerial style. He's definitely not a dictatorial superstar in the Whitey Herzog mold, which may explain why, as recently as 2000, he was the lowest-paid GM in the game.

For most of his career Jocketty did not lean heavily on statistical analysis—practically unheard of for a protégé of Sandy Alderson. But in recent years he has begun to hire more saber-friendly personnel. In the winter of 2003-04, Jocketty recruited the wonkish Jeff Luhnow to be his vice president of baseball development, signed Ron Shandler and his BaseballHQ analysts to serve as part of a six-man advisory board, trimmed the scouting staff and demoted farm director Bruce Manno—a definite shift away from the traditional observational mode of talent evaluation. The cumulative effect of these moves puts the Cardinals in a camp with teams like, say, the Padres and Indians—that is, neither heavily sabermetric nor scout-based, but a mix of each.

What kinds of managers does he hire? How closely does he work with them?

Jocketty has only hired one manager on his watch: Tony La Russa. Their relationship goes back to 1979, when La Russa managed Iowa in the American Association and Jocketty was in the team's front office. Since then they've engaged in some high-level logrolling; La Russa pulled strings with Charles O. Finley to get Jocketty hired by the Oakland A's, and Jocketty recommended La Russa to A's management when he lost his job with the White Sox.

Since La Russa took the helm as Cards skipper in 1996, his relationship with Jocketty has been as cozy as any manager-GM partnership in the game. In fact, it's difficult to tell where Jocketty stops and La Russa starts—they both share a taste for veteran pitchers, defense-minded catchers, power at the corners and "sturdy character" types. The current Cardinals team has been crafted very much in the image of both men.

Player Development

How does he approach the amateur draft? Does he prefer major league-ready players or "projects"? Tools or performance? High school or college? Pitchers or hitters?

Jocketty has a real yen for college talent. During his tenure, the Cards have used a first-round pick on a high schooler just three times, and never have they chosen a high school pitcher in the first round. Even after the first round, Jocketty and his scouting director, Marty Maier, are, as Bryan Smith of Baseball Analysts (www.baseballanalysts.com) has pointed out, "almost all college." In 2004, for example, the Cards signed only one high schooler among their 47 picks in the amateur draft.

This is not to suggest that Jocketty eschews high-ceiling, "toolsy" players. In recent years he's chosen a number of pitchers with both serious heaters and serious control problems (see '04 pick Chris Lambert or '05 selection Mark McCormick). He also made very splashy commitments to three superstuds—J.D. Drew, Rick Ankiel and Chad Hutchinson—when most teams wouldn't touch them for fear of getting priced out of the market. Note that all three of those players were clients of noted extortionist Scott Boras. Jocketty's close working relationship with Boras points to one of the hallmarks of his regime—that if the circumstances are right, he is willing to pay dearly for top-shelf talent.

Is there anywhere (either within or outside the US) where he tends to find talent?

Jocketty has taken more than a few flyers on players from Missouri—notably Kerry Robinson, Cliff Politte and a certain Albert Pujols. But just as the Braves have had great success drafting players from their own backyard, that's to be expected. Otherwise he finds players under the usual rocks: California, the South and so on.

In general, Jocketty has made few broad-based commitments to overseas scouting and development. Where some franchises have made inroads into untapped markets (e.g., the Astros in Venezuela, the Mariners in Japan), the Cardinals have more often been late to the party. What's more, Jocketty has funneled scant resources into Latin American development—in 2003, the club went so far as to shut down its development program in the Dominican Republic (although the program has been recently reinstated under the guidance of Jocketty's "stat guy," Jeff Luhnow).

Does he tend to rush guys to the majors or let them marinate?

There's no glaring trend here, but the record seems to indicate that Jocketty is more eager than most. J.D. Drew spent less than a year in the minors. Bud Smith was placed on the fast track throughout the minor leagues and started 14 games for the Cards at age 21. Matt Morris started only one game in Triple-A before reaching the majors, and both Ankiel and Pujols were in St. Louis the year after Single-A ball. (Despite the splash he made his rookie year, promoting Pujols to the majors out of spring training 2001 was not the no-brainer it seems in retrospect. Several publications—most famously *Baseball Prospectus*—urged the Cards to give him another year of seasoning.)

In general, though, there aren't many players whom Jocketty promoted who can be considered clearly over-cooked (like, say, Jonny Gomes) or under-cooked (like Jose Reyes). But he will push players with standout skills. As we've seen with the amateur draft, and as we're about to see with Jocketty's trading habits, the man has a clear-cut philosophy: go out of your way to get superstars into the lineup.

Roster Construction

Are there any types of players of whom he's especially fond? Does he like proven players or youngsters? Offensive players or glovemen? Power pitchers or finesse guys?

There are four things Jocketty looks for when assembling his teams:

1. Power Hitters

In 1995, with a team primarily built by Jocketty's predecessor Dal Maxvill, the Cards finished second to last in the league in home runs. Their five starting infielders, in fact, hit only 20 homers *combined*. That winter the club added Ron Gant and Gary Gaetti and climbed to 11th of 14 teams in home runs. The next year they climbed to eighth. Since then they've consistently finished near the top of the league: first, fifth, second, seventh (but only 14 homers behind the #2 team), third, third, and third. This year they actually tailed off to seventh place. But in general Jocketty has favored names (acquiring McGwire, Edmonds and Pujols and re-signing Lankford to a long-term contract) that are known for serious lumber.

2. Defense Up the Middle

Coming into 2005, Jocketty's teams have won 12 Gold Gloves combined at catcher, short, second and center field. While some of these guys were handy with the bat too (notably Edmonds and Renteria), Jocketty has no problem scrimping on offense up the middle, particularly catcher and second base. Compare, for example, the Cardinals' isolated powers at these two positions compared to the rest of the league over the last four years:

	Cardinals	League
Catcher	0.096	0.141
Second Base	0.094	0.137

At other positions Jocketty likes guys who are good with both the glove and the stick (Rolen, Walker and Pujols are good current examples), but at catcher and second he leans heavily in favor of defense, and this past winter he was content to put a light-hitting "bat twirler" type at shortstop in the person of David Eckstein.

3. Finesse Pitchers

On Jocketty's watch Cardinal pitchers have consistently finished at or near the bottom of the league in strikeouts, and only a few of their starters could be considered legit power pitchers (Rick Ankiel, Andy Benes, Chris Carpenter and, to a lesser degree, Todd Stottlemyre).

There seem to be two reasons why Jocketty seeks out these fluffballers. One is that La Russa and Dave Duncan, the pitching coach, seem more comfortable grooming "location" pitchers. The other is that finesse guys are, by and large, cheaper than power pitchers. Note, for example, that the Cards' entire 2005 starting rotation cost only $17 million, this after an offseason in which several fastballers (Pedro Martinez, Matt Clement and Jaret Wright among them) were rewarded with prodigious contracts.

4. "Proven" Talent

It can be said that for Jocketty, young talent is only valuable to the extent that it can be converted into established talent. He absolutely loves guys with track records, even if their success was not so recent. We'll get into this much more when we examine Jocketty's trading habits, but it's safe to say that he's the opposite of a guy like, say, Pirates GM Dave Littlefield, who will sign veteran players solely to convert them into promising young talent. Jocketty almost always operates in the opposite direction.

Does he tend to allocate resources primarily on impact players or role players? How does he flesh out his bullpen and his bench? Does he often work the waiver wire or sign minor league free agents or make Rule 5 picks?

Jocketty collects superstars, but he rarely overspends for them. Perhaps this is because he refuses to go all-in during bidding wars for players like Mike Hampton or Jason Giambi (both sought by Jocketty at one point). As a result, Jocketty's salary disbursements are not top-heavy. His four highest-paid players, for example, have eaten up between 40-45% of the payroll, which is fairly normal—and a far cry from a truly lopsided team like the 2005 Houston Astros (who doled out 72% of its payroll to the top four employees).

This is not to say that Jocketty doesn't go after impact players. But he is much more likely to lure them by giving up young talent on the trading market rather than handing out huge contracts on the free agent market. For the last few years, St. Louis' talent base has been heavily tied up in a handful of players, as this chart demonstrates:

Top four players, % Of Total Team Win Shares for the Last Three Years:

1.	St. Louis	41.2%
2.	Cincinnati	39.2%
3.	Philadelphia	39.0%

If you want to caricaturize the Cardinals' talent base over the last few years, try picturing an inverted pyramid.

As for the rest of the roster, Jocketty, like the Braves' John Schuerholz, tends to take the Dr. Frankenstein approach: He figures he can build a passable bench and bullpen out of spare parts. In 2004, for example, the Cards employed an unusual number of cheap, recycled arms in the bullpen. Four roster slots were taken up by veterans who hadn't even played major league baseball the year before (Lance Painter, Russ Springer, Cal Eldred and Pedro Borbon). This is a typical Jocketty strategy, the same way he fleshed out his bench in 2005 with a host of minor league free agents.

When will he release players? Who has he given up on? Who has he given a shot? Does he cut bait early or late?

Jocketty will almost always use La Russa as a weather vane when it comes to keeping or releasing players. The players Jocketty gave up on—Ron Gant, Royce Clayton, Fernando Tatis, Mike Crudale, Dustin Hermanson, Brett Tomko, J.D. Drew, Tino Martinez—all ran afoul of La Russa at some point. They all had reps as slackers or malcontents, and Jocketty shipped off most of them rather than waiting to see if they would gel with the team.

Conversely, Jocketty tends to stand by players who are seen as hardworking and upstanding, long past the point where other GMs might cut bait. So Taguchi was a disaster at first, but Jocketty stuck with him for years. Andy Benes was seen as a good guy, so Jocketty brought him back to St. Louis for a second go-round in 2000; he also kept Benes around after his calamitous 2001 campaign. He handled Benes's brother Alan much the same way, continually keeping him close to the organization despite his obvious troubles. Ditto for Ankiel, another pitcher with a rep for amiability and a good work ethic.

It's not clear whether Jocketty commits to these players out of sense or sentiment, but it should be pointed out that some of them—notably Chris Carpenter—will pay back Jocketty's loyalty by re-signing with the club well below market value.

Is he active or passive? An optimist or a problem solver? Does he tend to want to win now or wait out the success cycle?

Jocketty is primarily a problem solver, a fix-it guy. We see this most glaringly in his approach to the trading deadline—Jocketty rarely, if ever, sits back and tries to "dance with them what brung you." He's always working the phones, trying to tinker, upgrade.

Where he's an optimist is in his relationship with his manager. It's doubtful that Jocketty has ever seriously considered replacing La Russa. What's more, he frequently acquires talent to fit La Russa's predilections. Note, for example, the long list of older reclamation projects that Jocketty has added to his pitching staffs: Pat Hentgen, Andy Benes, Darryl Kile, Rick Honeycutt, Todd Stottlemyre, Dennis Eckersley, Mike Morgan, Chris Carpenter, Woody Williams. Jocketty lands these guys not because he's trying to shoehorn a particular type of pitcher on his manager. Rather, he figures that reclaiming these pitchers is what La Russa and Duncan are good at. To some extent he works with what he's got.

Does he favor players acquired via trade, development or free agency?

The Cardinals have only three starters that were developed internally—Albert Pujols, Yadier Molina and Matt Morris. That's the fewest of any team in the division. Needless to say, then, Jocketty favors players from other organizations. In the past he'd be more likely to fetch players via trade (especially guys like McGwire and Rolen whom he could trade for and then immediately sign to long-term contracts). But in recent years—partly due to an influx of money, partly due to a diminishing farm system—Jocketty has relied on free-agent signings. The Cards' current roster has six starters who were taken on as free agents, each in the last couple of years. That's about a third of all the free-agent starters that Jocketty signed in his first nine years as GM.

Trades and Free Agents

Is he an active trader? Does he tend to move talent or horde it? Whom does he trade and when?

Two things characterize Jocketty's behavior on the trading market. One we've already covered: he will consistently deal young, emerging, speculative talent in order to acquire older, proven, accomplished talent. There are only three exceptions to this rule. The first was in 1996, when Jocketty moved six-year veteran Bernard Gilkey in exchange for youngsters Eric Ludwick and Yudith Orozio. Perhaps burned by this experience—Gilkey went on to have a phenomenal season his first year away from St. Louis—Jocketty has traded older-for-younger only twice since: the first time in 1997 when he acquired Fernando Tatis for Stottlemyre and Clayton and the second time in 2003 when free-agent-to-be J.D. Drew was the centerpiece of a deal to get young Jason Marquis and prized pitching prospect Adam Wainwright. Jocketty has made no other significant trades that could be seen as an attempt to replenish the pipeline.

He has, however, made countless trades to obtain players who have *arrived*, and apart from the players named above, it was always, always at the expense of young talent. That's how he got Renteria, McGwire, Eckersley, Stottlemyre, Kile, Fernando Viña, Edmonds, Rolen, Hermanson, Hentgen, Mulder, Will Clark, Dave Veres, Steve Kline, Larry Walker, Chuck Finley, Jeff Brantley, Jason Christensen and just about everybody else. Occasionally these deals backfire (Jocketty would likely want Coco Crisp, Dmitri Young and Jack Wilson back, and possibly Danny Haren and Daric Barton as well), but it's unlikely that Jocketty will forgo his A1 trading tactic. In general he'd much rather roll the dice with someone who's "been there" than someone who hasn't.

This does not mean, however, that Jocketty hates youth or that he'll trade away farmhands willy-nilly. Two deals that did not come to pass show that even Jocketty has his limits. The first was in the summer of 1997, when Sandy Alderson was trying to pry 22-year-old Matt Morris from the Cardinals in the Mark McGwire deal. Jocketty refused to unload the young righthander and ended up dealing a bunch of lesser prospects instead. The second occurred in July 2000, when, according to *Baseball Prospectus*, Padres' GM Kevin Towers was looking for a minor leaguer in exchange for veteran Carlos Hernandez. He asked for one of two A-ball hitters: Ben Johnson and Albert Pujols. Jocketty mulled it over, but finally decided he'd rather keep Pujols. The rest, of course, is history.

The other dimension to Jocketty's trade strategy is this: buy low. Jeff Angus, a management consultant and baseball journalist, coined the phrase "Bounce Back Guy," which refers to a good player who bounces back after an off-year. Often organizations, believing that the apex of the bounce is either the beginning of a new uptick in accomplishment or a new assumed level of performance, will spend vast resources to acquire these guys. (A prime example is the Pittsburgh Pirates and Derek Bell. Bell had apparently bounced back with a solid 2000 campaign for the Mets, and the Pirates promptly rewarded him with a two-year, $9 million contract.)

Jocketty almost never takes chances on guys like that. In fact, he usually does the opposite, scouring the trade wire for guys on the presumed *downtick* of their careers. He went after Darryl Kile as he was coming off a 6.61 ERA in Coors Field. He pursued Jim Edmonds the year after an injury-riddled 1999 season that was marred by character controversies. He traded for Mark Mulder following the worst half-season of his career. Apart from Ron Gant in his first winter as general manager, Jocketty has generally avoided players whose career is spiking and has instead chosen to buy when their stock is low.

Will he make deals with other teams in-season? How does he usually approach the trading deadline?

Jocketty is probably the most aggressive deadline dealer in the history of baseball. McGwire, Tatis, Will Clark, Woody Williams, Chuck Finley, Scott Rolen and Larry Walker were all acquired at midseason—a huge haul of talent.

Unlike Billy Beane, who waits for the season to develop in order to identify and address his team's most pressing holes, Jocketty will frequently try to land players at the trading deadline that will help the team long-term. This is highly unusual, especially for clubs in contention (which the Cards usually are), but Jocketty takes those gambles anyway.

Are there any teams or GMs with whom he trades frequently?

Early in his tenure Jocketty would pull deals with his old mentor, Sandy Alderson—that's how he netted McGwire, Eckersley and Stottlemyre. But lately he's been more promiscuous, making major trades with over half the teams in baseball during his time in office. Jocketty is liked and respected by virtually all of his peers, and it's difficult to picture him ruffling feathers the way that Jim Bowden, Dan Duquette or even Beane has done.

Under what circumstances will he sign free agents?

Jocketty is not a major player on the free-agent market, and when he dabbles he usually goes after mid-priced bargains: guys like Gary Gaetti, Delino DeShields and Eric Davis.

Lately Jocketty has signed more free agents, but he hasn't been a frontrunner. Instead, he's waited until the end of the offseason—i.e., after the market has calmed down—to go bargain-shopping. Reggie Sanders, Jeff Suppan, Mark Grudzielanek, Julian Tavarez and David Eckstein were all acquired after most of their fellow position players were gobbled up. This follows Jocketty's pattern of buying low, which is also how he landed Jim Edmonds (trading for him only a week before the start of the regular season), as well as Larry Walker and Woody Williams (both obtained after the July 31 trade deadline). This might also explain his recent habit of acquiring minor league free agents throughout the offseason and regular season. Again, the pattern is familiar: lie in wait, don't overcommit and then pounce when the market dips.

Jocketty also likes to acquire guys at the tail end of their contracts, then circumvent free agency by signing them to long-term deals. That's precisely how he secured McGwire, Rolen, and Edmonds. Considering the Cards play in a smallish media market (26th among the 32 teams), this strategy is totally dependent on signing these players below market cost. Each of the above-named players has said he took less money to play in St. Louis, which Jocketty sells as a tranquil haven untroubled by the jostling and rancor you might find on the coasts. This is a far cry from the strategy of Jocketty's predecessor Dal Maxvill, who rarely cozied up to his players and experienced acrimonious partings with the likes of Jack Clark, Terry Pendleton, Willie McGee and Vince Coleman.

Contracts

Does he prefer long-term deals or short? Does he backload his contracts very often? Does he lock up players early in their career or is he more likely to practice brinksmanship? Does he like to avoid arbitration?

It's a mixed bag. Jocketty has no problem doling out long-term contracts for cornerstone players. Scott Rolen, for example, is locked up through 2010. Albert Pujols' contract runs out the same year, but the club has an option on him into 2011. Edmonds and Isringhausen are also products of long-term deals.

Otherwise there's nothing remarkable about Jocketty's contracts—generally they run one or two years, especially for pitchers. And yes, Jocketty also backloads his contracts rather extensively. Pujols, for example, will earn a paycheck from the Cardinals in the year 2029. Another way Jocketty tries to save money up front is by issuing incentive-laden contracts like the one he did with Chris Carpenter in '04 or Matt Morris in '05.

Anything unique about his negotiating tactics? Is he vocal? Does he prefer to work behind the scenes or through the media?

Apparently Jocketty is very personable with players and personnel, but he comes across as much more nondescript in public. Other general managers are easier to pigeonhole: there's Theo Epstein, the Thalberg-esque wunderkind; Billy Beane, the GM with the jawline of Superman and the mind of Clark Kent; and Brian Cashman, as wearied and funereal as a Charles Addams cartoon. Jocketty, on the other hand, seems like the great uncle whose name you keep forgetting. Perhaps that's why he's able to fly under the radar so often before he pulls off his biggest deals.

Bonus

What is his strongest point as GM?

Working within his limitations. In 1980 Jocketty was signed as the farm director for A's owner Charley O. Finley, a notorious skinflint. The experience taught Jock how to cobble together a team on a shoestring budget.

He brought these same lessons to St. Louis. Before Jocketty arrived, the Cardinals' front office was content to operate as a small- to mid-market team. More often than not, they sat back and tried to recapture the glory days of Whiteyball, overly preoccupied with aging legends like Ozzie Smith. But new ownership in the mid-1990s brought an influx of money, and Jocketty added a cutthroat style that put St. Louis at the forefront of the trade and free-agent markets.

Jocketty's first forays onto the big stage were more heat than light. Signees like Danny Jackson and Scott Radinsky and Ron Gant were busts—the byproduct of Jocketty's eagerness to sign a "name" above all else.

Jocketty turned a corner when he went out and got Mark McGwire at the trading deadline in 1997. Yes, McGwire was a big name—bigger than Gant or Radinsky or Jackson ever were. But Jocketty learned that you didn't have to throw money at him on the free-agent market to get him. Instead, you could sacrifice a few up-and-coming prospects to put him on the roster, then exploit the homeness of the Cards' Midwestern tradition to lock him into a long-term deal. This model later paved the way for the acquisitions of Scott Rolen and Jim Edmonds, both premier players at their positions.

In recent years Jocketty has continued to find creative ways to work within the limitations of his market. For example, he knows that he can't go out and sign marquee strikeout pitchers without blowing out his budget. So he gets finesse, groundball hurlers at a reasonable price, surrounds them with good defense up the middle (especially second basemen who are quick on the pivot, like Vina and Grudzielanek), and puts them under the tutelage of rehab artists like Dave Duncan and Tony La Russa. To pull this off takes a commitment to the big picture and an awareness of how each part fits with the other. But it can pay off handsomely—witness, for example, how the Cardinals led the league in ERA this year with an average starter's salary of only $3.4 million. Pretty impressive stuff.

What would he be doing if he weren't in baseball?

He would be an insurance salesman in his home state of Minnesota, very active in the Rotary and Kiwanis clubs, volunteering for the Republican Party come election time. He'd be the best salesman in his district for several years running—the type of guy who could convince you to buy earthquake insurance 2,000 miles from any fault line.

Getting with the Program
by Matt Welch

Mike Scioscia's system makes more sense than you think ... but can it work?

Most hard-core seamheads would probably agree that the writers of Baseball Prospectus (www.baseballprospectus.com) are some of the sharper tools in the analysis shed. While the preseason predictions of newspaper sportswriters rarely merit a second glance, the picks by the Prospectus bunch, like those at The Hardball Times (www.hardballtimes.com), ESPN.com (www.espn.com) and a scant few other outlets, are worth bookmarking and taking seriously.

In 2002, the year the Anaheim Angels would go on to win the World Series after racking up the best Pythagorean win-loss record in baseball, each and every one of the 11 Prospectus writers came to the exact same preseason conclusion: the team from Orange County would finish dead last.

Such are the many joys and delicious ironies of being both an avid Angels fan and consumer of sabermetric analysis. Year after year, Mike Scioscia's boys and their distasteful "productive outs" are picked to stumble; year after year, the widely scrutinized moves of Oakland's Billy Beane are picked to pay off with division titles, MVP Awards, even World Series rings.

The 2005 season was no different, despite the Angels' 2004 division banner and Beane's offseason off-loading of Tim Hudson and Mark Mulder. The 12 prognosticators at Baseball Prospectus picked the A's over the Angels (and Rangers) by 7 to 4 to 1; the exact same numbers, coincidentally enough, as the soothsayers from The Hardball Times. ESPN.com's Rob Neyer, inventor of "The Beane Count" (which measures teams' accumulation and prevention of homers and walks) predicted for the fourth time in five years that the A's would win the West (and the fifth year—2002, as it turns out—he had Oakland winning the Wild Card on the way to a World Championship). At least he didn't have the A's sweeping not just the World Series, but the three major individual awards as well, as he had in 2004. "You know," he wrote at the time, "the Angels aren't going to win the West. The A's are, and I'm saying that mostly because that's what the numbers say."

These elusive "numbers" have been predicting Angels failure for the past four years, even as they've won as many playoff series as any major league team except the St. Louis Cardinals and earned more finger jewelry than a thousand Derek Jeters. With a winning track record in the immediate past and a swollen farm system promising an excellent crop of prospects over the next three years, it may be time to stop asking when Los Angeles of Anaheim will pay for what it does so wrong and start asking what exactly it is that it does so right.

And what you'll find when you start looking on the bright side is a surprising amount of qualities and strategies that would look right at home in a Baseball Primer thread or a Bill James book, starting with manager Mike Scioscia.

"There is one indispensable quality of a baseball manager," James wrote in the introduction to *The Bill James Guide to Baseball Managers*. "The manager *must* be able to command the respect of his players. This is absolute; everything else is negotiable."

There is no question that Scioscia and his coaching staff, now heading into their seventh full year, command the full respect of their players. And not just on the big-league roster, but up and down the minor leagues, where players and coaches alike casually refer to the whole organization as "the program," with a clear understanding of what the single system entails.

"Being part of the organization makes [the playoffs] more fun," wrote second base phenom Howie Kendrick in an online dispatch from the Arizona Fall League, where he was busy spraying line drives while the big club was toppling the Yankees in the Division Series. Kendrick finished second in the entire minor leagues with a .367 batting average split between Singe-A ball and Double-A. "Seeing what they teach us down here and seeing it put to use with success at that level is exciting. What they teach fits their style of play," he said.

Set aside for the moment the *wisdom* of Scioscia's "program," there is no confusion about whether it exists or what it entails. Angel players are expected to cut down on strikeouts (especially with runners on base), avoid the double play, take extra bases aggressively but not recklessly, keep disputes within the clubhouse, take each game one day at a time and above all else submit their egos to the higher authority of the team. That many or most of these are well-worn clichés matters far less than that they're enforced by the players themselves and widely believed in (with a few notable exceptions).

The discipline makes deviants stick out like atheists at the Crystal Cathedral. Jim Edmonds and Chuck

Finley, two dyed-blond talents who were perceived as the flaky moral center of an underachieving franchise, were let go soon after Scioscia was hired after the 70-92 1999 season. Mo Vaughn, the first and most intransigent of the stars who have demanded (and received) special treatment from the former Dodger catcher (mainly in the form of being allowed to play first base badly while the defensively superior Darin Erstad and Scott Spiezio made 70 starts at DH in 2000), was traded away. Scott Schoeneweis complained about being demoted from the starting rotation during the magical 2002 year and as a result became that rarity of modern Angeldom—a midseason trade (in 2003) by General Manager Bill Stoneman. Jose Guillen called out his pitchers publicly for not retaliating when he got hit by pitches and confronted Scioscia in private, drawing the remarkable punishment of being banished from the team while it was one game down with a week to go in the 2004 season. The 100-mph fireballer Bobby Jenks never got with the program despite several interventions, so he was left unprotected on the 40-man roster while "organization-men" catchers like Wil Nieves and Josh Paul stayed put.

As that last example illustrates, there are drawbacks to the Angels' system, but suffice it to say that they *have* one, and every player on every level knows what it demands.

In terms of roster construction and managerial strategy, Scioscia and Bill Stoneman have so far adhered to at least seven principles that wouldn't be out of place at a SABR convention:

1) Don't be afraid to let a free agent walk, especially if a replacement is ready for his close-up.

Troy Percival was still an effective closer in 2004, but Stoneman let Detroit pay $6 million for Percy's career-threatening injury while Francisco Rodriguez led the league in saves for $440,000. Dallas McPherson (if not his hip) was ready by 2005, so the most prodigious slugger in team history was cut loose to sign with Arizona. Despite the heartfelt pleading of nostalgic fans, Scott Spiezio was allowed to have his career implosion financed by the Seattle Mariners. Kevin Appier was cut from the team in 2003 when he was still owed millions.

It's true, Stoneman did offer longer-than-productive extensions to the team's core of Erstad, Garret Anderson and Tim Salmon, but A) those three (plus Edmonds and Glaus) were about the only sources of proven and promising talent when Scioscia and Stoneman took over the club; B) the minors were then and are still now absolutely barren of outfield talent; and C)

they each in their own way personified the Program—Erstad the intense, Anderson the unflappable, Salmon the awkwardly effective; each with terrific and versatile defense in their primes.

The crucial test for Stoneman's free-agent unsentimentality will come this offseason, as Scioscia favorite Bengie Molina seeks a multi-year deal while catcher-of-the-future Jeff Mathis makes his final preparations for the Show, and Mark Grace-caliber first base prospect Casey Kotchman vies for a deserved starting job against either Erstad or an as-yet unsigned free agent such as Paul Konerko.

2) There is untested but promising talent lying around waiting to be acquired, even in the middle infield.

When Stoneman took over, the Angels double-play combination was a train wreck—a breaking-down Gary DiSarcina feeding non-entity pivot men like Trent Durrington and Jeff Huson, with no minor league help on the way. Within a five-month period, Stoneman signed Benji Gil, who hadn't played major league ball in more than two years; traded for Adam Kennedy, who had 33 games total under his belt, and claimed David Eckstein off waivers. By 2005, Anaheim had arguably the best defensive middle infield in baseball, a capable young backup in Maicer Izturis, and five or six legitimate big league prospects vaulting up through the minors.

3) There is untested but promising talent lying around waiting to join MLB's best bullpen.

Scioscia, Stoneman and pitching coach Bud Black have made an art form out of plucking unloved relievers with baffling deliveries from obscurity and converting them into solid contributors. Brendan Donnelly, a strikebreaker-turned 30-year-old rookie in 2002, is the best and most effective example (at least until 2005, when he declined significantly), but Black has also spun temporary gold out of such scrap as Ben Weber, Kevin Gregg and Joel Peralta, while developing 38th round pick Scot Shields into one of the most versatile and coveted relievers in the game.

4) Older Quadruple-A players can still contribute.

Where other organizations turn their noses up at career minor leaguers (such as the relievers mentioned above), the Angels see opportunity. Robb Quinlan's major league debut came at 26; he was forced to learn third base on the job, and he's managed a .291/.340/.446 line over three years. Jeff DaVanon's first season with more than 88 at-bats came at age 29. Zach Sorensen, the 28-year-old with just a 36-game cup of coffee in 2003 to his credit, played in some crucial September moments in 2005, just as 31-year-old Adam Riggs did in 2004. Shawn Wooten hit .277 with 18 HR and 83 RBI in 606 AB from 2001-03, when he was 28-30.

5) Depth matters, and few things increase depth like having a Chone Figgins-style rover.

As Dodgers GM Paul DePodesta can surely attest, there is value at having major league depth waiting in the wings should injuries strike. Stoneman built a 2005 roster with four different players (Figgins, DaVanon, Juan Rivera and Erstad in a pinch) who could play the outfield should one of the three starters go down. With a 40-year-old in center field, a 33-year-old arthritic in left field, and a guy who looks like a walking backache in right field, this was prudent. The three combined to miss 156 games in the field.

Figgins started the year as a credible replacement second baseman for a convalescing Adam Kennedy, switched to third base (which he defended marvelously) when McPherson went down, and played center field when Scioscia belatedly noticed that Finley couldn't hit. This type of permanent rover position is strangely absent in the modern game, despite Seattle's 302 victories during the three years Mark McLemore filled gaps on a daily basis. Figgins, like Junior Gilliam a half century before, acts like a shock absorber on the roster's system, smoothing out the effects of unplanned injury or underperformance.

It also can't have escaped Stoneman's notice that his two most successful years (2002 and 2005), were marked by terrific depth at the fourth and fifth slots in the rotation. Neither club had a truly dominating ace, but they were almost always in games.

6) The postseason is no time to manage like the regular season.

One of the only complaints about Atlanta Braves Manager Bobby Cox is that his strategies do not appreciably change in the playoffs. Not so Mike Scioscia.

In the last game of the American League Championship Series, the Angels' starting center fielder was Garret Anderson. *Anderson didn't play a single inning in center field all year long.* This move may have smacked of desperation—the team couldn't buy a hit against the White Sox, and Scioscia needed to get both Kotchman and Rivera in the lineup—but it also speaks to the manager's willingness to tear up the playbook in the postseason.

Francisco Rodriguez pitched all of five and two-thirds innings in the regular season of 2002. Yet not only was the 20-year-old placed on the postseason roster, he was given a crucial role, and he performed

brilliantly. Fellow rookie John Lackey started Game 7 of the World Series instead of staff ace Ramon Ortiz.

Scioscia's bullpen usage also adapts for the postseason, with K-Rod in 2002 and Kelvim Escobar in 2005 being brought in for dominating, two-plus-inning stints that recall the days of Goose Gossage and early Rollie Fingers.

7) Keep meticulous stats, and let coaches and players know how they're measuring up.

Though they might not be the stats you value. Jeff Angus, of the website Management By Baseball, published an intriguing two-part article in October 2005 detailing how the Angels obsess about three measurements in particular: batting with runners in scoring position, batting with runners in scoring position and two outs, and individual runners taking extra bases. As it happens, the team has performed particularly well on these fronts the last two years, leading the league last year in batting average with runners in scoring position and two outs.

Taken together, these tactics have produced a solid track record of success, while drastically overhauling the look and feel of the major league ball club. In 2000, Scioscia and Stoneman's first year, the team scored 864 runs, drew 608 walks, hit 236 homers and stole 93 bases; all while giving up 5.36 runs a game. By 2005, the offense was down to 761 runs, 447 walks, 147 homers and 161 stolen bases, while giving up just 3.97 runs per game. The Angels have gone from a team of bashers (four guys with at least 34 home runs) to a team of pepper-sprayers (only one guy with more than 17), from a team whose top starter pitched 170 innings to one whose fourth-best pitched 177. The "program" of pitching, defense and scrapping for runs seems to have become more, not less, timely, with the decline of offense and the advent of defensive scrappers like the White Sox and Astros. Meanwhile the farm is stocked with remarkable talent. What's not to like?

Plenty. The organization is at a crossroads before the 2006 season, as Stoneman chooses between loyalty to Scioscia's favorites, sane development of his young talent and media pressure to clog up the right side of the defensive spectrum with a right-handed masher like Manny Ramirez or Paul Konerko.

Put plainly, Casey Kotchman (with his 124 OPS+) is ready to play full-time right now, and any obstacle to that goal will be a sign that Stoneman lacks the nerve to tell Scioscia he can't continue deferring to his favored veterans.

Anderson will be 34, and his arthritis has triggered related knee and back injuries. He was never what you'd call much of a hard runner anyway, but now his legs are going, and he's just not much of a left fielder anymore. Yet Scioscia down the stretch refused to start him at DH, where he belongs, and play 27-year-old Juan Rivera in left field.

Erstad has been a below-average hitter for *five years* now, and a brutal one against left-handed pitchers—.232/.298/.316 in 2005, .248/.291/.321 from 2001-2005. Yet Scioscia has refused so far to even consider pinch-hitting for him once in a while, let alone giving him the platoon he so richly deserves. (Adam Kennedy, on the other hand, is a substantially better hitter against lefties, and a more valuable defender, yet he's forced into a semi-platoon because he's not Scioscia's pet.)

In addition to consciously fielding a worse lineup in order to placate his veterans, Scioscia exhibits little clue that they are too injured to contribute. Finley last year hurt his shoulder the first week of the season and then kept quiet about it for two awful months before finally being moved to the disabled list. Vladimir Guerrero played noticeably hurt for stretches of the season (including the playoffs), when he couldn't contribute at all. Erstad and Bengie Molina both played, and hit terribly, when their bodies were visibly aching.

Every successful manager eventually has to face the day when the players to whom he's loyal are no longer contributing enough to win. If no major acquisitions are made, Scioscia needs to play Kotchman every day at first, move Erstad back to the outfield, and transition Anderson to DH, where he can do less damage to the club while riding out the rest of his painfully long contract.

But that's not the worst of Anaheim's problems. The biggest curse may be the success they've already enjoyed.

Having the Angel "program" deliver the playoffs three years out of four masks its inherent weaknesses. The organization may truly believe it has succeeded through productive outs, "little things" and grit, but in fact it has become adept at preventing runs while building just enough offense around one legitimate superstar. If and when he breaks down—as in the playoffs last year—the results will be ugly.

And one reason the team is scraping for runs is precisely because it insists on players comporting themselves within the company guidelines. Jim Edmonds may be a bit goofy around the gills, but he's hit 220 home runs since leaving Anaheim (Adam Kennedy, his replacement, has 47 over that period). Jose Guillen may be a jerk, but he drove in 104 runs in 2004, while his two replacements (Rivera and Izturis) combined for 74. Troy Glaus's departure was accompanied with some whispers about his commitment, but he did manage to out-homer McPherson 37-8.

Perhaps of greater concern, the team has proven too quick to give up on promising young arms and too protective of journeymen catchers nobody else wants. While the Angels were busy keeping Wil Nieves and Josh Paul on the 40-man roster, the White Sox snapped up young head case Bobby Jenks and the Brewers picked closer Derrick Turnbow off waivers. Power arms don't grow on trees, and the team's magic in locating unheralded journeymen relievers seemed to run out with the over-expensive signing of Esteban Yan.

When your program is too narrow to include two major league closers, yet your bullpen suffers from overwork, it might be time re-evaluate the program. But after making the final four, the only lesson the Angels seem to have learned is that it's hard to win when you can't score.

This is all cause for concern, but nothing more than that. Stoneman has one of the league's best 1-4 rotations coming back intact, $25 million or so coming off the books, and what is looking like one of the best Triple-A teams in recent memory preparing for liftoff in Salt Lake. By 2007 we should see the beginning of long and productive careers for Jeff Mathis, Brandon Wood, Howie Kendrick, Kendry Morales and Jered Weaver, at minimum.

If Scioscia can transition from the decline of his favorites to the advent of the new generation, all while keeping the Angels' annual date with October baseball, he will vault from the managerial ranks of the very good to the great. And the rest of us will be left in the enviable pickle of examining how a program that feels so anathema can be so successful.

The DePo Era

by Jon Weisman

So I'm the fellow who's going to show you how bright the Dodgers' future was with Paul DePodesta as their general manager. And you're either someone who's going to say, "Right on" or "Give me a break."

Two seasons into his tenure in Los Angeles, DePodesta was a folk hero to some and a homewrecker to others; he was "The Graduate" in a world with Mrs. Robinsons waiting in every apartment. And they did not all want to shake his hand. In the end, the Mrs. Robinsons won: On October 28, DePodesta learned from a reporter that he was going to be fired by Dodger owner Frank McCourt, and the following day it was made official.

Was it deserved? To evaluate DePodesta, I'll use statistics, unfortunately feeding the phony mythology that statistics define DePodesta. In truth, the DePodesta Era in Los Angeles wasn't about statistics. It wasn't even really about DePodesta.

The DePodesta Era was about fear. Fear that any statistic that hasn't been in the public consciousness for a century is wool pulled over the eyes. Fear that DePodesta pushed a first-class franchise into second-class status. Fear that he turned the Dodgers into losers—unlovable losers. Fear that people like him will chase the personality out of baseball. It's about the self-appointed gatekeepers of baseball—the media and the fans—fearing a loss of control.

And it's a fear that predated DePodesta's February 16, 2004 arrival as the Dodgers' general manager.

For approximately half a century, until 1998, the O'Malley family owned the Dodgers. Unlike Brooklyn, where the O'Malley name is sour milk, Los Angeles drinks to fond memories of the O'Malley ownership. Neither Walter nor his son, Peter, who succeeded him, was an extravagant spender, least of all on ballplayers. Instead, they built and maintained an enchanting stadium, kept ticket prices among the lowest in the major leagues, and delivered winning teams on a mostly regular basis. Perhaps above all else, they created a home for Vin Scully.

The O'Malley's sale of the Dodgers placed the team's respectability before a wrecking ball. The first new owners, Rupert Murdoch and News Corp., traded the team's best and most popular player, Mike Piazza, without consulting general manager Fred Claire. Claire left shortly thereafter, and the new GM, Kevin Malone, came in and infamously announced there was a "new sheriff in town" before having misadventures at the position worthy of Lobo, squandering the burgeoning Dodger player payroll on extravagant contracts for such players as Darren Dreifort and Carlos Perez. The Dodgers fired Malone after he threatened to fight a spectator in San Diego. Though no punches were thrown, Dodger fans were scarred.

Under new team president Bob Daly, interim general manager Dave Wallace and permanent replacement Dan Evans restored some hope, some stability, some class. But then News ended its dalliance with baseball. The subsequent sale to McCourt, who by some accounts borrowed more money to fund his acquisition of the Dodgers than the purchase price itself, placed everyone back on grass needles. Fox was the frying pan, McCourt was the fire. People reasoned that McCourt, a real estate developer, was really using the Dodgers as an excuse to buy and develop the Chavez Ravine land beneath and around Dodger Stadium, and would treat the baseball team itself as a teardown project. A report in the *Los Angeles Times* that McCourt's debt-heavy ownership quest unraveled a potential Vladimir Guerrero signing supported this theory, and McCourt's belated public greeting to Los Angeles was ineffective in convincing many that he wasn't a carpetbagger.

Coincident to these travails, Michael Lewis published *Moneyball*, his account of how Oakland A's general manager Billy Beane survived and thrived with a low payroll by exploiting inefficiencies in the business of baseball—rounding up undervalued talent, often against what baseball scouts (much less sportswriters and fans) would have recommended. The book legitimately hit a nerve in the culture of baseball by questioning some of the value of anecdotal observation. Some extrapolated that *Moneyball* was a movement to rid baseball of its humanity. Humanity is an appealing quality, so this put more people on edge.

Shortly after McCourt completed his purchase of the Dodgers, he declared the team's general manager job open. To say this action, like his acquisition of the team, was also handled distastefully is a bit of an understatement, considering that he had not yet let go of Evans. Instead, he made Evans interview for his job like anyone else. Not for the first time, McCourt turned an employee into a martyr—even to his detractors.

More than a few speculated that Beane was McCourt's first choice, but ultimately it was Beane's assistant general manager, DePodesta, who ended up as Dodger GM. In any case, there it was: an evil owner had brought an evil *Moneyball*er to Los Angeles.

If the O'Malleys had hired someone like DePodesta, and if DePodesta had not been exposed by the *Moneyball* klieg lights, the move would easily have been blessed—a bright young man who spoke in reasonable tones, who could work within constraints, who could win without overspending. DePodesta's relative inexperience would hardly have mattered. Fans in Los Angeles had been raised in the legend of Walter Alston, anonymous when he was named Dodger manager and a Hall of Famer when he left. Heck, many had even grown fond of Wallace and Evans.

Instead, DePodesta was treated like a live grenade. Two seasons later, observers continue to debate whether DePodesta was the blast that was destroying the Dodgers or saving them.

Stripped of the emotional backstory, DePodesta was almost conventional. Like most general managers, DePodesta alternated between intense activity and dormancy. He made obvious moves and risky ones. He made bad moves and good ones.

And yes, they were mostly good. In reviewing every player transaction that DePodesta executed with the Dodgers, the cumulative effect is stunning. According to The Hardball Times' Win Shares Above Bench statistics (which represent all contributions a player makes toward his team's wins, compared to those an average bench player would have made), players that DePodesta traded or gave up rights to accumulated 12.2 WSAB after their departure. Players that DePodesta acquired accumulated 69.0 WSAB. Even while enduring more player injuries in 2005 than any other team in the majors, DePodesta multiplied many times over the offense and pitching production of the players he replaced.

Of course, there remains one huge statistic against DePodesta. Despite these improvements, the Dodgers went 71-91 in 2005, their second-worst record in 46 seasons in Los Angeles. It's hard enough to sell Win Shares to an unenthusiastic public—is it even worth the effort when the team victories don't correspond?

The answer is that had DePodesta not made the moves he did, the Dodgers would have been far more rancid than they appeared to the world at the end of 2005. DePodesta has been accused of gutting the Dodgers, but he was more like someone's fiancée evaluating each item in the bachelor apartment and deciding which fit into a grown-up house. A good deal of what DePodesta discarded, for simplification's sake, was crap. Crap with sentimental value, crap with a heartbeat, crap that had once been heroic, but ultimately crap with an expiration date.

This has been a surprisingly difficult concept for many people to swallow, but there's an apparent reason for it. People often need to see a disaster first-hand to appreciate it. Hideo Nomo, for example, was a true phenomenon in Los Angeles twice over—first as a mesmerizing strikeout pitcher, then enjoying a Frank Tanana-like renaissance while adjusting to declining arm strength. In both incarnations, Nomo was a fan favorite.

DePodesta allowed Nomo to leave as a free agent at the end of the 2004 season, and no one minded. That's because Dodger fans in 2004 suffered the almost physical discomfort of Nomo's 8.25 ERA (and -8.4 WSAB) in person. He was not a contributor to the 2004 division title—so there was no loss.

One could argue that Nomo was someone DePodesta should have signed to a minor league contract for 2005, as Tampa Bay did, and invited him to Spring Training. Starting pitching is always at a premium. Nomo had rebounded once before. He was eminently affordable, a no-risk proposition. And most of all, he was a classy guy, a true Dodger.

As it happens, DePodesta made the correct decision on Nomo, whose rebound in 2005 was non-existent (7.24 ERA, -4 WSAB). As it also happens, DePodesta made similarly correct decisions on a number of players—only with the added bonus of anticipating their declines. But the looming fear of DePodesta prevented complete acceptance of this.

Perhaps it was understandable for people to bemoan the end of Jose Lima Time in Los Angeles following his 14 victories in 2004—including the Dodgers' only playoff triumph in 16 seasons. It was almost pathological that some continued the rending of garments following the 2005 season, in which he was the single-worst starting pitcher in baseball, with a supersonic 7.47 ERA and -8 WSAB.

Eschewing sentimentality for pragmatism, DePodesta let go of Alex Cora, whose WSAB in 2005 was -1, and Cora's platoon partner Jose Hernandez, who declined to -3. In exchange for low-salaried catcher Jason Phillips, Kazuhisa Ishii went to New York, where the Mets paid him $2.6 million for 91 innings of a 5.14 ERA (-2 WSAB). DePodesta still gets grief for casting aside Steve Finley, which is galling not only because of Finley's .645 OPS (-2 WSAB) in 2005, but because

DePodesta acquired Finley in the first place. DePodesta milked Finley like a day trader selling Cisco before the collapse, earning 13 home runs and 4.3 WSAB from the center fielder in only 58 games, in exchange for three minor leaguers who since that time have built a combined 0.3 WSAB.

Furthermore, because of baseball's rules that force a team to offer eligible players arbitration or relinquish all negotiating rights to them until May 1 of the following season, DePodesta could not have signed some of these players as cheaply as other teams did. DePodesta could have been forced to work through baseball's arbitration process, which all but guarantees a raise based on past success, even if everyone in the world agrees that an older player is headed for a decline. Finley, for example, stood to earn a big boost from his 2004 salary of $7 million if he went through arbitration. Instead, after DePodesta declined to offer arbitration, Finley signed a two-year deal with Anaheim worth, on average, the same $7 million per year.

Paying Lima, Cora, Hernandez and Finley the $15 million or so that it would have taken to retain them in Los Angeles would have accessorized the Dodgers about as well as a fraternity mug in a china cabinet. But many castigate DePodesta to this day, again in part because of misdirected McCourt anger that wonders whether the saved money will be reinvested in the team.

Not every transaction by DePodesta was as black-and-white right as these. But some were still more virtuous than people realize.

Back in July 2004, the Dodgers had built a lead in the National League West, with DePodesta acquisitions like Milton Bradley and Jayson Werth blending nicely with the pre-existing talent. It was a feel-good summer, but DePodesta sensed that the Dodgers did not have enough to make them bulletproof in the playoffs. To be sure, he could have stood pat: the Dodgers hadn't won a division in nearly a decade, and people genuinely liked the team. But instead, DePodesta gave Dodger fans their rudest awakening since they rubbed their eyes to the Piazza trade, sending lovable Paul Lo Duca with Juan Encarnacion and Guillermo Mota to Florida for Brad Penny, Hee-Seop Choi and minor league pitcher Bill Murphy.

Even for some who discounted Lo Duca's heart and soul value (which took on legendary proportions after the trade), even for some who believed that victories would solve any chemistry problems Lo Duca left behind, the trade was risky. While the Dodgers appeared to have the outfield depth to withstand the loss of Encarnacion—who had already pretty much been benched for Werth anyway—and the relief pitch-

ing to thrive beyond Mota's departure (ace closer Eric Gagne pitched only 3.1 more innings after the All-Star break in 2004 than he did in 2003 or 2002, with Yhency Brazoban arriving from the minors to fill Mota's role), the trade exchanged a deficiency in starting pitching for a deficiency at catcher.

But after Penny was injured in his second Dodger start, DePodesta's thought process was validated when the Dodger starting pitching barely made it through September. Lo Duca's presence would have done little to solve a near-nightmare that found the Dodgers fighting off the Giants with Edwin Jackson, Jeff Weaver, Ishii and Nomo combining for 15 starts and an ERA of 6.12 in the final month. And it's hard to imagine that Lo Duca would have made much of a difference in a National League Division Series in which the Dodgers' three losses were by a combined score of 22-8.

This trade, DePodesta's most famous and most polarizing, the transaction that truly made him a protagonist in his own story, continues to defy final judgment. So far, there has been a net WSAB loss of 4.9—mainly because Encarnacion had something of a resurgence in 2005 (.795 OPS, 4.9 WSAB) that was vexing considering the injuries that befell the Dodger outfield in '05. Even though he missed most of his 2004 time with the Dodgers, Penny, the main reason for the trade, has outperformed Lo Duca in WSAB, 5.7 to 4. Mota (1.2 WSAB) has been a disappointment with the Marlins, while the semi-maligned Choi (-0.5 WSAB) has been a story unto himself.

Given the youth of Penny and Choi compared to whom they were traded for, the trade still figures to play out in DePodesta's favor. If Penny had Lo Duca's rags-to-riches story, local fans would already be just as thrilled with him.

For sure, this wasn't even the Dodgers' most costly deadline trade in 2004. Almost as an afterthought, DePodesta sent Dave Roberts to Boston for a minor league veteran, Henri Stanley. For someone accused of being a robot, DePodesta made a trade that was mostly a humanitarian gesture. Upon acquiring Finley and Choi to join Bradley, Werth and Shawn Green, the Dodgers appeared to have a surplus of outfielders and first basemen. Roberts' playing time was going to be slashed, so DePodesta rewarded him with a move to another contender where he might contribute more.

A year later, Finley wisely was not offered arbitration, Green was traded, and Bradley, Werth and newcomers J.D. Drew and Ricky Ledee were injured. DePodesta took major league outfield depth for granted and it cost him. The alternatives to Roberts—Jason Grabowski, Mike Edwards, Jason Repko—could not carry his spikes. Even with Roberts' usual injuries in 2005, the giveaway cost the Dodgers 6.2 WSAB. Other trades that DePodesta has made brought in younger players that could turn negatives into positives over the long haul (putting aside for the moment what they meant in 2004 or 2005). But with Stanley's arc almost certain to fall short of major league impact—a poor man's Roberts is he—the Roberts trade is DePodesta's clearest loser. Speaking to reporters in 2005, DePodesta correctly cited the Roberts trade, not the Lo Duca trade, as the one he'd most like to have back, and one can see why. He kept Grabowski (-1.3 WSAB as a Dodger), after all, as an alternative.

But think about this. DePodesta's biggest overall mistake, on paper, was trading Dave Roberts. *Dave Roberts*. It's not exactly like letting a 22-year-old Pedro Martinez go.

Still, it remains unclear whether gambling with Lo Duca was worth the social capital it cost DePodesta. Unlike others who became part of the Dodger group hug in 2004, trading Lo Duca kept DePodesta outside the embrace. The fears for the Dodgers' future began to telescope toward him. The trade and its rationale defined him and colored every move he made—even the ones that the numbers, common sense or both show to have been prudent.

DePodesta shied away from committing $50 million or more to Adrian Beltre and found the circumspection justified (for now, at least) when Beltre's first season in Seattle produced only a .716 OPS (3 WSAB). Yet after Lo Duca, the Beltre farewell is considered prime evidence for prosecutors against DePodesta. In contrast, the man who did receive Beltre's money, J.D. Drew, more than doubled Beltre's WSAB at 7 despite playing only 72 games. Beltre is a more valuable fielder, but even Drew is unlikely to play so few games in coming seasons.

The best remaining piece of Dodger furniture boxed for shipping in the 2004-2005 offseason was Shawn Green, whom DePodesta traded for four minor leaguers, including catcher Dioner Navarro. DePodesta threw in $10 million to make the trade but also saved the other $6 million of Green's 2005 salary. Green produced an OPS of .832 and 6 WSAB in 2005. The 21-year-old Navarro, called up for good in the summer, produced a .729 OPS (0 WSAB), while pitcher Derek Lowe, whose free agent signing came within 24 hours of the Green trade using the cash dividend, produced 5 WSAB. So the trade was just about an even exchange for 2005, while leaving the Dodgers with a promising catcher for years to come (to go with top minor league prospect Russell Martin).

In two years, DePodesta got rid of mostly the right people, broke even on some other moves, stands to profit on even more—including possibly the Lo Duca trade—and made only the Roberts blunder, such as it was. Meanwhile, we haven't yet talked about DePodesta's transcendent victories.

- Finding a taker in Tampa Bay for Jason Romano at the end of Spring Training 2004, DePodesta procured Antonio Perez and a WSAB reward of 4.4.

- Giovanni Carrara, picked up off the scrap heap for a second stint in Los Angeles (first under DePodesta), enjoyed a rebirth à la Nomo with a 2.18 ERA in 2004 and a total 7.7 WSAB in 1 1/2 seasons. Carrara was the last Dodger acquisition before Penny/Choi, and for the sake of argument, if Carrara had been a throw-in with that deal, the Dodgers would have already won it.

- In August deals one year apart, DePodesta sent off nondescript minor leaguers Jereme Milons and Tony Schrager for Elmer Dessens and Jose Cruz Jr., netting a swingman and an outfielder with a combined 6 WSAB.

- And at the top of the list, joined at the hip-check: Milton Bradley and Jeff Kent.

With all the angst that surrounds Bradley, his acquisition was a huge success for the Dodgers even if he never plays another game in Los Angeles. Bradley's WSAB in two seasons is 10.6. There is no evidence or anecdotal implication that his personality undermined the performance of his teammates or cost the team victories. And as for disgracing the Dodger uniform, Bradley would at worst have to get in line behind someone like Guillermo Mota, who pleaded no contest in July 2004 to a reckless driving charge stemming from an arrest for driving under the influence—yet whose trade by DePodesta that same month met with widespread lamentations. DePodesta has yet to pay a higher price in minor leaguers than he did for Bradley—outfielder Franklin Gutierrez and pitcher Andrew Brown—and with Bradley's Dodger career in doubt, it's possible DePodesta might lose this trade in the long run. But for two years, Bradley was a significant contributor.

Kent, meanwhile, replaced Beltre as the Dodgers' cleanup hitter and posted a WSAB six times as high in 2005: 18, second-highest of any position player with a new team behind Florida's Carlos Delgado. Kent was almost as valuable offensively in 2005 as Lo Duca, Beltre and Green combined, and of that group, only Beltre is above average defensively. The caveat with Kent is whether he contributed to Bradley's final downfall in Los Angeles, perhaps by goading him into either Bradley's divisive remarks inside and outside of the clubhouse or the extra bit of hustle that caused Bradley to further injure his ailing knee, irreparably as far as 2005 was concerned.

Overall, the period in which people commonly think DePodesta completed his destruction of the Dodgers was a triumph disguised by how likely many of the 2004 players were going to decline. DePodesta by far brought in more talent than he let go, all the while preserving and even adding to the Dodger cache of highly regarded prospects. While increasing the production of his major leaguers, DePodesta also augmented and preserved the top-rated farm system in baseball according to *Baseball America*. He improved the present without sacrificing the future. In 2005, DePodesta traded only one minor leaguer, 28-year-old Triple-A infielder Schrager, for major league talent.

During the 2004-2005 offseason, the period in which DePodesta supposedly completed his gutting of the Dodgers, DePodesta acquisitions tallied 24.9 WSAB in 2005. The players they replaced were in the negative: -10.0 WSAB. This statistic is not colored by underuse of ex-Dodgers by their new employers. The positive contributors played every day that they were healthy. Most of the negative contributors were benched or released before their seasons were over and they could do further damage. No one was held back the way, for example, a healthy Choi was held back by DePodesta's own manager.

DePodesta anticipated a decline in popular Dodgers. He saved the Dodgers money and brought all the heartache onto himself.

Meanwhile, Jim Tracy got off with his reputation intact. Little in a career in baseball bears resemblance to the 9-to-5 life, but the showdown between DePodesta and the Dodger manager, culminating in Tracy's departure the day after the 2005 season ended, speaks to a conventional workplace drama.

For Tracy, it was, "What do you do when your boss is an idiot?"

For DePodesta, it was, "But I'm not an idiot."

Ironically, both believed in the value of numbers; to his final days, Tracy regularly used statistics to align his players. But Tracy and DePodesta clashed over which statistics mattered and how much.

Over time, Tracy perceived his roster to have been infiltrated by a group of alien drones. Tracy disliked several of DePodesta's changes individually and in the aggregate. Furthermore, with DePodesta's moves came an expectation that the team would be managed in a manner accentuating the acquisitions' strengths, contrary to some tactics Tracy embraces.

Tracy was faced with a choice: fit himself into his supervisor's philosophy or stick to his own. Workplace etiquette makes the solution simple. If the boss says, "Do something," you do it. The exception is if the boss proposes something so nefarious that to go along would abet some legal, moral or ethical crime.

Buoyed by nearly 30 years of professional experience, Tracy rebelled.

Insubordination is taken seriously in baseball. Players who so much as swing when they're not supposed to are censured. Yet Tracy went ahead, at times going as far as to play a backup catcher (Phillips) at first base ahead of DePodesta's preferred starter or having DePodesta's top hitter (Drew) bunt.

The Dodgers addressed the conflict the way most organizations do. They held meetings. They got frustrated. Finally, Tracy was granted conscientious objector status and released from service.

In addition to the respect that is rightfully his for four winning seasons in Los Angeles, Tracy enjoys sympathy from those who believe him a latter-day Norma Rae, risking his livelihood for the greater good. However, it's dubious whether DePodesta's philosophy deserved such a war from within, or whether, once again, this was an issue of insecurity and fear. Consider the principal charges against DePodesta:

DePodesta undervalued workplace chemistry. It has never been proven that chemistry breeds success—at a minimum, success has also been shown to solve many a clubhouse chemistry problem, and failure has shattered the most congenial of teams.

DePodesta undervalued workplace character. This stems mainly from the mercurial actions of Bradley and to a lesser extent, the isolationism of a couple others. What it discounts is the commendable personalities of almost every current Dodger and the character deficiencies that predated DePodesta's arrival.

DePodesta undervalued workplace continuity. Though 60 percent of the Dodgers' 2004 playoff roster remained in 2005, significant pieces were gone. However, only one departee, Green, had anything approaching a decent season this year. Whether continuity is more important than talent is debatable. There are certainly a number of Dodgers who declined in 2005 despite remaining Dodgers.

But there is an under-told story here. Many DePodesta moves aimed for the chemistry, character and continuity that Tracy espouses—but over the long term. DePodesta was striving to remove obstacles that would prevent players raised in the organization from thriving cohesively for years at a time, while he found the most qualified veterans to compliment them that he can. The result was a mix of regrettable and shrewd moves—the same mix Tracy displayed as manager.

One might disagree with DePodesta's methods, but it was not madness.

There will always be bosses who are idiots and subordinates smarter than them, and time might prove DePodesta and Tracy prime examples. As much as possible, different views should be shared up the organizational ladder as well as down. But DePodesta was no evil leader. Tracy won't have trouble sleeping over his decisions, and workplace rebellion has its place, but this wasn't it.

Before he was fired, DePodesta faced a challenging offseason, with few quality free agents available and tension everywhere. A year removed from a division

title, the Dodgers appear a work in progress. But the vast majority of DePodesta's decisions were positives, and fear about him was misplaced. If the goal of Dodger fans is for their general manager to improve their team, DePodesta appeared to have been their man. He was a young general manager, and like any young prospect, on the field or off, the occasional misstep did not negate his potential.

When the Yankees barely win a division and then go out in the first round of the playoffs, New York goes ballistic. In Los Angeles, the same results happened in 2004 and it was cause for beatification. Fear of any tampering became overwhelming. DePodesta messed with a team that became sacred. The combination of history that pre-dated DePodesta and his refusal to be satisfied led him into the hottest of hot water.

"Right on."/"Give me a break."

DePodesta's Dodger Transaction Legacy			
When Transactions Took Place	WSAB Lost After Transactions	WSAB Gained After Transactions	Net WSAB After Transactions
Before 2004 Season	6.2	21.8	15.6
During 2004 Season	16.0	16.3	0.3
Between 2004 and 2005 Seasons	-10.0	24.9	34.9
During 2005 Season	0.0	6.0	6.0
Total	**12.2**	**69.0**	**56.8**

Never a Dull Moment

by Alex Belth

New York City has a lot of traditions and institutions, all of which are subject to change. If the late, great Penn Station could get ripped down, surely nothing is sacred. For a native, there is no other feeling quite like the sudden emptiness that overcomes you when you walk down the street to discover your favorite bookstore, restaurant or shop is no longer there. Woody Allen once said that "Change equals Death," and that sums up my feelings about how things evolve in New York. Yet as off-putting as they may initially seem, these changes are an integral part of New York's nature, so there is little use getting all heated about the fact that there is a Starbucks or a Duane Reade on every other block. The good old days? Yeah, you could afford to live in Manhattan 25 years ago, but you'd probably get mugged twice a month too. So what are you gonna do but try and accept things for what they are?

I often feel like this coping mechanism is what makes being a Yankees fan seem like second nature to me. You pretty much know what you are going to get from them—what the advantages and disadvantages will be—and try to accept them for what they are. The Yankees are a genuine New York institution and have been on top for a decade now. *Cats* might be the longest running show in Broadway history, but in the New York sports world, nothing beats *The Steinbrenner Follies*, 32 years and running at the end of the 2005 season. Since 1973, the Yankees have been in the World Series on ten occasions and have won it six times. This past year, they set an attendance record, and business is booming.

George Steinbrenner turned 75 this season, and despite persistent rumors about his failing health (both physically and mentally), he stands as the senior-ranking owner in the game. That is remarkable for the upstart who spearheaded the era of free agency in the mid 1970s. Steinbrenner's nose for showbiz made him the David Merrick of big league owners, and when I think back on the names that have come and gone over the years, they are like characters in a comic book or actors in a soap opera. The names change, but the story lines stay the same. If there has been some semblance of order established in the Joe Torre years, the Bronx Zoo is still alive and kicking behind the scenes. It's still crazy after all these years.

The fact that Torre has lasted this long under Steinbrenner is a small miracle that isn't appreciated as often as it should be. If manager years are like dog years—endangered-specific-years in George's world—then Torre's streak of ten seasons as the Yankee skipper should be regarded along with Cal Ripken's streak of consecutive games played as one of the great all time records. Twenty years ago what would you have been more impressed with: Ripken beating Gehrig's streak or any man lasting ten straight years as a manager for George Steinbrenner?

In Steinbrenner's first 23 years as owner of the Yankees, he employed 21 managers. Billy Martin, who had five separate stints, managed the most games during this period, with 941 (556-385, good for a .591 winning percentage). Buck Showalter, the organization man who took over the big league team during Steinbrenner's second exile from the game, was the Yankees manager for the longest consecutive stretch, four seasons, or 592 games (313-268, a .539 winning percentage). After ten years, Torre has been the most successful manager who has ever worked for Steinbrenner, with 1618 games (982-634, a .608 percentage), and trails only Joe McCarthy (1149-969, .623) and Casey Stengel (1460-867, .627) in Yankees history as the team's greatest manager.

There is a lot to be said for Torre as a strategist—and he deservedly took many jabs this year to be sure—but it is hard to argue with his appeal as a public figure. The calm stoicism he has projected under great stress has made him a beloved paternal figure. He's the stern but lovable uncle from Brooklyn everyone wishes they had. In fact, Torre has moved beyond baseball celebrity: He's an icon, the most popular coach in New York since Casey Stengel. Naturally, while Steinbrenner undoubtedly appreciates Torre, he is also insecure enough to envy Torre's adulation and has taken shots at his manager for the past several years now. It is the most interesting of power plays that Steinbrenner has been involved with one of his managers simply because Torre has so much leverage. The truth of the matter is Torre is even more charming than Steinbrenner can be, plus he's got something that George can never have: He's a native New Yorker. Torre is coddled and even protected in a way that an out-of-towner could never be. He's baseball's version of a made guy.

When the 2005 season ended with a first-round playoff defeat to the Angels, the Yankees had not won a title in five years. While some writers and many fans have jumped on the team's flaws—of which there are many—the current Yankees are competing against an almost mythical team. If anything, the Yankees are now more like the Braves than ever before, and I don't mean that as an insult. Their relative lack of success in the playoffs serves to highlight just how special the 1996-2000 teams were, not how bad the newer teams have necessarily been. (With the exception of 1998, they never did blow the league away, as Allen Barra noted in his article "Don't Blame the Yankees," which appeared in his collection of essays *Brushbacks and Knockdowns*.)

Were the Yankees players of those seasons magical? Did they posses more character or more heart than the more recent teams? The results make this an easy answer for some, but I don't regard Hideki Matsui or Gary Sheffield as mentally weak or lacking in personality, and I don't look back on Scott Brosius or Chad Curtis as if they could walk on water. The Yankees did have a lot of guys who did not accept losing during that era, and were wired so tight that they often were able to create their own fortune. (I've never felt so confident in a team after a playoff loss than I did in 1997. Watching that team, led by David Cone and Paul O'Neill standing red-faced in the dugout as the Indians celebrated, I thought, "Wow, these guys are even more upset than I am.") Those teams were characterized by an ability to play sound baseball; when the other team made a mistake, they pounced on it and made the opponent pay. Those Yankees were closers in a way that no team will likely be again for a sustained period of time for many years to come.

What truly distinguished those teams in my mind was their appreciation for how hard baseball is to play, and how difficult it is to win a championship. I always felt watching that team that they collectively understood how hard it all was. They took their jobs seriously and defended their title with pride and honor. Even when the strain of repeating started wearing them down in 2000, they held it together a little bit longer through an admirable 2001 postseason. Some of the Yankees' newer star players—Mike Mussina, Jason Giambi, Hideki Matsui and Alex Rodriguez—have been accused of coming to New York to pick up a ring as if it were something you could get with a cup of coffee at a bodega. While that might have been what attracted them here, I doubt that any of them thought it would be easy. And since none of them has won a title in New York, each has discovered the downside of not winning in here. (Just to make sure, the Yanks brought back some of the old faces from the glory days this year: Luis Sojo and Joe Girardi were coaches, and Tino Martinez, Mike Stanton and Ramiro Mendoza were all on the roster

at various points. Other than a last-hurrah home run streak in the spring by Martinez, none of the old guard was productive.)

The 2005 season was a cockamamie year for the Bronx Bombers, but I liked the team and came away once again marveling at just how difficult baseball is. It's hard to win the division and outlast everyone else to make the playoffs, and it is a chore to win the World Series. Heck, it was an ordeal for Al Leiter not to go 3-2 on every batter he faced. The Yankees didn't make it easy on themselves with a thoroughly misbegotten offseason from the front office, but they were able to overcome their (mostly self-imposed) flaws and rallied to win the American League East for the eighth straight year.

Writers have been anticipating the great Yankee decline for five or six years now, and while it hasn't exactly happened yet, the front office certainly put the team behind the eight-ball coming into the year. After their disastrous playoff loss to the Boston Red Sox in 2004, the Yankees needed pitching help, a second baseman and a center fielder. They came out of the winter handing out fat deals to Carl Pavano, Jaret Wright and signing Tony Womack to be their second baseman. They traded Kenny Lofton, who was underused in a platoon situation with Bernie Williams in 2004, to the Phillies for relief pitcher Felix Rodriguez. Carlos Beltran was available and willing to give the Yankees somewhat of a discount, and he would have been the ideal replacement for Williams, who has not been a good fielder in years and has rapidly deteriorated as a hitter too. But after signing Pavano and Wright, even the Yankees couldn't fork out another $100 million deal. They did not re-sign Jon Lieber, and of course, they traded for Randy Johnson.

During the first two months of the season, we watched the Yankees pay for their mistakes. Pavano was inconsistent and then hurt, Wright was hurt early, and then hurt again later—both were resounding busts. (Kevin Brown wasn't far behind them either.) Womack was flat-out bad, and eventually moved to the outfield before he found a more suitable position on the bench. I followed the early part of the year with a mixture of righteousness, frustration and finally, resignation. The Yankees were getting exactly what they paid for. The team couldn't do anything with any degree of reliability: pitch, field, or hit well with runners on base. Jorge Posada, generally a fine catcher, slumped horribly. Randy Johnson was tentative, and didn't look at all like the intimidating pitcher he had been just the year before (though he would recover nicely to have a solid season).

Maybe the writers were finally right. This was the year the Yankees would crumble. The team sure didn't look like they were enjoying themselves. They were 11-19 to start the season and then won ten straight games (18 out of 20 all told) only to lose 11 of their next 14. After a loss to the Twins dropped their record to 28-28 on June 6, Minnesota's center fielder Torii Hunter said, "They've got some great guys over there, but it just seems like they're not having any fun. Even when you're losing, you've got to have fun out here. It seems like it's all controlled over there … I know they've got a lot of expectations on them, and that makes it harder. But to me, that's no way to play."

Several days later, the Yankees were humiliated in St. Louis, putting forth such a weak effort in the first game that afterwards Torre told reporters, "It was an embarrassing game." Derek Jeter was visibly furious in the dugout as the team did its best Chico's Bail Bonds imitation. Afterwards, when Torre had conducted another of what would be a string of team meetings this year, the manager told reporters, "This was the worst. This one stands on its own … It's not the pitching coach's fault, it's not the hitting coach's fault," Torre said. "It's my fault. Ultimately it falls on me. I'm in charge of this team."

Yet six games after the Cards series, the Yankees rolled over the Cubs at the Stadium (after sweeping the Pirates), prompting Chicago's manager Dusty Baker to say, "The Yankees are the best team we've seen all season … I don't know why they're a couple games over .500." The Yanks lost five of their next six games. And so it went. The Yankees were foiled by bottom-feeders like the Royals and especially the Devil Rays. At some point the smug satisfaction that they were getting what they deserved became an unpleasant way to endure the rest of the season.

Fortunately, in the second half, the Yankees played very well. They survived and even prospered through the most arduous part of their schedule in the middle of the summer. Ignited by the likes of Aaron Small, Shawn Chacon, Chien-Ming Wang and Robinson Cano, and led by their stars Rodriguez, Rivera, Jeter, Sheffield and Matsui, the Bombers were still flawed and far from great, but they were good enough to get back in the playoff race. In fact, the final six weeks of the schedule were filled with nerve-racking "must-win" games, and the Yanks, aided by a poor finish by the Red Sox, managed to qualify for the playoffs on the second to last game of the regular season.

A quick first round exit at the hands of the Angels did not entirely come as a surprise. Each game they lost was all too familiar; they were the ways the team had been losing all year. In all, it was a fitting end. However, Joe Torre admitted to the media that he was more upset about losing this year than he had been in 2004. Torre has never had to work so hard to get a Yankees team into the playoffs. In fact, the last two weeks of the season felt like they were the playoffs. By the end of the year, the team seemed to come together and was able to win close games that they had lost in May and June.

You could sense how badly Torre wanted to win even before October. During the last week of the season, the Yankees held a big lead over the Orioles and yet their middle relief allowed Baltimore back in the game. At his wit's end, Torre was forced to bring Flash Gordon into the game. As the infielders huddled around the pitcher's mound during the pitching change, Jeter put his arm on Torre's shoulder, gave him a quick little massage and essentially told him not to worry. Torre, whose paternal relationship with Jeter was never more evident than later that weekend when the two men hugged on the infield at Fenway Park after the Yanks clinched the AL East, must have appreciated Jeter's efforts to cheer him up, but his expression did not change. He still had the blank look of a Brooklyn undertaker, and yet you knew he was just dying inside having to bring Gordon in the game.

Torre wasn't the only one who desperately wanted to win this year. During the ninth inning of Game 4 of the ALCS, a game in which Rivera pitched two scoreless innings, the Fox TV cameras showed Brian Cashman watching the game from his box. Cashman's arms were folded and it appeared as if his chest had caved in. He was hunched over, and I'll be damned if he was breathing at all. That image—of enervated, breathless, tension—summed up how I felt during the last weeks of the season. Of course I'm not working in the "Win or Else!" fishbowl, I just follow those that do.

I understand why the Yankees measure their success in World Championships, but as a fan, it's a losing proposition to view your team in such limited terms. The trick for a Yankees fan is to somehow not subscribe to the company line of "Win or Else!" It's tempting, believe me, but that sensibility makes it just too difficult to enjoy the game. There is nothing more vapid than the culture of entitlement that engulfs the Yankees. The worst part about it is that it discounts the really hard work that goes into winning. For years now, I've felt that many Yankee fans don't really appreciate what they've had—but once you are winning, you get greedy and begin to obsess over the end results and not the process. While 2005 was filled with plenty of frustration to go around, there were some memorable moments and performances. One thing that struck me towards the end of the year was that over the past two or three seasons, the Hall of Fame futures of several Yankees have played themselves out, with Bernie Williams and Mike Mussina likely falling short, and Gary Sheffield, Derek Jeter and Mariano Rivera virtually a lock to make it.

There is no Yankee whose career has given more satisfaction than Bernie Williams' has. Sure, he was the organization's top prospect in the early nineties, but when he first showed up in the Bronx, a cautious, passive-looking switch-hitter with glasses, I didn't think he'd last. He was just the kind of player who had never been given a chance on George's Yankees. If Jeter and Rivera have been the face of the Yankees during Joe Torre's Era, then Williams is the symbol of the transition years under Stick Michael and Buck Showalter. He not only matured into a very good player, he was the team's best hitter during the 1996-2000 run, and ultimately came close to being a Hall of Famer. That was more than I would have ever imagined from him. During the 2005 season, it was sad to witness Williams' slow bat and his slower first step in the outfield, but I tried to watch him more closely than ever, studying his mannerisms and ticks, knowing that he very well could have played his last games as a Yankee.

In order to be voted into the Hall, Mike Mussina desperately needs a 20-win season, or at least another couple of 17+ win campaigns, perhaps followed by a huge playoff performance. That didn't happen in '05, and while he's still an above-average pitcher, he is no longer an ace. Sheffield, on the other hand, has been tremendous in his two years in the Bronx. His numbers fell off toward the end of the summer due to injuries, but he continued to be a ferocious presence in the Yankees' line-up. No right-handed Yankee has hit the kind of searing line drives that come off Sheffield's bat since Dave Winfield. The fact that their swings are so different—Sheffield's short, compact, violent, Winfield's looping and long, thunderous—yet the results so similar had me remembering how much I enjoyed watching Winfield play during the 1980s.

Jeter and Rivera were probably already going to be Hall of Famers as early as two years ago, but they've now padded their career numbers to the point where there no longer are arguments against their candidacy. Jeter suffered through the worst slump of his career during the first half of the 2004 season, and as a result

his walk rate was low (46 on the year) while his sacrifices increased (16 in all, when he had 18 total in the previous five seasons combined). Yet at the same time, his power numbers jumped and he ended the season with a fine .292/.352/.471.

Better still, his fielding actually improved. Whether or not he deserved the Gold Glove is debatable, but considering the fact that Jeter's defensive reputation had been such a source of debate during the previous couple of years, it was an accomplishment nonetheless. Jeter's defense remained good in '05, and many observers feel that Rodriguez's range at third has allowed Jeter to cheat up-the-middle which cuts down on his greatest weakness, a lack of range. Offensively, Jeter hit .309/.389/.450 and scored 122 runs and collected over 200 hits for the fourth time in his career. In ten full seasons with the Yankees, Jeter has scored 100 or more runs nine times (he scored 87 in 119 games in 2003). So far, he has been blessed with relatively good health.

Speaking of the Captain, it is difficult to discuss Alex Rodriguez without noting his relationship with Jeter. Once good friends, the two evidently drifted apart over the years. Rodriguez was the greatest shortstop in the game when he came to New York but agreed to move to third because the Yankees would never ask Jeter to move (even if it would have been what was best for the team). On the field, they have existed peacefully enough. (There was an Internet rumor during the middle of the summer that the two had a nasty fight in the clubhouse, but that was never substantiated. While it is plausible that such an incident could have happened, it would have been surprising for two players as image-conscious as these two are to let anything like that become public.)

Even more than Reggie Jackson and Thurman Munson, Rodriguez and Jeter are paired together, possibly like no other Yankee duo since the days of Ruth and Gehrig. Rodriguez has far more talent than Jeter, yet Jeter is considered to possess a psychological, competitive edge that Rodriguez lacks. Rodriguez reminds me of a guy who could go 3-3 and then ask one of his teammates, "How does my swing look today?" Whereas Jeter could go 0-4 against a pitcher and walk back to the dugout with his face screwed up and tell his teammates, "This guy's got nothing."

One of the defining differences between the two men that I can tell is that Jeter seems to thoroughly enjoy himself on the field or in the dugout. Whether it is a blowout game in July against the Devil Rays or a playoff game in October, Jeter is smiling, enjoying the competition. Which isn't to say he's a clown or a flake, far from it, but he's involved in the moment and soaks it all up. (Before reaching on an infield dribbler, which drove in the winning run in Game 4 of the ALCS, there was Jeter, adjusting his batting gloves, smirking like there was no other place in the world he'd rather be.) Rodriguez on the other hand, doesn't look like he's having fun. He's not a loose guy and has developed a reputation as a player who presses in tense situations. To be fair, Jeter has never had to carry the burden that Rodriguez has, but instead of relaxing under pressure, Rodriguez tends to tighten up.

Some regard this tendency as some kind of moral flaw in Rodriguez, but if a guy fails because he's just trying too hard, it's difficult for me to get down on him too much. If anything, the fact that Rodriguez has any kind of flaw in his game makes him more appealing to me. He's vulnerable, which makes him even more interesting to follow because a) he's still got something to overcome, and b) proves that he's not an android. In spite of his looks and his bland public persona, there is something frail about Rodriguez, as if he somehow feels unsure of himself in some way.

In a way, he's the anti-Paul O'Neill, even though he's got more in common with Paulie O than any Yankee player since O'Neill retired. O'Neill was a hot head when he didn't succeed, and so is Rodriguez. But O'Neill was regarded as being unbridled, passionate and incorrigible, where as the hyper-aware Rodriguez comes off as a phony. (Even when he says the "right thing" like when he called himself a "dog" after the ALCS, there is something forced about it. He's trying too hard to say what he thinks people want to hear, where O'Neill didn't give a damn and was just being himself.)

His first year in New York was marked by uncertainty. In 2005, Alex Rodriguez had one of the ten best seasons ever by a third baseman, as he broke Joe DiMaggio's record for home runs hit by a right-handed Yankee. Early on his fielding was poor, and by the beginning of June, he told a reporter from *The Daily News* that he was positioning was all screwy:

"The perfect position would be, if anyone plays tennis, to be on the balls of your feet, able to go backward or forward," Rodriguez explained. "If you're on the balls of your feet, you're able to go back or forth. When you're back on your heels, any move you make is going to be slower. That's kind of what I was doing, being more passive, a step late instead of a step early …It's like driving in New York. If you stop, you're going to get in a car wreck. If you attack and drive like a maniac, you'll be fine. Take that from a frustrated driver in New York. That's the best example I can give."

Offensively, Rodriguez was the model of consistency. Here are his month-by-month splits:

	AVG	OBP	SLG
April	.304	.349	.618
May	.349	.513	.686
June	.337	.407	.481
July	.281	.400	.552
August	.324	.429	.733
September	.317	.419	.567
Total	.321	.421	.610

Rodriguez's walk and strikeout numbers switched by the middle of the year, going up incrementally in whiffs and dropping measure by measure in base on balls too. However, Rodriguez scored the most runs (24) in September, and hit the most homers (12) and doubles (7) in August. The most RBIs he had in a month (24) came in August and September. He also provided some memorable moments in the field—the game-ending double play against the Blue Jays late in September—as well as at the plate: the game-winning home run against Curt Schilling, his 500-foot home run against Juan Dominguez and the Rangers at the Stadium ("That was ridiculous," Tino Martinez told reporters, "I've never seen a ball hit that far"), and the three-home-runs game v. Bartolo Colon. Rodriguez was also far from just a home run or bust hitter late in games, taking his walks, and slapping base hits, instead of the all-or-nothing approach that characterized his first season in New York.

I've found myself rooting for Rodriguez to do well because he's such a gifted ballplayer and because I root emphatically for greatness on the baseball field. But it is not lost on me why so many fans find him easy to root against. He's the highest-paid player, he's good-looking, and he knows it. He also has the ability to make the game appear to be easy. His swing is so fluid, his arm so strong, that the game can look effortless to him. Furthermore, Rodriguez was blessed with the ability to hit a ball with the kind of power that few men have ever possessed. The ball jumps off his bat in a way that is just special, and I'm sure that inspires a good deal of envy from his peers. Even a great slugger like Sheffield, who hits for tremendous power, doesn't have the ball almost magically jump off his bat like Rodriguez does. When Sheffield or Giambi really get into one you know instantly at home watching on TV whether the ball will be gone or not. With Rodriguez, he'll hit what looks like a routine fly ball to the outfield, and it'll just keep on going and sail away for a homer. This year I was able to get adjusted to this phenomenon and can now call his homers based on the fly balls that look like they might be outs and know they are just gonna keep going.

Watching Rodriguez is like watching a super hero. He's perfectly drawn and his ups and downs have a comic book scale to them. When he fails, you can understand why some people want him to get it good, and when he shines you can see why he's irresistible— his talent is just too much. (That's why others recoil even—or especially—when Rodriguez does well.) Rodriguez is the most dramatic offensive presence the Yanks have had since Reggie. When A-Rod hits it *matters*. He strikes out a lot and hits the ball father and deeper than anyone on the team. He can do it all. And yet he doesn't have it all yet. He's still got something to prove, that he can rise to the occasion like Jackson did. The end of the 2005 season is a good cliffhanger for him. After a terrific season, there is still a void. So long as he remains healthy and has a few opportunities to play in October, he should be just fine. If Rodriguez has proved anything since signing his infamous $252 million deal, it is that he's up to the task of living up to being the highest-paid player in the league.

As impressive as Rodriguez was, perhaps Mariano Rivera had the finest season in New York. Not that it was necessarily worth more than Rodriguez's—though that is debatable—but because of Rivera's age, it helped cement the Yankees' closer as one of the best relievers ever. When Rivera was hurt during the 2002 season, I couldn't help but think that we'd be watching his decline soon enough. Instead, Rivera has posted three of the greatest seasons of his career.

After blowing two saves in the first series of the season against the Red Sox—which prompted every sportswriter in the vicinity to weigh in with a theory about how to fix him—Rivera saved a career-best thirty consecutive games. (He finally blew one to the White Sox on August 10.) In that span Rivera's record was 4-1 with a 0.57 ERA in 47. 1 innings (8 walks, 51 strike-outs). He recorded 18 of those saves on the road, where his ERA was 0.00 in 22.2 innings of work (2 walks, 22 strikeouts). Rivera ended the season with a record of 7-4, and a 1.38 ERA in 78.1 innings, recording 43 saves in 47 chances (18 walks, 80 strikeouts).

Against my better judgment, Rivera is one of the few players I am guilty of rooting for his numbers ahead of the team's performance. He is one of the only players I've done that with as an adult. The truth is, I never quite believed a pitcher with essentially one pitch could be this good for this long. And yet he has been. Rivera has a beautifully simple and easy delivery. I've given up trying to explain why he's so good. To be honest, his talent seems to be not of this world. So long as he and Jeter and Torre are still around, the Yankees will be the show to see. Whether or not they win another championship should not prevent us from admiring how good they and the rest of the Yankees have continued to be. Every fan should have such problems.

Leapers

by David Cameron

Have you ever seen something one way for a while, and then, as time passes, your impression of it changes, despite the object itself staying the same? Our history is full of changing perceptions. A few years ago, I took a road trip that led me through Eagle, Colorado. The local gas station was charging $2.12 per gallon for regular unleaded. I was so outraged, I took a picture and sent it to the regional manager of the station with a letter about the injustices of price gouging. Today, if I saw a gas station charging $2.12 per gallon, I'd likely give the cashier a hug. My interpretation of what now constitutes expensive gasoline has changed. Our interpretations of baseball players are no different.

For instance, in 1995, *Baseball America* ranked Scott Rolen 91st on their list of the best prospects in baseball. For comparison sakes, the immortal Dante Powell was 90th and Desi Relaford came in at 92nd. By the time the list was updated a year later, Rolen ranked 27th, directly behind Jason Kendall. Following closely behind Rolen were guys like Bobby Abreu, Jermaine Dye, Todd Helton, Edgar Renteria, and Nomar Garciaparra. The informed outlook for Scott Rolen got significantly more optimistic during the 1996 season, even though nothing about Rolen inherently changed. What caused the baseball world to sit up and take notice?

During the 1996 season, Scott Rolen took The Leap. We've all seen it. There are few things more enjoyable in baseball than watching one of "your guys" take that elevator to the top of the baseball world. The guy who was a solid role player is now a household name, appearing shirtless on the cover of *Sports Illustrated* and explaining how he's going to keep it real and not let the fame change him. But whether he changes or not, our perception and our expectations of him cannot stay the same.

It could be argued that the city of Chicago watched Derrek Lee take The Leap this season. Baltimore experienced it with Melvin Mora in 2003. Eric Gagne leapt in 2002. The changes in their performance were staggering, and, while they had shown flashes of ability before, the level of their achievements were so far out of the realm of reasonable expectations that you could do nothing but just shake your head. Often, these seasons get labeled as flukes, and occasionally they legitimately are. Richard Hidalgo, I'd like to introduce you to Brady Anderson.

Not every breakout season really is a start of a new trend. However, there are far too many players who

have sustained their success after what looked like a career year to write this effect off. The Leap is very real. And while it happens occasionally at the major league level, it is far more frequent in the minor leagues.

Prospects, by their nature, are still developing, and human beings grow at different stages. While you can build a nice arc depicting a normal development curve, there are always exceptions. When we want to sound geeky, we call them outliers. They blow our expectations away and make our bell curve do really funky things. We love them anyway. Watching a guy at 19 or 20 years old take The Leap is just more fun than we should be allowed to have. And in 2005, we had a lot of fun, because the line for The Leap ride got pretty long.

No one in recent history has taken The Leap to the same lengths that Brandon Wood took it this season. He was a first-round selection of the Angels in the 2003 draft as part of the new breed of shortstops. Standing 6'3", Wood looked the part of the offensive middle infielder, but his first year and a half of professional baseball were not what you expect from a phenom. Wood spent his first 720 professional at-bats looking kind of interesting, but he was certainly more potential than performance.

He hit decently in the Arizona Rookie League during his pro debut, but the AZL has only slightly better pitching than the local junior varsity high school team. His 2004 performance for Cedar Rapids in the full season Midwest League was not something he would write home to Mom about, finishing the year with a .251 batting average, .322 on-base percentage, .404 slugging percentage, and 117 strikeouts in 478 at-bats. He flashed a bit of power, hitting 11 home runs in one of the toughest leagues in the minors for offense, but he appeared to be on the slow track to the major leagues.

Wood had some adjustments to make, and with Erick Aybar and Alberto Callaspo ahead of him on the middle-infield depth chart, the Angels were in no hurry to rush him. As is the case with almost every tall shortstop prospect, the talk of moving Wood to third base began. Questions about both his bat and his future position followed him into the 2005 season.

As the year began, however, Wood took the normal development curve behind the woodshed and gave it a first-class beating. He was assigned to Rancho Cucamonga of the advanced Class-A California League, a promotion from his 2004 assignment. The

Cal League is known for having a few offensive band-boxes, but Rancho is not one of them. A nice uptick in his offensive performance would have been expected simply based on the context of the league Wood was in, but instead we got one of the most impressive minor league seasons in recent history.

He played 130 games for Rancho and hit .321 with *43 home runs.* Toss in his 51 doubles and four triples, and Wood amassed 98 extra-base hits. He finished the year with four games in Triple-A Salt Lake and whacked two more doubles and a triple there, giving him a total of 101 extra-base hits on the season. As best as anyone can figure, no player had recorded 100 extra-base hits in a minor league season in 50 years.

The questions about Wood's bat have disappeared. At 20 years old, he raised his batting average 28 percent and his slugging percentage increased by 67 percent. Wood's home run total increased 390 percent. That, ladies and gentlemen, isn't just taking The Leap. Brandon Wood's season redefined The Leap.

Wood wasn't the only player who took a big step forward, however, even if no one else could match his ridiculous numbers. In a different way, Jeremy Hermida also took The Leap. Like Wood, Hermida was a first-round selection, being taken 11th overall in the 2002 draft. Scouts fell in love with Hermida's swing in high school, and he got the rep for being the best hitting prospect in that draft. Comparisons ranged from Will Clark to Shawn Green, and everyone agreed that watching him hit was a thing of beauty.

Hermida showed off that swing and some terrific plate discipline in his full-season debut for Greensboro of the South Atlantic League in 2003, hitting .284 and drawing 80 walks. While moving to the pitcher-friendly Florida State League in 2004, Hermida continued to display his swing, posting a .297 average in a league that is famous for 2-1 pitcher's duels. However, during his first several professional seasons, he had yet to show much in the way of power potential. He had just 34 extra-base hits in 2003 while slugging .393, though the plate discipline was certainly encouraging. He let that patience slip a bit and managed to hit 10 home runs while playing in the FSL, but the fact that he had to steal from his strength to make up for his weakness wasn't what the Marlins were looking for. The Marlins drafted Hermida to be a complete hitter, and through his first two seasons he had yet to show that he could combine his variety of skills simultaneously.

The 2005 season brought Hermida to Double-A, where he put the package together and tied it with a nice little bow. He posted his normal .293 average, got on base at a ridiculous .453 clip, and slugged .518, far and away better than what he had done the previous two seasons. He drew 111 walks against 89 strikeouts and blew away his career high with 49 extra-base hits. He had fewer extra-base hits than Wood had doubles, showing just how ridiculous Wood's season was, but it was still a vast improvement over what he had shown previously.

For instance, when you look at Hermida's extra-base hits as a percentage of total hits, there is a marked change. In 2003, he had just 25 percent of his hits go for extra bases, a number comparable to what a player like Cristian Guzman puts up annually. Hermida improved that to 28 percent in 2004, still unacceptable for anyone not winning gold gloves. Then came 2005, when 44 percent of his hits went for two bases or better. For comparison, 46 percent of Adam Dunn's hits went for extra bases in his last season in the minors.

When any measure of your power was comparable to Cristian Guzman but now places you in a category with Adam Dunn, you took The Leap in a big way. Hermida finished off his breakout season by hitting like an All-Star in his major league debut. Twelve hits in 43 at-bats, four of them leaving the yard, assured everyone in Florida that this kid was there to stay.

Not all improvements are so easy to spot. Sometimes, a player takes a giant step forward and gets overlooked, often as a result of the raw numbers being deflated because of the environment the player is in. While Wood and Hermida stole most of the spotlight among players having huge seasons, Jarrod Saltalamacchia's performance was just as impressive, even if the numbers are not quite as glamorous. Salty, as almost everyone refers to him simply to save themselves the embarrassment of trying to pronounce his surname, was selected by the Braves with a supplemental first-round pick in the 2003 draft. As a 6'4", switch-hitting catcher with significant power, Atlanta had high hopes for his offensive abilities.

He debuted in the rookie-level Gulf Coast League in the summer of 2003 and hit just .239, but his peripheral numbers were terrific: 15 of his 32 hits went for extra bases and he drew 28 walks against 33 strikeouts. He moved to the South Atlantic League in 2004 and had a decent, unspectacular season. He hit .272/.348/.437 and saw his walk rate take a nosedive while his power remained more projection than performance. It was not a disappointing season by any stretch of the imagination, but the overall line did not portend what was to come the following season.

The Braves moved Salty up to advanced Single-A Myrtle Beach in the Carolina League for the 2005 season. Myrtle Beach is, without a doubt, one of the most pitcher-friendly ballparks in professional baseball. There's a stiff wind that blows off the water and kills long fly balls, making it nearly impossible to post huge numbers while taking half your hacks there. The park factors for Coastal Federal Field have been consistently among the lowest in baseball. Salty was barely fazed by it.

In 459 at-bats, he hit .314/.394/.519, which may not live up to the raw numbers posted by Wood and Hermida, but when placed in context, they constitute a super-human season. His .314 average ranked third in the Carolina League behind Winston-Salem's Social Security duo of 28-year-old Leo Daigle and Noah Hall, who is youthful by comparison at 26. His on-base and slugging percentages were good for sixth-best in the league, and like Hall and Daigle, the guys ahead of him aren't exactly major league prospects. Salty was far and away the most valuable player in the league, putting up near league-leading offensive numbers while playing catcher and doing so in the most oppressive park for offense that exists in professional baseball. In context-neutral terms, Salty's season was almost the offensive equal of Wood's. Just one season removed from a rather ho-hum performance in the SAL, that qualifies as taking The Leap.

So far, I've identified three hitters who look to have taken The Leap in the past year. I can hear those who make their living toeing the rubber preparing a class-action lawsuit for discrimination as we speak, but the fact of life is that pitchers are flaky. A consistent pitcher is like an honest lawyer; we know they're out there, but they cost more than most people can afford and there is only one for every few states in the union. Generally, when a pitcher has an out-of-the-blue amazing season in the minors, it isn't followed up by years and years of dominance. However, there are exceptions, and if ever a pitcher made the jump, it was probably Francisco Liriano.

Liriano was signed by the Giants out of the Dominican Republic in 2000 and spent several years pitching in the lower levels of their farm system, showing a good arm, poor mechanics that led to some control problems, and an inability to stay healthy. He pitched just 89 combined innings in 2002 and 2003 before the Giants agreed to include him as the third player in the A.J. Pierzynski trade. As if giving up Joe Nathan for one year of the least-likable catcher in the game wasn't enough, the Giants had to sit and watch as the guy they gave up turned into something far better than what they believed they had.

Liriano stayed mostly healthy in 2004 and continued to flash some potential, striking out 125 batters in 117

innings at Single-A Fort Myers, but his ERA of 4.00 in the Florida State League wasn't what you look for out of a future ace. His ratios were solid, however, and he pitched well in a late-season promotion to Double-A New Britain, allowing the Twins to be optimistic about his future.

Minnesota, like everyone else, didn't see his 2005 season coming, however. A minor mechanical change improved the bite on his slider and the command of his change-up, both of which can be devastating to hitters, and Liriano became unhittable. After pitching well at Double-A in the first half, Liriano moved up to Triple-A and posted a 1.78 ERA in 91 innings, while allowing just 80 base runners and striking out 112. In his last 10 starts for Rochester, he allowed eight earned runs.

Liriano was promoted to The Show to end the year, and while his 5.70 ERA isn't going to open any eyes, he pitched extremely well, walking seven and striking out 33 in 23.2 innings. His command of three pitches, including a terrific change-up, along with being left-handed and a member of the Twins organization, lead to inevitable comparisons to Johan Santana. He's not quite that good, but making that kind of comparison prior to this season would have gotten you laughed out of the baseball community. The fact that it's even considered slightly possible now shows just how far Liriano came in the past 12 months. Until proven otherwise, he is still a member of the flaky pitcher society, but it appears that Liriano just may have taken The Leap.

These four certainly aren't the only players who could lay claim to large improvements in the past year. Others that should receive honorable mentions include Scott Moore (Cubs), Adam Jones (Mariners), Brent Clevlen (Tigers), Rich Hill (Cubs), Kelly Johnson (Braves), and Ryan Doumit (Pirates). Certainly, not all of the players who had breakout seasons will continue to perform at their past season's levels, but it is very likely that a solid handful of these players will look back at the past season as the year they took The Leap.

I've identified a few players who appear to have turned a corner early in their career. They are certainly more highly valued now than they were a year ago. Looking ahead to 2006, I wonder if there are lessons we can learn from this group and from past seasons' leapers that might give us an indication that a player could be in for a breakout season? What should we be looking for if we want to identify the guy who will be the next Brandon Wood?

Based on the small sample we've looked at, the most common correlations are in draft status and age. Wood and Hermida were first-round selections. Saltalamacchia was a supplemental first-round selection. In the honorable mention category, Moore was a first rounder, Jones and Johnson were supplemental first-round picks, and Clevlen and Doumit were second-round picks. Other recent leapers were also high selections, such as David Wright, Rocco Baldelli, and going a little further back, the aforementioned Scott Rolen.

Perhaps more significantly, all of the aforementioned players were selected out of high school. A large percentage of the players whose performance improved rapidly are players who were selected at an early age by scouts as having upper-tier talent. Indeed, it's likely true that these players are not so much establishing new levels of their abilities as they are finally fulfilling their natural potential. While performance evaluations certainly have their place, we also can't ignore the fact that baseball is full of overachievers and underachievers. Past performance is not a perfect gauge of a player's talent, especially when a player is still developing physically. If scouts have evaluated the player positively based on his physical abilities, which draft status can serve as a good proxy for, a few seasons of mediocre performance should not be taken as the gospel truth of the player's actual talent level.

Beyond that, however, the criteria for finding potential breakouts get cloudy. One theory that has gained some popularity is that players who control the strike zone are good candidates, but the evidence simply doesn't support this claim. Hermida would fit the stereotype of a player with great plate discipline who found his power, but try using that model to explain this year's other breakout stars. Wood's plate discipline was poor in 2004 and nothing to write home about in 2005, but despite that, he became a monster. Jones still swings at almost everything he sees, but the quality of his contact is improved, if not the quantity.

Simply looking at players with good walk-to-strike-out ratios and extrapolating that "the power will come" is wish casting. In many circumstances, players who walk in the minor leagues do so because they lack the physical capability to actually hit the baseball with any regularity, so they take as many free passes as humanly possible. I have tried to find a correlation tying minor league walk and strikeout rates to breakout performances, but it simply is not there.

So, we have to simply acknowledge that trying to find the next group of potential leapers is a very inexact science. They come in all shapes and sizes, though they do tend to have similar backgrounds. Generally, they are in the 19-21 age range and have scouting reports that are more positive than their performance records. That's a wide net to cast, but let's go fishing anyway, shall we?

At the top of my list of guys to watch next year is Minnesota shortstop Trevor Plouffe. He was selected 20th overall in the 2004 draft but hasn't lived up to expectations to date. Assigned to the Midwest League this season, he hit a paltry .223/.304/.345 in 466 at-bats. However, there are some signs of hope. Thirty-one of his 104 hits were extra-base knocks, and his 50 walks against 78 strikeouts don't paint the picture of a guy who was simply overmatched at the plate. Essentially, the only thing missing from his offensive line is a lot of singles. There isn't a less consistent skill in baseball than hitting a single, and if Plouffe can convert 20-30 of his outs into singles going forward, he's a .280/.350/.400 hitter who plays a solid shortstop. That's a pretty nice prospect.

Another Midwest League teenage shortstop is on the list as well. Matt Tuiasasopo, hereafter referred to as Tui, had a significantly better year than Plouffe. His .276 average while playing in Wisconsin as a 19-year-old is well above what the Mariners saw from Adam Jones when they put him in the same situation in 2004. For him to qualify as a 2006 Leaper, he's going to have to have a pretty terrific season. There are legitimate reasons to think it may happen.

Tui was selected in the third round of the 2004 draft mostly due to the football scholarship the University of Washington had offered him. The M's bought him away from the gridiron because they fell in love with his stick. Tui has a similar physique to Wood, but his defensive abilities are far behind most professional shortstops. It is quite likely that Tui will begin the 2006 season at third base, or possibly even right field, as the organization attempts to allow his bat to develop by taking some of the pressure off him. Combine that with a move to the hitter-friendly California League, and the environment will be significantly more conducive to success. His power numbers in Wisconsin didn't live up to the juice that scouts have projected for him, but with an offseason of strength training, Tui could well be in for a large step forward next season.

Moving out of the Midwest League, we come to Greg Golson, the player selected one spot after Plouffe in the 2004 draft. Golson is the kind of player who can divide scouts and statistical analysts right down the middle. He is a superb athlete who runs well and has a cannon arm. He can also drive a fastball a long ways, and at times can look like a star in the making. His ability to hit an off-speed pitch is his undoing, however, and he has a very rudimentary approach at the plate, as evidenced by his 26 walks and 106 strikeouts in 375 at-bats for Lakewood in the South Atlantic League this season.

His raw line of .263/.322/.389 certainly doesn't stand out, but there were extenuating circumstances. He suffered through a sprained ankle and a sprained knee at separate points during the season, but was on the field as often as the doctors would let him. Despite playing through injuries, 31 of his 99 hits went for extra bases, showing some power that you may not anticipate for a guy who hit all of four home runs during the season. The player Golson is compared to most often, Torii Hunter, put up similar numbers on his trek through the minor leagues, and while Hunter never had a monstrous breakout season, Golson has similar potential.

Others on the watch list include Yankees third baseman Eric Duncan, Dodgers first baseman James Loney (who, in the interest of disclosure, I've been predicting big things for since 2003 with little success), Indians outfielder Franklin Gutierrez, and Devil Rays shortstop Reid Brignac. Clearly, not all of these guys will take The Leap next year, but in some vein, they do fit the profile and have shown similar flashes of potential that Wood, Hermida, and Saltalamacchia displayed in the past.

At some point, next year, we're going to look at a prospect or two a lot differently than we do now. It isn't so much that they have changed, however, as that their performance has caused us to view them in a different light. Scott Rolen, David Wright, and Brandon Wood were always great players. We just didn't always know it. I look forward to meeting the next great player that I currently underestimate.

Japanese Baseball in 2005
by Craig Burley

The Colonel's Curse

The Yomiuri Giants are the New York Yankees of Japanese professional baseball. In fact, the Giants are even bigger than the Yankees—if you merged the fan bases of the Yankees, the Los Angeles Lakers, the Dallas Cowboys, Nebraska football and Duke basketball together, you might start approaching the popularity of the Giants. But the second most-beloved team in Japanese pro ball, the Hanshin Tigers, is Japan's answer to the Chicago Cubs. In their 68-year existence, the Tigers (whose home field, Koshien Stadium, is Japanese baseball's greatest shrine) have only won three Japan Series titles, and just one in the last 40 years.

That title came in 1985. Many Tigers fans—who are known as obsessively fanatical even by the passionate standard of Japanese fandom—responded by leaping into the poison-, trash- and scum-infested Dotonbori River. In their zeal, seeking something resembling the Tigers' power-hitting hero, Randy Bass, a statue of Colonel Sanders was liberated from an Osaka Kentucky Fried Chicken outlet and was thrown into the river's murky depths. Naturally, as the Tigers have not won since, the legend has grown that the Tigers will never again win the Japan Series until the statue is recovered and replaced on its pedestal.

The plinth at the KFC remains empty, and so does the Tigers' trophy case.

This year, the Tigers teased their fans unmercifully. The best team in the Central League by miles, the Tigers cruised into the Japan Series but faced a 17-day layoff between the end of the regular season and the beginning of the Series while the Pacific League held its playoffs. Seventeen days for fans to hold their breath and think of what might be, seventeen days without a ballgame in which to lengthen out the tension.

At the end of all that, the Tigers were swept in the Japan Series by the Lotte Marines. The Colonel's Curse lives on.

Bobby, You Done Us Proud

It is not precisely accurate to say that Bobby Valentine is "respected" in Japan. Certainly, Valentine's time as a manager in Japan has been successful; in his first stint with the Marines, "*Barentain*" turned around a miserable and indifferent team and guided them into second place—and was fired for his pains. (There is an excel-lent account of this in Robert Whiting's fine book *The Meaning of Ichiro*). But despite this, Valentine has always been seen as someone who can work with Japanese players and within a Japanese system—his obvious respect for the game and the country is well-received in Japan. In Valentine's second go-around with the Marines, he began with an indifferent .500 record in 2004 before this year's heroics. With the Pacific League's playoff system in place, the Marines were able to beat Seibu in the first round and the SoftBank Hawks in the PL championship, before dusting off the Tigers, who barely put up any resistance. The first three games of the Series ended 10-1, 10-0, and 10-1, before a 3-2 win in Game 4. Toshiaki Imae, who hit .667 in the Series and ended it with a sparkling double play at third base, was named the Series MVP.

Interestingly for devotees of sabermetrics, Valentine's Lotte staff included a full-time data analyst, Paul Pupo.

The Year That Was

2005 saw some individual performances that took Japanese baseball by surprise. The Sawamura Award, given to Nippon Professional Baseball's top pitcher (the equivalent of the Cy Young Award in the States) went to Toshiya Sugiuchi of the Hawks, who led a very fine team to the best record in NPB. Sugiuchi, a lefthander and only 24, went 18-4 with a 2.11 ERA and 218 strikeouts in 196 innings. He missed the pitching Triple Crown in the Pacific League by just eight strikeouts, as Daisuke Matsuzaka of the Lions (who finished a disappointing 14-13) beat him out.

Also in the PL, Sugiuchi's Hawks teammate, Nobuhiko Matsunaka, also nearly won a repeat Triple Crown. After taking all three categories in 2004, Matsunaka won the home run (46) and RBI (121) titles in a walk, but finished seven points behind the Lions' Kazuhiro Wada for the batting title, .322 to .315.

Over in the Central League, with the Tigers running away with the pennant race, much of the September excitement concerned the Swallows' Norichika Aoki and his quest for 200 hits, which he achieved on the season's next-to-last day. Aoki, who hit .344, became only the second player to collect 200 hits in a season in NPB. (Ichiro was the first, and took only 130 games to collect 210 hits, versus 202 in 145 games for Aoki). Tomoaki Kanemoto of the Tigers was the league's best hitter, hitting .327 and blasting 40 home runs. The Tigers had both the best offense (Kanemoto was ably supported by Makoto Imaoka, who had 147 RBIs to lead NPB, and Norihiro Akahoshi) and the best defense in the Central League. They had some amazing days along the way, including a 21-2 victory over the Carp – the 21 runs were the most that the Tigers have ever scored.

New boys, Rakuten, for whom many had high hopes, fizzled in their first season as they won only 38 games and lost 97, the first team in decades to lose 90 or more games in the Pacific League.

Off The Field

A much quieter 2005 after a tumultuous 2004 was disturbed only by continuing debate over the World Baseball Classic, with the players being eventually won over to the idea.

The Year Ahead

Look for Rakuten to take a step forward in 2006. Not only will they have better opportunities to bring in some new players, they will also be managed by legendary player Katsuya Nomura, who has won three Pacific League pennants as a manager as well. Another interesting managerial hire is Atsuya Furuta of the Swallows—the first player-manager in Japan in many years and the first in top-level baseball of any kind since Pete Rose with the Cincinnati Reds.

Lions pitching ace Daisuke Matsuzaka elected at the end of the season not to seek a job in Major League Baseball, meaning that Japan's premier asset will be staying home. However, some very fine players, including Hawks catcher Kenji Johjima, have decided to follow the lead of world champion Tadahito Iguchi.

Final Standings

Central League

	W	L	T	PCT	GB
Hanshin Tigers	87	54	5	.617	-
Chunichi Dragons	79	66	1	.545	10
Yokohama BayStars	69	70	7	.496	17
Yakult Swallows	71	73	2	.493	17.5
Tokyo Yomiuri Giants	62	80	4	.437	25.5
Hiroshima Carp	58	84	4	.408	29.5

Pacific League

	W	L	T	PCT	GB
SoftBank Hawks	89	45	2	.664	-
Chiba Lotte Marines	84	49	3	.632	4.5
Seibu Lions	67	69	0	.493	23
Orix Blue Wave	62	70	4	.470	26
Nippon Ham Fighters	62	71	3	.466	26.5
Rakuten Golden Eagles	38	97	1	.281	51.5

The Steroids Scandal

by John Brattain

It was inevitable.

Generally a statement like that is made in retrospect. When something unexpected happens it takes us by surprise. When we look back at the ignored warning signs, however, we wonder why we didn't see it coming.

Just as someone doesn't wake up and think, "Today I've decided to become a drug addict," major league baseball players didn't decide to start juicing for the sake of juicing. A culture developed over decades, circumstances evolved and an environment was created that allowed steroids to walk into the game.

The "silly-ball" era may have begun after the strike of 1994; its first seeds, however, were sown decades ago. Some contributing factors include the traditional distrust between management and labor and ownership that often looked the other way when the stars got in trouble and more often than not got them out of jams. There was the whole philosophy of "if you ain't cheatin' you ain't tryin'," which led to corked bats and doctored baseballs. The emergence of a materialistic consumer culture, an overmedicated society that suggested that any problem can be solved by swallowing a pill, and the transformation of street drugs from "evil" to "recreational" all played a part.

And of course the billions of dollars that flowed into major league baseball—a good chunk of which flowed to the men who could play the game at the highest levels—was a crucial factor.

It's important to remember that the current steroids crisis in major league baseball is entirely consistent with how the sport has been played and run almost since its inception.

A quick example with which we're all familiar: the Black Sox scandal of 1919. What created the environment that led to the throwing of the World Series was simple: One, certain shady folks had almost unlimited access to the players. Second, although management knew about a gambling problem, rather than deal with it they swept it under the rug, lest it go public and hurt ticket sales. Third, the media were more concerned about staying on the good side of MLB, and the players they covered were largely mute on the subject. Fourth, if a star player was discovered to have been involved, team owners would help cover up the player's indiscretion to protect their "cash cows." Finally, players simply wanted more money and weren't shy about how they went about

it, even if it did involve violating some rule—regardless of whether it was written or unwritten.

Sound familiar?

Baseball has had a storied tradition of dealing with problems by simply ignoring them and hoping they'll disappear. That's how they handled gambling in the early part of the 20th century, how they handled the emergence of the players' union in the 1960s, how they handled the cocaine problem in the 1980s, and how they've handled the issue of performance-enhancing drugs. In each case it had to blow up in their faces to get them to deal constructively with the problem. The word "proactive" does not exist in the lexicon of major league baseball.

Anabolic substances, however, pose some unique problems that things like gambling and recreational drugs do not, and that really should be the focus of concern. A player who gambles or uses cocaine or marijuana is largely hurting only his own career prospects, opening the door for someone else to take the job. His behavior is not coercive; in fact, it's quite the opposite. But a player who uses performance-enhancing substances may well be taking a job that he truly does not deserve. Two players with roughly equal ability competing for one spot on a major league roster may well determine who gets that spot by using anabolic steroids, which then puts pressure on the other player to do likewise or be left languishing in the minors.

Furthermore, young people often look up to athletes. Athletes are not role models nor should they be treated as such. A talented teenager with big-league aspirations can look at a player who abuses recreational drugs and watch his career suffer. He would understand that emulating that particular behavior is inconsistent with his goals. On the other hand, when he watches a player use performance-enhancing drugs, become an All-Star, set new statistical records and be rewarded with adulation and a nine-digit contract, then it's going to have an impact. Citing studies about the possible negative health consequences of using anabolic steroids will not act as a deterrent because young adults feel they are bulletproof and invincible. We see this all the time in other avenues of life; every generation of teenagers struggles with the problems of teen pregnancy, sexually transmitted diseases, over-drinking, drinking and driving accidents and narcotic and tobacco addictions.

An aspiring big-leaguer will only see the immediate benefits and think that the potential consequences will pass him by. A young athlete considering using anabolic substances will see visions of playing in the major leagues, receiving adulation—especially from the opposite sex—a top-shelf lifestyle, multi-million dollar contracts, star treatment, all the bling he could ever want and a really fun job. The downside of getting caught or getting sick is too vague and too far off in the future to merit concern.

Major league baseball was late to the game when it came to anabolic steroids; it was right on time, however, with respect to the use of drugs and the drug culture. As drug issues became more prevalent in the 1960s, professional baseball couldn't stay out if its way. When Jim Bouton's *Ball Four* was published, it outed baseball's worst-kept secret: that players were using amphetamines, or greenies as they were better known. Management knew about it, and indeed a number of teams provided their players with the drug. With ownership approval, the media's willing silence and the public's blissful ignorance, the abuse of illegal drugs came swiftly and easily into the game. Both star and scrub alike used greenies, whether to recover from a night's revelries or to cope with the hectic pace of a 162-game season that required late nights, extensive travel and brutal scheduling.

Some players used it to be "up" for a game; others felt it gave them an edge. Regardless the message was crystal clear: If it helps you be ready for the game, do it. No one was going to stop you—not the commissioner, not the manager, not the police.

In the early days of the Major League Baseball Players Association—before *Ball Four*—the union had greater concerns than what the players were putting into their bodies. The executive director of the players' union, Marvin Miller, was more concerned with getting players the basic rights enjoyed by the average unionized worker in America: better wages, the right to impartial arbitration, a decent pension and the right to seek work elsewhere when a current work contract expired.

It wasn't until *Ball Four* came out that the drug issue even became an issue. Even though, in some cases, management provided amphetamines—or at the very least condoned their use—the players were the ones who would ultimately be criticized. The media in many cases became self-righteous, proclaiming, in effect, "won't somebody think about the children?" MLB did what it did best—nothing. The media was silenced, Bouton became a persona non grata in baseball circles, and eventually it blew over. It simply wasn't discussed much anymore, and the situation continued unabated.

As the 1970s progressed into the 1980s, the union grew in power, and ownership continued to try to reign in the gains made by Miller and the MLBPA. The players secured first salary arbitration and then free agency. Revenues skyrocketed and players' salaries did likewise. Profits could be higher if free agency and arbitration could somehow be reigned in or at the very least neutralized. The battles between MLB and the MLBPA were about control, especially control of the game's revenues. What players were putting into their bodies was the least of anyone's concern.

The tremendous salaries players were earning, however, meant that they had more disposable income. Young men, a celebrity lifestyle and a party atmosphere could spell problems.

And they did.

Beyond that, as the rewards grew, so did the stakes. Instead of just battling for a spot in the major leagues, players were also fighting over the difference between almost starvation wages in the minor leagues and the chance at being a multi-millionaire in the glamorous major leagues.

It was the use of recreational drugs by newly rich players that paved the way for the use of performance-enhancing anabolic steroids in MLB.

As cocaine found its way into major league clubhouses so did additional tensions between MLB and the MLBPA. In 1983, four members of the Kansas City Royals—Willie Aikens, Jerry Martin, Vida Blue and Willie Wilson—pleaded guilty to misdemeanor charges of attempted cocaine possession. All four received a three-month jail sentence. It was the first time in baseball history that active players served a prison sentence. Then-Commissioner Bowie Kuhn suspended the four for a year without pay for the "illegal use of drugs." The MLBPA under Miller filed a grievance, and the suspensions were substantially reduced through arbitration.

Atlanta Braves pitcher Pascual Perez was arrested in his native Dominican Republic on drug-related charges. Perez, like the four in Kansas City, served a three-month prison sentence for a misdemeanor cocaine possession. Upon his release Kuhn, mindful of how his suspensions of Aikens, Martin, Blue and Wilson were in arbitration, suspended Perez for one month, stating that "[w]hen players violate the law and baseball's drug rules, discipline must follow." The MLBPA and Perez filed a grievance and the suspension was completely overturned.

Dodgers relief pitcher Steve Howe was suspended for drug violations seven times, including a lifetime ban, yet the MLBPA went to bat for Howe each time, and even the lifetime ban didn't stick.

Regardless of the merits of the players' cases in arbitration it wasn't difficult to see how a player could view the situation; the old adage was becoming frighteningly close to the literal truth—if you could hit the curveball you could get away with murder. You could take illegal drugs, and even if the courts incarcerated you, chances were good that MLB couldn't do much to you beyond a token suspension and fine. No matter what you did, the MLBPA would stand by you and defend you with extreme prejudice. It wouldn't be difficult to see how a player might feel above accountability.

The question has to be raised though—when salaries started to explode, why was it that cocaine was such an issue and anabolic steroids weren't? Baseball was a bit behind when it came to how much weight training could affect a player's performance. For decades pumping iron was seen as a detriment to a player's game. After all, the one-time all-time home run king looked more at home in front of a buffet than he did at home plate. Joe DiMaggio and Ted Williams looked like the guy in Archie comics ads who got sand kicked in his face at the beach. Even in recent memory Reggie Jackson blamed the worst season of his career—1983 when he batted .194/.290/.340 with 14 home runs and 49 RBIs—on an offseason weight-training program which he claimed made him so muscle bound that it affected his swing. Even more recently, Ruben Sierra went from a potential Hall of Fame career by age 25 to "the Village Idiot," as manager Tony La Russa labeled him, after becoming a muscle-bound hulk. Weight training and anabolic steroids seemed about as wise a career move as a cocaine habit.

Still, some players' successes paved the way for acceptance of weight training as a way to improve. In the 1980s Brian Downing of the Angels forged a fine career as a catcher, outfielder and designated hitter. Lance Parrish of the Tigers was a Gold Glove-quality receiver and one of a handful of catchers to slug over 300 home runs. Jose Canseco burst on the scene as a bulking, intimidating slugger who could both play the outfield and steal bases, and he became the first 40-40 player in baseball history. The late 1980s to early 1990s were littered with weight-training success stories.

The 1990s also marked a seemingly minor event that would have seismic implications for MLB. In October 1994 U.S. President Bill Clinton signed into law the Dietary Supplements Health and Education Act (known as DSHEA), which was approved unanimously by both the House and the Senate. Sen. Orrin Hatch (R-Utah) had proposed the bill to provide American consumers with a larger selection of medicinal and pharmaceutical remedies. It ended up shifting the burden of proof concerning a product's safety from the manufacturer to the Food and Drug Administration (FDA). No longer would a company have to go through the arduous process of demonstrating that its newest supplements were safe; instead the overworked FDA was responsible for proving such products *weren't* safe. DSHEA spawned a billion-dollar supplement industry that created many body-building products that would catch fire with both amateur and professional athletes alike.

The fertile ground was ready for the seeding of the steroid scandal. It would be the strike that planted the bumper crop to come. But it wouldn't just be steroids in isolation. It would be part and parcel of a movement to recover from the effects of the strike of 1994.

It might sound like a conspiracy theory, but bear in mind that historically MLB has performed very well in the conspiracy department. There was never any written rule, signed document or codified legislation for six decades that said blacks could not play in major league baseball. The commissioner, any league president, any club owner, or any general manager would publicly deny that there was a rule that expressly forbid blacks from playing in the major leagues. All you had to do was look at the diamond and look at the color of the faces of the men who were playing.

In the 1980s there was no rule forbidding the signing of free agents—no written edict from the commissioner, no notation in the collective bargaining agreement, no stated penalties for signing free agents. But the results were obvious—unless you felt that a given team's least talented player was superior to Jack Morris, Tim Raines, Bob Boone, Rich Gedman and Bob Horner and couldn't use them.

Baseball could conspire and collude with the best of them.

Many things came into sharper focus after the strike: it appeared that the ball was "juiced." The traditional ash bat was in many cases being replaced by harder lacquer-treated Canadian maple. The strike zone was getting lower—even the best hitters couldn't consistently get around on the best high gas, and now they could lay off the high heat with impunity. Batters were coming up to the plate wearing padding that looked more like it belonged in the National Football League or the National Hockey League. Umpires were being instructed to crack down on pitchers who threw inside officially to cut down on beanballs, but it was more to protect team's investments in $10 million-a-year sluggers. It used to be a pitcher owned one side of the plate while the batter owned the other. Now MLB had conceded both sides to the hitter. A pitcher couldn't throw high, he couldn't throw inside, and the hitter could reach over and tee off on pitches on the outer half of the plate without fearing pitcher retaliation. Also a number of newer ballparks were playing like hitter's parks.

In short, there were a lot of changes in the game, and they always seemed to be geared toward increasing offense. In the post-strike world, baseball needed to build interest. Cal Ripken's successful chase to eclipse Lou Gehrig's consecutive games-played streak in 1995 was certainly a feel-good story that generated interest, but it wasn't a cure to baseball's self-inflicted malaise.

Then a certain nondescript outfielder for the Baltimore Orioles discovered the wonders of creatine. In 1995, after seven years in the majors, Brady Anderson had 72 home runs and a career line of .250/.349/.393. When he blasted 50 long balls in 1996, baseball took notice. Mark McGwire, who was suddenly healthy for the first time in years, ripped 52 homers. McGwire followed that up with a 58 HR campaign while splitting time between Oakland and St. Louis. The following year he not only bested Roger Maris's 37-year-old single-season home run record, he blew past it, clubbing 70 while Chicago Cubs outfielder Sammy Sosa went yard 66 times.

And the sporting public learned another new word: androstenedione—a steroid precursor discovered in McGwire's locker.

Following a brief but intense media furor—which was quashed fairly quickly—McGwire publicly forsook the use of "andro" (as androstenedione was commonly known). The following year he still crushed 65 dingers, and Sosa was right there with 63. Commissioner Bud Selig initiated a series of studies with the players' union on andro that all but gathered dust. Androstenedione remained legal in baseball. For the most part the media focused on the home run exploits and paid little attention to how they were achieved.

Things settled down a bit in 2000 as Sosa was the only hitter in either league to hit 50 home runs. But Barry Bonds—who by this time was already a first-ballot Hall of Famer—at age 35 enjoyed what could be argued as the finest offensive season of his career to that point, ripping a then-career high 49 home runs while posting a .306/.440/.688 line.

He was just getting warmed up. Over the subsequent four seasons Bonds literally rewrote the record book, setting single-season records for home runs, walks, intentional walks, on-base percentage, slugging percentage and on-base plus slugging, as well as several sabermetric measures. No matter how you sliced and diced the numbers, Bonds had a five-year run that no player in baseball history had ever enjoyed; not even Babe Ruth's amazing run of 1920-24 in which he rewrote baseball's record book was as good. And Bonds was 10 years older than Ruth had been.

Suspicions abounded that Bonds's achievements were a matter of "better baseball through chemistry." After all, during this amazing run came revelations from various players who followed in Bouton's steps and published their stories. Then-Yankees starter David Wells wrote *Perfect I'm Not! Boomer on Beer, Brawls, Backaches and Baseball*, in which he claimed half of all major leaguers used anabolic steroids. In *Juiced: Wild Times, Rampant 'Roids, Smash Hits, and How Baseball Got Big*, former slugger Jose Canseco wrote that 85 percent of players used steroids, and he named former teammates McGwire, Jason Giambi, Rafael Palmeiro, Ivan Rodriguez and Juan Gonzalez. Beyond that he credited steroids for his near-Hall of Fame career. This might have been dismissed as the ranting of a player of questionable character until retired former MVP Ken Caminiti told *Sports Illustrated* writer Tom Verducci that he credited his 1996 MVP award to the juice.

These admissions were not a mea culpa; the players proclaimed loud and clear that anabolic steroids worked and that the juice made them great. Other high-profile players like Curt Schilling, Frank Thomas and John Smoltz became more vocal about steroids too, stating that they had no place in the game.

The new collective bargaining agreement ratified in 2002 included the first drug-testing program at the major league level.

If baseball had any hopes that this would blow over like amphetamines and androstenedione, they were soon shattered when agents from the IRS's Criminal Investigations Unit and the San Mateo County Narcotics Task Force raided the Bay Area Laboratory Cooperative (BALCO). Initially it appeared to have very little to do with baseball until the names of Bonds and Giambi surfaced during the investigation. When Congress decided to get involved there was no hope that MLB could sweep this under the rug.

During a grand jury investigation into BALCO, Giambi admitted using anabolic substances, while Bonds said he had inadvertently used a non-detectable steroid (THG) called "the cream," believing it was flaxseed oil for his arthritic knee.

Four different MVP winners were now tainted by the steroid scandal. Senate hearings prompted by Henry Waxman (D-California) and Tom Davis (R-

Virginia) resulted in subpoenas for Frank Thomas, Mark McGwire, Rafael Palmeiro, Sammy Sosa, Curt Schilling, Jose Canseco, Don Fehr, Bob Manfred and Bud Selig, as well as baseball's drug testing program which had been renegotiated earlier that year.

It did not go well. McGwire left with his legacy in tatters. Palmeiro's vehement denial of steroids use would come back to haunt him as he would test positive for stanozolol just months later. The committee suggested that baseball needs a new commissioner. The MLBPA was painted as a major enabler of steroid use within the sport. Great pressure was put on both parties to again reopen the collective bargaining agreement and toughen penalties for the use of performance-enhancing substances.

Shortly thereafter, Selig sent a proposal to the MLBPA that suggested penalties of a 50-game suspension for a first offense, a 100-game suspension for a second offense and a lifetime ban for a third. In September 2005 the union finally countered with 20 games for the first offense (with the possibility of 30 games for extenuating circumstances) and 75 games for a second offense (also with the possibility of an arbitrator increasing it to 100 games). For the third offense, the commissioner could mete out any punishment at his discretion, including a lifetime ban, as long as it would be subject to arbitral review. MLB could also test for amphetamines.

In the fall of 2005, the Senate Commerce, Science and Transportation Committee (which includes Hall of Fame pitcher Jim Bunning, now a Republican Senator from Kentucky) commenced a hearing on legislation that would standardize steroid policies in professional sports: first offense a two-year suspension, second offense lifetime banishment. Fehr and Selig were called to testify, and they brought along former MLBPA members and Hall of Famers Ryne Sandberg, Phil Niekro, Robin Roberts, Lou Brock and Henry Aaron, all of whom endorsed Selig's plan. Sen. John McCain (R-Arizona) basically told Fehr to accept the Selig proposal or have Olympic-style testing legislated down his throat. Fehr said that a new testing agreement would be in place by the end of the World Series.

So how do we look back at the steroid era?

Probably the most disturbing trend so far has been the singling out of the players as the sole recipients of the punishments and scorn. It all hearkens back to the Black Sox scandal. The environment wasn't just the responsibility of the players; owners and league presidents alike knew of gambling within the sport and for the most part did nothing. The media were generally silent on the issue as well. It was White Sox owner

Charles Comiskey's pecuniary practices that embittered the Black Sox in the first place. Comiskey may well have known about the possible fix even before the World Series was played and said nothing. He certainly knew about it shortly thereafter and did his part to cover up—including re-signing the guilty players to play the following year.

It wasn't until the whole thing blew up in public that management and media decided to get on the right side of history. The Black Sox were banished from the game for life, while those who enabled the gambling culture were not only allowed to stay in the game—some even found their way into the Hall of Fame. Marvin Miller summed it up succinctly in his autobiography *A Whole Different Ballgame* when he said that the question isn't why "Shoeless" Joe Jackson isn't in the Hall of Fame but why Comiskey isn't out.

There's plenty of blame to be shared in the steroid scandal, but it appears just a few men will bear the brunt of history's wrath. It has become clear that a number of owners/general managers/managers/members of the media certainly knew what was going on and kept silent. Clubs lavished huge monetary rewards to players who could hit the long ball. Some teams even provided the muscle-building creatine for the players. Ownership was never willing to stand up to the union on the issue and stake a claim on the moral high ground, and the MLBPA repeatedly made it clear that even if players were breaking the law of the land that it was none of baseball's (or anyone else's) business. There were no tests, no penalties and plenty of rewards for those willing to use illegal performance-enhancing drugs. There was never a written directive that said as much, but it was clearly understood by all parties. It was as clear as the $120 million-contract the New York Yankees bestowed upon Giambi with a steroid clause that could void the deal crossed out.

The media could certainly tell that players of today were far different physically than their counterparts of just 20 years ago and were doing things that players had never before accomplished. Roger Maris and Babe Ruth were the only players with 60+ home run seasons, and Ruth was the only player to have back-to-back 50-home run campaigns. Suddenly Mark McGwire has four consecutive 50-home run seasons, topping 60 twice and hitting 70 once. Sammy Sosa also has four consecutive 50-home run seasons, topping 60 in three of those years. And Bonds, past the age considered a player's prime, outdoes Babe Ruth *in his prime*. In a sport that traditionally eschewed muscle, players suddenly looked like they belonged in the NFL.

As of right now, it appears that Palmeiro, McGwire and Sosa will take the fall for the previous decade by a possible exclusion to the Hall of Fame, while at the management end of the business no one is being discussed as unworthy of Cooperstown for his part in creating and perpetuating the steroid culture—history again repeating itself.

Probably the most difficult part of this era is how to put the accomplishments we've witnessed into some kind of perspective. To begin with, in the last 10 years players discovered the benefits of weight training, the ball was "juiced," bats got harder and lighter, the strike zone shrank, and batters came to the plate protected as never before. Pitchers were punished for throwing inside. Ballpark dimensions shrank. These are also factors that contributed to the offensive explosion. It wasn't just anabolic substances in isolation.

I've written before on Bonds's and Palmeiro's post-steroid revelation achievements and I'll just reiterate it here:

Barry Bonds

What to make of Barry Bonds's achievements? Are his totals tainted?

Sure—but nowhere near the extent that some claim. Tom Boswell opined:

"Let Bonds keep his 411 homers and three MVPs before he linked his fate to Anderson in '98, though we can't be sure what he might have used to aid his play before that. At least we now know what he's willing to use: anything that's put into his hands."

To completely discount almost 300 home runs and to say that Bonds wouldn't have hit a single dinger after 1998 is, to put it simply, absurd. Obviously his totals are skewed, and I'm guessing that Boz (Tom Boswell) is engaging in a little good old fashioned hyperbole. It also assumes that if you were to put Alex Rodriguez, Albert Pujols, Carlos Beltran or Vladimir Guerrero on Bonds's program, they too could go five seasons averaging .339/.530/.781 with 123 runs scored and 109 RBIs while blasting 258 home runs after their 35th birthdays. They can't produce a 1.100 OPS in their primes (Pujols did reach 1.106 in 2003), so what makes us think they could post a 1.421 OPS when they're 39 or 40, regardless of what they put into their bodies? Steroids won't turn a bum into a Hall of Famer any more than they could turn Neifi Perez into Alex Rodriguez. Bonds's achievements are due to a convergence

of several circumstances: an extremely gifted athlete, an otherworldly nutrition and fitness program and an era geared toward offense and performance-enhancing drugs. For laughs, let's deduct 30% of Bonds' totals since he turned 35: that makes him a .237 hitter, but his OBP is still a healthy .371 and his SLG is an excellent .547, and he hits not 258 but 181 HR, giving him a career total of 626 dingers. What kind of player posts an aggregate OPS of .918 and blasts 181 HR for five seasons after his 35th birthday?

One of the best ever.

Rafael Palmeiro

We know that Rafael Palmeiro has used steroids. How do we view his career numbers in light of that? Has his whole career been pharmaceutically driven? Unless some new evidence surfaces, it appears that Palmeiro's statements before Congress were lies; hence everything he says from this point on will be viewed with suspicion. Having said that, there are a number of things that have to be entered into the equation when re-evaluating Palmeiro's career.

With the exception of Barry Bonds, heavy use of steroids seems to take a toll on ballplayers' longevity. Those noted for their possible usage have had their bodies break down and have been out of the game by their late 30s: Mark McGwire retired at 37, Ken Caminiti made it to 38, Jose Canseco was gone at 36 and Sammy Sosa appears to be declining at 36. Palmeiro will be 41 at season's end. This can mean one of three things: he hasn't been using that long, he was on a well-regulated program, or he's just been very fortunate.

It's possible that he hasn't been using that long. His use of stanozolol rather than more sophisticated substances would indicate that his program hasn't been well-regulated, making it unlikely that he has simply been fortunate.

Palmeiro has been the mark of durability, playing at least 150 games in every non-strike year since 1988. A lack of physical breakdown is remarkable—all the more so if he's been a long-time user. According to Canseco's book Juiced, Palmeiro's usage stretches back over a decade. The amusing thing about Canseco's claims is that they implicated Palmeiro when he wasn't being tested, but now that Palmeiro has been tested and caught, Canseco says he's innocent. So do we believe Canseco or not? The bottom line is that there is no way of finding out conclusively. In the interest of fairness, the only evidence we have that Palmeiro was clean before is his testimony, but his credibility is lacking as well.

We don't know 100% how steroids improve a ballplayer's performance. It varies from person to person. In a sense, steroids are a lot like having a batting cage and a pitching machine in your backyard. It can improve your performance if you have the natural physical gifts to play the sport at the highest levels and you use the equipment correctly. Sticking a syringe into your backside will do you little good unless you have significant gifts to begin with and the work ethic to go along with it.

Personally I don't feel Canseco's word, coupled with a failed drug test in 2005, meets either the legal requirement of "guilty beyond a reasonable doubt" or the civil requirement of "preponderance of evidence" to discount everything Palmeiro has accomplished since 1993. If more evidence becomes available, we can readjust accordingly. Am I being naïve? Possibly, but those are the standards by which I'd want to be judged.

Let's assume for a moment that 1993 was Palmeiro's first "steroid" year. In his first 3,270 career at-bats (presumably before steroids) Palmeiro batted .296/.358/.457. Now we'll look at his first six "steroid" years from 1993-98 (3,446 at-bats): .292/.371/.547. Suspicious? Perhaps, but during those seasons Palmeiro was between the ages of 28 and 33, generally a power hitter's peak. So is the jump in power due to steroids, a normal power peak or both? Assuming steroids, Palmeiro's power improved, but unlike Bonds, his batting average did not (.296 to .292). Bonds batted .294 from 1995 to 1999 (2,462 at-bats). However, from the time it was assumed he started using (2000-2004, 2,122 at-bats), he jumped up to .339, and his slugging over those aforementioned stretches went from .600 to .781. Bonds's first assumed steroid year was at age 35; Palmeiro's first alleged steroid year was at age 28. Which would you assume was the steroid user, the 28-year-old whose subsequent batting average dropped six points while his slugging percentage jumped .090 or the 35-year-old whose subsequent batting average jumped .045 while his slugging vaulted .181?

Since he turned 34 (discounting this year's stats), Palmeiro is .280/.385/.545, which is pretty close to his age 28-33 seasons, but those totals are propped up from his years between his age-34 to age-37 years. In his past two full seasons, his age-38 and age-39 seasons, Palmeiro is .259/.357/.473, which looks like a normal decline phase.

When we look at Palmeiro's career, his first alleged "steroid" year came about the same time as a normal hitter's power peak. In other words, the numbers don't

scream "This is when he started using steroids" a la Barry Bonds.

If Palmeiro has indeed been a long-time user, the benefits to his game were primarily in the power department. His "pre-steroid" years featured his best batting averages, which might well mean—steroids or not—that he'd still be a member of the 3,000-hit club. Since the durability knife with regards to steroids cuts both ways—it can prolong or shorten careers, as well as make one more durable or more susceptible to injury—we cannot assume with any certainty that steroids contributed to the durability that allowed him to bang out 3,000 hits. If you wish to discount 25% of the home runs he hit since he allegedly started using, then he's left with 3,000 hits and over 450 home runs (and probably well over 600 doubles).

Ultimately we'll never know precisely who has used what. To expunge the stats of only those players who got caught is absurd. Some have suggested placing asterisks alongside some players' achievements, but history is littered with mental asterisks about every era: the low ERAs of the dead ball era, the big HR and RBI totals of the 1920s and 1930s, back to the low ERAs of the 1960s. We understand that records put up before 1947 were accomplished without the very best black and Latino players in the game. We have pre-expansion adjustments, post-expansion adjustments, strike-shortened season adjustments. For example, let's compare the best five seasons of two third basemen from the post-expansion era:

Player	AVG/OBP/SLG	HR	RBI
Player A	.275/.398/.576	199	522
Player B	.302/.348/.545	191	562

Player A is an inner-circle Hall of Famer, Player B probably will have trouble drawing any votes. The Hall of Famer is Mike Schmidt, the other Vinny Castilla. Castilla benefited from playing in the thin air of Colorado. We know that. There's no need to wonder if Castilla hit almost as well as Schmidt for five years. We've already mentally asterisked Castilla's totals due to playing in Denver.

It's the same today; folks will look back at Bonds's and McGwire's 70-home run seasons, Sosa's trio of 60-plus-home run seasons and think, "That was during the steroid era." It's the same way we look at Ed Walsh's career ERA record of 1.82 or Dutch Leonard's single-season ERA record of 0.96—"that was during the dead ball era." No one has ever suggested that Walsh was the greatest pitcher of all time or that Leonard had the greatest single season ever by a pitcher.

Records are set, records change, but legacies don't. Hank Aaron owns the all-time home run record, but Ruth is still considered the greatest home run hitter of all time. Pete Rose owns the all-time hits record, but Ty Cobb is considered a far superior hitter. Bonds currently holds the single-season record for OBP, SLG and walks and has over 700 HR, but folks still say Ted Williams was the greatest hitter ever.

You cannot manufacture a Hall of Fame player. To be a Hall of Famer, one needs unique physical gifts. One can goose the totals, to be sure, but all the pharmaceuticals in the world will not turn Barry Bonnell into Barry Bonds. McGwire slugged 49 home runs as a rookie, Bonds won three MVPs before BALCO, Sammy Sosa was a 30-30 player twice before 1998. There are many nondescript players in both the major and minor leagues who have used anabolic steroids who remain nondescript because they lack the talent of the game's elite.

History will give us the proper perspective to deal with this era. Make no mistake—performance-enhancing substances are here to stay. America fought the war on drugs and got its butt kicked badly. There's too much demand and too much money involved to ever make it go away. As long as the money is so big in baseball, as long as big-league dreams burn like fire in the soul, there will be athletes willing to make any sacrifice to get there. There will be chemists who will help develop ways to beat the tests. You cannot legislate morality. Does this mean that we should give up trying? Of course not. The good fight should always be fought. But we have to be realistic.

Business of Baseball Year in Review
by Brian Borawski

Baseball Team for Sale

On September 28, 2004, Major League Baseball announced that the league-owned Montreal Expos would relocate to Washington, D.C. This single announcement triggered a series of complicated developments over the next year—everything from government showdowns and lawsuits to backroom deals and land grabs.

The initial roadblock to the sale was city councilwoman and current mayoral hopeful Linda Cropp. A publicly financed stadium appeared to be a done deal at a December 14 city council meeting, but Cropp's last-minute curveball to add a provision requiring $142 million in private funding for the stadium nearly derailed the entire relocation. The idea came about when Cropp was approached by the owners of BW Realty Advisors LLC, who offered to pay for two-thirds of the stadium in exchange for exclusive rights to the stadium's construction. Cropp slipped the amendment into the proposed bill late in the evening once she knew that she had the deciding vote. In the end, the pro-stadium supporters were left with a bill radically different than the one agreed upon by Mayor Anthony Williams.

Commissioner Bud Selig and his chief lieutenant, MLB President and CEO Bob DuPuy, immediately went on the offensive. All business and promotional activities for the team were halted, and the unveiling of the new Nationals uniform was delayed indefinitely. Talk of moving the team began to circulate, even though most of the other prospective cities didn't have a viable interim stadium.

In the end, it appeared to be political posturing by Cropp, because at the following week's city council meeting, she backed off the private funding requirement. The final agreement was that private funding would be sought but would not necessarily be required. On December 29, just days before MLB's deadline for a stadium deal, Mayor Williams signed the stadium financing package into law. As long as the cost of acquiring the land didn't exceed $165 million, the Washington Nationals' new home would be on the Anacostia River waterfront, and the city would be allowed to issue $535 million in bonds to build the new stadium.

With the stadium taken care of, the league began the process of selling the Nationals. In January, eight prospective buyers were told that they had until January 31, 2005 to submit their applications and their $100,000 deposits.

The initial word was that the league was attempting to sell the Nationals by Opening Day, but as is usually the case with MLB deadlines, it came and went without a sale. The initial expected sales price was $300 million.

In the meantime, the league had to contend with the sole owner that opposed the relocation. Baltimore Orioles owner Peter Angelos felt that the move would cost him money and fans, and he even went as far as to threaten a lawsuit to prevent a club moving into what he saw as Orioles territory. At the end of March, the league took care of this by compensating Angelos for the various losses he might incur with another franchise in close proximity. The deal gave the Orioles a controlling interest in the newly created Mid-Atlantic Sports Network (MASN), which would hold the television rights for both the Orioles and the Nationals. The Orioles received a 90% stake in MASN while the league kept 10%; the league's stake increases incrementally to 33% over the next 28 years.

This resolution created a new problem. In late April, Comcast SportsNet, a subsidiary of Comcast Corporation, filed a lawsuit against the Orioles. They contended that the deal that Angelos struck with MLB violated the distribution agreement that Comcast has with the team. Even though Comcast's current deal with the Orioles is set to expire at the end of 2006, the company has an exclusive negotiating window with the Orioles until November 1, 2006. When the team announced that they'd be moving to MASN after the deal with Comcast expires, the cable giant filed a breach of contract lawsuit, claiming they weren't given this exclusive negotiating window with the team.

The ancillary effect of the lawsuit was that Comcast refused to air anything related to MASN, including Nationals games. It delayed a deal between DirecTV and MASN to air 70 Nationals games, and there was also speculation that the lawsuit could slow down the sale of the team even further. By Opening Day, the furthest the sale had gotten was that the league had given the prospective owners a second chance to look through the team's books in order to complete their due diligence.

It wasn't until early May that the Nationals finally got on television, at least on a limited basis. The DirecTV deal that was delayed because of the Comcast lawsuit finally got signed. At around the same time, the D.C. Sports and Entertainment Commission acquired a lien that protected Washington, D.C. in the event that the Nationals relocated. The lien gives the city legal authority to seek restitution on any outstanding debt for the proposed ballpark if the team were to move. Meanwhile, the sale of the team was moving slowly. In mid-May, Bud Selig revised his estimate on the sales date to "mid-summer." Bids on the team by the prospective ownership groups were due on May 31, 2005.

In the interim, the Orioles and Comcast continued their legal battle. The Orioles sought a protective order that would have put the entire case on hold, and they argued that MASN wasn't a third party in the case. The Orioles claimed that MASN was the equivalent of TCR, Inc., which is the Orioles' subsidiary that signed the TV deal with Comcast's predecessor, Home Team Sports. MLB and the Orioles had until early June to formally file their response to the lawsuit, and there were grumblings that the Orioles might even countersue, although it was unclear what their claim would be.

In late May, the bids began to come in for the team. Estimates on the ultimate sales price ran from $350 million to $400 million, with an estimate of $500 million if MLB threw in its 10% share in MASN. To sweeten the deal even more, it was announced that the Nationals were going to turn a profit of around $20 million for the year. The one thing that looked like it could hold up the sale was the Orioles and Comcast lawsuit. The Orioles filed a motion in late May alleging MASN wasn't a third party, so there wasn't any violation of the standing agreement.

In early June, news began to leak regarding the bids for the team. Political heavyweights like former Secretary of State Colin Powell and billionaire fund manager and Democratic supporter George Soros teamed up with different groups that were bidding on the team. The number floating around was now $400 million, and with the news that the team was going to post a nice profit, things were looking good for the other 29 owners who owned stakes in the team.

Around the same time, the Virginia Baseball Stadium Authority closed its office. With the Nationals firmly entrenched in Washington, D.C., the chances that either northern Virginia or Norfolk could land a team effectively became zero. In addition, the Orioles took the offensive in fending off Comcast in their lawsuit. The Orioles asked the Federal Communication Commission to force Comcast to carry Nationals games that were produced by MASN. Comcast was still blocking any attempt to have Nationals games on their cable network, and MASN had paid the team $20 million for broadcast rights. Until the games were broadcast by the largest cable company in the country, the Orioles and MASN would have a hard time recouping their up-front cost.

In mid-June, a few new developments affected the construction of the Nationals' future home. On June

15, the first installment of a gross receipts tax that is a pivotal piece of the Nationals' stadium bill came due. Many small business owners felt the tax hit small businesses more than it did large companies and that the tax was basically an unfair subsidy to MLB. The other development was a United States Supreme Court ruling allowing local governments to force property owners to sell their property to make way for private development if the land can be used to benefit the public. If the landowners on the proposed site balked at the city's offers to buy the land, the city had the teeth of the ruling to claim eminent domain.

In the meantime, the team went on a hot streak. In early June, the Nationals won 10 straight games, and they were in first place heading into the All-Star break. But they were having a huge shortfall in actual attendance compared to the number of tickets sold. The team estimated that about 7,000 tickets on average were going unused every game, which was around 25% of tickets sold. The league average is closer to 20%. So while the team did pocket the money from the sale of the unused tickets, the District was losing out. One of the provisions of the stadium bill was a 12% tax on parking and a 10% tax on food, beverages and merchandise. If people weren't going to the park, they weren't buying hot dogs and souvenirs, so there was concern of a shortfall in tax revenue along with a potential downgrade of the stadium's prospective debt.

In mid-July, three Anacostia River waterfront landowners filed lawsuits in federal court claiming that the District violated their civil rights by illegally attempting to seize their properties to expedite the construction of the stadium. The suit stemmed from an allegedly faulty study conducted by Washington, D.C. officials to determine the cost of the land. The stadium bill contained a provision saying the cost of the land for the stadium, including infrastructure and environmental remediation, couldn't exceed $165 million. The city's study estimated the cost of the land would be $161.4 million. The three landowners were alleging that the study was arbitrarily done and that the conclusion was indefensible.

In late July and early August, MLB began showing the prospective owners some of the perks of ownership. Each ownership group was allowed a visit with MLB's Advanced Media division. The division is estimated to make approximately $130 million a year from Internet game telecasts, online ticket sales and advertising. There was some speculation that the league was considering spinning off the division and turning it into a publicly traded company. Despite the fact that the proceeds from a public sale could net $2-4 billion dollars, the sale hasn't gone through because of the league's hesitance towards opening their books. Regardless, the next owner of the Nationals would own one-thirtieth of the Advanced Media division, so the road show was most likely done as an attempt to get the groups to raise their bids.

While this was happening, the Orioles and the Nationals caught a huge break. Montgomery County Circuit Court Judge Durke Thompson dismissed Comcast's lawsuit against MASN. Thompson sided with the Orioles by stating that MASN wasn't a third party, although he left the door open for Comcast by allowing the company 30 days to amend its suit. The decision didn't force Comcast to air Nationals games, so basic cable subscribers were still left in the dark.

By mid-August, the league announced that it hoped to set a sale price for the team soon. The latest price was rumored to be $450 million, well above the estimates thrown around in the spring. The league once again amended its deadline, now proclaiming that a new owner would be chosen by mid-September and that the sale would be closed by the end of the World Series.

Around the same time, the city received two pieces of good news as the process of paving the way for the Nationals' new stadium began. The city had collected more than $15 million in gross receipts tax to date; only $14 million had been expected for the whole year. In addition, sales tax receipts were up as well. The city had collected $6.7 million, which was ahead of the pace to meet the anticipated $10.5 million for the year. The other piece of good news was that District Court Judge Richard Roberts declined to impose an injunction on the city as it prepared to acquire the property to build the new stadium. He concluded that the suit filed by the three Anacostia River waterfront landowners wasn't strong enough and that the city's study wasn't arbitrary.

While it looked like the city was on track to begin construction of the stadium by spring 2006, the sale of the team continued at a snail's pace. With the Comcast/Orioles lawsuit in the background, the new holdup was the lease agreement between the current owner of the Nationals, MLB, and Washington, D.C. The league was hesitant to sell the team until annual lease payments were agreed upon, because it made coming up with a final sales price difficult. The league was at least moving forward with the bidding process by requesting additional information from the eight prospective bidders. The information included how much each group was willing to pay, the lead member of the group, and which banks would be providing financing for the purchase.

In early September, Washington, D.C. officials began making offers for the land where the stadium would be located. In order to begin construction in spring 2006, the city needed to acquire all of the land by the end of the year. Many landowners said the offers were too low. If the landowners can't settle with the city, then the city will likely take the land through eminent domain, and at that point the landowners would be entitled to have their case heard in court. They'd be arguing not whether they could keep their land, but only the ultimate sales price. The city would get the land but it could end up costing more than their initial offers.

In mid-September, MLB distributed detailed purchase agreements to each of the prospective owners. The agreements are binding documents, and if an agreement is signed and returned, the bidding group has officially put its price on the table for the team. Once again, the rumored price was $450 million. As usual, the league was being coy and blamed the holdup of the sale on the not-yet-agreed-upon lease terms with the city.

On September 21, the league finally announced the sale price of the team. As expected, the final number was $450 million. Bud Selig said he'd like to pick a new owner before the playoffs started, but the one major snag was the stadium lease with the city. A couple of weeks later, White Sox owner Jerry Reinsdorf, one of the key negotiators for the league with the D.C. city council, said that he wouldn't be able to get the lease deal done because he was following his team in the playoffs. He also said that he didn't expect a new owner until November. The major stumbling block is that the city wants the owner of the team to guarantee the $6 million that will be needed to cover the city's debt payments every year. In addition, Wall Street is declining to guarantee the debt until the guaranteed lease payment is set. In order to have financing in place by the December 31, 2005 deadline, the lease must be finished in November.

In early October, Judge Thompson once again dismissed Comcast's case against the Orioles. While he gave the cable giant a chance to bring forward more information to help its case, Comcast failed to present anything new to sway the judge.

By mid-October, a new owner had still not been selected. Bud Selig was now saying that an owner would be in place by the 2006 season, an unusually long-term hedge for him. In addition, the city council was revisiting last December's stadium deal. Councilwoman Cropp and Councilman Vincent B. Orange sparred over a private financing deal with Deutsche Bank that would give the city $246 million for the stadium. In return, the bank would receive revenue generated from the new stadium. Cropp endorsed the plan and said that if the deal doesn't go through, she'll resurrect her idea of building the new ballpark on the site of RFK Stadium, a move that could save the city $200 million. It was viewed as a political ploy because both Cropp and Orange seek to replace Mayor

Brown. Cropp eventually voted for Orange's proposal to allow the council to review the agreement with Deutsche Bank because it was a nonbinding agreement. In order to change the deal, someone on the council would have to propose new legislation. Orange also threatened to propose legislation that would force the league to choose an owner before the stadium lease negotiations were finalized. The threats didn't sit very well with Selig and DuPuy. To make matters worse, the city council could revisit the entire stadium deal because of concerns that Wall Street bonds raters might not give the city an investment-grade debt rating unless some technical problems in the bill were corrected. There is a good chance, however, that technical amendments could be added to the stadium bill that would remove the ability to amend the bill.

We've come a long way since the league announced the Expos' relocation, but as this book goes to print, there are still several unanswered questions. Who will be the owner of the Nationals and when will the sale close? Will construction of the stadium begin on time? Will the city run into problems acquiring the land for the new stadium site? Will the financing be completed so the city's bonds can be issued by December 31, 2005? Only time will tell.

The Los Angeles Angels of Anaheim

In November 2004, Bud Selig approved the request by Angels' owner Arte Moreno to change the name of the Anaheim Angels to the Los Angeles Angels. Once Moreno got wind of the fact that the city of Anaheim was contemplating a lawsuit over the name change, citing the lease agreement which states "Anaheim" must be in the name of the team, he settled on the Los Angeles Angels of Anaheim. By throwing the team's home at the end of the name, Moreno not only got the team mentioned in one of the largest markets in the country, but he also fulfilled his obligation to the city of Anaheim. Moreno hoped that the team could attract more fans and advertisers, and eventually better broadcasting contracts, by lining up with the much larger city of Los Angeles.

The city of Anaheim followed this up by filing a breach of contract lawsuit. It also asked for a restraining order that would have forced the team to change the name back to the Anaheim Angels. It claimed that the name change hurts the city's ability to market itself as a tourist destination and that it wasn't permitted by the lease. If the city of Anaheim prevailed, the city could terminate the lease, evict the Angels and collect $15 million plus any damages. Moreno claimed that the city was trying to rewrite the lease, and based on the exact wording provided in the agreement—"include the name of Anaheim therein"—he wasn't in violation.

On January 7, 2005, the Angels took round one. The judge in the case denied the city its temporary restraining order and for the time being allowed the name change. Later that month, the city tried again to stop the name change by getting a preliminary injunction against the Angels, but this was also shot down. The Los Angeles Angels of Anaheim would be the new team name until the city got its day in court, expected to be sometime in 2005. In the meantime, the court urged the team and the city to enter mediation in an attempt to resolve the dispute out of court.

By the end of April, mediation had resolved nothing. The team was a month into the baseball season, and the league had officially recognized the new name. At the end of June, the Fourth Circuit Court of Appeals upheld the same decision made by the Orange Count Superior Court, and a preliminary injunction that would have forced the team to change its name back was denied. In the meantime, the city attempted to force the team to include disclosures on tickets and advertisements that the team was actually located in Anaheim. The city eventually backed off of this around the All-Star break.

In late September, Orange County Superior Court Judge Peter Polos pushed the court date for the lawsuit back to January 9, 2006. He felt that trial preparations couldn't be completed by November, and he also ordered Angels team president Dennis Kuhl to answer questions that his lawyer had previously prevented him from answering during his deposition.

Ownership Changes

On January 13, 2005, Los Angeles investor Mark Attanasio was approved as the new owner of the Milwaukee Brewers. With the unanimous approval of the other league owners, one of the most blatant conflicts of interest ended. The former owner, Bud Selig, had put his 28% ownership of the interest in the team into a trust, and his daughter, Wendy Selig-Prieb ran the team when Selig took over as the baseball commissioner in 1998. Many felt that even though his interest was in a trust, he was never truly independent. Selig had owned the team since it relocated from Seattle in 1970; Attanasio bought it for $220 million.

While Selig exited the ownership club, his fraternity brother, Lewis Wolff, and a group of investors, including John Fisher, the son of Gap, Inc. founder David Fisher, were finishing up their purchase of the Oakland Athletics. The sale became official in late March, and the team was sold for a price of $175 million. Wolff had worked for the team as the vice president for venue development, where he had worked towards getting a new stadium for the Athletics.

The final ownership change happened shortly after the end of the season. Stuart Sternberg assumed control of the Tampa Bay Devil Rays from former managing general partner Vince Naimoli. Sternberg didn't waste any time in making changes; he dismissed general manager Chuck LaMar and announced that parking would be free for the 2006 season. Matt Silverman, who worked for the team as vice president for planning and development, was named the organization's new president. Sternberg purchased a 50% interest in the team in May 2004, but only just now attained control of the team. Naimoli, a 15% owner of the team and the general partner of the ownership group, stepped down so that he could spend time with his family.

The one developing story is the sale of three current owners' 51.5% stake in the Cincinnati Reds. The interest that's being sold does not include operating control, but a change in control could be a part of the negotiations. Part-owner Carl Lidner, as part of the current operating agreement, currently has control over the team until he either relinquishes it or passes away. There are five potential buyers and the expected sales price ranges from $250-275 million. The sale is expected to close in November 2005.

Stadium Developments

The Washington Nationals weren't the only team this season to try to garner public interest in a new home for their team. For over 10 years, Minnesota Twins owner Carl Pohlad had been trying to get some municipality in Minnesota to buck up and help him pay for a new home for the Twins. He finally struck a deal with Hennepin County. Pohlad agreed to put up $120 million of his own money, and the remaining $350 million would come from a sales tax increase in the county. The deal got county approval, but the sales tax bill stalled in the state legislature. The legislature's session ended at the end of May, and Pohlad lost the race against the clock.

The state government got mired in a nasty budget battle that led to a special legislative session. With the budget still unresolved, there was even a partial shutdown of the Minnesota government over the Independence Day weekend. While the state finally got its budget problems resolved, the stadium bill was never brought up again. At press time, a subsequent special session appeared very unlikely, so once again, Pohlad will have to wait for his new stadium.

The Florida Marlins fared even worse. While it looked like there was some hope for the Twins' stadium bill, the Marlins' $60 million sales tax bill didn't even make it to the floor of the state legislature before the session ended. In mid-May, MLB President Bob DuPuy issued an ultimatum to Miami-Dade County to get a deal done or else. He gave the county until June 9, but the date came and went without any development.

New Athletics owner Lew Wolff didn't waste much time in his attempt to procure a new stadium. In July he unveiled his plans for an intimate 35,000-seat stadium and while he's said that he'd like to stay in Oakland, he hasn't ruled out relocating the team if necessary.

Both New York teams made inroads toward building new stadiums. The city committed to helping the Mets build a new stadium, hoping to use the venue to entice the Olympic Committee to commit to the 2012 Summer Olympics in New York. The city eventually lost on its bid for the summer games, but it did agree to pay for $180 million in infrastructure improvements around the planned stadium in Queens. Mets owner Fred Wilpon is responsible for the construction of the estimated $600-million stadium set to open in 2009.

New York Yankees owner George Steinbrenner took matters into his own hands. Under the leadership of team president Randy Levine, Steinbrenner unveiled his plans for an $800 million-stadium just north of Yankee Stadium. In exchange, the state is expected to pay $300 million to build parking garages around the stadium from which they'll then receive revenue.

The St. Louis Cardinals closed "old" Busch Stadium and plan to open up "new" Busch Stadium in 2006. The $400 million-ballpark is nearing completion in the south end of downtown St. Louis, next to the old stadium. Important parts of the new park are located within the footprint of the current stadium. Demolition was to start as soon as the Cardinals' season was over.

Attendance Record

According to a press release from Major League Baseball, the official attendance for all games was a record 74,915,268. This is up 2.6% from the previous year's 73,022,969, which was the previous record. The Yankees led the way as they became only the third franchise to draw over four million fans in a single season. The previous franchises who topped the four million mark were the Toronto Blue Jays (1992 and 1993) and the Colorado Rockies (1993). The largest increase came from the relocation of the Nationals. The Nationals drew almost two million more fans than did the previous year's Montreal Expos, but attendance for the other 29 teams was effectively flat.

Minor league baseball also set a new attendance record for the second straight season. 41,333,279 fans showed up to watch the big league's minor league affiliates take the field, an increase of 3.6% from the previous season.

Crystal Ball: The 2006 CBA and the Battles Within It

by Maury Brown

The time-honored match-up between the snake and the mongoose approaches again. Bud Selig and Bob DuPuy vs. Don Fehr and Gene Orza. George Steinbrenner vs. David Glass. Strike and Lockout vs. the baseball fans.

On December 19, 2006, the current collective bargaining agreement expires. As with every other round of collective bargaining, the baseball world waits to see what changes are in store. In reality, most watch the monopoly that is MLB and the strongest union in the United States to see if they reach an impasse and throw baseball into work stoppage #9. As always, this is about money, but it's obviously more complicated than that. There's posturing. There's MLB looking out for MLB. There are 29 (soon to be 30) owners looking to stab one of their own in the back, if it means getting a leg up, moving up in the standings or pocketing some green. And then there's the Major League Baseball Players Association, which had consistently outmatched MLB since Marvin Miller became executive director of the union, but now has some chinks in its armor.

Since Miller came along in 1965, there have been a total of eight work stoppages totaling 366 days and 1,719 games lost. None was as painful as 1994-95 strike that canceled the World Series for the first time in history, a pain that still lingers in the hearts of the fans and is always present with both MLB and the MLBPA during collective bargaining. When the 2002 negotiations started, MLB and the MLBPA had a perfect record since 1972: eight negotiations—eight work stoppages. Maybe it was the anniversary of 9/11. Maybe it was that gnawing reminder of the 1994-95 strike. The two sides hammered out a deal and proved that they had the ability to not poke themselves in the eye for a ninth time.

Rolling the dice, looking at the tea leaves, sticking a finger in the air and reading which way the wind blows—it's impossible to say what's going to come out of this collective bargaining session. But, as 2006 rolls up on us, by looking at the last agreement and its structure, we get some clues as to the labor-management battles we might see after the end of the 2006 season.

Looking at where we're at, here's a good chance of what you'll see.

Contraction

In 2002, the clubs agreed to keep 30 teams through 2006 and have the option of electing to eliminate two clubs in 2007. The clubs may not take a vote relating to contraction effective for the 2007 season prior to April 1, 2006. They are, however, required to notify the players union no later than July 1, 2006. If the owners decide to contract in 2007, they are not beholden to the MLBPA to reveal which teams they plan to eliminate in the July 1, 2006 notification.

Despite this option's availability, "That's not on the table," Selig said in July 2005. "I'll never say never. But I don't see contraction. I certainly don't see expansion and I don't see contraction. As long as I'm commissioner, which is another four years, we have 30 teams and that's what we'll have."

Attempts at contraction in 2001, real or of the straw man variety, were done with MLB owning the Montreal Expos and Minnesota Twins owner, Carl Pohlad, offering up his franchise for contraction to balance out the league. But a few changes make the issue moot. The Expos have relocated to Washington, DC. And MLB saw the legal wrangling around the Twins' Metrodome lease that followed contraction talk in 2001—only a precursor to further legal problems that would have attached to contraction. Finally, Selig is no longer going up before Congress and the press to poor-mouth baseball's depressed state. If anything, the commissioner sounds nearly Pollyannaish trumpeting the game's unprecedented popularity.

Beyond that, MLB would actually *lose* money via contraction. The cost of purchasing the remaining balance on multi-year contracts and bonuses for those players who do not find homes on other teams, as well as day-of-game personnel, executives, managers, coaches, marketing and legal services, would cost tens of millions of dollars. When you add in the costs associated with dissolving all the minor league affiliates, the total costs could possibly run into the hundreds of millions of dollars.

No, contraction was a bargaining chip last time. It's not going to be considered in the next basic agreement.

Outcome for the 2006 CBA: Contraction dropped from the CBA.

Revenue Sharing

Before the union and its player representatives sit across from management to discuss matters, tough negotiations will already have occurred inside the house that is Major League Baseball. Owners like David Glass of the Kansas City Royals and Kevin McClatchy of the Pittsburgh Pirates will have to deal with George Steinbrenner and the likes of John Henry, Tom Werner and Larry Lucchino of the Red Sox over changes to the revenue sharing provisions. This isn't a matter of the bigger markets wanting simply to pocket more money, although they certainly aren't opposed to that notion. The ongoing issue is that an owner like Carl Pohlad of the Minnesota Twins is the richest owner in baseball, yet he continues to receive luxury tax and revenue sharing distributions under the current CBA. This behavior drives the likes of Steinbrenner nuts. And let's not kid ourselves. The amount of money that has flowed from the haves to the have-nots has increased steadily. Compared to 2002, the owners are all considerably richer than the last time this game was played.

In mid-September 2005, MLB inked a deal with ESPN for eight years that covers radio and digital highlights in addition to game broadcasts. The deal will add $337 million a year to MLB's coffers—$11.23 million annually for each of the 30 owners during the course of the agreement. This is on top of: 1) $60 million annually that XM Radio pays to broadcast games and content over satellite radio, 2) the money that will be collected and disbursed upon the sale of the Washington Nationals, 3) a restructured TBS deal that expires in 2008, 4) OLN/Comcast aggressively looking to get MLB programming on their network and 5) FOX's six-year deal that expires in 2006.

Already the Kansas City Royals and the Toronto Blue Jays have announced that they plan to increase payroll in 2006. Increased common revenues are finally affecting player personnel costs on the lowest payroll teams. In the case of the Royals, payroll will jump from $36.881 million to $50 million or more—an increase of at least 35%. "Because of the improving revenue picture in major league baseball," David Glass said, "we have more funds available to us. Now, we still can't go out and spend $100 million in a market like this, but we can go to $50 million-plus.

"That's what we're going to have next year. The opportunities are getting better, and that gives us some flexibility to go do some things that will allow us to put a competitive team on the field," he said.

So, with this in mind, revenue sharing should decrease and it's possible the luxury tax will be dropped. Right? Not so fast …

In the 1997-2001 CBA, local revenue sharing was 20%. That figure rose to 34% net of ballpark expenses for the 2002-2006 agreement with the monies equally distributed among the teams. The owners, however, had originally proposed 50%. With that in mind, look for a discussion of increases in the amount of local revenue sharing in the next CBA.

As for the money that will flow from the haves to the have-nots, under the 2002 agreement, $72.2 million (based on 2001 revenue figures) is taken annually from those franchises that are net payers into the base plan to net takers. The provision was phased in to prevent sticker shock—60% in 2003, 80% in 2004 and 100% in 2005-06. The disbursement formula is based on the franchise's distance from the average revenue. Beyond these numbers, some events have occurred over the last four years that would seem to point to more in the way of revenue sharing.

Does revenue sharing really create parity? Or more precisely, is the current revenue sharing system working to allow the franchises with lower payrolls a chance to get into the postseason? The teams that landed in the playoffs were ranked at the top of their divisions in payroll (see tables on adjacent page). Owners with lower team player payroll will point to this and ask for an increase in revenue sharing.

There are some other issues to consider when talking revenue sharing.

The Montreal Expos moved to Washington, D.C. A team that was a revenue taker is now going to be a revenue payer. In addition, several clubs are looking to build new stadiums and pay for the stadium construction out of their own pockets. The Yankees, Mets, Cardinals and Athletics all have offered up such plans. They have some incentive to do so. In the current CBA, clubs must make revenue-sharing payments on all baseball revenue. The exception is that clubs can deduct stadium operations expenses annually. MLB is allowing stadium construction to fall under this provision.

Under the system, clubs can deduct roughly 40% of their total stadium construction and operations expenses. With that in mind, if the Yankees move forward on a planned $750 million stadium, the club could write off roughly $15.6 million a year in revenue-sharing obligations. Over the course of 20 years, this amounts to over $300 million. There is nothing in the current CBA that

Postseason Teams – 2003-2005 by Opening Day Payroll

2003

Club	W	L	Pct.	Opening Day Payroll	Payroll Ranking by "Division"
NYA	101	61	.623	$149,710,995	1
ATL	101	61	.623	$104,622,210	1
BOS	95	67	.586	$96,631,677	2
SF	100	61	.621	$82,352,167	2
CHN	88	74	.543	$80,743,333	2
MIN	90	72	.556	$55,605,000	1
OAK	96	66	.562	$50,360,833	4
FL	91	71	.562	$48,368,298	5

2004

Club	W	L	Pct.	Opening Day Payroll	Payroll Ranking by "Division"
NYA	101	61	.623	$184,193,950	1
BOS	98	64	.605	$127,298,500	2
ANA	92	70	.568	$100,534,667	1
LA	93	69	.574	$92,902,001	1
ATL	96	66	.593	$90,182,500	2
STL	105	57	.648	$83,228,333	2
HOU	92	70	.568	$75,397,000	3
MIN	92	70	.568	$53,585,000	2

2005

Club	W	L	Pct.	Opening Day Payroll	Payroll Ranking by "Division"
NYA	95	67	.586	$208,306,817	1
BOS	95	67	.586	$123,505,125	2
LAA	95	67	.586	$97,725,322	1
STL	100	62	.617	$92,106,833	1
ATL	90	72	.556	$86,457,302	3
HOU	89	73	.549	$76,779,000	3
CHA	99	63	.611	$75,178,000	1
SD	82	80	.506	$63,290,833	3

* "Division" includes East, Central and West Divisions, along with "Wild Card"

allows for the loss of these obligations to be covered by some other source.

This will surely attract attention in the next CBA and may require some form of a cap on write-offs. Some adjustment to allow revenue sharing to remain static or increase will be demanded by the takers. This could create fractures in the ownership ranks as those considering new stadium construction look to write off these revenue-sharing dollars. Those clubs clamoring for the ability to compete with the high-revenue teams via these revenue-sharing dollars will look to keep the flow coming.

Luxury Tax

The luxury tax was added in the last CBA to keep payrolls down to a level at which small- and mid-market clubs could compete with large-market teams—specifically George Steinbrenner and the New York Yankees. For the luxury tax, payrolls are based on the average annual values of contracts for all players on the 40-man roster and include benefits. The rate at which the team is taxed depends on the number of times the club exceeds the threshold.

The luxury tax structure in the current CBA is as follows:

Threshold (Millions of dollars)

2003	2004	2005	2006
117.0	120.5	128.0	136.5

Tax Rate by Times Exceeding Threshold (Percent)

	1st	2nd	3rd	4th
2003	17.5			
2004	22.5	30.0		
2005	22.5	30.0	40.0	
2006	0	40.0	40.0	40.0

The current agreement on the luxury tax expires on the last day of the 2006 season. If the players and management go forward under the status quo, there is no luxury tax for 2007. The expiration date was a compromise by the union in the last round of collective bargaining. Management had pushed for the luxury tax for every year in the agreement. The union did not want the tax in 2007 and, for negotiating purposes, pushed for no tax in 2006. The compromise worked to the MLBPA's benefit. The luxury tax, of which

the MLBPA wanted no part, was a key sticking point in the last round of collective bargaining. Increased revenue sharing and the luxury tax represented to the players union a half step towards a soft cap on player salaries. Look for the MLBPA to, once again, push to drop the luxury tax altogether in the coming collective bargaining.

In 2003 the Yankees were the only club that went above the threshold of $117 million in player payroll. They paid $11.82 million, 17.5% of their $184.5 million-payroll.

In 2004, the Yankees, Red Sox and Angels broke through the $120.5 million-threshold. The Yankees paid a luxury tax of $25,026,352 on a $203.9 million-payroll at a higher 30% rate because they surpassed the threshold for a second time. The Red Sox paid $3,155,234 on a payroll of $134.5 million and the Angels paid $927,059 on a payroll of $124.6 million. The first-time offenders Red Sox and Angels paid at the 22.5% rate.

As for 2005, the Yankees, once again, topped the list. In 2005, $128 million marked the threshold. The Yankees, three-time losers, paid a 40% tax—$30,637,531—on an Opening Day payroll of $204.6 million. The Red Sox, the only other club to surpass the threshold, paid $969,177 on an Opening Day payroll of $131.2 million—a 30% tax rate for their second offense.

What do these numbers tell us? The luxury tax hits only a small fraction of the clubs. Those clubs that have no fear of nearing the tax threshold will push for a continuation of the tax. The Royals, Pirates and Devil Rays of the world will point to the luxury tax as a good method of stopping runaway spending by large market franchises, fostering some level of parity in the MLB. Steinbrenner will, of course, see things differently.

As payrolls look to increase for some clubs that have been at the bottom of the list, a continued internal battle over the luxury tax will surely occur. Look for contention on the issue in 2006 with some adjustments made. But the luxury tax will likely remain in some form in the next CBA.

Grabbing a Part of the MLBAM

One thing that has certainly changed since the 2002 agreement is the value of Major League Baseball Advanced Media, which is responsible for MLB.com and other electronic media used for broadcast purposes. The division also controls matters such as fantasy baseball licenses.

Advanced media revenue is split evenly among the 30 clubs. MLB.com was funded by the clubs in an agreement that had them each investing $1 million a year over four years. The cost was targeted at $120 million. To the joy of the owners and MLB, the website started generating excess revenue in only the second year of its existence, allowing them to invest only $70-$75 million before beginning to see a return on their investment.

MLB had considered an initial public offering of the Internet site in late September or early October. Wall Street analysts targeted the value of the IPO anywhere between $2 and $3 billion—a cool $100 million to each of the owners. MLB put the kibosh on the deal for a couple of reasons. One, it would require that MLB open its books; no company can go public without full disclosure. Second, it would give the MLBPA plenty of ammunition when the CBA comes due in December 2006. As Advanced Media continues to grow and possibly gobble up other businesses, as it did in its purchase of Tickets.com, it will be hard for the MLBPA to resist grabbing a part of this cash cow.

Look for the players association to try for a piece of this pie in 2006. Given the amount on the table, the owners won't readily agree to sharing with their players.

The Hawks Look at the NHL and Push for a Salary Cap

And then there was one....

In 2005, we saw an entire season of the NHL erased due to labor strife. When the NHL returned for the 2005-2006 season, it played to packed houses and owners were armed with a salary cap. That leaves MLB as the last of the Big-Four sports to not have a salary cap. Some owners, such as Jerry Reinsdorf of the Chicago White Sox, are hawks on labor issues. Reinsdorf is a key member of several committees in MLB, including the Executive Council—the main sounding board for the commissioner. Some of these hawkish owners may ally to push for a salary cap in the next CBA. Look for pushback on this idea by other owners. Avoiding a work stoppage in 2002 is paying substantial dividends. Cooler heads brought riches to everyone.

Worldwide Amateur Draft

In 2002, the sides agreed that there was insufficient time to discuss and negotiate a worldwide draft, but they outlined in Attachment 24 that a committee comprised of members of the MLBPA and the commissioner's office would convene to discuss implementation of the draft. In early May 2003, the committee had one and only one meeting on the topic. Not surprisingly, nothing was resolved. If it wasn't critical to the last CBA,

why would the parties move on the subject outside the collective bargaining pressure? So the concept of a worldwide amateur draft has been shelved but will come up in the 2006 CBA. Don't look for the MLBPA to be excited about this idea. After all, the more players that are signed in free agency, the more money is made by their constituency.

Drug Testing and Performance-Enhancing Drugs Policy

On March 17, 2005, representatives from MLB and the players association, as well as current and former MLB players, appeared on Capitol Hill at the request of the House of Representatives Committee on Government Reform to testify about baseball's position on testing for steroids. But it really was a chance for members of the committee to verbally beat up the likes of Bud Selig and Don Fehr over the lack of penalties for those in violation of what the committee members saw as a terribly weak drug policy. It was an embarrassing moment for Selig, who had been able to get the MLBPA to see the writing on the wall in late January 2005 and do the unthinkable: negotiate and open up the collective bargaining agreement before the contractual expiration in December 2006. MLB and the MLBPA announced new stricter penalties for those in violation of the joint drug and treatment program—a 10-day suspension for those testing positive for steroids for the first time, a public announcement, and stricter penalties for those in violation more than once. Selig went to D.C. feeling optimistic about matters, but he left with his tail between his legs.

Just a little over a month later, on April 25, Selig sent a letter to Fehr outlining proposed changes to the penalties for those in violation of the Drug Prevention and Treatment Program. As Selig wrote, "Discipline levels should be increased within the framework of a three strikes and you are out approach. First offenders should be suspended for 50 games. Second offenders should be suspended for 100 games. Third offenders should be banned permanently. I recognize the need for progressive discipline, but a third-time offender has no place in the game. Steroid users cheat the game. After three offenses, they have no place in it."

On May 1, Fehr responded: "To date both clubs and players have approached this subject in good faith and with no ill intentions. Our efforts have been productive. As you have acknowledged, the [Joint Drug Agreement] is, in fact, working well, as indicated by the very low number of positives from 2004, before the new provisions were agreed to for this year. The players support the current program and are confident that it will deter the unlawful use of steroids, while at the same time being both a fair and appropriate response to the matters at issue, and are understandably reluctant to renegotiate the existing agreements."

This perceived stonewalling by Fehr sent Congress into further posturing; no fewer than three proposed bills were in works to impose stringent federal penalties on all professional sports. In the meantime, Selig waited for Fehr and the Union to respond to proposed changes... and waited...and waited. Finally, five months later and two days before Selig and Fehr were again being called upon to testify before another committee on Capitol Hill, Fehr responded via letter saying:

"Our principal remaining disagreement is the penalty to be imposed for an initial positive test for steroids. You have publicly proposed a 50-game penalty, a position from which you have not wavered. Indeed, your current proposal provides for a presumptive 50-game penalty, but in appropriate circumstances permits you to impose 60 games and the player to argue before the arbitration panel for 40 games. We have proposed a presumptive penalty of 20 games, twice the current penalty, with the possibility that you may impose a suspension of up to 30 games if the facts and circumstances warrant, and the player may argue to an arbitrator that the facts justify a lower penalty, but not below 10 games."

How did Congress react? Senator John McCain (R-Arizona) laid into Fehr, a long-time acquaintance: "Don't you get it? We're at the end of the line. How many more Rafael Palmeiros is there going to be?" McCain said. Fehr, when pressed, seemed to buckle. "Can I give you a precise date? No," Fehr said. "Do I expect to know within the reasonably near future whether that will be done? Yes. Would I expect it to be by the end of the World Series? I would certainly hope so."

So, the 800-pound gorilla in the room in the next round of collective bargaining will surely center around the Joint Drug Agreement. With Selig on the offensive for nearly all of 2005 regarding tougher penalties and the MLBPA on the ropes since the last CBA in 2002, Selig can't lose on this topic. If the MLBPA agrees, Selig plays the part of the proactive leader of the sport. If the MLBPA balks at the agreement, Congress could force policy on baseball. At that point, Selig can wash his hands of the matter.

So it is very possible the union could accept the penalties outside of the collective bargaining window. Regardless, there surely will be further tweaks to the system. Possible changes could be clarification on whether a prior positive test with proven subsequent non-use but with lingering substance can trigger further penalties. This is the Mike Morse issue. The Seattle Mariners shortstop used steroids in 2003 which produced positive tests—and penalties—in three separate testings. Look for the MLBPA to push for protection of players who fall into this category.

In addition, there could be a faster arbitration process for those players who have been notified of testing positive and elected to file a grievance. One thing seems a near certainty: the MLBPA will look at the bending that they have done on the testing policy and seek to use it as leverage to get other concessions. But if you've already bent, what kind of leverage do you have?

Will there be a work stoppage?

So will there be a strike or a lockout? Will the owners, flush with knowledge that for the first time since the players association gained its power they have a slight edge, push for more than the players association is willing to accept? Will the MLBPA dig in its heels when the time arrives by saying that already it negotiated once—or possibly twice—outside of the collective bargaining window? Or will cooler heads on both sides of the table prevail and realize that everyone—players and owners—has a far better chance of becoming wealthy if baseball avoids a work stoppage? Look for the latter, happily. When the game is left alone to its own devices and work stoppages do not become commonplace, the game is almost always better for it.

The World Baseball Classic
by Craig Burley and Thomas Ayers

An event that has been years, if not decades, in the making, the first World Baseball Classic will take place this March in Japan, Puerto Rico and the United States. Semi-finals and the final will be played at San Diego's PETCO Park, with the final on March 20. The Classic will feature the best players of 16 countries fighting through two layers of four-team round-robin pools for the right to come to San Diego for a single-game elimination in the semis and the finals.

The event is sanctioned by IBAF (the International Baseball Federation), and each team will be chosen by its national sanctioning body. MLB will apparently be doing its utmost to ensure that all MLB players who want to will have the opportunity to play.

Two teams from each of the first-round pools will make the second round; two teams from each of those pools will make the semifinals. The first-round pools are:

Pool A (Japan) China, Chinese Taipei, Japan and South Korea

Pool B (Arizona) Canada, Mexico, United States and South Africa

Pool C (Puerto Rico) Cuba, the Netherlands, Panama and Puerto Rico

Pool D (Florida) Australia, Dominican Republic, Italy and Venezuela

It is difficult to write a preview of an event that at press time is still several months in the future. For example, we have just been blindsided by the retirement of Larry Walker, who will be unavailable for Canada at the Classic. Also, not all arrangements are set in stone; Cuba, for example, still hasn't accepted its invitation to play. We've done our best, however, to speculate what we may see this coming March. Enjoy.

Pool A

Japan

Rotation:
SP: Daisuke Matsuzaka (Seibu Lions)
SP: Toshiya Sugiuchi (Softbank Hawks)
SP: Fumiya Nishiguchi (Seibu Lions)
SP: Koji Uehara (Yomiuri Giants)
Bullpen:
RP: Hitoki Iwase (Chunichi Dragons)

RP: Akinori Otsuka (San Diego)
RP: Hirotoshii Ishii (Yakult Swallows)
RP: Kiyoshi Toyoda (Seibu Lions)
RP: Toyohiko Yoshida (Kinetsu Buffaloes)
RP: Ryoto Igarashii (Yakult Swallows)
RP: Kyuji Fujikawa (Hanshin Tigers)
RP: Shingo Takatsu (New York Mets)
RP: Shinya Okamoto (Chunichi Dragons)
Lineup:
C: Kenji Johjima (Softbank Hawks)
1B: Nobuhiko Matsunaka (Softbank Hawks)
2B: Tadahito Iguchi (Chicago White Sox)
SS: Kaz Matsui (New York Mets)
3B: Michihiro Ogasawara (Nippon Ham Fighters)
LF: Hideki Matsui (New York Yankees)
CF: Norichika Aoki (Yakult Swallows)
RF: Ichiro Suzuki (Seattle)
DH: Tomoaki Kanemoto (Hanshin Tigers)
Bench:
C: Atsuya Furuta (Yakult Swallows)
C: Shinnosuke Abe (Yomiuri Giants)
Backup IF: Akinora Iwamura (Yakult Swallows)
Backup IF: Norihiro Nakamura (Los Angeles)
Backup OF: Kosuke Fukudome (Chunichi Dragons)
Backup OF: Tomonori Maeda (Hiroshima Toyo Carp)
Utility: Toshiaki Imae (Chiba Lotte Marines)
Utility: Kazuhiro Wada (Seibu Lions)

For at least 40 years, Japanese fans have been eagerly awaiting a baseball matchup where the very best American professionals had the opportunity to face off against Japan's best professionals. This hasn't happened yet; although dozens of teams have toured Japan, both post-season All-Star groups and MLB club teams, never have the best played for bragging rights. So yes, the Classic is a very big deal for Japanese baseball fans—even if they seem a little apprehensive about it.

The Classic is not nearly as popular a choice for Japanese fans as a postseason face-off between MLB and NPB champions would be. The format of the Classic and the March timing are not particularly popular with players, fans or owners. In the end, however, the almighty dollar has spoken, and after years of holdups, mostly coming from Japan in one form or another, the tournament is on.

What we will see from Japan on the field is far more interesting, though, than machinations off of it. How will Japan stack up against the other teams? One thing is for certain: as the host for the first round in Pool A, Japan is a clear favorite to go 3-0 and cruise into the second round. There, the team has the distinct advantage of the weaker second-round group; with Korea and either Canada or Mexico in the group along with the USA, it should be easy for Japan to move along to the semifinals.

For the very first time at the Classic, Japanese MLB players and NPB players will play together on the same team. It will be interesting to see how many MLB players make the cut for the team; certainly Ichiro, Hideki Matsui and Tadahito Iguchi would seem like obvious choices, as would Akinori Otsuka in the pen. All-World catcher Kenji Johjima will also be a major leaguer by the time the Classic starts. However, we think that the Japanese federation may lean more towards the NPB players, and there are some good ones who may show up in the U.S. for the second round.

Who are the NPB players to watch? Pitcher Daisuke Matsuzaka of the Seibu Lions, only 25 years old, is one of the finest pitchers in the world and has decided to put off coming to MLB for another year at least. Equally young and successful is Toshiya Sugiuchi of the SoftBank Hawks, a left-hander (Matsuzaka's a righty) who is just 24 but has just won NPB's equivalent to the Cy Young, the Eiji Sawamura Award. Both pitchers were key pitchers on Japan's entry at the 2000 Sydney Olympics.

On the offensive side of the ball, first baseman Nobuhiko Matsunaka of the Hawks won the Triple Crown in 2004 and nearly repeated it in 2005. He is a well-built left-handed power hitter. Just the opposite is center fielder Norichika Aoki of the Yakult Swallows, a Juan Pierre clone who brings excitement to the basepaths and is the only player other than Ichiro to have a 200-hit season in NPB; this in nearly seven decades of play. Fifty-one of Aoki's 202 hits last season were of the infield variety; he gets down the line as well as anyone anywhere.

The Japanese team likely doesn't have the offensive firepower to win the tournament, but a park like PETCO with its wide-open spaces and low-scoring games may set up well for them.

South Korea

Korea will field an extremely strong team who should make it to the second round. In fact, you could argue that we should cover them in more detail. Silver medallists at the World Cup in the Netherlands, Korea didn't play that well in the tournament but won games when it counted. Add major leaguers like Hee Seop Choi and Shin-Soo Choo and half of a pretty good pitching staff in Sun-Woo Kim, Byung-Hyun Kim, Jung Bong, Dae-Sung Koo, Chan Ho Park and Jae Wong Seo, the team should beat out Chinese Taipei for a trip to the second round.

China

A baseball neophyte as countries go, both the IBAF and MLB are encouraging the sport's growth in China, which should in theory be quite receptive to the game. China's progress on the playing side has been not at all bad, and although its players are far from major league caliber, they went 3-5 in the Netherlands and played most of the good teams very tough, losing 12-8 to Cuba and 3-1 to South Korea. They will struggle not to be blown away by their competition in Pool A.

Chinese Taipei

Taiwan sent a very young team to the Netherlands for the last World Cup, and we would expect them to do the same at the Classic. This team did not play well in Holland, and despite being able to add some pitching depth (led by the Yankees' Chien-Min Wang) and Dodger farmhand Chin-Feng Chen in the outfield, they should be outclassed by Korea and Japan. Look for them to beat up on their mainland rivals though.

Pool B

Mexico

We meant to do a proper breakdown of Mexico. We really did. This is a very good team, one that will play its heart out against the U.S., give Canada all it can handle, and feast on the entrails of South Africa in Pool B action. Unfortunately, we never got around to breaking the team down in the detail it deserves.

There are quite a few talented Mexican major leaguers around the diamond. Tampa second baseman Jorge Cantu, who is of Mexican descent although he was born in Texas, is probably the best current Mexican position player. Rangers prospect Adrian Gonzalez would like to join him on the right side of the infield, with Alfredo Amezaga of the Angels, or possibly Juan Castro of the Twins, at shortstop and Vinny Castilla at third. Rod

Barajas hopes to play for Mexico and would be the starting catcher, with several able backstops, including Geronimo Gil, behind him. Erubiel Durazo is a natural for the DH role.

With Ismael Valdez and Esteban Loaiza to hold down starting spots, Mexico's chances of making the second round may depend upon Pirates starter Oliver Perez, who will likely start against Canada to exploit their weakness against lefthanders. If Perez can capture his 2004 form, Mexico may well make the second round.

South Africa

The South Africans face an impossible task in Pool B, facing three teams full of big-league talent. Outscored 76-15 in losing all eight games at the last World Cup in Holland, expect them to be the beneficiaries of whatever mercy rule the tournament adopts to stop slaughters. It says a lot when the nation's best player is quite possibly Seattle's Rookie League reliever Tyrone Lamont—it would have made much more sense to invite Nicaragua, Brazil, Colombia or even another European team.

United States

Rotation:
SP: Roger Clemens (Houston)
SP: Randy Johnson (New York Yankees)
SP: Dontrelle Willis (Florida)
SP: Andy Pettitte (Houston)
Bullpen:
RP: Brad Lidge (Houston)
RP: Joe Nathan (Minnesota)
RP: Billy Wagner (Philadelphia)
RP: Trevor Hoffman (San Diego)
RP: BJ Ryan (Baltimore)
RP: Huston Street (Oakland)
RP: Chad Cordero (Washington)
RP: John Smoltz (Atlanta)
RP: Chris Carpenter (St. Louis)
Lineup:
C: Jason Varitek (Boston)
1B: Todd Helton (Colorado)
2B: Jeff Kent (Los Angeles)
SS: Derek Jeter (New York Yankees—yes, it must be Jeter, no matter what!)
3B: Alex Rodriguez (New York Yankees)
LF: Adam Dunn (Cincinnati)
CF: Jim Edmonds (St. Louis)
RF: Lance Berkman (Houston)

DH: Jason Giambi (New York Yankees)
Bench:
C: Joe Mauer (Minnesota)
C: Michael Barrett (Chicago Cubs)
Backup IF: Chase Utley (Philadelphia)
Backup IF: Michael Young (Texas)
Backup OF: Gary Sheffield (New York Yankees)
Backup OF: Carl Crawford (Tampa Bay)
Utility: Travis Hafner (Cleveland)
Utility: Chipper Jones (Atlanta)

It's nearly impossible to predict Team USA's roster with any true degree of accuracy because there are so many talented players that could make the team. No other country has such an embarrassment of riches. We tried to limit it to the best of the best, and there are still plenty of legitimate candidates at every position. We went with our predictions for the roster, given that there will be pressure to select experienced veterans, but a lot of this will depend on the mindset of the manager and the other execs who select the team. How will they decide with regards to career vs. 2005 accomplishments? Will they prefer veterans or will they prefer youths?

If he's willing, the ageless and brilliant Roger Clemens will almost certainly anchor the rotation, and despite the Big Unit's mediocre year in New York, it will be difficult not to select his as well. The back of the rotation could be lefty-heavy with the exciting Dontrelle Willis and the veteran presence of Andy Pettitte, or could employ former teammates Roy Halladay and Chris Carpenter.

The bullpen for the United States will be the best in the competition. Brad Lidge will likely pitch the ninth and could be set up by Joe Nathan from the right and Billy Wagner from the left. The rest of the bullpen is nothing to sneeze at and consists of Trevor Hoffman, Huston Street, Chad Cordero, John Smoltz and southpaw BJ Ryan. Carpenter could make the team as the long man and, if necessary, spot starter. The entire bullpen is composed of ace relievers; it would hardly make a difference if the bullpen were managed by picking names out of a hat.

The lineup is no easier to sort out, as the large number of possible candidates can attest to. At each position, we went with the person who established a reputation over the last few years, but one can make legitimate arguments for several other candidates at every position. We selected a rather slow team with big bats but unsure gloves; any position could be improved by sliding in a better glove. An infield of Chavez, Crosby, Roberts and Teixeira might not hit as much as A-Rod/Jeter/Kent/Helton, but they would make up a little of that with the leather.

Based on his September Barry Bonds will have a spot on the team if his health allows it, but the odds of that seem remote enough that we didn't put him on the projected roster. The real wild card is Manny Ramirez, who is now a U.S. citizen but will likely end up playing for the Dominican Republic. Without Bonds or Ramirez around Adam Dunn should become America's left fielder, as it's hard to argue with his power. This will force Lance Berkman to slide over to right, while Jim Edmonds patrols center.

America may go with a bit more youth on the bench, and we expect to see Joe Mauer back up Jason Varitek in anticipation of the fact he will become the team's catcher before very long. Michael Young is familiar with both middle infield positions and swings a mean bat, while Chase Utley's breakout season will likely land him a roster spot ahead of Marcus Giles or Brian Roberts. Chipper Jones gives the U.S. a switch hitter off the bench, as well as someone who can back up third base and is familiar with the outfield. Travis Hafner's MVP-like numbers got lost in the Ortiz vs. A-Rod debate, but he's had two outstanding years in a row. Gary Sheffield gives the U.S. a right-handed bat to complement Hafner's left-handed approach, while Carl Crawford provides speed and defense, something the team badly needs. The lineup is as good as the pitching staff, and America has the luxury of constructing the bench according to need without losing any ability.

It's hard not to make the U.S. the favorites in this competition because of the depth and the lineup of sluggers. In a one-day competition, though, anything can happen. Like any team, the U.S. will need to get pitching to win.

Canada

Rotation:

SP: Rich Harden (Oakland)

SP: Erik Bedard (Baltimore)

SP: Jeff Francis (Colorado)

SP: Vince Perkins (Toronto/AA)

Bullpen:

RP: Eric Gagne (Los Angeles)

RP: Ryan Dempster (Chicago Cubs)

RP: Rheal Cormier (Philadelphia)

RP: Chris Reitsma (Atlanta)

RP: Jesse Crain (Minnesota)

RP: Paul Quantrill (Florida)

RP: Eric Cyr (Anaheim/AAA)

RP: Mike Meyers (Milwaukee/AAA)

RP: Adam Loewen (Baltimore/A)

Lineup:

C: Pete LaForest (Tampa Bay)

1B: Justin Morneau (Minnesota)

2B: Peter Orr (Atlanta)

SS: Chris Woodward (New York Mets)

3B: Corey Koskie (Toronto)

LF: Jason Bay (Pittsburgh)

CF: Adam Stern (Boston)

RF: Aaron Guiel (Kansas City)

DH: Matt Stairs (Kansas City)

Bench:

C: Russell Martin (Los Angeles/AA)

C: Cody McKay (St. Louis/AAA)

Backup IF: Danny Klassen (Houston/AAA)

Backup IF: Mark Teahen (Kansas City)

Backup OF: Ryan Radmanovich (Atlantic League)

Backup OF: Sebastien Boucher (Seattle/A)

Utility: Scott Thorman (Atlanta/AAA)

Utility: Joey Votto (Cincinnati/A)

The Canadian team has a solid pitching staff at the front, as Rich Harden is a legitimate ace. However, the rotation definitely suffers at the back end, as Jeff Francis and Vince Perkins will be overmatched by other contending teams' #3 and #4 starters.

A healthy Eric Gagne will be one of the best closers in the competition and is as good a bet as any in the competition to keep a small lead safe. Ryan Dempster is a good arm to have in the bullpen due to his ability to go multiple innings at a time in back-to-back appearances, and he will serve as Gagne's setup man. Minnesota's Jesse Crain was born in Toronto, but he has already played for the United States in international competition. Baseball USA has given him permission to play for Canada, and he will certainly strengthen Canada's right-handed short relief. However, the team is weak at long relief and left-handed short relief, as Rheal Cormier or Eric Cyr will be overmatched by the opposition's strong left-handed batters.

Like the pitching staff, the lineup has a few bright spots and is very mediocre thereafter. The star is Jason Bay, a legitimate MVP candidate. Larry Walker will be offered the cleanup spot in the lineup and the starting job in right field, but we don't think his health will allow him to play. After corrective eye surgery Aaron Guiel had a very solid year at Triple-A Omaha and hit well during a short stint with Kansas City. He'll take Walker's place and will be the number one outfield backup if Walker agrees to play. Despite his disappointing year, Justin Morneau will end up in the middle of Canada's lineup and needs to have a great tournament if Canada wants to seriously contend.

Canada's brightest future is at the position of catcher. Pete LaForest has power—he slugged .578 at Triple-A Durham—but his defensive skills are lacking. Russ Martin is one of the best catching prospects in baseball; he made the Futures Game as well as the Southern League All-Star Team after posting a .430 OBP in Double-A, and he should make the team to back up LaForest along with Triple-A veteran Cody McKay.

Once you get past Bay and Morneau the holes in the Canadian lineup are exposed. The middle infield is particularly weak; Pete Orr is a solid backup for the Braves, but a backup nevertheless. Chris Woodward, who met and married a woman from Toronto during his time with the Blue Jays, has applied for Canadian citizenship and hopes to play for Canada during the tournament. Assuming his request is granted in time, he will start at short for Canada; if not it will be Danny Klassen, a career minor leaguer coming off a good year at Triple-A Round Rock.

If Woodward's request is denied, he will be replaced by a player from the independent leagues or low minors, likely former first-round pick Kevin Nicholson. Joey Votto and Scott Thorman supply power off the bench and will inevitably pinch-hit for the middle infielders. Speedster Sebastien Boucher should stand out from the other outfield prospects, as with the tournament's deep bench Canada can pick someone who excels at something, which is in short supply on the rest of the roster.

One thing that likely manager Ernie Whitt will have to keep in mind when selecting the reserves is the fact that Canada's projected lineup is very lefty heavy, as only Bay and Woodward are right-handed. During the Athens Olympics, crafty Cuban lefty Adiel Palma started twice against Canada and shut the team down almost completely. After Palma left in the semifinal, Canada made an incredible comeback and almost won the game against Cuba's right-handed relievers. The message won't be lost on other teams, and Canada can expect to face a lefty almost every time out

Pool C

Panama

The best team of those we're not profiling in detail is probably Panama, who will be looking to upset Cuba in Pool C and might well do it with a team bolstered by several top professionals. Julio Zuleta and Fernando Seguignol are both hulking sluggers who ply their trade in Japan's Central League and are among that circuit's top

hitters. Carlos Lee mans left field and cleans up for the Milwaukee Brewers, and Mariano Rivera is well-known to the entire world as the Yankee closer destined for the Hall of Fame. Add in major league vets like Bruce Chen, Jose Macias, Olmedo Saenz and Einar Diaz, and this team has both arms and the lumber to do damage. They should push Cuba in their group game. Even without the major leaguers, Panama won the bronze medal at the World Cup, so there is plenty of depth in the team.

Netherlands

The Dutch are the makeweights in Pool C, but it's dangerous to overlook them. They went 7-1 in group play at the World Cup that they hosted last September and ended up fourth, and that was without Sidney Ponson (who may not play owing to personal problems, but will likely be looking to redeem himself) and All-World center fielder/slugger Andruw Jones. Look for Jones to cause Pool C pitchers some nervous moments but for the Dutch to go winless thanks to a weak pitching staff.

Puerto Rico
Rotation:
SP: Javier Vazquez (Arizona)
SP: Joel Pineiro (Seattle)
SP: J.C. Romero (Minnesota)
SP: Josue Matos (Philadelphia/AA);
Bullpen:
RP: Roberto Hernandez (New York Mets)
RP: Kiko Calero (Oakland)
RP: Juan Padilla (New York Mets)
RP: Fernando Cabrera (Cleveland)
RP: Javier Lopez (Arizona)
RP: Pedro Feliciano (Fukoka Hawks/Japan)
RP: Jose Santiago (New York Mets/AAA)
RP: Dicky Gonzalez (Yakult Swallows/Japan)
RP: Omar Olivares (Indios de Mayaguez/2005 Caribbean Series)
Lineup:
C: Javy Lopez (Baltimore)
1B: Carlos Delgado (Florida)
2B: Jose Vidro (Washington)
SS: Felipe Lopez (Cincinnati)
3B: Mike Lowell (Florida)
LF: Luis Matos (Baltimore)
CF: Carlos Beltran (New York Mets)
RF: Alex Rios (Toronto)
DH: Jorge Posada (New York Yankees)

Bench:

C: Ivan Rodriguez (Detroit)

C: Bengie Molina (Anaheim)

Backup IF: Alex Cintron (Arizona)

Backup IF: Jose Valentin (Los Angeles)

Backup OF: Ricky Ledee (Los Angeles)

Backup OF: Bernie Williams (New York Yankees)

Utility: Alex Cora (Boston)

Utility: Jose Cruz (Los Angeles)

The Puerto Rican offense is led by a core of talented hitters, notably Carlos Delgado and Carlos Beltran. Beltran, his struggles in 2005 notwithstanding, is a five-tool player who will likely bat third, ahead of Delgado. Delgado had another All-Star season this year and will be as feared as any hitter in the competition. Delgado and Beltran aren't the offense's only contributors, as two catchers, Javy Lopez and Jorge Posada, will also provide a spark in the lineup. Puerto Rico has a surplus of catchers and one will likely start at designated hitter, as they are better hitters than any of the other reserves. Aside from Lopez and Posada, Ivan Rodriguez and Bengie Molina should both make the team as backup catchers.

Felipe Lopez is finally harnessing the potential that made him a first-round pick in 1998, and if Jose Vidro is healthy, the pair should form one of the best double-play combinations in the tournament. The back of the lineup suffers with an aging Mike Lowell, Luis Matos and Alex Rios, although the latter two combine with Beltran to form one of the best defensive outfields in the competition. Aside from catcher, the bench isn't particularly strong, as Ricky Ledee and Bernie Williams do not compare to the bats that teams such as the United States and the Dominican Republic can call on in tough situations. There is also a noticeable drop-off from Vidro and Lopez to the reserve infielders, and if either of the two can't play, Alex Cintron or Alex Cora will likely be forced into starting duty.

The Puerto Rican team probably has the competition's biggest discrepancy between the skill of the offense and the quality of the pitching staff. It is a powerful offense, even if it's not the most dangerous in the tournament. The pitching staff, however, is very weak, and that's clear by looking at the rotation. Beyond Javier Vazquez and Joel Pineiro there aren't any other MLB-caliber pitchers in the scenario. It's very possible that Puerto Rico will try to stretch out J.C. Romero and Kiko Calero into starters, but neither is a particularly good candidate as they both averaged under an inning per appearance last year. The best bet from the rest of the staff may be Josue Matos, who pitched quite well at Double-A Reading in 2005 after being released from the Toronto organization.

The bullpen will probably be led by veteran Roberto Hernandez. If Romero and Calero are in the rotation, the setup duties will likely fall to Fernando Cabrera, Cleveland's good young reliever, and Juan Padilla, who quietly had a good half-season in the Mets' bullpen, albeit with a suspect K/BB ratio. Javier Lopez will handle the left-handed specialist duties, although he'll fall behind Romero on the depth chart if the latter is not in the rotation. Quadruple-A pitchers Jose Santiago, Dicky Gonzalez and Pedro Feliciano should also make the team; if there's one to watch it's probably Feliciano. The bullpen might also see the return of Omar Olivares, who pitched in the 2005 Caribbean World Series for Puerto Rico.

Puerto Rico's offense boasts some exciting names and perhaps the tournament's richest collection of catchers. But the pitching staff will be severely tested by most of the lineups in the event, and this will likely prevent Puerto Rico from mounting any serious challenge for the championship.

Cuba

Rotation:

SP: Yulieski Gonzalez

SP: Dany Betancourt

SP: Adiel Palma

SP: Frank Montieht

Bullpen:

RP: Pedro Luis Lazo

RP: Yunesky Maya

RP: Norberto Gonzalez

RP: Ormari Romero

RP: Yadier Pedroso

Lineup:

C: Ariel Pestano

1B: Eriel Sanchez

2B: Rudy Reyes

SS: Eduardo Paret

3B: Yulieski Gourriel

LF: Frederich Cepeda

CF: Carlos Tabares

RF: Osmani Urruita

DH: Michel Enriquez

Nine consecutive titles in the World Cup. Twenty-four World Cup titles in all, in 27 tries. Three Olympic gold medals. Undefeated against Team USA at the World Cup since 1970. Nine straight Pan American Games wins. The Cubans are the undisputed kings of international baseball, regularly running off long winning streaks in international play and routinely dominating its closest opponents.

The single most disappointing aspect of this tournament is not that it is too short, but that one of the world's most fanatical baseball nations will deprive itself of some of its best players. There is no way to satisfactorily resolve the problem that the Classic faces with Cuba; it would be unjust not to invite a team that clearly can play with the best teams in the world. At the same time, that team will not feature many of the country's best players. Because of their defections, players like Orlando and Livan Hernandez, Yuniesky Betancourt and Jose Contreras, are *persona non grata* in Cuban baseball. So Cuba will send a weakened but still strong team to Puerto Rico for the first round.

There they will face a tough test in the hosts and another tough test in Panama. How good is the Cuban team? Pitching-wise, they still produce some of the world's top talent, and Dany Betancourt, Adiel Palma, Pedro Luis Lazo and Yulieski Gonzalez carry on the tradition. Betancourt and Lazo's four-hit shutout in the gold medal game against Korea at the 2005 World Cup in the Netherlands was an example of the kind of work Cuba can do in tough games. Hitting-wise, their excellence is less certain. Cuban-groomed hitting talent has not been successful in professional baseball, and Cuba's traditional reliance on small ball betrays a lack of confidence in the lumber.

But in the last World Cup, the Cubans turned on their bats. Shortstop Eduardo Paret, probably the world's best amateur player, hit .632 in six games with five extra-base hits and eight stolen bases before getting hurt. The awesome young 21-year-old third baseman Yulieski Gourriel hit eight homers in just 11 games and will soon surpass Paret as the best player outside MLB or NPB. Cuba hit 18 home runs in 11 games at the World Cup; if they can maintain that power ability in the Classic, they will be tough to beat. One thing is for sure—their style sets up very well for PETCO Park, which hosts the semifinals and finals.

But all this talent will hardly be intimidating to the major league veterans they will be up against in the Classic. They face players as good as the Cubans' best on a daily basis; the Cuban team never plays teams as talented as theirs. And the Cubans can be beaten; at the 2004 Olympics Lazo almost blew a save against Canada when a two-out drive in the bottom of the ninth off the bat of minor leaguer Kevin Nicholson ended up two feet short of the wall and a three-run homer. In the same tournament, Cuba lost to Japan in the preliminary round and was lucky not to have to face Japan again in the final.

Pool D

Italy

Anyone who read Dave Bidini's magnificent book *Baseballissimo* will have a great deal of sympathy for Italy's best as they venture forth into three really tough games. Sympathy they will need, as even the Panamanians will vaporize a team that finished last at the Sydney Olympics.

Australia

The Australians aren't as talented as Venezuela or the Dominican Republic, and their players will certainly be going back to their big-league camps early. That said, a lot of Australian players will be at big-league camps this spring and their young talent is looking very good. Aussie prospects like Justin Huber, Chris Snelling and Travis Blackley mean that the team will be a lot tougher if this tournament ever gets played again in the future.

Venezuela

Rotation:
SP: Johan Santana (Minnesota)
SP: Freddy Garcia (Chicago White Sox)
SP: Felix Hernandez (Seattle)
SP: Carlos Zambrano (Chicago Cubs)
Bullpen:
RP: Francisco Rodriguez (Anaheim)
RP: Ugueth Urbina (Philadelphia)
RP: Rafael Betancourt (Cleveland)
RP: Juan Rincon (Minnesota)
RP: Kelvim Escobar (Anaheim)
RP: Gustavo Chacin (Toronto)
RP: Wilfredo Ledezma (Detroit)
RP: Carlos Silva (Minnesota)
RP: Yusmeiro Petit (New York Mets/AAA)
Lineup:
C: Victor Martinez (Cleveland)
1B: Alex Cabrera (Yakult Swallows/Japan)
2B: Marco Scutaro (Oakland)
SS: Carlos Guillen (Detroit)
3B: Melvin Mora (Baltimore)
LF: Magglio Ordonez (Detroit)
CF: Juan Rivera (Anaheim)
RF: Bobby Abreu (Philadelphia)
DH: Miguel Cabrera (Florida)
Bench:
C: Ramon Hernandez (San Diego)
C: Dioner Navarro (Los Angeles)

Backup IF: Jose Lopez (Seattle)
Backup IF: Cesar Izturis (Los Angeles)
Backup OF: Richard Hidalgo (Texas)
Backup OF: Franklin Gutierrez (Cleveland/AAA)
Utility: Edgardo Alfonzo (San Francisco)
Utility: Alex Escobar (Washington)

The only pitcher who can legitimately challenge Johan Santana as the best in the American League is Roy Halladay. But there soon will be a new challenger on the block, perhaps as early next spring, and it's no secret that that pitcher is Seattle's teenage phenom Felix Hernandez. Seattle will want the Venezuelan team to handle him with care, as one would with any teenage prospect, but on talent alone he'd be starter #1B on this team. Instead, he'll likely be slotted into a lower-pressure situation, such as the #3 starter behind Santana and Freddy Garcia.

With energetic righty Carlos Zambrano slotted in as the fourth starter, the Venezuelan starters are the tournament's best. The bullpen will be anchored by K-Rod, on his way to eclipsing Mariano Rivera as the AL's best reliever. There are several good right-handed short men from Rafael Betancourt to Juan Rincon. Yusmeiro Petit, the best Venezuelan pitching prospect, should find a spot on the team both to gain international experience and because it's hard to argue with his control. Because of the dearth of Venezuelan left-handed pitchers, Gustavo Chacin and Wilfredo Ledezma should make the bullpen. At some point, however, a manger has to sacrifice the platoon advantage and go with his best relievers. Venezuela's manager will probably turn to Rincon, Betancourt, Ugueth Urbina and Kelvim Escobar in key situations, regardless of the batters.

The Venezuelan lineup is also strong. The heart of the order is impressive with Miguel Cabrera, Bobby Abreu and Victor Martinez; those three batters will carry the load for the team. The big question marks are what the team can expect from Melvin Mora and the injury-prone Magglio Ordoñez. Defensively, the team is shakier, with only one above-average defender in Abreu. After Richard Hidalgo's poor injury-filled season, we expect Juan Rivera to win the center field job, and he's stretched there. Franklin Gutierrez, who will challenge for a starting spot, is another alternative in center. Nevertheless, Venezuela's defensive shortcomings won't hide their offensive prowess.

Ramon Hernandez and Dioner Navarro form one of the best backup catching tandems in the competition, and Navarro will gain valuable experience as Venezuela's third catcher. The future is quite bright behind the plate, and in a few years there could be four above-average Venezuelan catchers in the majors, and the country didn't even have to resort to a three-brother combo. Because of his youth and potential, 22-year-old Jose Lopez stands out from a plethora of candidates for the reserve middle infield positions, while it's hard to turn down Cesar Izturis's glove off the bench with the competition's expanded rosters. Edgardo Alfonzo is a shell of his former greatness, but he should make the team as the backup for the infield corners. Alex Escobar had a huge year in 2004 before spending 2005 injured, and if he is healthy, Escobar should make the team as a dangerous late-inning pinch-hitter.

As is the case with the Dominican Republic, the Venezuelan team is closely knit. Many of their players, especially Santana, have stated that they are passionately awaiting the Classic as an opportunity to show their national colors on the international stage. That immense pride, along with their killer starting pitching, makes them the toughest team to beat in the competition on any given day.

Dominican Republic

Rotation:
SP: Pedro Martinez (New York Mets)
SP: Bartolo Colon (Anaheim)
SP: Daniel Cabrera (Baltimore)
SP: Jorge Sosa (Atlanta)
Bullpen:
RP: Armando Benitez (San Francisco)
RP: Francisco Cordero (Texas)
RP: Damaso Marte (Chicago White Sox)
RP: Julian Tavarez (St. Louis)
RP: Luis Vizcaino (Chicago White Sox)
RP: Al Reyes (St. Louis)
RP: Jose Valverde (Arizona)
RP: Guillermo Mota (Florida)
RP: Ervin Santana (Anaheim)
Lineup:
C: Miguel Olivo (San Diego)
1B: Albert Pujols (St. Louis)
2B: Alfonso Soriano (Texas)
SS: Miguel Tejada (Baltimore)
3B: Aramis Ramirez (Chicago Cubs)
LF: Manny Ramirez (Boston)
CF: Wily Mo Pena (Cincinnati)
RF: Jose Guillen (Washington)
DH: David Ortiz (Boston)
Bench:
C: Alberto Castillo (Oakland)

C: Ronny Paulino (Pittsburgh/AAA)
Backup IF: Placido Polanco (Detroit)
Backup IF: Rafael Furcal (Atlanta)
Backup OF: Juan Encarnacion (Florida)
Backup OF: Willy Taveras (Houston)
Utility: Jhonny Peralta (Cleveland)
Utility: Adrian Beltre (Seattle)

Another outstanding team that will almost certainly contend for the title, the Dominican Republic's main question centers on Manny Ramirez. Manny was born on the island, but he grew up in New York City's Washington Heights neighborhood. He recently became a U.S. citizen, so it's unclear for which nation he'll play in the tournament. It seems likely that he'll want to join David Ortiz in a friendly Dominican clubhouse, particularly if he's no longer with the Red Sox next spring. While Ortiz, Albert Pujols, Miguel Tejada and Alfonso Soriano would make up for Manny's absence, it is nonetheless a noticeable downgrade to Juan Encarnacion. Another nation that may struggle on defense, the Dominican Republic has a very formidable lineup (outside of catcher) and will not struggle to score runs. Jose Guillen and Wily Mo Pena are both solid offensive players, and it's easy to forget Pena is only 23 years old.

The Dominican infield reserves are probably the strongest in the competition; there are outstanding players who will not make the team. The reserves, led by Jhonny Peralta, will likely be called upon frequently to pinch-hit for the offensively challenged catchers. Rafael Furcal and Willy Taveras both provide speed and defense off the bench, and both should be utilized frequently in late innings. The likely presence of Peralta, Furcal, Placido Polanco and Adrian Beltre will leave Robinson Cano and Jose Reyes, along with top prospects Hanley Ramirez and Andy Marte, on the outside looking in.

In 2005 Pedro Martinez proved that rumors of his demise were exaggerated, and while he'll never be the 1999-2000 Pedro again, he is still one of the best pitchers in baseball. Bartolo Colon similarly rebounded in 2005 to lead Anaheim to the AL West title and will fit in nicely behind Pedro at the top of the rotation. Daniel Cabrera held right-handed batters to an average under .200 last year, but he struggles mightily with his control, walking 4.85 per nine innings in 2005. This past year Jorge Sosa became the latest Leo Mazzone reclamation project, finishing the year with a 2.55 ERA in 44 appearances, 20 of which were starts. Despite his poor K/BB ratio this success should give him the last rotation spot, although Anaheim's Ervin Santana is also a viable contender.

The back of the bullpen consists of three hard throwers in Armando Benitez and Francisco Cordero from the right side and Damaso Marte from the left. Marte is basically the country's only reasonable lefty option, and he should perform the lefty-specialist role ahead of the setup man and closer. That leaves the rest of the spots open for right-handed middle relievers, and it's almost a guessing game as to who will fill the spots. We've assumed Guillermo Mota's past success will tempt the manager into taking him, and the present success of Jose Valverde, Al Reyes, Luis Vizcaino and the eccentric Julian Tavarez should give them the edge over other contenders. The bullpen is nothing outstanding, but it is a collection of fairly good relievers, and the offense should be more than enough to make people forget the pitching staff's shortcomings very quickly.

If you cast your mind back to the joyous, intense Dominican group at the All-Star Game's Home Run Derby, you will have a sense of what this tournament means to these players and how closely knit they are. Because of the circumstances of international baseball, the country has never before had a chance to show off the national colors on an American stage. Possibly more than any other team, the Dominican players will be burning to win and pulling as one man, and that motivation should not be underestimated.

Prediction

Predicting the outcome of a one-game event like the World Baseball Classic semifinals or finals is a mug's game. Likewise, predicting a three-game round-robin pool is pretty much impossible. So, if possible, we'd like to leave our options open.

But let us just say this. The pitching that Venezuela can bring to any one-game situation is fantastic. It may be the best starting pitching in the tournament. And despite that, Venezuela might not be the best team in that pool, because the hitting might of the Dominican Republic is so awesome.

If pressed to pick a winner, we'd take the United States, if only because the American manager can hit the bullpen in the sixth inning and bring in an awesome series of relievers. They also probably have the best hitters, though it is close.

There is no question that those three teams are the class of the field. But there are a lot of teams who can beat any of them with the right pitcher on the right day. Would you feel confident, knowing your back was against the wall, facing Rich Harden? Or the legendary Daisuke Matsuzaka? Or even Oliver Perez?

So let's make only one prediction—something will happen this spring at the World Baseball Classic that will shock and amaze everyone.

History

Night Sky: The 2005 Season in Historical Perspective

by Steve Treder

No offense intended to Chicago White Sox or Houston Astros fans. But it must be said: until the World Series, the 2005 baseball season was a rather forgettable one.

Not that there's anything wrong with that.

Great, historic, amazing things don't happen every year. Their very rarity is what makes them great, historic and amazing. Most years don't feature stunning play-off comebacks like that of the Boston Red Sox in 2004, or staggering individual performances such as that of Barry Bonds in 2001, or wire-to-wire juggernauts like the New York Yankees of 1998. Most years, indeed, are far more moderate in their offerings, their imprint on the record books soft and subtle.

The World Series match-up of the haven't-been-there-in-ages White Sox against the never-been-there-at-all Astros finally provided 2005, at the 11th hour, with a historically significant element. Until then, 2005 was proving to be just another one of those moderate seasons. In fact, if anything, 2005 was extreme in its moderation, historically notable for its lack of historic notability. This was one of the great non-great seasons.

Let's briefly review some of the non-events of 2005:

- **There were no long-shot or particular upset winners among the division or Wild Card champions.** The White Sox's regular-season performance surprised most of us, but not overwhelmingly. Everyone knew they'd be a good team, and the American League Central was widely expected to be a division in which the Sox would at least be a challenger. And among the seven other postseason qualifiers, six (the Angels, Red Sox, Yankees, Cardinals, Braves and Astros) were repeaters. The eighth playoff team, the San Diego Padres, hadn't been in the 2004 postseason, but like the White Sox they had been a good club in '04, and were expected to be contenders in '05.

- **There weren't any especially remarkable division or Wild Card races.** The one that might have been truly dramatic, the American League East battle between the perennial-rival Yankees and Red Sox, coming down to a final-weekend showdown at Fenway Park, was drained of much of its excitement by the failure of the Cleveland Indians in the final week to put up any kind of a Wild Card (or

Central Division) fight. The regular season's final Sunday match-up between the Yanks and Sawks, instead of a winner-take-all nail-biter to recall 1978 or 1949, became an it-doesn't-matter snoozer, with the Yankees already having been granted division-title status based on head-to-head results (a *ridiculous* rule!) and the Red Sox backing in to a Wild Card berth.

- **There were no particularly great team performances.** No team won more than 100 games (St. Louis went 100-62, .617), and only two teams won more than 95 (the White Sox were 99-63, .611).

- **There were no unusually bad team performances.** Only one team lost more than 95 games, and that club (the Kansas City Royals, at 56-106, .346) lost significantly fewer than the worst teams of 2004 and 2003 and no more than three teams did in 2002.

- **There were no record-setting individual performances.** No significant individual marks were even threatened. All the league-leading achievements in the major categories, for batters and pitchers alike, were at levels that have been exceeded (in most cases far exceeded) within recent seasons. Nor were any notable career milestones achieved, thanks primarily to the injury suffered by Barry Bonds.

It was, all in all, a bacchanalia of moderation, a rollicking feast of sensible portions. It might be, indeed, a symbol of the meekness, the timidity, of the 2005 season that the lone historic feat that was accomplished was a feat of non-accomplishment: The Padres won the National League West Division with the lowest winning percentage (.506) of any full-season division in history, and their division as a whole posted the most feeble performance (.459) of any full-season division in history.

So what are we to make of this triumph of mediocrity, this hog wallow in mildness? Well, being non-memorable isn't necessarily a bad thing. There's something to be said for the baseball season in which heart-stopping drama is absent. In fact, it's possible to take a particular enjoyment in such seasons, and not just in the sense that it's only through the experience of such ordinariness that we're able to recognize and appreciate the extraordinary when it occurs. Seasons such as 2005 can be valued for more than just spear-carrier functionality. Viewed from the proper perspective, a season such as 2005 can be appreciated as a particular splendor in its own right.

Intrinsic Beauty

The first way this can happen is in our real-time experience of the season itself. Obviously we all take huge enjoyment in a scintillating pennant race, and of course it makes for great drama when individual stars overtake, or simply approach, major records. But baseball offers many charms beyond those. Indeed, the glitz and flash of big games and superstar exploits may sometimes serve to blind us to more subtle, but perhaps more interesting, aspects of the sport. The game *itself*, in all its intricacy, balance, difficulty and beauty, can often be best *seen*, most acutely appreciated, when there's no historical legacy on the line.

A game watched for its own sake—valued for being nothing more or less than a simple contest between two ball clubs—can take on a compelling quality, offer a particular *joie de vivre*, that a game fraught with meta-meaning cannot. There's abundant, even special, reward to be found in the squaring-off of ordinary teams, the exertions of athletes Cooperstown will surely ignore, the sweating for victories little noted and quickly forgotten. A crisply executed double play, a curve that paints the corner, a liner whistling up the alley—the appreciative shout earned by these simple, wonderful feats is perhaps never more heartfelt than when it's expressed in recognition for absolutely nothing other than the feat itself. No other meaning, no deeper importance needs to be accorded.

A season like 2005 provides a particularly favorable view of such delights. In the sky above us the stars are always there, but we only see them, we only marvel and wonder at their timeless beauty, when the overbearing glare of the sun is removed. A 2005 is the glittering night sky of seasons.

The Pings of History

The other way in which such a superficially plain vanilla year as 2005 can reveal deeply complex flavors is in the subtle echoes it offers of seasons past. A high-profile event like the '04 Red Sox or '01 Bonds is obvious in its historical connection; indeed the enormous historical linkage is what it's all about. In contrast, a 2005 might be seen as eluding historical association, standing alone in obscurity, but that wouldn't be correct. The truth is that a 2005 has its own network of historical relations. They aren't the rich-and-famous ancestors, but that makes them no less connected, and as most any student of history will tell you, sometimes the lesser-known characters from the past are the most interesting.

The very facets of 2005 that were so flatly ordinary, so mildly unremarkable—the lack of upsets, wild races and record-threatening feats—all resound with historical precedent.

There were no long-shot or particular upset winners among the division or Wild Card champions.

By definition, long shots and upsets are surprises. But they aren't as rare as one might expect. Particularly in the current era, with eight postseason qualifiers each season, an upset winner of some proportion actually appears rather frequently. In 2004, for instance, the Anaheim Angels eclipsed the Oakland Athletics for the American League West Division championship after having been 77-85, 19 games behind the A's the previous year. In 2003, the Florida Marlins won the National League Wild Card berth (and went on to win the World Series) despite not having had a winning record since 1997 and having fired their manager in mid-May.

Still, the dynamic in 2005 is one with ample precedent. Several seasons from decades past demonstrated patterns of no-big-surprise among postseason qualifiers. In 1992, for example, three of the four divisions featured repeat champions: the Atlanta Braves in the NL West, the Pittsburgh Pirates in the NL East and the Toronto Blue Jays in the AL East. The only division without a repeater was the AL West, and that winner, the Oakland A's, had been the champ in 1988, 1989 and 1990 before pitching problems in 1991 held them to 84-78 and fourth place. Oakland was certainly expected to be a strong contender for 1992.

The period of 1976 through 1978 was one of particular stability among flag winners. In the American League, the Kansas City Royals (West) and New York Yankees (East) were division champs all three years. In the National League, the Philadelphia Phillies (East) were three-peaters, while the Cincinnati Reds won the West in 1976, and the Los Angeles Dodgers won in both '77 and '78. The Dodgers were no long shot in overtaking the Big Red Machine, as they had won the division in 1974 and finished second to the Reds in '73, '75 and '76.

Before 1969, in the pre-division era, there were oodles of seasons when the pennant winners in both leagues were a shock to no one. In the American League there were long periods in which the only surprising result was the rare event when the Yankees *didn't* win it. The Bronx Bombers and their World Series opponents *both* were making repeat appearances no fewer than seven times: in 1922 (versus the New York Giants), 1923 (the Giants again), 1937 (the Giants yet again), 1943 (versus the St. Louis Cardinals), 1953 (versus the Brooklyn Dodgers), 1956 (the Dodgers again) and 1958 (versus the Milwaukee Braves). Non-Yankees Fall Classic repeat match-ups occurred in 1908 (Detroit Tigers and Chicago Cubs) and 1931 (Philadelphia Athletics and St. Louis Cardinals).

There weren't any especially remarkable division or wild card races.

As we've said, remarkable events are remarkable precisely because they don't occur all the time. There's no guarantee a potboiler race will be delivered every year. But under the modern arrangement of three divisions per league, plus the Wild Card berth, there's more potential than ever before for close battles. (This is, of course, an intended feature of the current setup.) It can be the case, however, that eight races are all simultaneously rather ordinary, as we observed this year.

Another season that produced little in terms of memorable chases under the existing configuration was 1998. Five of the six divisions saw complete runaways: the Indians won by nine games, the Padres by 9.5, the Astros by 12.5, the Braves by 18 and the completely unstoppable Yankees by a staggering 22. Only one division featured a close race, and that was the American League West's slow-motion slog between the 88-74 Angels and the 85-77 Rangers—not exactly one for the ages. The AL Wild Card winner, the Red Sox, breezed in by a margin of seven games.

Only in the NL Wild Card race was there much to sweat about in '98, as the Cubs, Giants and Mets went right down to the wire. The Mets finished at 88-74, and the Cubs and Giants ended the season in a flat-footed tie at 89-73, necessitating a one-game playoff at Wrigley Field in which Steve Trachsel pitched 6.1 one-hit shutout innings to defeat San Francisco. That was pretty exciting (well, it was excruciating to us Giants' fans), but showdowns between 80-something-win ball clubs don't exactly transfix the nation.

In the two-divisions-per-league arrangement, 1992 was a year of little flag-race drama—a year which, as we just saw, was also similar to 2005 in its lack of surprising flag winners. The four races that season were won by margins of four, six, eight and nine games, and none was memorable. 1986 was even less harrowing: five, five-and-a-half, 10 and a whopping 21.5 (won by the raucous, stunningly talented Gooden-Strawberry-Hernandez Mets).

Back in 1981, a gent by the name of John Warner Davenport published a marvelous book entitled *Base-ball's Pennant Races: a Graphic View*. Presenting fascinating graphs illustrating every pennant race in history, Davenport's supporting commentary is brisk and informative. On the book's final page, Davenport salutes "Baseball's Pennant Non-Races," the *least* close and dramatic league-wide chases seen to that point: the 1901 American League, the 1903 National League, the 1909 NL, the 1930 AL, the 1942 AL, the 1951 AL, the 1974 NL West and the 1975 AL East. Davenport observes:

> *Finally, there are those serene summers when the thought of torrid pennant races seems wearying, when one would prefer, restfully, to savor all the quieter colors and sounds of the great national pastime as no other sport can be enjoyed. To those who like their baseball this way, adoring every moment and aspect of the game no matter what the score or the standings, the final multigraph—showing those wonderfully spaced-out seasons in which each team is tracking its course of destiny without contending for first place or anyplace—is dedicated. These pennant non-races may not have been the most gripping seasons, but graphically they are the most graceful.*

Indeed they are. May 2005 take its place in their graceful midst.

There were no particularly great team performances.

In a 30-team environment, a season has to really work hard to produce zero teams with more than 100 victories and only two over 95. In the eight 30-club years since 1998, something like that has taken place just once before: in 2000, when the winningest team in the majors was the San Francisco Giants, with 97, for a .599 winning percentage. (Don't get me started on that year's Division Series against the Mets.) Three teams that year (the Braves, Cardinals and White Sox) won 95.

There was one full season (1996) in the short-lived 28-team configuration in which no one managed to reach the century mark. But in the 1977-92 era of 26 big-league outfits—a period well-regarded for competitive balance—no one won 100 games (in completed seasons) six times: 1982, 1983, 1987, 1989, 1991 and 1992 (yes, that one again!). The most moderate of those years was 1982, in which the biggest winners were the "Harvey's Wallbangers" Milwaukee Brewers, at 95-67, .586: the lowest top win total since the introduction of the 162-game schedule, and the lowest top winning percentage in all of history.

From 1969 through 1976 there were 24 teams, and 1973 was the only non-strike-shortened season among them without a 100-victory ball club (the Cincinnati Reds won 99). That was also the year in which the New York Mets won the National League East Division at just 82-79 (.509), the record for fewest wins by a full-season division champion that the 2005 Padres matched with their 82-80 mark.

In the 20-team arrangement of 1962 through 1968, two seasons saw no 100-game winners: in 1964 the Yankees won the most at 99, and in 1966 the Orioles were the top winner with 97.

From 1904 through 1960 (except in the war-shortened seasons of 1918 and 1919), the schedule was 154 games, with 16 teams in operation over the entire period. Among those 55 complete seasons, there were just six in which no team in either league won as many as 95 games: 1916, 1922, 1924, 1926, 1958, and 1959. The year with the lowest top total was 1926, in which the winningest ball club in the major leagues was the New York Yankees at 91-63 (.591), while nobody else won as many as 90.

There were no unusually bad team performances.

To be frank, the 2005 Royals were a pretty doggone bad team. But still it's true that their 106-defeat total wasn't nearly as pitiful as that of either the 2004 Arizona Diamondbacks (51-111) or the historically horrendous 2003 Detroit Tigers (43-119). And three cellar-dwellers in 2002 matched the 106-loss mark: the Tigers, the Devil Rays and the Brewers. Especially when factoring in that the '05 Royals' Pythagorean record was "only" 60-102, they don't stand out as a particularly notable bad club of the current era. And no one else in 2005 was especially bad at all.

There have been two seasons in the 30-club configuration in which no team lost 100 games: 1999 (the Florida Marlins were the worst at 64-98) and 2000 (the Chicago Cubs and Philadelphia Phillies each lost 97). In 1997, none of the 28 major league teams lost 100, as the Oakland Athletics "led" at 65-97.

In that competitively balanced 26-team arrangement of 1977 through 1992, there were four full seasons (1984, 1986, 1990, and—you guessed it—1992) without a 100-game loser. The year with the "best" worst team was 1984, when the Johnnie LeMaster-led San Francisco Giants went 66-96 for a .407 winning percentage.

Never in the 24-club 1969-76 configuration was there a season without at least one 100-game loser (even the slightly strike-reduced 1972 produced the .217-hitting

Texas Rangers, at 54-100). And only one year in the 1960s saw no 100-loss teams: the worst team among the 20 in The Year of the Pitcher, 1968, was the new Washington Senators, at 65-96, .404.

Never in the 16-team, 154-game schedule setup had there been a season without at least one team losing 95 games until 1944, which had nobody worse than the Philadelphia Blue Jays (which the Phillies were called then, in a brief and unsuccessful effort to get fans to forget the franchise's legacy of futility), at 61-92, .399. Then those two seasons, 1958 and 1959, which as we saw didn't produce any 95-game winners, also had the distinction of generating zero 95-game losers. The worst team of 1959 (the old Washington Senators) had a record of 63-91: the fewest losses to lead the major leagues in a full season in history, and the least-bad winning percentage (.409) of any worst-in-the-majors ball club in history.

There were no record-setting individual performances.

Of all the immoderately moderate aspects of the 2005 season, this one is perhaps the most notable. Almost nothing of individual statistical significance happened in 2005:

- The league batting champions were at the bland levels of .335 and .331.

- The major league home run champ hit 51, which in the current era is hardly remarkable: it marked the 19th time a slugger has hit at least 50 since 1995, and he obviously never got within shouting distance of the record.

- The league RBI leaders were, at 148 and 128, entirely ho-hum totals in this era.

- The leagues' top winning pitchers were at 22 and 21, totals exactly in line with where they've been for the past 10 years.

- The strikeout kings were at 238 and 216, figures interesting only because they're slightly on the low side of modern normality. But they aren't even record-threatening lows, even within the current strikeout-happy era.

- Only in the ERA category was there something resembling a run at a record, as Roger Clemens wowed everyone through the summer. But he faded toward the end, and although his final marks of 1.87 ERA and 221 ERA+ were spectacular, neither threatened those compiled by Pedro Martinez and Greg Maddux within the past dozen seasons.

Recent seasons had seen all-time marks broken or threatened in a dazzling array of categories.

For batters:

- On-base percentage (Barry Bonds, 2002 and again in 2004)
- Slugging percentage (Bonds, 2001)
- OPS (Bonds, '02 and '04)
- OPS+ (Bonds, '01 and '02)
- At-bats (Ichiro Suzuki falling one shy of the record, 2004)
- Hits (Ichiro breaking the mark, '04)
- Singles (Ichiro, '04)
- Doubles (Todd Helton coming within five of the league record, 2000)
- Home runs (Bonds, '01)
- Walks (Bonds, '01, '02 and '04)
- Strikeouts (threatened by numerous batters in recent years, then broken by Adam Dunn, 2004)

For pitchers:

- ERA+ (the modern record, Pedro Martinez, 2000)
- WHIP (Pedro, '00)
- Hits-per-inning (threatened by Pedro, '00)
- Strikeouts (the modern record threatened by Randy Johnson, 2001)
- Strikeouts-per-inning (Pedro, 1999; Johnson, '01)
- Saves (threatened by John Smoltz, 2002, and Eric Gagne, 2003)
- Home runs allowed (threatened by Jose Lima, 2000)

All 2005 could muster was a single record-setting feat: Carlos Silva of the Minnesota Twins set a new modern mark for fewest walks allowed per nine innings, at .430 (he surrendered just 9 in 188 innings), shattering the standards set by Babe Adams (.616 in 1920) and Bret Saberhagen (.660 in 1994). Impressive? You bet. Something we'll tell our grandkids about? I'm guessing not.

For sheer not-threatening-anybody meekness in record setting, few seasons stand up to 2005. One milquetoast year that might top it is—you can see this one coming, can't you—1992. In '92, no one broke any records or even came close. It is interesting to note that Bob Tewksbury, one of the all-time great control artists, posted his career-best fewest-walks-per-nine mark in 2002, at .770.

Other seasons through the decades that you won't find much mention of in the record books include 1976 (though the skintight double-knit unis were at their zenith), 1967 (though the AL did feature a Triple Crown winner for an unprecedented second straight year), 1960 (though the World Series was wacky and full of records),

1940 (though ... nothing, it was just a dull year), 1926 (which was also without any powerhouse teams), 1917 (sorry again, White Sox fans) and 1910 (noted for little other than the Ty Cobb-Napoleon Lajoie batting championship controversy).

So What Does This Tell Us About 2005?

In comparing the events of 2005 to those of previous seasons, a few particular periods seem to keep coming up. The most obvious single year is 1992, although the overall shape of the 2005 season is generally similar to several in the 1982-92 period, as well as to some in the early-to-mid-1970s, the 1958-59-60 triplet and to some in the mid-1920s. All of these are phases that stand in the shadows cast by much flashier nearby seasons. The mid-1920s are the rather obscure middle ground between the tumultuous 1919-21 period (the Black Sox scandal and the sudden Ruth-led offensive transformation) and the record-setting batting exploits of 1930. The early-to-mid 1950s "Golden Era" Yankees-Dodgers and the high-profile exploits of Roger Maris, Maury Wills and Casey Stengel's hapless early Mets bracket the mild 1958-60 period. The early-to-mid-1970s featured little high-powered offense, followed the Miracle Mets, and pre-staged the Reggie/Billy/Guidry Yankee show. And 1982-92 was the interregnum between that Yankee-fueled boisterous late 1970s and the even more boisterous, ultra-high-scoring 1990s.

It's significant that none of these periods similar to 2005 featured particularly high levels of offensive performance. The records that command our attention and loom large in our memory tend to be batting marks, and like 2005, these periods produced few. 2005, while a high-scoring year compared to the historical average, was a slightly low-scoring season within the context of its era: the 4.59 runs per team/game produced major league-wide in 2005 puts it just barely behind 1993 (4.60) and 2002 (4.62), and thus renders it the lowest-scoring year since—wait for it—1992.

There are surely those who will rush to conclude that the reduced scoring of 2005 is a direct result of MLB's stricter steroid-testing regimen. While obviously it's impossible to know that this isn't true, there are a multitude of reasons to be quite skeptical of such a conclusion, not the least of which is that the slight decline in scoring witnessed in 2005 is well within the range of year-to-year variation we see all the time. Still, it remains the case that 2005 wasn't a great sluggers' year, though it was by no means a year featuring extraordinary pitching achievements, either.

The dearth of great-winning or great-losing teams in 2005 is an indication of general parity, or competitive balance. One should be exceedingly hesitant to draw a firm conclusion about that regarding 2005, however, given that it's followed right on the heels of a cluster of seasons that featured extremely dominant winners (the 2001 Seattle Mariners, at 116-46; the 1998 New York Yankees, at 114-40) as well as extremely dominated losers (the '04 Diamondbacks; the '03 Tigers). Sustained parity isn't the sort of thing that's likely to just suddenly come about, and there's little reason to expect that it has here. But it is the case that the periods the standings of 2005 recall were generally lacking unbeatable dynasties or hopeless doormats. It thus might not be unreasonable to imagine that seasons to come may produce more somewhat-surprising success stories along the lines of the 2005 Chicago White Sox.

So How About Those White Sox, Huh?

Only the most staunch North Side Windy City loyalist couldn't have been charmed by the story of the erstwhile ne'er-do-well Southsiders—who, fittingly, featured a few characters with checkered pasts (Carl Everett, A.J. Pierzynski, Jose Contreras) coming through big time.

Though the superficial similarity is obvious, the White Sox's breaking of their ancient "curse" had little in common with the 2004 Boston Red Sox's victory. The differences in the stories were major. The Red Sox's frustrations over the decades centered around the fact that they were often an extremely good team, tantalizingly close to claiming the ultimate prize, but always finding a way to fall short at the end, whereas the White Sox over the years were rarely a strong contender, usually finding a way to fall short by mid-June. In addition, the Red Sox were almost insanely beloved, not only in their hometown but pretty much across the country (with the notable exception of New York, of course), while the White Sox were anything but widely loved, the perennial second banana even in their hometown, saddled (fairly or not) with a coarse, tough, outlaw image.

Actually the franchise most comparable to the White Sox is probably the Philadelphia Phillies. Like the White Sox, the Phils are a very old franchise whose long history is mostly a tedious discourse in defeat, and like the White Sox, the Phillies have developed an understandably frustrated fan base that (again, fairly or not) has a reputation for booing and fighting more than cheering and smiling.

Thus the World Series match-up that 2005 brought to mind was that of 1980. That year, the long-denied Phillies finally won the National League pennant, for the first time since 1950, and the second time since 1915. In 1980, the Phillies' World Series opponent was a far younger expansion franchise from a smaller city in a warmer climate, making its very first Fall Classic appearance: the Kansas City Royals. This year, the White Sox's World Series opponent was a far younger expansion franchise from a smaller city (well, a smaller metro area, for sure) in a warmer climate, making its very first Fall Classic appearance: the Houston Astros.

There were even some similarities between the teams themselves. None of the ball clubs in either Series featured an especially overpowering offense, and each was anchored by very strong front-line starting pitching. (At the risk of carrying this too far, isn't there a striking similarity between Willie Wilson and Willy Taveras?) At any rate, both Series demonstrated the same patterns of play: the games were consistently close, in general neither especially high- nor low-scoring. The expansion sunny-climate team tended to get itself into trouble with sloppy fielding and an inability to capitalize on scoring opportunities, while the old-franchise big-city team wasn't overpowering but impressed everyone with its fundamentally sound, generally mistake-free performance.

The 1980 Phillies won the World Series four games to two, though with a break or two going the other way, the Royals might have beaten them. The 2005 White Sox won the World Series in a four-game sweep, though with a break or two going the other way, the Astros might have made it a far more competitive outcome. In both 1980 and 2005, the outcome that did occur was greeted with a thunderous outburst of joy in the bigger, older city, as a lugubrious ball and chain was smashed to bits, at last.

The Low-Profile Legacy

There's every reason to suspect that decades from now, when fans recall memorable seasons of the past, 2005 won't be among those they tout. In so many ways, 2005 is destined to become one of those in-between years, a non-dog-eared page in the encyclopedia, historical fly-over country.

Well, so be it. Let the snobs fly over. Those of us who are here in 2005 don't need their shallow affirmation, anyway. Let the blinding glare of the sun stay away, at least for now, while we enjoy the twinkling marvels of 2005.

The Big Postseason Blasts

In "Postseason Review," where we offered a Win Probability view of the World Series, we mentioned that Paul Konerko's grand slam in the second game was the biggest blow of the Series. How does Konerko's big homer (61 WPA) compare to some of the other big blows of past postseasons? A number of THT readers have been pitching in, developing their own WPA research, and one intrepid reader sent us this list of big postseason plays:

Kirk Gibson's home run in the 1988 World Series:	86
Pujols' HR in this year's NLCS:	73
Francisco Cabrera's single in the 1992 NLCS:	73
Dane Iorg's single in Game 6 of the 1985 Series:	73
Joe Carter's walk-off home run in the 1993 Series:	65
Bill Buckner's error in the 1986 Series:	-39
Bob Stanley's wild pitch in the same inning:	-41
Bernie Carbo's home run in the 1975 Series: .	44
Carlton Fisk's better-known home run in the same game:	35

Young Pitchers
by Bill James

I. The Royals

Although I am no longer a Kansas City Royals fan, I still live in the area, attend many Royals games, and spend about two and a half hours a day, on average, listening to my friends try to put their finger on what it is exactly that the Royals are doing wrong. We have a lot of theories about it, many of which are difficult or impossible to document, perhaps because they're just wrong.

We used to complain about their drafting high school pitchers, but somebody did a study which showed that the number of high school pitchers they drafted wasn't really unusual. It drives me crazy when they shift pitchers back and forth between starting and relieving a la Jeremy Affeldt, but when I tried to document this it didn't seem that they were doing any more of it than many other teams, some of them successful teams. They have repeatedly brought pitchers to the major leagues after about 45 innings at Double-A, skipping Triple-A entirely, and this seems silly, but again, it's not clear that it is unusual; a lot of teams now warehouse sub-marginal major league veterans at Triple-A, and promote prospects from Double-A.

The Royals walk less than Stephen Hawking, but the offense is another issue … don't get me started. I was talking about the pitching. In 2005 the Royals turned loose the veteran Darrell May, who had made 84 starts for them over the previous three seasons, to turn their pitching chores over to a number of young pitchers who were, as it turns out, demonstrably worse than Darrell May, and perhaps worse than Stephen Hawking. The Royals in the winter of 2004/2005 thought that what they needed was to clear out the mediocre veterans like Darrell May and Joe Randa, when in reality what they needed was a lot more mediocre veterans like Darrell May and Joe Randa. This is a theory, not a proven truth, but I am trying to trace the logic that led me to this research.

What the Royals need right now is a working platform. They need a scaffold to stand on as they build a team. The point of having Darrell May and Raul Ibanez and Michael Tucker around is not that those guys are going to win the pennant for you, but that they stabilize the situation so that you can work on developing the guys who might win the pennant for you. When the Royals haughtily dismissed Darrell May and Joe Randa as no longer worthy to wear the blue, they left themselves so short of talent that they were forced to throw into the breach players who were not prospects, players who simply had no business being on a major league roster. They tore down the scaffolding, and found themselves with no way to construct the walls of their redemption.

Young pitchers will break your heart. I call it Sam's Law, after Sam Reich. There are many, many young pitchers who look like they might be outstanding, but who just don't produce results. To have a couple of young pitchers on your staff, hoping they will develop, is one thing. To have an entire kiddie staff is something else. What the Royals need to do, I found myself arguing, is to stabilize the rotation with two or three veterans, and then put their best pitching prospects into the other two slots. What they have done instead is to get rid of the veterans, and turn over the entire staff to young pitchers. This just basically creates chaos.

That's my latest effort to put my finger on what the Royals are doing wrong, but how do you document it? I decided to focus simply on the amount of young pitching that the organization uses, over a period of years—not on the quality of the pitching, not on the process of drafting them or promoting them, but just on the question "how many young pitchers did the team put on the mound, over a period of years?"

II. The Study

I studied major league organizations, by decade, and asked about each organization in each decade one simple question: what percentage of their innings pitched were worked by pitchers aged 25 or younger? Let's take the Pittsburgh Pirates in the years 1930 to 1939:

a) How many innings did they play? (13,697)

b) How many of those innings were pitched by pitchers aged 25 or younger? (3,237.2)

c) What percentage is that? (24%)

d) What was the won-lost record of the team? (812 wins, 718 losses)

e) How was their pitching? (184 runs better than average, according to the *Sabermetric Encyclopedia*, which applies park adjustments.)

I asked those questions for every team in every decade since 1900, no Federal League.

A summary of this research in one sentence is that everything I thought would be true turned out to be true, but perhaps less true than I would have guessed. First, it *is* true that the Royals have used more young pitching in recent years than most other major league teams. Since 2000 (2000 through 2004), 45% of the Royals' innings pitched have been by pitchers aged 25 or younger. This is the third-highest percentage in baseball for this decade, behind the White Sox and the Marlins.

In the 1990s the Royals had 33% of their innings pitched by pitchers aged 25 or younger, which was the fifth-highest percentage in baseball. In the 1980s they were also at 33%, which was the seventh-highest percentage in baseball. So it is true, first of all, that

1) The Royals have used more young pitchers than most other teams, and

2) This tendency is accelerating over time.

Second, it is true, generally speaking, that using lots of young pitching is characteristic of losing teams.

I sorted the team decades into four groups by the amount of young pitching they had used.

Group	Wins	Losses	W Pct.	ERA
>50% young	6,796	7,525	.475	3.93
35-49% young	41,118	42,623	.491	3.82
20-35% young	89,375	88,254	.503	3.79
<20% young	24,441	23,286	.512	3.73

The less young pitching an organization used during the decade, the more successful they were.

However, while this is not a trivial bias in the data, neither is it an overpowering pattern. There are many teams, like the White Sox of 2000-2004, who used a large number of young pitchers just because they had a large number of very good young pitchers. The Red Sox of the years 1910-1919, a tremendously successful organization, used 60% young pitchers, the second-highest figure of all time. The Orioles of the 1960s, another highly successful organization, used 54% young pitching, the fourth-highest percentage of all time.

Nor is it anything like universally true that perennially bad organizations always use lots of young, inexperienced pitchers. In fact, many of the worst organizations in baseball history did it with veterans. The Boston Braves of the 1930s used only 9% young pitchers. The St. Louis Browns used only 17% young pitching in the 1930s, and only 15% in the 1940s. The hapless Philadelphia Phillies of the 1920s and 1930s, whose inept pitching is legendary, used only 19% young pitching in each decade.

This could be interpreted as a hopeful sign for the Royals, which I think would make a total of one, but there are many organizations in history who used a lot of young pitching while they were getting better. The Cubs of the 1960s, who were hopeless at the start of the decade but very good by decade's end, used 54% young pitching, eventually finding the pitchers they needed to be

competitive. The A's of the same decade, going through the same process except going from more hopeless to more competitive, used 50% young pitching. The Brewers lost a lot of games in the 1970s with 50% young pitching, but they were building the team that came together in the early 1980s. The Mets of the 1960s and the Blue Jays of the 1970s were truly horrible teams, but they used 45% young pitching, and by decade's end they were ready to go. There is an argument that losing a lot of games with young pitching is just a stage you go through if you don't want to become the Browns of the 1940s or the Philadelphia Phillies of the 1930s.

III. Interesting Stuff I Accidentally Learned by Doing This Study

Has the amount of young pitching in the major leagues declined over time?

Well, yes, but not really. I would have guessed that the percentage of innings pitched by pitchers aged 25 and younger might have declined steadily over the last century, but actually it has declined, or may have declined, very erratically. This is the decade by decade

Decade of ...	Young %
1900 – 1909	34%
1910 – 1919	42%
1920 – 1929	24%
1930 – 1939	23%
1940 – 1949	20%
1950 – 1959	27%
1960 – 1969	37%
1970 – 1979	36%
1980 – 1989	29%
1990 – 1999	27%
2000 – 2004	27%

chart:

Why did the percentage of young pitching rocket upwards in the teens, then drop sharply in the 1920s? Believe it or not, because I did that book with Neyer about pitching, I actually understand that. The pitching patterns of the 1910-1919 era were abnormally simple. At that time the pitcher was allowed to abuse the baseball—scratch it, rub it in the dirt, spit licorice on it—and then pitch with it. I may have overstated it; there *were* some limitations on abuse of the ball, but it wasn't like now, when clean baseballs are kept in play as much as possible.

Well, who's going to mess around throwing a fork ball or a slider/hard curve in a game like that? You just rear back and throw hard, and the baseball itself will take care of the rest. Pitchers in that era threw fewer breaking pitches and fewer off-speed pitches than ever before or since, and this obviously worked to the advantage of young, inexperienced pitchers.

After 1920 the salaries of players grew rapidly, which probably accelerated the trend away from younger pitchers. A pitcher who had made $2,000 a year in his prime may have been reluctant to retire when he could make $5,000 a year hanging around in the bullpen. That changed the age pattern, too.

Why the numbers shot back up again in the 1960s is a harder question. Expansion certainly contributed to it—expansion teams *do* use a large number of young pitchers in their formative years—but if you work the numbers, you can see that it is obviously impossible for expansion to have caused the increase in young pitching from 23% (before the war) to 37%. Something else happened.

As to what it was, I would say that the best answer I can give is that there was a dramatic example of successful young pitching. Paul Richards took over the Baltimore Orioles when they were losing 100 games a year, and built them into a competitive team, basically on the backs of young pitchers. The 1960 Baltimore Orioles went 89-65, and led the league in ERA. Their starting rotation was Chuck Estrada (22), Milt Pappas (21), Jack Fisher (21), Steve Barber (21), and Jerry Walker (21), plus a couple of aging spot starters. I think that destroyed the idea that young pitchers *had* to be seasoned with several years in the minor leagues, and perhaps even fed the idea that young pitching was preferable to veteran pitching—much as the Royals' success in 1985, with a collection of young hard throwers, has left them perpetually trying to repeat 1985.

If you look at the chart above, there appears to be a kind of a pattern that, when the conditions of the game favor the pitcher, the percentage of young pitching shoots up, whereas when the conditions of the game favor the hitter, the teams look more for veteran pitchers. When pitching is easy, young pitchers take over; when pitching is hard, veteran pitchers rule. There may be a lesson in this for the Colorado Rockies or other teams trying to win in pitching parks, I don't know, and this actually may be the most interesting thing I learned from doing this research.

Perhaps I should stop there, but I will stumble forward blindly. What is the best pitching staff any team ever had, for a decade?

Measured by Runs Saved Against Average, the *worst* pitching staff ever was that of the Philadelphia/Kansas City Athletics in the 1950s—873 runs worse than average. That was mostly a veteran staff. The only other team worse than negative 750 was the Boston Braves in the 1920s.

The *best* pitching staff ever—this is not a surprise—was the Atlanta Braves of the 1990s, +963 runs, narrowly edging out the Cardinals of the 1940s, +955 runs. The Cardinals of the 1940s had phenomenal depth, with the first great farm system churning out arms like IHOP frying pancakes. Behind them are the Tigers of the 1940s (Hal Newhouser, Dizzy Trout, Fred Hutchinson and Virgil Trucks), followed by the Cubs of Three Finger Brown's decade (Brown, Reulbach, Carl Lundgren, Jack Pfiester, Orval Overall and Jack Taylor), and the Cardinals of the 1960s (Bob Gibson and Steve Carlton, Curt Simmons and Ray Sadecki.)

The great surprise, however, is that in ninth place on the list of teams with great pitching for a decade are the Boston Red Sox in the 1950s.

What? Ike Delock is a Hall of Famer?

It is sure funny how numbers will fool you sometimes. Asked to grade the pitching of the Boston Red Sox in the 1950s, I would have guess-graded them somewhere about a C-, maybe a D+. Looking at it analytically, I guess I can kind of see why they do better. There are two powerful illusions. First, Fenway Park was, in the 1950s, the best hitter's park in baseball, which of course has the effect of making the hitters look better than they ought to, the pitchers look worse. In 1955 Fenway Park had a Park Run Index of 156. In spite of this, the Red Sox' team ERA was 3.72, 24 points better than the league average.

Second, the Red Sox had no one or two starters who were there throughout the decade, as the Yankees did (Ford) or the Braves did (Spahn, Burdette and Buhl). They rotated pitchers in and out, which makes it hard to "see" them as a quality staff.

But if you look at them year by year, there are a lot of pitchers here having very good years. Mel Parnell was 18-10, 18-11 and 21-8 in the 1950s (also had some good years in the 1940s.) Mickey McDermott was 18-10 one year. Frank Sullivan was 18-13 one year—a whopping 62 runs better than league—and also had four other seasons with 13 to 15 wins, winning records and very good ERAs. (Neither Bob Gibson nor Sandy Koufax was ever 62 runs better than the league average. Sullivan's 1955 figure is the highest total between Lefty Gomez in 1937 and Grëg Maddux in 1995.) Tom Brewer was 19-9 in 1956. Joe Dobson, Ellis Kinder, Chuck Stobbs, Willard Nixon and even Ike Delock had some very decent seasons as third starters. I guess if I look at it just right I can see that their pitching may have been underrated, although I don't know that I'm really convinced that it was historically good, either.

The Hall of Merit

by Joe Dimino
(with help from John Murphy)

I absolutely love baseball history. As far back as I can remember it's been my favorite part of the game. The Hall of Fame has been central to this ever since the first time I visited the shrine for my 11th birthday during the 1983 World Series. As I walked through the Plaque Room back then, I just assumed that these were the greatest players of all time.

John and I started questioning the conventional wisdom after reading Bill James's *Baseball Abstract* in the mid-1980s. I received my first *MacMillan Encyclopedia* for my 16th birthday, picked up a copy of *The Historical Baseball Abstract* a few years later, and more and more of the Hall of Fame selections came into question in my mind.

Then came *The Politics of Glory*, another great book from James. The Veterans' Committee's dark periods, 1945-6 and the early 1970s, were especially disturbing; most of the mistakes and arbitrary decisions came from these two periods.

Lee Allen, who was a contributor to the Veterans' Committee in the 1960s—a period when many of the mistakes of omission from the mid-1940s were corrected—became one of my baseball heroes. At this point, I was convinced that I needed to come up with something better, even if it was just for my own benefit.

So the Hall of Something came to mind. I couldn't think of a good name, and other than some 1980s baseball cards and a Bobby Ramos–autographed Tommy John replica glove, I didn't have much memorabilia to draw visitors to my basement. But I started working on it anyway. I re-worked my way through the *Politics of Glory* and came up with a list of "mistake players." I also came up with a list of unjustly overlooked players.

Then I thought of going back to 1935 and seeing who should have been chosen in each election, but I would take the top players each year based on actual voting whether or not they garnered 75% of the vote. By the late 1940s, satisfied that the 65 years of baseball history before my elections start had been made up for, I cut it to two per season. I also tweaked my annual 'elections' by allowing Bill James's top 100 lists to override the Baseball Writers Association of America vote when appropriate. This list came out better than what is in the Hall presently but still missed the 19th century players and Negro Leaguers.

At that point, I stumbled onto Baseball Reference (www.baseball-reference.com). A few months later, I noticed Sean Forman's now defunct Outside the Box blog and discovered that I wasn't the only baseball lunatic out there. I started talking with Robert Dudek, and over several months, we refined these ideas. He came up with a name that made a lot of sense. Fame shouldn't be the criteria for selection; merit should be. We should label our shrine for what it takes to get in, not the reward for getting in. We had a name—the Hall of Merit.

The basic premise is not that there are too many people in the Hall of Fame but that there are too many mistakes. Add Ron Santo and Stan Hack and remove George Kell and Freddy Lindstrom, for example, and the Hall looks better. Get rid of Tommy McCarthy and put Deacon White in and it goes up another notch. A few more of these "trades" and suddenly the whole thing starts looking much better. Everybody knows that Ruth, Mantle and Mays are the greats. The key is honoring the correct players who were just a notch below them. By starting over, we can correct the mistakes of Cooperstown's past.

So we decided to travel through time, selecting the greatest players in the history of baseball, learning plenty in the process. It took about a year and a half from when it was introduced (12/2001) until the first vote (4/2003), but that worked out well, because we had picked up 29 contributors by then. We peaked at 54 and currently (1961) have 49. We also have some non-voting contributors.

John was there from the beginning. Gradually, he emerged as the go-to guy whenever I was too busy for something (the job doesn't pay well), and at this point he does all of the day-to-day work involved with the site, including posting new threads for discussion, tallying the votes (we have a few who do that, as a check), writing the 'plaques'—and basically everything else. He's largely responsible for the bios you'll read throughout this piece as well. At this point I just guide the project, vote and discuss.

We've set up a plaque room as well on the Baseball Think Factory site (everything can be found at http://www.baseballthinkfactory.org/files/hall_of_merit/, click the 'important links' link in the intro), where people can go to view a short career synopsis of the "HoMers". We even decide which hat they wear.

Before we could get started, we had to correct the flaws in the Hall of Fame voting system. In an article called "Honors" in the *Historical Abstract*, James talks about how well constructed the MVP ballot is (the voters aren't great, but the system is solid), and how poorly constructed the

Hall of Fame voting system is. The major drawbacks are that there is no way to express degrees in voting (it's yes or no) and the election cutoff is arbitrary (75%), not absolute (say two per year). We did keep the five-year waiting period intact, but that was about it.

Players' contributions *on the field* are the main criteria for selection; off-field actions should only be taken into account for the effect they had on the players' teams on the field of play. Pete Rose and Joe Jackson are eligible; however many voters decided to dock Jackson credit for his entire 1919 season because of his involvement in the Black Sox scandal.

Players will never lose eligibility. This is crucial, because it means that if new information about a player comes to light, that player can benefit. (As an example, we offer Bill James's reassessment of Phil Rizzuto based on Win Shares evaluation of his defensive prowess.) Also, if a voter thinks there were more great players from one era than another, he can vote for a player who might have been squeezed out by his contemporaries in a future election. Since the inherent structure of the vote forces the best to the top, there is no reason to remove players from the process artificially.

As for the number of people elected in any given year, we take 'team seasons' into account and scale accordingly. We started with four in 1898 and two every year through 1905 to catch up. After that we'll elect anywhere from one to three per season.

We've designed it so that we will have 213 honorees after the 2001 ceremony. The Hall of Fame had 213 members after 2001 as well. Since then, the Hall of Fame has only added seven players in four years. Our schedule will call for 12 additional players over those four years. Most of us think the Hall of Fame has gotten a little too tight over the past few years. As you will see, there are plenty of qualified candidates the Veterans' Committee could elect.

We decided to start with elections in 1898, meaning the first elections encompassed careers ending in 1892 or earlier. We chose to start this early to force ourselves to put the great players of the 1870s and 1880s on the first few ballots. Nineteenth century baseball is largely forgotten, but with the statistical advances of the last 36 years we can evaluate them fairly now. Great players of that era deserve to be remembered. Even if you could somehow put them on the same field and find they weren't as great as today's stars, they still have a place in history—pennants were still won and lost during that time.

For this article we'll cover the Hall of Merit through 1925. So who did we elect that first year? We passed over three Hall of Fame players and three pioneer/exec-utives. Among those elected for on-the-field accomplishments, Old Hoss Radbourn finished fifth, Pud Galvin finished 12th and Mickey Welch finished 17th. Pioneers George Wright (sixth), Al Spalding (ninth) and Candy Cummings (33rd) also drew votes, although we only considered their playing careers.

We chose to honor Deacon White, Paul Hines, George Gore and Ross Barnes instead. White, Hines and Gore were the only players named on all 29 ballots, despite each voter having 15 available choices. Thirty-three players received at least one vote.

So who are these guys? As we walk through history here, we'll elaborate on the players that we've elected that aren't Hall of Famers (we'll use HoFer to denote them), and we'll also mention why we've dismissed someone who's in the Hall of Fame.

We'll mention something called season-length adjusted Win Shares (slaWS) from time to time also. Twenty WS in a 70-game season in 1876 are much more valuable than 20 in a 162-game season. WS aren't the be-all, end-all—they're just an easy way for us to give some perspective in terms the modern fan can understand.

White was the greatest all-around catcher of the 19th century. He racked up 500 slaWS if you include estimates of his National Association (NA) seasons. During his 20-year career he posted an OPS+ of 126 and was a standout defensively. He would have won the 1877 MVP Award if it existed, and he was a key cog on six pennant winners (1873-77, 1887).

Hines was narrowly beaten by White for the top spot in the inaugural election. A terrific hitter, he won the Triple Crown in 1878. Hines was a lifetime .300 hitter, with a 131 OPS+ over a 20-year career. He was also a great fielder. Like White, he is a ridiculously over-qualified candidate with 507 career slaWS.

Gore was the best all-around center fielder of the 1880s. "Piano Legs" had an impressive peak, including six years of more than 30 slaWS and two over 40. One of the greatest offensive stars of his era (career OPS+ 136), he was also a terrific base stealer (he stole seven in one game in 1881) and an amazing fielder; he finished his career with 376 slaWS.

Barnes's qualifications were eye-popping at first glance. The undisputed MVP of the 1871-76 period (240 slaWS in six years), the second baseman hit over .400 four times and owns many of the major offensive records for the National Association. His candidacy was questioned because he excelled at utilizing the fair-foul hit as a major part of his offensive attack. The abolishment of the fair-foul hit and an injury that zapped his power in 1877 gave us pause, but in the end that six-year run (in addition to his being a fine player in the pre-NA days of 1868-70) was enough to push him over the hump.

The 1898 election also established a pecking order for future elections. After Radbourn and Wright, third baseman Ezra Sutton, second baseman Hardy Richardson, pitcher Al Spalding, third baseman Ed Williamson, first baseman Joe Start, pitcher Pud Galvin and catcher/first baseman/outfielder Cal McVey were named on at least 19 of the 29 ballots and received from 198 to 427 points.

In 1899 we elected two first-year eligible 'slam dunks:' Jim O'Rourke and King Kelly, both HoFers. Wright, a 1898 holdover, was a distant third. Pitcher Tim Keefe and non-HoFer first baseman/left fielder Harry Stovey also appeared prominently, pulling fourth and fifth place, dropping Radbourn to sixth. Non-HoFers pitcher/right fielder Bob Caruthers, catcher Charlie Bennett and center fielder Pete Browning also debuted in the top 15.

Pitcher John Clarkson and John Ward, both HoFers, were elected in the first ballot in 1900. Ward edged Keefe for the second spot, 617-582. At this point we were up to 35 ballots.

Backlog candidates were first elected in 1901; Tim Keefe and George Wright joined the fraternity, narrowly edging the only strong first-year candidate shortstop Jack Glasscock.

Wright is in the Hall of Fame as a contributor, but he should be in there as a player. He was the premier defensive shortstop in the game and was second in the NA in OPS+ in 1871 and 1873. He was second or third in his league in runs scored six times and played for seven pennant winners. He had 329 slaWS from 1871-79 and was also a star of the pre-NA era; his career spanned 1867-82.

In 1902 four HoFers became eligible. Dan Brouthers was elected easily with 39 of 42 first-place votes. Buck Ewing edged Glasscock, 752.5-704 for the second spot. Right fielder Sam Thompson debuted in ninth place, between Spalding and Galvin. Tommy McCarthy tallied one 15th-place vote among the 42 ballots cast. That was generous.

McCarthy was a corner outfielder with a career OPS+ of 102. He popularized some things like the hit-and-run and signals, but he only played regularly for nine seasons. He was a smarter Mickey Rivers, not a player worthy of the game's highest honor.

The backlog would have to wait in 1903, when two Hall of Famers—first baseman Roger Connor and Cap Anson—were elected in their first year of eligibility. Anson was only named on 38 of 44 ballots, which may seem strange at first. The Hall of Merit

has a morals clause that allows voters to refrain from voting for a player in his first year of eligibility for off-field issues. Six voters chose to exercise this option on Anson due to his involvement in the establishment of the color line.

Glasscock, Radbourn and Richardson were the runners up. Pud Galvin made a surge, leap-frogging three candidates into seventh place, as evidence of his teammates' poor fielding came to the forefront.

In 1904 Jack Glasscock's four-year wait ended. HoFer Amos Rusie was also elected in his first year of eligibility. Al Spalding jumped over two candidates into a strong seventh place, just two points behind Joe Start, as voters became more comfortable with just how important the contribution of pitching, as opposed to fielding, was to the NA game.

Glasscock was the star defensive shortstop of the 1880s; he played barehanded and popularized backing up throws to second base. "Pebbly Jack" was also an above-average hitter at his position, winning the NL batting title in 1890, and played for 17 seasons. He tallied 367 slaWS, including four seasons over 30.

1905 was a backlog year, with one HoFer, Old Hoss Radbourn elected. He was joined by Hardy Richardson. Another second baseman, 2000 HoF electee Bid McPhee, debuted in fourth place behind Galvin. Ten players received a first-place vote. The backlog was especially tight, with just 29 points separating third and seventh places. Right fielder Mike Tiernan finished 13th in his first election, between Browning and Caruthers.

Richardson was a versatile performer considered the best second baseman of the 19th century by our group. He was a valued member of the Buffalo and Detroit teams in the 1880s. A stellar hitter who batted leadoff and cleanup, he was MVP material with his .351/.402/.504 line in 1886. Richardson tallied 342 slaWS over his 13-year career.

1906 was the first year we elected only one candidate; Al Spalding edged Ezra Sutton 758-749.5. Galvin, McPhee and Start were not far behind. Though Spalding was honored by the Hall of Fame, it was more for his pioneer status in forming the NL than his pitching. We elected him based solely on his mound exploits as the game's greatest pitcher of the 1870s and the first 200-game winner. He was also a great hitter (116 OPS+) for a pitcher.

Over the 1903-6 period, Lip Pike started to break from the pack he was in with Williamson and Welch, establishing himself as a serious candidate down the line. His emergence came as questions about his defense were answered.

In 1907 Hall of Fame center fielder Billy Hamilton was easily elected 203 points ahead of Sutton. There was a slight shakeup at the top; McPhee moved ahead of Galvin and Start moved ahead of them both into third place. Hall of Fame outfielder Hugh Duffy debuted in ninth place. Second baseman Cupid Childs also entered the ballot, in 11th place.

Mickey Welch fell off a cliff this year, as eight of the 17 that voted for him in 1906 withdrew their support. Despite 307 wins, his candidacy has stalled because most of us think he simply doesn't stack up to his contemporaries.

In 1908, another holdover from the first ballot was elected: Ezra Sutton. Sutton's career does not jump out at first, but that's entirely due to context issues such as short seasons and perception of his defensive value. We pushed his candidacy as hard as we could.

Sutton ends up with 444 slaWS, including seven years over 30. He was a star in 1871-75 and then had a second peak in 1883-85. He had a 119 career OPS+, good for a modern third baseman but not great. However, he was manning the hot corner when the position was more like second base is viewed today in terms of value. Sutton also played the equivalent of about three years at shortstop as well.

He was greatest third baseman of the 19th century; he combined good offense and defense over an 18-year career. HoFer Hughie Jennings debuted in 1908 as well finishing 10th.

Right fielder Ed Delahanty, another slam-dunk HoFer, was inducted in his first year of eligibility in 1909. Several prominent players debuted that year—Jimmy Ryan finished eighth. Frank Grant, our first serious Negro League candidate, was ninth and George Van Haltren was 12th. John McGraw debuted 22nd. His candidacy never took off because his career was short, and he wasn't particularly durable in-season either.

With the new debuts, Browning and Tiernan's candidacy took a serious hit—they didn't look nearly as good when compared to Ryan and Van Haltren. By this time Williamson (23rd) and Welch (26th) had vanished from the radar.

We consider Negro Leaguers right along with their white counterparts; there is not a separate wing or separate ballot. Because of this we need as much information as possible to assess them. Neither of us is a Negro League expert; fortunately we have a few in our group. Brent Moulton provides great biographies to supplement our numbers. Chris Cobb, Eric Chaleek and Kevin Johnson provide statistics and translate them into something we can all understand. Without their contributions, this part of the project wouldn't have been nearly as successful.

There was a slight upset in 1910 when HoFer Pud Galvin leapfrogged Start, winning 780-743. Galvin had deeper support; he was only omitted from one ballot, while Start was left off five.

Start is an interesting candidate (Joe's pet candidate actually). He played from 1862 to 1886, one of the longest careers ever. But we don't have stats before 1871, and this was an issue for several voters. If you only look at the record after 1871, a case could be made that he's only a borderline candidate. He had 342 slaWS, a good number, but not an eye-popping one.

It's easy to forget that those numbers fail to include anything he did before the age of 28. His career high is only 31 slaWS—but he managed that at age 34. (He also had 30 at age 38.) He also had two terrible years in 1872-73, which hurt his candidacy. He's underrated when looking at the stats because first base was much less of an offensive position in his day—imagine the beating the hands took playing first base without a glove. WS does not account for this.

A player who had that much value in his 30s would generally have been a great player in his 20s. This is entirely backed up by the non-statistical record in Start's case—he was generally thought of as one of the best players through the 1860s.

Start would have to wait at least another year, however, as two HoFers joined the ballot at the top in 1911. Kid Nichols was elected, falling two first-place votes short of unanimous election. Jesse Burkett was a strong second, beating Start 765-634.

Both Joe Start and Jesse Burkett were elected in 1912, the first year scheduled for two electees since 1905. Pitcher Clark Griffith was the only significant debut, entering the ballot in 17th place, but ahead of all of the backlogged pitchers.

Through 1912, we had elected 26 players, eight were pitchers. The 29% was in line with what we'd expected, but it did cause some concern that there were none in queue.

In 1913 Bid McPhee sneaked past McVey in the closest election ever, winning 751-747. HoFer Jake Beckley debuted at ninth, narrowly edging Pike.

Dickey Pearce, my pet candidate and a star 1860s shortstop who had been eligible since the first election, started to make serious progress, being named on 20 of 42 ballots after appearing on just 13 of 42 two years before. His candidacy started to take off as voters became more comfortable with his being eligible since most of his career took place before 1871.

As a group we've decided that if a player has a 'significant' post-1871 career, we'll then take everything he did (even pre-1871) into account. This was the key with both Start and Pearce.

Cal McVey rolled to election in 1914 after his near-miss in 1913. A major offensive star of the NA and early NL, he never had a bad season. While he played every position during his career, his greatest seasons were behind the plate. He finished his major league career with 320 slaWS, which does not include his 1869 and 1870 seasons. He also went on to star in the minor leagues out west for most of the next decade.

Three HoFers also joined the ballot in 1914. Left fielder Joe Kelley debuted at third, while third baseman Jimmy Collins was fifth and pitcher Joe McGinnity was eighth.

1915 saw the election of two of the 10 greatest shortstops of all time. George Davis, who was elected to the HoF in 1998, finished first. The second spot went to non-HoFer Bill Dahlen.

Dahlen was an outstanding defensive shortstop and a 21-year veteran. "Bad Bill" could also do the job offensively via a walk, good power and aggressive base running. Dahlen had a career 110 OPS+ and an eye-popping 452 slaWS.

In 1915 we also summarily dismissed HoFer Jack Chesbro, who was named on the back of just two ballots. Chesbro only pitched for about 9.5 years. He had a nice run in 1901-07, but he only had four years with an ERA+ over 120 and just one over 140.

It's amazing that the Veterans' Committee was completely restructured after the 2001 election. Sure there were a couple of clunkers, but the committee did great work through the 1990s. They honored several 19th century stars and several overlooked Negro Leaguers. It appears the voters on that committee actually listened to some of the things James wrote in *The Politics of Glory*.

Harry Stovey was inducted in 1916 after 18 years on the ballot in the closest HoM election in its history. He nipped Joe Kelly by just two points. First-timers Elmer Flick and Willie Keeler (both HOFers) were right on their heels. Other notable debuts were HoFers Rube Waddell (12th), Addie Joss (21st) and Vic Willis (22nd). Bob Caruthers jumped up from 14th to eighth. His candidacy moved forward largely because voters began to understand just how valuable his pitching/hitting combination was in terms of a high peak.

The greatest combination of power and speed during the 19th century, Stovey's merging of prodigious strength (the greatest home run hitter of the 1880s with 122) and blazing speed (his introduction of the sliding pad helped him amass his many stolen bases) created a mother lode of runs for his teams during his heyday (363 slaWS).

Joss was elected to the HoF by the Veterans' Committee in 1977. He was a great pitcher, but our group felt his career was simply too short (8.5 seasons). He also wasn't particularly durable in-season; he only finished in the top 10 in his league in Innings Pitched twice—and those were just eight-team leagues.

Willis joined the HoF in 1995, via the Veterans' Committee. He was a very good pitcher and not a terrible choice for Cooperstown. Our electorate, however, feels there are *better* Negro League pitchers and major league position players who have been slighted over the years. That's the key to our project: finding the best available player, not just players we think are good enough to be honored.

Cy Young's name was at the top of all 45 ballots in the 1917 election. Another newbie and HoFer, Fred Clarke, easily took the second spot. Frank Chance, a HoFer himself, debuted at 24th.

Chance's case for induction is similar to Joss's. There is no doubting how great he was when he played, but he just didn't play enough—he surpassed 130 games just once in his career and only played 100 six times. Even with his 136 career OPS+, a 1,287-game career just isn't enough.

Elmer Flick achieved HoM immortality in his third year on the ballot in 1918, narrowly besting Willie Keeler by 36 points with Joe Kelly not that far behind.

HoF outfielders Willie Keeler and Joe Kelley were inducted in 1919. Jimmy Collins was only 50 points behind, and Jimmy Sheckard made an impressive debut at sixth.

Ed Walsh became a first-ballot HoMer 1920. HoF shortstop Bobby Wallace entered at a healthy fourth. Negro League second baseman Bill Monroe debuted at 19th. Hugh Duffy's up-and-down candidacy jumped, as he moved from 18th to 12th. Duffy's candidacy, like those of Ryan, Van Haltren, Thompson, Pike and Browning, has been slowed by being part of a glut of outfielders that has split the ballot. None has been able to break out of it—yet.

The two runners-up from 1920 found their way to the top in 1921: Jimmy Collins took the top spot in his eighth year on the ballot. Charlie Bennett, who waited a record 23 years, also received the honor. McGinnity trailed Bennett by only 42 points, while Negro Leaguer "Home Run" Johnson nabbed the fourth spot—the most impressive Negro League candidate to date. Other prominent new candidates were HoFers Roger Bresnahan (12th) and Joe Tinker (39th); Tommy Leach debuted at 21st.

The 1880s' most durable catcher, Bennett was also its greatest defensive backstop, both for his terrific play behind the plate and his handling of pitchers. Among catchers, Bennett was second only to Buck Ewing as a hitter during the decade. He was a member of the Detroit Wolverines' only pennant winner in 1887; the popular Bennett was also part of the great Boston dynasty of 1891-93.

Two "inner circle" HoFers joined our group in 1922: Nap Lajoie and Christy Mathewson. Mordecai "Three Finger" Brown, also newly eligible, finished third.

Honus Wagner, in the HoM class of 1923, was our second unanimous selection. Sam Crawford was one of the strongest runner-ups ever in his debut. Another HoFer, Eddie Plank, had a strong first showing at third. Two more HoFers, Rube Foster (21st) and Johnny Evers (36th), made the ballot from the newly eligible. Chief Bender didn't receive a vote.

Evers was a good player, but he was only a regular for 12 years. Second base was a hitter's position in his era, and his career OPS+ is 106. After 1907 he walked a lot and was undoubtedly a great fielder, but he shouldn't have a plaque in Cooperstown.

Bender was a good pitcher from 1906 to 1914, but he never made as many as 30 starts in a season during that period. He pitched for very good teams as well, distorting his win-loss record. Despite pitching relatively few innings, he only cracked the top five in ERA+ once.

Sam Crawford and Eddie Plank made it to the HoM easily in 1924 in their second tries. In 1925, Home Run Johnson became the first Negro Leaguer elected to the HoM.

Three Finger Brown got the nod with his fourth attempt. It was a wide-open election, as 16 players received first-place votes.

The greatest Negro League shortstop prior to John Henry Lloyd, Johnson was arguably the finest player at the turn of the 20th century. A terrific slugger during the dead ball era, he also possessed impressive strike zone judgment, was an outstanding contact hitter and an excellent fielder. He also formed one of the all-time great keystone combinations as a second baseman with the young Lloyd late in his career.

The next few years don't present many no-brainer candidates (Home Run Baker and Joe Jackson—who will surely have to wait a year due to the morals clause), so we'll be electing several backlog candidates from 1926 until 1930.

A quick rundown of where we stand:

Non Hall of Famers (as players) that we've elected:

- Deacon White C/3B
- Paul Hines CF
- George Gore CF
- Ross Barnes 2B
- George Wright SS
- Jack Glasscock SS
- Hardy Richardson 2B
- Al Spalding P
- Ezra Sutton 3B
- Joe Start 1B
- Cal McVey C/1B/OF
- Bill Dahlen SS
- Harry Stovey OF/1B
- Charlie Bennett C
- Home Run Johnson SS

And a list of HoFers that we won't elect (with their year of election to the HoF):

- Tommy McCarthy (1946)
- Mickey Welch (1973)
- Jack Chesbro (1946)
- Addie Joss (1978)
- Vic Willis (1995)
- Frank Chance (1946)
- Joe Tinker (1946)
- Johnny Evers (1946)
- Chief Bender (1953)

Hall of Famers that aren't in yet, but still have a chance (with 1925 finish):

- Joe McGinnity (3rd)
- Bobby Wallace (4th)
- Sam Thompson (8th)
- Jake Beckley (13th)
- Rube Waddell (15th)
- Hughie Jennings (16th)
- Roger Bresnahan (17th)
- Hugh Duffy (18th)
- Clark Griffith (19th) (HoF as a pioneer/executive)

And finally a list of non-HoFers who are strong candidates (with 1925 finish):

- Frank Grant (5th)
- Sherry Magee (6th)
- Jimmy Sheckard (7th)
- Bob Caruthers (9th)
- Dickey Pearce (10th)
- Lip Pike (11th)
- George Van Haltren (12th)
- Jimmy Ryan (14th)

The Nasty Dutchman
by Bill James

A couple of years ago I did a television show which consisted on the air of being yelled at by Alan Dershowitz, which wasn't fun, but off the air of sitting in a room for eight hours with Steve Garvey and Dave Parker and Bill Lee and a couple of other guys, which was a lot of fun. Lee and Parker and Garvey spent an hour or more telling stories about the Nasty Dutchman, most of which I can't repeat, and who knows whether they are true or not?

For many years I have been wanted to do a definitive study of the Bert Blyleven problem. The Bert Blyleven problem, simply stated, is that Blyleven's win-loss record does not jibe with his innings pitched and ERA. Blyleven pitched just short of 5,000 innings in his career, with a 3.31 ERA. Other pitchers with comparable combinations won 300 games, 310, 320. Blyleven didn't.

This shortfall is well known, and Bert Blyleven has been left out of the Hall of Fame because of it. Life isn't always fair. Other pitchers with 280 wins, and some with 220 wins, and some with less, have made the Hall of Fame—and with the same ERA.

Alright; life's a bitch.

Bert Blyleven is an intriguing figure because he is the most conspicuous victim of what most of us regard as a malicious fiction. You ask any baseball writer from Blyleven's era why Bert hasn't been bronzed, and the guy will tell you "He wasn't a winner. His team scored three runs, he gave up four. They scored one, he gave up two. He had good numbers, but he didn't win the tough games."

Most of us don't believe that this ability to win the close games really exists, and many of us kind of resent Blyleven being discriminated against because he fails a doofus test. Still, in theory, Bert's detractors *could* be on to something. Suppose that you have two pitchers. One, whom we will call Ferguson Winner, loses a game 6-0, but wins six others 1-0, 2-1, 3-2, 4-3, 5-4 and 6-5. The other, whom we will call Bert Loser, wins a game 6-0, but loses six others by the same scores (1-0, 2-1, etc.)

The run support for both pitchers is exactly the same: 21 runs in seven games. Their runs allowed are exactly the same: 21 runs in seven games. The average is the same; the distribution of the runs is the same. But Ferguson has gone 6-1 and Bert has gone 1-6, because Ferguson has matched his effort to the runs he has to work with. My point is, there *could* be something there

that isn't measured by run support and isn't measured by runs allowed. We'll call it the ability to match.

If Blyleven in fact had an inability to match the effort needed, it must be possible to document this by examining his career log game-by-game alongside that of comparable pitchers. Beyond that, it must possible to place a value on it, or to measure the cost of it. The Sabermetric Encyclopedia estimates that Blyleven was 344 runs better than an average pitcher over the course of his career. How many of those 344 runs should be offset because of this inability to match the effort needed?

As a rule of thumb, a pitcher can be expected to be about one game over .500 for each three to five runs that he saves. Luis Tiant was 57 games over .500 (229-172) and saved 172 runs. Carl Hubbell saved 355 runs—about the same number as Blyleven—and was 99 games over .500 (253-154). Roger Clemens through 2004 has saved 645 runs and is 164 games over .500. Pedro Martinez through 2004 has saved 477 runs and is 106 games over .500. Bret Saberhagen saved 241 runs and was 50 games over .500. These are normal ratios.

Blyleven, however, saved 344 runs but was only 37 games over .500. Among the 25 other pitchers in major league history who were at least 300 runs better than league in ERA, most (15 of the 25) were more than 100 games over .500, and all were at least 44 games over .500. Phil Niekro was only 44 games over, but the reasons for that are fairly obvious; Niekro pitched most of his career for bad teams, and also allowed more than 300 unearned runs, many of them because of Passed Knuckleballs. Blyleven did neither of those things. He pitched for as many good teams as bad teams, and he allowed less than 200 unearned runs.

If Blyleven were one game over .500 for each four runs saved, he would have finished with about 311 career wins (311-226). The *Sabermetric Encyclopedia* credits Blyleven with 313 "Neutral Wins" (313-224). He's actually 287-250.

Blyleven's win-loss record is about 196 runs worse than his ERA. He is 37 games over .500; that's equivalent to 148 runs. He should be 344 runs better than average. That's a 196-run discrepancy. These odd ratios create a *prima facie* case that Blyleven was guilty of the failure to match the effort needed. I'm skeptical, but … we'll never know unless we look.

I. The Method

Suppose that we form a group of pitchers who are similar to Blyleven in terms of games started, innings pitched and ERA, but different from Blyleven in terms of wins and losses.

The group that I formed has seven pitchers—Steve Carlton, Tommy John, Jim Kaat, Ferguson Jenkins, Don Sutton and Phil Niekro, plus Blyleven. Carlton, Jenkins, Sutton and Niekro are in the Hall of Fame; Kaat and John aren't, but then their other stats aren't quite as good as Blyleven's, and besides, haven't you ever heard Kaat broadcast? Anyway, these seven pitchers made an average of 684 starts in their careers. Blyleven made 685. They pitched an average of 4,945 innings; Blyleven pitched 4,970. They allowed an average of 2,073 runs, 1,835 of them earned; Bert allowed 2,029 runs, 1,840 of them earned. They had an average ERA of 3.32; Blyleven's was 3.31. These pitchers, then, are on average very, very similar to Bert Blyleven. But whereas Blyleven won 287 games and is 37 games over .500, the other six won an average of 304 and are more than 60 games over.. Among the seven pitchers, Blyleven is first in runs saved against average (because he played in a slightly higher run context than the others), but last in winning percentage.

These pitchers are very similar to Blyleven in the aggregate, and they are also generally similar to him individually, particularly with regard to ERA. All of the pitchers have career ERAs within a few points of Blyleven's.

The key question is, why did Blyleven not win the games he should have won? There are two possible explanations:

1. Blyleven's run support was weaker than the other pitchers', and
2. Blyleven did a poorer job than the other pitchers of matching the effort.

What we mean, specifically, by failing to match the effort is that, given two runs to work with, he was less likely to deliver a victory than were the other pitchers in the group. Given three runs to work with, he was less likely to deliver a victory than were the other pitchers in the group. Given six runs to work with, he was more likely than the others to blow up and let the other team win anyway.

I compiled game-by-game pitching logs for the careers of each of these seven pitchers. Obviously, I used Retrosheet data to do this, and I am very grateful to Retrosheet for making this available, and also to several individuals (Dave Smith, Clem Comley and others) who responded to my request for help when I was missing a few appearances for Jim Kaat. Also my son Isaac helped me with this project.

Anyway, my purpose in doing this was to be able to look at all of the games started by Bert Blyleven and the other pitchers, and ask two questions:

1. When supported by X runs, how often did Blyleven deliver a win?
2. How does this compare to the other pitchers in the group?

I wanted to take a range of issues off the table, to focus directly on the ability to match the effort. Ferguson Jenkins was a better hitter than Blyleven, thus had more runs to work with? Doesn't matter. How he got the runs is not relevant to what we are talking about right now. Since these other pitchers allowed runs at the same rate that Blyleven did, then, given a certain number of runs to work with, he should have the same ability to win as they do—regardless of where the runs come from.

Don Sutton pitched in much lower run contexts than Blyleven? It doesn't matter. Their career ERAs are essentially the same. If two pitchers have the same ERA, one would expect them to have the same ability to win, given a certain level of run support. The fact that one of them works in a hitter's park and one in a pitcher's park doesn't change that. It changes their expected run support, but not their expected win-loss record with a fixed level of run support. Nothing should change the pitcher's ability to win with a given level of run support, except, to a minor extent, unearned runs. And we're not worrying about the unearned runs because Blyleven didn't allow many unearned runs, which therefore can't be the reason he didn't win more.

II. Data Point

Before giving you the straight results, let me first report on one rather stunning data point from the study.

When given three runs to work with—not three or more but three exactly—Don Sutton had a career win-loss record of 52-33, and his teams had a win-loss record of 65-51.

When given three runs to work with, Bert Blyleven had a career win-loss record of 29-48, and his teams had a career record of 35-62..

Sutton's winning percentage, working with three runs, was .612. Blyleven's was .377.

In other words, just in this one data point—three runs to work with—Don Sutton was a whopping 19 games better than Blyleven, and his teams were 20 ½ games better. If that data were representative of the entire study to even a tiny extent, we would have to conclude that Sutton was massively better than Blyleven at matching the effort needed to win the game.

III. Actual Results of the Study

Blyleven's relatively poor win-loss records are primarily a result of poor offensive support. He was below the group average in terms of his ability to match the effort of the opposing pitcher, and this did cost him a few games over the course of his career—somewhere between 7 and 11 games. But most of the discrepancy is caused by sub-standard offensive support.

In Blyleven's 685 major league starts, his team scored 2,869 runs, or 4.19 runs per start. This is the data for the seven pitchers in the study:

Pitcher	GS	Tm Runs	Average
Jenkins	594	2605	4.39
Kaat	625	2737	4.38
Carlton	709	3096	4.37
John	700	2969	4.24
Niekro	716	3022	4.22
Blyleven	685	2869	4.19
Sutton	756	3130	4.14

Blyleven's offensive support was the second-poorest among the group of seven pitchers—and it is actually worse than the average reveals (although not worse than Sutton's). The next chart gives the winning percentage of their teams with one of these pitchers on the mound and a given number of runs to work with:

Offensive Support		Wpct
More than 12	runs	1.000
12	runs	.959
11	runs	.964
10	runs	.963
9	runs	.916
8	runs	.857
7	runs	.882
6	runs	.805
5	runs	.734
4	runs	.579
3	runs	.474
2	runs	.347
1	runs	.151
0	runs	.000

The average number of runs per start can be misleading in this way: that 10 runs in one game and a shutout in the next are not the same as five runs in each start. If you give one of these pitchers five runs in each of two starts, that creates an expectation of 1.468 wins. If you give him 10 runs in one start but none in the next, that creates an expectation of 0.963 wins—a large difference. Blyleven's offensive support is actually worse than it looks, because he had a disproportionate number of games when he was denied those critical first few runs which have an exaggerated impact on the win total.

This chart gives the number of times in his career that Blyleven was supported by each number of runs:

Support		G
More than 12	runs	11
12	runs	8
11	runs	6
10	runs	16
9	runs	19
8	runs	36
7	runs	43
6	runs	46
5	runs	90
4	runs	82
3	runs	97
2	runs	104
1	runs	85
0	runs	42

Blyleven was shut out 42 times in his career, which is a little below the group average. But he was forced to work with one or two runs 189 times in his career, or 28% of his career starts. By contrast, Ferguson Jenkins was limited to one or two runs in only 22% of his career starts, Phil Niekro 23%, and no other pitcher in the group more than 26%.

We can figure, for each pitcher, his "expected team winning percentage", based on the charts above. If the pitcher's team scores seven runs, this creates an expectation of .882 wins, since the winning percentage of their teams with one of these pitchers on the mound and 7 runs on the scoreboard was .882. But if the team scores only one run, that creates an expectation of only .151 wins.

Blyleven's teams, by the number of runs they scored, had an expectation of 371 wins, 313 losses and one tie in 685 starts. Their actual record was 364-321. Blyleven fell short by seven and a half games, and it may be appropriate to dock him somewhere between 60 and 85 runs for that shortfall.

But of the 196-run discrepancy in Blyleven's career (the discrepancy between his runs saved and his win-loss record), about two-thirds is explained by poor offensive support. Only about one-third is attributable to his failure to match the effort needed.

I highlighted before the remarkable difference between Sutton and Blyleven in working with three runs. But only Sutton was that effective with three runs. Niekro, Kaat and Steve Carlton, given three runs to work with, had losing records.

Working with just one run, Blyleven tied Carlton for the best winning percentage in the group (.188). Blyleven's 15 career 1-0 victories is one of the highest totals of all time; this is well known. Working with four runs, six runs, seven runs or eight runs, Blyleven was better than Sutton. This narrows the gap between them.

Blyleven was stuck with just one run to work with 85 times in his career—compared to 57 times for Ferguson Jenkins, 69 for Kaat, 71 for Carlton and 59 for Phil Niekro. Since those games are almost automatic losses, that in itself is a huge difference between Blyleven and his peers. (Only Don Sutton had as many one-run challenges as Blyleven.) But in the "nearly automatic victory" categories of six runs and up, Blyleven had only 185 in his career—as opposed to 208 for Niekro, 220 for Carlton, 219 for Sutton, 200 for Jim Kaat, and 207 for Tommy John. Only Ferguson Jenkins had fewer than Blyleven—and he had far more as a percentage of his starts. Blyleven had six or more runs to work with in only 27% of his career starts, whereas all of the other pitchers in the study had six or more in at least 29% of their starts.

It may sound like a small thing, but Steve Carlton had 151 wins those games; he was 151-11. Blyleven had a better percentage, but he had only 128 wins (he was 128-6). He's short by 23 wins, 18 if you adjust for games started. It's the difference between 288 wins and 300-

plus. Thus, that's what's keeping him out of the Hall of Fame—a documented shortage of easy wins.

IV. Other Studies of the Issue

On a blog, someone named Chris posted this comment:

His toughest loss was on September 22, 1972 when the eventual champion Athletics beat him 1-0 in the 11th inning. His game score was 82. Twice he got the loss with a game score over 80, seventeen times when it was over 70, 47 times when it was over 60, and 118 times when it was over 50. Though the number of tough losses always is far greater than the number of cheap wins for the six pitchers I've checked so far, Blyleven still has a very high number of tough losses.

Defining a "Cheap Win" as any win in which the pitcher had a Game Score under 50 and a "Tough Loss" as any loss in which the pitcher had a Game Score over 50, Blyleven had 26 Cheap Wins and 109 Tough Losses. The chart on the bottom of the page gives the data for the seven comparable pitchers:

Blyleven did have more tough losses than the comparable pitchers. It doesn't seem to me that this is all that helpful in the discussion. First, there is the problem of strikeouts figuring into Game Scores, which is a pretty minor problem but some people will choose to worry about it. A bigger problem is that it seems to me that if a pitcher did have an "inability to match", this might well result in a larger number of tough losses—not as a result of tough luck, but as a result of his inability to pitch well at the times he most needs to pitch well. The most striking thing on the chart, really, is the very small number of cheap wins by Steve Carlton.

On Baseball Think Factory (www.baseballthinkfactory.org/), Mike Emeigh wrote.

I have checked the numbers. I looked at his run support on the basis of the game situation at the time of his departure, not a full game or per-nine-

	GS >50 W-L	GS<50 W-L	Cheap Wins	Tough Losses
Blyleven	257-109	26-130	26	109
John	245- 67	33-157	33	67
Jenkins	250- 97	25-117	25	97
Kaat	223- 70	35-142	35	70
Sutton	289-102	29-143	29	102
Carlton	311-101	15-133	15	101
Niekro	272-102	27-157	27	102

inning basis; IOW, if Blyleven got three runs of batting support through seven innings in which his team batted (he could have pitched anywhere from 6 innings to 7 2/3 innings in those games, depending on location and when he was removed from the game).

Well, but what if Blyleven pitched five innings and left with the score 2-1, then his team scored two more runs in the seventh inning, making the score 4-1. Are those runs scored in support of Blyleven, or aren't they?

It seems to me that they are. As long as Blyleven is the pitcher of record, runs scored by his team are scored in support of his win-loss record. I don't see how carving those runs out of the study makes for a more accurate study, and in fact I would argue that it doesn't.

Or consider this situation: Blyleven pitches six innings and leaves the game trailing 3-2. In the eighth inning his team scores 3 runs to take a 5-3 lead. Should those runs be counted in Blyleven's account, or shouldn't they?

Well, of course they should, because without them, Blyleven is charged with a defeat. Runs scored which have the effect of taking a loss away from the pitcher, it seems to me, obviously should not excluded.

How do we decide which runs to count in Blyleven's support and which not? I don't know. It's a confusing issue, and I don't have an answer. But here's what I think about it.

First, the rules by which major league baseball credits wins and losses to individual pitchers are objectively silly, and there is no reason for a serious analyst to pay much attention to them in the process of figuring out what a pitcher's "true" value has been. The more appropriate thing to do is to study the impact of Blyleven on the win-loss record of his team.

Second, Blyleven averaged 7.24 innings pitched per start throughout his career.

Unless we have real evidence that something weird is going on, like a colossal collapse of the bullpen or a bunch of runs being scored in a very few innings after Blyleven left, aren't we better off assuming that the entire game represents a Blyleven game, rather than enter into a speculative and uncertain analysis based on questionable attribution of runs scored in support of Blyleven as an individual pitcher?

Third, Blyleven's individual winning percentage was .534. The winning percentage of his teams in games that he started was .531—a lower figure than for any of the comparable pitchers except Niekro (also .531).

What reason is there to believe that studying the innings specifically charged to Blyleven—even if we did know how to do that accurately—would give us a different answer than studying the entire games?

Emeigh concludes:

Ergo, the difference between Blyleven and Hunter, Tiant, et. al. is almost entirely due to the fact that those other pitchers were better supported on a game-by-game basis.

I didn't deal with Hunter and Tiant, but I don't think that is quite true. I think that it is more the offense than the failure to match the effort needed, but it seems clear to me that there is also some actual failure to match on Blyleven's part.

Another researcher, Eric Chalek, studied Blyleven's bullpen support. A summary of Chalek's research by some unidentifiable blogger is as follows:

(Chalek) found that there were 28 games in which Blyleven left the game losing only to be let off the hook as the offense came back for him. His record in those games was 1-0. Three times when he left a tie game the bullpen allowed inherited runners to score go ahead runs for the opposition. Blyleven ended up losing all those games. In another 47 games he left leading only to see the bullpen blow the lead. Blyleven got tagged for the loss in 3 of those games. Altogether his record was 1-6 in which the score changed hands after he left the game.

How un/lucky is that? Hard to say without a way to measure it. A record of 1-6 does sound rather unlucky though. Those games represent 11.4% of his starts. I have no idea if that's a high or low percentage for something like this because a sample size of one is tough to draw conclusions from. Also, in those 71 no-decisions, there's 17 more games where a lead was blown than gained. That's high but for a good pitcher it should be high (he should hand off more leads than deficits to the bullpen).

Sorting out 3 relief decision he had, and his complete games, it appears that Blyleven handed 164 leads over to his bullpen and 196 times he handed them a deficit. By blowing 47 leads, his bullpen preserved 71.3% of his leads, but they preserved 85.7% of the deficits (168/196 — you get 168 by subtracting the 196 deficits mentioned here from the 28 rallies listed in the previous paragraph). Again, that sounds high.

I didn't study Blyleven's bullpen support, so I can't comment on that directly. However, Chalek apparently didn't study any comparable pitchers in this regard, so his data is without context, and maybe I can suggest a little context.

Blyleven made 685 career starts, and pitched 4,957.1 innings in those starts. If we assume that those games lasted nine innings on average—an assumption which carries a substantial degree of risk—that would suggest that his bullpen may have pitched about 1,207.2 innings after he left the game.

Blyleven was charged with 2,021 runs allowed as a starting pitcher. The total runs scored by the opposition in games that he started were 2,547. Thus, Blyleven's bullpens allowed 526 runs to score in approximate-ly 1,207.2 innings, a number that could be seriously in error. But, as best I can estimate, Blyleven's bullpens allowed about 3.91 runs per nine innings.

Blyleven was 286-248 as a starting pitcher; his teams were 364-321 in those games. His bullpen, then, was 78 and 73.

These numbers do not appear to be remarkably different from the bullpen numbers of the compa-rable pitchers. As you can see on the following chart, Blyleven's bullpens had fewer wins and more losses and a higher estimated runs allowed average than the group norms, but not remarkably so. His bullpen support was probably a little bit on the weak side.

Pitcher	Innings	Runs	R Avg	Wins	Losses
Blyleven	1207.1	526	3.92	78	73
Carlton	1215.2	502	3.72	76	65
Jenkins	987.1	403	3.67	59	38
John	1677.2	725	3.89	102	85
Kaat	1487.1	589	3.56	85	60
Niekro	1294.1	641	4.46	77	73
Sutton	1555.2	634	3.67	98	84
Average	1346.5	574	3.84	79.5	65.7

V. One-Run Games

One-run games have an obvious bearing on this study. Remember the what-if example I gave in part one of this admittedly too long study?

One, whom we will call Ferguson Winner, loses a game 6-0, but wins six others 1-0, 2-1, 3-2, 4-3, 5-4 and 6-5. The other, whom we will call Bert Loser, wins a game 6-0, but loses six others by the same scores (1-0, 2-1, etc.)

In that example, Ferguson Winner has a record of 6-0 in one-run games, while Bert Loser has a record of 0-6 in one-run games. If there were a pitcher who had an inability to win the close, low-scoring games, obvi-ously that should be reflected in his record in one-run games.

Blyleven has the poorest record in one-run games of any pitcher in this study. The chart below gives:

A) the pitcher's individual wins in one-run games,

B) his losses,

C) his winning percentage,

D) his team's wins,

E) his team's losses.

Pitcher	A	B	C	D	E
Carlton	68	58	.540	113	104
Sutton	69	63	.523	138	121
Kaat	64	60	.516	118	103
John	63	63	.500	124	120
Niekro	62	64	.492	115	107
Jenkins	63	71	.470	103	95
Blyleven	56	75	.427	113	122

VI. Conclusion

Although Blyleven's critics have made too much of his disappointing win-loss record, there *is* something there. Blyleven did not do an A+ job of matching his effort to the runs that he had to work with.

However, this probably should not be keeping him out of the Hall of Fame. Blyleven was 344 runs better than an average pitcher. The largest penalty that we could reasonably charge him for failing to match his best games with the games that he had a chance to win would be about 83 runs. (That leaves him 261 runs better-than-league. I explained earlier how I derived the 83-run figure, but it used up three pages with boring math, so I cut it. Sorry.)

There are ten pitchers in history who are 240 to 280 runs better than league: Bob Feller, Eddie Plank, Ferguson Jenkins, Jack Stivetts, Ed Walsh, Clark Griffith, Rube Waddell, Old Hoss Radbourn, Juan Marichal and Dazzy Vance. All except Stivetts are in the Hall of Fame.

Also, look at it this way. Suppose that Blyleven has a seven-game stretch during which he wins games 13-0 and 5-2, but then loses 3-2, 4-3, 3-2, 7-4 and 3-2. Those are the actual scores of Blyleven's games from May 3 to June 4, 1977. Blyleven was supported by 4.43 runs per game during that stretch and allowed 3.14, but he lost five of the seven games.

One *can* look at that and say that Blyleven failed to match his efforts to the runs he had to work with—but why is that all Blyleven's fault? Isn't it equally true that his offense failed to match *their* efforts to Bert's better games? It seems to me that it is.

So why do we hold Blyleven wholly responsible for this? Wouldn't it be equally reasonable to say that this was half Blyleven's fault, and half his team's fault?

That would cut the 83-run penalty to a 42-run penalty, and that would put Blyleven back over 300—over 300 wins, and over 300 runs saved against average. That's Hall of Fame territory. All the guys over 300 are Hall of Famers except Tommy Bridges (301) and the guys who are still active. Blyleven probably should be in there, too.

Analysis

What's So Magic about 100 Pitches?

by John Dewan

This business of managers watching pitch counts so closely seems silly to me. As the starting pitcher approaches 100 pitches, it's like a time bomb ticking. Any time a pitcher gets his pitch count up into the 90s—one walk and he's out of there.

What's so magic about 100 pitches? Is it simply because it's a three-digit number? I don't think there's a mechanism in a pitcher's arm that triggers at 100 pitches.

My theory for years has been that managers baby their starting pitchers. Back in my day I used to walk five miles to school … in the snow … each way. And managers used to stay with their starters deep into the game. These pitchers were men. The work made their arms stronger. Who cares about pitch count?

It makes sense, doesn't it? If you want to get stronger you work out. You lift weights in a repetitive motion. The harder you work, the stronger you get. You do have to rest—when you're building muscle, you're actually causing small injuries in the muscle. The body cures those injuries and builds muscle. Resting allows the body to do that. Of course, starting pitchers rest too. That's been done for 100 years in baseball.

Now White Sox manager Ozzie Guillen has proven my point. Four straight complete game wins in one playoff series. That's completely unheard of. Ozzie has the slowest hook in baseball. I'm not just saying that; here are the numbers:

Most Slow Hooks, American League, 2005 Season

Ozzie Guillen	CWS	55
Terry Francona	Bos	55
Lou Piniella	TB	54
Mike Hargrove	Sea	45
Joe Torre	NYY	44

Source: *Bill James Handbook 2006*

This is a new definition by Bill James, replacing an older one he developed many years ago. This definition is based on pitch count and runs allowed. If a manager pulls the starter after fewer pitches and fewer runs than other managers, that's a quick hook. If he leaves him in after more pitches and more runs, that's a slow hook.

Only one manager in baseball had more slow hooks than Ozzie last year. Clint Hurdle had 60 for the Colorado Rockies. But he really has no choice; with all the hitting at Coors Field, he has to keep his starters in longer.

What we have here then is a manager who allows his pitchers to grow stronger during the season by keeping them in the game. They reward him at the end of the year by doing their best work. Their arms have gotten stronger, not weaker, because of the extra work. Ozzie Guillen, genius!

All right, I admit it. This is anecdotal evidence. I just want to gloat a bit … about the World Champion Chicago White Sox!

Let's see if we can find more data to support my position. Baseball Info Solutions (BIS) has pitch count data from 2002 to 2005. Unfortunately I don't have access to the data going back to the late 1980s at my old company, STATS, Inc, but we do have boxscore data from the good folks at Retrosheet (www.retrosheet.org) going back to 1974. Using the pitcher line scores, and information from BIS (like the average number of pitches on a walk is 5.62), we can come up with a very good pitch count estimate for every game and every pitcher going back to 1974.

Were men really men back in the mid-'70s? Yes, and here's proof:

Seasons	Avg Number of Pitches By Starters
1974-1975	102.4
1976-1978	99.9
1979-1980	98.4
1981-1988	97.5
1989-2005	96.0

There's been a steady decline in pitch counts over the last 30 years. Maybe it's not quite as dramatic as I might have expected, but it's clearly there.

But the real question I want to ask is: Do starters get stronger later in the season if they work deeper into games (i.e. throw more pitches) early in the season?

Let's look at that 100-pitch mark going back to 1974. Here's a chart that compares pitchers who averaged 100 or more pitches in the first half of the season to those who averaged fewer than 100:

Ave Pitches per Start First Half of Season	First Half ERA	Second Half ERA
Less than 100	5.05	4.67
100 or More	3.87	4.16

Starting Pitchers 1974-2005

Whoa! Wait a minute. That's not what I expected. It shows the opposite of what I expected. I thought that pitchers who worked deep into games in the first half (averaged 100 or more pitches) would have their ERA improve in the second half. Their ERA actually got worse. And those who didn't pitch deep into games actually improved in the second half.

What's going on here? We can find a clue if we look at the first-half ERA for the two groups. Pitchers who average fewer than 100 pitches had an ERA more than a full run higher than those with more pitches (5.05 vs. 3.87). I believe we have a problem of cause and effect. The pitchers with the 5.05 ERA are being pulled before 100 pitches because they are ineffective, not to protect their arms.

When I asked Bill James for his opinion on the chart, he pretty much said the same thing. In his e-mail he wrote,

> *There's a selection problem. Pitchers who are pitching well in the first half of the season will be much, much more likely to exceed the 100-pitch threshold consistently … thus will tend to pitch less well in the second half. Pitchers who are pitching badly in the first half of the season will less often reach the 100-pitch threshold, and also (incidentally) are more likely to pitch better in the second half. You need to sort by ERA in the first half to get a different look at the picture … that is, pitchers with ERAs of 4.00 the first half of the season … those who have 100-pitch games, those who don't…*

Let's do exactly that. First, let's look at all pitchers comparing first-half ERAs to second-half ERAs regardless of pitch count. We'll put all pitchers into groups based on their first-half ERA. One group is all those pitchers who had an ERA under 3.00 in the first half. A second group includes all those with first-half ERAs between 3.00 and 3.99. Another group is for ERAs in the fours, and a final group for ERAs in the fives. We'll ignore pitchers with first-half ERAs over 6.00 for two reasons: there are far fewer of them compared to other groups, and they

are generally ineffective and not of as much interest. Here's the chart:

First Half ERA Group	# of First Half Starts	First Half ERA	Second Half ERA
Under 3.00	8,227	2.53	3.58
3.00 to 3.99	15,925	3.50	3.82
4.00 to 4.99	13,813	4.44	4.11
5.00 to 5.99	5,952	5.42	4.41

Starting Pitchers 1974-2005

The first thing to note is that we have a lot of data here. We have a least 5,000 first-half starts in each group. The second thing is "regression towards the mean." Namely, pitchers who pitch well in the first half tend to pitch less effectively in the second half and pitchers who don't pitch as well improve in the second half. This makes sense. Over a half season, all players will tend to perform at greater extremes than they will for a whole season. They tend to even out as the season progresses. Nevertheless, we do also see that pitchers who have a good first half also tend to perform better in the second half than pitchers who don't have a good first half.

So, what are we looking for relative to 100-pitch starts? Within each ERA group we'll break the data down between pitchers averaging above and below 100 pitches. If my theory has merit we should see, within each ERA group, second half ERAs that are better for those pitchers who average 100 or more pitches in the first half. Here's the data:

First-Half ERA Group	Ave First Half Pitches per Start	First-Half ERA	Second-Half ERA
Under 3.00	100 or More	2.52	3.47
	Less than 100	2.55	3.90
3.00 to 3.99	100 or More	3.47	3.73
	Less than 100	3.54	3.97
4.00 to 4.99	100 or More	4.38	3.99
	Less than 100	4.48	4.19
5.00 to 5.99	100 or More	5.37	4.36
	Less than 100	5.43	4.43

Starting Pitchers 1974-2005

Now that's more like it. The pattern I wanted to see is there. Maybe it's not quite as strong as I would like, but it's clearly there. In each of the first three ERA groups, pitchers with higher first-half pitch counts perform better in the second half. The final ERA group is neutral. There's a trend as well. The second half improvement is strongest for the best pitchers. Here's how I would summarize the improvement:

First-Half ERA Group:
Improvement due to Averaging 100
or More pitches in the First Half

Under 3.00	40 ERA points
3.00 to 3.99	20 ERA points
4.00 to 4.99	10 ERA points
Over 4.99	No change

All in all, there seems to be some evidence here that managers should be less concerned about pulling pitchers at the 100-pitch mark. It appears that the better pitchers will tend to remain stronger in the second half if they work a little harder in the first half.

This is only the tip of the iceberg. As with the first chart we discussed, there can be other factors at work here. Maybe the data has some kind of bias that I haven't considered. Or maybe injuries are a factor. Maybe there are more injuries by pitching deeper into games that negate the second half improvement. These are all things that can be researched in future studies.

But I do like what I'm seeing here!

Are You Feeling Lucky?
by Dan Fox

The element of luck in baseball is significant ... The result is a game that can be studied, scrutinized, and understood to the minutest detail, and yet one still has to play the games, and watch them, because no one can predict what will actually happen.

– Author Cecilia Tan

It is often said that "baseball is a game of inches." What lies just under the surface of that bit of conventional wisdom is the element of luck that pervades baseball as described in Tan's quote. In the last few years the role of luck has come to the forefront of the performance analysis community in at least three ways I'll briefly review.

First, in 2001 there was Voros McCracken's Defense Independent Pitching (DIPs) system: The core idea is that pitchers generally don't have as much control over whether batted balls (other than perhaps home runs) become hits as is commonly perceived. McCracken demonstrated this by examining the correlation between the batting average on balls in play against a pitcher, again minus home runs, across seasons. What he found was that essentially there was no correlation from year to year, so he concluded that chance and not skill rules once a pitcher releases the ball. This insight revolutionized the way in which pitching statistics have been viewed. For example, in the stats section of this book is a simpler variant of DIPs called Fielding Independent Pitching (FIP) that we calculate for each pitcher that attempts to measure all of those things for which a pitcher is specifically responsible. You'll notice hits are not included in the formula.

Other researchers such as Tom Tippett subsequently showed that some pitchers, particularly knuckleballers, do have an ability to influence batting average on balls in play but that there is still a large element of luck involved. And our own David Gassko moved the ball forward with some further and more complex work on DIPs this season which can be found at http://www.hardballtimes.com/main/article/batted-balls-and-dips/.

The flip side of DIPs is the increasing visibility of the idea that a hitter's batting average is more variable than most casual fans, and some media members, understand. In other words, luck also plays a significant role in seasonal batting averages. In April 2004 Jim Albert, co-author of *Curve Ball*, published an article titled "A Batting Average: Does It Represent Ability or Luck?" In that article Albert showed that measures such as strikeout rate, walk rate, home run rate and on-base percentage were all much more strongly correlated from year to year than batting average on balls in play (removing the effect of strikeouts) as well as batting average itself. In short, as much as 50% of the difference in batting average among players can be attributed to luck, while 50% can be attributed to differences in their hitting abilities.

This conclusion is reinforced when you discover that balls hit on the ground are converted into outs around 75% of the time and that 45% of all singles are ground balls while line drives are converted into outs just 26% of the time and 50% of doubles hit are line drives. Because ground balls are inherently easier to convert into outs, it stands to reason that there is a much larger element of luck in determining which ground balls end up getting through the infield for singles and which are turned into outs.

As an aside, this is one reason (and only one since there are obviously personal and personnel factors that would be thrown into the mix) that if I were a GM I would rather have the Phillies' Ryan Howard over the Astros' Willy Taveras. While Taveras played very well, offensively I would view him as a bigger risk because much more of his value is tied up in his .291 batting average which may prove to contain a larger element of luck. Howard's value, on the other hand, is tied up in the less variable measures of slugging percentage (.567) and on base percentage (.356).

Finally, Bill James published an article entitled "Underestimating the Fog" in the *2005 Baseball Research Journal* that stirred the waters in the debate over the role of luck. In the article James challenged the almost 30-year practice of devising studies to determine if a particular effect (clutch hitting or hitting left-handed pitchers for example) persisted across seasons or was simply transient and therefore the result of chance.

James argued that in many of these cases the negative conclusion—the phenomena is not real—is flawed because there is too much variability in the data used to make that conclusion. For example, the conclusion that there is no specific ability to hit well or poorly against left-handed pitching is based on platoon differentials where the number of plate appearances against left-handed pitchers is around 120 per season. The randomness involved in such a small sample size tends to swamp the differential itself, thereby making the results meaningless. His subtler point was that sometimes the magnitude of the phenomena under study—if it exists—is smaller than the magnitude of the normal variation in the statistics we use to try and study it. In other words, while a skill like clutch hitting may indeed exist in the real world, the noise or fog in the data used to try and measure it will obscure our finding and measuring that skill.

The long-held belief that clutch hitting is essentially random was one of those conclusions that James now believes was perhaps too quickly adopted. Several articles in *By The Numbers,* a response from James and a very comprehensive study by Tom Ruane kept the debate going this summer. Although good points were made on both sides, the fundamental issue was the role that chance plays in the game and how to measure it.

Lucky or Good?

All of these cases illustrate that luck plays a role in the outcomes of individual games and in the performances of individual players in a season. But what role does luck play at the team level over an entire season? And since you're reading a book recapping the 2005 season, specifically what role, if any, did luck play over the course of last season?

In order to attempt to answer that question I stood on the shoulders of others and was inspired to write this article based on the notes from Phil Birnbaum's presentation given at the annual Society for American Baseball Research convention in Toronto titled "Were the 1994 Expos Just Lucky?" In that presentation Phil noted that there are five ways that teams can be lucky:

- Hitters having unexpected career years
- Pitchers having unexpected career years
- A team scoring more runs than expected by their batting line
- A team allowing fewer runs than expected by the opposition's batting line
- A team winning more games than expected by its ratio of runs scored to runs allowed

While all five of these are certainly valid, for a single-year analysis like the one in this article we'll have to throw out hitters and pitchers having unexpected career years, because when analyzing the most recent season it's difficult to tell whether the performance of a player is an outlier or whether he's established a new performance level for himself. This is especially the case for younger players on teams like the Indians. The other three, however, we can take a look at for 2005 and add a few interesting twists along the way.

Scoring More Runs than Expected

Estimating the number of runs a team will score based on their offensive elements has been a favorite pastime of performance analysts for 35 years. For this article I've used the most recent Base Runs (BsR) formula published by David Smyth last June and adjusted for the 2005 season. Like Bill James's better-known Runs Created (RC) formula, BsR is a multiplicative formula, but I prefer it because its underlying model is more intuitive than RC.

Using that formula I've ranked the teams in order by the biggest negative difference between their actual runs scored and their BsR estimate.

Team	Lg	BsR	R	Diff
Diamondbacks	NL	764	696	68
Cubs	NL	753	703	50
Padres	NL	710	684	26
Indians	AL	814	790	24
Orioles	AL	752	729	23
Pirates	NL	698	680	18
Marlins	NL	733	717	16
Astros	NL	707	693	14
Brewers	NL	740	726	14
Mets	NL	732	722	10
Reds	NL	830	820	10
Tigers	AL	732	723	9
Giants	NL	658	649	9
Nationals	NL	648	639	9
Phillies	NL	813	807	6
Devil Rays	AL	750	750	0
Dodgers	NL	683	685	-2
White Sox	AL	739	741	-2
Braves	NL	765	769	-4
Rockies	NL	734	740	-6
Yankees	AL	879	886	-7
Rangers	AL	854	865	-11
Twins	AL	674	688	-14
Red Sox	AL	887	910	-23
Mariners	AL	665	699	-34
Royals	AL	666	701	-35
Cardinals	NL	766	805	-39
Angels	AL	721	761	-40
Blue Jays	AL	734	775	-41
Athletics	AL	727	772	-45

In other words, the Diamondbacks scored 68 fewer runs than would have been expected given the combination of their offensive elements while the A's outperformed their estimate of runs scored by 45. (Isn't it a little scary that the Royals outperformed their estimate by 35 runs?)

Are the differences here purely the result of luck? Well, that depends on how you define luck.

As mentioned previously, one of the debates in the performance analysis community that heated up this summer is the role luck plays in measures such as clutch hitting. One of the reasons the Diamondbacks scored fewer runs than expected is certainly their .237 average with runners in scoring position (the major league average was .267) and their .250 batting average with runners on base (league average was .271). Meanwhile the Blue Jays hit .287 with runners on and had a RISP batting average of .267, while the Angels hit .280 with runners on with a .296 RISP average. And as you would expect, in 2005 there was a positive, if not particularly strong, correlation between both batting average with runners on base and RISP batting average and runs scored above a team's Base Runs estimate.

If you believe that clutch hitting is essentially good fortune, then you would conclude that the Diamondbacks were unlucky offensively while the Blue Jays, A's, Cardinals and Angels, among others, were fortunate to bunch their hits and therefore score more runs than expected given their talent as indicated by their BsR estimate. On the other hand if you believe that clutch hitting is a real, albeit hard to measure, skill then you might try and factor RISP or similar statistics into the run estimation formula much like James does when computing RC for individual players. My own view, and following most of the performance analysis community, is that if clutch hitting exists at all, its effects are so small that they needn't be considered at the individual or the team level, so I didn't make any adjustments for them here.

Obviously, there are also other factors that one might reasonably guess go into whether or not a team exceeds their BsR estimates such as managerial skill, good base running (or a lack thereof) and the ability to move runners. But again the consensus of the performance analysis community has been that there is no evidence that these make a significant difference in the course of a season.

Allowing Fewer Runs than Expected

Of course the same approach can be used when analyzing the pitching side of the ledger. The Base Runs formula can be applied to the aggregate pitching statistics for each team in order to see which pitching staffs were greater than the sum of their parts and which weren't. The following table lists the differences between BsR and runs allowed ranked by largest positive difference.

Team	Lg	BsR	RA	Diff
Braves	NL	709	674	35
Angels	AL	673	643	30
Reds	NL	914	889	25
Giants	NL	698	673	25
White Sox	AL	668	645	23
Blue Jays	AL	728	705	23
Rockies	NL	884	862	22
Astros	NL	629	609	20
Brewers	NL	715	697	18
Nationals	NL	663	648	15
Cardinals	NL	642	634	8
Phillies	NL	726	726	0
Cubs	NL	708	714	-6
Indians	AL	739	745	-6
Padres	NL	720	726	-6
Marlins	NL	744	751	-7
Red Sox	AL	797	805	-8
Dodgers	NL	745	755	-10
Diamondbacks	NL	846	856	-10
Twins	AL	650	662	-12
Pirates	NL	757	769	-12
Mets	NL	720	732	-12
Mariners	AL	628	642	-14
Athletics	AL	637	658	-21
Yankees	AL	751	789	-38
Tigers	AL	746	787	-41
Orioles	AL	759	800	-41
Royals	AL	890	935	-45
Rangers	AL	801	858	-57
Devil Rays	AL	868	936	-68

Here the Braves came out on top, having outperformed their BsR estimate by 35 runs, while the Devil Rays gave up 68 more runs than would have been expected given the offensive events that opposing batters racked up.

The same arguments about RISP can be applied to pitching if you assume that some pitchers have the ability to turn it up a notch when the game is on the line or that others are perennial choke artists. Once again, however, there is little evidence that this is a skill that can be differentiated from simple luck, so I didn't make any adjustments for a team's performance in clutch situations.

But what about DIPs? Shouldn't the concept of batting average on balls in play being governed to a large extent by luck be applied at the team level?

Keep in mind that all types of hits figure prominently in the Base Runs formula, so it is only concerned with estimating run scoring assuming those hits have already been recorded. Applying DIPs theory to team pitching statistics (or for that matter hitting statistics) would take the analysis back a step to consider how many of those hits might otherwise have been outs given a little luck here and there or vice versa.

And while it's true that factors out of a pitcher's control play a significant role in batting average on balls in play for individual pitchers, they do not do so to the same extent for teams. The rationale is that part of the reason a ground ball becomes an out or a hit is the quality of the defense—a quality that is often measured using Defensive Efficiency Ratio (DER), which is the ratio of batted balls other than home runs that were converted into outs. You can find team DER listed in the team totals later in this book.

Scoring Runs When They Count

The final non-overlapping aspect where we might be able to detect some good fortune is by comparing a team's record with their estimated record based on the ratio of the runs scored and the runs allowed. The relationship between the two and a team's record was dubbed the Pythagorean method by Bill James in an early Baseball Abstract. In all its forms the method looks as follows:

$$\text{Expected W\%} = R^x / (R^x + RA^x)$$

where x is an exponent with values ranging from 1.83 to 2 depending on your preference. A more refined version has been published by U.S. Patriot and dubbed Pythagenpat where the exponent x is calculated as:

$$X = ((R+RA)/G)^{2.85}$$

which for 2005 comes out to 1.881.

One can then compare this estimated winning percentage with a team's actual winning percentage to determine how many games above or below the estimate they were. The following table lists each team's record followed by their Pythagenpat record and how the two compare.

Team	Lg	W	PythW	Diff
Nationals	NL	81	69	12
Diamondbacks	NL	77	65	12
Indians	AL	93	85	8
White Sox	AL	99	92	7
Padres	NL	82	76	6
Yankees	AL	95	90	5
Red Sox	AL	95	90	5
Devil Rays	AL	67	64	3
Angels	AL	95	94	1
Cardinals	NL	100	99	1
Orioles	AL	74	74	0
Cubs	NL	79	80	-1
Twins	AL	83	84	-1
Braves	NL	90	91	-1
Phillies	NL	88	89	-1
Reds	NL	73	75	-2
Astros	NL	89	91	-2
Rockies	NL	67	69	-2
Dodgers	NL	71	74	-3
Rangers	AL	79	82	-3
Brewers	NL	81	84	-3
Mets	NL	83	86	-3
Tigers	AL	71	75	-4
Royals	AL	56	60	-4
Pirates	NL	67	72	-5
Athletics	AL	88	93	-5
Marlins	NL	83	89	-6
Giants	NL	75	82	-7
Blue Jays	AL	80	88	-8
Mariners	AL	69	77	-8

So based on the ratio of their runs scored and runs allowed, the Nationals would have been expected to win just 69 games when in fact they broke even with 81 wins. On the other end of the spectrum, the Blue Jays actually were one game below .500 when they would have been expected to be 7 games over.

What can account for these differences between teams?

The biggest aspect likely relates to how a team performs in games decided by one run. For example, the Diamondbacks went an amazing 28-18 in one-run games when they would have been expected to have gone more like 21-25 based on their runs scored and runs allowed given a Pythagorean-inspired formula developed by Bill James in 2002. Other teams of note include the White Sox, who won six more one-run games (35-19) than would have been expected (29-25), and the Padres, who won five more (29-20) than expected (24-25). On the reverse side, the Blue Jays were just 16-31 in one-run games when they would have been expected to go 24-23.

Among all teams there is a clear correlation between wins above Pythagenpat estimate and one-run wins above expected as shown in the following graph.

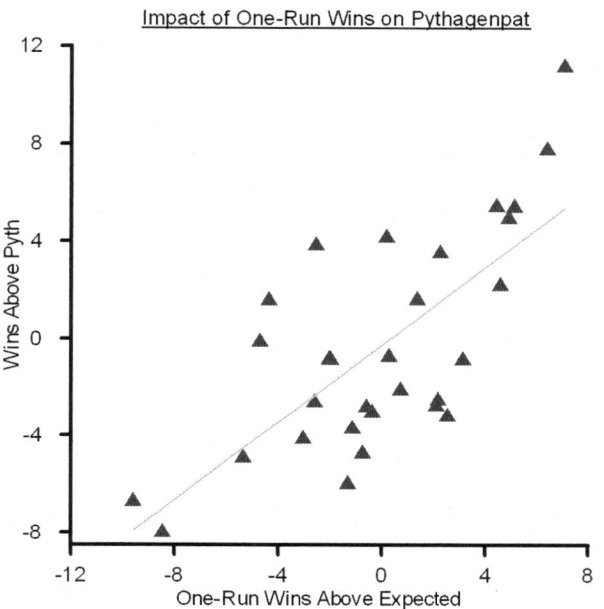

The general consensus in the performance analysis community has been that one-run wins (above those expected based on runs scored and runs allowed) are probably not a team skill but rather are governed mostly by luck.

A second but lesser factor is one our own Dave Studenmund pointed out earlier this season. He noted that the White Sox were doing very well in consistently scoring between two and seven runs which, with a decent pitching staff, enables teams to not only win lots of games, but with a little luck, many close ones as well. And as it turns out, for the season the White Sox won 17 of the 24 one-run games in which they scored between four and six runs.

Overall, their scoring distribution looked as follows for the year, where the dotted line indicates the major league average.

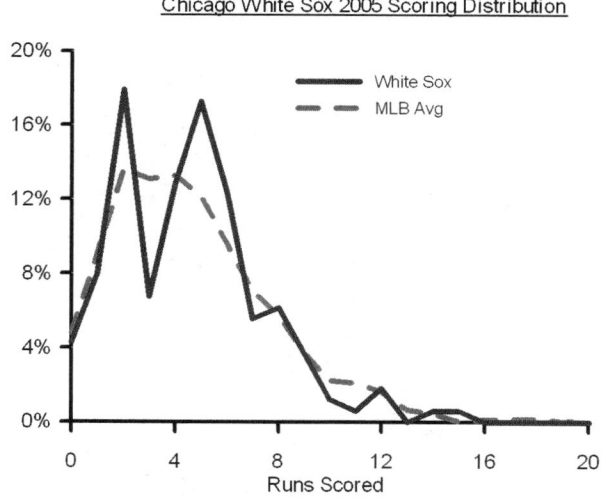

Teams that didn't fare so well in meeting their Pythagorean estimates tended to have trouble consistently scoring runs; for example, the Blue Jays who were just 16-31 in one-run games recorded the scoring distribution shown below.

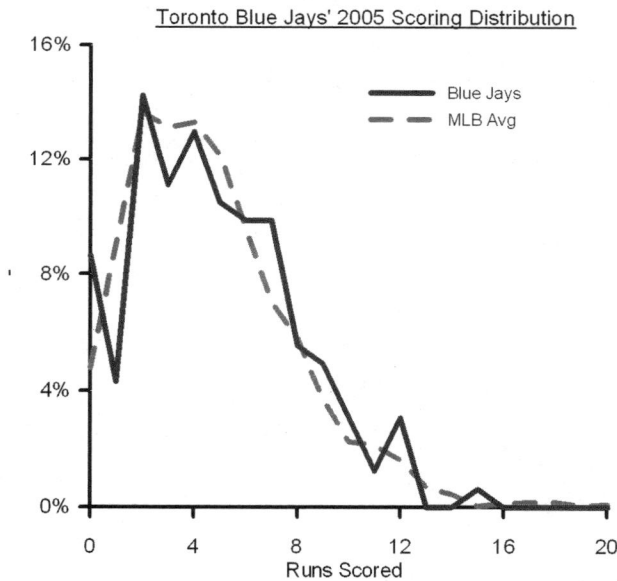

As you can see, the Blue Jays had trouble scoring between three and six runs a game, but they scored seven or more in excess of the league average. In other words, they often scored just enough runs to lose and then won other games in blowouts. They didn't score their runs when they most needed them. And they were unlucky in the one-run games they did play when they scored between four and six runs, going just 7-14 in those contests.

Adding It Up

With our three categories, we can now try and assess which teams were the most fortunate in 2005 and then estimate what their records might have looked like had that luck been factored out.

First, in order to convert our wins above Pythagenpat estimate to runs we'll calculate how many runs it takes to pick up an additional win using Pete Palmer's formula found in *The Hidden Game of Baseball*. There he calculated that number as:

Runs Per Win=10*SQRT(RPG/9)

For 2005, 9.18 runs were scored per game, so the number of runs per win comes out to 10.1. We'll then take the wins above Pythagenpat and multiply them by this number to convert them to runs. For example, the Diamondbacks were actually 11.6 wins above expected, so that equates to just over 117 runs. In other words, scoring their runs at the right time was worth about 117 runs.

The following table lists the number of runs in each category and the total runs that might be attributed in large part to luck followed by their record had that luck not been present.

The Luckiest and Unluckiest Teams of 2005									
		Actual		Runs				Projected	
Team	Lg	W	L	Hitting	Pitching	Pyth	Total	W	L
Nationals	NL	81	81	-9	15	117	124	69	93
White Sox	AL	99	63	2	23	76	101	89	73
Angels	AL	95	67	40	30	13	83	87	75
Red Sox	AL	95	67	23	-8	47	63	89	73
Cardinals	NL	100	62	39	8	11	58	94	68
Indians	AL	93	69	-24	-6	82	52	88	74
Diamondbacks	NL	77	85	-68	-10	117	39	73	89
Braves	NL	90	72	4	35	-10	29	87	75
Padres	NL	82	80	-26	-6	56	23	80	82
Yankees	AL	95	67	7	-38	53	22	93	69
Rockies	NL	67	95	6	22	-25	4	67	95
Twins	AL	83	79	14	-12	-9	-8	84	78
Reds	NL	73	89	-10	25	-23	-8	74	88
Phillies	NL	88	74	-6	0	-10	-16	90	72
Astros	NL	89	73	-14	20	-24	-18	91	71
Blue Jays	AL	80	82	41	23	-83	-19	82	80
Athletics	AL	88	74	45	-21	-51	-28	91	71
Brewers	NL	81	81	-14	18	-31	-28	84	78
Dodgers	NL	71	91	2	-10	-26	-34	74	88
Devil Rays	AL	67	95	0	-68	27	-41	71	91
Royals	AL	56	106	35	-45	-36	-46	61	101
Giants	NL	75	87	-9	25	-69	-53	80	82
Mets	NL	83	79	-10	-12	-34	-56	89	73
Orioles	AL	74	88	-23	-41	1	-64	80	82
Cubs	NL	79	83	-50	-6	-8	-64	85	77
Mariners	AL	69	93	34	-14	-86	-65	75	87
Rangers	AL	79	83	11	-57	-26	-72	86	76
Pirates	NL	67	95	-18	-12	-47	-78	75	87
Marlins	NL	83	79	-16	-7	-57	-80	91	71
Tigers	AL	71	91	-9	-41	-36	-86	79	83

Based on this analysis the Nationals were fortunate to the tune of 124 runs and 12 wins while the Tigers were unlucky by 86 runs and eight wins.

There are several interesting aspects of this table:

- The range in this analysis is from eight fewer wins than expected for the Tigers, Marlins and Pirates to 12 more for the Nationals, with over half the teams clustered between +5 and -5. Part of the reason, of course, is that at times the three categories tend to cancel each other out.

- The Nationals, as many hard-core fans (although not many in the media) predicted, came back to earth after a hot start, which they parlayed into a 50-32 record and a 22-7 record in one-run games through July 4. The rest of the way they went 31-49 and 8-24 in one-run contests. Their tremendous luck in winning those close games early even overcame an offense that was nine runs under their estimate. You'll also notice that their 124 run total is almost 25% higher than any other team's.

- The White Sox, by overshooting their Pythagenpat estimate and outperforming their runs allowed, picked up an extra 10 wins. What hasn't gotten the attention, however, is that the Indians were also fortunate in their Pythagenpat estimate 82 runs. Factoring these things out, the Sox still would have wound up one game better than the Indians. A small consolation for those Sox fans who have heard all season (and from yours truly) that their team was not as good on paper as it looked.

- The Padres were fortunate (and looked so in the beating they took at the hands of the Cardinals in the NLDS) in scoring runs and winning one-run games, which allowed them to win those two extra games that they needed to stay ahead of the Giants. However, had the Giants been a bit luckier (and gotten Barry Bonds back sooner) in both hitting and pitching, they could have wound up with 80 wins as well, which would have put them in a tie with the Padres.

- In the NL East the Braves finished with an 87-75 estimate. The Braves won by getting the most out of their pitching (an additional 35 runs which some might attribute to Leo Mazzone rather than luck) while the Phillies, given a little luck, might have won 90 games. The Marlins, however, were the unluckiest team in the division, winning just 83 games when they could have won 91, in part because they underperformed their Pythagenpat by playing poorly in one-run games (20-22). Had things fallen a bit differently the division-winning streak might have come to an end.

- The Royals, although a really bad team, were also unlucky, especially in the pitching department, and could have won a handful more games with a little fortune on their side. Royals fans are neither surprised nor amused.

- The A's were also unlucky and in this analysis actually come out four games better than the Angels who used a combination of great hitting with runners in scoring position (.296) and winning their expected number of close games (33-26) to take the division.

- The eight playoff teams given their projected records would have been: Marlins (NL East), Cardinals (NL Central), Giants or Padres (NL West), Astros (Wild Card), Yankees (AL East), White Sox (AL Central), A's (AL West) and Red Sox (Wild Card). So five or six of the eight teams would have been the same.

- Some things never change, and the Cardinals, although not a 100-win team, still come out as the most dominating team in baseball.

So to answer our question at the outset of this article, does luck play a role at the season level and did it do so in 2005?

One of the beauties of baseball being "a game of inches" is that there is plenty of room for luck to play a role. As fans we're also fortunate that players come to the plate and pitch enough innings and teams play enough games that an individual's or a team's performance can be influenced by luck but not totally determined by it. In the end, luck certainly plays a role and can even make the difference between playing in October and sitting at home. But even so there are plenty more factors of which the teams themselves have control.

Following are some of the web articles referenced in this article:
- *Voros McCracken's original DIPs article: http://baseballprospectus.com/article.php?articleid=878*
- *Tom Tippett's subsequent research: http://www.diamond-mind.com/articles/ipavg2.htm*
- *Jim Alpert's article "A Batting Average: Does it Represent Ability or Luck?": http://bayes.bgsu.edu/papers/paper_bavg.pdf*
- *Phil Birnbaum's Toronto presentation entitled "Were the 1994 Expos Just Lucky?": http://www.philbirnbaum.com/luck.ppt*
- *David Smyth's Base Runs formula: http://mlb7.scout.com/fbaseballfrm8.show/Message?topicID=1045.topic*
- *Bill James's Pythagorean formula for one-run games: http://www.diamond-mind.com/articles/james_onerun.htm*

What's a Batted Ball Worth?

by Dave Studenmund

This past summer, Tom Ruane posted a study on Retrosheet (www.retrosheet.org) called "The Value-Added Approach to Evaluating Performance." Don't be intimidated by the title; the idea behind the article was to determine how much each event on a baseball field was worth, and then add up the number of times each batter or pitcher did one of those things. Saying that the article does this well is like saying that Albert Pujols had a pretty good year.

For example, here is a table of how much each of the following events was worth from 2002 through 2004:

Event	Runs
Single	.465
Double	.772
Triple	1.055
Home Run	1.394
Non-Intentional Walk	.315
Intentional Walk	.176
Hit by Pitch	.342
Sacrifice Hit	-.127
Sacrifice Fly	-.052
Double Play	-.839
Strikeout	-.287
Other kinds of outs	-.250

Tom developed this list by evaluating the impact of every play in every game on the number of runs each team eventually scored. As you can see, there is a whole lot of information packed into these little bitty numbers, to wit …

- A home run is worth about three times as much as a single. This is why slugging percentage is not a great stat, though it's still a lot better than batting average (in which a home run is the same as a single).
- A walk is worth about two-thirds of a single. But intentional walks, dictated by game strategy, usually yield about half as many runs as a regular walk.
- In general, sacrifice bunts and sacrifice flies add more outs than runs.
- A strikeout really is worse than a regular out (or better, if you're pitching).

At The Hardball Times, we also publish a lot of baseball information collected by our friends at Baseball Info Solutions (BIS). One of the most unique items they collect is something called "batted-ball type." For each plate appearance, BIS notes whether the batter hit a ground ball, fly ball or line drive. On our website, for instance, you can see how many line drives each batter has smashed, or how many each pitcher has allowed.

Recently, we started playing around with the outcome (otherwise known as the baseball event) of every type of batted ball from 2002 through 2005. Using this data, we asked a bunch of questions, such as "How many times does a fly ball become a hit? Or a home run? What about line drives? Why do you park your car on a driveway but drive your car on a parkway?"

To answer some of those questions, we looked at the results of each kind of batted ball from 2002 through 2005:

	Outfield Fly	Groundball	Line Drive	Infield Fly	Bunt
Fair Out	74.4%	60.6%	25.4%	53.3%	67.1%
Foul Out	3.0%	0.0%	0.0%	45.3%	2.1%
Double Play	0.2%	6.4%	0.8%	0.1%	1.3%
Error	0.3%	2.5%	0.2%	0.3%	2.8%
Fielders' Choice	0.1%	7.8%	0.2%	0.1%	7.8%
Single	4.1%	20.7%	51.4%	0.3%	18.6%
Double	6.1%	1.9%	18.3%	0.0%	0.0%
Triple	0.9%	0.1%	1.6%	0.0%	0.0%
Home Run	11.0%	0.0%	2.0%	0.1%	0.0%

Take some time with this table, because there is a lot here. And while you're looking, allow me to make a few points:

- Flies to the outfield are either really good or really bad. They're caught for outs three quarters of the time, but they make it over the fence 11% of the time. Outfield flies are the dramatic flourishes of the baseball bat. Only when the ball lands do you know if you've witnessed a tragedy or comedy.

- If you include double plays and fielder's choices, ground balls are turned into outs about as often as outfield flies. Most other times, ground balls are singles. In fact, a batter is more likely to reach on a ground ball error than a ground ball double.

- Line drives are pure baseball. They're either caught for outs (a quarter of the time) or batted for singles and doubles.

- The infield fly is a pitcher's secret weapon, an automatic out. They are caught for outs nearly 99% of the time, almost half of those in the foul area.

- Bunts are almost as productive as regular ground balls. Of course, this depends on who's doing the bunting.

So we have runs per event and events per batted ball. Like peanut butter and chocolate or horses and carriages, these are two things that really go together. By simply multiplying the two previous tables, we have a new kind of table: the value of each type of batted ball.

Batted Ball	Run Value
Line Drive	.356
HBP	.342
Non-Intentional Walk	.315
Intentional Walk	.176
Outfield Fly	.035
Groundball	-.101
Bunts	-.103
Infield Fly	-.243
Strikeout	-.287

I threw in batting events that don't involve batted balls, such as strikeouts and walks. Otherwise, this table is simply the product of multiplying the value of each type of event times the number of times it occurred for each batted ball.

As you can see, on average the best thing for a batter to do is to hit a line drive. The best thing for a pitcher is a strikeout. There is a lot of nuance in between, however. For instance, this table shows the power of the walk (and hit by pitch)—it is second to only the line drive in its value.

On the other hand, an infield fly is almost as good as a strikeout. To the extent pitchers can induce infield flies from batters, they are almost as effective as power strikeout pitchers.

Bunts aren't really much worse than ground balls. And the true difference between the outfield fly (a somewhat positive value) and the ground ball (negative value) is the home run.

Batted ball information like this allows you to look at the baseball diamond a little differently. It adds another dimension to what's happening on the field. Keep this chart in the back of your mind next time you watch a game. It will give you some brand new insights.

Batted-ball information also permits you to investigate a few things you might be curious about, such as …

- Why are some parks pitcher's parks and other parks batter's parks?

- Do pitchers and batters have a consistent ability to hit line drives, induce infield flies and other cool things?

- What does the batted-ball data tell us about fielders?

Read on.

Retrosheet is a wonderful website, containing detailed box scores, stats and research for the entire history of baseball. It is a nonprofit site, meaning that you won't run into a single ad or popup window. Donations are tax-deductible.

You can read Tom Ruane's article at http://www.retrosheet.org/Research/RuaneT/valueadd_art.htm. The article includes detailed lists of the best batters and pitchers from 1960 through 2004, as determined by the value added by the events on the field.

They Play in Parks

by Dave Studenmund

Ballparks have long been the "invisible hand" of the ol' ballgame. From the crazy dimensions of the Polo Grounds inflating Mel Ott's home run totals to Sandy Koufax's lifetime 1.37 ERA at Dodger Stadium, ballparks have had a huge impact on baseball games and the players that have played in them. And I haven't even mentioned the "House that Ruth Built."

In today's baseball world, ballparks range from the rarefied atmosphere of Denver's Coors Field to the low-scoring environment of PETCO Park in San Diego. Various ballparks have turf, ivy, short porches, deep alleys, roofs, retractable roofs and Green Monsters. Ballplayers spend a lot of time getting to know each angle off every wall, and general managers spend a lot of energy figuring out which type of player will feel most at home in their parks.

As a result, baseball fans sometimes like to track something called a "park factor," which is a ratio that represents the level of offense at each park compared to other parks. According to last year's *Bill James Handbook*, park factors ranged from 82 at PETCO to 136 at Coors. Since 100 represents average, this means that runs scored 36% more often at Coors and 18% less often at PETCO. It also means that runs scored 65% more often at Coors than PETCO (136 divided by 82).

But sometimes park factors are impish, inconstant measures. For instance, the park factors at Cincinnati's Great American Ballpark (GAB) each of the three years since it opened have been 99, 85 and 114 (according to my simple calculations), a swing of almost 30 points. Someone once e-mailed me to say (and I'm paraphrasing) "Well, the GAB was a pitcher's ballpark last year, but it's a hitter's park this year." But how can a ballpark fundamentally change like that?

Typical culprits include the weather (wind and humidity, for instance, are two meteorological conditions that influence what happens to a ball), or maybe something subtle (the slope of the mound, for instance). Maybe the players themselves started playing differently at home for whatever reason.

But if park factors can change so much, can they be helpful at all?

I'd like to partially answer this question by discussing a complex mathematical calculation called regression to the mean. I promise I'll be quick.

Statisticians, baseball and otherwise, engage in sample sizes. When statisticians want to predict which candidate is likely to win the next election, they don't ask everyone. They only ask some of the voters, and they're careful to make sure the sample size is large enough and that the folks they poll are representative of the greater voting population. In baseball, we don't have that luxury.

In baseball, we get 162 games a year, like it or not. We get unbalanced schedules, which means that external comparisons between teams aren't the same. And yes, we get weather and changing mound slopes.

So think of a baseball season as an imperfect sample of a ballpark's tendencies. It takes more than 162 games to really know the impact of a park, weather or not. For instance, Arizona's Chase Field, a domed stadium in the desert, has ranged from 107 to 121 in each of the past four years. Weather had nothing to do with it.

To get a better handle on park factors, baseball statisticians can do three things (at least!):

- Use multiple years for park factors. The more years, the better—unless something has changed in the park (such as moving the fences in). The *Bill James Handbook* calculates three-year park factors, for instance.

- Adjust the sample. The *Handbook* excludes interleague games, because the designated hitter skews AL ballparks to higher offense. Great point but, unfortunately, steps like this decrease the sample size.

- Regress the sample to the mean.

Here's what you do to regress to the mean: Using regression analysis, you find out how much one-year park factors are correlated. You can also find out how much two-year average factors correlate with a third year, and how much three-year factors correlate with a fourth year, etc. etc. Correlation is measured with something called a correlation coefficient, or "R" (read "Do Players Control Batted Balls?" for a definition of R), where one (1) means that you can exactly predict next year's park factor from the previous year's.

Here's the mathematical paragraph: One-year park factors typically have an R of about .6, two-year factors are around .7 and three-year factors are around .8. So to regress a one-year park factor to the mean, you multiply it by the relevant R (.6 in this case) and you multiply the average by 1-R. Since average equals 100 for park factors, the math is PF*.6 + 100*.4. If your park factor is 120, your one-year regressed factor is 112, your two-year factor is 114 and your three-year factor is 116. So you can see how larger sample sizes increase your confidence in the factors.

Going from 120 to 112 might not sound like a big change, but go back and calculate Cincinnati's regressed park factor at the end of its first two years. You'll see that a two-year regressed park factor will cut down the error by a third, as opposed to just using a one-year factor.

I learned all of this from an Internet baseball wonk who calls himself U.S. Patriot. Patriot maintains his own website with a host of useful (albeit highly mathematical) essays and spreadsheets (gosu02.tripod.com/id7.html). With his permission, we are reprinting his Run and Home Run Park Factors for 2006. They include up to five years' worth of data, if appropriate, and they're regressed to the mean. Please note that Patriot has taken the added step of essentially cutting his park factors in half, because teams play only half their games at home. In other words, you can multiply or divide these factors directly onto a player's stats since a player plays half his games at home.

Team	Run PF	HR PF	Team	Run PF	HR PF
ARI	105	106	BAL	97	101
ATL	100	99	BOS	102	97
CHN	100	104	CHA	102	113
CIN	99	106	CLE	98	96
COL	115	114	DET	97	93
FLA	96	93	KC	98	91
HOU	102	104	LAA	98	97
LA	94	101	MIN	101	95
MIL	100	104	NYA	99	103
NYN	97	95	OAK	99	101
PHI	103	107	SEA	95	96
PIT	100	95	TB	99	96
SD	94	91	TEX	106	107
SF	97	89	TOR	103	105
STL	98	96			
WAS	96	94			

I'm sometimes asked what THT's park factors are. There's your answer.

Park factors like these are extremely important but, in some ways, they're only the tip of the iceberg. Ballparks have quirks, like big walls in left field, short fences in right, low air pressure, bad infields, poor sight lines, artificial turf, etc. Park factors pick up the sum impact of these quirks, but they miss the details. And one of the reasons park factors change is that different batters and pitchers have different styles of play themselves. Sometimes they match the ballpark, sometimes they don't.

So we've done something at The Hardball Times that I haven't seen before. We took the batted-ball information from our buddies at Baseball Info Solutions and looked at what happened in every park over the last four years. Essentially, we developed annual park factors for every type of batted ball in each ballpark. We looked at how often batters struck out and walked, or how often they hit flies, line drives and grounders at each park. We also looked at how often each batted ball was an out or a hit (single, double, triple or home run). We even looked at how often there were errors on each type of batted ball.

We found some things that we expected, but we found some other things that blew us away. Here are some of those things …

Strikeouts per Plate Appearance

In our data, the most persistent trait of a ballpark was its strikeout ratio. We correlated three years of data against the fourth year, to see how predictable trends were, and strikeout factors were highest at .79. Average strikeout park factors ranged from 88 at Coors to 112 at Florida's Dolphins Stadium. In fact, the most important aspect of Dolphins Stadium is its strikeout ratio.

Why does this happen? I'm guessing factors like sight lines and heavy atmosphere causing balls to break more. Whatever the reason, the data is fairly clear.

Outs and Home Runs Per Outfield Fly

These two factors were the second and third most persistent ones, which is not really a surprise. The outcome of an outfield fly has the biggest impact on park factors in general. As you can imagine, outs and home run factors are related, because the more outfield flies go over the fence, the fewer are caught for outs.

Some of the exceptions to this rule are…

- Fenway, where the monster wall in left field turns both would-be home runs and outs into singles and doubles,
- Yankee Stadium, a relatively average home run park where outfield flies are caught for outs more often than any other park, and
- Dolphins Stadium, again. Dolphins Stadium is an average park for outs per outfield fly but the second lowest in home runs per outfield fly. Home runs

don't turn into outs at Dolphins Stadium; they turn into singles, doubles and triples.

Foul Outs Per Outfield Fly

It's fairly well known that parks have different foul areas, and our data showed this. But I was a little surprised to find that foul outs per outfield flies have a much stronger pattern than foul outs per infield flies. The three-year correlation for foul out per outfield fly was .637 but was only .316 for infield flies. By the way, BIS considers anything beyond the base running paths to be an outfield fly, regardless of who catches it.

In addition, some of the differences were extreme. The factor at Oakland's Network Associates Coliseum is 192, and it's 160 at Tampa Bay's Tropicana Field. On the low end, it's 40 at Yankee Stadium and 46 at Fenway.

Extra Base Hits per Ground ball

This was initially a surprise to me. We looked at the factor of doubles and triples per ground ball at each park and found a three-year correlation of .64, a higher factor than I expected. Upon closer inspection, however, we found that the ballparks with the highest factors in this were mostly turf parks, where grounders can skip through infields and into corners very quickly. These parks were Rogers Centre in Toronto (137), the Humphrey Dome in Minnesota (126), Tampa Bay's Tropicana (123) and Chase Field in Arizona (123). That last park doesn't have turf, by the way.

On the other end of the spectrum, here are the parks where it is least likely that a ground ball will be a double or triple: Yankee Stadium (69), Comerica Park in Detroit (80) and Baltimore's Camden Yards (80).

There was also a good correlation in doubles and triples per line drive (.54) and most of the same parks made the best and worst lists. One exception is Milwaukee's Miller Park, which has the second-highest factor (117) for line drives. I have no idea why.

Ground Balls and Line Drives Per Batted Ball

Speaking of being clueless, this finding truly shocked me. Essentially, we found that ballparks have a persistent trend in the types of batted balls that are hit. In other words, a batted ball is more likely to be a ground-ball in some parks, or a line drive in others. The impact isn't huge in most cases, but it's persistent.

I'd never heard of this before, so I double-checked the findings many times. I put out feelers to various folks asking if they had heard of such a thing and received a negative reply in each case. In fact, when I mentioned the results on The Hardball Times website, one reader

said that I "had gone horribly wrong." Maybe, but let me share the results with you.

Line drives per batted ball have a three-year correlation of .59 and ground balls per batted ball have a three-year correlation of .54. We didn't leave home runs out of the equation, so different home run factors are not to blame. The foul area does have some impact, because parks with large foul areas will wind up with more fly balls as more of them are caught for outs. But that impact is relatively small.

The highest line drive factors are at Coors (116) and Texas's Ameriquest Field (105), while the lowest line drive factors are at Dodger Stadium (93) and Dolphins Stadium (95).

The highest ground ball factors are at Cleveland's Jacobs Field (107) and Dodger Stadium (104), and the lowest ground ball factors belong to Yankee Stadium (96), US Cellular Field in Chicago (97) and Safeco in Seattle (97).

In each of the four years we examined, for both batters and pitchers, Jacobs Field was a ground ball park. This was the single most surprising finding to me. The ground ball factor is Jacobs's most important ballpark influence.

I don't know why this is, but I do know that it could have implications for building a team in Cleveland. With more ground balls, the Indians can put a relatively higher value on infield defense and less of an emphasis on outfield defense. In other words, if you're going to sacrifice defense for offense, the Indians should do it in the outfield. This is a good example of how strategy can evolve from a careful analysis of park factors.

Please note that we only considered ballparks that have been around, unaltered, for four straight years. We left a number of new parks out of the analysis, including PETCO, Citizen's Bank and the Great American Ballpark, as well as Kansas City's Kauffman Stadium, which had its fences moved out after the 2003 season. In retrospect, we shouldn't have included Detroit in our sample, because they lowered their fences after the 2003 season. As proof, here is their HR/OF park factors from 2002 to 2005: 70, 77, 85 and 92. Better, but it's still not the Polo Grounds.

So, that's what we found. I haven't mentioned every ballpark or finding, just the highlights. I know you probably have a favorite team you're wondering about. So following is a table of commentary and statistics for each major league ballpark. There are two stats, Run Impact and Ball Factor.

Run Impact shows the value of each batted ball type relative to the major league average. In other words, an outfield fly in Fenway has a run impact of 0.043, because of the net effect of lots more singles and doubles but fewer triples and home runs off the Green Monster yields a total run impact of .078 per fly ball, or .043 runs more than the MLB average of .035. You can find average run values of all batted ball types in the article "What's a Batted Ball Worth?"

Ball Factor is kind of like Park Factors, only for batted balls. This is a number that represents the relative impact of both changes in frequency (such as more ground balls in Jacobs) and run impact for a type of batted ball. I've expressed ball factor in the same format as park factor.

By the way, these figures aren't regressed to the mean. They're raw four-year averages (or less, where noted). We thought you might like to see the raw data in this case.

In the following shorthand comments, "rate" is the word I use for a true rate, such as strikeouts per plate appearance, while "factor" is the word I use for each type of park/ball factor, where 100 is average. K stands for strikeouts, OF for outfield flies, GB for ground balls and LD for line drives. Notations such as "2B/OF" stand for doubles per outfield flies, for instance. And where I say "OF factor" or "GB factor," I'm referring to the factor of how often a certain type of batted ball occurs relative to other types of batted balls.

AMERICAN LEAGUE BALLPARKS

Baltimore Orioles Camden Yards		K	OF	GB	LD
	Run Impact:		-0.008	-0.005	-0.020
	Ball Factor:	103	98	99	96

Comments: K rate of 93%, which helps offset the higher out factors of batted balls. Avg HR/OF park, but fewer other types of hits from OF.

Boston Red Sox Fenway		K	OF	GB	LD
	Run Impact:		0.043	0.001	-0.010
	Ball Factor:	101	109	100	100

Comments: It's all about the Green Monster: 2B/OF factor is 176

Chicago White Sox U.S. Cellular		K	OF	GB	LD
	Run Impact:		0.040	-0.014	0.014
	Ball Factor:	100	110	97	101

Comments: HR/OF factor is 127, second highest behind Coors. Also, OF factor is 105. Hence the fireworks.

Cleveland Indians Jacobs		K	OF	GB	LD
	Run Impact:		-0.001	-0.009	-0.021
	Ball Factor:	97	99	95	96

Comments: Ground balls. Higher frequency, plus they're turned into outs more often. Also, Out/LD factor is 110.

Detroit Tigers Comerica		K	OF	GB	LD
	Run Impact:		-0.037	-0.010	-0.001
	Ball Factor:	103	92	97	102

Comments: Out/OF factor is 103 fair, 112 foul. In addition to changing HR/OF factors, 2B factor is 80 or less for all types of batted balls.

Kansas City Royals Kauffman		K	OF	GB	LD
	Run Impact:		-0.049	-0.010	0.001
	Ball Factor:	104	89	96	100

Comments: Two years of data, since they moved fences back. HR/OF factor is 73. 3B/OF factor is 143.

Anaheim Angels Edison Park:		K	OF	GB	LD
	Run Impact:		-0.014	-0.002	-0.011
	Ball Factor:	100	97	99	97

Comments: HR/OF is 90, 3B/OF is 83, but 3B/GB is 221. Small sample size flukes, but interesting. 1B/OF factor is 120.

Minnesota Twins		K	OF	GB	LD
Humphrey Dome	Run Impact:		-0.013	0.013	-0.001
	Ball Factor:	97	97	104	99

Comments: Strikeout rate is 107%, tendency to be ground ball park (factor of 102). 3B/GB factor is 428.

New York Yankees		K	OF	GB	LD
Yankee Stadium	Run Impact:		-0.007	-0.002	0.001
	Ball Factor:	98	99	101	100

Comments: Overall average, but a lot going on underneath. Induces outfield flies more than ground balls. HR factors OK, but 2B and 3B factors are low.

Oakland Athletics		K	OF	GB	LD
Network Associates	Run Impact:		-0.015	-0.013	0.024
	Ball Factor:	101	97	97	105

Comments: Huge foul area, even for line drives. Foul out per LD factor is 342. But Fair out/LD factor is only 93.

Seattle Mariners		K	OF	GB	LD
Safeco	Run Impact:		-0.033	0.012	-0.014
	Ball Factor:	96	93	105	95

Comments: Fly ball park, OF factor is 106, Out per OF is 103, foul out per OF is 114. All base hits off OF are 90 or lower.

Tampa Bay Devil Rays		K	OF	GB	LD
Tropicana	Run Impact:		-0.042	0.022	0.007
	Ball Factor:	99	91	107	99

Comments: Foul outs per OF factor is 160 and fair outs factor is 103. Favors ground ball hitters: 106 for 1B/GB, 121 for 2B/GB, 183 for 3B/GB.

Texas Rangers		K	OF	GB	LD
Ameriquest	Run Impact:		0.057	-0.004	0.017
	Ball Factor:	102	113	98	106

Comments: Masher's park: only 62 factor foul out per OF, 97 for fair outs. LD factor is 105 and are outs/LD factor is 95.

Toronto Blue Jays		K	OF	GB	LD
Rogers Centre	Run Impact:		0.026	0.021	0.011
	Ball Factor:	100	105	106	101

Comments: OF factors are a mixed bag: OF factor is 97, foul out is 118, 1B factor is 87, HR factor is 118. GB hit more often (103) and have much more run value.

NATIONAL LEAGUE BALLPARKS

Arizona Diamondbacks		K	OF	GB	LD
Chase Field	Run Impact:		0.015	0.004	0.025
	Ball Factor:	102	104	101	105

Comments: Hitter's park across all batted balls. Out/LD factor only 91. 2B/GB is 121. 3B factors for both OF and LD above 150.

Atlanta Braves		K	OF	GB	LD
Turner Field	Run Impact:		-0.017	0.007	-0.012
	Ball Factor:	101	96	103	100

Comments: OF trap. Rate is 102, fair outs 101, foul outs 116. 3B come from GB (235) not OF (73). May be due to Andruw effect.

Chicago Cubs		**K**	**OF**	**GB**	**LD**
Wrigley	Run Impact:		0.045	-0.006	-0.017
	Ball Factor:	98	110	99	95

Comments: OF factor is 101, but fair out per OF factor is 96 and foul out per OF is 81. HR/OF factor is 117. Not a great place for a fly ball pitcher.

Cincinnati Reds		**K**	**OF**	**GB**	**LD**
Great American	Run Impact:		0.016	-0.021	0.005
	Ball Factor:	100	104	95	102

Comments: Three years of data says: Death to ground balls. GB factor is 96, and Out per GB is 105. HR/OF factor is 111. Find GB pitchers!

Colorado Rockies		**K**	**OF**	**GB**	**LD**
Coors Field	Run Impact:		0.077	0.003	0.016
	Ball Factor:	106	117	101	113

Comments: It's Coors. More line drives, fewer outs.

Florida Marlins		**K**	**OF**	**GB**	**LD**
Dolphins Stadium	Run Impact:		-0.012	-0.001	-0.012
	Ball Factor:	94	97	102	94

Comments: K rate is biggest issue. High OF factor, with fewer HR per OF (83) but more 1B, 2B and 3B. LD factor only 95.

Houston Astros		**K**	**OF**	**GB**	**LD**
Minute Maid Park	Run Impact:		0.019	0.001	0.014
	Ball Factor:	100	105	99	101

Comments: Low LD out factor (92) and high HR/OF factor (108) are key.

Los Angeles Dodgers		**K**	**OF**	**GB**	**LD**
Dodger Stadium	Run Impact:		0.008	-0.004	-0.008
	Ball Factor:	97	101	98	95

Comments: Favors GB (104), not LD (93), which is why there are fewer 2B and 3B in general. Still, 2B/OF factor is 90 and 2B/ LD is 89. HR/OF is actually 110.

Milwaukee Brewers		**K**	**OF**	**GB**	**LD**
Miller Park	Run Impact:		-0.008	0.001	0.018
	Ball Factor:	98	98	101	101

Comments: K rate is 105, OF out factor is 102, but foul out factor/OF is 77. All OF hit factors below 90 except HR/OF (104). 2B/LD is 116, 3B per LD is 121 and HR/LD is 155. All small samples, but line drives appear to pay off a bit more here.

New York Mets		**K**	**OF**	**GB**	**LD**
Shea Stadium	Run Impact:		-0.014	-0.001	0.003
	Ball Factor:	100	97	99	99

Comments: OF factors: 1B: 124, 2B: 108, 3B: 67, HR: 88. LD factor is 97, though Out/LD factor is 94.

Philadelphia Phillies		**K**	**OF**	**GB**	**LD**
Citizens Bank	Run Impact:		-0.002	0.011	0.024
	Ball Factor:	102	100	103	107

Comments: Only open for two years. LD factor is 105. K rate is 95%. Foul outs on OF factor is 135.

Pittsburgh Pirates		**K**	**OF**	**GB**	**LD**
PNC Park	Run Impact:		-0.021	0.009	-0.011
	Ball Factor:	103	95	103	101

Comments: OF out factor is 103, HR factor is 89. More LDs are hit (104) but more are outs (105).

St. Louis Cardinals		K	OF	GB	LD
Busch Stadium	Run Impact:		-0.020	0.007	0.000
	Ball Factor:	100	96	102	98

Comments: OF factor is 103, HR/OF is 90. LD factor is low at 97. Will next year's park be different?

San Diego Padres		K	OF	GB	LD
PETCO Park	Run Impact:		-0.043	-0.009	-0.025
	Ball Factor:	96	90	98	94

Comments: Favors all kinds of pitchers. Higher OF factor (102) and lower LD (97) factor; Very high out factors: OF (104), GB (106), LD (108). Two years of data.

San Francisco Giants		K	OF	GB	LD
Pac Bell Park	Run Impact:		-0.029	-0.006	0.027
	Ball Factor:	101	93	96	105

Comments: Groundball (104) much stronger than fly ball (95) factors. HR/OF only 82. Hitter's opening: Out/LD is 89.

Washington Nationals		K	OF	GB	LD
RFK	Run Impact:		-0.056	0.013	-0.033
	Ball Factor:	96	87	107	92

Comments: Only open one year, extreme park. K rate is 109, OF factor is 110 vs. GB factor of 93. Out per OF factor was 105, per LD was 117. Best hitter strategy: stay out of town.

Batted Ball Fielding Stats

by Dave Studenmund

I've noticed a disturbing trend in baseball columns these days. More and more writers are referring to something called Defense Efficiency Ratio (or DER) to describe a team's fielding prowess. This is disturbing to me, because DER has some serious flaws.

The calculation for DER, which was introduced by Bill James over 20 years ago, is relatively simple. Take all the balls in play given up by a pitching staff (batters faced minus strikeouts, walks, batters hit by pitches and home runs) and then figure out how often the team's fielders recorded an out off those balls in play. The second part is a little tricky, because you don't want to include outs that occurred in other ways, such as a runner caught stealing or the first out of a double play. But you can usually find a way to get the right stats.

It's true that good fielders get to more balls than bad fielders. But it's also true that many other things can affect DER, such as:

- The ballpark. Try catching an easy fly ball 15 feet up the Green Monster in Fenway.
- The type of batted ball. Line drives are hard to catch; infield flies are easy. Outfield flies, ground balls and bunts are in-between.
- Where the ball goes. Balls in the shortstop hole are harder to field than balls hit directly at the shortstop. I won't name names.
- How hard the ball is hit. Even Rafael Furcal will have trouble with a ball hit hard in the shortstop hole.

So when you see a columnist use DER to announce that one team's fielders are better than another's, you should be skeptical. It's not that DER is wrong; it's just not always right. Let me give you an example.

Last year, the Yankees' DER was .691, according to our stats from Baseball Info Solutions; 69% of qualified batted balls were fielded for outs. That would place the Yankee fielders slightly below the major league average DER of .695. But the Yankee fielders were actually much worse than that.

You see, the much-maligned Yankee staff actually yielded the most fieldable batted balls in the majors last year. If you add up all of their batted-ball types and assume that each type was turned into an out at the average major league rate, their DER would be .721. So when judging the Yankees fielders, you should compare them to .721, not .695.

Luckily, The Hardball Times can help. We used our batted-ball data to develop better fielding stats for 2005, and we found that the Yankees were actually the third-worst fielding team in the majors last year.

Here's what we did.

- We added up the number of batted balls allowed by each team's pitching staffs. The Yankees allowed 2,161 ground balls, 1,280 outfield flies (not including home runs), 798 line drives (also not including home runs), 188 infield flies and 57 bunts for a total of 4,484 batted balls in play.
- We then applied the major league average out percentage for each type of batted ball (such as 99% for infield flies and 25% for line drives) to each total to generate the number of expected outs from the batted balls. We also adjusted the out percentage for each team based on the ballpark factors discussed in the previous article. (The fielding impact of Yankee Stadium is pretty small). This produced a total of 3,235 expected outs off those batted balls.
- Next, we compared the expected total to the actual number of batted balls turned into outs: 3,146, or 89 fewer than expected.
- Finally, we converted each "unfielded" ball into a run value, based on how often each type of batted ball hit is a single, double or triple, on average. As you can imagine, an unfielded outfield fly does more damage than an unfielded bunt.

We're still missing two important elements, where the ball was hit and how hard it was hit. But with just the stats we have, we find that Yankee fielders allowed 51 runs below average. When you consider that every nine-to-ten runs equal a win, this means that their fielders cost them at least five wins compared to the average major league team.

I don't mean to pick on the Yankees; they're just the example I chose. Actually, the Reds (57 runs below average) and Royals (67 runs below average) were worse. The best fielding teams were the Indians (49 runs above average), Athletics (46) and Phillies (40). The difference between the best (Cleveland) and worst (Kansas City) fielding teams was 116 runs.

To put that in perspective, the difference between the best and worst defensive teams (pitching and fielding) last year was 302 runs. (Tampa Bay allowed 936 runs and the Cardinals allowed 634.) Pitching is still the most important aspect of total defense, but fielding matters too.

The following table has more information than you can shake a stick at. By team, it shows the number of runs allowed above/below average for each type of batted ball and in total, as well as each team's rank in DER and their fielding runs above/below average in 2004. Let me lay it out for you and add comments afterward:

DER			Fielding Runs Above/Below Average							
Rank	Rank	Team	IF	OF	LD	GB	Bunt	Total	2004	Diff
1	3	Indians	0.10	-22.52	21.52	4.19	0.76	49.09	-11.1	60.2
2	1	Athletics	0.58	9.41	13.48	22.11	0.40	45.97	4.7	41.3
3	5	Phillies	0.05	13.50	5.76	20.85	-0.11	40.04	0.1	39.9
4	2	White Sox	-0.38	21.23	4.53	13.78	0.64	39.79	5.0	34.8
5	4	Astros	-0.06	5.35	9.21	21.00	1.33	36.82	-4.6	41.4
6	19	Braves	-1.06	24.66	4.81	-3.43	0.87	25.84	17.1	8.7
7	8	Mets	0.47	19.29	-11.55	12.58	4.03	24.81	29.7	-4.8
8	11	Cubs	-0.09	6.97	11.60	2.08	3.22	23.79	19.8	3.9
9	6	Cardinals	-0.61	-17.26	2.86	27.61	3.48	16.08	39.8	-23.7
10	10	Blue Jays	-0.45	7.64	-6.88	15.51	-0.77	15.05	8.7	6.4
11	20	Orioles	-0.48	12.09	6.06	-7.07	-3.67	6.94	-14.3	21.3
12	15	Brewers	0.56	-3.75	11.61	-2.05	0.29	6.65	1.9	4.7
13	18	Pirates	0.55	-16.35	2.75	20.26	-1.70	5.51	-13.5	19.0
14	16	Nationals	0.15	-5.00	9.42	-3.17	0.82	2.22	15.9	-13.7
15	7	Twins	0.12	-3.73	-6.63	9.83	2.16	1.75	-23.5	25.3
16	12	Dodgers	-0.96	3.19	-5.44	-2.19	4.61	-0.80	28.6	-29.4
17	14	Giants	-0.29	-8.38	7.33	-3.15	3.17	-1.33	0.5	-1.8
18	9	Mariners	0.58	15.72	-5.17	-17.88	-0.74	-7.49	9.0	-16.5
19	23	Diamondbacks	0.00	-12.70	-1.71	4.00	2.09	-8.33	3.9	-12.2
20	22	Padres	0.04	-10.05	-3.43	4.93	-2.13	-10.64	5.0	-15.6
21	17	Tigers	0.55	-2.15	-7.25	0.04	-2.24	-11.04	-21.7	10.6
22	13	Angels	0.08	-10.73	-0.18	4.93	-6.71	-12.61	-40.5	27.9
23	24	Red Sox	-0.34	2.31	-17.71	-0.44	-0.86	-17.04	18.5	-35.5
24	26	Rangers	0.51	4.52	5.31	-32.48	-2.51	-24.65	-3.6	-21.0
25	25	Devil Rays	0.13	7.83	-3.99	-26.99	-2.71	-25.73	10.5	-36.2
26	29	Rockies	-0.03	-11.61	-10.19	-3.07	-2.31	-27.21	-33.3	6.1
27	27	Marlins	0.07	-13.54	-2.88	-14.74	3.82	-27.28	12.5	-39.8
28	21	Yankees	0.56	-25.62	2.05	-24.00	-3.68	-50.69	-32.8	-17.9
29	28	Reds	-0.37	-27.16	-18.86	-9.82	-0.56	-56.75	-4.6	-52.1
30	30	Royals	0.02	-14.89	-16.41	-35.24	-0.97	-67.49	-32.2	-35.3

It's really not that bad; let me point out a few things.

The first two columns show each team's rank in Fielding Runs and its rank in DER. As you can see, DER is close, but it misses badly on a few teams, such as the Braves, Orioles, Mariners, Angels and Twins.

The five middle columns show each team's Fielding Runs by batted-ball type. This allows you to say a few things about each team's outfield and infield defense.

Outfields

- The Braves, with Andruw Jones in center and Jeff Francoeur in right, had the best outfield in the majors last year. The Indians and White Sox also had great outfields.

- On the other hand, the worst outfields were the Reds' and Yankees'. Bernie Williams' outfield limitations are fairly well known, but it appears that Mr. Griffey Jr. has lost his outfield panache as well.

Infields

- Even though the Cardinals' infield almost had a complete turnover this year at second, shortstop and third base, they still had the best infield defense in the majors. Findings like this make you wonder if the ballpark is having some sort of impact, but no such impact is apparent in the data.

- There were a number of other fine infields last year, including the A's, Astros, Phillies and Pirates.

- The Royals' and Rangers' infields were truly terrible in 2005. A number of teams had big differences between their infields and outfields, but the Royals were really, really bad in both.

By the way, research shows that when line drives are caught for outs, the outfield accounts for a little more than half of those outs. This makes it tough to say whether a good record at turning line drives into outs is the result of good plays by the outfield or infield, or just plain good luck.

The last two columns list each team's 2004 Fielding Runs, as well as the difference between this year and last. The team with the greatest improvement from 2004 to 2005 was the Cleveland Indians, the best story in the American League the second half of the season. During the Indians' mad run for the Wild Card slot, a lot of attention was paid to their improved pitching and second-half hitting. Not many people mentioned their improved fielding.

In retrospect, it should have been obvious. The Indians allowed 857 runs in 2004 and only 642 in 2005—a difference of 215 runs. It's hard to make that much of an improvement in pitching alone. Indeed, the Indians' fielders contributed 60 of that 215-run difference.

So here's a salute to the Indians' reconfigured outfield of left fielder Coco Crisp, center fielder Grady Sizemore and right fielder Casey Blake. I nominate them for the unsung fielding heroes of 2005.

Do Players Control Batted Balls?

by J.C. Bradbury and David Gassko

Several articles in this year's *THT Annual* use batted ball type data provided by Baseball Info Solutions (BIS). For most of baseball history, baseball fans have gauged player performance according to officially scored outcomes such as singles, doubles, and triples. The BIS data provides a new tool for fans of the game to evaluate player performance. Why would we want to do this? Because random bounces can do funny things to the metrics we have long used to judge pitchers and hitters.

One way to determine the part of the player's performance that is skill and the part that is the product of random chance is to see how much certain outcomes persist from season to season. Random events should not persist over time, but skill should. While finding a lack of a statistically significant correlation between performances over time does not mean players necessarily lack ability in the area in question, where such correlations do exist it likely does reflect the existence of ability. And while the scientific method does not permit us to reject non-findings—that a year-to-year correlation is no different from random chance—it most certainly is an inference that there is no such skill in the area. This is just one step in the search for knowledge, and we encourage future investigators to continue to look for evidence of abilities that we are unable to identify.

The method for generating meaningful correlations requires a sample of players who played regularly in consecutive years. The large sample is necessary to meet a minimum sample-size requirement and to ensure batters and pitchers experienced many instances of a variety of situations (e.g, runner configurations, left-right match-ups, and pitcher/batter quality). Therefore, we examined the performances of pitchers and hitters who faced more than 350 batters or pitchers in two consecutive seasons from 2002-2004. This gave us a large sample of players—217 pitchers and 319 hitters—with a large number of pitcher-batter contests in consecutive seasons. We did not park-correct the numbers because we are looking mainly at hit types, not outcomes like hits or home runs, and any influence of parks on how players hit the ball should be minor.

Our main tool for examining how players' metrics were associated from year to year is to calculate a correlation coefficient ("r") between the performance of players in a year and the year prior. The correlation coefficient, which is continuous and ranges from -1 to one, measures the degree to which two variables move in relation to one another. A correlation of one indicates the variables correlate perfectly in the same direction, a correlation of zero means there is no correlation between changes in the variables, and a correlation of -1 indicates the variables correlate perfectly in the opposite direction. The further away from zero a correlation coefficient is, the more closely the two variables being tested are related.

Before we discuss the specific results for the players, let's take a quick glance at the year-to-year correlations of some of the standard performance metrics for players. Table 1 displays the correlations from year to year as well as the sample averages for each metric. The main focus of our analysis was the hit-type data provided by BIS, in order to observe how useful this new information can be for evaluating players; however, we used this method to look at other traditional statistics as well. The variables in the first group are defense independent … meaning, they are the product of interactions between only pitchers and hitters. The second group lists the frequency of hit types allowed and produced. The next three groups look at the outcomes according to three hit types in terms of outs, singles, doubles and triples (a measure used by Michael Schell in *Baseball's All-Time Best Sluggers*), and home runs. We do not report the results for infield flies in the table, because they almost always result in outs.

Both pitchers and hitters perform similarly from year to year in defense independent areas; however, batters seem to have greater control over being hit by pitchers and hitting home runs than pitchers do at preventing them. Both also control the frequency of outfield flies, ground balls, and infield flies. Pitchers seem to have no control over line drives while batters have some, but not nearly as much as they do for the other hit types. Pitchers have almost no control over what batting outcome results for a particular hit type, such as a line drive, as opposed to batters, who do seem to be able to control the outcomes that result from hit types. In the next two sections we examine the effects on hitters and pitchers more closely.

Table 1. Season-to-Season Correlations for Pitchers and Hitters (2002-2004)

Statistic	Year-to-Year Correlation		Mean Frequency of Occurrence	
	Pitchers	Hitters	Pitchers	Hitters
Defense Independent (per plate appearance)				
Strikeout Rate	0.77[1]	0.84[1]	16.27%	15.17%
Walk Rate	0.69[1]	0.81[1]	8.06%	7.24%
Hit by Pitch Rate	0.38[1]	0.71[1]	0.91%	0.90%
Home Run Rate	0.28[1]	0.76[1]	2.78%	3.11%
Batted-Ball Type (per ball in play)				
Line Drives	-0.03	0.10[5]	20.34%	20.77%
Ground Balls	0.79[1]	0.73[1]	42.37%	41.74%
Fly Balls (IF+OF)	0.73[1]	0.73[1]	34.88%	35.91%
Outfield Flies	0.69[1]	0.71[1]	30.64%	31.65%
Infield Flies	0.50[1]	0.60[1]	4.23%	4.26%
Infield Flies per Fly Ball	0.24[1]	0.46[1]	11.65%	11.91%
Outfield Flies Outcomes (per outfield fly)				
Outs	0.05	0.60[1]	78.02%	77.15%
Singles	-0.08	0.03	4.08%	4.03%
Doubles + Triples	0.08	0.22[1]	6.62%	6.64%
Home Runs	0.08	0.77[1]	10.70%	11.61%
Line Drives Outcomes (per line drive)				
Outs	0.08	0.14[1]	24.53%	23.75%
Singles	0.15[5]	0.11[5]	51.67%	52.02%
Doubles + Triples	0.05	0.14[1]	20.15%	20.34%
Home Runs	0.04	0.37[1]	2.22%	2.41%
Ground Ball Outcomes (per ground ball)				
Outs	0.17[1]	0.46[1]	61.25%	59.94%
Singles	0.12	0.16[1]	20.27%	20.83%
Doubles + Triples	0.02	0.14[1]	2.16%	2.16%
Observations	217	319	217	319

Statistical significance:

1 = Significant at the 1% level

5 = Significant at the 5% level

Pitcher Control over Balls in Play

In many ways, batted ball information is the holy grail of pitching analysis. When Voros McCracken discovered that pitchers have little influence on whether or not a ball in play falls in for a hit, the need to know batted ball information became great, because only by knowing what kind of batted balls a pitcher allows is it possible to figure out his subtle effects on batting average on balls in play (BABIP).

In August of 2005, David made a contribution to the topic of Defensive Independent Pitching Statistics (DIPS), a term that was coined by McCracken in his original article on the subject. Having performed a regression on batted ball data versus RA (runs allowed per nine innings), he published his own system.

The idea behind David's system is that more granular data, based on batted-ball type, gives us a better idea of how DIPS works, and improves the statistic's predictive quality. While McCracken's basic assumption was generally correct, many (including McCracken) have shown that pitchers do indeed have *some* effect on BABIP (see "Solving DIPS" by Erik Allen and Arvis Hsu and "Can Pitchers Prevent Hits on Balls in Play?" by Tom Tippett), but it is small. However, J.C. (see "Another Look at DIPS") found that much of the skill pitchers have in preventing hits on balls in play is reflected by the DIPS metrics. It's no wonder that McCracken found almost no correlation in BABIP from year to year.

David's system, inspired by earlier analysis from Mitchel Lichtman, used batted ball data in the hope that we could better understand what factors contributed to a pitcher's BABIP. What made some pitchers better than others at preventing hits on balls in play? We know, for example, that line drives are only caught roughly 26% of the time, so a pitcher who allows many line drives will tend to have a high BABIP. We know that infield flies are caught about 97% of the time, so pitchers who get a lot of pop-ups will have a lower BABIP.

But how much control do pitchers actually have over the types of batted balls they allow? Quite a bit.

The Original DIPS Categories

McCracken's versions of DIPS both relied on the four defense-independent plate appearance outcomes: hit batters, strikeouts, walks, and home runs. The idea was that fielders have no impact on these outcomes, and they are stable from year to year. Is this true?

Outcome (DIPS)	Correlation
Strikeout Rate	0.77[1]
Walk Rate	0.69[1]
Hit by Pitch Rate	0.38[1]
Home Run Rate	0.28[1]

[1] = *Significant at the 1% level*

Strikeouts and walks are highly predictable from year to year, so McCracken was definitely right on that issue. Hit batters probably have a relatively low correlation coefficient because of how rare they are; rare occurrences allow for more randomness in the data. Nonetheless, the correlation is still statistically significant. What is interesting here is the last row: home runs. That correlation is low—significant, but low. What does this mean? It is possible that the relatively low occurrence of home runs plays a role here, as with hit batters, and park factors could be important as well. But even then, there may be other factors involved. As you will see, once fly ball tendencies are accounted for, home runs actually have *no* significant correlation from year to year. This discovery is not only very important in determining in what areas pitchers were lucky, but it is also key to identifying who got lucky and who did not.

Outfield Flies

Outfield fly balls have a strong year-to-year correlation (r = .69), which is similar to the correlation for walks. This helps explain why home runs have a decent year-to-year "r": if home runs are a function of fly balls, and fly ball rate is stable, then home run rate should correlate somewhat as well. But are home runs purely a function of fly ball rate, or do pitchers have individual control over the percentage of outfield flies that become home runs?

The main critical response given to David about his system was that he should not have omitted home runs from the regression. David based the omission on the assumption that homers are just another batted ball, and therefore just a function of outfield flies. Many people responded that different pitchers had differing impacts on what percentage of outfield flies become home runs. Upon further review, this does not appear to be true, as shown on the following graph.

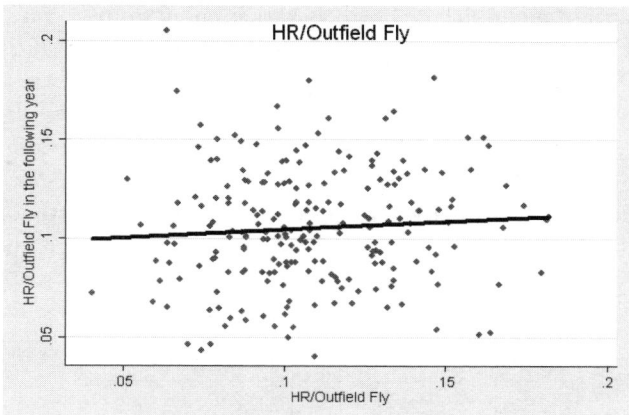

This is a picture of almost total randomness. The low correlation between home runs per outfield flies from year to year means that the number of home runs a pitcher allows depends almost solely on outfield flies allowed, with ballpark and luck thrown into the mix as well. Thus, when evaluating a pitcher, we should care more about the number of outfield fly balls he allows than home runs.

But how much control do pitchers have over other outcomes of fly balls? If we accept that pitchers have strong control over the *types* of batted balls they allow, is the next logical step to say that they have control over the *outcomes* as well? Not necessarily.

In fact, and this is actually intuitively logical, pitchers have *no* control over the outcomes of fly balls they allow. Fly balls are generally in the air for a few seconds, so almost all of them are catchable. The balls that aren't caught are generally hit either between outfielders or over the defenders' heads. As you might imagine, the placement of a ball in play is largely a product of luck (at least from the pitcher's side); thus, we expect a low correlation between fly ball outcomes from year to year.

Outcome (OF Fly)	Correlation
Outs	0.05
Singles	-0.08
Doubles + Triples	0.08
Home Runs	0.08

Infield Flies

Anyone who has watched a ball game or two in his or her life knows that infield flies, otherwise known as pop-ups, are almost always caught. Thus, a pitcher with the ability to induce many infield flies prevents additional hits on balls in play, and consequently, runs.

While it seems that some pitchers have the ability to "jam" batters and get a lot of pop-ups (Mariano Rivera is the most prominent example), Lichtman found almost no year-to-year correlation for infield flies. The results below show something different.

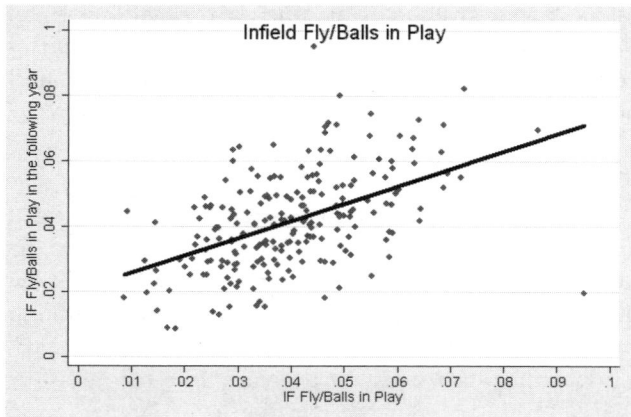

A distinct linear trend is visible in the above graph. It's not perfect (r = .5), but it's clearly there. However, when looking at the percentage of fly balls that are infield flies, the correlation is a little smaller, but still statistically significant. The correlations indicate that pitchers do seem to have some control over the rate of infield flies they allow, which in turn explains some of the differences in BABIP between pitchers. Since almost all infield flies are caught, pitchers who can consistently induce them will allow many fewer hits on balls in play.

Ground Balls

Ground balls are sort of the inverse of outfield flies. They actually correlate more strongly (r = .79); in fact, they have a higher "r" than any other element. A possible reason that ground balls correlate better than outfield flies is because of the singularity of their outcome. That is, if a ball is put on the ground, it will be a ground ball. A ball hit in the air could be an infield fly or a line drive as well as an outfield fly. There's a little more wiggle room there and that is why grounders have a slightly stronger correlation.

But what's really interesting about ground balls is that pitchers seem to have some slight ability to affect hits in this area.

Outcome (GB)	Correlation
Outs	0.17[1]
Singles	0.12
Doubles + Triples	0.02

[1] = Significant at the 1% level

The preceding table indicates that while pitchers have no impact on *what kind* of hits their ground balls turn into, they do seem to have some small ability to impact whether or not the grounders they allow become hits. Lichtman concluded that pitchers who stay with the same team had a .23 correlation for Outs/GB while pitchers who switched teams had a correlation of .06, so it is possible (and perhaps even likely) that fielders and park are the main reasons for the correlation found here.

Line Drives

We mentioned earlier that BABIP is, in large part, a function of infield flies. But line drives also greatly impact BABIP; the reason being the fact that so few line drives are caught. In fact, Dave Studenmund published a simple formula to predict BABIP—.120 + LD%—that shows just how greatly line drives affect the DIPS theory. But the question is, if pitchers have seemingly little control over their BABIP, do they have any control over the number of line drives they allow? The answer seems to be no.

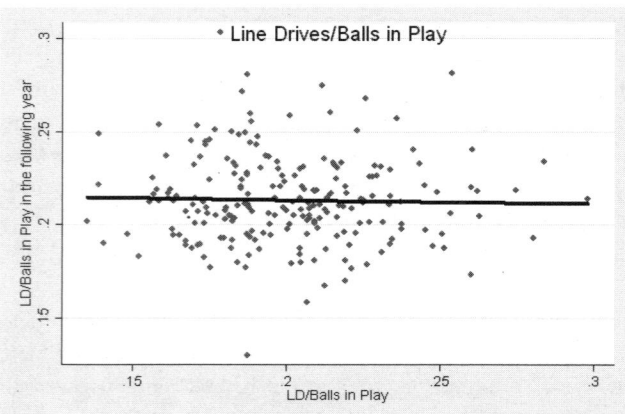

The regression line in the preceding figure slopes slightly negatively (r = -.03), but there is basically no trend whatsoever. This indicates a mistake in David's system, which uses a pitcher's actual line drive rate. What we want to be doing is substitute in the league average rate, as McCracken did with BABIP in his original DIPS. And if BABIP is largely a function of line drives, it becomes clear why it does not correlate well from year to year.

Perhaps of interest here is the pitcher's effect on the outcome of line drives. What the table below indicates is that while pitchers seem to have no effect on what percentage of line drives become hits, or extra-base hits, they do have some small effect on what percentage become singles. Lichtman found that pitchers do

affect the number of line drives that fall in for hits, with better pitchers allowing fewer hits per line drive. While this data reveals something different, the correlation for singles does seem to imply some pitcher control. It is possible, or even likely, that this correlation is a false positive, that is that the correlation is caused by luck, fielding, or ballpark effects. Without further investigation, it is safer to assume simply that pitchers have no control over line drives.

Outcome	Correlation
Outs	0.08
Singles	0.15[5]
Doubles + Triples	0.05
Home Runs	0.04

[5] = *Significant at the 5% level*

So What Does This Tell Us?

Plenty of things, actually. Having done this research, it becomes obvious why McCracken's original postulate works so well. While pitchers exhibit great control over the types of balls in play they allow, they show little overall control on the two batted ball types that impact BABIP the most—infield flies (where there is some year-to-year correlation) and line drives (where there is none). More so, as infield flies occur relatively rarely (constituting only slightly more than 4% of all balls in play), they will not have enough of an overall impact for any strong year-to-year relationship in year-to-year BABIP. You can make sense of a pitcher's season just by looking at his home run, strikeout, and walk rates. But you'll get a better and more detailed picture by using batted ball data.

Hitter Control over Balls in Play

Like pitchers, batters have a lot of control over the defense independent outcomes and the hit types on balls they put into play; however, hitters seem to have more control in these areas and over the result produced by different hit types. This explains why DIPS have strong predictive power for pitchers but not hitters. Pitchers don't have near as much control over hits on balls in play as hitters do.

In terms of the defense independent variables, hitters have a little more control than pitchers over strikeouts and walks, but have much greater control over home runs and hit batters. Home runs are more skewed for hitters than pitchers. Hitting lots of home runs is a skill that is confined to a few hitters, while giving up home runs is something that pitchers are more similar in. Batters who hit lots of home runs continue to hit lots of home runs, while pitchers experience more season-to-season variation. It's also quite interesting that batters have more skill in getting hit by a pitch than pitchers do at preventing it. Maybe pitchers should start charging the plate after batters get hit.

Outcome (DIPS)	Correlation
Strikeout Rate	0.84[1]
Walk Rate	0.81[1]
Hit by Pitch Rate	0.71[1]
Home Run Rate	0.76[1]

[1] = Significant at the 1% level

Batters also have quite a bit of control over the types of balls they put into play. There is a strong relationship between the frequency of grounders and fly balls hit; however, the persistence of line drive hitting is less correlated across seasons. This is not surprising. Hitting a dancing 80-100 mph pitch on the nose is quite difficult to do, and even the best players have trouble hitting line drives consistently. But some players do seem to be able to do it better than others, and the relationship is statistically significant.

Outcome (Hit Type)	Correlation
Outfield Flies	0.71[1]
Line Drives	0.10[5]
Ground Balls	0.73[1]
Infield Flies	0.60[1]

[1] = Significant at the 1% level
[5] = Significant at the 5% level

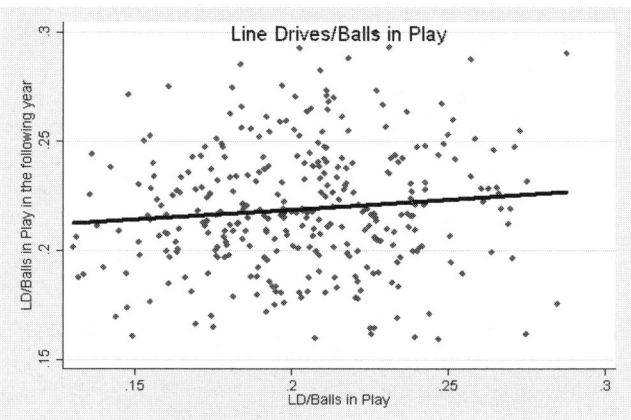

While the relationship is weaker for line drives than the other hit types, it is still real and meaningful. For this sample of hitters, about 20% of the balls put into play were line drives, and a 10% increase in line drives increased a hitter's BABIP by approximately 4%. Even though the skill persists in small doses, even small changes in line drives can have a big effect on BABIP. As we noted earlier, about three-fourths of line drives fall in safely for hits.

Outcome (OF Fly)	Correlation
Outs	0.60[1]
Singles	0.03
Doubles + Triples	0.22[1]
Home Runs	0.77[1]

[1] = Significant at the 1% level

However, the biggest difference from pitchers is that hitters appear to have some control over outcomes of different hit types. For outfield flies, batters seem to be able to control all outcomes other than singles, which normally result from poor contact or a broken bat. Long fly balls that generate extra-base hits are more likely to be the product of skill in hitting the ball hard. And, unlike pitchers, hitters seem have a skill generating home runs from outfield flies. Contrast the figure below with the one above for pitchers.

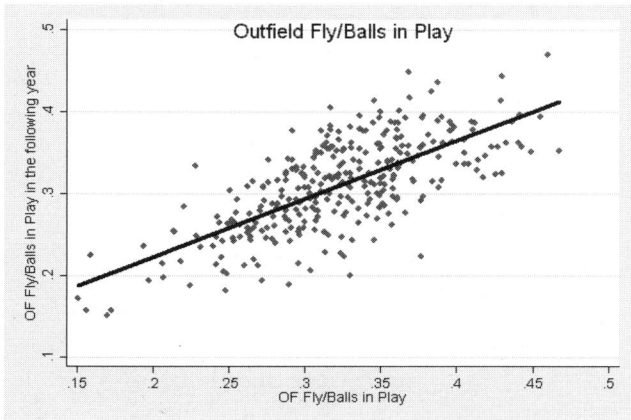

For hits on line drives, the correlations are smaller than for outfield flies, but they are all statistically significant. Not only do batters have some skill in hitting line drives, but in the type of line drives they hit. In particular, line drive home runs correlate more strongly than the other measures.

Outcome (LD)	Correlation
Outs	0.14[1]
Singles	0.11[5]
Doubles + Triples	0.14[1]
Home Runs	0.37[1]

[1] = *Significant at the 1% level*

[5] = *Significant at the 5% level*

In terms of ground balls, hitters do have some ability to reach base safely and possess a slightly lesser skill in the terms of the types of hits they get. This is important since a ground ball is the most common type of ball in play. In fact, when I regressed the impact of player hit types and outs per hit types from the previous season on current BABIP, outs on grounders had a statistically significant impact. This is something that was not true for outs generated from outfield flies or line drives. Players who are good at getting on base via the ground ball continue to do so. This might be a product of player speed, but the fact that the impact on singles and extra-base hits is about the same indicates that it has something to do with the way players hit the ball (e.g., hitting the ball hard, through infield gaps, and down the lines).

Outcome (GB)	Correlation
Outs	0.46[1]
Singles	0.16[1]
Doubles + Triples	0.14[1]

[1] = *Significant at the 1% level*

What does this mean for Predictive OPS (PrOPS) (discussed on page 294)? PrOPS relies on hit types, not scorebook outcomes, to predict batting performances of players. It's designed to remove some of the random bounces on balls in play that pollute hitting statistics. Given that batters seem to have a degree of skill in not only the types of balls they put in play, but also to generate hits among the different batted-ball types, recording the way in which players hit the ball is an important step in cleansing the data of luck. But PrOPS could go further. As it's currently constructed, PrOPS relies on a player's propensity to hit balls only in terms of line drives, ground balls, and fly balls; however, there seems to be a reason to include hit outcomes from each hit type. While we don't know if this will drastically alter the predictions, perhaps this is something that should be addressed in the further development of PrOPS.

Conclusion

This essay is merely a summary of our preliminary analysis of the newly available hit-type data. Though our work looked at only one of the important topics available for study with this new information, we have learned quite a bit about how much control pitchers and hitters exhibit. We expect new discoveries from this data in the future, and as more data comes in and becomes even more detailed we expect the sabermetric quest for truth about the game of baseball to progress even further.

Giving Players Their PrOPS:
A Platonic Measure of Hitting

by J.C. Bradbury

"[W]hat is a double? It really isn't enough to say that a double is when a runner hits the ball and gets to second base without a fielder's error. Anyone who has seen a baseball game knows that all doubles are not alike. There are doubles that should have been caught—just as there are balls that are hit that should have been doubles but were plucked from the air by preternaturally gifted fielders. There are lucky doubles and unlucky outs. To strip out the luck what you need, really, is something like a Platonic idea of a double."

- Michael Lewis, *Moneyball*, p. 134.

Baseball fans have always loved to judge players by the numbers they generate. Over the course of any given time period—most commonly it's a season or a career—numbers help us evaluate the quality of performance of the players who post the statistics. And once a few simple things such as parks, platoon splits, etc. are accounted for, statistics provide an objective unbiased record of performance. Fans may differ in the value they place on different stats, but there is little argument that players with higher batting, slugging and on-base averages performed better than players with lower numbers. Maybe there should be.

A problem with many of the statistics that we use is highlighted in the passage from *Moneyball* quoted above. Statistics generated from scorebook outcomes (single, double, etc.) are more than just a product of player skill; they include luck as well. The hitter who reaches base on a swinging bunt is credited as getting a hit. Conversely, a hitter who has a line drive to the gap erased by a spectacular defensive effort records an out. In these cases, one player is rewarded for poor hitting while the other is punished for good hitting. Yet players who hit the ball hard are preferred to those who dink the ball around the infield, because in the long run, the former will produce more runs than the latter. When we view raw player statistics over the course of the season, we often assume these things cancel out for each player. But the fact is that sometimes they don't. Every season, some players experience runs of good bounces, while others experience the opposite. Even though we know these runs of luck exist, it's hard to know who these people are from the outcome stats on which we normally rely.

The fact that any player is the beneficiary or victim of random chance isn't really an injustice. Stats are just a record of events, nothing more. As a practical matter, however, it's useful to know which players did the things that typically result in good outcomes and which avoided the things that cause bad outcomes. If we can identify players doing good things (e.g. hitting line drives) and bad things (e.g. hitting lazy pop-flies), then we can better evaluate and predict future performance of all players.

The data provided to *The Hardball Times* by *Baseball Info Solutions* provides a possible way to tease out some of the luck from player stats. This data includes not just officially scored results but also a record of the types of batted balls that players hit. In May 2004, I used this hit-type data to develop a new statistic called "PrOPS" to evaluate hitters. PrOPS (from Predicted On-base Plus Slugging) is a metric that projects a player's OPS using the composition of batted-ball types that a player hits over the course of a season. It is an attempt to capture Platonic performance, as opposed to outcome performance. By looking at how a large sample of players performed based on their batted-ball types as well as a few other important factors, I was able to estimate the typical OPS of players with similar hit-types. PrOPS is similar to the component ERA used to judge pitchers, which predicts the expected ERAs of pitchers based on their allowed hits, walks and strikeouts. Actual ERAs and component ERAs can differ quite a bit, and, as I'll show in a moment, so can PrOPS and OPS.

PrOPS rewards each player for the way he hits the ball, not for the actual outcome on balls put into play. If a player hits line drives 22% of the time, he is counted as having produced the outcomes typically generated from players with this same line-drive rate. Whether or not that particular player achieved the same outcome is not important.

To generate PrOPS I took every player season from 2002 to 2005—the sample of BIS data available to The Hardball Times—in which a player had over 400 plate appearances. I then used linear regression analysis to estimate the impact of several factors on a player's batting average (AVG), on-base percentage (OBP) and isolated power (ISO). Separately, these factors generate OPS (OPS=AVG+OBP+ISO); therefore, adding the projected statistics together creates a projected OPS or

PrOPS. I used the following factors to estimate the predicted values that go into PrOPS.

- Percentage of batted balls that were line drives
- Ground ball-to-fly ball ratio
- Walks per plate appearance
- Hit-by-pitches per plate appearance
- Strikeouts per at-bat
- Home runs per at-bat
- Home park of the player
- Season

Rather than directly making typical park-effect corrections, I estimated the impact of a player's home park using a regression "indicator variable" technique to explain how much a home park affected batting performance in terms of AVG, OBP and ISO. I used the same technique to tease out differences from year to year. In the end, PrOPS is a model that estimates how well a player performed in terms of scorebook outcomes that generate OPS, based on how he hit the ball when he put it in play (line drives, fly balls and ground balls) plus his defense independent performance (walks, hit-by-pitches strikeouts, and home runs). The odd bounces that pollute OPS occur mainly when the ball is put into play; therefore, replacing scorebook outcomes with hit types should remove much of this bias. Additionally, the defense independent outcomes measure not just a player's direct impact of these events on his batting statistics, but they also capture factors that may affect how batters control hits on balls in play. For example, a batter who walks a lot may be more likely to see good pitches to hit, such that when he does put the ball in play, on the ground or in the air, he's more likely to get a hit than someone who walks less.

But how reliable is PrOPS? Just because it came out of a computer doesn't make it useful. If PrOPS contains meaningful information, then it's something that players should be able to repeat from season to season. Additionally, it ought to correlate well with OPS. It turns out that PrOPS does both nicely.

As the next paired graphs show, PrOPS and OPS predicted OPS in the following season similarly. (Of course, Barry Bonds's 2002-2003 and 2003-2004 seasons are the extreme observations in the upper-right of the graphs. And no, excluding them from the sample does not alter the analysis significantly.) The lines over the scatter plots map the best linear predicted fits of the data. It turns out that PrOPS actually predicted the OPS of a player in the following season slightly better than OPS. OPS explained approximately 43% of the variance in OPS in the following year, while PrOPS explained about 46%.

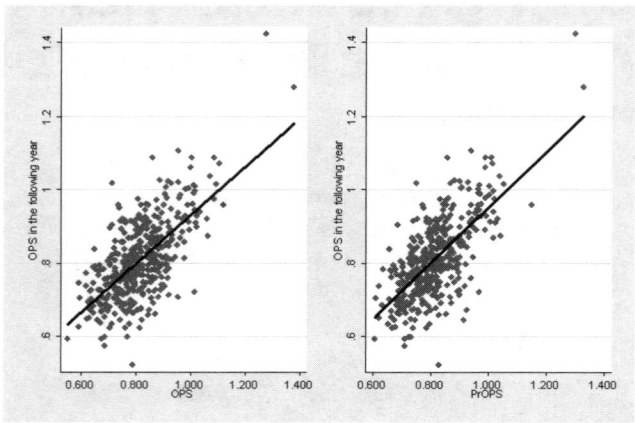

Also, PrOPS correlated more strongly from season to season than OPS did, with PrOPS explaining 53% of the variance of PrOPS in the following season. As the tighter fit of the points on the next graph indicates, PrOPS explained 10% more variance from year to year than OPS.

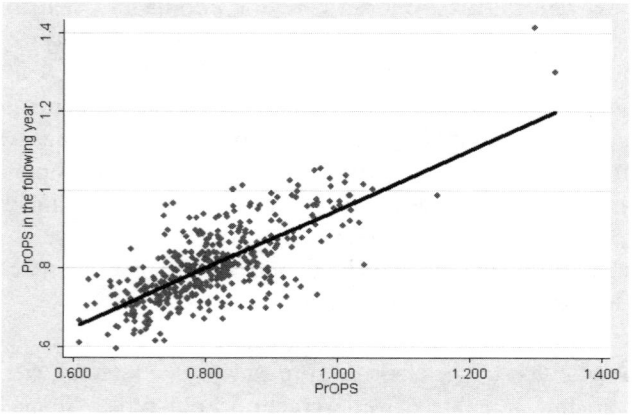

The next step was to observe how players with PrOPS that were very different from their OPS did in the following season. If PrOPS removes some luck, then a divergence of PrOPS from OPS ought to be associated with reversion of OPS towards PrOPS in the following year. The skill, and not the random bounces, will persist over time.

The table on the next page (Table 1) lists the top 25 "over performers" in terms of OPS from 2002-2004. That is, their OPS exceed their PrOPS predictions. If PrOPS correctly separates out some of the luck that pollutes OPS, then these players' OPS ought to decline in the following season. Of the top 25 over performers, 20 players had a lower OPS in the following season.

Table 1. Top 25 Over Performances (2002-2004)

02-04 Rank	02-05 Rank	Player	Team	Current Season				Following Season		
				Year	OPS	PrOPS	Over Performance	Team	OPS	Improvement/ Decline
1	1	Scott Podsednik	Brewers	2003	0.817	0.706	0.110	Brewers	0.674	-0.143
2	3	Adam Kennedy	Angels	2002	0.791	0.692	0.099	Angels	0.742	-0.049
3	5	Albert Pujols	Cardinals	2003	1.106	1.013	0.093	Cardinals	1.072	-0.034
4	6	J.T. Snow	Giants	2004	0.956	0.868	0.088	Giants	0.707	-0.249
5	7	Travis Hafner	Indians	2004	0.991	0.903	0.088	Indians	1.003	0.012
6	9	Milton Bradley	Indians	2003	0.923	0.836	0.087	Dodgers	0.785	-0.138
7	8	Ichiro Suzuki	Mariners	2004	0.868	0.781	0.087	Mariners	0.783	-0.085
8	10	Melvin Mora	Orioles	2004	0.977	0.889	0.087	Orioles	0.814	-0.163
9	11	Marcus Giles	Braves	2003	0.911	0.825	0.086	Braves	0.819	-0.092
10	14	Bobby Abreu	Phillies	2002	0.934	0.851	0.083	Phillies	0.877	-0.058
11	16	Randy Winn	Devil Rays	2002	0.820	0.737	0.083	Mariners	0.767	-0.053
12	20	Brad Wilkerson	Expos	2002	0.836	0.754	0.081	Expos	0.843	0.007
13	18	Edgar Renteria	Cardinals	2003	0.873	0.792	0.081	Cardinals	0.725	-0.148
14	23	Larry Walker	Rockies	2002	1.023	0.945	0.078	Rockies	0.898	-0.125
15	21	Garret Anderson	Angels	2003	0.885	0.808	0.078	Angels	0.789	-0.097
16	22	Aaron Rowand	White Sox	2004	0.902	0.824	0.078	White Sox	0.734	-0.168
17	24	Junior Spivey	Diamondbacks	2002	0.864	0.787	0.077	Diamondbacks	0.759	-0.105
18	25	Rocco Baldelli	Devil Rays	2003	0.741	0.663	0.077	Devil Rays	0.760	0.020
19	26	Ray Durham	Giants	2003	0.804	0.728	0.076	Giants	0.846	0.042
20	27	Todd Helton	Rockies	2003	1.088	1.011	0.076	Rockies	1.088	0.001
21	29	Jack Wilson	Pirates	2004	0.790	0.716	0.075	Pirates	0.663	-0.128
22	31	Bernie Williams	Yankees	2002	0.908	0.835	0.073	Yankees	0.778	-0.131
23	32	Kevin Millar	Marlins	2002	0.875	0.802	0.073	Red Sox	0.820	-0.055
24	33	Magglio Ordonez	White Sox	2002	0.977	0.905	0.072	White Sox	0.923	-0.054
25	35	Derek Jeter	Yankees	2003	0.841	0.771	0.071	Yankees	0.815	-0.026

Table 2: Top 25 Under Performances (2002-2004)

02-04 Rank	02-05 Rank	Player	Current Season Team	Year	OPS	PrOPS	Under Performance	Following Season Team	OPS	Improvement/ Decline
1	1	Paul Konerko	White Sox	2003	0.704	0.821	-0.117	White Sox	0.894	0.190
2	2	Matt Lawton	Indians	2003	0.762	0.875	-0.113	Indians	0.787	0.025
3	3	Jason Phillips	Mets	2004	0.622	0.732	-0.110	Dodgers	0.647	0.025
4	5	Bobby Higginson	Tigers	2003	0.688	0.792	-0.104	Tigers	0.741	0.053
5	7	Bengie Molina	Angels	2002	0.593	0.689	-0.096	Angels	0.745	0.152
6	9	Tony Batista	Orioles	2003	0.663	0.758	-0.094	Expos	0.726	0.063
7	10	Rafael Palmeiro	Orioles	2004	0.796	0.890	-0.094	Orioles	0.786	-0.010
8	12	Chipper Jones	Braves	2004	0.847	0.939	-0.092	Braves	0.956	0.110
9	13	Steve Finley	Diamondbacks	2004	0.823	0.914	-0.090	Angels	0.644	-0.180
10	14	Brad Ausmus	Astros	2003	0.592	0.680	-0.088	Astros	0.626	0.035
11	15	Vinny Castilla	Braves	2002	0.616	0.703	-0.087	Braves	0.772	0.156
12	16	Toby Hall	Devil Rays	2003	0.675	0.762	-0.086	Devil Rays	0.666	-0.010
13	18	Matt Lawton	Indians	2002	0.740	0.823	-0.083	Indians	0.762	0.022
14	21	Brad Ausmus	Astros	2004	0.626	0.705	-0.079	Astros	0.694	0.067
15	25	Sammy Sosa	Cubs	2004	0.849	0.923	-0.074	Orioles	0.671	-0.178
16	26	Deivi Cruz	Orioles	2003	0.643	0.717	-0.073	Giants	0.746	0.103
17	30	Rondell White	Yankees	2002	0.665	0.736	-0.071	Padres	0.795	0.129
18	33	Ben Broussard	Indians	2003	0.753	0.821	-0.068	Indians	0.857	0.104
19	34	Pat Burrell	Phillies	2003	0.713	0.779	-0.065	Phillies	0.821	0.107
20	35	Brian Schneider	Expos	2004	0.721	0.785	-0.064	Nationals	0.739	0.018
21	36	Craig Counsell	Brewers	2004	0.638	0.702	-0.064	Diamondbacks	0.726	0.088
22	37	Carlos Delgado	Blue Jays	2004	0.907	0.970	-0.063	Marlins	0.986	0.079
23	46	Tino Martinez	Cardinals	2002	0.775	0.835	-0.060	Cardinals	0.780	0.004
24	47	Melvin Mora	Orioles	2002	0.741	0.801	-0.060	Orioles	0.915	0.173
25	42	Adam Dunn	Reds	2003	0.819	0.879	-0.060	Reds	0.956	0.138

Among this group are some seasons you may recall: Podsednik's 2003 (an .822 OPS from a career .733 OPS hitter), Ichiro's record-breaking 262-hit 2004, and Marcus Giles's "breakout" 2003 season.

The second table (Table 2) includes a list of the top 25 "under performers" from 2002-2004. These players put up OPS worse than what PrOPS says they should have and therefore may have been victims of bad luck. Of the 25 under performers, 21 improved their OPS in the following season.

This seems to indicate that PrOPS is picking up some useful information not captured by OPS. To see whether or not this phenomenon is isolated at the extremes, I looked at the entire sample to determine if there is a relationship between a player's over/under performance and the decline/improvement in the following season. It turns out that there is. The next graph maps the relationship.

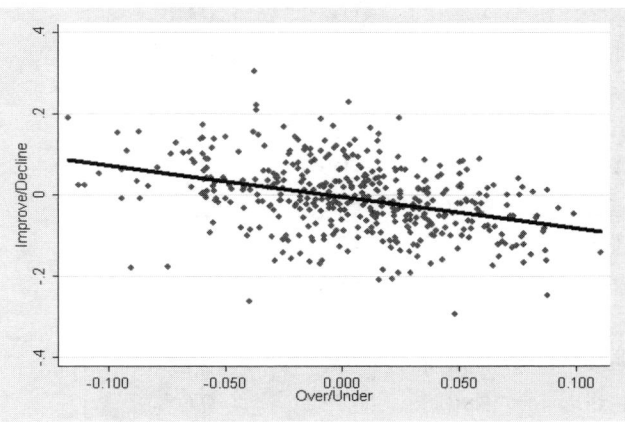

There is a highly statistically significant relationship—meaning the observed correlation is not likely the result of random variation—between a player's over/under performance and his decline/improvement. And the greater the deviation between PrOPS and OPS, the larger the reversion is in the following season. For every 0.01 increase/decrease in a player's over/under performance, his OPS is likely to fall/rise by 0.008 the following season. For example, a player with an OPS 10 "points" above his PrOPS, can expect his OPS to fall by eight points in the following season. That is quite a reversion. Again, this is more evidence that PrOPS successfully separates some luck from skill.

Now that we have some confidence in the usefulness of PrOPS, what can it tell us about player performances during the 2005 season? Tables 3 and 4 on the next two pages list the top 25 over/under performances of 2005 for players with more than 400 plate appearances. There are some interesting players on both lists. Some players with uncharacteristically good seasons, such as Bill Hall, Robinson Cano and Brian Roberts, appear to have over performed their PrOPS. I expect these players to take a step backwards in 2006. And some players who performed below expectations, like Aaron Boone, Luis Castillo and Austin Kearns, appear to have under performed their PrOPS. It's likely these players will progress towards their previous form in 2006.

It's also interesting to see that several players with exceptionally good and bad seasons played better and worse than their PrOPS indicate. Jason Giambi, Manny Ramirez and Andruw Jones all played better than their OPS, and their seasons were pretty good, while Willy Taveras, Jose Reyes and Alex Gonzalez were lucky that their weak bats didn't look as bad as they were.

I want to make it clear that, at its current state of development, PrOPS is not designed to predict performance accurately from one season to the next. It certainly might help projections by stripping some luck from past performance; however, other corrections (such as age) are needed to build a full-blown projection system. And even then, I don't know if it would predict better than any of the existing projection systems out there. These systems also strip away luck using different methods. What we have learned from PrOPS is that luck does play a non-trivial role in biasing player statistics that we ought to be aware of. PrOPS ought to help us identify large swings in performance as flukes or reality. With the BIS data, hopefully PrOPS can be refined to more accurately reflect player skills and to assist us in our quest to capture Platonic performance.

05 Rank	02-05 Rank	Player	Team	OPS	PrOPS	Over Performance
1	2	Mark Ellis	Athletics	0.868	0.759	0.109
2	4	Carl Crawford	Devil Rays	0.800	0.708	0.093
3	12	Hideki Matsui	Yankees	0.854	0.769	0.085
4	13	Bill Hall	Brewers	0.837	0.752	0.085
5	15	Mike Sweeney	Royals	0.864	0.781	0.083
6	17	Coco Crisp	Indians	0.816	0.733	0.082
7	19	Marcus Giles	Braves	0.831	0.750	0.081
8	28	Derrek Lee	Cubs	1.089	1.012	0.076
9	30	Miguel Tejada	Orioles	0.869	0.794	0.075
10	34	Sean Casey	Reds	0.795	0.722	0.072
11	39	Alex Gonzalez	Marlins	0.686	0.616	0.070
12	40	Scott Podsednik	White Sox	0.706	0.637	0.069
13	45	Jose Reyes	Mets	0.688	0.621	0.066
14	46	Jhonny Peralta	Indians	0.889	0.822	0.066
15	50	Todd Walker	Cubs	0.833	0.769	0.064
16	52	Willy Taveras	Astros	0.663	0.600	0.063
17	59	Alex Rodriguez	Yankees	1.025	0.964	0.060
18	60	Michael Young	Rangers	0.901	0.840	0.060
19	66	Robinson Cano	Yankees	0.777	0.719	0.057
20	67	Miguel Cabrera	Marlins	0.947	0.892	0.056
21	70	Luis Matos	Orioles	0.710	0.653	0.056
22	72	David DeJesus	Royals	0.804	0.749	0.055
23	73	Frank Catalanotto	Blue Jays	0.806	0.752	0.054
24	76	Brian Roberts	Orioles	0.903	0.848	0.054
25	78	Jimmy Rollins	Phillies	0.764	0.711	0.053

Table 3: Top 25 Over Performers 2005*

*Based on first 160 games.

05 Rank	02-05 Rank	Player	Team	OPS	PrOPS	Under Performance
		Table 4: Top 25 Under Performers 2005*				
1	4	Jason Giambi	Yankees	0.986	1.093	-0.107
2	6	Manny Ramirez	Red Sox	0.960	1.057	-0.097
3	17	Rafael Palmeiro	Orioles	0.786	0.872	-0.086
4	19	Aaron Boone	Indians	0.677	0.759	-0.082
5	20	Andruw Jones	Braves	0.925	1.004	-0.079
6	22	Luis Castillo	Marlins	0.765	0.841	-0.077
7	23	Paul Konerko	White Sox	0.907	0.983	-0.076
8	24	Austin Kearns	Reds	0.766	0.840	-0.074
9	28	Cristian Guzman	Nationals	0.573	0.645	-0.072
10	29	Yadier Molina	Cardinals	0.659	0.731	-0.072
11	31	Mark Loretta	Padres	0.708	0.777	-0.069
12	32	Jason Phillips	Dodgers	0.647	0.716	-0.069
13	38	Mike Matheny	Giants	0.702	0.765	-0.063
14	39	Steve Finley	Angels	0.644	0.706	-0.062
15	40	Gregg Zaun	Blue Jays	0.729	0.790	-0.062
16	41	A.J. Pierzynski	White Sox	0.730	0.791	-0.061
17	44	Abraham Nunez	Cardinals	0.700	0.760	-0.060
18	45	Justin Morneau	Twins	0.737	0.797	-0.060
19	49	Adam LaRoche	Braves	0.775	0.835	-0.059
20	59	Sammy Sosa	Orioles	0.671	0.729	-0.058
21	61	Juan Pierre	Marlins	0.671	0.727	-0.057
22	72	Casey Blake	Indians	0.744	0.797	-0.053
23	74	Dan Johnson	Athletics	0.818	0.871	-0.053
24	75	Brad Ausmus	Astros	0.694	0.746	-0.052
25	76	Rickie Weeks	Brewers	0.731	0.783	-0.052

*Based on first 160 games.

Around the Bases One More Time
by Dan Fox

The new phone books are here! The new phone books are Here!

– Steve Martin as "The Jerk", 1979

For a baseball geek like me, the feeling that Steve Martin's character had was duplicated when, just before press time, I was able to get a hold of play-by-play data (yes, all 191,823 plays) for the newly minted 2005 season. And with that data comes a plethora of ideas for analysis of the 2005 season.

While you'll have to wait for those to appear on The Hardball Times website because we're rushing to get this book out, one for which I already had the tools assembled is the base running framework I described in three articles this summer under the heading "Circle the Wagons." For those who haven't read the explanations I'll provide a short synopsis in this article and then reveal the results for the 2005 season.

The Methodology

The methodology I use derives from looking at three specific scenarios in a ballgame.

- Runner on first, second not occupied and the batter singles
- Runner on second, third not occupied and the batter singles
- Runner on first, second not occupied and the batter doubles

After isolating these scenarios, I then calculate the number of bases that runners advanced in each scenario, grouped by the number of outs there were at the start of the play and which fielder fielded the ball. I take these into consideration because both the number of outs and the location of the fielded ball play a large role in determining whether and how many bases the runner will advance. For example, as I showed in part I of my series, with two outs and a man on first when the batter doubles, the runner scores 80% of the time when the ball is fielded by the center fielder, but just 43% of the time when fielded by the left fielder. By using the position that fielded the ball, the differences in left-handed or right-handed hitters hitting behind certain base runners is also taken into account.

To illustrate the magnitude of the differences involved, consider the situation when the runner is on first, no one on second and the batter singles with nobody out. Here's a chart of how far the runner advances, based on where the ball is hit:

Hit to...	To 2nd	To 3rd
Left	85%	14%
Center	73%	26%
Right	57%	41%

What this indicates is that the probability of advancing can vary by as much as 30% depending on the field to which the ball is hit. If a particular player is typically followed in the lineup by a left-handed hitter, his chances of moving from first to third on a single, and therefore accumulating more bases, increases.

What this approach gives us is a baseline we can use to measure individual base runners against the average runner in each of the three scenarios. In other words, we can now see just how often Derek Jeter takes third when Alex Rodriguez singles and how that compares to the average runner given the number of outs and the player who fielded the ball. Totaling across all the dimensions can then yield both the total number of bases gained (EB) and the total number of bases above expected—what I call Incremental Bases (IB).

But simply counting bases, while helpful in comparing players, isn't what we're really after. Our preference is to try and convert those bases gained into runs—"the currency with which runs are purchased" in the words of Bill James. This approach was also used in an excellent article by James Click in the *2005 Baseball Prospectus*.

To do that we use Run Expectancy tables like the one shown here modeled for the 2005 National League.

Runners	0	1	2
No one on	0.528	0.279	0.107
Runner on first	0.887	0.536	0.232
Runner on second	1.135	0.690	0.331
Runners on first and second	1.503	0.916	0.448
Runner on third	1.380	0.961	0.368
Runners on first and third	1.762	1.168	0.496
Runners on second and third	1.980	1.405	0.589
Bases loaded	2.303	1.548	0.766

These tables represent the eight states in which you can find base runners and the expected number of runs in the remainder of the inning, given the number of outs. In other words, when the bases are empty with nobody out, the average team scored just over half a run (.528) in the remainder of the inning, while with the bases loaded and one out teams average 1.548 runs.

So if a base runner moves from first to third on a single with one out, he's helped transition his team from a state where they were expected to score .536 runs to one where the expectation is 1.169 runs. But of course we can't give full credit to the runner for the additional .633 runs. After all, the hitter does play a role, and in the vast majority of the cases the base runner could have jogged to second without a play.

In order to count the runner's contribution appropriately we look at what would have normally occurred and compare it to what actually did occur. In this case we'll assume the runner would have gotten to second anyway, making it first and second and one out (.916), and subtract it from the actual situation (1.168). This allows us to credit the runner with his contribution (.252) to increasing the Run Expectancy. Likewise, if a runner gets thrown out, he'll receive negative credit because he cost the team a scoring opportunity. For example, getting thrown out at third on a single with nobody out cost the team .967 runs, calculated as the new situation (.536 = a runner on first with one out) minus the situation had he not tried to advance (1.503 = runners on first and second with nobody out). By following this method we can build derivative tables of run values for the various outcomes in the three base running scenarios I've used to measure base running performance. It should be noted that in these calculations, I did not give any credit to a runner for advancing the "standard" number of bases, e.g. one base for a single and two for a double.

For example, with a runner on first and the batter singles the derivative table for 2005 would look as follows:

	Advance		
Outs	To 3rd	Scores	Out
0	0.259	0.384	-0.967
1	0.252	0.620	-0.685
2	0.048	0.784	-0.448

Each cell indicates the run value that will be credited to a base runner based on his advancement in this scenario.

Those derivative tables can then be applied to each actual opportunity in which a base runner finds himself. So if Jeter moved from first to third on a single with nobody out, we'll credit him with .259 runs for that opportunity, and so on. I call the total across all opportunities Base Runner Runs (BRR).

But just as with measuring the total number of bases gained, BRR needs to be compared against some baseline since the number of runs (a good analogy here is RBIs) has a lot to do with the number of opportunities a runner has in addition to the number of outs and field to which the ball is hit in those opportunities. To adjust for this I also used the derivative table to calculate the number of runs the runner would be expected to contribute given the opportunities he had.

Putting all of this together we can then report a few new measures that include:

- **EB**—the expected number of bases a base runner should have gained given his opportunities in our three scenarios above.

- **IB**—the difference between the actual and expected bases gained. Negative values indicate that the base runner did not advance as many bases as an average player would have given the same opportunities

- **Base Runner Runs or BRR**—the total number of runs a runner can be attributed given his base running performance in the opportunities he had (given our three scenarios above).

- **Expected Runs or ExR**—the total number of runs a runner should have contributed given his opportunities in our three scenarios.

- **Incremental Runs or IR**—the difference between the BRR and ExR. Negative values indicate that the runner performed poorly in his opportunities by not taking as many bases and therefore contributing fewer runs than he should have.

- **Incremental Run Percentage (IRP)**—a rate statistic calculated as the ratio of IR to BRR. IRP is akin to OPS+ in that it shows at what rate players contribute runs with their base running. Values over 100 indicate players who contributed above what would have been expected while values under 100 indicate a poor performance. IRP is needed for player comparisons since IR, like RBIs, is weighted by opportunity.

Run Expectancy is superior to simply counting bases for several reasons. First, it at least quantifies the contribution base running makes in terms of runs and therefore wins and losses. And second, when looking at individuals, it weights base running decisions more accurately because getting to third with two outs is much less valuable (over six times less) than doing so with nobody out. Simply counting bases does not capture this dimension. The weakness of this approach is that it doesn't take into account the score. Teams that find themselves ahead a lot or behind a lot may have their base runners underestimated since they'll often play station-to-station.

Finally, I then take BRR, ExR and IR and park adjust them using a three year moving average based on the ratio of actual bases gained to expected bases. I weight each of the three years identically and take into consideration teams that moved into different parks. For example, the 2005 park factor I calculate for the Padres (.977) includes only 2004 and 2005 since they moved into PETCO Park to start the 2004 season. The list of park factors I've used for 2005 are listed at the end of the article.

The Results

First let's take a look at the leaders in IR for 2005. Note that OA represents "out advancing."

Name	Opp	OA	BRR	IR	IRP
Carlos Beltran	45	1	9.56	3.95	170
Robinson Cano	54	1	10.27	3.37	149
David Wright	41	0	10.65	3.26	144
Scott Podsednik	45	0	10.25	3.19	145
Julio Lugo	58	0	10.35	3.12	143
Edgar Renteria	49	0	12.08	3.10	135
Darin Erstad	59	0	11.14	3.05	138
Rafael Furcal	52	0	10.92	3.05	139
David DeJesus	50	0	9.75	3.03	145
Chone Figgins	58	3	11.44	3.02	136
Grady Sizemore	59	0	13.19	3.01	130
Juan Pierre	56	0	8.39	2.97	155
Jerry Hairston	32	0	6.88	2.74	166
Eric Chavez	56	0	11.44	2.68	131
Ryan Freel	28	0	5.70	2.63	186
Nook Logan	26	0	6.78	2.59	162
Terrence Long	37	1	6.51	2.51	163
Randy Winn	48	0	7.63	2.50	149
Ruben Gotay	21	0	7.54	2.44	148
Marcus Giles	42	0	10.49	2.44	130

So as shown in the part III article this summer, good base runners tend to contribute an additional 3 to 5.5 runs over the course of a season. In other words, a good base runner, at least in these three scenarios, is worth at most around a half win per season.

Over the last six years (2000-2006) Juan Pierre leads in IR at 15.374 while his teammate Luis Castillo is a close second at 15.368.

It is interesting that even though Carlos Beltran had an otherwise substandard year, he led the league while his teammate David Wright came in third. Beltran has also improved each year in IR with consecutive seasons of 0.23, 0.55, 1.67, 2.21 and 2.27 from 2000 to 2004.

You'll also notice that the Royals' Ruben Gotay contributed 2.44 additional runs in only 21 opportunities and that Chone Figgins came out three runs more than expected despite being thrown out three times in 58 opportunities. The matrix shown previously indicates just how costly getting thrown out is.

Those at the bottom in IR are shown in the following table.

Name	Opp	OA	BRR	IR	IRP
Luis Gonzalez	44	4	-0.24	-5.52	-5
Pat Burrell	34	4	1.69	-5.20	25
Lance Berkman	37	3	0.06	-4.52	1
David Ortiz	41	1	1.33	-4.24	24
Bengie Molina	34	0	1.17	-4.10	22
Mark Loretta	46	4	5.74	-3.99	59
Matt Lawton	49	3	2.54	-3.75	40
Kevin Millar	47	1	1.99	-3.60	36
Johnny Estrada	27	1	1.05	-3.06	26
Aramis Ramirez	45	2	3.82	-3.03	56
Carlos Delgado	48	0	4.08	-3.00	58
Rickie Weeks	30	5	2.51	-2.83	47
Carlos Lee	29	2	0.56	-2.79	17
Tino Martinez	30	2	0.69	-2.69	20
Jason Phillips	29	2	1.79	-2.68	40
Hank Blalock	32	2	1.73	-2.65	40
Paul Konerko	55	3	6.02	-2.53	70
Jim Thome	23	2	0.72	-2.52	22
Milton Bradley	21	4	2.30	-2.50	48
Mike Piazza	26	1	0.69	-2.46	22

This list is populated by players who were frequently thrown out, like Brewers rookie Rickie Weeks, who was nabbed an astounding five times in 30 opportunities, tops in baseball.

As an aside I should mention that in early October I wrote a post on my blog congratulating broadcaster Tim McCarver on his intuition when he noted that Derek Jeter never gets thrown out on the bases. In that post I noted that in 248 opportunities from 2000 through 2004, Jeter was thrown out only twice (once each in

2003 and 2004). However, in 2005 Jeter was thrown out three times in 69 opportunities, so now has been nabbed five times in 317 chances. Still, that's a far cry better than Weeks.

The list is also populated by players who are simply slow, like David Ortiz and Bengie Molina, and those like Lance Berkman who suffered through injuries in 2005. Berkman has never been outstanding on the bases, but his 2005 performance was more than a run and a half worse than his previous low of -2.91 in 2001.

This list also indicates that a bad runner can cost his team around a half win per season, so the spread is between eight and 10 runs per season between the best and worst.

Over the course of the last six seasons, Carlos Delgado takes the bottom spot at -13.8 with Edgar Martinez at -12.7.

But measuring by IR alone isn't sufficient to see who actually might be the best runner. For that we need to rank by IRP, our rate statistic.

Here are the top 20 in 2005 by IRP for those who had 25 or more opportunities.

Name	Opp	OA	BRR	IR	IRP
Ryan Freel	28	0	5.70	2.63	186
Carlos Beltran	45	1	9.56	3.95	170
Jerry Hairston	32	0	6.88	2.74	166
Terrence Long	37	1	6.51	2.51	163
Nook Logan	26	0	6.78	2.59	162
Aaron Miles	28	0	6.27	2.31	158
Juan Pierre	56	0	8.39	2.97	155
Robinson Cano	54	1	10.27	3.37	149
Randy Winn	48	0	7.63	2.50	149
Tadahito Iguchi	37	0	6.95	2.26	148
Scott Podsednik	45	0	10.25	3.19	145
David DeJesus	50	0	9.75	3.03	145
Jay Payton	33	0	5.99	1.85	145
David Wright	41	0	10.65	3.26	144
Clint Barmes	36	0	8.05	2.43	143
Julio Lugo	58	0	10.35	3.12	143
Tike Redman	31	0	5.58	1.65	142
Eric Byrnes	25	0	5.51	1.61	141
Jeremy Reed	31	0	7.04	2.06	141
Eric Hinske	35	1	7.47	2.14	140

Here you can see that Freel's 186 IRP indicates that he netted 86% more runs than expected given his 28 opportunities. You'll also notice that Gotay doesn't

make this list with his 148 IRP since he had only 21 opportunities. I restricted the number of opportunities to avoid the random effects of small sample sizes.

Gotay is also an example of why it's important to look both at IR and IRP. Remember that he racked up an IR of 2.44 in just 21 opportunities. A rate that high might lead you to believe that he's a Ty Cobb on the bases. Looking more closely, however, you see that his 148 IRP, while very good, does not crack the top 10 because he was *expected* to contribute 7.54 runs in those 21 opportunities. In other words, he just happened to be on base in situations where the run expectancy was already high and which he cashed in and then some.

Over the last six seasons Dusty Baker favorite Calvin Murray ranks first in IRP at 165 with Timo Perez second at 156 among those players with 50 or more opportunities (they each had 53).

The trailers in IRP for 2005 were:

Name	Opp	OA	BRR	IR	IRP
Luis Gonzalez	44	4	-0.24	-5.52	-5
Lance Berkman	37	3	0.06	-4.52	1
Carlos Lee	29	2	0.56	-2.79	17
Tino Martinez	30	2	0.69	-2.69	20
Mike Piazza	26	1	0.69	-2.46	22
Bengie Molina	34	0	1.17	-4.10	22
David Ortiz	41	1	1.33	-4.24	24
Pat Burrell	34	4	1.69	-5.20	25
Johnny Estrada	27	1	1.05	-3.06	26
Kevin Millar	47	1	1.99	-3.60	36
Daryle Ward	28	1	1.43	-2.19	40
Hank Blalock	32	2	1.73	-2.65	40
Jason Phillips	29	2	1.79	-2.68	40
Matt Lawton	49	3	2.54	-3.75	40
Rickie Weeks	30	5	2.51	-2.83	47
Toby Hall	31	2	2.02	-2.17	48
Juan Encarnacion	32	2	2.58	-2.38	52
Aramis Ramirez	45	2	3.82	-3.03	56
Phil Nevin	29	3	2.90	-2.24	56
Ramon Hernandez	28	1	2.21	-1.66	57

This list is interesting as it shows that the Diamondbacks' Luis Gonzalez not only had a negative IR but also a negative BRR. In other words, in absolute, not just in relative terms, he cost his team runs when on the bases.

Over the past six seasons among those players with 50 or more opportunities, two players rank quite a bit lower than everyone else: Jose Canseco ranks last in IR at .27 and Ken Harvey is next to the bottom at .36.

Finally, we'll turn to teams and rank them by IR.

Name	Opp	OA	BRR	IR	IRP
TBA	447	6	84.15	13.20	119
OAK	478	3	87.63	10.52	114
ATL	392	4	70.25	8.38	114
NYN	372	5	59.15	7.35	114
SEA	403	5	61.74	6.78	112
KCA	453	7	72.45	6.76	110
CHN	422	8	66.27	4.98	108
COL	449	7	80.12	4.33	106
CLE	437	7	70.81	3.79	106
SLN	448	6	73.91	3.09	104
TOR	453	10	61.43	2.86	105
CHA	420	11	64.92	2.67	104
DET	445	5	64.62	2.49	104
NYA	485	11	67.62	2.45	104
ANA	474	10	77.67	2.26	103
TEX	402	6	66.79	1.30	102
SFN	440	8	65.39	0.12	100
CIN	377	8	53.51	0.10	100
MIN	449	7	61.34	-1.18	98
MIL	383	12	55.24	-2.74	95
HOU	413	11	60.43	-4.85	93
ARI	394	7	53.05	-5.52	91
WAS	392	7	56.91	-5.63	91
PIT	458	13	69.29	-5.69	92
SDN	427	13	66.56	-5.86	92
BAL	436	11	62.82	-6.11	91
FLO	447	10	59.31	-7.82	88
LAN	396	12	45.62	-9.87	82
BOS	501	7	59.43	-13.64	81
PHI	448	19	56.16	-15.17	79

The spread here is around 30 runs, or three wins, from Tampa Bay to Philadelphia. Incidentally, the Phillies illustrate a factor not taken into account in this system—the effect of third base coaching. Those 19 times the Phils were thrown out on the bases were fairly evenly distributed, as shown in the table below, which is an indication that coaching (as with the 2003 Cubs and "Waving" Wendell Kim) may be involved.

Name	Opp	OA
Pat Burrell	34	4
David Bell	37	3
Mike Lieberthal	25	2
Bobby Abreu	56	2
Jason Michaels	35	2
Jim Thome	23	2
Jimmy Rollins	63	2
Chase Utley	38	1
Kenny Lofton	35	1

Although much was made in the postseason regarding the Angels' taking extra bases while "Moneyball" teams such as the A's waited for walks, this analysis indicates that it was the A's, not the Angels, that took advantage of their opportunities to a greater degree and were able to plate an additional 10 runs over what would have been expected. The Angels were at just over two, thanks to the trio of Bengie Molina, Dallas McPherson and Adam Kennedy who combined for an IR of around -8.

Heading Home

Certainly this system could use some refinements, as mentioned in my articles, including park factors for various scenarios and the addition of the advancement on outs, to name a couple. But at least it moves the ball forward and begins to quantify an area that has escaped or defied analysis for most of baseball history.

Addendum

Here are the 2005 baserunning park factors:

Team	Park	BRPF
TEX	The Ballpark at Arlington	105
COL	Coors Field	103
CHN	Wrigley Field	103
WAS	RFK Stadium	103
KCA	Royals Stadium	103
LAN	Dodger Stadium	103
BOS	Fenway Park II	102
MIL	Miller Park	102
DET	Comerica Park	101
ARI	Chase Field	101
BAL	Oriole Park at Camden Yards	100
OAK	Network Associates Coliseum	100
ATL	Turner Field	100
TBA	Tropicana Field	100
SFN	SBC Park	100
TOR	Rogers Centre	100
MIN	Hubert H Humphrey Metrodome	100
NYN	Shea Stadium	100
PIT	PNC Park	99
HOU	Minute Maid Park	99
SLN	Busch Stadium II	99
CHA	U.S. Cellular Field	99
CIN	Great American Ball Park	98
CLE	Jacobs Field	98
SDN	Petco Park	98
ANA	Edison International Field	98
SEA	Safeco Field	97
PHI	Citizen's Bank Park	97
FLO	Dolphins Stadium	96
NYA	Yankee Stadium II	96

The park factors in this table are used only when calculating the various statistics for performance in the home park. In other words, these are not overall factors but apply only to data captured in a particular park.

Following are some of the web addresses referenced in the article:

Circling the Bases Part I

http://www.hardballtimes.com/main/article/circling-the-wagons-running-the-bases-part-i/

Circling the Bases Part II

http://www.hardballtimes.com/main/article/circle-the-wagons-running-the-bases-part-ii/

Circling the Bases Part III

http://www.hardballtimes.com/main/article/circle-the-wagons-running-the-bases-part-iii/

Dan's blog is located at http://danagonistes.blogspot.com/

Net Win Shares Value
by Dave Studenmund

Jason Bay of the Pittsburgh Pirates had a great year in 2005. A one-time minor-league reject from the Mets and Padres, Bay batted .306/.402/.559 and created 34 Win Shares for the Bucs, production that would have qualified him for the MVP in many previous seasons.

To top it off, the "small-market" Pirates only paid him $355,000 last year because he was not eligible for arbitration. By my reckoning, that made his contract the most valuable in all of major league baseball. He may not win the MVP, but he does win THT's "Most Valuable Contract" award. It's going to take me a couple of paragraphs to explain why.

I use Win Shares to calculate the value of a major league contract, and the reason is simple. Ball clubs pay players to win ball games. Hitting home runs and throwing strikeouts is nice, but they're just a means to an end: winning games. Economic research has shown that each game a contending baseball team wins adds about $2 million in additional revenue, depending on the market. So if you want to figure out how much a player helped his team's bottom line, figure out how many wins he contributed. That's what Win Shares does.

For instance, Sidney Ponson was paid $8.5 million last year, due to a contract he signed with the Orioles before the 2004 season. He logged a miserable 6.21 ERA before the Orioles finally released him, creating one Win Share for the year. The Orioles paid him $8.5 million for one measly Win Share. On the other hand, the Pirates only paid Bay $10,441 per Win Share.

$8.5 million vs. $10 thousand. Big difference.

However, I like to take this analysis several steps further and calculate something called Net Win Shares Value. It's more complicated, but it results in a better, fairer way to evaluate contracts. To make this article bearable, I'll put a short example of the system here and the long, boring definition at the end. For my example, I'm going to refer to Derrek Lee, who would have been a free agent this year if he hadn't signed a long-term contract two years ago.

Lee was paid $7.7 million last year, or $7.4 million above the minimum of $316,000. He created 37 Win Shares, or 24 above what a typical bench player would have provided in his playing time (we call that WSAB, or Win Shares Above Bench). Net Win Shares Value assumes that major league teams can find average bench players at the major league minimum.

The average free agent was paid $1.3 million for each WSAB last year so, at $7.4 million, Lee was "expected" to create 5.6 WSAB ($7.4 divided by $1.3). At 24 WSAB, he was 18 WSAB above expectations.

In total, major league teams paid $789,000 for each WSAB, including all types of players (free agents, arbitration-eligible and non-arbitration). So to calculate how much value Lee brought to the Cubs, we multiply Lee's 18 "extra" WSAB by $789,000 for a total Net Win Share Value of $14.6 million. (You will get a slightly different figure due to rounding.)

If you still have questions, check out the addendum. Classifying players into different types was the trickiest part of the process.

OK, so who were the best values in 2005? The top 10 were:

Best 2005 Net Win Shares Values					
Name	Status	Pos	WSAB	Salary	Net WS Value
Bay, J.	NA	OF	20.4	$355,000	$16,091,580
Willis, D.	NA	SP	19.2	$378,500	$15,120,052
Hafner, T.	NA	1B	18.9	$500,000	$14,753,071
Lee, D.	FA	1B	24.1	$7,666,667	$14,602,644
Ortiz, D.	FA	DH	22.0	$5,250,000	$14,343,907
Roberts, B.	NA	2B	17.1	$390,000	$13,410,248
Delgado, C.	FA	1B	19.7	$4,000,000	$13,351,563
Ensberg, M.	NA	3B	16.9	$450,000	$13,218,179
Cabrera, M.	NA	OF	16.8	$370,000	$13,172,528
Giles, B.	FA	OF	22.7	$8,333,333	$13,044,900

FA stands for Free Agent, NA stands for Not Arbitration eligible and A stands for Arbitration eligible.

You might have assumed that the top ten values would all be players not eligible for arbitration, but Net Win Shares Value levels the comparisons between types. You also might be surprised to see Carlos Delgado, who signed a four-year, $52 million contract this offseason, on the list. Delgado's contract calls for most of his salary to be "backloaded." He made only $4 million in 2005, but he'll make $15 million a year for the next three years. In other words, he'll never be this valuable again.

This type of salary accounting is not a good way to evaluate long-term contracts. But it's a logical way to approach one-year evaluations.

How about the lowest values, you ask? On the next table, you will find the usual suspects, including Sammy Sosa, Kevin Brown and Chan Ho Park. There's a whole lot of pain on this list, mostly seriously injured players and general managers with ulcers.

To show you how much an injury can turn value around, consider that Barry Bonds was the best contractual value in baseball just a year ago (as listed in last year's *THT Annual*) at $23 million. On the other hand, Chan Ho Park has made the worst-value list two years in a row.

Lowest 2005 Net Win Shares Values					
Name	Status	Pos	WSAB	Salary	Net WS Value
Sosa, Sammy	FA	OF	-3.3	$17,000,000	-$12,721,992
Bonds, Barry	FA	OF	1.5	$22,000,000	-$11,920,375
Brown, Kevin	FA	SP	-2.2	$15,714,286	-$11,056,221
Bagwell, Jeff	FA	1B	1.3	$18,000,000	-$9,685,736
Park, Chan Ho	FA	SP	0.5	$15,000,0000	-$8,523,669
Schilling, Curt	FA	SP	0.3	$14,500,000	-$8,340,268
Thome, Jim	FA	1B	-0.4	$13,166,667	-$8,142,938
Mussina, Mike	FA	SP	4.5	$19,000,000	-$7,788,930
Ponson, Sidney	FA	SP	-3.6	$8,500,000	-$7,787,717
Gagne, Eric	A	RP	1.5	$8,000,000	-$7,443,508

The 2004 Free-Agent Class

Last year's free agents are on everybody's minds, so here's a list of the best and worst values based on the first year of those contracts:

Best 2004 Free-Agent Deals		Worst 2004 Free-Agent Deals	
Name	Net WS Value	Name	Net WS Value
Delgado, Carlos	$13,351,563	Ortiz, Russ	-$7,375,000
Kent, Jeff	$9,994,216	Leiter, Al	-$7,000,000
Eckstein, David	$9,888,064	Pavano, Carl	-$5,879,313
Clark, Tony	$9,817,827	Milton, Eric	-$5,333,333
Sexson, Richie	$8,406,559	Finley, Steve	-$4,776,882
Matheny, Mike	$7,129,353	Beltre, Adrian	-$4,656,317
Counsell, Craig	$6,849,084	Wright, Jaret	-$4,493,238
Jones, Todd	$6,325,570	Guzman, Cristian	-$4,200,000
Polanco, Placido	$6,281,047	Garciaparra, Nomar	-$4,198,257
Aurilia, Rich	$5,925,171	Percival, Troy	-$4,110,794

Reds' fans may be shaking their heads at Rich Aurilia's place on the "best value" list. Aurilia's value is high, compared to other free agents, because he was a free-agent sign for $600,000, and his bat did contribute to the Reds' cause (8 WSAB). The man who replaced Aurilia at shortstop, Felipe Lopez, created $8.3 million Net Win Shares Value.

For all you Mets fans, Carlos Beltran's Net Win Shares Value was $1.7 million positive. He was paid only about $11 million in 2005, the first year of his seven-year $115 million deal.

The Worst Free-Agent Class

Long-term free-agent contracts can be real killers, so I looked at the 2005 Net Win Shares value of every free-agent contract based on when it was signed.

Year	WSAB	Net WS Value
1998	4	-$22,571,135
1999	42	$13,359,560
2000	79	-$7,384,640
2001	75	-$62,599,181
2002	117	-$22,928,350
2003	373	$69,772,011
2004	411	$121,112,713

2001 was a bad year for free-agent contracts in 2005. Deals signed that year included many of the top 10 worst values of this year, such as Sosa's, Bonds's, Bagwell's and Park's, as well as the notorious contract of Bret Boone. The Yankees signed Jason Giambi to his megadeal in 2001, but he was a true value in 2005, to the tune of $5.1 million.

Arbitration Years

According to the collective bargaining agreement between MLB owners and players, players in arbitration are supposed to be compared to players with only one more year of major league service, as opposed to all players, and players with five years of service can be compared to free agents. In other words, there is a natural ladder of salaries built into the system. So I wondered, does this play out in Net Win Shares Value? The next table looks at Net Win Shares Value for arbitration-eligible players only. "MLS" stands for Major League Service and "SalAbMin" stands for Salary Above Minimum.

MLS	WSAB	SalAbMin	Net WS Value
2-3	26	$13,367,000	$18,645,769
3-4	191	$91,882,000	$75,777,865
4-5	212	$161,990,167	$9,429,808
5-6	169	$152,709,000	-$26,482,612

As you can see, very few players with two to three years of major league service go through the arbitration process. If you focus on the last three years of arbitration, you see that player salaries do rise (and Net Win Share Value falls) with longer major league service.

One of the reasons the free-agent class of this offseason will be so weak is that many of the final-year arbitration players (5-6 years) had poor years. Some of the players in this category include Byung-Hyun Kim, Erubiel Durazo and Octavio Dotel.

Ideally, Net Win Shares Value would adjust the expected WSAB by the number of years of major league service for those players in arbitration. But the sample size is just a little too small for that.

Position

Next, I wondered if we would discern any differences in Net Win Shares Value by position. Major league general managers took a lot of flak this past offseason for paying a lot of money to starting pitchers, and I was curious to see if they deserved it. Here's a table of Net Win Shares Value by position. I divided Net Win Shares Value by "expected WSAB" to standardize the comparison by playing time and player status.

	WSAB	Net WS Value	Per WSAB
2B	182	$95,887,093	$1,149,707
SS	156	$74,215,032	$949,638
RP	292	$162,980,670	$808,980
1B	305	$117,115,339	$651,046
OF	632	$205,348,374	$485,748
C	127	$46,764,194	$472,517
3B	154	$41,269,635	$343,573
SP	564	$115,979,144	$215,320

As you can see, major league starting pitchers are way overpaid by this measure. In the past, some commentators have criticized Win Shares for not valuing starting pitching highly enough. I made a correction for this in WSAB by setting bench levels at 60% of expected Win Shares for starting pitchers vs. 70% for all other positions. Even with this correction, starting pitchers appear to be extremely overpaid.

This doesn't tell the entire story, however, because it includes all pitchers, regardless of whether they were free agents, arbitration-eligible or not. For another view, here is a table of Net Win Share Value per WSAB by each category, for starting pitchers only:

	WSAB	Net WS Value	Per WSAB
NA	183	$183,817,969	$1,005,572
A	176	($7,690,846)	($43,638)
FA	205	($60,147,980)	($292,796)

Wow. As a category, free-agent starters created negative value of $60 million. The only other categories that are significantly negative are free-agent third basemen ($16 million: Mike Lowell, Adrian Beltre, David Bell) and free-agent relief pitchers (Graves, Foulke, Remlinger, Percival, yada yada yada).

Why is this happening? I can think of a few reasons:

- Recent outcomes have made it clear that starting pitching is perhaps the number one success factor in postseason play. Their postseason value is higher than their regular-season value.

- Pitchers are risky propositions. Their production is erratic, and their injury risk is high.

- Major league general managers just don't understand that there are good alternatives available to them without having to overpay below-average free agents.

- At the same time, GMs hope to catch lightning in a bottle. If Buzz Capra (circa 1974) can lead the league in ERA, then by gum anyone can lead the league in ERA! Which, of course, is exactly why you shouldn't overpay for a pitcher.

- High demand and low supply. Major league teams needs five starting pitchers, but they only need one regular for every other position. On the other hand, only 36% of all WSAB from starting pitchers came through the free-agent market last year, the third-lowest total behind only free agent third basemen and relief pitchers.

With the postseason success of the White Sox and Astros, a relative paucity of starting pitching in the free-agent market, and major league owners flush with cash from new media deals, look for this situation to get worse before it gets better.

Addendum

Here's the detailed explanation of Net Win Shares Value.

First of all, you run into simple mathematical problems when you divide salary by Win Shares. For instance, if you divide salary by Win Shares, and the player created zero Win Shares, how do you handle the "infinite" result? It's better to look at incremental value, as in dollars above or below an expected level.

To calculate an expected level, you could include all major league ballplayers. For instance, major league teams paid about $2.3 billion last year for 7,290 Win Shares, or about $315,000 per Win Share (or $945,000 per win, since each Win Share equals one-third of a win).

Even a bare-bones team, however, composed mostly of what's called "replacement players" (remember the strike years?) would win 30% to 40% of their games. The difference between an established major league player and a good Triple-A player is not that big.

So we differentiate Win Shares above a level we call "Bench," (or, WSAB) and salary paid above the major league minimum of $316,000 in 2005. Also, we differentiate between free agents (FA), arbitration-eligible players (A) and players not yet eligible for arbitration (NA). To do otherwise isn't really fair to the player or to management.

There are only so many great ballplayers who are not yet eligible for arbitration. General managers can't be expected to fill their roster with players like Jason Bay. At the same time, players fought hard for the right to control their lives and be paid according to their market value. To say a player didn't provide good value because he exercised this simple right isn't fair to the player or the GM who negotiated his contract. So our approach considers the conditions under which the player signed his contract.

To show you what a difference this makes, let me list how much major league teams paid above the minimum for each WSAB for each class of player:

Not arbitration eligible:	$16,000
Arbitration eligible:	$702,000
Free agent:	$1,303,000
Average:	**$789,000**

Speaking economically, these are three different player "markets," and any cohesive contract analysis has to level the playing field between them.

Here's the example of how the math works. Derrek Lee was paid $7.7 million last year, or $7.4 million above minimum. He created 37 Win Shares, or 24 above a bench player. The average free agent was paid $1.3 million for each WSAB so, at $7.4 million, Lee was "expected" to create 5.7 WSAB. At 24 WSAB, he was 18 above expectations.

Since major league teams paid $789,000 across all markets for each WSAB, we multiply Lee's 18 by that figure for a total Net Win Share Value of $14.6 million. (You will get a slightly different figure due to rounding.)

The approach is slightly different for players who are not eligible for arbitration. We assume that their expected WSAB is zero (since they're paid the minimum, or slightly more), so we first multiply each player's actual WSAB total by $789,000. Then we subtract any amount paid over the major league minimum (almost always $100,000 or less).

We use the "all market" figure for our final step because this puts all player contributions in the same context. In other words, expectations are set by the "market" in which the player signed, and incremental value is set by the average across all markets. This approach allows you to directly compare one player's value to another.

Two final notes: The calculation is set so that a player cannot have a negative Net Win Share Value greater than his salary. Without this "maximum allowable," you get some very strange results. Also, I used salary figures as published by Major League Baseball. These reflect only the current year payouts, not the full value of a long-term contract.

The key to this system is properly classifying players as free agents, arbitration-eligible and not eligible for arbitration. This is much trickier than it seems. Let me list some of the judgment calls I made:

- A few players, such as Rickie Weeks and Mark Prior, signed major league contracts when they were drafted even though they are not yet eligible for arbitration. I classified these players as free agents, because they effectively had free-agent leverage at the time they signed due to their talent (and agent).

- The same thinking applies to players from other countries who did not go through the draft, such as Jose Contreras, Ichiro Suzuki and the Matsuis. I classified them as free agents.

- There are many players who have not yet played for six years in the majors (and so aren't eligible to file for free agency) but were free agents because they were released by their teams. I did my best to identify all players who were in this situation when they signed their contract for 2005 and label them free agents. One of the best examples is A.J. Pierzynski, who was released by the Giants during the offseason and subsequently signed by the White Sox.

- If a player had played at least six years in the majors but was playing under a contract signed before he was eligible to be a free agent, I still classified him as a free agent.

- Two players, Roger Clemens and Placido Polanco, filed for arbitration instead of entering the free-agent market, as is their right. After much gnashing of the teeth, I decided to classify them as free agents. You could argue either way.

We have made a Net Win Shares Value spreadsheet available for those who have purchased this book. The spreadsheet lists all major-league players, their Net Win Shares Value and other information, such as years of major league service as of the beginning of the year. The spreadsheet is available at http://www.hardball-times.com/THT2005Annual/. The username is "reader" and the password is "kaline".

Statistics

Welcome to Our Stats

There are a lot of baseball statistics in *The Hardball Times Annual*, just around the page. You've read a lot of words so far, but baseball's language includes both letters and numbers. All we're really trying to do is tell the story of baseball, and tell it well.

At The Hardball Times, we publish all the standard baseball stats. We also publish "new" stats that have been invented by other people, such as Runs Created and Win Shares (Bill James), Pitching Runs (John Thorn and Pete Palmer) and Fielding-Independent Pitching, or FIP (Tangotiger). We have also introduced our own simple stat called Gross Production Average (GPA), which is a variation of OPS, and we publish some baseball data you can't get anywhere else, such as the number of line drives, ground balls and fly balls for every batter and pitcher. But we're not really interested in adding a bunch of new stats and acronyms to the mix.

We do think that presentation is a big issue. The way baseball stats were published in newspapers was so wrong for so many years that bad habits formed. Thankfully, this is changing. For instance, it's becoming common for baseball writers to express a batter's stats like this: .333/.444/.555, to represent his batting, on-base and slugging averages. I made those numbers up, but the point is that this is an insightful way to present batting stats.

So most of the statistics you're about to see are pretty simple, some of them are kind of complex, but we like to think that all of them are presented in a way that helps you easily see the big picture. Here's a little more info about each section...

League/Team Statistics

At the beginning of the section, we've laid out team stats for both leagues. The first thing you'll see in each section is a graph, just like this one...

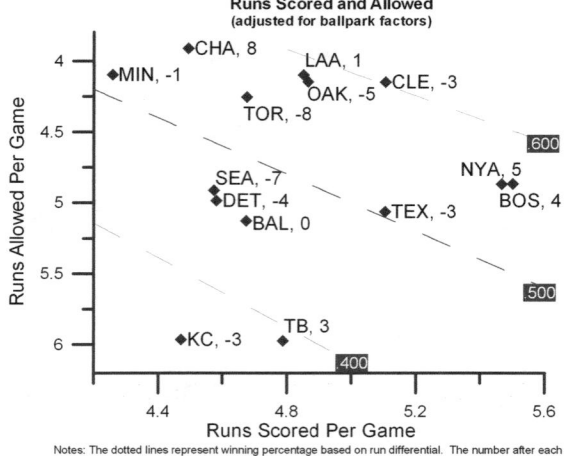

Runs Scored and Allowed
(adjusted for ballpark factors)

Notes: The dotted lines represent winning percentage based on run differential. The number after each team name represents the difference between the team's actual record and its run differential record.

Don't worry, the actual graph is bigger. The concept behind this graph is simple; Teams win when they score more runs and allow fewer runs, so the graph is based on runs scored and allowed. Teams to the right have scored more runs and teams on the top have allowed fewer runs. That makes teams in the upper right the best teams, and those in the lower left the worst.

We've also added three dotted lines to the graph, showing the points at which a team would be playing .400, .500 and .600 ball. If a team is on the lower-right end of the line, that means its strength is batting. If it's on the upper-left end of the line, its strength is pitching and fielding.

However, a team's win-loss record doesn't always reflect its runs scored and allowed. So we've added a number next to each team's name in the graph representing the number of victories by which it outperformed its projected win-loss record. In other words, that number represents how far away the team's actual victories were from the position on the graph.

Below the graph will be a table of each team's vital stats. The first five columns present basic wins and runs stuff. The next two sections of the table offer key stats regarding how teams score runs and how they allow them. For instance, the run-scoring stats are at-bats with runners in scoring position, batting average with runners in scoring position and home runs. If you think about it, scoring runs is all about getting to second or third and having someone bat you home, or hitting home runs. Teams differentiate themselves this way. The Angels, for example, only hit 147 home runs (league average of 174) but they had 1,400 at-bats with runners in scoring position (about average) and batted .291 in those at-bats (exceptional).

The runs allowed section describes how teams stop runs from being scored against them: Earned Run Average (ERA), home runs allowed (HRA) and strikeouts (K) are pitching stats. Defense Efficiency Ratio (DER), the number of batted balls converted to outs by fielders (see "Batted Ball Fielding Stats" for more information), is the responsibility of both pitchers and fielders. For example, Baltimore struck out lots of batters (1,052, third in the league) but their DER was below average at .693. This indicates that their fielders weren't up to task and/or their pitchers allowed too many hard-hit balls, and that's why they gave up 800 runs.

Finally, Pwin stands for "Projected Wins" or "Pythagorean Wins" depending on how technical you want to get. VAR stands for variance, the difference between each team's actual wins and its projected wins.

See Dan Fox's article "Are You Feeling Lucky?" for more background on this information.

The team batting stats are pretty straightforward, so I won't go into the details. Above the table is a graph of each team's on-base percentage and isolated power (which is slugging average minus batting average). This graph tells you whether a team scored by getting on base more often or by slugging more often.

The third page contains each team's pitching stats. The graph on the top of the page shows each team's FIP (a measure of those things pitchers control completely: strikeouts, walks and home runs) and DER (which is shared by pitchers and fielders). A quick look at this graph should tell you which teams were led by great pitching or great fielding. Or both. Or neither.

The stats below the graphs are pretty straightforward, too. You may not be familiar with some of them, but there is a comprehensive glossary coming up.

Finally, we've inserted a page of useful stats that didn't fit in the first three tables.

- Base running and batting stats. This table includes stolen base information as well as batted ball data, such as LD% (the percent of batted balls that were line drives), BABIP (or batting average on balls in play; the number of batted balls, not including home runs, that fell in for hits) and G/F (the ratio of batted ground balls to fly balls; line drives not included).

- Win Shares stats. On this table you'll find basic Win Shares info for each team, including total Win Shares, batting, pitching and fielding totals, the total number of career Win Shares on each team (as of the end of the year), and Win Shares Age, an effective way to measure the age of a team.

- Fielding and pitching stats, including batted ball information.

League Leaderboards

Leaderboards are a popular item, so we've listed the top 10 players for a bunch of statistics. You can find the definition of all the leaderboard stats in our glossary, which immediately follows this article.

There are a number of statistics in the leaderboards that aren't included in our individual player stats. However, you can find complete player listings of all stats on our website, at http://www.hardballtimes.com/main/stats.

Team/Player Stats

Specific stats for players are laid out by team in alphabetical order. Each team section begins with a graphical review of that team's wins and losses during the year, shown as running 10-game totals. The graphs also show each team's 10-game averages in runs scored and allowed, so you can visualize how each team's batters and pitchers performed throughout the year. In addition, we've listed some of the season's highlights below the graph. There's also a table under the graph that shows the team's monthly vital stats (Wins, losses, OBP and SLG for the offense and FIP and DER for the defense).

On the following three pages, individual player stats are listed for batters, pitchers and fielders. These are relatively straightforward stats, and you can find the definitions in the glossary. The statistics that are italicized have been adjusted for the home park.

There are also two unique tables for each team's players:

- Win Shares stats for every player with at least four expected Win Shares, including the player's Win Shares Above Bench (WSAB), expected Win Shares, Win Shares Percentage (WSP), career Win Shares (CWS) and Net Win Shares Value. You can find definitions of these items in the glossary. Please note that our Win Shares calculations differ somewhat from Bill James's original formulas.

- Baserunning stats for all players, based on Dan Fox's article "Around the Bases One More Time."

Composite Statistics

At the very end of the book, we've listed two sets of unique player stats:

- Fielding Range, which is the number of runs above or below average that each fielder contributed with his glove. We've listed every player who played at least 600 innings at a position. This stat was contributed by David Gassko.

- Plate Appearance Outcomes, the specific batted ball outcomes (strikeout, walk, ground ball, outfield fly ball, infield fly ball, line drive and other) for all batters with at least 400 plate appearances and pitchers with at least 300 batters faced.

We think you'll find a lot of interesting stuff in these last two tables.

Remember that we'll have 2006 statistics updated daily on our site throughout the next season. Yes, we're already looking ahead to next year. Can't wait.

Statistical Glossary

In the tables, stats that have been adjusted for the impact of the home park are italicized.

A: Assists. The number of times a fielder makes a throw that results in an out.

AB: At-Bats

AB/RSP: At-Bats with Runners in Scoring Position (second and/or third base)

BA: Batting Average; Hits divided by At-Bats

BA/RSP Batting Average with Runners in Scoring Position (second and/or third base)

BABIP Batting Average on Balls in Play. This is a measure of the number of batted balls that safely fall in for hits (not including home runs). The exact formula we use is (H-HR)/(AB-K-HR). This is similar to DER, but from the batter's perspective.

BB: Bases on Balls, otherwise known as walks

BB/G: Walks Allowed per games pitched. This stat is based on the number of walks allowed divided by total number of batters faced, times the average number of batters per game in that specific league (generally around 38 batters a game).

BFP: Batters Faced by Pitcher; the pitching equivalent of Plate Appearances for batters

CS: Caught Stealing

CWS: Career Win Shares

DER Defense Efficiency Ratio. The percent of times a batted ball is turned into an out by the team's fielders, not including home runs. The exact formula we use is (BFP-H-K-BB-HBP-0.6*E)/(BFP-HR-K-BB-HBP). This is similar to BABIP, but from the defensive team's perspective.

DP: Double Plays

DPS: Double Plays Started, in which the fielder typically gets only an assist

DPT: Double Plays Turned, in which the fielder records both an assist and an out

ERA: Earned Run Average. Number of earned runs allowed divided by innings pitched multiplied by nine.

ERA+: ERA measured against the league average and adjusted for ballpark factors. An ERA+ over 100 is better than average, less than 100 is below average.

ExpWS: Expected Win Shares. See the Win Shares section for a fuller discussion.

FE: Fielding Errors, as opposed to Throwing Errors (TE)

FIP: Fielding Independent Pitching, a measure of all those things for which a pitcher is specifically responsible. The formula is (HR*13+(BB+HBP)*3-K*2)/IP, plus a league-specific factor (usually around 3.2) to round out the number to an equivalent ERA number. FIP helps you understand how well a pitcher pitched, regardless of how well his fielders fielded. FIP was invented by Tangotiger.

FPct: Fielding Percentage, or the number of fielding chances handled without an error. The formula is (A+PO)/(A+PO+E).

G: Games played

G/F: G/F stands for Ground ball to Fly ball Ratio. It is the number of ground balls divided by the number of fly balls (but not line drives) hit by the batter or allowed by the pitcher. It includes all batted balls, not just outs.

GIDP (or GDP): The number of times a batter Grounded Into Double Plays

GPA: Gross Production Average, a variation of OPS, but more accurate and easier to interpret. The exact formula is (OBP*1.8+SLG)/4, adjusted for ballpark factor. The scale of GPA is similar to BA: .200 is lousy, .265 is around average and .300 is a star.

GS: Games Started, a pitching stat.

Holds: A bullpen stat. According to MLB.com, *A relief pitcher is credited with a hold any time he enters a game in a save situation, records at least one out and leaves the game never having relinquished the lead. A pitcher cannot finish the game and receive credit for a hold, nor can he earn a hold and a save in the same game.*

HRA: Home Runs Allowed, also a pitching stat

HR/Fly or HR/F: Home Runs as a percent of outfield fly balls. The home run totals are adjusted by the home ballpark's historic home run rates. Research has shown that about 11% to 12% of outfield flies are hit for home runs.

HR/G: Home Runs Allowed per games pitched. This stat is based on the number of home runs allowed divided by total number of batters faced, times the average number of batters per game in that specific league (generally around 38 batters a game).

IBB: Intentional Base on Balls.

IF/Fly or IF/F: The percent of fly balls that are infield flies.

IR and IRP: Base running stats created by Dan Fox for *The Hardball Times Annual*. IR stands for the incremental runs a base runner added by advancing on base hits, and IRP stands for Incremental Run Percentage, which expresses the rate at which a batter advanced compared to his opportunities. Average is 100; above 100 is good and below 100 is not so good. You can read more about these stats in his article "Around the Bases One More Time."

ISO: Isolated Power, which measures the "true power" of a batter. The formula is SLG-BA.

K: Strikeouts

K/G: Strikeouts per games pitched. This stat is based on the number of strikeouts divided by total number of batters faced, times the average number of batters per game in that specific league (generally around 38 batters a game).

L: Losses

LD%: Line Drive Percentage. Baseball Info Solutions tracks the trajectory of each batted ball and categorizes it as a ground ball, fly ball or line drive. LD% is the percent of batted balls that are line drives. Line drives are not necessarily the hardest hit balls, but they do fall for a hit around 75% of the time.

LOB and LOB%: LOB stands for Left On Base. It is the number of runners that are left on base at the end of an inning. LOB% is slightly different; it is the percentage of base runners allowed that didn't score a run. LOB% is used to track a pitcher's luck or effectiveness (depending on your point of view). The exact formula is (H+BB+HBP-R)/(H+BB+HBP-(1.4*HR)).

Net Stolen Bases: The effective impact of a player's stolen bases. For batters, the formula is SB-(2*CS) because being caught stealing hurts twice as much as a stolen base helps. For pitchers, the formula is (SB+balks)-2*(CS+pickoffs).

Net Win Shares Value: A dollar figure that represents the relative value of a player's contract, given how much the player contributed. See the article of the same name for more information.

OBP: On Base Percentage, the proportion of plate appearances in which a batter reached base successfully, including hits, walks and hit by pitches.

Op: Save Opportunities

OPS: On Base plus Slugging Percentage, a crude but quick measure of a batter's true contribution to his team's offense. See GPA for a better approach.

OPS+: OPS measured against the league average, and adjusted for ballpark factors. An OPS+ over 100 is better than average, less than 100 is below average.

Outs: Outs. Not just outs at bat, by the way, but also outs when caught stealing. Two outs are included when hitting into a double play.

P/PA: Pitches per Plate Appearance.

PA: Plate Appearances, or AB+BB+HBP+SF+SH.

PO: Putouts, the number of times a fielder recorded an out in the field. First basemen and catchers get lots of these. From a pitching perspective, PO stands for

pickoffs—the number of times a pitcher picks a base runner off a base.

POS: Position played in the field

PR: Invented by John Thorn and Pete Palmer, this is a measure of the number of runs a pitcher saved compared to average. The formula is league-average RA/IP minus the player's park-adjusted RA/IP, times total innings pitched.

Pythagorean Record: A formula for converting a team's Run Differential into a projected win-loss record. The formula is $RS^2/(RS^2+RA^2)$. Teams' actual win-loss records tend to mirror their Pythagorean records, and variances can usually be attributed to luck.

You can improve the accuracy of the Pythagorean formula by using a different exponent (the 2 in the formula). In particular, a sabermetrician named US Patriot discovered that the best exponent can be calculated this way: $(RS/G+RA/G)^{.285}$, where RS/G is Runs Scored per game and RA/G is Runs Allowed per game. This is called the PythagoPat formula.

PWins: Pythagorean Wins. See the previous entry.

R: Runs Scored and/or Allowed.

R/G: Runs Scored Per Game. Literally, R divided by games played.

RA: Runs Allowed or Runs Allowed Per Nine Innings. Just like ERA, but with unearned runs, too.

RBI: Runs Batted In

RC: Runs Created. Invented by Bill James, RC is a very good measure of the number of runs a batter truly contributed to his team's offense. The basic formula for RC is OBP*TB, but it has evolved into over 14 different versions. We use the most complicated version, which includes the impact of hitting well with runners in scoring position, and we adjust for ballpark impact.

RCAA: Runs Created Above Average. A stat invented and tracked by Lee Sinins, the author of the *Sabermetric Baseball Encyclopedia*. Lee calculates each player's Runs Created and then compares it to the league average, given that player's number of plate appearances.

RF: Range Factor, a measure of the total chances fielded in a player's playing time. The formula we use is 9*(PO+A)/Innings in Field.

RS: Runs Scored

RSAA: Runs Saved Above Average. This stat, which is also tracked and reported by Lee Sinins, is a measure of a pitcher's effectiveness and contribution. Also see Pitching Runs (PR).

Run Differential: Runs Scored minus Runs Allowed

SB: Stolen Bases

SB%: The percent of time a runner stole a base successfully. The formula is SB/SBA.

SBA: Stolen Bases Attempted.

SBA/G: Stolen Base Attempts per nine innings played.

ShO: Shutouts

Situational Hitting Runs: The portion of Bill James's Runs Created formula that includes the impact of a batter's batting average with runners in scoring position and the number of home runs with runners on. The specific formula is Hits with RISP minus (overall BA times at bats with RISP), plus HR with runners on minus ((all HR/AB) times at-bats with runners on). We call this stat "Clutch" on our website. While it is not a definitive description of "clutch hitting," it is one way of looking at it.

SLG and SLGA: Slugging Percentage. Total Bases divided by At-Bats. SLGA stands for Slugging Percentage Against. It represents SLG from the pitcher's perspective.

SO: Strikeouts

Sv: Saves. According to MLB.com, *A pitcher is credited with a save when he finishes a game won by his club, is not the winning pitcher, and either (a) enters the game with a lead of no more than three runs and pitches for at least one inning, (b) enters the game with the potential tying run either on base, or at bat, or on deck, or (c) pitches effectively for at least three innings.*

Sv%: Saves divided by Save Opportunities

TB: Total Bases, calculated as 1B+2B*2+3B*3+HR*4

TBA: Total Bases Allowed. A pitching stat.

TE: Throwing Errors, as opposed to Fielding Errors (FE)

UER: Unearned Runs

UERA: Unearned Run Average, or the number of unearned runs allowed for each nine innings pitched.

W: Wins

WHIP: Walks and Hits Per Inning Pitched, a variant of OBP for pitchers. This is a popular stat in rotisserie baseball circles.

WPA: Win Probability Added. A system in which each player is given credit toward helping his team win, based on play-by-play data and the impact each specific play has on the team's probability of winning.

WP+PB/G: Wild Pitches and Passed Balls per Nine Innings played. A fielding stat for catchers

Win Shares Definitions

WS: Win Shares. Invented by Bill James. Win Shares is a very complicated statistic that takes all the contributions a player made toward his team's wins and distills them into a single number that represents the number of wins he contributed to the team, times three.

There are three subcategories of Win Shares: batting, pitching and fielding.

We have tweaked James' original formula in two ways:

1) We allow players to accumulate negative Win Shares. Adding an artificial "floor" at zero (which the original formula does) has unfortunate repercussions for all player's totals.

2) We have somewhat de-emphasized the portion of Win Shares that credits relief pitchers. We feel this is appropriate in today's "save-happy" environment.

CWS: Career Win Shares. Each player's career Win Shares includes Bill James's totals through 2003 and our totals for the last two years.

WSAge: The average age of a team, weighted by each player's total Win Shares contribution.

NetWSValue: A dollar figure that represents the relative value of a player's contract, given how much the player contributed. See the article of the same name for more information.

ExpWS: Expected Win Shares. This figure represents a player's average baseline, or the number of Win Shares he would have contributed if he were an average player. To calculate this, we include the number of each player's plate appearances, innings in the field, innings pitched and relief innings pitched.

WSAB: Win Shares Above Bench. WSAB is a refined approach to Win Shares, in which each player's total Win Shares are compared to the Win Shares an average bench player would have received, given that player's time at bat, on the mound or in the field.

Our research indicates that this is an important adjustment to Win Shares, because it gives greater context to the Win Shares totals. The impact is similar to adding "Loss Shares" for each player.

The bench player is defined as 75% of Expected Win Shares for all players except starting pitchers, for whom it is 60% of Expected Win Shares.

WSP: Win Shares Percentage is a rate stat, calculated as WS/(2*ExpWS). WSP is similar to winning percentage in that .500 is average, but WSP ranges above 1.000 and below .000.

American League Team Stats

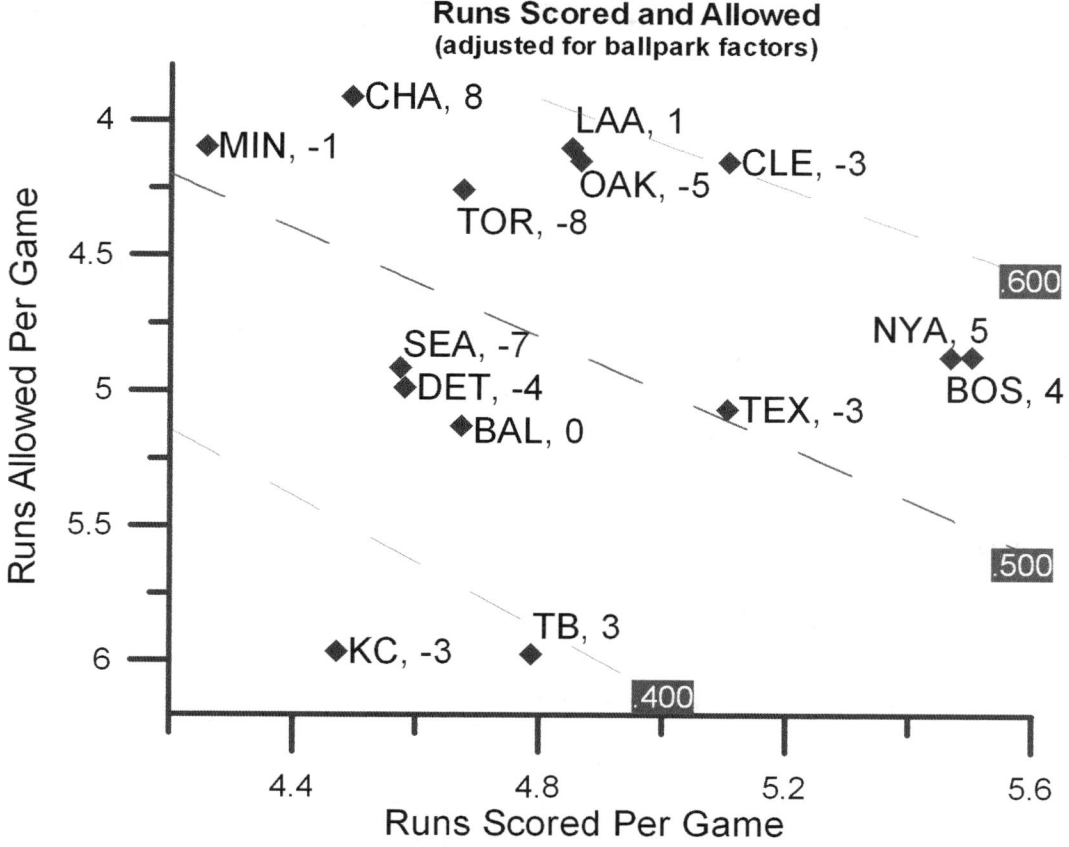

Runs Scored and Allowed
(adjusted for ballpark factors)

Notes: The dotted lines represent winning percentage based on run differential. The number after each team name represents the difference between the team's actual record and its run differential record.

	Team Record					Scoring Runs			Preventing Runs				Projection	
Team	W	L	RS	RA	RS-RA	AB/RSP	BA/RSP	HR	ERA	HRA	K	DER	PWINS	VAR
BAL	74	88	729	800	-71	1,315	.268	189	4.57	180	1,052	.693	74	0
BOS	95	67	910	805	105	1,509	.291	199	4.74	164	959	.683	91	4
CHA	99	63	741	645	96	1,245	.259	200	3.61	167	1,040	.713	91	8
CLE	93	69	790	642	148	1,375	.259	207	3.61	157	1,050	.711	96	-3
DET	71	91	723	787	-64	1,337	.273	168	4.51	193	907	.696	75	-4
KC	56	106	701	935	-234	1,340	.265	126	5.50	178	924	.667	59	-3
LAA	95	67	761	643	118	1,400	.296	147	3.68	158	1,126	.700	94	1
MIN	83	79	688	662	26	1,373	.271	134	3.71	169	965	.703	84	-1
NYA	95	67	886	789	97	1,490	.272	229	4.52	164	985	.691	90	5
OAK	88	74	772	658	114	1,423	.275	155	3.69	154	1,075	.717	93	-5
SEA	69	93	699	751	-52	1,367	.260	130	4.49	179	892	.702	76	-7
TB	67	95	750	936	-186	1,353	.285	157	5.39	194	949	.682	64	3
TEX	79	83	865	858	7	1,326	.271	260	4.96	159	932	.682	82	-3
TOR	80	82	775	705	70	1,440	.267	136	4.06	185	958	.701	88	-8
Average	**82**	**80**	**771**	**758**	**12**	**1,378**	**.273**	**174**	**4.35**	**172**	**987**	**.696**	**81**	**1**

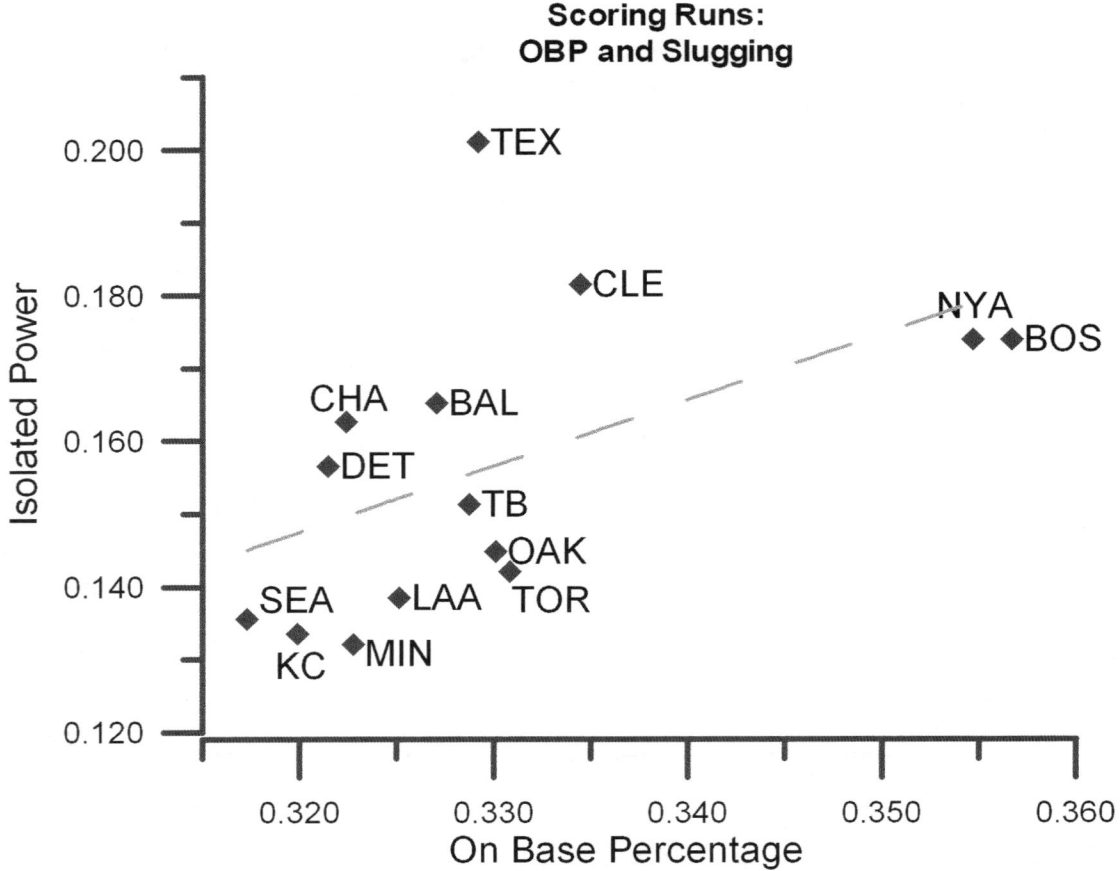

Scoring Runs:
OBP and Slugging

The dotted line shows the relationship between ISO and OBP.

Batting Statistics

Team	Runs	PA	H	1B	2B	3B	HR	TB	SO	BB	HBP	SH	SF	BA	OBP	SLG	GPA	ISO
BAL	729	6,134	1,492	980	296	27	189	2,409	902	447	54	40	42	.269	.327	.434	.256	.165
BOS	910	6,403	1,579	1,020	339	21	199	2,557	1,044	653	47	14	63	.281	.357	.454	.274	.174
CHA	741	6,146	1,450	974	253	23	200	2,349	1,002	435	79	53	49	.262	.322	.425	.251	.163
CLE	790	6,255	1,522	948	337	30	207	2,540	1,093	503	54	39	50	.271	.334	.453	.264	.181
DET	723	6,136	1,521	1,025	283	45	168	2,398	1,038	384	53	44	52	.272	.321	.428	.252	.157
KC	701	6,086	1,445	996	289	34	126	2,180	1,008	424	63	46	50	.263	.320	.396	.243	.134
LAA	761	6,186	1,520	1,065	278	30	147	2,299	848	447	29	43	39	.270	.325	.409	.249	.139
MIN	688	6,192	1,441	1,006	269	32	134	2,176	978	485	59	42	42	.259	.323	.391	.243	.132
NYA	886	6,406	1,552	1,048	259	16	229	2,530	989	637	73	28	43	.276	.355	.450	.272	.174
OAK	772	6,275	1,476	991	310	20	155	2,291	819	537	52	19	40	.262	.330	.407	.250	.145
SEA	699	6,095	1,408	955	289	34	130	2,155	986	466	48	37	37	.256	.317	.391	.241	.136
TB	750	6,120	1,519	1,033	289	40	157	2,359	990	412	69	34	51	.274	.329	.425	.254	.151
TEX	865	6,301	1,528	928	311	29	260	2,677	1,112	495	48	9	32	.267	.329	.468	.265	.201
TOR	775	6,233	1,480	998	307	39	136	2,273	955	486	89	21	56	.265	.331	.407	.251	.142
Average	771	6,212	1,495	998	294	30	174	2,371	983	487	58	34	46	.268	.333	.424	.256	.157

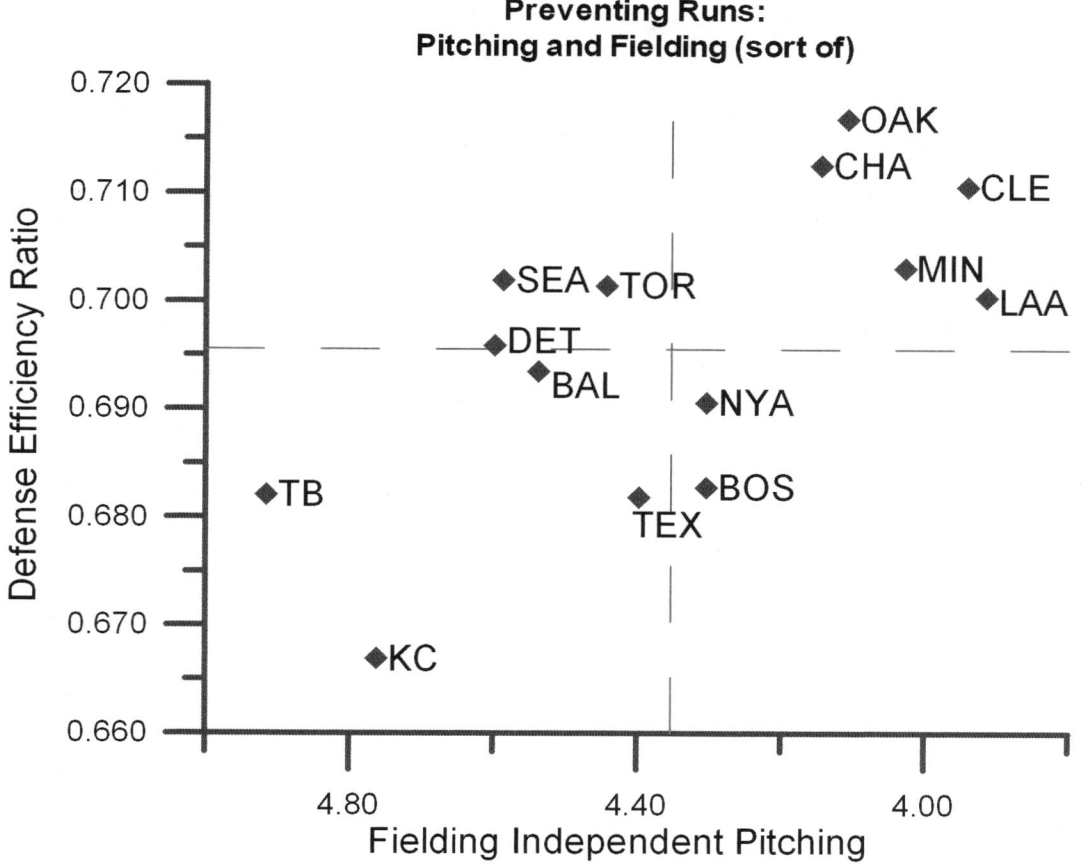

Preventing Runs:
Pitching and Fielding (sort of)

The dotted lines represent the league averages.

Pitching Statistics

Team	RA	IP	BFP	H	HRA	TBA	K	BB	ShO	Sv	Op	%Save	Holds	ERA	FIP	UERA	DER
BAL	800	1427.0	6,242	1,458	180	2,302	1,052	580	9	38	57	67%	70	4.57	4.54	0.48	.693
BOS	805	1429.0	6,227	1,550	164	2,478	959	440	8	38	57	67%	59	4.74	4.30	0.33	.683
CHA	645	1475.0	6,176	1,392	167	2,217	1,040	459	10	54	73	74%	79	3.61	4.14	0.32	.713
CLE	642	1452.0	6,048	1,363	157	2,133	1,050	413	10	51	66	77%	74	3.61	3.94	0.37	.711
DET	787	1435.0	6,139	1,504	193	2,411	907	461	2	37	57	65%	56	4.51	4.60	0.43	.696
KC	935	1413.0	6,370	1,640	178	2,605	924	580	4	25	43	58%	55	5.50	4.76	0.45	.667
LAA	643	1464.0	6,158	1,419	158	2,240	1,126	443	11	54	71	76%	55	3.68	3.91	0.28	.700
MIN	662	1464.0	6,072	1,458	169	2,278	965	348	8	44	60	73%	52	3.71	4.03	0.36	.703
NYA	789	1430.0	6,182	1,495	164	2,344	985	463	14	46	67	69%	69	4.52	4.30	0.45	.691
OAK	658	1450.0	6,080	1,315	154	2,080	1,075	504	12	38	56	68%	47	3.69	4.11	0.40	.717
SEA	751	1427.0	6,172	1,483	179	2,331	892	496	7	39	59	66%	73	4.49	4.59	0.25	.702
TB	936	1421.0	6,384	1,570	194	2,549	949	615	4	43	69	62%	66	5.39	4.92	0.54	.682
TEX	858	1440.0	6,371	1,589	159	2,441	932	522	6	46	68	68%	48	4.96	4.40	0.40	.682
TOR	705	1447.0	6,166	1,475	185	2,333	958	444	8	35	56	63%	66	4.06	4.44	0.32	.701
Average	758	1,441.0	6,199	1,479	172	2,339	987	483	8	42	61	68%	62	4.35	4.35	0.38	.696

Running and Miscellaneous Batting Stats

Team	SB	CS	SB%	GDP	P/PA	LD%	BABIP	G/F
BAL	83	37	69%	145	3.65	.195	.292	1.17
BOS	45	12	79%	135	3.86	.225	.315	1.15
CHA	137	67	67%	123	3.77	.197	.289	1.25
CLE	62	36	63%	128	3.82	.200	.305	1.28
DET	66	28	70%	138	3.67	.191	.308	1.28
KC	53	33	62%	139	3.69	.189	.302	1.29
LAA	161	57	74%	126	3.66	.198	.297	1.19
MIN	102	44	70%	156	3.72	.182	.294	1.64
NYA	85	27	76%	125	3.74	.172	.300	1.32
OAK	31	22	58%	149	3.86	.201	.284	1.20
SEA	102	47	68%	116	3.75	.199	.291	1.37
TB	151	49	76%	133	3.61	.194	.309	1.29
TEX	67	15	82%	123	3.80	.199	.292	1.03
TOR	72	35	67%	125	3.72	.199	.299	1.34
Average	87	36	71%	133	3.74	.196	.298	1.26

Win Shares Stats

Team	Bat	Pitch	Field	WS	CWS	WSAge
BAL	113	72	36	222	2,373	29.8
BOS	163	85	37	285	3,329	32.5
CHA	107	138	52	297	1,761	28.7
CLE	126	105	48	279	1,550	27.4
DET	106	69	37	213	1,707	28.5
KC	106	36	27	168	973	28.1
LAA	121	116	48	285	1,918	29.1
MIN	85	112	52	249	1,459	27.4
NYA	165	83	37	285	4,631	32.8
OAK	108	105	51	264	1,382	27.3
SEA	96	73	38	207	1,937	29.7
TB	127	47	27	201	1,184	26.9
TEX	123	80	34	237	1,696	28.6
TOR	100	95	45	240	1,102	28.2
Average	118	87	41	245	1,929	28.9

Fielding and Miscellaneous Pitching Stats

Team	DER	Fld %	UER	SBA	CS	%CS	PO	Err	TE	FE	DP	GIDP	LD%	G/F	IF/Fly
BAL	.693	.982	76	149	34	23%	8	107	51	54	154	126	.200	1.37	12.3%
BOS	.683	.982	53	117	29	25%	12	109	51	56	135	122	.209	1.16	12.9%
CHA	.713	.985	53	128	25	20%	11	94	35	56	167	144	.203	1.24	14.6%
CLE	.711	.983	60	136	33	24%	7	106	45	61	156	136	.205	1.31	14.0%
DET	.696	.982	68	109	49	45%	15	110	58	51	172	148	.185	1.33	14.7%
KC	.667	.979	71	114	44	39%	11	125	51	73	163	139	.194	1.29	13.3%
LAA	.700	.985	45	110	42	38%	6	87	45	40	139	114	.192	1.08	12.5%
MIN	.703	.984	58	80	36	45%	9	102	41	59	171	142	.188	1.29	15.0%
NYA	.691	.984	71	175	50	29%	6	95	40	53	151	127	.173	1.34	12.6%
OAK	.717	.986	64	134	25	19%	8	88	35	50	166	137	.203	1.30	15.9%
SEA	.702	.986	39	132	43	33%	12	86	39	45	145	118	.191	1.07	13.0%
TB	.682	.979	85	113	45	40%	11	124	53	69	140	101	.207	1.01	13.7%
TEX	.682	.982	64	95	26	27%	2	108	45	61	149	126	.197	1.40	13.9%
TOR	.701	.985	52	135	35	26%	13	95	47	45	155	134	.191	1.37	15.0%
Average	.696	.983	61	123	37	30%	9	103	45	55	155	130	.196	1.25	13.8%

American League Leaderboards
Batting Leaders

Runs Created

1	M. Teixeira	TEX	142
2	A. Rodriguez	NYA	138
3	D. Ortiz	BOS	136
4	M. Ramirez	BOS	134
5	G. Sheffield	NYA	131
6	M. Young	TEX	125
7	R. Sexson	SEA	122
7	T. Hafner	CLE	122
9	B. Roberts	BAL	114
9	I. Suzuki	SEA	114

Runs Scored

1	A. Rodriguez	NYA	124
2	D. Jeter	NYA	122
3	D. Ortiz	BOS	119
4	J. Damon	BOS	117
5	M. Young	TEX	114
6	C. Figgins	LAA	113
6	M. Ramirez	BOS	112
8	M. Teixeira	TEX	112
8	I. Suzuki	SEA	111
10	G. Sizemore	CLE	111

Runs Batted In

1	D. Ortiz	BOS	148
2	M. Ramirez	BOS	144
2	M. Teixeira	TEX	144
4	A. Rodriguez	NYA	130
5	G. Sheffield	NYA	123
6	R. Sexson	SEA	121
7	J. Cantu	TB	117
8	H. Matsui	NYA	116
9	V. Guerrero	LAA	108
9	T. Hafner	CLE	108

Gross Production Average (GPA)

1	T. Hafner	CLE	.348
2	A. Rodriguez	NYA	.341
3	J. Giambi	NYA	.331
4	V. Guerrero	LAA	.330
5	D. Ortiz	BOS	.323
6	R. Sexson	SEA	.321
7	M. Ramirez	BOS	.317
8	B. Roberts	BAL	.316
9	J. Peralta	CLE	.308
10	V. Martinez	CLE	.303

Batting Average

1	M. Young	TEX	.331
2	A. Rodriguez	NYA	.321
3	V. Guerrero	LAA	.317
4	J. Damon	BOS	.316
5	B. Roberts	BAL	.314
6	D. Jeter	NYA	.309
7	V. Martinez	CLE	.305
8	T. Hafner	CLE	.305
9	H. Matsui	NYA	.305
10	M. Tejada	BAL	.304

On Base Percentage

1	J. Giambi	NYA	.440
2	A. Rodriguez	NYA	.421
3	T. Hafner	CLE	.408
4	D. Ortiz	BOS	.397
5	V. Guerrero	LAA	.394
6	D. Jeter	NYA	.389
7	M. Ramirez	BOS	.388
8	B. Roberts	BAL	.387
9	M. Young	TEX	.385
10	G. Sheffield	NYA	.379

Slugging Percentage

1	A. Rodriguez	NYA	.610
2	D. Ortiz	BOS	.604
3	T. Hafner	CLE	.595
4	M. Ramirez	BOS	.594
5	M. Teixeira	TEX	.575
6	V. Guerrero	LAA	.565
7	R. Sexson	SEA	.541
8	J. Giambi	NYA	.535
9	P. Konerko	CHA	.534
10	J. Peralta	CLE	.520

OPS (On Base Plus Slugging)

1	A. Rodriguez	NYA	1.031
2	T. Hafner	CLE	1.003
3	D. Ortiz	BOS	1.001
4	M. Ramirez	BOS	.982
5	J. Giambi	NYA	.975
6	V. Guerrero	LAA	.959
7	M. Teixeira	TEX	.954
8	R. Sexson	SEA	.910
9	P. Konerko	CHA	.909
10	B. Roberts	BAL	.903

Plate Appearances

1	D. Jeter	NYA	752
2	I. Suzuki	SEA	739
3	M. Young	TEX	732
4	M. Teixeira	TEX	730
5	C. Figgins	LAA	720
6	A. Rodriguez	NYA	715
7	D. Ortiz	BOS	713
8	G. Sizemore	CLE	706
9	H. Blalock	TEX	705
10	2 tied with		704

Outs

1	H. Blalock	TEX	477
2	I. Suzuki	SEA	473
3	A. Soriano	TEX	466
4	E. Chavez	OAK	457
5	C. Figgins	LAA	456
6	B. Inge	DET	455
6	M. Tejada	BAL	455
6	G. Sizemore	CLE	455
9	V. Wells	TOR	453
10	D. Jeter	NYA	452

Hits

1	M. Young	TEX	221
2	I. Suzuki	SEA	206
3	D. Jeter	NYA	202
4	M. Tejada	BAL	199
5	J. Damon	BOS	197
6	C. Crawford	TB	194
6	A. Rodriguez	NYA	194
6	M. Teixeira	TEX	194
9	H. Matsui	NYA	192
10	C. Figgins	LAA	186

Total Bases

1	M. Teixeira	TEX	370
2	A. Rodriguez	NYA	369
3	D. Ortiz	BOS	363
4	M. Young	TEX	343
5	M. Tejada	BAL	337
6	M. Ramirez	BOS	329
7	A. Soriano	TEX	326
8	H. Matsui	NYA	312
9	G. Sizemore	CLE	310
10	P. Konerko	CHA	307

Singles

1	I. Suzuki	SEA	158
2	D. Jeter	NYA	153
3	M. Young	TEX	152
4	J. Damon	BOS	146
5	C. Figgins	LAA	143
6	J. Lugo	TB	134
6	J. Kendall	OAK	134
8	C. Crawford	TB	131
9	A. Berroa	KC	127
10	E. Renteria	BOS	124

Doubles

1	M. Tejada	BAL	50
2	B. Roberts	BAL	45
3	H. Matsui	NYA	45
4	A. Soriano	TEX	43
5	C. Crisp	CLE	42
5	T. Hafner	CLE	42
7	M. Teixeira	TEX	41
8	E. Chavez	OAK	40
8	M. Young	TEX	40
8	J. Cantu	TB	40
8	D. Ortiz	BOS	40

Triples

1	C. Crawford	TB	15
2	I. Suzuki	SEA	12
3	G. Sizemore	CLE	11
4	C. Figgins	LAA	10
5	B. Inge	DET	9
6	B. Roberts	BAL	7
7	7 Tied with		6

Home Runs

1	A. Rodriguez	NYA	48
2	D. Ortiz	BOS	47
3	M. Ramirez	BOS	45
4	M. Teixeira	TEX	43
5	P. Konerko	CHA	40
6	R. Sexson	SEA	39
7	A. Soriano	TEX	36
8	G. Sheffield	NYA	34
9	T. Hafner	CLE	33
10	V. Guerrero	LAA	32
10	J. Giambi	NYA	32

Italicized stats have been adjusted for home park. The leaders for "rate stats" include only those who played enough to qualify per MLB rules.

Walks

	Player	Team	
1	J. Giambi	NYA	108
2	D. Ortiz	BOS	102
3	A. Rodriguez	NYA	91
4	R. Sexson	SEA	89
5	P. Konerko	CHA	81
6	M. Ramirez	BOS	80
7	T. Hafner	CLE	79
8	G. Sheffield	NYA	78
9	D. Jeter	NYA	77
10	D. Dellucci	TEX	76

Intentional Walks

	Player	Team	
1	V. Guerrero	LAA	26
2	I. Suzuki	SEA	23
3	A. Huff	TB	13
4	J. Jones	MIN	12
4	J. Mauer	MIN	12
6	P. Konerko	CHA	10
7	M. Ramirez	BOS	9
7	V. Martinez	CLE	9
7	D. Ortiz	BOS	9
10	3 tied with		8

Hit By Pitches

	Player	Team	
1	S. Hillenbrand	TOR	22
2	A. Rowand	CHA	21
3	J. Kendall	OAK	20
4	J. Giambi	NYA	19
5	A. Rodriguez	NYA	16
5	L. Ford	MIN	16
7	A. Berroa	KC	14
7	J. Gomes	TB	14
9	A. Pierzynski	CHA	12
10	D. Jeter	NYA	11

Pitches per Plate Appearance

	Player	Team	
1	C. Blake	CLE	4.3
2	P. Konerko	CHA	4.2
3	G. Zaun	TOR	4.2
4	J. Giambi	NYA	4.2
5	D. Dellucci	TEX	4.2
6	T. Hafner	CLE	4.2
7	M. Ramirez	BOS	4.1
8	J. Varitek	BOS	4.1
9	N. Swisher	OAK	4.1
10	M. Mora	BAL	4.0

Stolen Bases

	Player	Team	
1	C. Figgins	LAA	62
2	S. Podsednik	CHA	59
3	C. Crawford	TB	46
4	J. Lugo	TB	39
5	I. Suzuki	SEA	33
6	A. Soriano	TEX	30
7	T. Womack	NYA	27
7	B. Roberts	BAL	27
9	T. Hunter	MIN	23
9	N. Logan	DET	23

Caught Stealing

	Player	Team	
1	S. Podsednik	CHA	23
2	C. Figgins	LAA	17
3	J. Lugo	TB	11
4	J. Reed	SEA	11
5	B. Roberts	BAL	10
6	G. Sizemore	CLE	10
7	A. Rios	TOR	9
7	L. Matos	BAL	9
7	J. Rivera	LAA	9
10	3 tied with		8

Net Stolen Bases

	Player	Team	
1	C. Crawford	TB	30
2	C. Figgins	LAA	28
2	A. Soriano	TEX	26
4	J. Lugo	TB	17
4	I. Suzuki	SEA	17
4	O. Cabrera	LAA	17
7	J. Damon	BOS	16
8	S. Podsednik	CHA	13
9	V. Guerrero	LAA	11
9	J. Mauer	MIN	11

Grounded into Double Plays

	Player	Team	
1	J. Kendall	OAK	27
2	M. Tejada	BAL	26
3	J. Cantu	TB	24
4	B. Mueller	BOS	22
4	S. Hatteberg	OAK	22
6	S. Hillenbrand	TOR	21
7	M. Ramirez	BOS	20
7	M. Young	TEX	20
9	I. Rodriguez	DET	19
9	M. Cuddyer	MIN	19

Isolated Power (ISO)

	Player	Team	
1	D. Ortiz	BOS	.304
2	M. Ramirez	BOS	.302
3	T. Hafner	CLE	.290
4	A. Rodriguez	NYA	.289
5	R. Sexson	SEA	.278
6	M. Teixeira	TEX	.274
7	J. Giambi	NYA	.264
8	D. Dellucci	TEX	.262
9	P. Konerko	CHA	.251
10	V. Guerrero	LAA	.248

BA on Balls in Play (BABIP)

	Player	Team	
1	M. Young	TEX	.356
2	D. Jeter	NYA	.353
3	A. Rodriguez	NYA	.349
4	J. Peralta	CLE	.349
5	T. Hafner	CLE	.348
6	B. Roberts	BAL	.343
7	J. Damon	BOS	.343
8	S. Podsednik	CHA	.340
9	D. DeJesus	KC	.335
10	G. Sizemore	CLE	.335

Batting Average with RISP

	Player	Team	
1	M. Young	TEX	.368
2	M. Teixeira	TEX	.366
3	G. Sheffield	NYA	.364
4	M. Ramirez	BOS	.358
5	D. Ortiz	BOS	.354
6	M. Kotsay	OAK	.346
7	J. Kendall	OAK	.344
8	B. Mueller	BOS	.338
9	V. Guerrero	LAA	.338
10	T. Hafner	CLE	.333

Situational Hitting Runs

	Player	Team	
1	M. Ramirez	BOS	19.8
2	G. Sheffield	NYA	19.1
3	M. Teixeira	TEX	18.7
4	G. Anderson	LAA	11.0
5	R. Sexson	SEA	10.6
6	F. Catalanotto	TOR	10.2
7	J. Cantu	TB	9.6
8	J. Kendall	OAK	9.3
9	S. Hatteberg	OAK	8.5
10	M. Kotsay	OAK	7.9

Line Drive Percentage

	Player	Team	
1	B. Roberts	BAL	27.0%
2	B. Mueller	BOS	25.5%
3	M. Young	TEX	25.5%
4	P. Konerko	CHA	24.5%
5	M. Kotsay	OAK	24.5%
6	H. Blalock	TEX	24.5%
7	E. Brown	KC	24.1%
8	G. Sizemore	CLE	24.1%
9	M. Ramirez	BOS	24.0%
10	E. Renteria	BOS	23.3%

Groundball/Flyball Ratio

	Player	Team	
1	D. Jeter	NYA	2.94
2	S. Podsednik	CHA	2.39
3	I. Suzuki	SEA	2.23
4	J. Jones	MIN	2.22
5	J. Mauer	MIN	2.17
6	J. Kendall	OAK	1.99
7	A. Rowand	CHA	1.87
8	L. Ford	MIN	1.82
9	R. Cano	NYA	1.71
10	T. Iguchi	CHA	1.64

Infield Fly per Flyball

	Player	Team	
1	D. Jeter	NYA	0.03
2	J. Mauer	MIN	0.05
3	T. Hafner	CLE	0.06
4	J. Peralta	CLE	0.06
5	J. Cantu	TB	0.06
6	M. Ramirez	BOS	0.07
7	A. Soriano	TEX	0.07
8	J. Kendall	OAK	0.07
9	I. Suzuki	SEA	0.07
10	H. Matsui	NYA	0.07

Home Run per Outfield Fly

	Player	Team	
1	M. Ramirez	BOS	0.28
2	T. Hafner	CLE	0.27
3	R. Sexson	SEA	0.25
4	A. Rodriguez	NYA	0.25
5	J. Jones	MIN	0.23
6	D. Ortiz	BOS	0.22
7	J. Varitek	BOS	0.21
8	J. Giambi	NYA	0.21
9	J. Peralta	CLE	0.20
10	D. Young	DET	0.19

Italicized stats have been adjusted for home park. The leaders for "rate stats" include only those who played enough to qualify per MLB rules.

Extra Base Hits				Sacrifice Hits				Sacrifice Flies				Strikeouts			
1	D. Ortiz	BOS	88	1	C. Crisp	CLE	13	1	C. Monroe	DET	12	1	R. Sexson	SEA	167
2	M. Teixeira	TEX	87	2	N. Logan	DET	12	2	J. Uribe	CHA	10	2	B. Inge	DET	140
3	A. Soriano	TEX	81	3	J. Uribe	CHA	11	2	C. Everett	CHA	10	3	A. Rodriguez	NYA	139
3	M. Tejada	BAL	81	3	T. Iguchi	CHA	11	4	J. Damon	BOS	9	4	H. Blalock	TEX	132
5	A. Rodriguez	NYA	78	5	A. Berroa	KC	10	4	E. Chavez	OAK	9	4	G. Sizemore	CLE	132
6	M. Ramirez	BOS	76	5	N. Green	TB	10	4	D. Ortiz	BOS	9	6	E. Chavez	OAK	129
6	R. Sexson	SEA	76	7	C. Figgins	LAA	9	7	6 tied with		8	7	J. Peralta	CLE	128
8	T. Hafner	CLE	75	7	J. Castro	MIN	9					8	A. Soriano	TEX	125
9	H. Matsui	NYA	71	9	M. Mora	BAL	8					9	M. Teixeira	TEX	124
10	B. Roberts	BAL	70	9	R. Belliard	CLE	8					9	D. Ortiz	BOS	124
10	G. Sizemore	CLE	70												

Pitching Leaders

Pitching Runs				Earned Run Average (ERA)				Runs Allowed Per 9 Innings (RA)				Fielding Independent Pitching (FIP)			
1	J. Santana	MIN	45	1	K. Millwood	CLE	2.86	1	J. Santana	MIN	2.99	1	J. Santana	MIN	2.84
2	R. Halladay	TOR	35	2	J. Santana	MIN	2.87	2	J. Washburn	LAA	3.35	2	J. Lackey	LAA	3.14
3	K. Millwood	CLE	31	3	M. Buehrle	CHA	3.12	3	K. Millwood	CLE	3.38	3	M. Buehrle	CHA	3.46
4	J. Washburn	LAA	29	4	J. Washburn	LAA	3.20	4	J. Lackey	LAA	3.66	4	C. Sabathia	CLE	3.73
5	J. Lackey	LAA	26	5	C. Silva	MIN	3.44	5	J. Garland	CHA	3.75	5	K. Millwood	CLE	3.77
5	R. Harden	OAK	26	6	J. Lackey	LAA	3.44	6	M. Buehrle	CHA	3.76	6	B. Colon	LAA	3.79
7	M. Buehrle	CHA	25	7	K. Rogers	TEX	3.46	7	B. Colon	LAA	3.76	7	S. Kazmir	TB	3.80
7	B. Colon	LAA	25	8	B. Colon	LAA	3.48	8	J. Blanton	OAK	3.84	8	R. Johnson	NYA	3.82
7	H. Street	OAK	25	9	J. Garland	CHA	3.50	9	K. Rogers	TEX	3.96	9	C. Lee	CLE	3.84
10	J. Garland	CHA	24	10	J. Blanton	OAK	3.53	10	C. Silva	MIN	3.97	10	C. Young	TEX	3.85

Innings Pitched				Batters Faced				Pitches				Pitches per Plate Appearances			
1	M. Buehrle	CHA	236.7	1	M. Buehrle	CHA	971	1	B. Zito	OAK	3804	1	C. Silva	MIN	3.1
2	J. Santana	MIN	231.7	2	B. Zito	OAK	953	2	J. Lackey	LAA	3489	2	J. Johnson	DET	3.4
3	B. Zito	OAK	228.3	3	T. Wakefield	BOS	943	3	M. Buehrle	CHA	3477	3	J. Towers	TOR	3.4
4	F. Garcia	CHA	228.0	4	F. Garcia	CHA	943	4	R. Johnson	NYA	3426	4	P. Byrd	LAA	3.5
5	R. Johnson	NYA	225.7	5	R. Johnson	NYA	920	5	F. Garcia	CHA	3395	5	B. Radke	MIN	3.5
6	T. Wakefield	BOS	225.3	6	R. Lopez	BAL	918	6	T. Wakefield	BOS	3393	6	R. Franklin	SEA	3.5
7	B. Colon	LAA	222.7	7	J. Santana	MIN	910	7	D. Haren	OAK	3372	7	N. Robertson	DET	3.5
8	J. Garland	CHA	221.0	8	B. Colon	LAA	906	8	J. Santana	MIN	3335	8	R. Lopez	BAL	3.6
9	D. Haren	OAK	217.0	9	J. Garland	CHA	901	9	J. Garland	CHA	3315	9	T. Wakefield	BOS	3.6
10	J. Westbrook	CLE	210.7	10	D. Haren	OAK	897	10	B. Arroyo	BOS	3300	10	M. Buehrle	CHA	3.6

Italicized stats have been adjusted for home park. The leaders for "rate stats" include only those who played enough to qualify per MLB rules.

Strikeouts

1	J. Santana	MIN	238
2	R. Johnson	NYA	211
3	J. Lackey	LAA	199
4	S. Kazmir	TB	174
5	B. Zito	OAK	171
6	D. Haren	OAK	163
7	C. Sabathia	CLE	161
8	B. Colon	LAA	157
9	D. Cabrera	BAL	157
10	J. Contreras	CHA	154

Walks (Most)

1	S. Kazmir	TB	100
2	B. Zito	OAK	89
3	D. Cabrera	BAL	87
4	J. Contreras	CHA	75
5	G. Meche	SEA	72
6	J. Lackey	LAA	71
7	G. Chacin	TOR	70
7	R. Hernandez	KC	70
9	T. Wakefield	BOS	68
9	M. Clement	BOS	68

Strikeouts Per Game

1	J. Santana	MIN	10.0
2	R. Johnson	NYA	8.8
3	J. Lackey	LAA	8.5
4	S. Kazmir	TB	8.1
5	C. Sabathia	CLE	7.5
6	C. Young	TEX	7.5
7	M. Mussina	NYA	7.1
8	K. Millwood	CLE	7.0
9	D. Haren	OAK	7.0
10	B. Zito	OAK	6.9

Walks Per Game (Least)

1	C. Silva	MIN	0.5
2	D. Wells	BOS	1.0
3	B. Radke	MIN	1.1
4	P. Byrd	LAA	1.3
5	J. Towers	TOR	1.3
6	M. Buehrle	CHA	1.6
7	B. Colon	LAA	1.8
8	J. Santana	MIN	1.9
9	R. Johnson	NYA	2.0
10	J. Garland	CHA	2.0

Strikeout/Walk Ratio

1	C. Silva	MIN	7.9
2	J. Santana	MIN	5.3
3	D. Wells	BOS	5.1
4	B. Radke	MIN	5.1
5	R. Johnson	NYA	4.5
6	J. Towers	TOR	3.9
7	M. Buehrle	CHA	3.7
8	B. Colon	LAA	3.7
9	P. Byrd	LAA	3.6
10	D. Haren	OAK	3.1

Walks+Hits per Inning (WHIP)

1	J. Santana	MIN	0.97
2	R. Johnson	NYA	1.13
3	B. Colon	LAA	1.16
4	J. Garland	CHA	1.17
5	C. Silva	MIN	1.17
6	B. Radke	MIN	1.18
7	M. Buehrle	CHA	1.19
8	P. Byrd	LAA	1.20
9	B. Zito	OAK	1.20
10	C. Lee	CLE	1.22

LOB% -- best

1	J. Washburn	LAA	81.8%
2	K. Millwood	CLE	79.0%
3	B. Chen	BAL	77.5%
4	K. Lohse	MIN	76.8%
5	J. Santana	MIN	76.3%
6	J. Garland	CHA	75.8%
7	J. Lackey	LAA	75.4%
8	G. Chacin	TOR	75.3%
9	J. Blanton	OAK	75.3%
10	B. Colon	LAA	74.8%

LOB% -- worst

1	J. Lima	KC	60.7%
2	M. Hendrickson	TB	62.2%
3	J. Westbrook	CLE	62.9%
4	Z. Greinke	KC	65.2%
5	B. Arroyo	BOS	65.9%
6	J. Pineiro	SEA	66.2%
7	J. Johnson	DET	66.8%
8	R. Lopez	BAL	67.0%
9	C. Fossum	TB	67.7%
10	M. Maroth	DET	68.0%

Wins

1	B. Colon	LAA	21
2	J. Garland	CHA	18
2	C. Lee	CLE	18
4	R. Johnson	NYA	17
5	T. Wakefield	BOS	16
5	M. Buehrle	CHA	16
5	J. Santana	MIN	16
8	5 tied with		15

Losses

1	Z. Greinke	KC	17
2	J. Lima	KC	16
2	N. Robertson	DET	16
4	J. Westbrook	CLE	15
2	R. Franklin	SEA	15
6	M. Maroth	DET	14
6	R. Hernandez	KC	14
8	5 tied with		13

Shutouts

1	J. Garland	CHA	3
2	J. Santana	MIN	2
2	M. Mussina	NYA	2
2	R. Halladay	TOR	2
5	14 tied with		1

Games

1	M. Timlin	BOS	81
2	S. Schoeneweis	TOR	80
3	B. Howry	CLE	79
3	T. Gordon	NYA	79
5	S. Shields	LAA	78
6	J. Rincon	MIN	75
6	J. Crain	MIN	75
8	T. Williams	BAL	72
9	M. Batista	TOR	71
9	M. Rivera	NYA	71

Games Finished

1	M. Rivera	NYA	67
2	D. Baez	TB	64
3	M. Batista	TOR	62
4	B. Ryan	BAL	61
5	F. Cordero	TEX	60
6	J. Nathan	MIN	58
6	F. Rodriguez	LAA	58
8	B. Wickman	CLE	55
8	E. Guardado	SEA	55
10	M. MacDougal	KC	53

Saves

1	B. Wickman	CLE	45
1	F. Rodriguez	LAA	45
3	M. Rivera	NYA	43
3	J. Nathan	MIN	43
5	D. Baez	TB	41
6	F. Cordero	TEX	37
7	B. Ryan	BAL	36
7	E. Guardado	SEA	36
9	D. Hermanson	CHA	34
10	M. Batista	TOR	31

Blown Saves

1	M. Batista	TOR	8
1	D. Baez	TB	8
1	F. Cordero	TEX	8
4	T. Gordon	NYA	7
4	M. Timlin	BOS	7
6	S. Shields	LAA	6
6	F. Rodney	DET	6
8	11 tied with		5

Holds

1	S. Shields	LAA	33
1	T. Gordon	NYA	33
3	B. Howry	CLE	29
4	J. Rincon	MIN	25
5	M. Timlin	BOS	24
6	C. Politte	CHA	23
7	D. Marte	CHA	22
8	S. Schoeneweis	TOR	21
8	J. Putz	SEA	21
10	J. Borowski	TB	19

Italicized stats have been adjusted for home park. The leaders for "rate stats" include only those who played enough to qualify per MLB rules.

Groundball/Flyball Ratio				Infield Fly per Flyball				Line Drive Percent				Defense Efficiency Ratio (DER)			
1	J. Westbrook	CLE	3.38	1	M. Maroth	DET	24%	1	J. Santana	MIN	16.1%	1	B. Zito	OAK	.757
2	J. Johnson	DET	1.68	2	B. Zito	OAK	19%	2	R. Franklin	SEA	16.3%	2	J. Blanton	OAK	.752
3	N. Robertson	DET	1.63	3	G. Chacin	TOR	19%	3	J. Blanton	OAK	16.6%	3	T. Wakefield	BOS	.742
4	C. Sabathia	CLE	1.61	4	J. Santana	MIN	19%	4	M. Maroth	DET	16.6%	4	J. Contreras	CHA	.742
5	D. Wells	BOS	1.60	5	J. Johnson	DET	18%	5	R. Johnson	NYA	16.7%	5	B. Chen	BAL	.741
6	F. Garcia	CHA	1.59	6	J. Garland	CHA	18%	6	T. Wakefield	BOS	16.9%	6	J. Santana	MIN	.738
7	C. Silva	MIN	1.58	7	B. Colon	LAA	17%	7	J. Johnson	DET	17.1%	7	J. Garland	CHA	.737
8	D. Haren	OAK	1.52	8	J. Westbrook	CLE	17%	8	B. Colon	LAA	17.3%	8	S. Elarton	CLE	.732
9	J. Garland	CHA	1.50	9	M. Hendrickson	TB	17%	9	M. Mussina	NYA	17.6%	9	C. Lee	CLE	.723
10	M. Hendrickson	TB	1.45	10	B. Chen	BAL	17%	10	C. Young	TEX	17.7%	10	B. Arroyo	BOS	.722
												11	B. Radke	MIN	.722

Home Runs Allowed				Home Runs Allowed Per Game				*Home Runs per Outfield Fly*				Slugging Average Allowed			
1	T. Wakefield	BOS	35	1	S. Kazmir	TB	0.56	1	K. Rogers	TEX	0.07	1	J. Santana	MIN	.350
2	B. Radke	MIN	33	2	J. Lackey	LAA	0.56	2	M. Buehrle	CHA	0.08	2	B. Zito	OAK	.360
3	B. Chen	BAL	33	3	K. Rogers	TEX	0.69	3	C. Young	TEX	0.08	3	J. Lackey	LAA	.360
4	R. Johnson	NYA	32	4	M. Buehrle	CHA	0.79	4	S. Kazmir	TB	0.08	4	C. Sabathia	CLE	.370
5	S. Elarton	CLE	32	5	J. Westbrook	CLE	0.81	5	J. Lackey	LAA	0.08	5	J. Contreras	CHA	.370
6	J. Lima	KC	31	6	M. Clement	BOS	0.83	6	P. Byrd	LAA	0.09	6	S. Kazmir	TB	.370
7	M. Maroth	DET	30	7	C. Sabathia	CLE	0.88	7	B. Arroyo	BOS	0.09	7	M. Buehrle	CHA	.380
8	D. Waechter	TB	29	8	G. Chacin	TOR	0.88	8	G. Chacin	TOR	0.09	8	K. Millwood	CLE	.390
9	R. Lopez	BAL	28	9	J. Santana	MIN	0.93	9	J. Washburn	LAA	0.10	9	J. Blanton	OAK	.390
9	R. Franklin	SEA	28	10	K. Millwood	CLE	0.96	10	M. Clement	BOS	0.10	10	J. Garland	CHA	.400
9	N. Robertson	DET	28	11	B. Arroyo	BOS	0.96								

Grounded into Double Plays				Total Double Plays				Wild Pitches				Batters Hit by Pitch			
1	C. Silva	MIN	36	1	C. Silva	MIN	43	1	F. Garcia	CHA	20	1	C. Fossum	TB	18
2	M. Buehrle	CHA	29	2	M. Buehrle	CHA	35	2	J. Contreras	CHA	20	2	M. Clement	BOS	16
3	D. Haren	OAK	26	3	D. Haren	OAK	30	3	J. Lackey	LAA	18	3	B. Arroyo	BOS	14
4	J. Johnson	DET	25	4	J. Washburn	LAA	29	4	J. Johnson	DET	17	4	B. Zito	OAK	13
5	J. Westbrook	CLE	25	5	J. Johnson	DET	29	5	M. Clement	BOS	13	5	Z. Greinke	KC	13
6	F. Garcia	CHA	25	6	F. Garcia	CHA	29	6	S. Shields	LAA	12	6	D. Bush	TOR	13
7	J. Pineiro	SEA	25	7	K. Rogers	TEX	29	7	J. Julio	BAL	10	7	R. Johnson	NYA	12
8	K. Rogers	TEX	25	8	J. Garland	CHA	28	8	S. Ponson	BAL	10	8	O. Hernandez	CHA	12
9	J. Washburn	LAA	24	9	J. Pineiro	SEA	28	9	D. Cabrera	BAL	9	9	4 tied with		11
10	J. Garland	CHA	24	10	K. Saarloos	OAK	28	10	5 tied with		8				

Stolen Bases Allowed				Runners Caught Stealing				Pickoffs				Net Stolen Bases Allowed			
1	K. Millwood	CLE	33	1	R. Johnson	NYA	14	1	M. Maroth	DET	10	1	M. Maroth	DET	-40
2	J. Contreras	CHA	28	2	M. Maroth	DET	12	2	M. Buehrle	CHA	5	2	G. Chacin	TOR	-22
3	J. Moyer	SEA	27	3	G. Chacin	TOR	10	3	M. Hendrickson	TB	5	3	M. Hendrickson	TB	-19
4	R. Johnson	NYA	23	4	S. Kazmir	TB	9	4	G. Chacin	TOR	5	4	J. Washburn	LAA	-14
5	R. Lopez	BAL	22	5	J. Johnson	DET	8	5	R. Johnson	NYA	4	5	K. Lohse	MIN	-14
6	B. Zito	OAK	22	6	B. Chen	BAL	8	6	B. Chen	BAL	4	6	S. Kazmir	TB	-14
7	O. Hernandez	CHA	19	7	G. Meche	SEA	8	7	D. Wells	BOS	4	7	R. Johnson	NYA	-12
8	F. Garcia	CHA	19	8	J. Lackey	LAA	8	8	K. Lohse	MIN	3	8	J. Garland	CHA	-9
9	D. Haren	OAK	19	9	5 tied with		7	9	D. Brazelton	TB	3	9	D. Wells	BOS	-9
10	T. Wakefield	BOS	18					10	18 tied		2	10	J. Lackey	LAA	-9

Italicized stats have been adjusted for home park. The leaders for "rate stats" include only those who played enough to qualify per MLB rules.

National League Team Stats

Runs Scored and Allowed
(adjusted for ballpark factors)

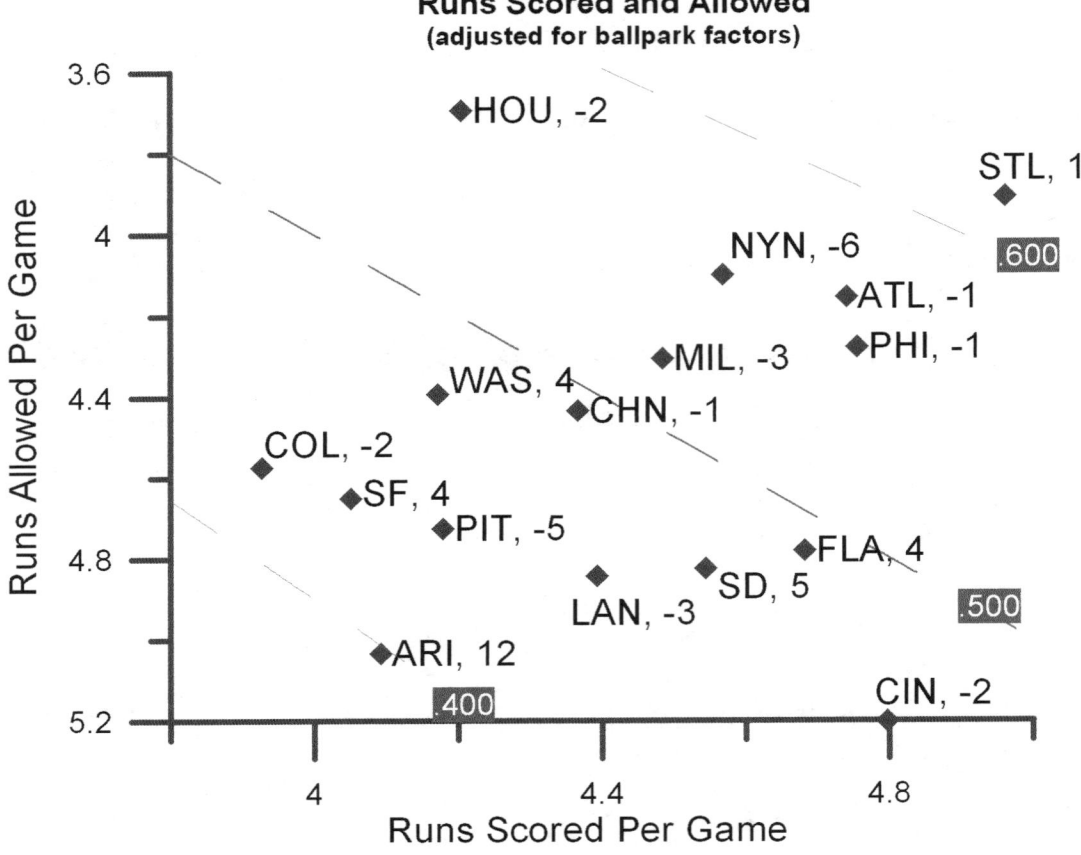

Notes: The dotted lines represent winning percentage based on run differential. The number after each team name represents the difference between the team's actual record and its run differential record.

Team	Team Record					Scoring Runs			Preventing Runs				Projection	
	W	L	RS	RA	RS-RA	AB/RSP	BA/RSP	HR	ERA	HRA	K	DER	PWINS	VAR
ARI	77	85	696	856	-160	1,378	.237	191	4.84	193	1,038	.684	65	12
ATL	90	72	769	674	95	1,400	.249	184	3.99	145	929	.694	91	-1
CHN	79	83	703	714	-11	1,355	.258	194	4.19	186	1,256	.701	80	-1
CIN	73	89	820	889	-69	1,375	.256	222	5.15	219	955	.678	75	-2
COL	67	95	740	862	-122	1,422	.265	150	5.13	175	981	.671	69	-2
FLA	83	79	717	732	-15	1,451	.276	128	4.16	116	1,125	.678	79	4
HOU	89	73	693	609	84	1,342	.261	161	3.51	155	1,164	.706	90	-1
LAN	71	91	685	755	-70	1,347	.263	149	4.38	182	1,004	.700	74	-3
MIL	81	81	726	697	29	1,347	.241	175	3.97	169	1,173	.698	84	-3
WAS	81	81	639	673	-34	1,322	.253	117	3.87	140	997	.698	77	4
NYN	83	79	722	648	74	1,364	.253	175	3.76	135	1,012	.702	89	-6
PHI	88	74	807	726	81	1,465	.278	167	4.21	189	1,159	.705	89	-1
PIT	67	95	680	769	-89	1,372	.270	139	4.42	162	958	.695	72	-5
STL	100	62	805	634	171	1,426	.290	170	3.49	153	974	.704	99	1
SD	82	80	684	726	-42	1,388	.260	130	4.13	146	1,133	.690	77	5
SF	75	87	649	745	-96	1,349	.268	128	4.33	151	972	.700	71	4
Average	80	82	721	732	-11	1,381	.261	161	4.22	164	1,052	.694	81	-1

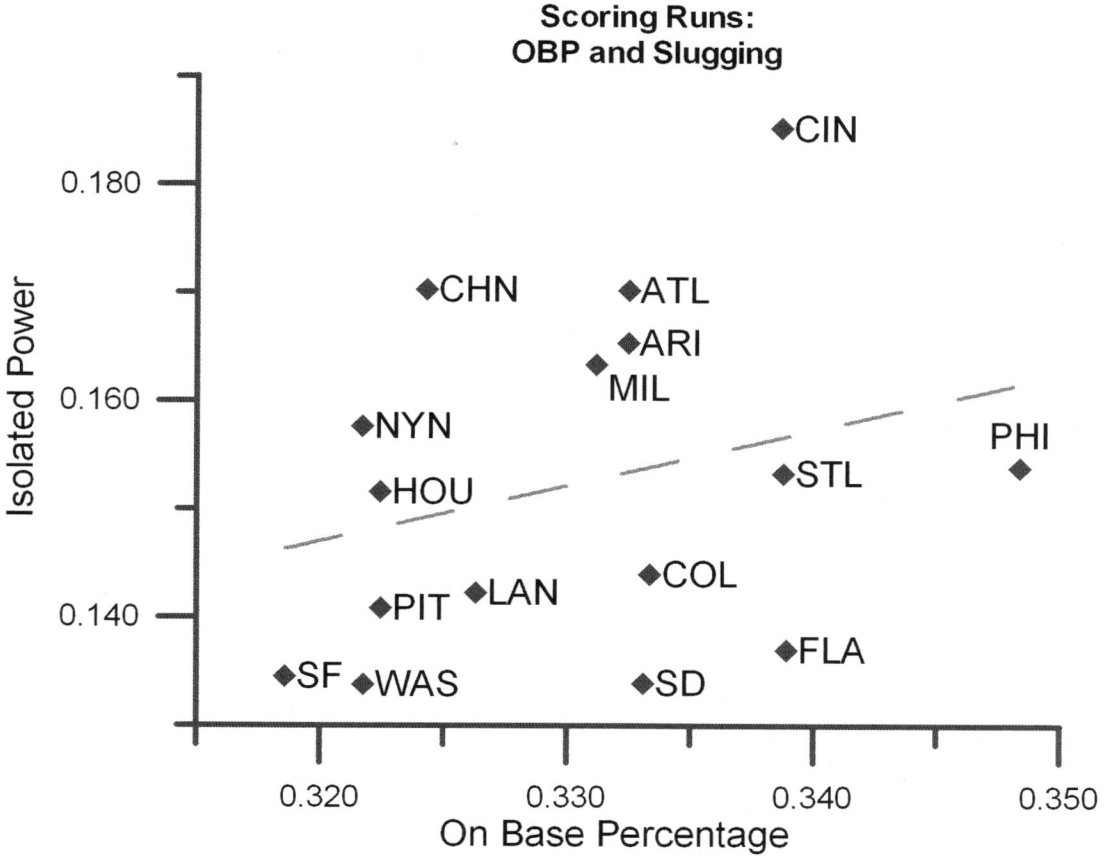

Scoring Runs: OBP and Slugging

The dotted line shows the relationship between ISO and OBP.

Batting Statistics

Team	Runs	PA	H	1B	2B	3B	HR	TB	SO	BB	HBP	SH	SF	BA	OBP	SLG	GPA	ISO
ARI	696	6,327	1,419	910	291	27	191	2,337	1,094	606	55	71	45	.256	.332	.421	.255	.165
ATL	769	6,186	1,453	924	308	37	184	2,387	1,084	534	45	75	46	.265	.333	.435	.258	.170
CHN	703	6,161	1,506	966	323	23	194	2,457	920	419	50	69	37	.270	.324	.440	.256	.170
CIN	820	6,321	1,453	881	335	15	222	2,484	1,303	611	62	43	39	.261	.339	.446	.264	.185
COL	740	6,238	1,477	1,013	280	34	150	2,275	1,103	509	64	88	34	.267	.333	.411	.253	.144
FLA	717	6,214	1,499	1,033	306	32	128	2,253	918	512	67	82	50	.272	.339	.409	.255	.137
HOU	693	6,139	1,400	926	281	32	161	2,228	1,037	481	72	82	42	.256	.322	.408	.247	.152
LAN	685	6,134	1,374	920	284	21	149	2,147	1,094	541	67	57	33	.253	.326	.395	.246	.142
MIL	726	6,156	1,413	892	327	19	175	2,303	1,162	531	73	66	38	.259	.331	.423	.255	.163
WAS	639	6,142	1,367	907	311	32	117	2,093	1,090	491	89	91	45	.252	.322	.386	.241	.134
NYN	722	6,146	1,421	935	279	32	175	2,289	1,075	486	48	69	38	.258	.322	.416	.249	.158
PHI	807	6,345	1,494	1,010	282	35	167	2,347	1,083	639	56	62	46	.270	.348	.423	.263	.154
PIT	680	6,221	1,445	976	292	38	139	2,230	1,092	471	72	56	49	.259	.322	.400	.245	.141
STL	805	6,246	1,494	1,011	287	26	170	2,343	947	534	62	77	35	.270	.339	.423	.258	.153
SD	684	6,271	1,416	978	269	39	130	2,153	977	600	49	72	48	.257	.333	.391	.248	.134
SF	649	6,077	1,427	974	299	26	128	2,162	901	431	49	91	44	.261	.319	.396	.242	.135
Average	721	6,208	1,441	954	297	29	161	2,281	1,055	525	61	72	42	.262	.330	.414	.252	.152

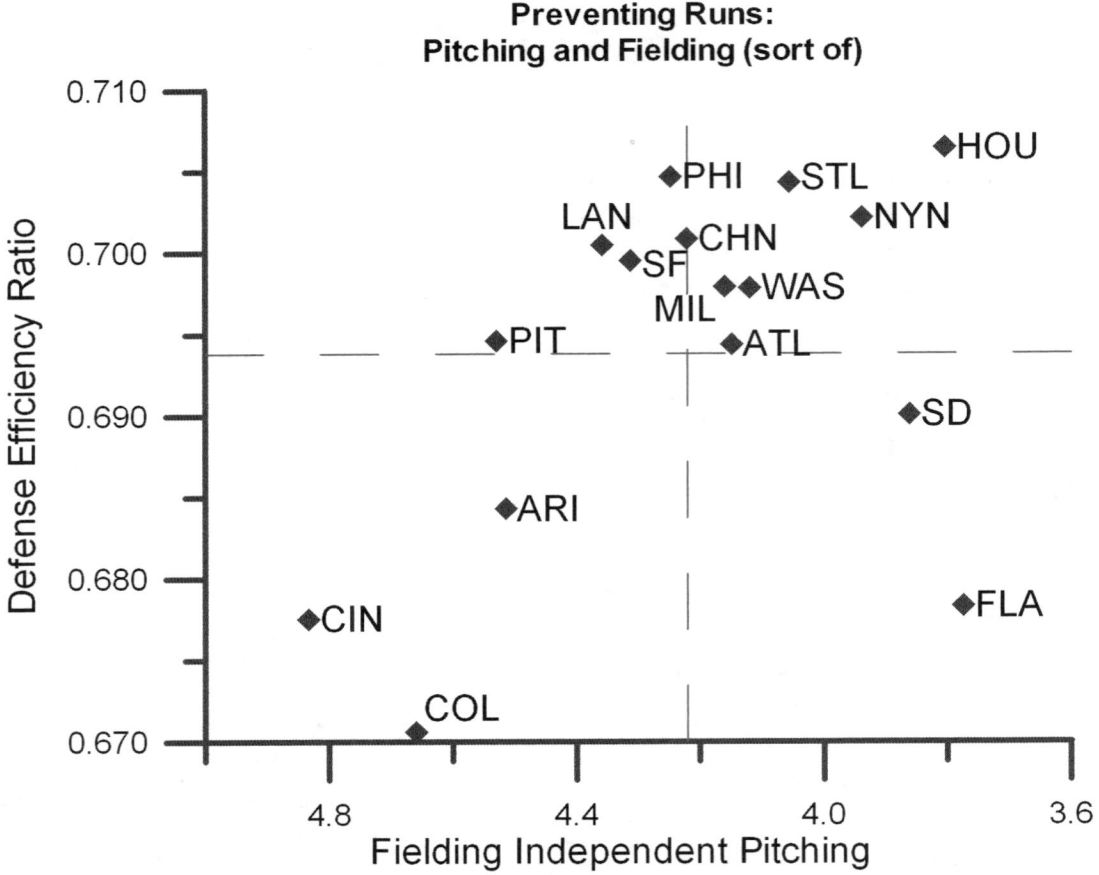

Preventing Runs:
Pitching and Fielding (sort of)

The dotted lines represent the league averages.

Pitching Statistics

Team	RA	IP	BFP	H	HR	TBA	K	BB	ShO	Sv	Op	%Save	Holds	ERA	FIP	UERA	DER
ARI	856	1456.0	6,402	1,580	193	2,582	1,038	537	10	45	62	73%	64	4.84	4.51	0.45	.684
ATL	674	1443.0	6,186	1,487	145	2,251	929	520	12	38	62	61%	73	3.99	4.15	0.22	.694
CHN	714	1440.0	6,185	1,357	186	2,211	1,256	576	10	39	58	67%	69	4.19	4.22	0.27	.701
CIN	889	1433.0	6,397	1,657	219	2,758	955	492	1	31	47	66%	63	5.15	4.83	0.43	.678
COL	862	1418.0	6,385	1,600	175	2,546	981	604	4	37	63	59%	68	5.13	4.66	0.34	.671
FLA	732	1442.0	6,236	1,459	116	2,205	1,125	563	15	42	60	70%	55	4.16	3.77	0.41	.678
HOU	609	1443.0	6,023	1,336	155	2,114	1,164	440	11	45	58	78%	66	3.51	3.80	0.29	.706
LAN	755	1427.0	6,113	1,434	182	2,337	1,004	471	9	40	59	68%	66	4.38	4.36	0.38	.700
MIL	697	1438.0	6,208	1,382	169	2,249	1,173	569	6	46	67	69%	61	3.97	4.16	0.39	.698
WAS	673	1458.0	6,286	1,456	140	2,197	997	539	9	51	69	74%	69	3.87	4.12	0.28	.698
NYN	648	1435.0	6,121	1,390	135	2,114	1,012	491	11	38	59	64%	49	3.76	3.94	0.31	.702
PHI	726	1435.0	6,119	1,379	189	2,321	1,159	487	6	40	63	63%	78	4.21	4.25	0.34	.705
PIT	769	1436.0	6,264	1,456	162	2,318	958	612	14	35	47	74%	59	4.42	4.53	0.39	.695
STL	634	1445.0	6,047	1,399	153	2,167	974	443	14	48	65	74%	86	3.49	4.05	0.46	.704
SD	726	1455.0	6,253	1,452	146	2,292	1,133	503	8	45	65	69%	70	4.13	3.86	0.36	.690
SF	745	1444.0	6,280	1,456	151	2,277	972	592	8	46	74	62%	89	4.33	4.31	0.31	.700
Average	**732**	**1440.5**	**6,219**	**1,455**	**164**	**2,309**	**1,052**	**527**	**9**	**42**	**61**	**68%**	**68**	**4.22**	**4.22**	**0.35**	**.694**

Running and Miscellaneous Batting Stats

Team	SB	CS	SB%	GDP	P/PA	LD%	BABIP	G/F
ARI	67	26	72%	132	3.83	.193	.288	1.34
ATL	92	32	74%	147	3.71	.205	.301	1.30
CHN	65	39	63%	131	3.61	.205	.294	1.29
CIN	72	23	76%	116	3.85	.207	.305	1.30
COL	65	32	67%	125	3.73	.218	.309	1.33
FLA	96	38	72%	144	3.77	.219	.308	1.35
HOU	115	44	72%	116	3.69	.190	.291	1.18
LAN	58	35	62%	139	3.84	.207	.292	1.26
MIL	79	34	70%	137	3.82	.214	.301	1.25
WAS	45	45	50%	131	3.71	.209	.296	1.39
NYN	153	40	79%	104	3.75	.201	.293	1.28
PHI	116	27	81%	107	3.84	.234	.309	1.23
PIT	73	30	71%	130	3.63	.195	.301	1.39
STL	83	36	70%	127	3.69	.206	.299	1.42
SD	99	44	69%	123	3.78	.214	.293	1.18
SF	71	35	67%	147	3.56	.200	.293	1.27
Average	84	35	71%	129	3.74	.207	.298	1.30

Win Shares Stats

Team	Bat	Pitch	Field	WS	CWS	WSAge
ARI	111	80	40	231	1,898	29.8
ATL	128	98	44	270	2,372	28.5
CHN	108	87	43	237	2,322	29.0
CIN	150	43	27	219	1,678	29.1
COL	90	75	36	201	1,092	27.6
FLA	133	81	35	249	2,275	28.8
HOU	105	113	50	267	2,463	31.1
LAN	117	65	31	213	1,750	29.5
MIL	114	88	41	243	1,168	28.5
NYN	114	94	41	249	2,628	29.6
PHI	133	88	42	264	2,584	29.7
PIT	96	68	37	201	1,169	27.6
SD	133	78	35	246	2,381	31.3
SF	102	82	41	225	3,259	31.8
STL	149	103	47	300	2,415	30.4
WAS	106	92	45	243	2,058	28.9
Average	118	83	40	241	2,095	29.4

Fielding and Miscellaneous Pitching Stats

Team	DER	Fld %	UER	SBA	CS	%CS	PO	Err	TE	FE	DP	GIDP	LD%	G/F	IF/Fly
ARI	.684	.985	73	106	28	26%	14	94	50	44	159	141	.215	1.42	13.8%
ATL	.694	.986	35	125	36	29%	8	86	34	50	170	144	.220	1.52	11.2%
CHN	.701	.983	43	130	40	31%	9	101	41	58	136	118	.204	1.39	10.4%
CIN	.678	.983	69	111	35	32%	9	103	53	49	133	121	.200	1.12	15.0%
COL	.671	.981	54	139	37	27%	19	118	66	51	158	132	.214	1.33	11.3%
FLA	.678	.983	66	156	38	24%	9	103	49	54	177	154	.214	1.38	14.1%
HOU	.706	.985	46	84	31	37%	9	89	38	50	146	122	.209	1.45	11.6%
LAN	.700	.983	60	164	34	21%	10	106	41	63	141	119	.192	1.34	13.4%
MIL	.698	.980	62	120	34	28%	25	119	55	61	138	108	.204	1.13	13.4%
WAS	.698	.985	46	117	41	35%	10	92	38	52	157	125	.221	1.07	12.9%
NYN	.702	.983	49	132	25	19%	5	106	42	61	146	128	.206	1.27	10.1%
PHI	.705	.985	54	108	26	24%	4	90	41	47	132	111	.223	1.34	12.8%
PIT	.695	.981	63	100	36	36%	11	117	51	64	193	164	.200	1.30	14.5%
STL	.704	.984	74	65	33	51%	10	100	40	58	196	181	.191	1.73	11.8%
SD	.690	.982	58	119	25	21%	4	109	56	53	137	117	.206	1.22	13.5%
SF	.700	.985	50	132	54	41%	13	90	24	64	146	118	.202	1.17	15.8%
Average	.694	.983	56	119	35	29%	11	101	45	55	154	131	.208	1.31	12.9%

197

National League Leaderboards
Batting Leaders

Runs Created

1	D. Lee	CHN	144
2	A. Pujols	STL	142
3	J. Bay	PIT	136
4	B. Giles	SD	130
5	C. Delgado	FLA	126
6	M. Cabrera	FLA	123
7	B. Abreu	PHI	117
8	J. Kent	LAN	113
9	M. Ensberg	HOU	110
9	P. Burrell	PHI	110
9	D. Wright	NYN	110

Runs Scored

1	A. Pujols	STL	129
2	D. Lee	CHN	120
3	J. Rollins	PHI	115
4	J. Bay	PIT	110
5	A. Dunn	CIN	107
6	M. Cabrera	FLA	106
7	M. Giles	ATL	104
7	B. Abreu	PHI	104
9	R. Furcal	ATL	100
9	J. Kent	LAN	100

Runs Batted In

1	A. Jones	ATL	128
2	P. Burrell	PHI	117
2	A. Pujols	STL	117
4	M. Cabrera	FLA	116
5	C. Delgado	FLA	115
6	C. Lee	MIL	114
7	D. Lee	CHN	107
8	J. Kent	LAN	105
8	C. Utley	PHI	105
10	B. Abreu	PHI	102
10	D. Wright	NYN	102

Gross Production Average (GPA)

1	D. Lee	CHN	.355
2	A. Pujols	STL	.344
3	C. Delgado	FLA	.344
4	B. Giles	SD	.337
5	M. Cabrera	FLA	.332
6	J. Bay	PIT	.318
7	N. Johnson	WAS	.317
8	D. Wright	NYN	.313
9	L. Berkman	HOU	.312
10	M. Ensberg	HOU	.311

Batting Average

1	D. Lee	CHN	.335
2	A. Pujols	STL	.330
3	M. Cabrera	FLA	.323
4	T. Helton	COL	.320
5	S. Casey	CIN	.312
6	C. Tracy	ARI	.308
7	M. Holliday	COL	.307
8	B. Clark	MIL	.306
9	J. Bay	PIT	.306
10	D. Wright	NYN	.306

On Base Percentage

1	T. Helton	COL	.445
2	A. Pujols	STL	.430
3	B. Giles	SD	.423
4	D. Lee	CHN	.418
5	L. Berkman	HOU	.411
6	N. Johnson	WAS	.408
7	B. Abreu	PHI	.405
8	J. Bay	PIT	.402
9	C. Delgado	FLA	.399
10	L. Castillo	FLA	.391

Slugging Percentage

1	D. Lee	CHN	.662
2	A. Pujols	STL	.609
3	C. Delgado	FLA	.582
4	K. Griffey Jr.	CIN	.576
5	A. Jones	ATL	.575
6	A. Ramirez	CHN	.568
7	M. Cabrera	FLA	.561
8	J. Bay	PIT	.559
9	M. Ensberg	HOU	.557
10	C. Tracy	ARI	.553

OPS (On Base Plus Slugging)

1	D. Lee	CHN	1.080
2	A. Pujols	STL	1.039
3	C. Delgado	FLA	.981
4	T. Helton	COL	.979
5	J. Bay	PIT	.961
6	M. Cabrera	FLA	.947
7	K. Griffey Jr.	CIN	.946
8	M. Ensberg	HOU	.945
9	L. Berkman	HOU	.934
10	A. Dunn	CIN	.927

Plate Appearances

1	J. Reyes	NYN	733
2	J. Rollins	PHI	732
3	J. Pierre	FLA	719
3	B. Abreu	PHI	719
5	D. Eckstein	STL	713
6	J. Bay	PIT	707
7	A. Pujols	STL	700
8	D. Lee	CHN	691
9	R. Furcal	ATL	689
10	C. Lee	MIL	688

Outs

1	J. Reyes	NYN	506
2	J. Rollins	PHI	481
3	J. Pierre	FLA	475
4	C. Lee	MIL	454
5	J. Burnitz	CHN	449
6	D. Eckstein	STL	445
7	R. Furcal	ATL	441
8	J. Wilson	PIT	436
9	C. Biggio	HOU	434
10	A. Jones	ATL	432

Hits

1	D. Lee	CHN	199
2	M. Cabrera	FLA	198
3	J. Rollins	PHI	196
4	A. Pujols	STL	195
5	J. Reyes	NYN	190
6	D. Eckstein	STL	185
7	B. Clark	MIL	183
7	J. Bay	PIT	183
9	J. Pierre	FLA	181
10	D. Wright	NYN	176

Total Bases

1	D. Lee	CHN	393
2	A. Pujols	STL	360
3	M. Cabrera	FLA	344
4	A. Jones	ATL	337
5	J. Bay	PIT	335
6	C. Delgado	FLA	303
7	C. Lee	MIL	301
7	D. Wright	NYN	301
9	A. Dunn	CIN	293
9	M. Ensberg	HOU	293

Singles

1	W. Taveras	HOU	152
2	J. Pierre	FLA	147
3	D. Eckstein	STL	144
3	J. Reyes	NYN	142
5	B. Clark	MIL	138
6	J. Rollins	PHI	135
7	S. Casey	CIN	124
8	R. Furcal	ATL	121
9	M. Cabrera	FLA	120
10	O. Vizquel	SF	119

Doubles

1	D. Lee	CHN	50
2	M. Giles	ATL	45
2	T. Helton	COL	45
3	J. Bay	PIT	44
5	M. Cabrera	FLA	43
5	J. Randa	SD/C	43
7	G. Jenkins	MIL	42
7	B. Wilkerson	WAS	42
7	D. Wright	NYN	42
10	2 tied with		41

Triples

1	J. Reyes	NYN	17
2	J. Pierre	FLA	13
3	R. Furcal	ATL	11
3	J. Rollins	PHI	11
5	D. Roberts	SD	10
6	B. Giles	SD	8
7	D. Eckstein	STL	7
7	B. Wilkerson	WAS	7
7	J. Wilson	PIT	7
7	M. Holliday	COL	7

Home Runs

1	A. Jones	ATL	51
2	D. Lee	CHN	46
3	A. Pujols	STL	41
3	A. Dunn	CIN	40
5	T. Glaus	ARI	37
6	M. Ensberg	HOU	36
7	K. Griffey Jr.	CIN	35
8	C. Floyd	NYN	34
9	C. Delgado	FLA	33
9	M. Cabrera	FLA	33

Italicized stats have been adjusted for home park. The leaders for "rate stats" include only those who played enough to qualify per MLB rules.

Walks

1	B. Giles	SD	119
2	B. Abreu	PHI	117
3	A. Dunn	CIN	114
4	T. Helton	COL	106
5	P. Burrell	PHI	99
6	A. Pujols	STL	97
7	J. Bay	PIT	95
8	L. Berkman	HOU	91
8	J. Edmonds	STL	91
10	D. Lee	CHN	85
10	M. Ensberg	HOU	85

Intentional Walks

1	A. Pujols	STL	27
2	D. Lee	CHN	23
3	T. Helton	COL	22
4	C. Delgado	FLA	20
5	B. Abreu	PHI	15
6	A. Dunn	CIN	14
6	M. Lieberthal	PHI	14
8	A. Jones	ATL	13
8	C. Floyd	NYN	13
10	3 tied with		12

Hit By Pitches

1	J. Guillen	WAS	19
1	G. Jenkins	MIL	19
3	B. Clark	MIL	18
4	C. Biggio	HOU	17
4	C. Delgado	FLA	17
6	A. Jones	ATL	15
7	D. Eckstein	STL	13
7	R. Doumit	PIT	13
7	J. LaRue	CIN	13
10	3 tied with		12

Pitches per Plate Appearance

1	B. Abreu	PHI	4.4
2	P. Burrell	PHI	4.3
3	A. Dunn	CIN	4.2
4	B. Wilkerson	WAS	4.2
5	J. Edmonds	STL	4.2
6	B. Hall	MIL	4.2
7	T. Glaus	ARI	4.1
8	C. Counsell	ARI	4.1
9	T. Helton	COL	4.1
10	N. Johnson	WAS	4.1

Stolen Bases

1	J. Reyes	NYN	60
2	J. Pierre	FLA	57
3	R. Furcal	ATL	46
4	J. Rollins	PHI	41
5	R. Freel	CIN	36
6	W. Taveras	HOU	34
7	B. Abreu	PHI	31
8	C. Counsell	ARI	26
9	O. Vizquel	SF	24
10	D. Roberts	SD	23

Caught Stealing

1	J. Pierre	FLA	17
2	J. Reyes	NYN	15
3	B. Clark	MIL	13
4	D. Roberts	SD	12
5	W. Taveras	HOU	11
6	R. Furcal	ATL	10
6	O. Vizquel	SF	10
6	B. Wilkerson	WAS	10
6	R. Freel	CIN	10
10	B. Abreu	PHI	9
10	Hairston Jr.	CHN	9

Net Stolen Bases

1	J. Reyes	NYN	30
2	J. Rollins	PHI	29
3	R. Furcal	ATL	26
4	J. Pierre	FLA	23
5	J. Bay	PIT	19
6	B. Abreu	PHI	13
7	C. Counsell	ARI	12
7	A. Pujols	STL	12
7	W. Taveras	HOU	12
10	M. Giles	ATL	10
10	C. Utley	PHI	10

Grounded into Double Plays

1	S. Casey	CIN	27
2	D. Bell	PHI	24
3	N. Perez	CHN	22
4	P. Feliz	SF	20
4	M. Cabrera	FLA	20
6	A. Jones	ATL	19
6	R. Clayton	ARI	19
6	R. Durham	SF	19
6	J. Kent	LAN	19
6	A. Pujols	STL	19

Isolated Power (ISO)

1	D. Lee	CHN	.327
2	A. Jones	ATL	.312
3	A. Dunn	CIN	.293
4	C. Delgado	FLA	.281
5	A. Pujols	STL	.279
6	K. Griffey Jr.	CIN	.275
7	M. Ensberg	HOU	.274
8	J. Edmonds	STL	.270
9	A. Ramirez	CHN	.266
10	T. Glaus	ARI	.264

BA on Balls in Play (BABIP)

1	M. Cabrera	FLA	.363
2	J. Bay	PIT	.355
3	G. Jenkins	MIL	.352
4	T. Helton	COL	.350
5	D. Lee	CHN	.349
6	W. Taveras	HOU	.348
7	D. Wright	NYN	.343
8	P. Burrell	PHI	.341
9	B. Hall	MIL	.339
10	C. Delgado	FLA	.338

Batting Average with RISP

1	D. Eckstein	STL	.373
2	J. Kent	LAN	.366
3	B. Giles	SD	.360
4	J. Bay	PIT	.346
5	J. Encarnacion	FLA	.331
6	O. Vizquel	SF	.331
7	D. Lee	CHN	.331
8	A. Pujols	STL	.329
9	C. Delgado	FLA	.327
10	J. Rollins	PHI	.325

Situational Hitting Runs

1	D. Eckstein	STL	12.3
2	S. Taguchi	STL	9.6
3	C. Beltran	NYN	9.2
4	C. Delgado	FLA	8.7
5	J. Encarnacion	FLA	8.6
6	J. Kent	LAN	8.6
7	Y. Molina	STL	8.3
8	O. Vizquel	SF	8.2
9	P. Burrell	PHI	7.0
10	J. Bay	PIT	6.1

Line Drive Percentage

1	G. Jenkins	MIL	26.7%
2	B. Clark	MIL	25.5%
3	D. Wright	NYN	25.4%
4	T. Helton	COL	24.4%
5	M. Cabrera	FLA	24.3%
6	P. Burrell	PHI	24.1%
7	B. Abreu	PHI	24.0%
8	C. Tracy	ARI	23.9%
9	D. Bell	PHI	23.8%
10	G. Atkins	COL	23.7%

Groundball/Flyball Ratio

1	L. Castillo	FLA	4.13
2	J. Pierre	FLA	2.8
3	R. Clayton	ARI	2.71
4	W. Taveras	HOU	2.09
5	F. Lopez	CIN	2.03
6	L. Overbay	MIL	1.88
7	S. Casey	CIN	1.76
8	M. Grudzielanek	STL	1.74
9	R. Mackowiak	PIT	1.69
10	S. Green	ARI	1.65

Infield Fly per Flyball

1	B. Abreu	PHI	0.04
2	D. Wright	NYN	0.04
3	M. Giles	ATL	0.06
4	S. Casey	CIN	0.06
5	F. Lopez	CIN	0.06
6	R. Clayton	ARI	0.07
7	G. Jenkins	MIL	0.07
8	B. Wilkerson	WAS	0.07
9	L. Overbay	MIL	0.07
10	K. Griffey Jr.	CIN	0.08
10	J. Reyes	NYN	0.08

Home Run per Outfield Fly

1	A. Jones	ATL	0.26
2	C. Delgado	FLA	0.24
3	D. Lee	CHN	0.22
4	A. Pujols	STL	0.22
5	A. Dunn	CIN	0.21
6	J. Edmonds	STL	0.20
7	M. Cabrera	FLA	0.20
8	T. Glaus	ARI	0.19
9	C. Floyd	NYN	0.19
10	M. Ensberg	HOU	0.19

Italicized stats have been adjusted for home park. The leaders for "rate stats" include only those who played enough to qualify per MLB rules.

Extra Base Hits				Sacrifice Hits				Sacrifice Flies				Strikeouts			
1	D. Lee	CHN	99	1	O. Vizquel	SF	20	1	C. Lee	MIL	11	1	A. Dunn	CIN	168
2	J. Bay	PIT	82	2	L. Castillo	FLA	18	2	J. Guillen	WAS	9	2	P. Burrell	PHI	160
3	A. Pujols	STL	81	3	A. Pettitte	HOU	15	2	M. Lowell	FLA	9	3	P. Wilson	WAS	159
4	A. Jones	ATL	78	4	L. Hernandez	WAS	14	4	S. Green	ARI	8	4	B. Wilkerson	WAS	147
4	M. Cabrera	FLA	78	5	J. Carroll	WAS	13	4	B. Abreu	PHI	8	5	T. Glaus	ARI	145
6	A. Dunn	CIN	77	5	B. Webb	ARI	13	4	B. Giles	SD	8	6	J. Bay	PIT	142
6	C. Delgado	FLA	77	7	J. Smoltz	ATL	12	4	D. Ward	PIT	8	7	J. Edmonds	STL	139
8	C. Lee	MIL	73	7	N. Perez	CHN	12	4	P. LoDuca	FLA	8	8	G. Jenkins	MIL	138
8	C. Utley	PHI	73	7	M. Cairo	NYN	12	9	7 tied with		7	9	B. Abreu	PHI	134
10	D. Wright	NYN	70	10	N. Lowry	SF	12					10	M. Cabrera	FLA	125

Pitching Leaders

Pitching Runs				Earned Run Average (ERA)				Runs Allowed Per 9 Innings (RA)				Fielding Independent Pitching (FIP)			
1	R. Clemens	HOU	56	1	R. Clemens	HOU	1.87	1	R. Clemens	HOU	2.17	1	R. Clemens	HOU	2.85
2	A. Pettitte	HOU	47	2	A. Pettitte	HOU	2.39	2	A. Pettitte	HOU	2.67	2	J. Peavy	SD	2.87
3	D. Willis	FLA	44	3	D. Willis	FLA	2.63	3	P. Martinez	NYN	2.86	3	C. Carpenter	STL	2.88
4	P. Martinez	NYN	43	4	P. Martinez	NYN	2.82	4	D. Willis	FLA	3.01	4	P. Martinez	NYN	2.93
5	C. Carpenter	STL	41	5	C. Carpenter	STL	2.83	5	C. Carpenter	STL	3.05	5	D. Willis	FLA	2.97
6	R. Oswalt	HOU	38	6	J. Peavy	SD	2.88	6	J. Peavy	SD	3.10	6	A. Pettitte	HOU	3.05
7	J. Peavy	SD	36	7	R. Oswalt	HOU	2.94	7	R. Oswalt	HOU	3.17	7	A. Burnett	FLA	3.09
8	J. Smoltz	ATL	34	8	J. Smoltz	ATL	3.06	8	J. Patterson	WAS	3.22	8	R. Oswalt	HOU	3.14
9	J. Patterson	WAS	31	9	J. Patterson	WAS	3.13	9	J. Smoltz	ATL	3.25	9	J. Beckett	FLA	3.25
10	C. Zambrano	CHN	26	10	C. Zambrano	CHN	3.26	10	C. Zambrano	CHN	3.55	10	J. Smoltz	ATL	3.26

Innings Pitched				Batters Faced				Pitches				Pitches per Plate Appearances			
1	L. Hernandez	WAS	246.3	1	L. Hernandez	WAS	1065	1	L. Hernandez	WAS	4009	1	G. Maddux	CHN	3.3
2	R. Oswalt	HOU	241.7	2	R. Oswalt	HOU	1002	2	D. Davis	MIL	3726	2	J. Lieber	PHI	3.4
3	C. Carpenter	STL	241.7	3	D. Willis	FLA	960	3	C. Capuano	MIL	3641	3	R. Ortiz	CIN	3.5
4	D. Willis	FLA	236.3	4	C. Carpenter	STL	953	4	R. Oswalt	HOU	3600	4	J. Smoltz	ATL	3.5
5	J. Smoltz	ATL	229.7	5	C. Capuano	MIL	949	5	C. Zambrano	CHN	3562	5	J. Wright	COL	3.5
6	B. Webb	ARI	229.0	6	D. Davis	MIL	946	6	D. Willis	FLA	3556	6	T. Hudson	ATL	3.5
7	G. Maddux	CHN	225.0	7	B. Webb	ARI	943	7	N. Lowry	SF	3547	7	C. Lidle	PHI	3.5
8	J. Weaver	LAN	224.0	8	G. Maddux	CHN	936	8	B. Myers	PHI	3474	8	M. Mulder	STL	3.5
9	C. Zambrano	CHN	223.3	9	D. Lowe	LAN	934	9	A. Harang	CIN	3413	9	B. Lawrence	SD	3.5
10	D. Davis	MIL	222.7	10	J. Smoltz	ATL	931	10	C. Carpenter	STL	3395	10	M. Morris	STL	3.5

Strikeouts				Walks (Most)				Strikeouts Per Game				Walks Per Game (Least)			
1	J. Peavy	SD	216	1	K. Wells	PIT	99	1	M. Prior	CHN	10.3	1	G. Maddux	CHN	1.5
2	C. Carpenter	STL	213	2	D. Davis	MIL	93	2	J. Peavy	SD	10.2	2	J. Lieber	PHI	1.7
3	P. Martinez	NYN	208	3	C. Capuano	MIL	91	3	P. Martinez	NYN	9.5	3	M. Morris	STL	1.7
3	B. Myers	PHI	208	4	C. Zambrano	CHN	86	4	B. Myers	PHI	8.8	4	J. Weaver	LAN	1.8
3	D. Davis	MIL	208	5	J. Schmidt	SF	85	5	J. Patterson	WAS	8.7	5	R. Oswalt	HOU	1.8
6	C. Zambrano	CHN	202	6	L. Hernandez	WAS	84	6	J. Beckett	FLA	8.7	6	A. Pettitte	HOU	1.8
7	A. Burnett	FLA	198	7	J. Wright	COL	81	7	A. Burnett	FLA	8.7	7	C. Lidle	PHI	1.9
8	J. Vazquez	ARI	192	8	A. Burnett	FLA	79	8	C. Carpenter	STL	8.6	8	J. Vazquez	ARI	2.0
9	M. Prior	CHN	188	9	V. Zambrano	NYN	77	9	C. Zambrano	CHN	8.5	9	P. Martinez	NYN	2.1
10	J. Patterson	WAS	185	10	N. Lowry	SF	76	10	R. Clemens	HOU	8.5	10	B. Penny	LAN	2.1
10	R. Clemens	HOU	185												

Italicized stats have been adjusted for home park. The leaders for "rate stats" include only those who played enough to qualify per MLB rules.

Strikeout/Walk Ratio				Walks+Hits per Inning (WHIP)				LOB% -- best				LOB% -- worst			
1	P. Martinez	NYN	4.4	1	P. Martinez	NYN	0.95	1	R. Clemens	HOU	80.0%	1	E. Milton	CIN	64.6%
2	J. Peavy	SD	4.3	2	R. Clemens	HOU	1.01	2	A. Pettitte	HOU	79.7%	2	C. Lidle	PHI	65.4%
3	J. Vazquez	ARI	4.2	3	A. Pettitte	HOU	1.03	3	J. Patterson	WAS	79.4%	3	M. Redman	PIT	66.1%
4	A. Pettitte	HOU	4.2	4	J. Peavy	SD	1.04	4	T. Hudson	ATL	78.8%	4	J. Wright	COL	66.9%
5	C. Carpenter	STL	4.2	5	C. Carpenter	STL	1.06	5	R. Oswalt	HOU	78.2%	5	B. Lawrence	SD	68.2%
6	G. Maddux	CHN	3.8	6	D. Willis	FLA	1.14	6	B. Myers	PHI	77.9%	6	A. Burnett	FLA	68.3%
7	R. Oswalt	HOU	3.8	7	C. Zambrano	CHN	1.15	7	M. Prior	CHN	77.8%	7	K. Wells	PIT	68.4%
8	J. Weaver	LAN	3.7	8	J. Smoltz	ATL	1.15	8	C. Capuano	MIL	77.3%	8	M. Morris	STL	68.5%
9	J. Lieber	PHI	3.6	9	J. Weaver	LAN	1.17	9	P. Martinez	NYN	76.9%	9	J. Fogg	PIT	68.6%
10	J. Smoltz	ATL	3.2	10	J. Beckett	FLA	1.18	10	J. Peavy	SD	76.9%	10	J. Francis	COL	69.4%

Wins				Losses				Shutouts				Games			
1	D. Willis	FLA	22	1	K. Wells	PIT	18	1	D. Willis	FLA	5	1	S. Eyre	SF	86
2	C. Carpenter	STL	21	2	J. Wright	COL	16	2	C. Carpenter	STL	4	2	D. Sanchez	LAN	79
3	R. Oswalt	HOU	20	3	G. Maddux	CHN	15	3	J. Peavy	SD	3	2	G. Majewski	WAS	79
4	C. Capuano	MIL	18	3	D. Lowe	LAN	15	4	D. Lowe	LAN	2	4	B. Fuentes	COL	78
5	J. Lieber	PHI	17	3	M. Redman	PIT	15	4	J. Weaver	LAN	2	4	K. Mercker	CIN	78
5	A. Pettitte	HOU	17	3	E. Milton	CIN	15	4	A. Burnett	FLA	2	4	S. Torres	PIT	78
7	J. Suppan	STL	16	3	J. Vazquez	ARI	15	4	M. Mulder	STL	2	4	R. Madson	PHI	78
7	M. Mulder	STL	16	3	B. Lawrence	SD	15	8	Many tied with		1	8	R. King	STL	77
9	P. Martinez	NYN	15	3	B. Tomko	SF	15					8	C. Qualls	HOU	77
9	J. Beckett	FLA	15	10	J. Marquis	STL	14					10	C. Reitsma	ATL	76
9	L. Hernandez	WAS	15												

Games Finished				Saves				Blown Saves				Holds			
1	B. Wagner	PHI	70	1	C. Cordero	WAS	47	1	C. Reitsma	ATL	9	1	J. Tavarez	STL	32
2	B. Lidge	HOU	65	2	T. Hoffman	SD	43	2	B. Looper	NYN	8	1	S. Eyre	SF	32
3	D. Turnbow	MIL	62	3	B. Lidge	HOU	42	3	J. Mesa	PIT	7	1	R. Madson	PHI	32
3	C. Cordero	WAS	62	4	T. Jones	FLA	40	3	D. Kolb	ATL	7	4	S. Linebrink	SD	26
5	B. Fuentes	COL	55	5	J. Isringhausen	STL	39	3	C. Cordero	WAS	7	5	G. Majewski	WAS	24
5	T. Jones	FLA	55	5	D. Turnbow	MIL	39	3	R. Madson	PHI	7	6	L. Ayala	WAS	22
7	B. Looper	NYN	54	7	B. Wagner	PHI	38	7	5 tied with		6	6	A. Otsuka	SD	22
7	T. Hoffman	SD	54	8	R. Dempster	CHN	33					6	C. Qualls	HOU	22
9	R. Dempster	CHN	53	9	B. Fuentes	COL	31					9	K. Mercker	CIN	20
10	J. Isringhausen	STL	52	10	B. Looper	NYN	28					10	3 tied with		18

Italicized stats have been adjusted for home park. The leaders for "rate stats" include only those who played enough to qualify per MLB rules.

Groundball/Flyball Ratio

1	B. Webb	ARI	3.99
2	D. Lowe	LAN	3.03
3	M. Mulder	STL	2.88
4	T. Hudson	ATL	2.83
5	A. Burnett	FLA	2.63
6	C. Carpenter	STL	2.09
7	J. Wright	COL	1.95
8	C. Lidle	PHI	1.95
9	G. Maddux	CHN	1.94
10	A. Pettitte	HOU	1.87

Infield Fly per Flyball

1	R. Ortiz	CIN	21%
2	J. Fogg	PIT	21%
3	B. Claussen	CIN	20%
4	N. Lowry	SF	20%
5	J. Schmidt	SF	19%
6	J. Vazquez	ARI	17%
7	C. Capuano	MIL	17%
8	J. Francis	COL	17%
9	J. Marquis	STL	15%
10	J. Patterson	WAS	14%

Line Drive Percent -- best

1	D. Lowe	LAN	15.1%
2	J. Marquis	STL	16.5%
3	R. Ortiz	CIN	16.8%
4	P. Martinez	NYN	16.9%
5	M. Mulder	STL	18.2%
6	B. Webb	ARI	18.4%
7	B. Claussen	CIN	19.0%
8	K. Benson	NYN	19.0%
9	A. Burnett	FLA	19.1%
10	C. Carpenter	STL	19.2%

Defense Efficiency Ratio (DER)

1	R. Clemens	HOU	.757
2	P. Martinez	NYN	.752
3	C. Zambrano	CHN	.748
4	K. Benson	NYN	.740
5	J. Marquis	STL	.734
6	A. Pettitte	HOU	.734
7	J. Weaver	LAN	.727
8	H. Ramirez	ATL	.726
9	B. Myers	PHI	.724
10	J. Peavy	SD	.724

Home Runs Allowed

1	E. Milton	CIN	40
2	J. Weaver	LAN	35
2	J. Vazquez	ARI	35
4	R. Ortiz	CIN	34
5	J. Lieber	PHI	33
6	H. Ramirez	ATL	31
6	B. Myers	PHI	31
6	C. Capuano	MIL	31
9	G. Maddux	CHN	29
9	J. Marquis	STL	29

Home Runs Allowed Per Game

1	D. Willis	FLA	0.44
2	R. Clemens	HOU	0.50
3	T. Glavine	NYN	0.51
4	A. Burnett	FLA	0.53
5	V. Zambrano	NYN	0.62
6	R. Oswalt	HOU	0.69
7	C. Carpenter	STL	0.72
8	J. Smoltz	ATL	0.74
9	J. Beckett	FLA	0.74
10	A. Pettitte	HOU	0.75

Home Runs per Outfield Fly

1	D. Willis	FLA	0.06
2	T. Glavine	NYN	0.07
2	R. Clemens	HOU	0.07
4	P. Martinez	NYN	0.09
4	R. Oswalt	HOU	0.09
4	V. Zambrano	NYN	0.09
4	A. Harang	CIN	0.09
8	5 tied with		0.10

Slugging Average Allowed

1	R. Clemens	HOU	.280
2	P. Martinez	NYN	.330
3	A. Burnett	FLA	.330
4	C. Zambrano	CHN	.340
5	A. Pettitte	HOU	.350
6	C. Carpenter	STL	.350
7	D. Willis	FLA	.350
8	J. Patterson	WAS	.360
9	J. Smoltz	ATL	.360
10	J. Peavy	SD	.360

Grounded into Double Plays

1	H. Ramirez	ATL	32
1	M. Mulder	STL	32
3	B. Webb	ARI	30
4	J. Marquis	STL	29
4	J. Suppan	STL	29
6	A. Burnett	FLA	26
6	E. Loaiza	WAS	26
8	M. Redman	PIT	24
8	L. Hernandez	WAS	24
10	D. Willis	FLA	23

Total Double Plays

1	H. Ramirez	ATL	36
2	B. Webb	ARI	34
3	M. Mulder	STL	33
4	J. Marquis	STL	31
4	M. Redman	PIT	31
6	J. Suppan	STL	30
6	L. Hernandez	WAS	30
6	E. Loaiza	WAS	30
9	A. Burnett	FLA	28
10	3 tied with		26

Wild Pitches

1	B. Webb	ARI	14
2	A. Burnett	FLA	12
3	B. Kim	COL	11
4	J. Marquis	STL	10
5	J. Patterson	WAS	9
5	M. Mulder	STL	9
5	D. Turnbow	MIL	9
8	8 tied with		8

Batters Hit by Pitch

1	J. Weaver	LAN	18
2	J. Wright	COL	15
2	V. Zambrano	NYN	15
4	B. Kim	COL	14
5	L. Hernandez	WAS	13
6	K. Wells	PIT	12
6	C. Capuano	MIL	12
8	B. Myers	PHI	11
8	B. Lawrence	SD	11
8	L. Hudson	CIN	11

Stolen Bases Allowed

1	G. Maddux	CHN	32
2	J. Patterson	WAS	26
2	B. Webb	ARI	26
4	J. Wright	COL	25
4	V. Zambrano	NYN	25
6	A. Burnett	FLA	24
6	J. Schmidt	SF	24
8	J. Weaver	LAN	20
8	J. Sosa	ATL	20
10	3 tied with		19

Runners Caught Stealing

1	J. Patterson	WAS	11
1	L. Hernandez	WAS	11
1	J. Francis	COL	11
4	C. Zambrano	CHN	9
4	A. Harang	CIN	9
4	C. Capuano	MIL	9
7	5 tied with		8

Pickoffs

1	C. Capuano	MIL	12
2	J. Wright	COL	6
3	J. Fassero	SF	5
3	M. Mulder	STL	5
3	D. Davis	MIL	5
3	J. Francis	COL	5
7	L. Cormier	ARI	4
7	B. Halsey	ARI	4
9	J. Williams	CHN	4
10	8 tied with		3

Net Stolen Bases Allowed

1	C. Capuano	MIL	-36
2	M. Mulder	STL	-24
3	C. Zambrano	CHN	-23
4	C. Carpenter	STL	-13
4	J. Francis	COL	-13
6	R. Ortiz	CIN	-11
6	D. Davis	MIL	-11
8	4 tied with		-10

Italicized stats have been adjusted for home park. The leaders for "rate stats" include only those who played enough to qualify per MLB rules.

Arizona Diamondbacks

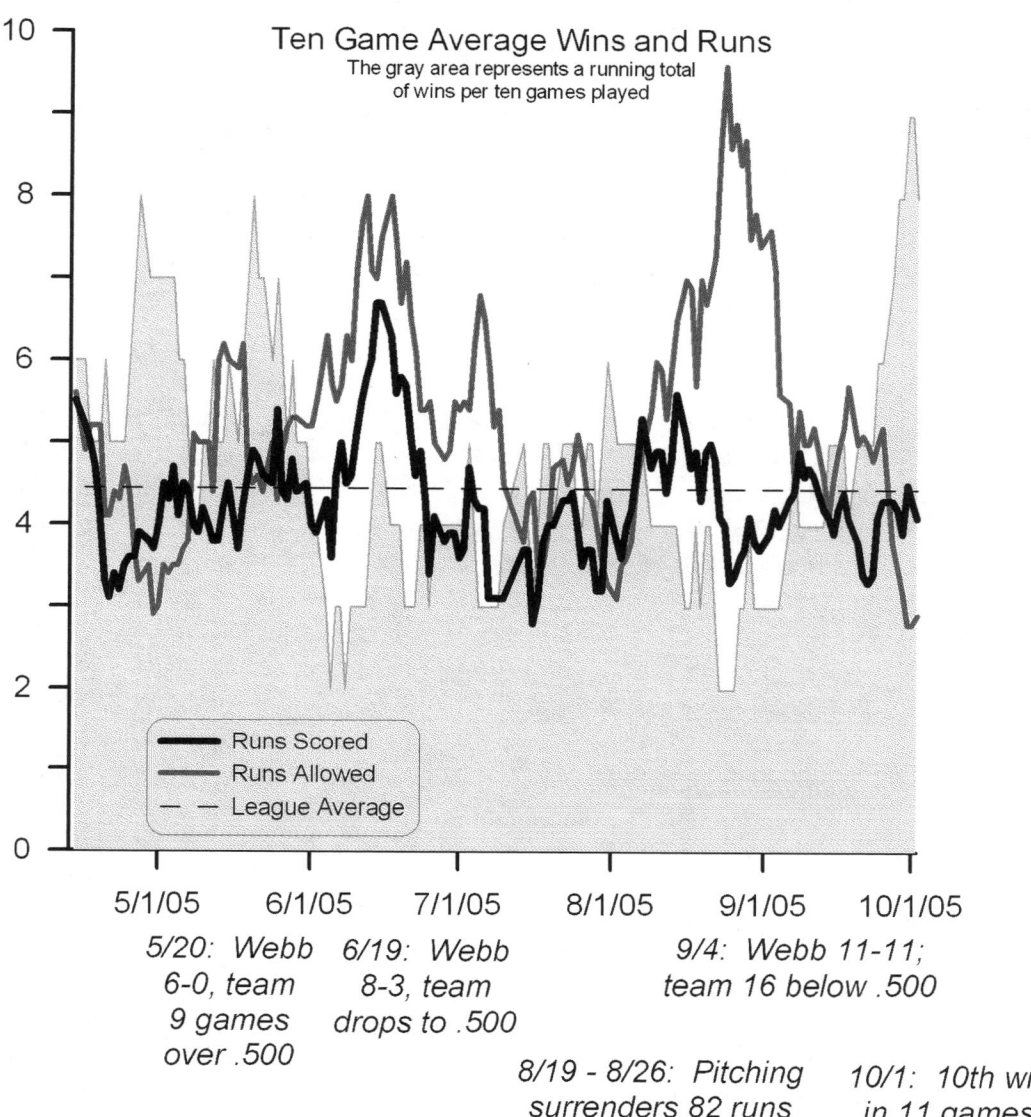

Ten Game Average Wins and Runs
The gray area represents a running total
of wins per ten games played

Runs Scored
Runs Allowed
— — League Average

5/1/05   6/1/05   7/1/05   8/1/05   9/1/05   10/1/05

*5/20: Webb
6-0, team
9 games
over .500*

*6/19: Webb
8-3, team
drops to .500*

*9/4: Webb 11-11;
team 16 below .500*

*8/19 - 8/26: Pitching
surrenders 82 runs
in 8-game span*

*10/1: 10th win
in 11 games
clinches 2nd place*

Team Batting and Pitching/Fielding Stats by Month						
	April	May	June	July	Aug	Spt/Oct
Wins	14	16	9	13	9	16
Losses	10	12	19	14	19	11
OBP	.328	.339	.336	.336	.322	.332
SLG	.412	.401	.455	.418	.424	.415
FIP	4.40	4.28	4.81	4.36	5.49	4.29
DER	.706	.673	.678	.719	.685	.724

Batting Stats

Player	RC	Runs	RBI	PA	Outs	P/PA	H	2B	3B	HR	TB	K	BB	IBB	HBP	SH	SF	SB	CS	GDP	BA	OBP	SLG	GPA
Gonzalez L.	89	90	79	672	437	3.95	157	37	0	24	266	90	78	12	11	0	4	4	1	14	.271	.366	.459	.280
Glaus T.	88	78	97	634	408	4.12	139	29	1	37	281	145	84	2	7	0	5	4	2	7	.258	.363	.522	.294
Tracy C.	83	73	72	553	359	3.84	155	34	4	27	278	78	35	4	8	1	6	3	1	10	.308	.359	.553	.300
Counsell C.	81	85	42	670	445	4.08	148	34	4	9	217	69	78	4	8	2	4	26	7	8	.256	.350	.375	.251
Green S.	79	87	73	656	437	3.61	166	37	4	22	277	95	62	6	5	0	8	8	4	18	.286	.355	.477	.279
Clark T.	72	47	87	393	253	3.92	106	22	2	30	222	88	37	6	1	0	6	0	0	10	.304	.366	.636	.324
Clayton R.	56	59	44	573	403	3.85	141	28	4	2	183	105	38	0	1	10	2	13	3	19	.270	.320	.351	.232
Cintron A.	35	36	48	348	250	3.18	90	19	2	8	137	33	12	3	1	2	3	1	2	8	.273	.298	.415	.238
Snyder C.	26	24	28	373	267	4.01	66	14	0	6	98	87	40	5	4	3	0	0	1	6	.202	.297	.301	.209
Cruz J.	26	23	28	245	166	3.89	43	9	0	12	88	54	42	2	0	0	1	0	1	6	.213	.347	.436	.265
McCracken Q.	20	23	13	246	168	3.80	51	4	3	1	64	35	23	4	1	6	1	4	0	4	.237	.313	.298	.215
Terrero L.	17	23	20	184	131	3.73	37	6	1	4	57	40	14	0	6	2	1	3	2	5	.230	.313	.354	.229
Stinnett K.	9	15	12	143	101	3.87	32	4	0	6	54	32	12	3	1	1	0	0	0	4	.248	.317	.419	.247
Jackson C.	6	8	8	99	74	3.83	17	3	0	2	26	11	12	0	1	0	1	0	0	6	.200	.303	.306	.213
Hill K.	6	6	6	91	62	3.63	17	5	0	0	22	27	11	0	0	0	2	0	1	0	.218	.308	.282	.209
Vazquez J.	4	2	2	72	48	3.72	15	1	0	1	19	10	3	0	0	6	0	0	0	0	.238	.273	.302	.198
Green A.	3	5	2	39	25	4.08	7	1	0	0	8	3	7	0	0	0	1	0	0	1	.226	.359	.258	.226
Ortiz R.	3	1	1	43	28	3.47	7	1	0	0	8	9	3	0	0	6	0	0	0	1	.206	.270	.235	.180
Kata M.	2	6	0	38	26	3.79	6	2	1	0	10	4	5	0	0	2	0	0	1	0	.194	.306	.323	.218
Cormier L.	1	0	1	7	5	2.86	2	0	0	0	2	1	0	0	0	1	0	0	0	1	.333	.333	.333	.233
Nippert D.	1	0	0	5	3	3.40	1	0	0	0	1	3	1	0	0	0	0	0	0	0	.250	.400	.250	.243
Bruney B.	-0	0	0	1	1	2.00	0	0	0	0	0	0	0	0	0	0	0	0	0	0	.000	.000	.000	.000
Medders B.	-0	0	0	1	1	5.00	0	0	0	0	0	0	0	0	0	0	0	0	0	0	.000	.000	.000	.000
Ligtenberg K	-0	0	0	1	1	3.00	0	0	0	0	0	1	0	0	0	0	0	0	0	0	.000	.000	.000	.000
Worrell T.	-0	0	0	1	1	3.00	0	0	0	0	0	1	0	0	0	0	0	0	0	0	.000	.000	.000	.000
Koplove M.	-0	0	0	2	2	3.00	0	0	0	0	0	1	0	0	0	0	0	0	0	0	.000	.000	.000	.000
Gosling M.	-1	0	0	7	6	4.29	0	0	0	0	0	4	0	0	0	1	0	0	0	0	.000	.000	.000	.000
Vargas C.	-1	1	3	43	33	2.91	3	0	0	0	3	7	2	0	0	7	0	0	0	2	.088	.139	.088	.085
Halsey B.	-1	2	2	60	45	3.88	3	0	0	0	3	18	6	0	0	6	0	0	0	0	.063	.167	.063	.091
Hairston S.	-1	0	0	20	19	3.55	2	1	0	0	3	6	0	0	0	0	0	0	0	1	.100	.100	.150	.083
Estes S.	-1	2	0	31	28	2.87	2	0	1	0	4	7	0	0	0	2	0	1	0	1	.069	.069	.138	.066
Webb B.	-2	0	2	76	56	3.04	6	0	0	0	6	30	1	0	0	13	0	0	0	0	.097	.111	.097	.074

Win Shares Stats

Player	WS	Bat	Pitch	Field	ExpWS	WSP	WSAB	CWS	NetWSValue
Glaus, T	23	19.6	0.0	4.0	17	.703	12	128	$4,090,725
Gonzalez, L	22	18.6	0.0	3.3	18	.619	10	289	$1,580,309
Tracy, C	21	18.9	0.0	2.0	15	.722	11	31	$8,490,500
Counsell, C	21	14.8	0.0	6.9	17	.622	9	93	$6,849,084
Clark, T	20	18.9	0.0	0.8	10	.995	13	123	$9,817,827
Webb, B	19	-3.2	22.8	0.0	11	.873	13	48	$9,745,573
Green, S	18	14.6	0.0	4.1	17	.534	6	217	$530,136

Continued on the next page.

Pitching Stats

Player	PR	IP	BFP	G	GS	P/PA	K	BB	IBB	HBP	H	HR	DP	DER	SB	CS	PO	W	L	Sv	Op	Hld	RA	ERA	FIP
Webb B.	23	229.0	943	33	33	3.58	172	59	4	2	229	21	34	.698	26	4	1	14	12	0	0	0	3.85	3.54	3.47
Valverde J.	16	66.3	268	61	0	4.08	75	20	1	2	51	5	3	.723	1	1	1	3	4	15	17	7	2.58	2.44	2.70
Medders B.	10	30.3	122	27	0	3.93	31	11	0	1	21	2	1	.753	1	1	0	4	1	0	0	2	1.78	1.78	2.98
Worrell T.	4	31.7	137	32	0	3.62	22	9	2	1	30	4	0	.743	1	0	0	1	1	0	1	9	3.69	2.27	4.18
Vazquez J.	3	215.7	904	33	33	3.67	192	46	4	5	223	35	23	.700	6	2	1	11	15	0	0	0	4.67	4.42	4.02
Almanza A.	1	4.0	19	6	0	3.74	2	3	0	0	5	1	1	.692	0	0	0	0	0	0	1	2	2.25	2.25	7.48
Groom B.	0	15.3	70	23	0	4.06	7	5	1	0	19	2	0	.696	0	0	0	0	1	1	1	4	4.70	4.70	4.74
Bulger J.	-1	10.0	48	9	0	3.90	9	5	1	0	14	1	0	.606	0	0	0	1	0	0	0	0	5.40	5.40	3.98
Villarreal O	-1	13.7	57	11	0	3.19	5	6	2	1	11	2	2	.791	1	0	0	2	0	0	2	2	5.27	5.27	5.69
Nippert D.	-1	14.7	68	3	3	3.91	11	13	0	1	10	1	1	.786	3	0	0	1	0	0	0	0	5.52	5.52	5.23
Vargas C.	-2	119.7	520	21	19	3.84	90	40	3	7	124	21	9	.715	6	3	0	9	6	0	0	0	4.96	4.81	4.94
Gosling M.	-3	32.3	154	13	5	3.75	14	19	2	0	40	2	8	.681	1	1	0	0	3	0	0	0	5.57	4.45	4.68
Choate R.	-3	7.0	35	8	0	3.34	4	5	1	1	8	0	0	.680	0	0	0	0	0	0	0	2	9.00	9.00	4.41
Gonzalez E.	-4	0.3	5	1	0	5.20	1	2	0	0	2	1	0	.000	0	0	0	0	0	0	0	0	108.00	108.00	53.98
Estes S.	-4	123.7	535	21	21	3.62	63	45	0	4	132	15	21	.713	4	1	1	7	8	0	0	0	5.09	4.80	4.73
Koplove M.	-4	49.7	217	44	0	3.53	28	20	3	6	48	6	8	.732	2	1	0	2	1	0	2	9	5.62	5.07	5.00
Lopez J.	-7	14.3	74	29	0	3.81	11	11	3	1	19	2	2	.653	0	0	0	1	1	2	3	6	9.42	9.42	5.77
Cormier L.	-7	79.3	356	67	0	3.85	63	43	5	5	86	7	9	.668	4	3	4	7	3	0	1	13	5.67	5.11	4.36
Herges M.	-7	8.0	42	7	0	3.57	3	5	0	1	12	4	0	.724	0	0	0	0	0	0	0	0	13.50	13.50	10.98
Lyon B.	-9	29.3	144	32	0	3.49	17	10	2	2	44	6	1	.651	2	0	0	0	2	14	15	1	7.67	6.44	5.71
Ligtenberg K	-9	9.7	48	7	0	3.19	5	4	0	0	16	4	0	.657	0	1	0	0	0	0	0	0	13.97	13.97	8.57
Aquino G.	-12	31.3	155	35	0	3.55	34	17	1	4	42	7	2	.624	1	1	2	0	1	1	3	3	8.33	7.76	5.73
Bruney B.	-14	46.0	230	47	0	4.12	51	35	2	5	56	6	4	.624	2	0	0	1	3	12	16	4	7.63	7.43	5.07
Halsey B.	-15	160.0	700	28	26	3.45	82	39	3	9	191	20	20	.689	15	4	4	8	12	0	0	0	5.68	4.61	4.48
Ortiz R.	-29	115.0	551	22	22	3.77	46	65	3	4	147	18	10	.691	2	5	0	5	11	0	0	0	7.20	6.89	6.02

Win Shares Stats (cont.)

Player	WS	Bat	Pitch	Field	ExpWS	WSP	WSAB	CWS	NetWSValue
Vazquez, J	14	-0.7	14.8	0.0	10	.678	8	99	($278,535)
Valverde, J	12	0.0	11.8	0.0	5	1.223	8	25	$6,652,907
Clayton, R	11	6.1	0.0	4.8	15	.357	0	147	($469,254)
Cintron, A	7	4.4	0.0	2.3	9	.380	1	30	$382,827
Vargas, C	6	-1.8	8.0	0.0	6	.531	3	14	$1,791,146
Estes, S	6	-1.4	7.2	0.0	6	.466	2	65	$302,012
Halsey, B	6	-2.2	7.9	0.0	8	.367	1	6	$822,803
Cormier, L	5	0.2	4.6	0.0	4	.559	2	4	$1,413,080
Cruz, J	5	4.1	0.0	1.1	6	.408	1	116	$2,050,310
Snyder, C	5	0.1	0.0	5.1	10	.249	-2	8	($318,000)
Terrero, L	4	1.8	0.0	2.0	5	.374	0	7	$185,957
McCracken, Q	2	1.1	0.0	0.9	6	.165	-2	50	($750,000)
Stinnett, K	1	-0.1	0.0	1.1	4	.117	-2	45	($316,000)
Ortiz, R	-1	-0.0	-1.5	0.0	6	-.136	-5	76	($7,375,000)
Bruney, B	-2	-0.0	-2.6	0.0	4	-.368	-5	0	($322,500)

Fielding and Baserunning Stats

Name	POS	Inn	SBA/G	CS%	ERA	WP+PB/G	PO	A	TE	FE
Snyder	C	915.7	0.57	21%	4.54	0.472	679	44	2	0
Stinnett	C	329.3	0.66	17%	5.41	0.273	237	15	5	1
Hill	C	211.3	0.60	14%	5.45	0.468	144	13	0	0

Name	POS	Inn	PO	A	TE	FE	FPct	RF	DPS	DPT
C Tracy	1B	652.7	706	47	1	2	.996	10.38	14	0
T Clark	1B	642.7	663	45	0	2	.997	9.91	8	1
C Jackson	1B	161.0	171	11	3	2	.973	10.17	1	2
C Counsell	2B	1244.0	304	458	5	3	.990	5.51	32	66
A Cintron	2B	144.7	31	39	0	1	.986	4.35	6	5
A Green	2B	39.3	10	11	0	0	1.000	4.81	1	3
M Kata	2B	28.0	8	12	0	0	1.000	6.43	2	4
R Clayton	SS	1177.0	180	404	6	5	.982	4.47	43	47
A Cintron	SS	271.0	44	99	1	4	.966	4.75	13	7
A Green	SS	7.0	1	4	0	0	1.000	6.43	0	0
C Counsell	SS	1.0	0	0	0	0	0.000	0.00	0	0
T Glaus	3B	1264.0	113	310	15	9	.946	3.01	27	2
A Cintron	3B	192.3	15	41	0	2	.966	2.62	9	0
L Gonzalez	LF	1318.0	270	7	0	3	.989	1.89	2	0
C Tracy	LF	40.7	7	0	0	0	1.000	1.55	0	0
Q McCracken	LF	38.3	8	0	0	0	1.000	1.88	0	0
J Cruz	LF	17.7	3	0	0	0	1.000	1.53	0	0
A Green	LF	17.0	3	0	0	0	1.000	1.59	0	0
S Hairston	LF	13.3	3	0	0	0	1.000	2.03	0	0
C Jackson	LF	9.0	0	0	0	0	0.000	0.00	0	0
L Terrero	LF	2.0	0	0	0	0	0.000	0.00	0	0
L Terrero	CF	419.7	121	1	0	2	.984	2.62	0	0
J Cruz	CF	415.0	87	1	0	2	.978	1.91	0	0
S Green	CF	315.0	80	2	0	0	1.000	2.34	1	0
Q McCracken	CF	306.0	66	2	1	1	.971	2.00	0	0
S Hairston	CF	0.7	0	0	0	0	0.000	0.00	0	0
S Green	RF	1031.0	232	2	0	0	1.000	2.04	0	0
C Tracy	RF	376.0	86	2	0	2	.978	2.11	0	0
J Cruz	RF	35.7	8	1	0	0	1.000	2.27	0	0
L Terrero	RF	10.3	3	0	0	0	1.000	2.61	0	0
Q McCracken	RF	3.0	1	0	0	0	1.000	3.00	0	0

Incremental Baserunning Runs		
Name	IR	IRP
Shawn Green	1.84	121
Royce Clayton	1.16	125
Craig Counsell	1.14	117
Alex Cintron	1.13	132
Matt Kata	0.38	138
Javier Vazquez	0.29	541
Andy Green	0.21	126
Chad Tracy	0.16	102
Jose Cruz	0.12	105
Conor Jackson	0.10	109
Dustin Nippert	-0.03	0
Brandon Webb	-0.04	0
Koyie Hill	-0.10	0
Troy Glaus	-0.13	97
Quinton McCracken	-0.15	91
Brad Halsey	-0.17	0
Russ Ortiz	-0.19	0
Claudio Vargas	-0.67	0
Kelly Stinnett	-0.90	54
Tony Clark	-1.04	60
Luis Terrero	-1.28	-22
Chris Snyder	-1.83	45
Luis Gonzalez	-5.52	-5

Atlanta Braves

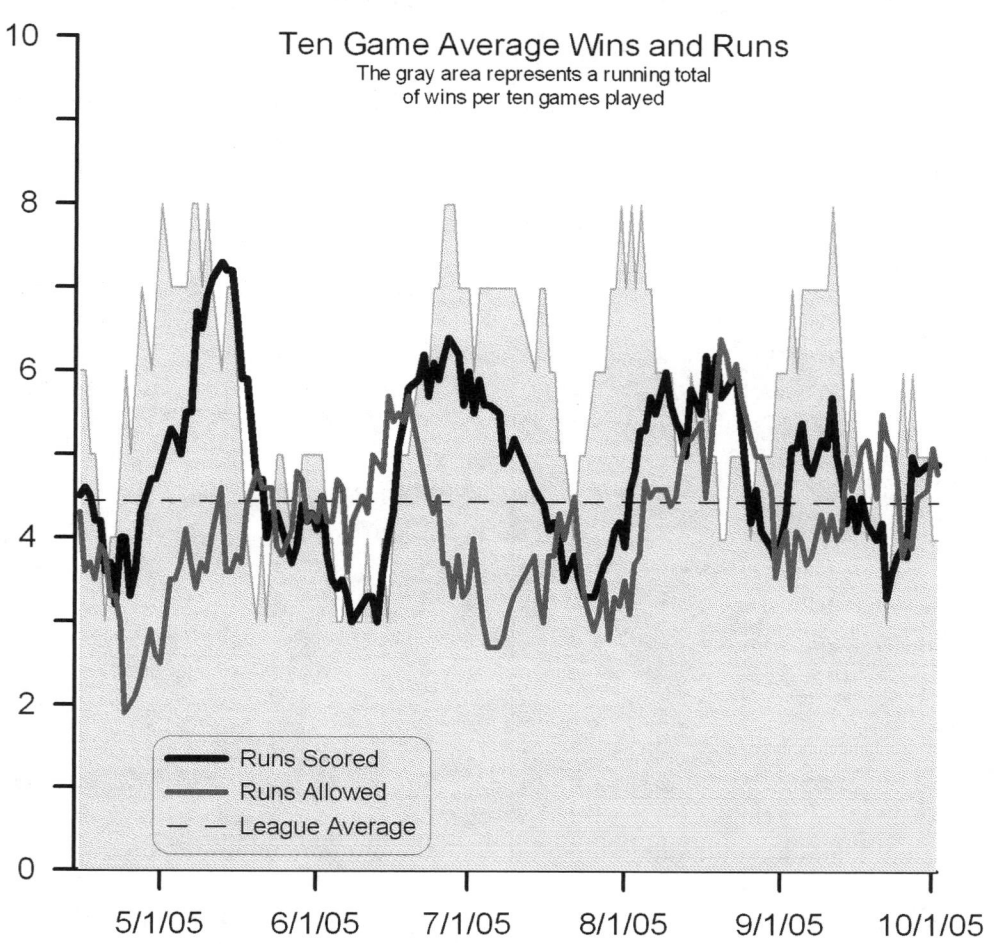

Ten Game Average Wins and Runs
The gray area represents a running total
of wins per ten games played

- Runs Scored
- Runs Allowed
- League Average

4/5: Smoltz makes
first start since 2001

7/7: Francoeur plays
first game; hits .884
OPS rest of season

7/31: Pick up
Farnsworth, who
saves 10 of 10
opportunities

9/14: - Andruw Jones
becomes first Atlanta
Brave to hit 50 HR

7/26: Take over
first place for good

Team Batting and Pitching/Fielding Stats by Month						
	April	May	June	July	Aug	Spt/Oct
Wins	14	14	15	18	14	15
Losses	10	13	13	8	14	14
OBP	.312	.313	.352	.335	.351	.326
SLG	.390	.427	.466	.443	.438	.440
FIP	4.03	4.17	4.78	4.21	4.29	4.27
DER	.714	.697	.702	.737	.696	.692

Batting Stats

Player	RC	Runs	RBI	PA	Outs	P/PA	H	2B	3B	HR	TB	K	BB	IBB	HBP	SH	SF	SB	CS	GDP	BA	OBP	SLG	GPA
Furcal R.	96	100	58	689	462	3.82	175	31	11	12	264	78	62	3	1	5	5	46	10	11	.284	.348	.429	.264
Giles M.	94	104	63	654	426	3.72	168	45	4	15	266	108	64	1	5	4	4	16	3	14	.291	.365	.461	.279
Jones A.	90	95	128	672	454	3.82	154	24	3	51	337	112	64	13	15	0	7	5	3	19	.263	.347	.575	.300
Jones C.	77	66	72	432	262	4.02	106	30	0	21	199	56	72	5	0	0	2	5	1	9	.296	.412	.556	.324
LaRoche A.	62	53	78	502	351	3.47	117	28	0	20	205	87	39	7	4	2	6	0	2	15	.259	.320	.455	.258
Langerhans R	53	48	42	373	243	3.75	87	22	3	8	139	75	37	3	5	2	3	0	2	2	.267	.348	.426	.263
Francoeur J.	49	41	45	274	186	3.41	77	20	1	14	141	58	11	3	4	0	2	3	2	4	.300	.336	.549	.288
Johnson K.	40	46	40	334	232	4.13	70	12	3	9	115	75	40	1	1	2	1	2	1	11	.241	.334	.397	.250
Franco J.	35	30	42	265	179	4.09	64	12	1	9	105	57	27	1	1	1	3	4	0	10	.275	.348	.451	.269
Betemit W.	35	36	20	274	179	3.93	75	12	4	4	107	55	22	4	0	4	2	1	3	5	.305	.359	.435	.270
Estrada J.	35	31	39	383	277	3.30	93	26	0	4	131	38	20	6	3	0	3	0	0	13	.261	.303	.367	.228
McCann B.	24	20	23	204	136	3.73	50	7	0	5	72	26	18	5	1	4	1	1	1	5	.278	.345	.400	.255
Jordan B.	23	25	24	251	179	3.52	57	8	2	3	78	46	14	0	3	0	3	2	0	5	.247	.295	.338	.217
Orr P.	17	32	8	162	108	3.14	45	8	1	1	58	23	6	0	1	5	0	7	1	2	.300	.331	.387	.246
Mondesi R.	10	17	17	155	118	3.72	30	7	1	4	51	35	12	3	0	0	1	0	1	5	.211	.271	.359	.212
Perez E.	5	3	6	39	31	3.08	8	2	0	2	16	5	1	0	0	0	0	0	0	1	.211	.231	.421	.209
Hampton M.	2	4	1	29	19	3.03	8	1	0	1	12	9	0	0	1	3	0	0	0	2	.320	.346	.480	.276
Thomson J.	2	2	2	36	20	3.14	5	2	0	0	7	12	2	0	0	9	0	0	0	0	.200	.259	.280	.187
Davies K.	2	0	4	28	12	2.96	3	0	0	0	3	3	2	0	0	10	1	0	0	0	.200	.278	.200	.175
Hollandswort	1	3	1	40	31	3.98	6	0	0	1	9	13	5	0	0	0	0	0	1	1	.171	.275	.257	.188
Marte A.	1	3	4	66	52	4.18	8	2	1	0	12	13	7	0	0	0	2	0	1	2	.140	.227	.211	.155
Ramirez H.	1	4	2	77	59	3.13	16	3	0	0	19	17	1	0	0	3	0	0	0	2	.219	.230	.260	.168
James C.	1	0	1	1	0	2.00	1	0	0	0	1	0	0	0	0	0	0	0	0	0	1.000	1.000	1.000	.700
Bernero A.	1	0	0	2	0	2.00	1	0	0	0	1	0	0	0	0	1	0	0	0	0	1.000	1.000	1.000	.700
Reitsma C.	-0	0	0	1	1	1.00	0	0	0	0	0	0	0	0	0	0	0	0	0	0	.000	.000	.000	.000
Kolb D.	-0	0	0	1	1	5.00	0	0	0	0	0	1	0	0	0	0	0	0	0	0	.000	.000	.000	.000
Vasquez J.	-0	0	0	1	1	6.00	0	0	0	0	0	1	0	0	0	0	0	0	0	0	.000	.000	.000	.000
Devine J.	-0	0	0	1	1	5.00	0	0	0	0	0	1	0	0	0	0	0	0	0	0	.000	.000	.000	.000
Pena B.	-0	2	4	40	33	3.55	7	2	0	0	9	7	1	1	0	0	0	0	0	1	.179	.200	.231	.148
Greisinger S	-0	0	0	2	2	4.00	0	0	0	0	0	1	0	0	0	0	0	0	0	0	.000	.000	.000	.000
Colon R.	-1	0	0	8	7	2.63	0	0	0	0	0	5	0	0	0	1	0	0	0	0	.000	.000	.000	.000
Sosa J.	-1	1	0	35	29	3.23	3	0	0	0	3	15	1	0	0	3	0	0	0	1	.097	.125	.097	.080
Hudson T.	-1	2	6	72	60	3.44	9	2	1	0	13	26	3	0	0	4	0	0	0	4	.138	.176	.200	.129
Smoltz J.	-2	1	3	83	61	3.78	10	2	1	0	14	26	3	0	0	12	0	0	0	3	.147	.183	.206	.134

Win Shares Stats

Player	WS	Bat	Pitch	Field	ExpWS	WSP	WSAB	CWS	NetWSValue
Furcal, R	27	18.6	0.0	8.1	18	.722	14	119	$4,888,060
Giles, M	25	19.0	0.0	5.7	18	.701	12	85	$7,498,586
Jones, A	23	17.6	0.0	5.8	18	.639	11	215	$675,195
Jones, C	20	18.7	0.0	1.4	12	.862	12	282	($156,071)
Smoltz, J	18	-2.8	21.1	0.0	11	.832	12	252	$4,004,686
Sosa, J	14	-1.2	15.5	0.0	7	1.038	10	24	$7,607,662
Francoeur, J	13	11.3	0.0	2.0	8	.879	8	13	$6,325,526

Continued on the next page.

Pitching Stats

Player	PR	IP	BFP	G	GS	P/PA	K	BB	IBB	HBP	H	HR	DP	DER	SB	CS	PO	W	L	Sv	Op	Hld	RA	ERA	FIP
Smoltz J.	34	229.7	931	33	33	3.54	169	53	7	1	210	18	19	.722	10	6	0	14	7	0	0	0	3.25	3.06	3.23
Sosa J.	26	134.0	577	44	20	3.75	85	64	8	0	122	12	11	.736	20	1	0	13	3	0	0	4	2.82	2.55	4.31
Hudson T.	19	192.0	817	29	29	3.54	115	65	5	9	194	20	24	.714	10	7	2	14	9	0	0	0	3.70	3.52	4.29
Farnsworth K	8	27.3	103	26	0	4.01	32	7	0	2	15	4	3	.810	3	0	0	0	0	10	10	4	1.98	1.98	3.53
Hampton M.	7	69.3	284	12	12	3.58	27	18	0	0	74	5	12	.705	3	2	0	5	3	0	0	0	3.63	3.50	3.92
Boyer B.	6	37.7	157	43	0	3.94	33	17	0	2	32	1	3	.702	1	1	0	4	2	0	2	9	3.11	3.11	3.09
Reitsma C.	5	73.3	307	76	0	3.50	42	14	3	0	79	3	8	.694	5	0	0	3	6	15	24	13	3.93	3.93	2.94
James C.	2	5.7	23	2	0	4.00	5	3	0	0	4	0	0	.733	0	0	0	0	0	0	0	0	1.59	1.59	2.81
Powell J.	2	3.3	15	5	0	4.53	1	4	0	0	1	0	0	.900	0	0	0	0	0	0	0	1	0.00	0.00	5.98
Brower J.	1	30.0	138	37	0	4.02	28	17	3	3	33	6	3	.679	1	1	0	1	2	0	0	7	4.20	4.20	5.72
Gryboski K.	1	21.3	99	31	0	3.67	8	12	3	2	24	0	4	.688	0	0	0	0	0	0	2	2	4.22	2.95	4.20
Foster J.	1	34.7	150	62	0	4.04	32	19	0	2	27	3	2	.745	3	0	0	4	2	1	2	12	4.41	4.15	4.08
Vasquez J.	1	9.0	42	7	0	3.88	9	5	0	0	11	2	2	.654	1	0	0	1	0	0	0	0	4.00	3.00	5.54
Greisinger S	1	5.0	21	1	1	3.29	2	1	0	0	7	1	1	.647	0	0	0	0	0	0	0	0	3.60	3.60	5.38
Brooks F.	0	0.3	1	1	0	8.00	0	0	0	0	1	0	0	.000	0	1	0	0	0	0	0	0	0.00	0.00	2.98
Childers M.	0	4.0	21	3	0	3.71	2	3	0	1	5	1	0	.714	0	0	0	0	0	0	0	0	4.50	4.50	8.23
Lerew A.	-1	8.0	37	7	0	4.05	5	5	2	0	9	1	0	.692	1	0	0	0	0	0	1	0	5.63	5.63	5.23
Thomson J.	-2	98.7	427	17	17	3.66	61	28	2	2	111	6	11	.682	9	6	1	4	6	0	0	0	4.74	4.47	3.45
Martin T.	-4	2.3	14	4	0	3.36	0	2	0	0	6	1	1	.545	0	0	0	0	0	0	0	0	19.29	19.29	11.13
McBride M.	-4	14.0	68	23	0	4.50	22	7	0	0	18	0	0	.538	0	0	0	1	0	1	1	6	7.07	5.79	1.34
Devine J.	-4	5.0	26	5	0	3.88	3	5	1	0	6	2	0	.750	1	0	0	0	1	0	0	1	12.60	12.60	9.98
Ramirez H.	-5	202.3	847	33	32	3.60	80	67	4	2	214	31	36	.726	12	6	3	11	9	0	0	0	4.80	4.63	5.21
Colon R.	-5	44.3	191	23	4	3.52	30	14	1	0	47	10	3	.730	6	1	0	1	5	0	0	2	5.68	5.28	5.51
Davies K.	-6	87.7	403	21	14	4.01	62	49	5	1	98	8	9	.682	0	4	2	7	6	0	1	2	5.24	4.93	4.47
Kolb D.	-10	57.7	271	65	0	3.77	39	29	5	1	78	5	14	.629	3	0	0	3	8	11	18	6	6.09	5.93	4.32
Bernero A.	-11	47.0	216	36	0	3.51	37	12	3	4	61	5	4	.646	0	0	0	4	3	0	1	4	6.70	6.51	3.81

Win Shares Stats (cont.)

Player	WS	Bat	Pitch	Field	ExpWS	WSP	WSAB	CWS	NetWSValue
Hudson, T	13	-2.2	15.5	0.0	9	.729	8	119	($748,698)
Langerhans, R	13	10.6	0.0	2.7	10	.644	6	13	$4,804,011
LaRoche, A	12	10.7	0.0	1.4	14	.441	2	20	$1,939,643
Johnson, K	9	6.7	0.0	2.6	9	.517	3	9	$2,374,708
Estrada, J	9	3.8	0.0	5.7	11	.445	2	34	$1,441,819
Ramirez, H	8	-1.5	9.2	0.0	10	.408	2	21	$1,570,540
Reitsma, C	7	-0.0	7.1	0.0	6	.603	3	32	$841,850
Franco, J	7	6.6	0.0	0.6	7	.522	2	275	$1,442,020
Betemit, W	7	6.2	0.0	1.3	8	.495	2	7	$1,719,154
McCann, B	6	3.8	0.0	2.7	6	.570	3	6	$1,977,047
Thomson, J	4	-0.2	4.3	0.0	5	.438	1	60	($1,355,805)
Jordan, B	4	2.3	0.0	1.8	7	.302	-1	165	($600,000)
Davies, K	3	-0.0	3.5	0.0	4	.391	1	3	$640,972
Orr, P	3	2.3	0.0	0.8	4	.382	0	3	$203,690
Mondesi, R	1	-0.1	0.0	0.9	4	.086	-2	183	($1,000,000)
Kolb, D	0	-0.0	-0.8	0.0	4	-.096	-4	23	($3,400,000)

Fielding and Baserunning Stats

Name	POS	Inn	SBA/G	CS%	ERA	WP+PB/G	PO	A	TE	FE
Estrada	C	826.3	0.86	27%	3.99	0.294	574	51	2	0
McCann	C	449.3	0.54	19%	3.91	0.300	310	21	1	1
Perez	C	87.0	0.41	75%	2.17	0.414	38	4	0	0
Pena	C	81.0	1.00	11%	6.33	0.444	46	5	0	0

Name	POS	Inn	PO	A	TE	FE	FPct	RF	DPS	DPT
A LaRoche	1B	1019.0	1070	77	2	5	.994	10.13	12	1
J Franco	1B	423.3	450	37	0	4	.990	10.35	2	0
T Hollandswo	1B	1.0	0	0	0	0	0.000	0.00	0	0
M Giles	2B	1276.0	266	468	5	7	.984	5.18	38	56
P Orr	2B	159.7	35	57	0	5	.948	5.19	4	7
W Betemit	2B	8.0	1	3	0	0	1.000	4.50	0	0
R Furcal	SS	1306.0	255	504	7	8	.981	5.23	66	52
W Betemit	SS	136.3	24	40	0	1	.985	4.22	2	7
P Orr	SS	1.0	0	0	0	0	0.000	0.00	0	0
C Jones	3B	830.3	80	169	0	5	.980	2.70	16	2
W Betemit	3B	431.0	26	94	2	4	.952	2.51	5	0
A Marte	3B	130.7	4	14	2	1	.857	1.24	2	0
P Orr	3B	45.7	2	14	1	0	.941	3.15	3	0
M Giles	3B	6.0	0	6	0	0	1.000	9.00	0	0
K Johnson	LF	648.3	166	6	0	0	1.000	2.39	2	0
R Langerhans	LF	379.3	91	0	0	0	1.000	2.16	0	0
B Jordan	LF	358.3	74	5	0	0	1.000	1.98	2	0
T Hollandswo	LF	32.7	8	0	0	0	1.000	2.20	0	0
P Orr	LF	25.0	5	0	0	0	1.000	1.80	0	0
A Jones	CF	1366.0	365	11	0	2	.995	2.48	2	0
R Langerhans	CF	77.3	28	0	0	0	1.000	3.26	0	0
J Francoeur	RF	589.0	131	13	2	3	.966	2.20	6	0
R Langerhans	RF	356.0	75	3	0	1	.987	1.97	2	0
R Mondesi	RF	339.0	67	2	0	1	.986	1.83	0	0
B Jordan	RF	141.7	38	1	0	0	1.000	2.48	0	0
T Hollandswo	RF	18.0	2	0	0	0	1.000	1.00	0	0

Incremental Baserunning Runs		
Name	IR	IRP
Rafael Furcal	3.05	139
Marcus Giles	2.44	130
Pete Orr	2.24	166
Brian Jordan	1.69	144
Kelly Johnson	1.68	134
Ryan Langerhans	1.34	135
Andruw Jones	0.75	119
Wilson Betemit	0.35	108
Julio Franco	0.33	139
Tim Hudson	0.22	128
Todd Hollandsworth	0.22	125
Jeff Francoeur	0.19	109
John Smoltz	0.16	127
Raul Mondesi	0.10	123
Brayan Pena	-0.00	0
Eddie Perez	-0.07	0
Jorge Sosa	-0.08	0
Chipper Jones	-0.11	98
Andy Marte	-0.18	0
Horacio Ramirez	-0.24	61
Kyle Davies	-0.26	0
Adam LaRoche	-0.68	78
Brian McCann	-1.70	-35
Johnny Estrada	-3.06	26

Baltimore Orioles

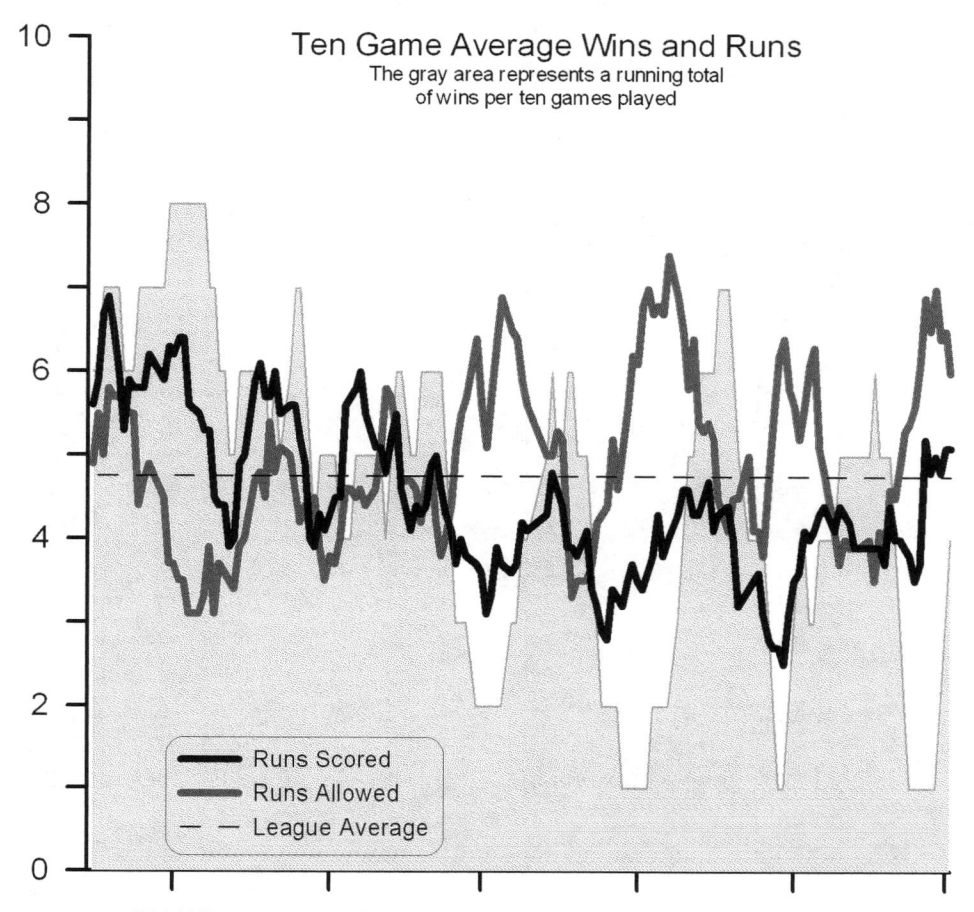

Ten Game Average Wins and Runs
The gray area represents a running total
of wins per ten games played

Runs Scored
Runs Allowed
League Average

4/23 - Beat Jays to take
first place, stay there until 6/24

5/17 - Roberts hits 11th
homer in 157 ABs, had 12
homers in 1,472 ABs before

5/27 - Bedard (5-1, 2.08 ERA)
goes on DL and posts 5.44 ERA
after returning in July

8/1 - Palmeiro suspended
for steroids, will go 2-for-28
in 7 games rest of season

8/25 - Sosa's last
day (toe injury)

9/2 - Ponson (6.21
ERA) released
for violating terms
of contract

Team Batting and Pitching/Fielding Stats by Month						
	April	May	June	July	Aug	Spt/Oct
Wins	16	15	12	8	11	12
Losses	7	13	15	18	17	18
OBP	.354	.334	.325	.316	.311	.325
SLG	.497	.466	.457	.422	.383	.389
FIP	4.22	3.90	4.62	4.65	5.28	4.78
DER	.691	.728	.705	.677	.726	.717

Batting Stats

Player	RC	Runs	RBI	PA	Outs	P/PA	H	2B	3B	HR	TB	K	BB	IBB	HBP	SH	SF	SB	CS	GDP	BA	OBP	SLG	GPA
Roberts B.	114	92	73	640	401	3.68	176	45	7	18	289	83	67	5	3	5	4	27	10	6	.314	.387	.515	.303
Tejada M.	110	89	98	704	482	3.55	199	50	5	26	337	83	40	8	7	0	3	5	1	26	.304	.349	.515	.286
Mora M.	94	86	88	664	438	3.98	168	30	1	27	281	112	50	0	10	8	3	7	4	9	.283	.348	.474	.275
Gibbons J.	78	72	79	518	368	3.57	135	33	3	26	252	56	28	3	1	0	1	0	0	15	.277	.317	.516	.272
Lopez J.	60	47	49	423	296	3.44	110	24	1	15	181	68	19	2	7	0	2	0	1	10	.278	.322	.458	.259
Palmeiro R.	59	47	60	422	280	3.65	98	13	0	18	165	43	43	4	2	0	8	2	0	9	.266	.339	.447	.264
Matos L.	55	53	32	433	293	3.56	109	20	2	4	145	58	27	0	10	3	4	17	9	4	.280	.340	.373	.246
Sosa S.	39	39	45	424	312	3.66	84	15	1	14	143	84	39	3	2	0	3	1	1	15	.221	.295	.376	.227
Surhoff B.	30	30	34	321	231	3.51	78	11	2	5	108	32	11	1	1	2	4	0	0	6	.257	.282	.356	.216
Gomez C.	26	27	18	254	173	3.73	61	11	0	1	75	17	27	1	1	6	1	2	1	14	.279	.359	.342	.247
Bigbie L.	24	22	21	234	160	3.79	51	9	1	5	77	49	21	1	0	5	2	3	3	2	.248	.314	.374	.235
Newhan D.	21	31	21	249	178	3.55	44	9	0	5	68	45	22	1	2	5	2	9	2	2	.202	.279	.312	.203
Fasano S.	18	25	20	174	125	3.60	40	3	0	11	76	41	9	0	5	0	0	0	0	5	.250	.310	.475	.258
Castro B.	14	14	7	89	59	3.55	23	3	1	0	28	10	9	0	0	0	0	6	2	0	.288	.360	.350	.249
Byrnes E.	9	17	11	181	140	3.71	32	7	1	3	50	33	11	0	1	2	0	3	0	5	.192	.246	.299	.185
Marrero E.	7	8	10	56	40	4.07	11	3	2	3	27	20	4	0	0	0	2	0	0	1	.220	.268	.540	.256
Gil G.	6	7	17	134	111	3.78	24	3	0	4	39	23	5	0	0	2	2	0	0	10	.192	.220	.312	.177
Young Jr. W.	6	2	3	37	24	3.49	10	1	0	1	14	7	4	1	0	0	0	0	0	1	.303	.378	.424	.276
Freire A.	6	7	4	72	53	4.01	16	3	0	1	22	17	6	0	1	0	0	0	0	4	.246	.319	.338	.228
Fiorentino J	2	7	5	47	33	3.81	11	2	0	1	16	10	2	0	0	0	1	1	0	0	.250	.277	.364	.215
Nivar R.	2	1	1	15	10	3.40	4	0	0	0	4	2	0	0	1	1	0	0	1	0	.308	.357	.308	.238
Reed K.	1	1	1	6	4	3.67	1	0	0	0	1	2	1	0	0	0	0	0	0	0	.200	.333	.200	.200
Ponson S.	0	0	0	4	3	2.75	1	1	0	0	2	0	0	0	0	0	0	0	0	0	.250	.250	.500	.238
Whiteside E.	0	1	1	12	10	3.42	3	0	0	0	3	2	0	0	0	0	0	0	0	1	.250	.250	.250	.175
Chen B.	0	0	0	4	2	2.75	1	0	0	0	1	0	1	0	0	0	0	0	0	0	.333	.500	.333	.308
Penn H.	0	0	0	3	1	3.67	0	0	0	0	0	0	1	0	0	1	0	0	0	0	.000	.500	0.000	.225
Rogers E.	0	4	2	1	2	2.00	1	0	0	1	4	0	0	0	0	0	0	0	2	0	1.000	1.000	4.000	1.450
Calzado N.	-0	0	0	5	4	2.80	1	0	0	0	1	1	0	0	0	0	0	0	0	0	.200	.200	.200	.140
Baldwin J.	-0	0	0	1	1	3.00	0	0	0	0	0	0	0	0	0	0	0	0	0	0	.000	.000	.000	.000
Cabrera D.	-0	0	0	1	1	3.00	0	0	0	0	0	1	0	0	0	0	0	0	0	0	.000	.000	.000	.000
Cummings M.	-0	0	0	2	2	2.50	0	0	0	0	0	1	0	0	0	0	0	0	0	0	.000	.000	.000	.000
Lopez R.	-0	0	0	4	4	4.00	0	0	0	0	0	2	0	0	0	0	0	0	0	0	.000	.000	.000	.000

Win Shares Stats

Player	WS	Bat	Pitch	Field	ExpWS	WSP	WSAB	CWS	NetWSValue
Roberts, B	28	23.5	0.0	5.0	16	.873	17	63	$13,410,248
Tejada, M	26	20.0	0.0	6.1	18	.717	13	188	$4,061,874
Mora, M	19	15.7	0.0	3.6	17	.568	7	99	$3,753,212
Gibbons, J	16	13.8	0.0	1.8	12	.635	7	55	$2,966,870
Chen, B	13	-0.1	13.5	0.0	10	.644	7	36	$5,420,761
Ryan, B	12	0.0	11.8	0.0	8	.737	6	39	$2,350,171
Lopez, J	12	10.0	0.0	2.3	10	.604	5	190	($262,190)

Continued on the next page.

Pitching Stats

Player	PR	IP	BFP	G	GS	P/PA	K	BB	IBB	HBP	H	HR	DP	DER	SB	CS	PO	W	L	Sv	Op	Hld	RA	ERA	FIP
Ryan B.	16	70.3	290	69	0	4.29	100	26	2	2	54	4	4	.684	8	1	0	1	4	36	41	0	2.56	2.43	2.13
Chen B.	6	197.3	832	34	32	3.78	133	63	0	9	187	33	17	.741	17	8	4	13	10	0	0	0	4.29	3.83	4.96
Bedard E.	6	141.7	606	24	24	4.07	125	57	1	5	139	10	18	.685	8	4	2	6	8	0	0	0	4.19	4.00	3.51
Ray C.	6	40.7	174	41	0	3.87	43	18	3	1	34	5	3	.729	1	1	0	1	3	0	4	8	3.32	2.66	3.93
Williams T.	5	76.3	321	72	0	3.69	38	26	4	3	72	5	15	.731	6	1	0	5	5	1	3	18	4.01	3.30	4.04
Parrish J.	3	17.3	86	14	0	4.40	25	17	1	0	19	1	1	.581	1	1	0	1	0	0	0	1	3.12	3.12	3.85
Baldwin J.	2	39.3	162	20	0	3.55	20	9	0	2	36	5	5	.754	2	0	0	0	0	0	0	0	4.12	3.20	4.52
Rakers A.	2	13.7	55	10	0	3.45	11	3	0	0	11	3	0	.789	1	0	0	1	0	0	0	1	3.29	3.29	4.95
Byrdak T.	-1	26.7	131	41	0	3.91	31	21	1	1	27	1	1	.662	1	0	0	0	1	1	1	11	4.73	4.05	3.68
Kline S.	-3	61.0	263	67	0	3.66	36	30	5	0	59	11	8	.742	2	2	0	2	4	0	3	9	5.02	4.28	5.68
Grimsley J.	-4	22.0	93	22	0	3.52	10	9	2	0	24	5	7	.725	2	1	0	1	2	0	3	3	6.14	5.73	6.32
Bauer R.	-5	8.3	40	5	0	4.10	5	4	0	0	13	2	2	.621	0	0	0	0	0	0	0	0	9.72	9.72	6.40
DuBose E.	-6	29.3	135	15	3	3.84	17	19	0	1	28	4	2	.745	1	1	0	2	3	0	0	3	6.44	5.52	5.70
Reed S.	-8	32.7	149	30	0	3.64	15	11	2	4	41	5	4	.684	1	0	0	1	2	0	0	4	6.61	6.61	5.49
Maine J.	-10	40.0	184	10	8	4.01	24	24	0	1	39	8	3	.756	5	0	0	2	3	0	0	0	6.75	6.30	6.32
Cabrera D.	-11	161.3	716	29	29	4.00	157	87	2	11	144	14	10	.709	16	7	0	10	13	0	0	0	5.13	4.52	4.05
Penn H.	-11	38.3	178	8	8	3.77	18	21	3	0	46	6	4	.699	3	0	0	3	2	0	0	0	7.04	6.34	5.78
Julio J.	-14	71.7	314	67	0	3.68	58	24	4	2	76	14	6	.713	9	0	0	3	5	0	2	12	6.28	5.90	5.05
Lopez R.	-21	209.3	918	35	35	3.59	118	63	1	7	232	28	21	.709	22	6	2	15	12	0	0	0	5.42	4.90	4.66
Ponson S.	-32	130.3	595	23	23	3.48	68	48	1	3	177	16	23	.650	9	1	0	7	11	0	0	0	6.70	6.21	4.77

Win Shares Stats (cont.)

Player	WS	Bat	Pitch	Field	ExpWS	WSP	WSAB	CWS	NetWSValue
Matos, L	12	7.9	0.0	4.2	12	.522	4	34	$2,373,724
Palmeiro, R	11	9.3	0.0	1.4	11	.505	3	395	$966,331
Bedard, E	9	0.0	8.8	0.0	7	.587	4	15	$3,368,387
Lopez, R	9	-0.1	8.7	0.0	11	.387	2	41	($794,947)
Williams, T	7	0.0	6.7	0.0	5	.618	3	13	$2,272,825
Cabrera, D	7	-0.0	7.4	0.0	9	.435	2	15	$1,801,022
Gomez, C	4	2.2	0.0	1.4	7	.276	-1	89	($850,000)
Sosa, S	4	2.5	0.0	1.2	10	.185	-3	313	($12,721,992)
Kline, S	3	0.0	3.0	0.0	4	.350	0	55	($1,323,009)
Fasano, S	3	1.9	0.0	0.7	5	.272	-1	22	($316,000)
Bigbie, L	3	2.3	0.0	1.2	6	.280	-1	26	($380,000)
Surhoff, B	3	1.9	0.0	1.5	8	.204	-2	230	($1,100,000)
Newhan, D	2	1.1	0.0	1.1	6	.170	-2	16	($365,000)
Gil, G	1	-1.4	0.0	2.1	4	.089	-2	14	($342,500)
Julio, J	1	0.0	1.0	0.0	5	.098	-2	26	($2,500,000)
Ponson, S	1	0.2	0.3	0.0	7	.042	-4	63	($7,787,717)
Byrnes, E	0	-1.6	0.0	0.8	5	-.078	-4	38	($2,200,000)

Fielding and Baserunning Stats

Name	POS	Inn	SBA/G	CS%	ERA	WP+PB/G	PO	A	TE	FE
Lopez	C	628.7	0.90	17%	4.71	0.487	500	27	3	0
Fasano	C	417.0	0.91	12%	5.09	0.540	284	25	3	1
Gil	C	349.3	0.82	28%	3.74	0.567	264	26	2	0
Whiteside	C	32.7	1.11	25%	3.86	0.551	21	4	2	0

Name	POS	Inn	PO	A	TE	FE	FPct	RF	DPS	DPT
R Palmeiro	1B	748.3	748	58	0	4	.995	9.69	10	0
C Gomez	1B	241.0	253	15	1	1	.993	10.01	3	0
J Gibbons	1B	164.3	171	8	1	0	.994	9.80	3	0
B Surhoff	1B	113.0	117	8	1	0	.992	9.96	3	1
A Freire	1B	103.0	101	4	0	1	.991	9.17	0	0
W Young Jr.	1B	54.0	55	6	0	0	1.000	10.17	1	0
S Fasano	1B	2.0	0	0	0	0	0.000	0.00	0	0
J Lopez	1B	2.0	1	0	0	0	1.000	4.50	0	0
B Roberts	2B	1208.0	238	413	2	5	.988	4.85	32	53
C Gomez	2B	123.7	31	39	0	1	.986	5.09	5	8
B Castro	2B	96.0	17	31	0	3	.941	4.50	4	4
M Tejada	SS	1394.0	251	479	9	13	.971	4.71	52	50
C Gomez	SS	31.0	5	8	1	0	.929	3.77	3	0
E Rogers	SS	2.0	0	0	0	0	0.000	0.00	0	0
M Mora	3B	1289.0	96	302	10	8	.957	2.78	24	0
C Gomez	3B	120.0	11	23	0	1	.971	2.55	1	0
D Newhan	3B	18.0	1	3	0	0	1.000	2.00	1	0
L Bigbie	LF	480.3	98	3	0	0	1.000	1.89	0	0
E Byrnes	LF	382.0	91	2	1	2	.969	2.19	0	0
B Surhoff	LF	367.3	76	3	0	0	1.000	1.94	0	0
D Newhan	LF	132.0	18	1	0	0	1.000	1.30	0	0
E Marrero	LF	48.0	10	0	0	0	.909	1.88	0	0
N Calzado	LF	8.0	2	0	0	0	1.000	2.25	0	0
B Castro	LF	7.0	1	0	0	1	.500	1.29	0	0
M Cummings	LF	2.0	0	0	0	0	0.000	0.00	0	0
A Freire	LF	1.0	0	0	0	0	0.000	0.00	0	0
L Matos	CF	990.0	298	7	0	5	.984	2.77	4	0
D Newhan	CF	234.7	61	0	0	0	1.000	2.34	0	0
J Fiorentino	CF	96.0	29	0	0	0	1.000	2.72	0	0
L Bigbie	CF	45.0	10	0	0	0	1.000	2.00	0	0
E Marrero	CF	26.0	10	0	0	0	1.000	3.46	0	0
R Nivar	CF	25.0	10	0	0	0	1.000	3.60	0	0
K Reed	CF	8.0	0	0	0	0	0.000	0.00	0	0
E Byrnes	CF	2.0	0	0	0	0	0.000	0.00	0	0
N Calzado	CF	1.0	0	0	0	0	0.000	0.00	0	0

Name	POS	Inn	PO	A	TE	FE	FPct	RF	DPS	DPT
S Sosa	RF	577.0	121	3	0	3	.976	1.93	2	0
J Gibbons	RF	558.7	133	6	2	0	.986	2.24	2	0
B Surhoff	RF	118.0	33	0	0	1	.971	2.52	0	0
D Newhan	RF	116.0	20	0	1	0	.952	1.55	0	0
E Marrero	RF	46.0	8	0	0	0	1.000	1.57	0	0
K Reed	RF	11.0	3	0	0	0	1.000	2.45	0	0
E Byrnes	RF	1.0	0	0	0	0	0.000	0.00	0	0

Incremental Baserunning Runs		
Name	IR	IRP
Luis Matos	1.66	132
Eric Byrnes	0.82	148
Alejandro Freire	0.71	147
Sal Fasano	0.70	162
Larry Bigbie	0.37	113
Jeffrey Fiorentino	0.36	186
Miguel Tejada	0.35	103
Bernie Castro	0.29	133
Eli Whiteside	0.14	204
Javy Lopez	0.13	103
Ed Rogers	0.08	458
Keith Reed	0.06	120
Bruce Chen	-0.07	0
Geronimo Gil	-0.52	0
David Newhan	-0.57	84
Brian Roberts	-0.63	93
Chris Gomez	-0.73	81
Jay Gibbons	-1.06	79
BJ Surhoff	-1.80	15
Sammy Sosa	-2.01	41
Rafael Palmeiro	-2.14	50
Melvin Mora	-2.25	75

Boston Red Sox

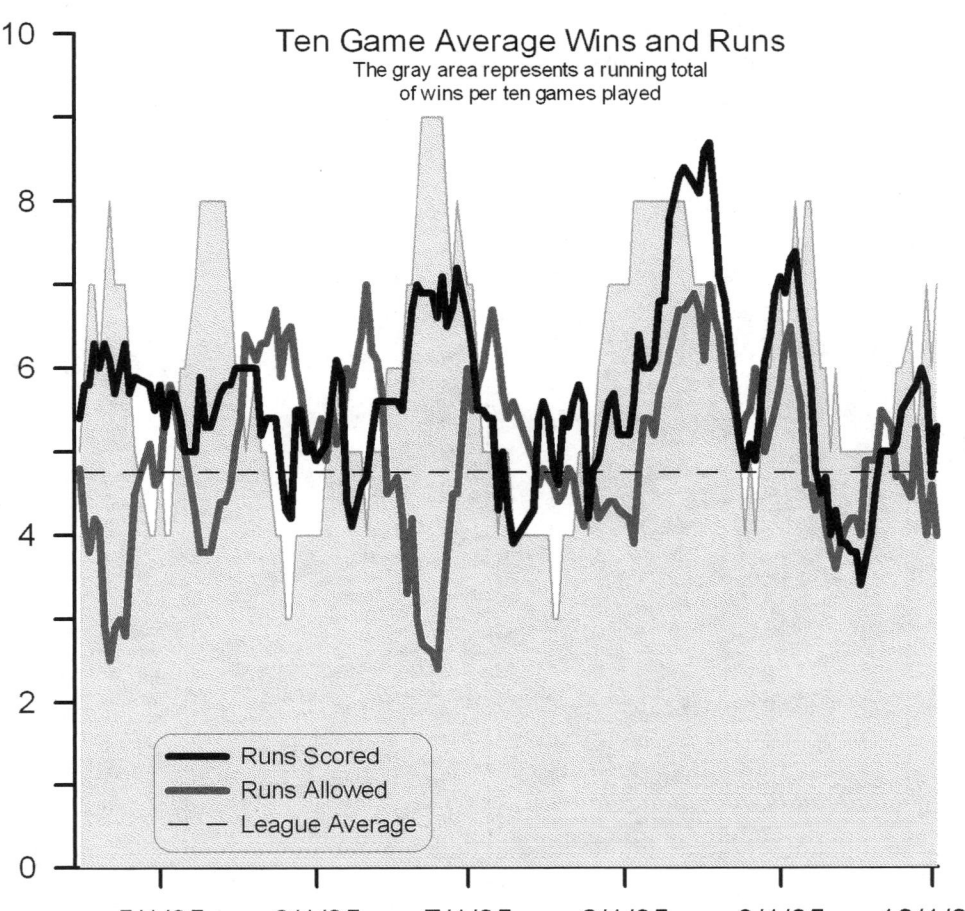

Ten Game Average Wins and Runs
The gray area represents a running total
of wins per ten games played

Runs Scored
Runs Allowed
League Average

5/1/05 6/1/05 7/1/05 8/1/05 9/1/05 10/1/05

*6/24 - Move into first,
where they spend all
but one day until 9/21*

*7/19 - Trade for
Graffanino, who hits
.319/.355/.457*

*7/7 - Foulke (6.23 ERA)
put on DL, pitches
just six more games*

*9/9 - Ramirez homers
vs. Yankees, first of
nine homers in final
20 games*

*7/14 - Schilling returns from
DL, but is ineffective*

Team Batting and Pitching/Fielding Stats by Month						
	April	May	June	July	Aug	Spt/Oct
Wins	12	16	17	14	18	18
Losses	11	12	9	13	9	13
OBP	.358	.367	.354	.354	.371	.337
SLG	.451	.431	.501	.431	.489	.425
FIP	4.08	4.29	4.23	4.65	4.10	4.27
DER	.675	.719	.696	.715	.665	.709

Batting Stats

Player	RC	Runs	RBI	PA	Outs	P/PA	H	2B	3B	HR	TB	K	BB	IBB	HBP	SH	SF	SB	CS	GDP	BA	OBP	SLG	GPA
Ortiz D.	136	119	148	713	434	4.00	180	40	1	47	363	124	102	9	1	0	9	1	0	13	.300	.397	.604	.330
Ramirez M.	134	112	144	650	412	4.06	162	30	1	45	329	119	80	9	10	0	6	1	0	20	.292	.388	.594	.323
Damon J.	105	117	75	688	433	3.72	197	35	6	10	274	69	53	3	2	0	9	18	1	5	.316	.366	.439	.275
Renteria E.	82	100	70	692	470	3.65	172	36	4	8	240	100	55	0	3	6	5	9	4	15	.276	.335	.385	.247
Mueller B.	81	69	62	590	388	3.64	153	34	3	10	223	74	59	3	6	0	6	0	0	22	.295	.369	.430	.274
Varitek J.	78	70	70	539	348	4.14	132	30	1	22	230	117	62	3	3	1	3	2	0	10	.281	.366	.489	.287
Nixon T.	70	64	67	470	304	3.69	112	29	1	13	182	59	53	3	3	0	6	2	1	7	.275	.357	.446	.272
Millar K.	58	57	50	519	340	3.90	122	28	1	9	179	74	54	0	8	0	8	0	1	12	.272	.355	.399	.259
Olerud J.	31	18	37	192	129	3.84	50	7	0	7	78	20	16	2	0	0	3	0	0	6	.289	.344	.451	.267
Bellhorn M.	28	41	28	335	226	4.23	61	20	0	7	102	109	49	1	0	0	3	3	0	4	.216	.328	.360	.238
Graffanino T	26	39	20	200	137	3.42	60	12	1	4	86	23	9	1	2	0	1	4	1	8	.319	.355	.457	.274
Mirabelli D.	18	16	18	152	107	4.10	31	7	0	6	56	48	14	0	2	0	0	2	0	2	.228	.309	.412	.242
Payton J.	16	24	21	144	102	3.43	35	7	0	5	57	14	10	0	0	0	1	0	0	4	.263	.313	.429	.248
Youkilis K.	13	11	9	95	58	4.69	22	7	0	1	32	19	14	0	2	0	0	0	1	0	.278	.400	.405	.281
Cora A.	12	14	16	116	81	3.92	28	3	2	2	41	12	6	0	1	3	2	1	2	3	.269	.310	.394	.238
Kapler G.	7	15	9	104	74	3.71	24	7	0	1	34	15	3	0	2	1	1	1	0	1	.247	.282	.351	.214
Petagine R.	4	4	9	36	26	4.03	9	2	0	1	14	5	4	0	0	0	0	0	0	3	.281	.361	.438	.272
Vazquez R.	3	6	4	66	49	3.52	12	2	0	0	14	14	3	0	0	2	0	0	0	0	.197	.234	.230	.163
McCarty D.	2	2	2	6	2	4.67	2	0	0	0	2	0	2	0	0	0	0	0	0	0	.500	.667	.500	.425
Wakefield T.	1	1	1	9	6	3.67	2	0	0	0	2	2	0	0	0	1	0	0	0	0	.250	.250	.250	.175
Cruz J.	1	0	0	13	9	3.77	3	1	0	0	4	4	1	0	0	0	0	0	0	0	.250	.308	.333	.222
Stern A.	1	4	2	16	14	3.19	2	0	0	1	5	4	0	0	1	0	0	1	1	0	.133	.188	.333	.168
Wells D.	0	1	1	7	6	3.14	1	0	0	0	1	2	0	0	0	0	0	0	0	0	.143	.143	.143	.100
Miller W.	0	0	0	3	1	2.67	2	0	0	0	2	1	0	0	0	0	0	0	0	0	.667	.667	.667	.467
Machado A.	0	4	0	6	4	5.33	1	1	0	0	2	1	1	0	0	0	0	0	0	0	.200	.333	.400	.250
Clement M.	-0	0	0	4	3	4.50	0	0	0	0	0	2	1	0	0	0	0	0	0	0	.000	.250	0.000	.113
Wooten S.	-0	0	0	1	1	3.00	0	0	0	0	0	0	0	0	0	0	0	0	0	0	.000	.000	.000	.000
Arroyo B.	-0	0	0	1	1	3.00	0	0	0	0	0	1	0	0	0	0	0	0	0	0	.000	.000	.000	.000
Ramirez H.	-0	0	0	2	2	5.50	0	0	0	0	0	2	0	0	0	0	0	0	0	0	.000	.000	.000	.000
Hyzdu A.	-0	1	0	18	12	3.22	4	1	0	0	5	3	2	0	0	0	0	0	0	0	.250	.333	.313	.228
Shoppach K.	-1	1	0	16	15	4.06	0	0	0	0	0	7	0	0	1	0	0	0	0	0	.000	.063	.000	.028

Win Shares Stats

Player	WS	Bat	Pitch	Field	ExpWS	WSP	WSAB	CWS	NetWSValue
Ramirez, M	34	30.9	0.0	2.9	17	1.018	22	310	$4,359,565
Ortiz, D	31	31.4	0.0	0.2	14	1.149	22	108	$14,343,907
Damon, J	25	19.9	0.0	5.7	17	.739	13	195	$5,815,121
Varitek, J	19	14.6	0.0	4.9	14	.696	10	99	$2,999,081
Mueller, B	18	14.0	0.0	4.5	16	.595	8	136	$4,687,172
Wakefield, T	16	0.1	16.1	0.0	12	.675	9	137	$4,482,434
Nixon, T	16	13.0	0.0	2.9	12	.652	7	100	$1,455,114
Renteria, E	14	11.3	0.0	2.7	18	.398	2	163	($3,317,013)
Timlin, M	13	0.0	13.1	0.0	7	.879	8	110	$4,730,518
Wells, D	13	-0.2	12.8	0.0	10	.643	7	205	$3,047,218

Continued on the next page.

Pitching Stats

Player	PR	IP	BFP	G	GS	P/PA	K	BB	IBB	HBP	H	HR	DP	DER	SB	CS	PO	W	L	Sv	Op	Hld	RA	ERA	FIP
Timlin M.	20	80.3	342	81	0	3.42	59	20	5	2	86	2	6	.676	6	1	1	7	3	13	20	24	2.58	2.24	2.72
Wakefield T.	8	225.3	943	33	33	3.60	151	68	4	11	210	35	18	.742	18	7	1	16	12	0	0	0	4.51	4.15	4.77
Papelbon J.	7	34.0	148	17	3	3.98	34	17	2	3	33	4	3	.678	1	4	0	3	1	0	1	4	2.91	2.65	4.34
Myers M.	6	37.3	151	65	0	3.97	21	13	2	2	30	3	7	.759	4	0	0	3	1	0	1	9	3.38	3.13	4.17
Wells D.	4	184.0	780	30	30	3.56	107	21	0	9	220	21	23	.680	8	5	4	15	7	0	0	0	4.65	4.45	3.85
Bradford C.	2	23.3	104	31	0	3.59	10	4	1	3	29	1	3	.674	5	0	0	2	1	0	1	8	3.86	3.86	3.64
Dinardo L.	2	14.7	62	8	1	3.97	15	5	1	0	13	1	3	.707	1	0	0	0	1	0	0	0	3.68	1.84	2.91
Delcarmen M.	2	9.0	41	10	0	4.44	9	7	0	1	8	0	2	.667	0	0	0	0	0	0	0	0	3.00	3.00	3.71
Clement M.	1	191.0	830	32	32	3.83	146	68	1	16	192	18	22	.701	6	2	0	13	6	0	0	0	4.81	4.57	4.06
Stanton M.	1	1.0	3	1	0	4.00	1	0	0	0	1	0	0	.500	0	1	1	0	0	0	0	0	0.00	0.00	1.04
Hansen C.	-0	3.0	16	4	0	4.00	3	1	0	0	6	1	0	.545	0	0	0	0	0	0	1	0	6.00	6.00	6.38
Perisho M.	-1	0.0	1	1	0	3.00	0	0	0	0	1	0	0	.000	0	0	0	0	0	0	0	0	0.00	0.00	3.04
Harville C.	-1	7.0	30	8	0	3.77	3	3	0	1	7	1	0	.727	0	1	0	0	1	0	0	0	6.43	6.43	5.76
Cassidy S.	-3	0.7	6	1	0	3.83	0	0	0	0	4	0	0	.333	0	0	0	0	0	0	0	0	40.50	40.50	3.04
Alvarez A.	-3	2.3	13	2	0	4.00	1	0	0	0	6	1	0	.545	0	0	0	0	0	0	0	0	15.43	15.43	7.76
Miller W.	-4	91.0	414	16	16	4.04	64	47	0	3	96	8	7	.699	9	3	2	4	4	0	0	0	5.24	4.95	4.43
Neal B.	-5	8.0	41	8	0	3.17	3	3	0	0	15	2	1	.606	2	0	0	0	1	0	0	0	10.13	9.00	6.67
Foulke K.	-5	45.7	210	43	0	3.91	34	18	1	5	53	8	2	.690	3	0	0	5	5	15	19	1	5.91	5.91	5.34
Arroyo B.	-6	205.3	878	35	32	3.76	100	54	3	14	213	22	17	.722	5	3	1	14	10	0	0	0	5.08	4.51	4.46
Meredith C.	-6	2.3	18	3	0	3.39	0	4	0	1	6	1	0	.583	0	0	0	0	0	0	0	0	27.00	27.00	15.04
Mantei M.	-6	26.3	125	34	0	4.30	22	24	1	5	23	1	3	.699	2	1	0	1	0	0	0	8	6.84	6.49	5.17
Schilling C.	-9	93.3	418	32	11	3.70	87	22	0	3	121	12	5	.629	4	0	1	8	8	9	11	0	5.69	5.69	3.65
Gonzalez J.	-9	56.0	244	28	3	4.16	28	16	2	2	64	7	6	.702	9	0	1	2	1	0	0	1	6.27	6.11	4.63
Halama J.	-9	43.7	205	30	1	3.68	26	9	3	7	56	5	3	.677	1	0	0	1	1	0	0	0	6.80	6.18	4.44
Remlinger M.	-10	6.7	41	8	0	4.24	5	5	0	0	15	2	0	.552	0	0	0	0	0	0	0	0	18.90	14.85	7.69
Embree A.	-13	37.7	163	43	0	3.55	30	11	2	1	42	8	4	.699	4	1	0	1	4	1	3	4	7.88	7.65	5.17

Win Shares Stats (cont.)

Player	WS	Bat	Pitch	Field	ExpWS	WSP	WSAB	CWS	NetWSValue
Clement, M	12	-0.1	12.1	0.0	10	.594	6	60	$956,511
Arroyo, B	12	-0.0	12.2	0.0	11	.561	6	29	$2,743,307
Millar, K	10	8.0	0.0	2.3	13	.388	1	99	($1,130,068)
Olerud, J	7	5.9	0.0	1.0	5	.670	3	301	$2,603,135
Mirabelli, D	5	2.8	0.0	2.0	4	.608	2	36	$894,718
Graffanino, T	5	4.1	0.0	1.4	5	.525	2	54	$3,300,968
Bellhorn, M	5	2.3	0.0	2.6	9	.277	-1	55	($2,750,000)
Miller, W	4	-0.0	4.2	0.0	5	.434	1	55	$310,593
Schilling, C	4	0.0	3.8	0.0	6	.328	0	228	($8,340,268)
Payton, J	3	2.0	0.0	1.2	4	.414	0	66	($538,086)
Foulke, K	2	0.0	1.7	0.0	5	.193	-1	106	($5,481,202)

Fielding and Baserunning Stats

Name	POS	Inn	SBA/G	CS%	ERA	WP+PB/G	PO	A	TE	FE
Varitek	C	1089.0	0.67	20%	5.03	0.413	783	33	8	0
Mirabelli	C	309.0	0.76	19%	3.73	0.466	224	17	3	0
Shoppach	C	29.0	0.62	0%	4.97	0.931	14	0	0	0
Wooten	C	2.0	0.00	0%	0.00	0.000	0	0	0	0

Name	POS	Inn	PO	A	TE	FE	FPct	RF	DPS	DPT
K Millar	1B	796.3	799	85	2	5	.992	9.99	9	0
J Olerud	1B	431.0	416	40	0	1	.998	9.52	6	0
D Ortiz	1B	78.0	69	11	0	2	.976	9.23	2	0
R Petagine	1B	53.7	51	6	0	1	.983	9.56	0	0
K Youkilis	1B	47.0	48	0	0	0	1.000	9.19	0	0
D McCarty	1B	23.0	19	3	0	0	1.000	8.61	1	0
M Bellhorn	2B	712.0	148	253	2	4	.985	5.07	19	35
T Graffanino	2B	424.7	90	140	1	2	.987	4.87	11	16
A Cora	2B	209.3	52	62	2	0	.983	4.90	6	12
B Mueller	2B	43.0	10	13	0	1	.958	4.81	0	1
R Vazquez	2B	25.0	3	6	0	2	.818	3.24	0	1
A Machado	2B	8.0	0	0	0	0	0.000	0.00	0	0
K Youkilis	2B	7.0	0	2	0	0	1.000	2.57	0	0
E Renteria	SS	1293.0	227	398	13	17	.954	4.35	43	44
R Vazquez	SS	70.0	16	15	1	0	.969	3.99	1	2
A Cora	SS	48.3	9	24	0	0	1.000	6.14	5	0
M Bellhorn	SS	9.0	1	3	1	0	.800	4.00	0	0
H Ramirez	SS	6.0	0	1	0	0	1.000	1.50	0	0
A Machado	SS	2.7	1	1	0	0	1.000	6.75	0	0
B Mueller	3B	1209.0	87	265	8	1	.972	2.62	19	0
K Youkilis	3B	139.0	10	29	0	0	1.000	2.53	3	0
R Vazquez	3B	56.0	6	11	0	0	1.000	2.73	3	0
A Cora	3B	24.7	2	7	3	0	.750	3.28	0	0
M Ramirez	LF	1225.0	243	17	0	7	.974	1.91	0	0
K Millar	LF	119.0	19	0	0	0	1.000	1.44	0	0
J Payton	LF	51.0	8	1	0	0	1.000	1.59	0	0
G Kapler	LF	15.0	1	0	0	0	1.000	0.60	0	0
R Petagine	LF	5.7	0	0	0	0	0.000	0.00	0	0
A Stern	LF	4.0	0	0	0	0	0.000	0.00	0	0
A Machado	LF	4.0	1	0	0	0	1.000	2.25	0	0
A Hyzdu	LF	3.3	0	0	0	1	0.000	0.00	0	0
D McCarty	LF	2.0	0	0	0	0	0.000	0.00	0	0
J Damon	CF	1225.0	394	5	0	6	.985	2.93	1	0
G Kapler	CF	80.0	19	0	0	0	1.000	2.14	0	0
J Payton	CF	80.0	20	0	0	0	1.000	2.25	0	0
A Hyzdu	CF	18.7	8	0	0	0	1.000	3.86	0	0
A Stern	CF	18.0	3	0	0	0	1.000	1.50	0	0
A Machado	CF	7.3	2	0	0	0	1.000	2.45	0	0

Name	POS	Inn	PO	A	TE	FE	FPct	RF	DPS	DPT
T Nixon	RF	935.3	240	8	0	1	.996	2.39	5	0
J Payton	RF	181.0	54	2	0	0	1.000	2.78	0	0
G Kapler	RF	144.7	45	0	0	0	1.000	2.80	0	0
K Millar	RF	87.0	22	1	0	0	1.000	2.38	0	0
J Cruz	RF	31.0	2	0	0	0	1.000	0.58	0	0
A Stern	RF	27.0	7	0	0	0	1.000	2.33	0	0
A Hyzdu	RF	22.0	2	0	0	0	1.000	0.82	0	0
A Machado	RF	1.0	0	0	0	0	0.000	0.00	0	0

Incremental Baserunning Runs		
Name	IR	IRP
Edgar Renteria	3.10	135
Tony Graffanino	0.74	126
Jay Payton	0.73	135
Gabe Kapler	0.54	189
Adam Stern	0.34	198
Kevin Youkilis	0.34	130
Adam Hyzdu	0.13	120
Alex Cora	0.09	119
David McCarty	0.01	131
Johnny Damon	-0.24	98
Doug Mirabelli	-0.28	53
Ramon Vazquez	-0.41	50
John Olerud	-0.50	9
Wade Miller	-0.54	0
Roberto Petagine	-0.68	0
David Wells	-0.72	0
Trot Nixon	-0.78	88
Manny Ramirez	-0.99	87
Mark Bellhorn	-2.07	-69
Bill Mueller	-2.26	62
Jason Varitek	-2.36	72
Kevin Millar	-3.60	36
David Ortiz	-4.24	24

Chicago Cubs

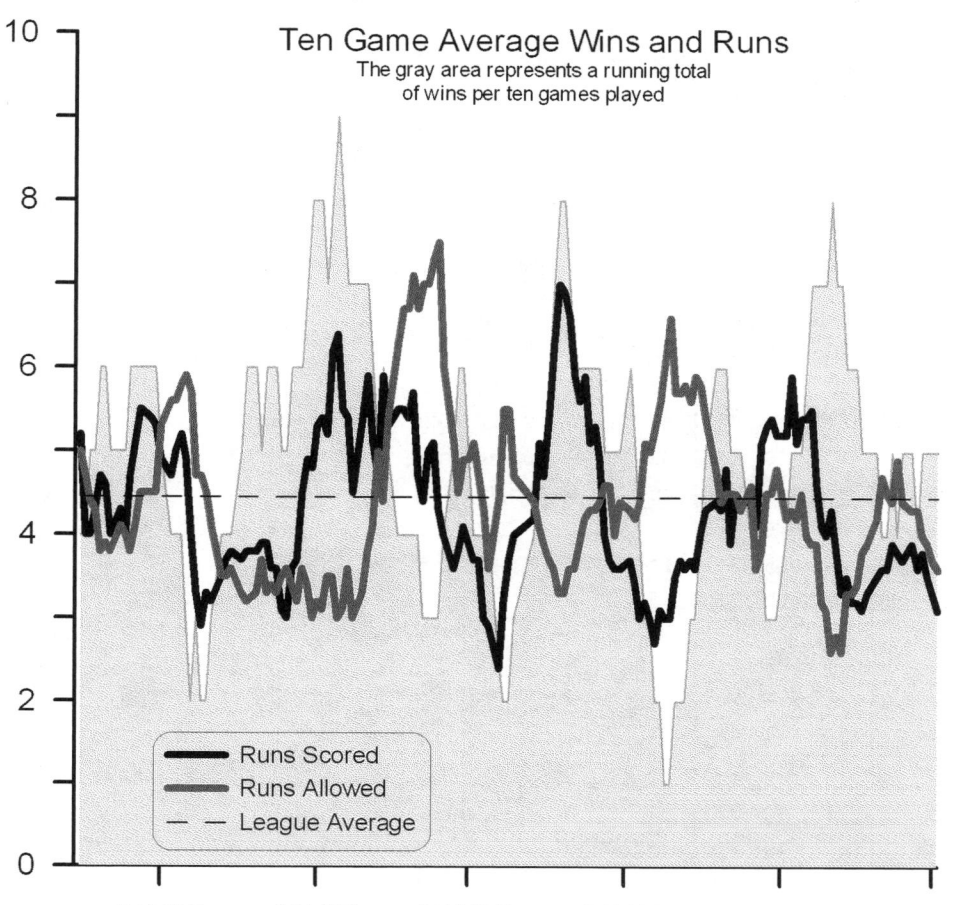

Ten Game Average Wins and Runs
The gray area represents a running total
of wins per ten games played

Legend: Runs Scored, Runs Allowed, League Average

4/20: Garciaparra's last game until 8/5 due to torn groin muscle

5/17: Dempster's first of 33 saves. Becomes closer.

7/7: Patterson sent to minors

7/22: Last day that Lee leads in all Triple Crown categories

7/26: Maddux reaches career mark of 3,000 K's

8/29: Wood's last game (only 66 IP for season) before right shoulder surgery

Team Batting and Pitching/Fielding Stats by Month						
	April	May	June	July	Aug	Spt/Oct
Wins	12	14	14	13	10	16
Losses	11	13	13	15	18	13
OBP	.336	.315	.328	.335	.328	.306
SLG	.461	.424	.466	.458	.438	.397
FIP	4.42	4.05	4.94	4.59	4.26	3.81
DER	.698	.739	.708	.717	.714	.715

Batting Stats

Player	RC	Runs	RBI	PA	Outs	P/PA	H	2B	3B	HR	TB	K	BB	IBB	HBP	SH	SF	SB	CS	GDP	BA	OBP	SLG	GPA
Lee D.	145	120	107	691	410	4.03	199	50	3	46	393	109	85	23	5	0	7	15	3	12	.335	.418	.662	.354
Ramirez A.	85	72	92	506	339	3.62	140	30	0	31	263	60	35	4	6	0	2	0	1	15	.302	.358	.568	.303
Burnitz J.	84	84	87	671	465	3.96	156	31	2	24	263	109	57	3	3	1	5	5	4	12	.258	.322	.435	.254
Barrett M.	72	48	61	477	317	3.57	117	32	3	16	203	61	40	3	7	2	4	0	3	7	.276	.345	.479	.275
Perez N.	62	59	54	609	441	3.24	157	33	1	9	219	47	18	3	3	12	4	8	4	22	.274	.298	.383	.230
Walker T.	60	50	40	433	285	3.64	121	25	3	12	188	40	31	1	1	2	2	1	1	8	.305	.355	.474	.278
Hairston Jr.	50	51	30	430	295	3.80	99	25	2	4	140	46	31	0	12	7	0	8	9	5	.261	.336	.368	.243
Patterson C.	34	47	34	483	364	3.37	97	15	3	13	157	118	23	3	1	5	1	15	5	5	.215	.254	.348	.201
Garciaparra	30	28	30	247	171	3.20	65	12	0	9	104	24	12	0	2	0	3	0	0	6	.283	.320	.452	.257
Hollandswort	29	23	35	290	208	3.36	68	17	2	5	104	53	18	1	1	1	2	4	4	4	.254	.301	.388	.232
Murton M.	20	19	14	160	100	3.46	45	3	2	7	73	22	16	4	0	2	2	2	1	4	.321	.386	.521	.304
Dubois J.	19	15	22	152	112	3.61	34	12	0	7	67	49	7	1	3	0	0	0	1	3	.239	.289	.472	.248
Blanco H.	18	16	25	178	128	3.80	39	6	0	6	63	24	11	1	0	4	2	0	0	6	.242	.287	.391	.227
Macias J.	12	15	13	190	141	3.48	45	8	0	1	56	24	6	0	0	4	3	4	3	6	.254	.274	.316	.202
Cedeno R.	12	13	6	89	60	3.48	24	3	0	1	30	11	5	1	2	2	0	1	0	4	.300	.356	.375	.254
Zambrano C.	5	8	6	84	58	3.25	24	6	2	1	37	25	0	0	0	4	0	0	0	2	.300	.300	.463	.251
Lawton M.	5	8	5	83	62	3.81	19	2	0	1	24	8	4	0	1	0	0	1	0	3	.244	.289	.308	.207
Prior M.	5	5	3	56	37	3.71	11	2	0	0	13	14	2	0	0	6	0	0	0	0	.229	.260	.271	.185
Mitre S.	2	2	1	12	7	2.25	4	1	0	0	5	1	0	0	0	1	0	0	0	0	.364	.364	.455	.277
Grieve B.	2	1	1	25	15	4.16	5	0	0	0	5	7	5	1	0	0	0	0	0	0	.250	.400	.250	.243
Wilson E.	1	1	0	25	19	3.32	3	2	0	0	5	1	3	0	0	0	0	0	0	0	.136	.240	.227	.165
Fontenot M.	1	4	0	5	2	4.40	0	0	0	0	0	0	2	0	1	0	0	0	0	0	.000	.600	.000	.270
Wood K.	1	0	2	21	16	3.62	2	2	0	0	4	6	1	0	0	2	0	0	0	0	.111	.158	.222	.127
Bartosh C.	1	0	0	1	0	4.00	1	0	0	0	1	0	0	0	0	0	0	0	0	0	1.000	1.000	1.000	.700
Wellemeyer T	0	1	0	4	3	4.25	1	0	0	0	1	2	0	0	0	0	0	0	0	0	.250	.250	.250	.175
Theriot R.	0	3	0	14	11	4.07	2	1	0	0	3	2	1	0	0	0	0	0	0	0	.154	.214	.231	.154
Hill R.	0	1	0	6	4	4.17	2	0	0	0	2	2	0	0	0	0	0	0	0	0	.333	.333	.333	.233
Leicester J.	0	0	0	1	0	0.00	0	0	0	0	0	0	0	0	0	1	0	0	0	0	.000	.000	.000	.000
Greenberg A.	0	0	0	1	0	0.00	0	0	0	0	0	0	0	0	1	0	0	0	0	0	.000	1.000	.000	.450
Novoa R.	-0	0	0	1	1	2.00	0	0	0	0	0	0	0	0	0	0	0	0	0	0	.000	.000	.000	.000
Soto G.	-0	0	0	1	1	5.00	0	0	0	0	0	0	0	0	0	0	0	0	0	0	.000	.000	.000	.000
Koronka J.	-0	0	0	5	4	4.00	0	0	0	0	0	3	1	0	0	0	0	0	0	0	.000	.200	.000	.090
McClain S.	-0	1	1	16	13	3.25	2	1	0	0	3	2	2	0	0	0	0	0	0	1	.143	.250	.214	.166
Wuertz M.	-0	0	0	2	2	4.00	0	0	0	0	0	2	0	0	0	0	0	0	0	0	.000	.000	.000	.000
Gerut J.	-0	1	0	16	13	4.13	1	1	0	0	2	3	2	0	0	0	0	0	0	0	.071	.188	.143	.120
Dempster R.	-1	0	0	14	13	3.29	1	0	0	0	1	5	0	0	0	0	0	0	0	0	.071	.071	.071	.050
Rusch G.	-1	2	0	43	37	3.33	6	2	0	0	8	9	1	0	1	0	0	0	0	2	.146	.186	.195	.133
Williams J.	-1	1	0	36	27	3.58	3	1	0	0	4	16	0	0	0	6	0	0	0	0	.100	.100	.133	.078
Maddux G.	-1	4	5	83	67	2.87	13	0	0	1	16	15	0	0	0	7	0	1	0	4	.171	.171	.211	.130

Pitching Stats

Player	PR	IP	BFP	G	GS	P/PA	K	BB	IBB	HBP	H	HR	DP	DER	SB	CS	PO	W	L	Sv	Op.	Hld	RA	ERA	FIP
Zambrano C.	25	223.3	909	33	33	3.92	202	86	3	8	170	21	23	.748	1	9	3	14	6	0	0	0	3.55	3.26	3.66
Dempster R.	12	92.0	401	63	6	3.92	89	49	7	4	83	4	14	.690	6	2	0	5	3	33	35	0	3.42	3.13	3.34
Prior M.	11	166.7	701	27	27	4.03	188	59	2	4	143	25	8	.722	5	6	0	11	7	0	0	0	3.94	3.67	3.81
Ohman W.	8	43.3	187	69	0	4.01	45	24	3	3	32	6	4	.761	4	0	0	2	2	0	3	13	2.91	2.91	4.57
Williams J.	4	106.0	459	18	17	3.65	59	45	0	9	98	12	10	.743	6	1	3	6	8	0	0	1	4.25	3.91	4.87
Wuertz M.	2	75.7	319	75	0	4.16	89	40	7	0	60	6	6	.707	7	4	0	6	2	0	3	18	4.28	3.81	3.25
Maddux G.	2	225.0	936	35	35	3.31	136	36	4	7	239	29	25	.712	32	8	0	13	15	0	0	0	4.48	4.24	4.02
Wood K.	1	66.0	273	21	10	3.88	77	26	0	2	52	14	2	.753	3	4	1	3	4	0	0	4	4.36	4.23	4.68
Van Buren J.	1	6.0	27	6	0	4.63	3	9	2	0	2	0	1	.867	0	1	0	0	2	0	0	0	3.00	3.00	6.48
Hawkins L.	1	19.0	80	21	0	3.69	13	7	0	0	18	4	3	.750	1	0	0	1	4	4	8	0	4.26	3.32	5.46
Novoa R.	1	44.7	205	49	0	3.91	47	25	6	0	47	4	1	.667	0	0	0	4	5	0	5	14	4.43	4.43	3.72
Williamson S	-2	14.3	65	17	0	3.82	23	6	0	1	15	3	1	.613	1	0	0	0	0	0	0	3	5.65	5.65	4.17
Fox C.	-2	8.0	38	11	0	4.61	11	8	0	0	8	2	1	.647	0	0	0	0	0	1	1	3	6.75	6.75	6.48
Remlinger M.	-2	33.0	141	35	0	3.81	30	12	2	2	31	5	2	.717	0	2	0	0	3	0	1	5	5.18	4.91	4.41
Borowski J.	-2	11.0	47	11	0	3.98	11	1	0	0	12	5	0	.767	2	0	0	0	0	0	0	1	6.55	6.55	7.16
Bartosh C.	-3	19.7	91	19	0	4.19	15	11	0	0	23	7	6	.714	1	0	0	0	2	0	0	1	5.95	5.49	8.07
Koronka J.	-5	15.7	76	4	3	3.80	10	8	0	0	19	2	0	.696	3	0	0	1	2	0	0	0	7.47	7.47	4.90
Leicester J.	-5	9.0	46	6	1	3.78	7	9	0	2	11	2	3	.654	0	0	0	0	2	0	0	0	10.00	9.00	7.98
Rusch G.	-6	145.3	655	46	19	3.92	111	53	8	1	175	14	14	.662	3	2	1	9	8	0	1	3	4.89	4.52	3.82
Mitre S.	-7	60.3	268	21	7	3.72	37	23	2	3	62	11	5	.737	8	1	1	2	5	0	0	0	5.52	5.37	5.42
Wellemeyer T	-7	32.3	146	22	0	3.92	32	22	1	0	32	7	4	.706	1	0	0	2	1	1	1	3	6.40	6.12	5.86
Hill R.	-12	23.7	115	10	4	4.13	21	17	1	1	25	3	3	.699	6	0	0	0	2	0	0	0	9.13	9.13	5.14

Win Shares Stats

Player	WS	Bat	Pitch	Field	ExpWS	WSP	WSAB	CWS	NetWSValue
Lee, D	37	34.3	0.0	3.0	19	.993	24	151	$14,602,644
Zambrano, C	19	-0.1	19.5	0.0	10	.948	13	61	$6,603,303
Barrett, M	19	13.3	0.0	5.5	13	.715	10	69	$4,422,906
Ramirez, A	19	17.1	0.0	1.6	14	.682	9	98	($2,502,184)
Burnitz, J	17	12.7	0.0	4.6	18	.471	4	163	$980,188
Walker, T	14	10.3	0.0	3.3	12	.584	5	112	$2,963,261
Prior, M	13	0.1	12.6	0.0	8	.791	8	49	$4,264,418
Perez, N	12	5.7	0.0	6.4	17	.365	0	93	($23,111)
Dempster, R	10	-0.7	10.8	0.0	7	.709	5	45	$2,998,102
Maddux, G	10	-2.8	12.6	0.0	11	.455	3	369	($2,637,506)
Hairston J, J	10	6.6	0.0	3.4	12	.431	2	56	($194,364)
Wuertz, M	6	-0.1	6.4	0.0	4	.711	3	8	$2,557,378
Rusch, G	6	-1.4	7.0	0.0	7	.384	1	49	($45,876)
Williams, J	5	-1.3	6.7	0.0	5	.520	2	20	$924,753
Blanco, H	5	1.8	0.0	3.6	5	.534	2	37	$933,052
Garciaparr, N	5	4.3	0.0	1.2	7	.407	1	187	($4,198,257)
Murton, M	4	3.0	0.0	0.8	4	.430	1	4	$553,774
Hollandswo, T	4	2.9	0.0	1.4	8	.269	-1	80	($900,000)
Patterson, C	4	-0.1	0.0	4.0	13	.150	-5	47	($2,800,000)
Dubois, J	3	2.7	0.0	0.7	4	.424	1	4	($278,939)
Macias, J	1	-0.6	0.0	1.3	5	.066	-3	32	($825,000)

Fielding and Baserunning Stats

Name	POS	Inn	SBA/G	CS%	ERA	WP+PB/G	PO	A	TE	FE
Barrett	C	1017.7	0.80	22%	4.45	0.433	870	51	5	0
Blanco	C	422.3	0.83	49%	3.58	0.298	407	31	0	1

Name	POS	Inn	PO	A	TE	FE	FPct	RF	DPS	DPT
D Lee	1B	1386.0	1323	122	0	6	.996	9.38	17	0
T Walker	1B	31.0	26	4	0	0	1.000	8.71	0	0
S McClain	1B	16.0	15	0	0	0	1.000	8.44	0	0
E Wilson	1B	6.0	7	0	0	0	1.000	10.50	0	0
T Hollandswo	1B	1.0	3	0	0	0	1.000	27.00	0	0
T Walker	2B	797.7	164	242	2	4	.985	4.58	17	24
J Hairston J	2B	331.7	69	111	1	4	.973	4.88	10	12
N Perez	2B	160.0	32	47	0	2	.975	4.44	6	4
J Macias	2B	112.3	27	34	0	0	1.000	4.89	4	4
R Theriot	2B	18.7	3	9	0	0	1.000	5.79	0	0
E Wilson	2B	18.7	4	9	0	1	.929	6.27	3	3
R Cedeno	2B	1.0	0	1	0	0	1.000	9.00	0	0
N Perez	SS	1063.0	175	385	4	6	.982	4.74	36	38
N Garciaparr	SS	206.0	41	51	4	2	.939	4.02	6	9
R Cedeno	SS	158.7	30	39	1	0	.986	3.91	2	5
E Wilson	SS	10.0	2	6	0	0	1.000	7.20	1	0
J Hairston J	SS	2.0	1	1	0	0	1.000	9.00	0	1
A Ramirez	3B	1020.0	70	218	6	10	.947	2.54	13	3
N Garciaparr	3B	295.7	20	65	4	2	.934	2.59	1	0
J Macias	3B	98.7	6	15	1	1	.913	1.92	1	0
S McClain	3B	10.3	1	1	0	0	1.000	1.74	0	0
E Wilson	3B	9.0	0	0	0	0	0.000	0.00	0	0
N Perez	3B	6.0	0	1	0	0	1.000	1.50	0	0
T Hollandswo	LF	566.3	95	2	1	0	.990	1.54	0	0
M Murton	LF	329.0	62	1	1	1	.969	1.72	2	0
J Dubois	LF	285.3	47	2	0	1	.980	1.55	0	0
M Lawton	LF	140.0	29	0	0	1	.967	1.86	0	0
J Hairston J	LF	92.7	22	1	0	0	1.000	2.23	0	0
J Gerut	LF	12.3	6	0	0	0	1.000	4.38	0	0
J Macias	LF	7.3	3	0	0	1	.750	3.68	0	0
B Grieve	LF	7.0	0	0	0	0	0.000	0.00	0	0
C Patterson	CF	986.7	239	6	2	3	.980	2.23	4	0
J Hairston J	CF	386.0	90	2	0	2	.979	2.15	0	0
J Macias	CF	47.7	20	1	0	1	.955	3.97	0	0
J Burnitz	CF	19.7	8	1	0	0	1.000	4.12	0	0

Name	POS	Inn	PO	A	TE	FE	FPct	RF	DPS	DPT
J Burnitz	RF	1359.0	303	5	1	3	.984	2.04	3	0
J Macias	RF	27.3	3	1	0	0	1.000	1.32	0	0
T Hollandswo	RF	19.3	1	0	0	1	.500	0.47	0	0
M Lawton	RF	18.7	4	0	0	0	1.000	1.93	0	0
J Gerut	RF	8.0	3	0	0	0	1.000	3.38	0	0
J Hairston J	RF	7.0	2	0	0	0	1.000	2.57	0	0

Incremental Baserunning Runs

Name	IR	IRP
Jerry Hairston	2.74	166
Neifi Perez	1.41	121
Derrek Lee	1.16	113
Michael Barrett	0.87	125
Todd Walker	0.76	119
Matt Murton	0.71	140
Jose Macias	0.71	140
Sergio Mitre	0.46	275
Corey Patterson	0.39	113
Mike Fontenot	0.39	256
Greg Maddux	0.29	525
Ronny Cedeno	0.20	113
Jody Gerut	0.11	119
Matt Lawton	0.09	107
Carlos Zambrano	0.01	101
Scott McClain	-0.03	63
Ben Grieve	-0.07	0
Henry Blanco	-0.11	92
Ryan Theriot	-0.16	83
Todd Hollandsworth	-0.18	85
Glendon Rusch	-0.19	0
Jason Dubois	-0.20	88
Rich Hill	-0.21	0
Nomar Garciaparra	-0.26	80
Mark Prior	-0.37	66
Jeromy Burnitz	-0.51	93
Aramis Ramirez	-3.03	56

Chicago White Sox

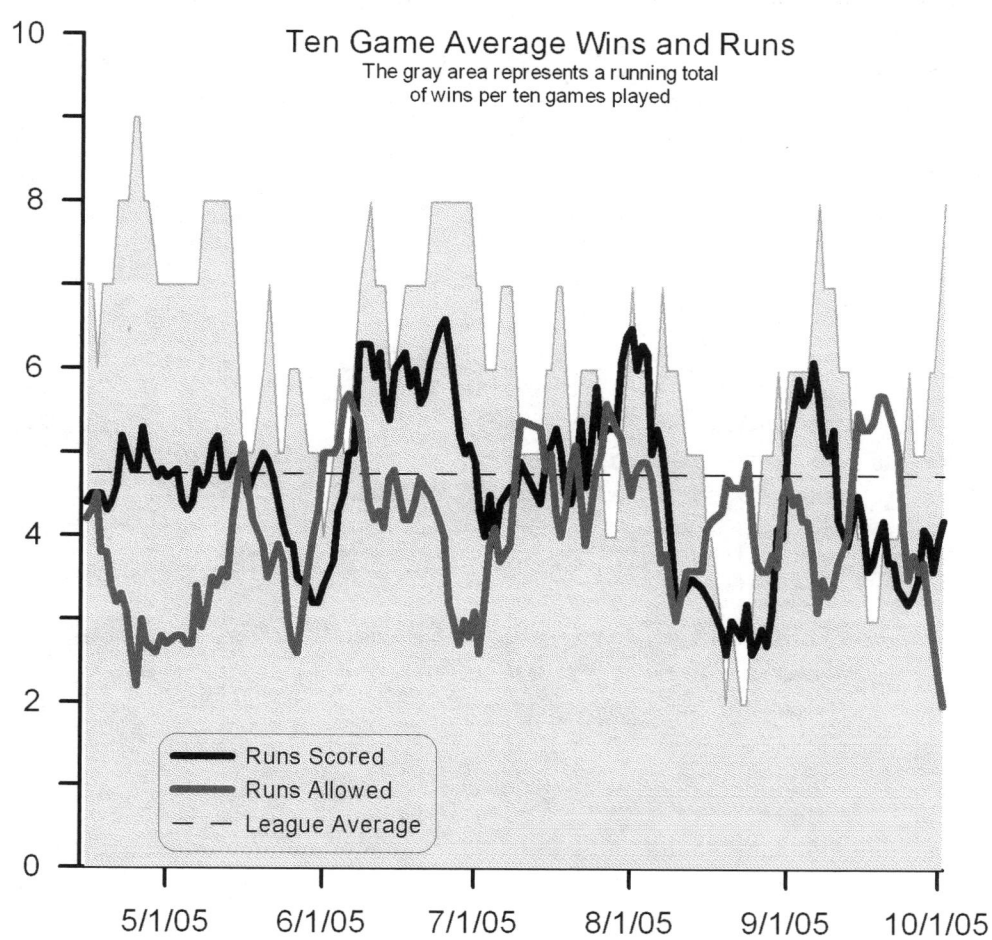

Ten Game Average Wins and Runs
The gray area represents a running total
of wins per ten games played

Runs Scored
Runs Allowed
— — League Average

*5/1: Garland shuts
out DET, has 1.39 ERA*

*5/11: Hermanson
replaces Takatsu
as closer, saves 34
with 2.04 ERA*

*7/5: Jenks called
up from AAA;
posts 2.75 ERA*

*7/20: Thomas plays
final game due
to ankle injury*

*8/10: Win back-to-back
2-1 games over NYY*

*9/29: Beat Tigers 4-2,
clinch AL Central title*

Team Batting and Pitching/Fielding Stats by Month						
	April	May	June	July	Aug	Spt/Oct
Wins	17	18	18	15	12	19
Losses	7	10	7	11	16	12
OBP	.316	.326	.327	.338	.294	.332
SLG	.375	.428	.454	.448	.410	.431
FIP	3.84	4.22	4.18	4.59	4.16	4.14
DER	.740	.723	.735	.701	.736	.720

Batting Stats

Player	RC	Runs	RBI	PA	Outs	P/PA	H	2B	3B	HR	TB	K	BB	IBB	HBP	SH	SF	SB	CS	GDP	BA	OBP	SLG	GPA
Konerko P.	103	98	100	664	422	4.17	163	24	0	40	307	109	81	10	5	0	3	0	0	10	.283	.375	.534	.302
Dye J.	78	74	86	579	403	4.01	145	29	2	31	271	99	39	3	9	0	2	11	4	15	.274	.333	.512	.278
Rowand A.	76	77	69	640	444	3.61	156	30	5	13	235	116	32	3	21	5	4	16	5	17	.270	.329	.407	.250
Iguchi T.	72	74	71	582	390	3.86	142	25	6	15	224	114	47	0	6	11	6	15	5	16	.278	.342	.438	.264
Everett C.	69	58	87	547	383	3.73	123	17	2	23	213	99	42	2	5	0	10	4	5	11	.251	.311	.435	.249
Podsednik S.	62	80	25	568	390	3.90	147	28	1	0	177	75	47	0	3	6	5	59	23	7	.290	.351	.349	.245
Crede J.	60	54	62	471	331	3.62	109	21	0	22	196	66	25	3	8	2	4	1	1	7	.252	.303	.454	.250
Uribe J.	58	58	71	540	373	3.54	121	23	3	16	198	77	34	0	4	11	10	4	6	7	.252	.301	.412	.238
Pierzynski A	53	61	56	497	357	3.57	118	21	0	18	193	68	23	5	12	1	1	0	2	13	.257	.308	.420	.244
Ozuna P.	20	27	11	217	159	3.18	56	7	2	0	67	26	7	0	4	3	0	14	7	5	.276	.313	.330	.223
Thomas F.	17	19	26	124	84	4.24	23	3	0	12	62	31	16	0	0	0	3	0	0	2	.219	.315	.590	.289
Harris W.	15	17	8	139	94	3.94	31	2	1	1	38	25	13	0	1	4	0	10	3	1	.256	.333	.314	.229
Perez T.	13	13	15	196	145	3.57	39	8	0	2	53	25	12	1	0	4	1	2	2	3	.218	.266	.296	.194
Widger C.	12	18	11	154	114	3.77	34	8	0	4	54	22	10	0	1	2	0	0	2	5	.241	.296	.383	.229
Blum G.	4	6	3	99	78	3.63	19	2	1	1	26	15	4	0	0	0	0	0	1	1	.200	.232	.274	.173
Gload R.	2	2	5	44	36	3.75	7	2	0	0	9	9	2	0	0	0	0	0	0	1	.167	.205	.214	.146
Lopez P.	2	1	2	8	5	2.63	2	0	0	0	2	1	0	0	0	1	0	0	0	0	.286	.286	.286	.200
Borchard J.	2	0	0	12	8	3.67	5	2	0	0	7	4	0	0	0	0	0	0	1	0	.417	.417	.583	.333
Anderson B.	2	3	3	35	30	3.80	6	1	0	2	13	12	0	0	0	1	0	1	0	2	.176	.176	.382	.175
Garland J.	1	0	1	2	1	4.50	1	0	0	0	1	1	0	0	0	0	0	0	0	0	.500	.500	.500	.350
Casanova R.	1	0	0	5	4	4.00	1	0	0	0	1	1	0	0	0	0	0	0	0	0	.200	.200	.200	.140
Politte C.	1	1	1	1	0	3.00	1	0	0	0	1	0	0	0	0	0	0	0	0	0	1.000	1.000	1.000	.700
Hernandez O.	0	0	0	3	2	4.33	1	0	0	0	1	1	0	0	0	0	0	0	0	0	.333	.333	.333	.233
Contreras J.	-0	0	0	4	3	4.25	0	0	0	0	0	2	1	0	0	0	0	0	0	0	.000	.250	.000	.113
Burke J.	-0	0	0	1	1	1.00	0	0	0	0	0	0	0	0	0	0	0	0	0	0	.000	.000	.000	.000
McCarthy B.	-0	0	0	2	2	6.50	0	0	0	0	0	2	0	0	0	0	0	0	0	0	.000	.000	.000	.000
Buehrle M.	-0	0	0	3	3	2.67	0	0	0	0	0	1	0	0	0	0	0	0	0	0	.000	.000	.000	.000
Garcia F.	-1	0	0	9	7	3.22	0	0	0	0	0	1	0	0	0	2	0	0	0	0	.000	.000	.000	.000

Pitching Stats

Player	PR	IP	BFP	G	GS	P/PA	K	BB	IBB	HBP	H	HR	DP	DER	SB	CS	PO	W	L	Sv	Op	Hld	RA	ERA	FIP
Buehrle M.	27	236.7	971	33	33	3.58	149	40	4	4	240	20	35	.710	8	3	5	16	8	0	0	0	3.76	3.12	3.44
Garland J.	26	221.0	901	32	32	3.68	115	47	3	7	212	26	28	.737	3	6	0	18	10	0	0	0	3.75	3.50	4.26
Politte C.	21	67.3	262	68	0	3.89	57	21	4	3	42	7	7	.799	6	2	0	7	1	1	2	23	2.00	2.00	3.77
Garcia F.	20	228.0	943	33	33	3.60	146	60	2	3	225	26	29	.719	19	5	1	14	8	0	0	0	4.03	3.87	4.07
Contreras J.	18	204.7	857	32	32	3.70	154	75	2	9	177	23	17	.742	28	2	2	15	7	0	0	0	4.00	3.61	4.23
Cotts N.	16	60.3	248	69	0	4.03	58	29	5	4	38	1	6	.763	2	1	1	4	0	0	2	13	2.39	1.94	2.98
Hermanson D.	13	57.3	228	57	0	3.65	33	17	4	1	46	4	9	.757	0	0	0	2	4	34	39	5	2.67	2.04	3.74
Vizcaino L.	7	70.0	305	65	0	3.82	43	29	6	2	74	8	10	.704	3	2	0	6	5	0	3	9	3.86	3.73	4.63
Jenks R.	6	39.3	168	32	0	3.86	50	15	3	1	34	3	1	.687	7	0	0	1	1	6	8	3	3.43	2.75	2.71
McCarthy B.	6	67.0	277	12	10	3.95	48	17	0	2	62	13	6	.751	2	0	0	3	2	0	0	0	4.03	4.03	4.98
Marte D.	3	45.3	213	66	0	4.25	54	33	4	3	45	5	4	.661	4	1	1	3	4	4	8	22	4.17	3.77	4.48
Bajenaru J.	-1	4.3	18	4	0	3.83	3	0	0	0	4	2	0	.846	0	0	0	0	0	0	0	0	6.23	6.23	7.66
Sanders D.	-2	2.0	10	2	0	3.90	1	1	0	0	3	1	0	.714	0	0	0	0	0	0	0	0	13.50	13.50	10.04
Walker K.	-3	7.0	35	9	0	3.51	5	5	1	0	10	1	1	.625	0	0	0	0	1	0	1	0	9.00	9.00	5.61
Adkins J.	-3	8.3	42	5	0	3.71	1	4	2	1	13	0	1	.639	0	0	0	0	1	0	0	0	8.64	8.64	4.60
Takatsu S.	-4	28.7	130	31	0	4.22	32	16	1	0	30	9	0	.712	2	1	0	1	2	8	9	3	5.97	5.97	6.57
Hernandez O.	-8	128.3	568	24	22	3.96	91	50	1	12	137	18	13	.700	19	2	1	9	9	1	1	1	5.40	5.12	4.90

Win Shares Stats

Player	WS	Bat	Pitch	Field	ExpWS	WSP	WSAB	CWS	NetWSValue
Konerko, P	24	21.5	0.0	2.9	17	.712	12	113	$4,692,444
Buehrle, M	23	-0.1	23.2	0.0	13	.922	16	94	$5,905,637
Garland, J	21	0.3	21.1	0.0	12	.914	14	60	$7,860,074
Rowand, A	19	11.4	0.0	7.6	17	.558	7	58	$3,703,511
Contreras, J	18	-0.1	18.2	0.0	11	.834	12	30	$4,201,445
Garcia, F	18	-0.6	18.6	0.0	12	.740	11	95	$3,800,523
Dye, J	18	14.2	0.0	3.9	15	.589	7	109	$3,582,419
Iguchi, T	17	11.2	0.0	5.9	15	.562	6	17	$3,893,533
Uribe, J	17	7.4	0.0	9.3	15	.563	6	61	$2,939,432
Crede, J	14	9.8	0.0	4.7	13	.560	5	42	$4,216,685
Politte, C	12	0.3	11.7	0.0	5	1.206	9	33	$5,976,400
Hermanson, D	12	0.0	11.6	0.0	7	.880	7	74	$4,515,874
Everett, C	12	11.0	0.0	0.6	11	.525	4	147	$826,362
Podsednik, S	12	8.2	0.0	4.2	15	.419	2	50	$1,227,755
Pierzynski, A	11	6.8	0.0	4.6	13	.428	2	82	$480,660
Cotts, N	9	0.0	9.3	0.0	4	1.098	6	12	$4,992,362
Vizcaino, L	7	0.0	6.6	0.0	5	.684	3	24	$1,422,209
McCarthy, B	5	-0.1	5.1	0.0	4	.700	3	5	$2,253,621
Hernandez, O	5	-0.1	5.6	0.0	7	.399	1	68	($850,990)
Marte, D	4	0.0	3.7	0.0	4	.446	1	37	($421,426)
Ozuna, P	4	1.2	0.0	2.4	6	.314	-0	6	($330,000)
Harris, W	3	1.9	0.0	1.6	4	.473	1	16	$650,348
Widger, C	2	0.3	0.0	1.4	4	.203	-1	33	($500,000)
Perez, T	1	-0.4	0.0	1.3	5	.093	-3	32	($1,000,000)

Fielding and Baserunning Stats

Name	POS	Inn	SBA/G	CS%	ERA	WP+PB/G	PO	A	TE	FE
Pierzynski	C	1117.7	0.79	19%	3.74	0.419	805	46	1	0
Widger	C	344.0	0.68	8%	3.30	0.549	252	12	3	1
Casanova	C	14.0	0.00	0%	1.29	0.643	9	0	0	0

Name	POS	Inn	PO	A	TE	FE	FPct	RF	DPS	DPT
P Konerko	1B	1272.0	1322	79	1	4	.996	9.91	8	3
R Gload	1B	89.0	71	4	0	1	.987	7.58	0	1
G Blum	1B	89.0	92	6	0	0	1.000	9.91	0	0
T Perez	1B	11.0	13	1	0	1	.933	11.45	0	0
J Dye	1B	9.0	7	1	0	0	1.000	8.00	0	0
P Ozuna	1B	3.0	2	1	0	0	1.000	9.00	0	0
J Burke	1B	1.0	0	0	0	0	0.000	0.00	0	0
C Widger	1B	1.0	0	0	0	0	0.000	0.00	0	0
T Iguchi	2B	1171.0	234	375	5	9	.978	4.68	35	51
W Harris	2B	248.3	58	78	1	1	.986	4.93	12	8
P Ozuna	2B	29.0	6	6	0	1	.923	3.72	0	0
G Blum	2B	18.0	3	4	0	0	1.000	3.50	0	1
P Lopez	2B	9.0	3	5	0	0	1.000	8.00	2	1
J Uribe	SS	1293.0	250	422	7	9	.977	4.68	49	47
P Ozuna	SS	99.0	19	35	0	1	.964	4.91	6	6
G Blum	SS	41.0	6	10	0	0	1.000	3.51	1	0
W Harris	SS	25.0	1	9	0	0	1.000	3.60	1	0
P Lopez	SS	9.0	0	2	0	0	1.000	2.00	0	0
J Crede	SS	8.0	1	3	0	0	1.000	4.50	1	1
J Dye	SS	0.3	0	0	0	0	0.000	0.00	0	0
J Crede	3B	1120.0	95	243	6	4	.971	2.72	27	1
P Ozuna	3B	261.0	29	67	1	4	.941	3.31	5	0
G Blum	3B	86.0	4	29	0	3	.917	3.45	1	1
C Widger	3B	8.3	1	1	0	0	1.000	2.16	0	0
S Podsednik	LF	1061.0	260	3	0	3	.989	2.23	2	0
T Perez	LF	175.7	33	3	0	1	.973	1.84	0	0
C Everett	LF	117.3	16	1	0	0	1.000	1.30	2	0
P Ozuna	LF	65.0	10	0	0	0	1.000	1.38	0	0
B Anderson	LF	42.0	10	1	0	0	1.000	2.36	2	0
R Gload	LF	14.0	3	0	0	0	1.000	1.93	0	0

Name	POS	Inn	PO	A	TE	FE	FPct	RF	DPS	DPT
A Rowand	CF	1367.0	388	3	1	2	.992	2.57	2	0
S Podsednik	CF	55.0	14	0	0	0	1.000	2.29	0	0
B Anderson	CF	36.0	7	0	0	0	1.000	1.75	0	0
T Perez	CF	17.0	7	0	0	0	1.000	3.71	0	0
J Dye	RF	1235.0	259	9	2	6	.971	1.95	4	0
T Perez	RF	152.3	35	2	0	2	.949	2.19	2	0
C Everett	RF	70.0	18	0	0	0	1.000	2.31	0	0
B Anderson	RF	7.0	2	0	0	0	1.000	2.57	0	0
J Borchard	RF	7.0	3	0	0	0	1.000	3.86	0	0
P Ozuna	RF	2.0	0	0	0	0	0.000	0.00	0	0
R Gload	RF	2.0	2	0	0	0	1.000	9.00	0	0

Incremental Baserunning Runs		
Name	IR	IRP
Scott Podsednik	3.19	145
Tadahito Iguchi	2.26	148
Aaron Rowand	1.91	128
Joe Crede	1.57	137
Pablo Ozuna	1.52	179
Juan Uribe	1.25	120
Willie Harris	0.20	108
Timo Perez	0.12	120
Orlando Hernandez	-0.03	0
Ross Gload	-0.14	0
Geoff Blum	-0.30	25
Joe Borchard	-0.45	0
Frank Thomas	-0.73	0
Carl Everett	-1.03	84
AJ Pierzynski	-1.08	76
Jermaine Dye	-1.27	75
Chris Widger	-1.79	1
Paul Konerko	-2.53	70

Cincinnati Reds

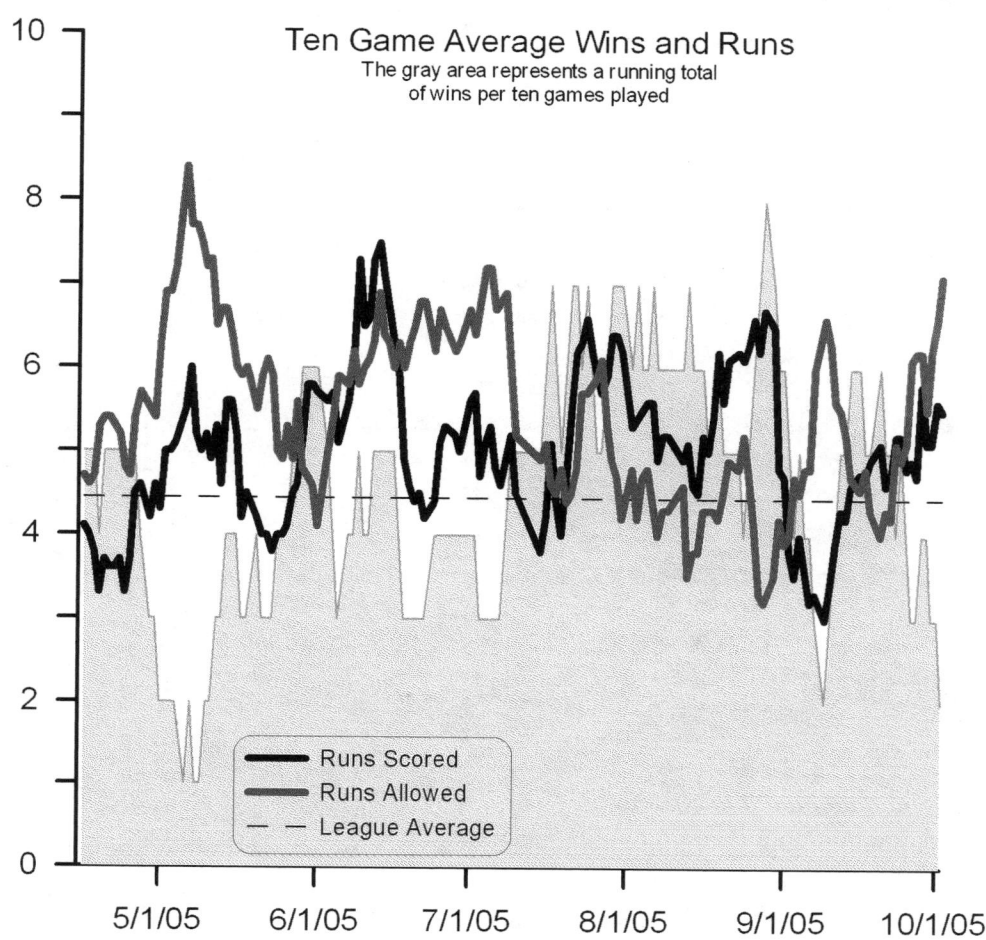

Ten Game Average Wins and Runs
The gray area represents a running total
of wins per ten games played

— Runs Scored
— Runs Allowed
– – League Average

*5/4: Lopez replaces
Aurilia as regular SS*

*6/24: Encarnacion
debuts at 3B*

*9/4: Griffey's last game
after spraining left foot*

*6/21: Manager Miley fired,
replaced by Jerry Narron
Were 27-43, go 46-46
rest of season*

*9/13: Milton yields 40th
HR for 2nd straight season*

Team Batting and Pitching/Fielding Stats by Month						
	April	May	June	July	Aug	Spt/Oct
Wins	10	11	9	17	15	11
Losses	13	18	16	11	12	19
OBP	.341	.328	.344	.341	.341	.338
SLG	.417	.432	.477	.501	.437	.412
FIP	5.35	4.91	5.58	4.51	4.25	4.87
DER	.703	.669	.678	.709	.705	.685

Batting Stats

Player	RC	Runs	RBI	PA	Outs	P/PA	H	2B	3B	HR	TB	K	BB	IBB	HBP	SH	SF	SB	CS	GDP	BA	OBP	SLG	GPA
Dunn A.	109	107	101	671	417	4.24	134	35	2	40	293	168	114	14	12	0	2	4	2	6	.247	.387	.540	.309
Lopez F.	93	97	85	648	426	3.96	169	34	5	23	282	111	57	2	1	3	7	15	7	8	.291	.352	.486	.280
Griffey Jr.	87	85	92	555	353	3.79	148	30	0	35	283	93	54	3	3	0	7	0	1	9	.301	.369	.576	.310
Casey S.	71	75	58	587	391	3.53	165	32	0	9	224	48	48	3	5	0	5	2	0	27	.312	.371	.423	.273
Aurilia R.	68	61	68	468	314	3.74	120	23	2	14	189	67	37	2	1	1	3	2	0	8	.282	.338	.444	.263
LaRue J.	61	38	60	422	275	3.80	94	27	0	14	163	101	41	7	13	5	2	0	0	8	.260	.355	.452	.273
Freel R.	54	69	21	432	288	4.07	100	19	3	4	137	59	51	0	8	3	0	36	10	9	.271	.371	.371	.260
Kearns A.	54	62	67	448	302	3.99	93	26	1	18	175	107	48	2	8	0	5	0	0	8	.240	.333	.452	.263
Randa J.	49	44	48	368	242	3.71	96	26	1	13	163	52	33	2	2	0	1	0	0	6	.289	.356	.491	.283
Valentin J.	40	36	50	254	164	3.76	62	11	0	14	115	37	30	3	0	0	3	0	0	5	.281	.362	.520	.293
Pena W.	39	42	51	335	240	3.77	79	17	0	19	153	116	20	0	3	0	1	2	1	7	.254	.304	.492	.260
Encarnacion	24	25	31	234	170	3.99	49	16	0	9	92	60	20	2	3	0	0	3	0	8	.232	.308	.436	.247
Cruz J.	17	12	18	145	97	3.97	30	10	0	4	52	46	16	1	1	0	1	0	0	0	.236	.324	.409	.248
Jimenez D.	9	14	5	119	83	3.92	24	7	0	0	31	23	14	0	0	0	0	2	1	1	.229	.319	.295	.218
Olmedo R.	6	10	4	88	61	3.68	17	4	1	1	26	22	6	0	1	3	1	4	0	1	.221	.282	.338	.211
Romano J.	5	3	3	34	22	4.03	8	2	0	1	13	9	3	0	1	0	0	0	0	0	.267	.353	.433	.267
Hudson L.	3	7	3	29	17	3.52	8	2	0	0	10	9	2	0	0	2	0	0	0	0	.320	.370	.400	.267
Denorfia C.	3	8	2	44	29	3.84	10	3	0	1	16	9	6	0	0	0	0	1	0	1	.263	.364	.421	.269
Milton E.	2	7	4	64	48	3.56	8	1	0	2	15	25	3	0	0	5	0	0	0	0	.143	.186	.268	.151
Holbert A.	2	3	2	32	22	3.47	6	3	0	0	9	8	3	1	0	1	1	1	0	1	.222	.290	.333	.214
Lopez L.	2	0	2	28	22	4.00	6	3	0	0	9	6	1	0	0	0	0	0	0	1	.222	.250	.333	.196
Keisler R.	1	3	2	15	11	3.67	4	2	0	1	9	4	0	0	0	0	0	0	0	0	.267	.267	.600	.270
Kelly K.	1	2	2	9	7	3.44	3	0	0	0	3	3	0	0	0	0	0	0	1	0	.333	.333	.333	.233
Belisle M.	1	0	0	8	6	4.00	1	0	0	0	1	3	0	0	0	1	0	0	0	0	.143	.143	.143	.100
Wilson P.	0	1	1	19	14	4.11	3	0	0	0	3	11	0	0	0	2	0	0	0	0	.176	.176	.176	.124
Wagner R.	-0	1	0	2	1	3.50	0	0	0	0	0	1	0	0	0	1	0	0	0	0	.000	.000	.000	.000
Shackelford	-0	0	0	1	1	4.00	0	0	0	0	0	1	0	0	0	0	0	0	0	0	.000	.000	.000	.000
Stone R.	-0	0	0	2	2	2.50	0	0	0	0	0	1	0	0	0	0	0	0	0	0	.000	.000	.000	.000
Machado A.	-0	0	0	2	2	4.50	0	0	0	0	0	1	0	0	0	0	0	0	0	0	.000	.000	.000	.000
Sardinha D.	-0	0	0	3	3	3.00	0	0	0	0	0	1	0	0	0	0	0	0	0	0	.000	.000	.000	.000
Perez M.	-0	0	0	3	3	5.00	0	0	0	0	0	1	0	0	0	0	0	0	0	0	.000	.000	.000	.000
Coffey T.	-0	0	0	3	3	4.67	0	0	0	0	0	3	0	0	0	0	0	0	0	0	.000	.000	.000	.000
Bergolla W.	-1	3	1	38	34	3.26	5	0	0	0	5	10	0	0	0	0	0	0	0	1	.132	.132	.132	.092
Ramirez E.	-1	0	0	8	9	3.88	0	0	0	0	0	3	0	0	0	0	0	0	0	1	.000	.000	.000	.000
Claussen B.	-2	3	0	64	50	3.86	5	0	0	0	5	22	3	0	0	6	0	0	0	0	.091	.138	.091	.085
Ortiz R.	-3	1	0	61	50	3.23	4	2	0	0	6	23	1	0	0	6	0	0	0	0	.074	.091	.111	.069
Harang A.	-5	1	3	78	72	3.50	2	0	0	0	2	39	0	0	0	4	0	0	0	0	.027	.027	.027	.019

Pitching Stats

Player	PR	IP	BFP	G	GS	P/PA	K	BB	IBB	HBP	H	HR	DP	DER	SB	CS	PO	W	L	Sv	Op	Hld	RA	ERA	FIP
Harang A.	19	211.7	887	32	32	3.85	163	51	3	8	217	22	19	.697	9	9	0	11	13	0	0	0	3.95	3.83	3.63
Shackelford	6	29.7	119	37	0	3.81	17	9	1	6	21	2	3	.776	1	1	2	1	0	0	0	3	2.73	2.43	4.23
Mercker K.	6	61.7	265	78	0	3.55	45	19	4	3	64	8	8	.705	2	1	1	3	1	4	7	20	3.94	3.65	4.28
Weathers D.	5	77.7	331	73	0	3.71	61	29	2	2	71	7	3	.724	4	3	0	7	4	15	19	8	4.17	3.94	3.78
Hancock J.	3	14.0	54	11	0	3.13	5	1	0	0	11	1	1	.787	0	0	1	1	0	0	0	0	2.57	1.93	3.41
Standridge J	2	31.0	140	32	0	3.46	17	16	7	1	38	3	8	.660	1	0	0	2	2	0	0	5	4.06	4.06	4.79
Claussen B.	-0	166.7	731	29	29	3.89	121	57	5	7	178	24	13	.705	12	1	1	10	11	0	0	0	4.81	4.21	4.55
Simpson A.	-1	6.7	28	9	0	4.46	6	5	0	1	3	1	1	.867	0	0	0	0	1	0	1	0	6.75	6.75	5.83
Coffey T.	-2	58.0	265	57	0	3.50	26	11	2	5	84	5	6	.638	3	2	0	4	1	1	2	3	5.12	4.50	4.03
Belisle M.	-3	85.7	382	60	5	3.58	59	26	6	6	101	11	9	.679	7	2	0	4	8	1	4	8	5.15	4.41	4.39
Weber B.	-4	12.3	66	10	0	3.62	8	9	1	1	20	0	1	.583	3	0	0	0	0	0	0	0	8.03	8.03	4.12
Booker C.	-7	2.0	15	3	0	4.87	2	4	0	0	6	2	0	.429	1	0	0	0	0	0	0	0	36.00	31.50	19.98
Valentine J.	-7	14.3	76	16	0	4.12	9	11	0	2	18	4	0	.720	2	0	0	0	1	0	1	2	9.42	8.16	8.08
Stone R.	-7	30.7	143	23	0	3.31	15	7	2	2	48	8	5	.640	0	0	0	0	0	0	0	2	7.04	6.75	6.28
Graves D.	-8	18.3	99	20	0	3.38	8	12	3	0	30	4	2	.653	0	0	0	1	1	10	12	0	8.84	7.36	6.91
Wagner R.	-8	45.7	210	42	0	3.65	39	17	1	4	56	4	6	.644	1	1	0	3	2	0	1	12	6.50	6.11	3.79
Ramirez E.	-10	22.3	110	6	4	3.39	9	10	2	2	33	5	3	.667	1	0	0	0	3	0	0	0	8.87	8.46	6.70
Keisler R.	-14	56.0	262	24	4	3.64	43	28	2	1	64	10	5	.700	2	0	0	2	1	0	0	0	7.23	6.27	5.32
Wilson P.	-16	46.3	224	9	9	3.40	30	17	1	4	68	10	5	.644	0	0	0	1	5	0	0	0	7.96	7.77	5.85
Hudson L.	-16	84.7	380	19	16	3.79	53	50	2	11	83	14	14	.726	10	6	1	6	9	0	0	0	6.59	6.38	6.04
Ortiz R.	-18	171.3	755	30	30	3.49	96	51	1	7	206	34	18	.697	6	6	3	9	11	0	0	0	5.78	5.36	5.46
Milton E.	-40	186.3	855	34	34	3.70	123	52	2	7	237	40	3	.689	11	3	0	8	15	0	0	0	6.81	6.47	5.40

Win Shares Stats

Player	WS	Bat	Pitch	Field	ExpWS	WSP	WSAB	CWS	NetWSValue
Dunn, A	28	26.5	0.0	1.8	18	.794	16	103	$7,687,208
Griffey Jr, K	22	20.1	0.0	1.9	15	.756	12	361	$1,978,751
Lopez, F	22	19.9	0.0	2.6	17	.663	11	45	$8,298,856
LaRue, J	18	13.3	0.0	4.4	11	.773	10	68	$4,643,560
Aurilia, R	16	14.3	0.0	2.1	12	.662	8	144	$5,925,171
Casey, S	14	12.3	0.0	1.7	15	.451	3	135	($2,056,779)
Valentin, J	12	8.9	0.0	2.7	7	.851	7	25	$5,263,965
Randa, J	12	10.1	0.0	1.6	10	.599	5	128	$2,904,333
Freel, R	12	10.0	0.0	2.3	11	.548	4	34	$3,419,957
Kearns, A	12	10.2	0.0	1.7	12	.502	4	45	$2,160,716
Harang, A	10	-3.9	13.9	0.0	10	.484	4	20	$2,868,009
Pena, W	8	6.8	0.0	1.0	9	.435	2	24	$1,074,079
Weathers, D	7	0.0	7.3	0.0	6	.652	3	61	$2,099,069
Claussen, B	6	-2.3	8.6	0.0	8	.393	1	6	$1,178,543
Mercker, K	5	0.0	5.1	0.0	4	.611	2	82	$1,155,745
Encarnacio, E	5	3.4	0.0	1.2	6	.368	0	5	$180,188
Belisle, M	4	0.1	3.6	0.0	5	.398	0	4	$355,182
Hudson, L	1	0.5	0.3	0.0	4	.088	-2	6	($318,000)
Ortiz, R	1	-2.7	4.2	0.0	8	.092	-3	46	($3,550,000)
Milton, E	-1	-0.9	-1.0	0.0	9	-.102	-7	62	($5,333,333)

Fielding and Baserunning Stats

Name	POS	Inn	SBA/G	CS%	ERA	WP+PB/G	PO	A	TE	FE
LaRue	C	914.7	0.72	30%	5.30	0.384	646	52	4	1
Valentin	C	508.3	0.60	26%	4.92	0.407	341	28	2	1
Sardinha	C	8.0	0.00	0%	7.88	0.000	7	0	0	0
Perez	C	2.0	0.00	0%	0.00	0.000	2	0	0	0

Name	POS	Inn	PO	A	TE	FE	FPct	RF	DPS	DPT
S Casey	1B	1138.0	1153	55	0	2	.998	9.55	3	1
A Dunn	1B	251.3	244	11	0	3	.985	9.13	3	0
J Cruz	1B	20.0	15	1	0	0	1.000	7.20	1	0
J Valentin	1B	18.0	21	0	0	0	1.000	10.50	0	0
A Holbert	1B	5.0	4	0	0	0	1.000	7.20	0	0
R Aurilia	2B	547.3	127	176	2	4	.981	4.98	14	25
R Freel	2B	382.7	91	127	2	4	.973	5.13	11	14
D Jimenez	2B	211.7	56	63	1	1	.983	5.06	5	11
R Olmedo	2B	137.3	38	40	0	2	.975	5.11	1	8
W Bergolla	2B	62.0	11	29	0	0	1.000	5.81	3	3
F Lopez	2B	48.0	15	11	0	0	1.000	4.88	1	3
A Holbert	2B	28.0	11	8	1	0	.950	6.11	2	1
L Lopez	2B	16.0	3	5	0	0	1.000	4.50	0	0
F Lopez	SS	1175.0	188	357	11	6	.970	4.17	44	25
R Aurilia	SS	237.7	29	86	1	2	.975	4.35	7	7
R Olmedo	SS	19.0	4	6	0	0	1.000	4.74	1	1
W Bergolla	SS	1.0	0	1	0	0	1.000	9.00	0	0
J Randa	3B	716.7	76	148	2	4	.974	2.81	12	0
E Encarnacio	3B	478.0	54	116	8	2	.944	3.20	10	0
R Aurilia	3B	129.3	12	33	0	1	.978	3.13	3	0
R Freel	3B	69.0	5	25	2	0	.938	3.91	1	0
L Lopez	3B	29.0	5	4	0	1	.900	2.79	0	0
A Holbert	3B	10.0	0	5	0	0	1.000	4.50	0	0
F Lopez	3B	1.0	0	1	0	0	1.000	9.00	0	0
A Dunn	LF	1090.0	246	6	0	5	.981	2.08	0	0
R Freel	LF	164.3	45	6	0	0	1.000	2.79	0	0
W Pena	LF	73.7	12	0	0	2	.857	1.47	0	0
J Cruz	LF	48.0	5	1	0	0	1.000	1.13	2	0
J Romano	LF	39.0	5	1	0	0	1.000	1.38	0	0
C Denorfia	LF	9.3	3	0	0	0	1.000	2.89	0	0
K Kelly	LF	8.0	2	0	0	0	1.000	2.25	0	0
K Griffey Jr	CF	1065.0	285	6	2	1	.990	2.46	2	0
W Pena	CF	192.7	57	0	0	1	.983	2.66	0	0
R Freel	CF	101.3	41	1	0	0	1.000	3.73	0	0
C Denorfia	CF	43.0	13	0	1	0	.929	2.72	0	0
J Romano	CF	26.0	10	0	1	0	.909	3.46	0	0
K Kelly	CF	2.3	2	0	0	0	1.000	7.71	0	0
A Kearns	CF	2.0	1	0	0	0	1.000	4.50	0	0

Name	POS	Inn	PO	A	TE	FE	FPct	RF	DPS	DPT
A Kearns	RF	890.0	236	8	1	1	.992	2.47	6	0
W Pena	RF	401.7	92	2	0	1	.989	2.11	0	0
R Freel	RF	69.7	23	0	0	0	1.000	2.97	0	0
J Cruz	RF	48.3	7	0	0	0	1.000	1.30	0	0
C Denorfia	RF	16.3	9	0	0	0	1.000	4.96	0	0
K Kelly	RF	3.0	0	0	0	0	0.000	0.00	0	0
J Romano	RF	3.0	0	0	0	0	0.000	0.00	0	0
J LaRue	RF	1.0	1	0	0	0	1.000	9.00	0	0

Incremental Baserunning Runs		
Name	IR	IRP
Ryan Freel	2.63	186
Felipe Lopez	1.59	124
Austin Kearns	1.20	142
Ray Olmedo	0.72	150
William Bergolla	0.35	201
Jacob Cruz	0.29	153
Kenny Kelly	0.27	143
Wily Mo Pena	0.16	119
Javier Valentin	0.14	106
Chris Denorfia	0.10	115
Aaron Holbert	0.00	101
Adam Dunn	0.00	100
Jason LaRue	-0.00	100
Ramon Ortiz	-0.01	0
Jason Romano	-0.01	0
Eric Milton	-0.02	0
Randy Keisler	-0.03	0
Brandon Claussen	-0.04	0
Ryan Wagner	-0.06	0
Paul Wilson	-0.10	0
D'Angelo Jimenez	-0.16	93
Joe Randa	-0.48	85
Luke Hudson	-0.89	0
Sean Casey	-0.91	78
Ken Griffey	-1.30	81
Rich Aurilia	-1.66	67
Edwin Encarnacion	-1.66	1

Cleveland Indians

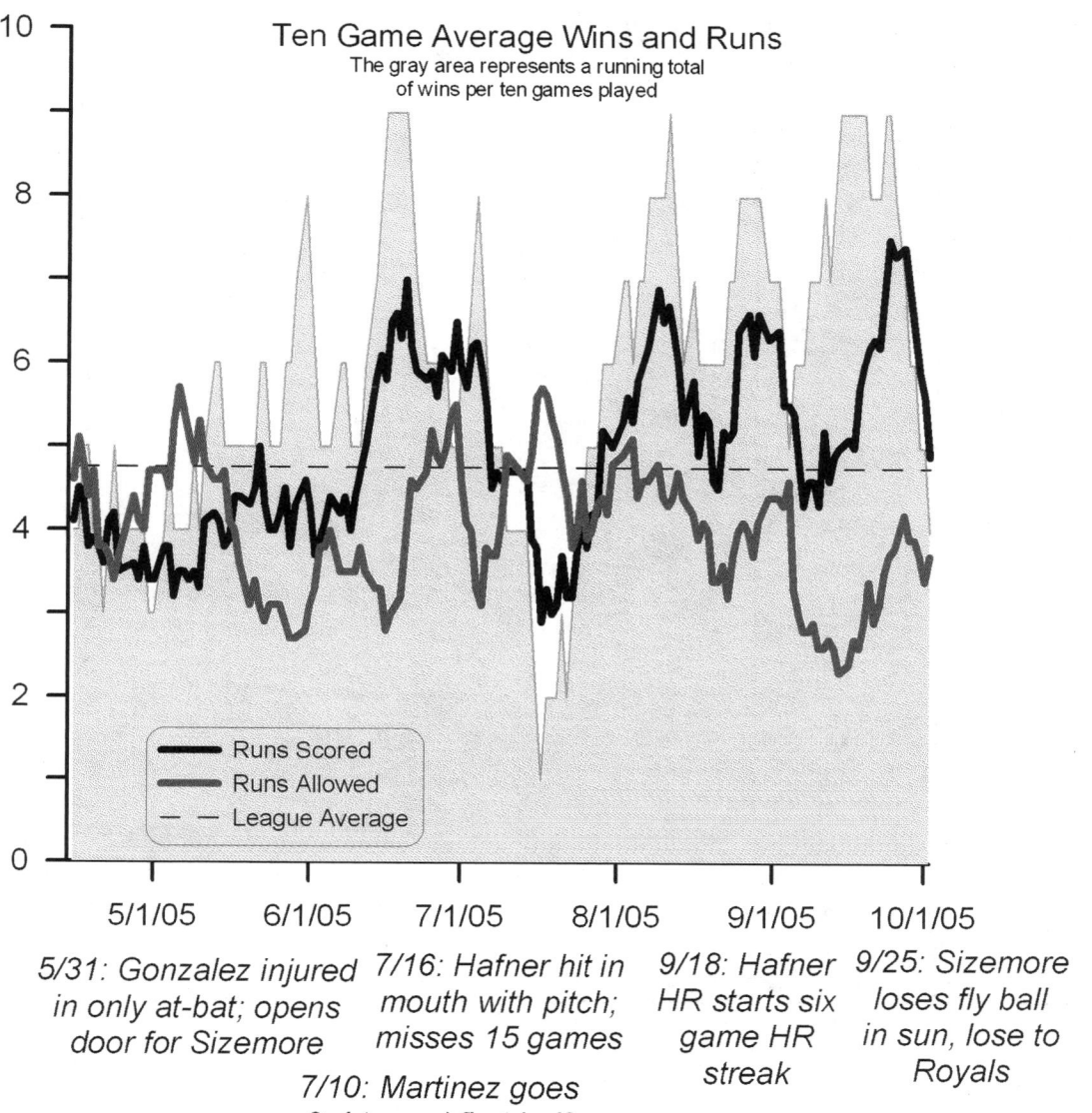

Ten Game Average Wins and Runs
The gray area represents a running total
of wins per ten games played

— Runs Scored
— Runs Allowed
– – League Average

5/31: Gonzalez injured in only at-bat; opens door for Sizemore

7/16: Hafner hit in mouth with pitch; misses 15 games

7/10: Martinez goes 0-4 to end first half at .236; hits .380 in second half

9/18: Hafner HR starts six game HR streak

9/25: Sizemore loses fly ball in sun, lose to Royals

9/28: Lose 1-0 to TB for 3rd straight loss

Team Batting and Pitching/Fielding Stats by Month						
	April	May	June	July	Aug	Spt/Oct
Wins	9	16	17	13	19	19
Losses	14	11	10	16	8	10
OBP	.293	.326	.345	.336	.349	.349
SLG	.376	.423	.477	.433	.493	.498
FIP	3.64	4.12	4.13	4.39	4.14	3.60
DER	.731	.726	.712	.723	.730	.730

Batting Stats

Player	RC	Runs	RBI	PA	Outs	P/PA	H	2B	3B	HR	TB	K	BB	IBB	HBP	SH	SF	SB	CS	GDP	BA	OBP	SLG	GPA
Hafner T.	122	94	108	578	347	4.17	148	42	0	33	289	123	79	7	9	0	4	0	0	9	.305	.408	.595	.332
Sizemore G.	107	111	81	706	482	3.81	185	37	11	22	310	132	52	1	7	5	2	22	10	17	.289	.348	.484	.278
Crisp C.	97	86	69	656	429	3.48	178	42	4	16	276	81	44	1	0	13	5	15	6	7	.300	.345	.465	.272
Martinez V.	96	73	80	622	397	3.79	167	33	0	20	260	78	63	9	5	0	7	0	1	16	.305	.378	.475	.289
Peralta J.	92	82	78	570	371	4.00	147	35	4	24	262	128	58	3	3	1	4	0	2	12	.292	.366	.520	.294
Belliard R.	75	71	78	587	403	3.52	152	36	1	17	241	72	35	0	1	8	7	2	2	17	.284	.325	.450	.259
Broussard B.	64	59	68	505	353	3.67	119	30	5	19	216	98	32	5	4	0	3	2	2	4	.255	.307	.464	.254
Blake C.	56	72	58	583	411	4.28	126	32	1	23	229	116	43	3	10	2	5	4	5	9	.241	.308	.438	.248
Boone A.	55	61	60	565	406	3.64	124	19	1	16	193	92	35	3	9	4	6	9	3	16	.243	.299	.378	.229
Hernandez J.	21	28	31	256	194	3.71	54	7	0	6	79	60	14	0	2	3	3	1	3	11	.231	.277	.338	.209
Gerut J.	18	12	12	157	104	3.98	38	9	1	1	52	14	18	1	0	0	1	1	1	3	.275	.357	.377	.255
Cora A.	10	11	8	157	119	3.80	30	5	2	1	42	18	5	0	4	1	1	6	0	3	.205	.250	.288	.184
Bard J.	8	6	9	95	69	3.48	16	4	0	1	23	11	9	0	0	1	2	0	0	2	.193	.266	.277	.189
Liefer J.	4	5	8	57	46	3.46	11	2	0	1	16	15	1	0	0	0	0	0	0	1	.196	.211	.286	.166
Ludwick R.	3	8	5	48	34	4.15	9	0	0	4	21	13	7	0	0	0	0	0	1	1	.220	.333	.512	.278
Sabathia C.	3	1	4	6	4	3.50	2	1	0	1	6	1	0	0	0	0	0	0	0	0	.333	.333	1.000	.400
Dubois J.	2	6	2	50	35	4.46	10	0	0	2	16	25	5	0	0	0	0	0	0	0	.222	.300	.356	.224
Vazquez R.	2	1	1	26	18	4.35	6	3	0	0	9	3	2	0	0	0	0	0	0	0	.250	.308	.375	.232
Gutierrez F.	0	2	0	2	1	4.00	0	0	0	0	0	0	1	0	0	0	0	0	0	0	.000	.500	.000	.225
Howry B.	-0	0	0	1	1	3.00	0	0	0	0	0	0	0	0	0	0	0	0	0	0	.000	.000	.000	.000
Gonzalez J.	-0	0	0	1	1	3.00	0	0	0	0	0	0	0	0	0	0	0	0	0	0	.000	.000	.000	.000
Garko R.	-0	0	0	1	1	4.00	0	0	0	0	0	1	0	0	0	0	0	0	0	0	.000	.000	.000	.000
Davis J.	-0	0	0	3	2	3.33	0	0	0	0	0	2	0	0	0	1	0	0	0	0	.000	.000	.000	.000
Millwood K.	-0	0	0	2	2	4.00	0	0	0	0	0	1	0	0	0	0	0	0	0	0	.000	.000	.000	.000
Elarton S.	-0	0	0	2	2	3.50	0	0	0	0	0	1	0	0	0	0	0	0	0	0	.000	.000	.000	.000
Westbrook J.	-0	0	0	2	2	6.00	0	0	0	0	0	2	0	0	0	0	0	0	0	0	.000	.000	.000	.000
Lee C.	-1	0	0	8	8	3.25	0	0	0	0	0	2	0	0	0	0	0	0	0	0	.000	.000	.000	.000
Phillips B.	-1	1	0	9	9	4.00	0	0	0	0	0	4	0	0	0	0	0	0	0	0	.000	.000	.000	.000

Pitching Stats

Player	PR	IP	BFP	G	GS	P/PA	K	BB	IBB	HBP	H	HR	DP	DER	SB	CS	PO	W	L	Sv	Op	Hld	RA	ERA	FIP
Millwood K.	26	192.0	799	30	30	3.71	146	52	0	4	182	20	21	.719	33	6	0	9	11	0	0	0	3.38	2.86	3.75
Wickman B.	15	62.0	257	64	0	3.65	41	21	3	1	57	9	11	.741	11	0	0	0	4	45	50	0	2.47	2.47	4.67
Howry B.	14	73.0	277	79	0	4.01	48	16	1	0	49	4	7	.785	4	1	1	7	4	3	5	29	2.84	2.47	3.10
Betancourt R	12	67.7	272	54	0	3.80	73	17	2	0	57	5	3	.706	3	4	0	4	3	1	3	10	3.06	2.79	2.60
Lee C.	11	202.0	838	32	32	3.70	143	52	1	0	194	22	16	.723	7	4	0	18	5	0	0	0	4.05	3.79	3.82
Miller M.	9	29.7	118	23	0	3.52	23	10	3	3	22	1	5	.741	4	0	0	1	0	1	2	4	1.82	1.82	3.25
Rhodes A.	9	43.3	175	47	0	3.98	43	12	2	1	33	2	4	.735	0	0	0	3	1	0	3	16	2.70	2.08	2.56
Riske D.	9	72.7	288	58	0	3.61	48	15	0	4	55	11	7	.790	2	1	0	3	4	1	1	0	3.47	3.10	4.47
Cabrera F.	9	30.7	124	15	0	3.48	29	11	1	0	24	1	4	.723	3	0	0	2	1	0	0	1	2.05	1.47	2.65
Sabathia C.	7	196.7	823	31	31	3.83	161	62	1	7	185	19	21	.711	11	7	2	15	10	0	0	0	4.21	4.03	3.71
Tadano K.	1	4.0	16	1	0	3.25	1	0	0	0	4	0	0	.733	1	0	0	0	0	0	0	0	2.25	2.25	2.54
Sauerbeck S.	-0	35.7	157	58	0	3.66	35	16	2	4	35	4	5	.684	0	1	1	1	0	0	2	14	4.54	4.04	4.22
Guthrie J.	-1	6.0	29	1	0	2.83	3	2	0	0	9	2	1	.682	0	0	0	0	0	0	0	0	6.00	6.00	7.38
Tallet B.	-2	4.7	24	2	0	3.50	2	3	0	1	6	2	0	.750	0	0	0	0	0	0	0	0	7.71	7.71	10.33
Davis J.	-2	40.3	182	11	4	3.75	32	20	0	3	44	4	7	.675	7	1	0	4	2	0	0	0	4.91	4.69	4.46
Elarton S.	-9	181.7	774	31	31	3.69	103	48	1	6	189	32	17	.732	4	4	1	11	9	0	0	0	4.95	4.61	5.09
Westbrook J.	-16	210.7	895	34	34	3.59	119	56	3	7	218	19	27	.713	13	4	2	15	15	0	0	0	5.17	4.49	3.98

Win Shares Stats

Player	WS	Bat	Pitch	Field	ExpWS	WSP	WSAB	CWS	NetWSValue
Hafner, T	27	26.8	0.0	0.0	11	1.190	19	56	$14,753,071
Peralta, J	25	17.0	0.0	8.1	15	.813	14	29	$11,274,826
Sizemore, G	25	18.2	0.0	6.4	19	.663	12	30	$9,182,636
Martinez, V	22	16.6	0.0	5.8	16	.679	11	47	$8,149,267
Crisp, C	21	16.3	0.0	4.4	17	.600	9	45	$6,768,734
Belliard, R	17	10.5	0.0	6.7	16	.544	6	92	$2,383,784
Millwood, K	15	-0.1	15.3	0.0	10	.752	9	100	$3,197,811
Lee, C	14	-0.5	14.5	0.0	11	.645	7	25	$5,848,328
Sabathia, C	13	0.8	12.1	0.0	10	.618	7	63	($288,221)
Broussard, B	11	9.1	0.0	1.6	14	.395	1	36	$922,760
Howry, B	10	-0.0	9.7	0.0	6	.836	6	49	$3,782,125
Blake, C	9	5.2	0.0	4.0	16	.291	-2	39	($2,250,000)
Boone, A	9	4.3	0.0	4.5	15	.286	-2	95	($3,000,000)
Wickman, B	8	0.0	7.7	0.0	7	.539	3	105	$655,154
Westbrook, J	8	-0.1	8.6	0.0	11	.385	2	34	($1,413,421)
Betancourt, R	7	0.0	6.7	0.0	5	.715	3	17	$2,677,875
Elarton, S	7	-0.1	7.5	0.0	10	.388	2	36	$1,012,648
Riske, D	5	0.0	5.5	0.0	5	.614	2	27	$627,000
Gerut, J	3	2.4	0.0	0.9	4	.393	0	27	($356,200)
Cora, A	2	-0.6	0.0	2.4	4	.223	-1	59	($1,300,000)
Hernandez, J	2	0.4	0.0	1.5	7	.131	-3	109	($1,800,000)

Fielding Stats

Name	POS	Inn	SBA/G	CS%	ERA	WP+PB/G	PO	A	TE	FE
Martinez	C	1233.0	0.88	21%	3.68	0.190	905	58	4	1
Bard	C	219.7	0.37	22%	3.20	0.246	164	10	1	2

Name	POS	Inn	PO	A	TE	FE	FPct	RF	DPS	DPT
B Broussard	1B	1050.0	1085	57	2	7	.992	9.79	12	1
J Hernandez	1B	339.0	337	27	1	1	.995	9.66	6	0
C Blake	1B	30.0	28	5	0	1	.971	9.90	0	0
J Liefer	1B	26.0	17	2	1	0	.950	6.58	0	0
T Hafner	1B	7.0	6	2	0	0	1.000	10.29	0	0
R Belliard	2B	1243.0	259	413	0	13	.981	4.87	42	49
A Cora	2B	119.0	24	45	0	0	1.000	5.22	7	3
R Vazquez	2B	45.0	17	10	0	0	1.000	5.40	2	3
J Hernandez	2B	27.0	6	9	0	0	1.000	5.00	2	4
B Phillips	2B	18.0	5	4	0	0	1.000	4.50	1	1
J Peralta	SS	1232.0	207	412	10	9	.970	4.52	54	50
A Cora	SS	197.3	28	83	3	0	.974	5.06	4	7
R Vazquez	SS	17.0	2	5	0	0	1.000	3.71	1	0
J Hernandez	SS	3.0	1	1	0	0	1.000	6.00	0	0
B Phillips	SS	3.0	1	2	1	0	.750	9.00	0	1
A Boone	3B	1249.0	81	298	9	9	.955	2.73	22	0
J Hernandez	3B	163.0	16	35	0	0	1.000	2.82	2	0
C Blake	3B	40.0	4	9	1	0	.929	2.93	1	0
C Crisp	LF	1200.0	294	3	0	4	.987	2.23	0	0
J Gerut	LF	143.7	24	1	0	0	1.000	1.57	0	0
R Ludwick	LF	59.0	16	0	0	1	.941	2.44	0	0
J Dubois	LF	26.0	6	0	0	0	1.000	2.08	0	0
J Hernandez	LF	23.0	3	0	0	0	1.000	1.17	0	0
A Cora	LF	1.0	0	0	0	0	0.000	0.00	0	0
G Sizemore	CF	1370.0	373	3	0	3	.992	2.47	1	0
C Crisp	CF	79.7	21	0	1	0	.955	2.37	0	0
F Gutierrez	CF	3.0	1	0	0	0	1.000	3.00	0	0
C Blake	RF	1188.0	287	3	1	7	.973	2.20	0	0
J Gerut	RF	176.0	34	0	0	0	1.000	1.74	0	0
R Ludwick	RF	34.0	6	0	0	0	1.000	1.59	0	0
J Dubois	RF	30.0	8	0	0	0	1.000	2.40	0	0
J Liefer	RF	16.0	4	0	0	0	1.000	2.25	0	0
J Hernandez	RF	8.0	1	0	0	0	1.000	1.13	0	0

Incremental Baserunning Runs		
Name	IR	IRP
Grady Sizemore	3.01	130
Coco Crisp	2.34	125
Casey Blake	1.97	133
Aaron Boone	1.02	113
Jhonny Peralta	0.77	112
Ramon Vazquez	0.28	503
Jose Hernandez	0.22	136
Franklin Gutierrez	0.17	251
Brandon Phillips	-0.02	0
Alex Cora	-0.03	97
Jeff Liefer	-0.03	0
Jason Dubois	-0.05	53
Jody Gerut	-0.22	77
Travis Hafner	-0.26	97
Ryan Ludwick	-0.42	0
Ronnie Belliard	-0.79	83
Josh Bard	-1.14	-327
Victor Martinez	-1.40	76
Ben Broussard	-1.65	64

Colorado Rockies

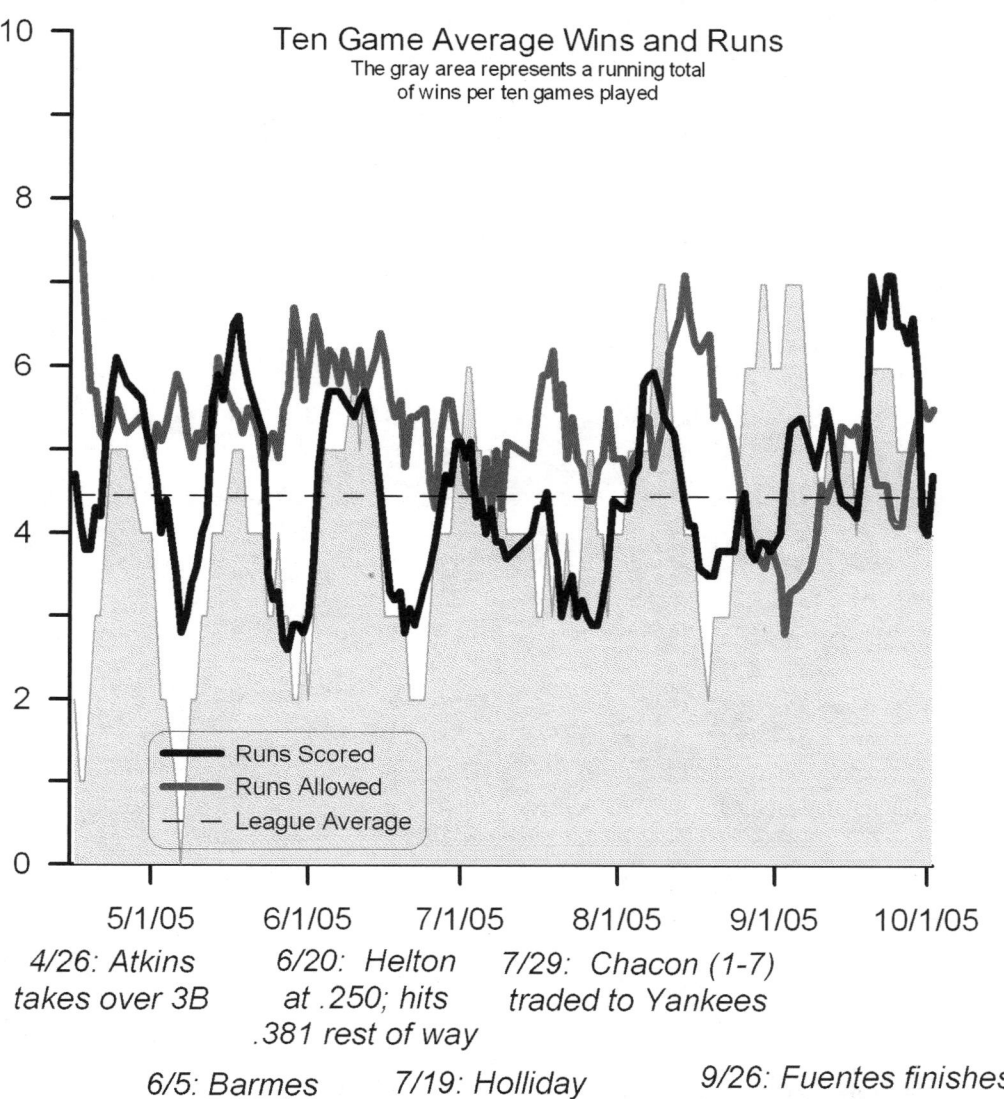

Ten Game Average Wins and Runs
The gray area represents a running total
of wins per ten games played

Runs Scored
Runs Allowed
League Average

4/26: Atkins
takes over 3B

6/20: Helton
at .250; hits
.381 rest of way

7/29: Chacon (1-7)
traded to Yankees

6/5: Barmes
breaks collarbone,
out til Sept

7/19: Holliday
returns after
missing 5 weeks

9/26: Fuentes finishes
with 2.91 ERA, best
ever for Rockie closer

Team Batting and Pitching/Fielding Stats by Month						
	April	May	June	July	Aug	Spt/Oct
Wins	6	9	12	10	15	15
Losses	15	20	15	17	14	14
OBP	.348	.319	.343	.320	.323	.351
SLG	.435	.400	.416	.396	.406	.416
FIP	5.72	5.11	4.15	4.11	4.13	5.20
DER	.688	.696	.654	.675	.702	.699

Batting Stats

Player	RC	Runs	RBI	PA	Outs	P/PA	H	2B	3B	HR	TB	K	BB	IBB	HBP	SH	SF	SB	CS	GDP	BA	OBP	SLG	GPA
Helton T.	100	92	79	626	360	4.13	163	45	2	20	272	80	106	22	9	1	1	3	0	14	.320	.445	.534	.334
Holliday M.	78	68	87	526	346	3.63	147	24	7	19	242	79	36	1	7	0	4	14	3	11	.307	.361	.505	.289
Atkins G.	66	62	89	573	390	3.61	149	31	1	13	221	72	45	1	5	0	4	0	2	18	.287	.347	.426	.263
Sullivan C.	47	64	30	424	276	3.89	111	15	4	4	146	83	28	0	3	10	5	12	3	6	.294	.343	.386	.251
Gonzalez L.	43	51	44	442	297	3.31	118	25	0	9	170	63	20	0	6	8	3	3	4	7	.292	.333	.421	.255
Barmes C.	43	55	46	377	257	3.56	101	19	1	10	152	36	16	1	6	4	1	6	4	4	.289	.330	.434	.257
Hawpe B.	39	38	47	351	232	3.89	80	10	3	9	123	70	43	3	0	0	3	2	2	5	.262	.350	.403	.259
Miles A.	37	37	28	347	241	3.31	91	12	3	2	115	38	8	1	4	10	1	4	2	6	.281	.306	.355	.226
Wilson P.	29	39	47	296	208	3.97	69	15	1	15	131	77	25	0	1	1	2	3	2	8	.258	.322	.491	.268
Mohr D.	23	34	38	293	214	3.81	57	10	3	17	124	94	23	2	2	0	2	1	2	3	.214	.280	.466	.242
Closser J.	21	31	27	272	194	4.01	52	12	2	7	89	48	32	1	1	1	1	1	0	9	.219	.314	.376	.235
Ardoin D.	19	28	22	248	171	3.92	48	10	0	6	76	69	20	2	9	7	2	1	1	8	.229	.320	.362	.234
Piedra J.	17	19	16	124	80	3.44	35	8	1	6	63	15	10	0	1	0	1	2	1	2	.313	.371	.563	.308
Relaford D.	17	24	16	238	167	3.95	47	13	2	1	67	42	22	2	4	1	1	3	3	1	.224	.308	.319	.218
Greene T.	17	10	23	134	99	3.46	32	4	0	7	57	21	7	0	1	0	0	0	0	5	.254	.299	.452	.247
Garabito E.	13	15	8	102	65	3.92	27	5	0	1	35	12	8	0	3	3	0	3	2	2	.307	.384	.398	.272
Shealy R.	12	14	16	104	67	4.21	30	7	0	2	43	22	13	0	0	0	0	1	0	6	.330	.413	.473	.304
Quintanilla	8	16	7	143	104	3.45	28	1	1	0	31	15	9	0	0	6	0	2	1	3	.219	.270	.242	.182
Bigbie L.	5	5	2	70	52	3.73	14	1	1	0	17	18	3	0	1	0	0	2	0	0	.212	.257	.258	.180
Restovich M.	4	5	3	34	24	3.21	9	2	0	1	14	5	3	0	0	0	0	0	0	2	.290	.353	.452	.272
Byrnes E.	4	2	5	60	44	3.68	10	2	0	0	12	11	7	0	0	0	0	2	0	1	.189	.283	.226	.184
Baker J.	3	6	4	43	31	4.14	8	4	0	1	15	12	5	0	0	0	0	0	0	1	.211	.302	.395	.235
Freeman C.	2	6	0	22	16	3.91	6	1	1	0	9	5	0	0	0	0	0	0	0	0	.273	.273	.409	.225
Wright J.	1	2	3	59	47	3.34	8	1	0	0	9	21	1	0	0	3	0	0	0	0	.145	.161	.164	.113
Carvajal M.	1	0	2	4	3	4.25	1	0	0	0	1	3	0	0	0	0	0	0	0	0	.250	.250	.250	.175
Spilborghs R	1	0	1	4	2	5.25	2	0	0	0	2	1	0	0	0	0	0	0	0	0	.500	.500	.500	.350
Chacon S.	1	0	1	25	18	3.08	3	0	0	0	3	8	2	0	0	3	0	0	0	1	.150	.227	.150	.140
Kim S.	0	2	3	20	13	3.45	2	0	0	0	2	4	0	0	0	4	1	0	0	0	.133	.125	.133	.090
Cook A.	0	3	0	36	25	3.08	5	0	1	0	7	12	1	0	0	5	0	0	0	0	.167	.194	.233	.145
Acevedo J.	0	0	0	11	7	3.64	1	0	0	0	1	6	1	0	1	1	0	0	0	0	.125	.300	.125	.166
Esposito M.	0	0	0	6	4	4.17	1	0	0	0	1	0	0	0	0	1	0	0	0	0	.200	.200	.200	.140
Olson T.	0	0	0	3	2	4.00	0	0	0	0	0	2	1	0	0	0	0	0	0	0	.000	.333	.000	.150
Amezaga A.	0	1	0	3	2	2.67	1	0	0	0	1	0	0	0	0	0	0	0	0	0	.333	.333	.333	.233
Day Z.	0	1	0	3	2	3.00	1	0	0	0	1	0	0	0	0	0	0	0	0	0	.333	.333	.333	.233
Lopez A.	-0	1	0	1	1	1.00	0	0	0	0	0	0	0	0	0	0	0	0	0	0	.000	.000	.000	.000
Dohmann S.	-0	0	0	1	1	7.00	0	0	0	0	0	0	0	0	0	0	0	0	0	0	.000	.000	.000	.000
Neal B.	-0	0	0	1	1	5.00	0	0	0	0	0	1	0	0	0	0	0	0	0	0	.000	.000	.000	.000
Cortes D.	-0	0	0	2	2	2.50	0	0	0	0	0	0	0	0	0	0	0	0	0	0	.000	.000	.000	.000
Speier R.	-0	0	0	2	2	2.00	0	0	0	0	0	0	0	0	0	0	0	0	0	0	.000	.000	.000	.000
Machado A.	-0	1	2	13	10	4.85	0	0	0	0	0	5	2	0	0	0	1	0	0	0	.000	.154	0.000	.069
Jennings J.	-0	0	1	44	32	3.36	6	1	0	0	7	12	2	0	0	4	0	0	0	0	.158	.200	.184	.136
Kennedy J.	-1	1	1	35	25	2.91	5	0	0	0	5	8	1	0	0	5	0	0	0	1	.172	.200	.172	.133
Francis J.	-1	7	4	71	53	4.18	6	2	0	0	8	27	7	0	0	6	0	0	0	1	.103	.200	.138	.124
Kim B.	-1	0	2	45	35	3.40	3	0	0	0	3	6	2	0	0	4	1	0	0	0	.079	.122	.079	.075

Pitching Stats

Player	PR	IP	BFP	G	GS	P/PA	K	BB	IBB	HBP	H	HR	DP	DER	SB	CS	PO	W	L	Sv	Op	Hld	RA	ERA	FIP
Fuentes B.	16	74.3	321	78	0	4.17	91	34	4	10	59	6	8	.706	2	1	1	2	5	31	34	6	3.03	2.91	3.36
Cook A.	10	83.3	357	13	13	3.32	24	16	2	2	101	8	17	.697	3	0	0	7	2	0	0	0	4.10	3.67	4.30
Witasick J.	9	35.7	148	32	0	3.88	40	12	3	3	27	2	3	.725	3	1	0	0	4	0	1	11	2.78	2.52	2.73
Chacon S.	9	72.7	322	13	12	3.69	39	36	4	8	69	7	7	.733	4	0	2	1	7	0	0	0	4.09	4.09	4.98
DeJean M.	7	36.7	151	38	0	3.82	35	12	1	2	26	0	0	.745	2	0	0	2	3	0	3	18	3.44	3.19	2.22
Cortes D.	6	52.7	213	50	0	3.71	36	10	2	1	50	9	4	.739	5	1	0	2	0	2	3	4	4.10	4.10	4.46
Kim S.	5	53.3	228	12	8	3.48	38	13	0	1	56	7	5	.710	1	0	0	5	1	0	0	0	4.39	4.22	4.05
Kim B.	5	148.0	668	40	22	3.86	115	71	8	14	156	17	13	.692	12	5	1	5	12	0	2	1	4.99	4.86	4.64
Speier R.	2	24.7	111	22	0	3.56	10	13	1	1	26	0	1	.701	1	3	1	2	1	0	1	2	4.38	3.65	3.87
Lopez A.	1	4.0	15	1	0	4.07	6	0	0	0	3	0	0	.667	0	0	0	0	0	0	0	0	2.25	2.25	-0.02
Carvajal M.	1	53.0	229	39	0	3.82	47	21	0	3	52	8	6	.707	4	0	0	0	2	0	1	0	5.09	5.09	4.53
Jennings J.	-1	122.0	551	20	20	3.60	75	62	4	5	130	11	19	.701	8	1	1	6	9	0	0	0	5.39	5.02	4.57
Miceli D.	-1	18.3	86	19	0	4.33	19	13	0	1	19	1	1	.654	2	1	0	1	2	0	2	5	5.89	5.89	3.91
Neal B.	-1	14.7	70	11	0	3.43	8	9	2	0	20	2	2	.647	0	0	0	1	2	0	2	0	6.14	6.14	5.51
Tsao C.	-1	11.0	56	10	0	3.52	4	5	1	1	16	3	0	.698	3	0	0	1	0	3	4	0	6.55	6.55	7.44
Williams R.	-2	22.0	100	30	0	3.96	19	9	3	0	26	4	1	.676	0	0	0	2	1	0	2	4	6.14	5.73	4.85
Esposito M.	-2	14.7	73	3	3	3.16	5	9	1	0	21	3	0	.679	0	1	0	0	2	0	0	0	6.75	6.75	6.80
Dohmann S.	-2	31.0	143	32	0	4.15	35	19	1	0	33	6	2	.675	4	0	0	2	1	0	3	7	6.10	6.10	5.08
Lopez J.	-3	2.0	13	3	0	3.08	1	0	0	0	7	0	0	.417	1	0	0	0	0	0	1	0	22.50	22.50	1.98
Seay B.	-4	11.7	57	17	0	4.05	11	8	1	0	18	3	2	.571	0	0	0	0	0	0	1	1	8.49	8.49	6.50
Day Z.	-4	11.3	59	5	3	3.83	7	7	1	0	20	2	3	.581	0	0	0	0	1	0	1	0	8.74	7.15	5.89
Simpson A.	-4	0.7	8	2	0	4.25	0	3	0	0	3	0	0	.400	0	0	0	0	0	0	0	0	67.50	67.50	16.48
Acevedo J.	-9	64.0	292	36	5	3.55	31	16	3	1	86	13	3	.684	0	3	1	2	4	1	2	6	6.75	6.47	5.45
Francis J.	-9	183.7	828	33	33	3.80	128	70	5	8	228	26	21	.661	19	11	5	14	12	0	0	0	5.83	5.68	4.70
Anderson M.	-10	10.0	62	12	0	3.81	4	11	0	2	19	3	1	.619	0	1	0	0	0	0	0	2	15.30	12.60	9.98
Wright J.	-15	171.3	782	34	27	3.49	101	81	4	15	201	22	26	.682	25	7	6	8	16	0	0	1	6.25	5.46	5.15
Kennedy J.	-23	92.0	442	16	16	3.58	52	44	4	6	128	12	13	.646	3	1	1	4	8	0	0	0	7.92	7.04	5.18

Win Shares Stats

Player	WS	Bat	Pitch	Field	ExpWS	WSP	WSAB	CWS	NetWSValue
Helton, T	26	23.6	0.0	2.7	17	.796	15	211	$4,195,778
Holliday, M	19	16.0	0.0	2.7	14	.669	9	29	$6,962,874
Atkins, G	13	10.2	0.0	2.9	15	.430	2	15	$1,918,574
Fuentes, B	12	0.0	11.8	0.0	7	.903	7	27	$5,674,937
Sullivan, C	10	7.1	0.0	3.3	11	.468	3	10	$2,048,640
Barmes, C	9	6.7	0.0	2.4	10	.467	2	12	$1,794,986
Gonzalez, L	9	5.7	0.0	3.1	12	.380	1	16	$556,634
Hawpe, B	8	6.1	0.0	2.1	9	.440	2	9	$1,311,121
Kim, B	7	-1.5	8.1	0.0	8	.439	2	67	($5,382,017)
Miles, A	7	4.7	0.0	2.6	9	.411	1	18	$846,884
Francis, J	6	-2.0	8.0	0.0	9	.338	1	8	$530,658
Wilson, P	6	4.1	0.0	1.6	8	.366	0	83	($3,198,906)
Wright, J	4	-1.2	5.6	0.0	8	.263	-1	52	($550,000)
Ardoin, D	4	0.9	0.0	2.7	7	.262	-1	4	($316,000)
Mohr, D	4	1.9	0.0	2.1	8	.260	-1	32	($950,000)
Closser, J	3	1.6	0.0	1.4	7	.203	-2	6	($317,000)

Fielding and Baserunning Stats

Name	POS	Inn	SBA/G	CS%	ERA	WP+PB/G	PO	A	TE	FE
Ardoin	C	591.0	0.62	44%	4.90	0.426	452	48	5	1
Closser	C	565.7	0.95	12%	5.35	0.493	410	25	7	1
Greene	C	262.0	0.93	4%	5.22	0.687	151	7	4	0

Name	POS	Inn	PO	A	TE	FE	FPct	RF	DPS	DPT
T Helton	1B	1229.0	1236	118	2	3	.996	9.92	21	2
R Shealy	1B	152.7	155	8	0	0	1.000	9.61	2	0
L Gonzalez	1B	36.3	37	3	0	0	1.000	9.91	1	0
A Miles	2B	602.0	154	206	1	5	.984	5.38	20	28
L Gonzalez	2B	579.3	119	197	0	0	1.000	4.91	15	22
E Garabito	2B	132.3	33	37	0	1	.986	4.76	4	8
D Relaford	2B	73.7	10	31	1	1	.953	5.01	2	2
O Quintanill	2B	31.3	10	10	0	0	1.000	5.74	2	3
C Barmes	SS	681.7	139	247	8	9	.958	5.10	32	28
D Relaford	SS	281.3	45	100	4	2	.960	4.64	11	6
O Quintanill	SS	268.7	42	89	0	1	.992	4.39	8	5
L Gonzalez	SS	132.0	28	34	3	1	.939	4.23	4	8
A Machado	SS	34.0	7	6	1	0	.929	3.44	0	1
E Garabito	SS	18.0	3	5	0	0	1.000	4.00	0	0
A Miles	SS	3.0	0	0	0	1	0.000	0.00	0	0
G Atkins	3B	1161.0	78	262	10	7	.950	2.64	21	1
D Relaford	3B	124.0	9	22	1	1	.939	2.25	1	0
J Baker	3B	79.0	3	20	0	1	.958	2.62	1	0
L Gonzalez	3B	51.0	6	7	0	0	1.000	2.29	1	0
A Amezaga	3B	3.0	0	0	0	0	0.000	0.00	0	0
M Holliday	LF	1049.0	236	5	2	5	.972	2.07	4	0
C Sullivan	LF	149.3	32	2	1	0	.971	2.05	0	0
D Mohr	LF	122.3	25	3	0	0	1.000	2.06	1	0
J Piedra	LF	47.3	5	1	0	0	1.000	1.14	0	0
E Byrnes	LF	33.0	9	0	0	0	1.000	2.45	0	0
M Restovich	LF	9.0	4	0	0	0	1.000	4.00	0	0
L Gonzalez	LF	8.0	2	0	0	0	1.000	2.25	0	0
C Sullivan	CF	617.7	172	4	1	1	.989	2.56	4	0
P Wilson	CF	580.0	140	2	0	3	.979	2.20	0	0
L Bigbie	CF	91.0	28	0	0	0	1.000	2.77	1	0
D Mohr	CF	63.0	19	1	0	0	1.000	2.86	0	0
C Freeman	CF	41.0	12	2	0	0	1.000	3.07	2	0
E Byrnes	CF	25.0	11	0	0	0	1.000	3.96	0	0
D Relaford	CF	1.0	0	0	0	0	0.000	0.00	0	0
B Hawpe	RF	693.0	148	10	2	1	.981	2.05	4	0
D Mohr	RF	382.7	103	0	1	1	.981	2.42	0	0
J Piedra	RF	121.7	22	0	0	0	1.000	1.63	0	0
E Byrnes	RF	59.0	19	1	1	0	.952	3.05	2	0
M Restovich	RF	53.0	14	0	0	0	1.000	2.38	0	0
L Gonzalez	RF	43.3	14	0	0	0	1.000	2.91	0	0
L Bigbie	RF	38.0	8	0	0	0	1.000	1.89	0	0

Name	POS	Inn	PO	A	TE	FE	FPct	RF	DPS	DPT
C Sullivan	RF	16.0	7	0	0	0	1.000	3.94	0	0
R Spilborghs	RF	8.0	6	1	0	0	1.000	7.88	2	0
D Relaford	RF	4.0	0	1	0	0	1.000	2.25	0	0

Incremental Baserunning Runs		
Name	IR	IRP
Clint Barmes	2.43	143
Aaron Miles	2.31	158
Preston Wilson	1.25	144
Omar Quintanilla	0.89	194
Luis Gonzalez	0.87	118
Jorge Piedra	0.75	153
Dustan Mohr	0.69	230
Garrett Atkins	0.67	111
JD Closser	0.55	112
Danny Ardoin	0.36	110
Desi Relaford	0.29	115
Aquilino Lopez	0.27	494
Cory Sullivan	0.19	102
Eric Byrnes	0.19	124
Michael Restovich	0.13	123
Jamey Wright	0.12	109
Alfredo Amezaga	0.06	109
Todd Greene	0.06	107
Anderson Machado	0.03	105
Aaron Cook	0.03	104
Sunny Kim	0.01	102
Jeff Baker	0.01	103
Zach Day	-0.01	0
Jason Jennings	-0.01	0
Joe Kennedy	-0.04	0
Choo Freeman	-0.10	33
Jeff Francis	-0.12	0
Larry Bigbie	-0.12	90
Mike Esposito	-0.32	0
Brad Hawpe	-0.60	77
Ryan Shealy	-0.99	54
Eddy Garabito	-1.01	21
Jose Acevedo	-1.09	0
Matt Holliday	-1.28	79
Todd Helton	-1.69	80

Detroit Tigers

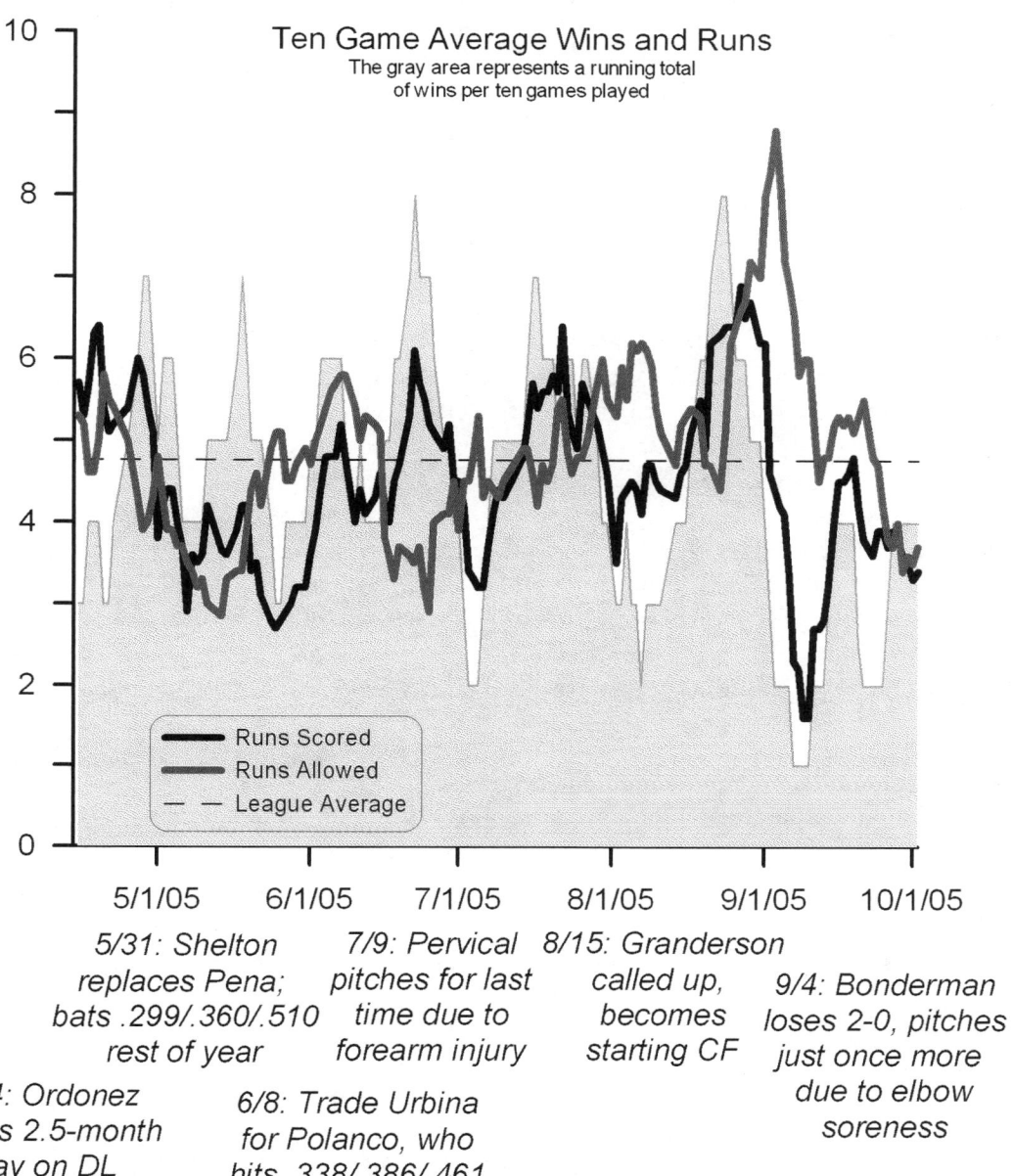

Ten Game Average Wins and Runs
The gray area represents a running total
of wins per ten games played

Legend:
— Runs Scored
— Runs Allowed
– – League Average

5/14: Ordonez begins 2.5-month stay on DL with hernia

5/31: Shelton replaces Pena; bats .299/.360/.510 rest of year

6/8: Trade Urbina for Polanco, who hits .338/,386/.461 for Tigers

7/9: Pervical pitches for last time due to forearm injury

8/15: Granderson called up, becomes starting CF

9/4: Bonderman loses 2-0, pitches just once more due to elbow soreness

Team Batting and Pitching/Fielding Stats by Month						
	April	May	June	July	Aug	Spt/Oct
Wins	11	12	13	14	13	8
Losses	11	15	13	15	13	24
OBP	.341	.309	.315	.349	.326	.292
SLG	.434	.398	.405	.463	.462	.405
FIP	4.76	4.06	4.20	4.83	5.18	4.82
DER	.731	.710	.718	.700	.701	.708

Batting Stats

Player	RC	Runs	RBI	PA	Outs	P/PA	H	2B	3B	HR	TB	K	BB	IBB	HBP	SH	SF	SB	CS	GDP	BA	OBP	SLG	GPA
Inge B.	88	75	72	694	475	4.01	161	31	9	16	258	140	63	1	3	6	6	7	6	14	.261	.330	.419	.253
Monroe C.	82	69	89	623	429	3.60	157	30	3	20	253	95	40	4	3	1	12	8	3	16	.277	.322	.446	.256
Shelton C.	70	61	59	431	284	4.26	116	22	3	18	198	87	34	0	5	0	4	0	0	12	.299	.360	.510	.289
White R.	65	49	53	400	265	3.53	117	24	3	12	183	48	17	0	5	0	4	1	0	8	.313	.348	.489	.279
Polanco P.	64	58	36	378	239	3.46	116	20	2	6	158	16	21	0	8	2	4	4	3	9	.338	.386	.461	.289
Young D.	64	61	72	509	358	3.62	127	25	3	21	221	100	29	7	9	0	1	1	0	16	.271	.325	.471	.264
Ordonez M.	55	38	46	343	221	3.51	92	17	0	8	133	35	30	1	1	0	7	0	0	8	.302	.359	.436	.270
Rodriguez I.	47	71	50	525	387	3.33	139	33	5	14	224	93	11	2	2	1	7	7	3	19	.276	.290	.444	.242
Pena C.	42	37	44	295	203	3.93	61	9	0	18	124	95	31	2	4	0	0	0	1	3	.235	.325	.477	.266
Guillen C.	42	48	23	361	239	3.70	107	15	4	5	145	45	24	3	2	0	1	2	3	9	.320	.368	.434	.274
Infante O.	41	36	43	434	321	3.52	90	28	2	9	149	73	16	0	2	8	2	8	0	5	.222	.254	.367	.206
Logan N.	35	47	17	356	250	3.38	83	12	5	1	108	52	21	3	1	12	0	23	6	5	.258	.305	.335	.221
Granderson C	27	18	20	174	121	4.11	44	6	3	8	80	43	10	0	0	2	0	1	1	2	.272	.314	.494	.265
Wilson V.	14	18	19	173	128	3.75	30	4	0	3	43	26	11	0	6	2	2	0	0	6	.197	.275	.283	.194
Thames M.	11	11	16	118	87	4.03	21	2	0	7	44	38	9	1	1	0	1	0	0	1	.196	.263	.411	.221
Martinez R.	7	4	5	62	42	3.52	15	1	0	0	16	4	3	0	0	2	1	0	0	1	.268	.300	.286	.206
McDonald J.	6	10	4	78	58	3.55	19	3	1	0	24	12	5	0	0	0	0	1	1	3	.260	.308	.329	.221
Smith J.	4	4	2	63	48	3.05	11	1	2	0	16	16	0	0	1	4	0	2	1	0	.190	.203	.276	.160
Giarratano T	3	4	4	47	37	3.36	6	0	0	1	9	7	5	0	0	0	0	1	0	1	.143	.234	.214	.159
Maroth M.	1	0	1	6	2	4.00	2	0	0	0	2	2	1	0	0	1	0	0	0	0	.500	.600	.500	.395
Johnson J.	1	1	1	2	1	2.50	1	0	0	1	4	0	0	0	0	0	0	0	0	0	.500	.500	2.000	.725
Gomez A.	1	2	1	18	13	3.61	3	0	0	0	3	2	2	0	0	0	0	0	0	0	.188	.278	.188	.172
Hooper K.	1	0	0	7	4	3.00	1	0	0	0	1	1	0	0	0	2	0	0	0	0	.200	.200	.200	.140
Douglass S.	-0	0	0	2	2	2.00	0	0	0	0	0	0	0	0	0	0	0	0	0	0	.000	.000	.000	.000
Robertson N.	-0	0	0	4	3	4.75	0	0	0	0	0	1	0	0	0	1	0	0	0	0	.000	.000	.000	.000
Higginson B.	-0	1	1	27	24	3.48	2	0	0	0	2	5	1	0	0	0	0	0	0	0	.077	.111	.077	.069
Bonderman J.	-1	0	0	6	6	2.83	0	0	0	0	0	2	0	0	0	0	0	0	0	0	.000	.000	.000	.000

Win Shares Stats

Player	WS	Bat	Pitch	Field	ExpWS	WSP	WSAB	CWS	NetWSValue
Inge, B	17	12.2	0.0	4.5	18	.456	4	42	$1,896,198
Polanco, P	15	11.8	0.0	2.9	10	.749	8	96	$6,281,047
Monroe, C	14	12.2	0.0	2.3	17	.432	3	37	$2,081,137
Shelton, C	13	12.8	0.0	0.8	11	.623	6	13	$4,679,064
White, R	13	11.7	0.0	0.9	10	.658	6	150	$2,873,210
Ordonez, M	11	9.7	0.0	1.1	9	.605	5	151	($575,082)
Rodriguez, I	11	3.1	0.0	8.0	14	.406	2	274	($3,451,622)
Young, D	10	9.2	0.0	0.5	11	.436	2	101	($3,145,582)
Bonderman, J	9	-0.5	9.5	0.0	10	.449	3	19	$2,277,788
Johnson, J	9	0.3	8.5	0.0	11	.396	2	45	($543,986)
Maroth, M	9	0.2	8.5	0.0	11	.393	2	31	$1,539,131

Continued on the next page.

Pitching Stats

Player	PR	IP	BFP	G	GS	P/PA	K	BB	IBB	HBP	H	HR	DP	DER	SB	CS	PO	W	L	Sv	Op	Hld	RA	ERA	FIP
Farnsworth K	10	42.7	174	46	0	4.03	55	20	0	1	29	1	3	.711	5	2	0	1	1	6	8	15	2.53	2.32	2.25
Rodney F.	9	44.0	185	39	0	4.19	42	17	3	2	39	5	4	.714	2	1	0	2	3	9	15	3	2.86	2.86	3.91
Spurling C.	6	70.7	284	56	0	3.57	26	22	6	2	58	8	12	.779	2	1	0	3	4	0	1	11	3.82	3.44	4.80
Urbina U.	5	27.3	116	25	0	4.66	31	14	2	1	21	4	1	.742	1	0	0	1	3	9	11	3	2.96	2.63	4.32
Darensbourg	5	22.3	96	22	0	3.46	9	7	2	0	24	2	3	.718	1	0	0	1	1	0	0	1	2.82	2.82	4.34
German F.	4	59.0	270	58	0	3.85	38	34	4	7	63	7	11	.696	6	0	0	4	0	1	3	4	3.97	3.66	5.38
Walker J.	3	48.7	208	66	0	3.54	30	13	3	2	49	5	2	.722	2	1	0	4	3	0	2	14	4.07	3.70	4.07
Dingman C.	2	32.0	128	34	0	3.66	24	9	0	1	30	5	6	.719	3	0	0	2	3	4	5	4	3.94	3.66	4.51
Grilli J.	2	16.0	63	3	2	3.37	5	6	0	0	14	1	3	.745	1	1	0	1	1	0	0	0	3.38	3.38	4.36
Woodyard M.	2	6.0	22	3	0	3.95	3	0	0	0	4	1	0	.833	1	0	0	0	0	0	0	0	1.50	1.50	4.21
Karnuth J.	-0	1.7	7	3	0	3.57	0	0	0	0	2	0	0	.714	0	0	0	0	0	0	0	0	5.40	5.40	3.04
Good A.	-0	5.0	20	2	0	3.90	7	1	0	0	4	1	0	.727	0	0	0	0	0	0	0	0	5.40	5.40	3.44
Percival T.	-3	25.0	107	26	0	3.82	20	11	3	2	19	7	0	.821	1	0	0	1	3	8	11	0	5.76	5.76	6.64
Verlander J.	-3	11.3	54	2	2	3.37	7	5	0	1	15	1	0	.650	1	0	0	0	2	0	0	0	7.15	7.15	4.54
Bonderman J.	-4	189.0	801	29	29	3.56	145	57	0	4	199	21	26	.690	4	5	0	14	13	0	0	0	4.81	4.57	3.92
Colon R.	-4	25.0	115	12	3	3.91	17	7	0	0	35	7	3	.667	0	0	0	1	1	0	1	0	6.12	6.12	6.16
Creek D.	-7	22.3	101	20	0	4.05	18	7	0	0	27	7	0	.710	0	1	1	0	0	0	0	1	7.25	6.85	6.45
Ginter M.	-7	35.0	157	14	1	3.40	15	9	1	2	49	6	7	.656	2	4	1	0	1	0	0	0	6.43	6.17	5.36
Johnson J.	-10	210.0	888	33	33	3.38	93	49	4	6	233	23	29	.707	11	8	0	8	13	0	0	0	5.01	4.54	4.37
Robertson N.	-13	196.7	846	32	32	3.46	122	65	2	7	202	28	25	.721	8	5	1	7	16	0	0	0	5.17	4.48	4.75
Douglass S.	-13	87.3	374	18	16	3.90	55	33	2	2	92	13	13	.708	2	4	1	5	5	0	0	0	5.87	5.56	4.92
Maroth M.	-16	209.0	889	34	34	3.66	115	51	1	9	235	30	21	.700	4	12	10	14	14	0	0	0	5.30	4.74	4.67
Ledezma W.	-21	49.7	234	10	10	4.01	30	24	0	2	61	10	3	.696	3	4	1	2	4	0	0	0	8.34	7.07	6.02

Win Shares Stats (cont.)

Player	WS	Bat	Pitch	Field	ExpWS	WSP	WSAB	CWS	NetWSValue
Guillen, C	8	5.3	0.0	2.4	9	.418	1	79	($1,254,214)
Pena, C	7	6.9	0.0	0.4	7	.513	2	41	($697,417)
Robertson, N	7	-0.1	7.3	0.0	10	.346	1	16	$711,082
Infante, O	7	3.3	0.0	3.9	12	.306	-1	26	($355,000)
Farnsworth, K	6	0.0	5.9	0.0	4	.783	3	31	$3,227,024
Granderson, C	6	4.8	0.0	1.6	5	.679	3	6	$2,417,789
Rodney, F	5	0.0	5.2	0.0	4	.631	2	6	$1,831,495
Spurling, C	5	0.0	5.5	0.0	5	.582	2	9	$1,729,566
Logan, N	5	2.7	0.0	2.8	10	.280	-1	8	($320,000)
German, F	4	0.0	4.5	0.0	4	.563	2	6	$1,331,256
Walker, J	4	0.0	4.1	0.0	4	.571	2	23	$587,291
Wilson, V	3	0.4	0.0	2.5	5	.300	-0	22	($760,000)
Douglass, S	2	-0.1	1.9	0.0	5	.197	-1	3	($316,000)

Fielding and Baserunning Stats

Name	POS	Inn	SBA/G	CS%	ERA	WP+PB/G	PO	A	TE	FE
Rodriguez	C	1032.7	0.51	44%	4.45	0.383	702	60	4	0
Wilson	C	403.0	0.80	25%	4.69	0.290	234	29	3	0

Name	POS	Inn	PO	A	TE	FE	FPct	RF	DPS	DPT
C Shelton	1B	738.3	779	59	2	4	.993	10.21	6	3
C Pena	1B	429.3	418	35	0	3	.993	9.50	5	0
D Young	1B	257.0	265	22	0	3	.990	10.05	5	0
J Smith	1B	8.0	10	1	0	0	1.000	12.38	0	0
R Martinez	1B	3.0	3	0	0	0	1.000	9.00	0	0
P Polanco	2B	716.0	187	248	2	1	.993	5.47	22	46
O Infante	2B	591.7	153	186	3	1	.988	5.16	17	33
J Smith	2B	51.0	8	16	0	1	.960	4.24	4	0
J McDonald	2B	34.0	6	9	0	0	1.000	3.97	1	2
R Martinez	2B	34.0	10	12	0	2	.917	5.82	2	1
K Hooper	2B	9.0	2	1	0	0	1.000	3.00	0	0
C Guillen	SS	625.0	85	227	5	2	.978	4.49	23	22
O Infante	SS	389.3	82	149	4	2	.975	5.34	22	12
J McDonald	SS	151.3	29	69	3	2	.951	5.83	8	8
T Giarratano	SS	110.0	16	40	1	2	.949	4.58	4	2
R Martinez	SS	92.3	13	29	0	2	.955	4.09	3	1
J Smith	SS	62.7	14	27	0	0	1.000	5.89	3	3
K Hooper	SS	5.0	2	3	0	1	.833	9.00	0	0
B Inge	3B	1399.0	128	378	11	11	.957	3.26	42	3
J Smith	3B	17.0	5	6	0	0	1.000	5.82	3	0
J McDonald	3B	9.0	2	0	0	0	1.000	2.00	0	0
P Polanco	3B	9.0	1	3	0	0	1.000	4.00	0	0
R Martinez	3B	1.0	0	0	0	0	0.000	0.00	0	0
R White	LF	534.7	119	0	0	0	1.000	2.00	0	0
C Monroe	LF	501.7	99	6	1	0	.991	1.88	6	1
M Thames	LF	153.0	31	0	0	0	1.000	1.82	0	0
D Young	LF	142.3	35	1	0	0	1.000	2.28	0	0
C Granderson	LF	54.7	10	0	0	0	1.000	1.65	0	0
A Gomez	LF	28.0	7	0	0	0	1.000	2.25	0	0
B Higginson	LF	9.0	2	1	0	0	1.000	3.00	0	0
B Inge	LF	6.0	2	0	0	0	1.000	3.00	0	0
K Hooper	LF	4.3	1	0	0	0	1.000	2.08	0	0
C Shelton	LF	2.0	0	0	0	0	0.000	0.00	0	0

Name	POS	Inn	PO	A	TE	FE	FPct	RF	DPS	DPT
N Logan	CF	874.3	282	3	1	5	.979	2.93	4	0
C Granderson	CF	320.0	119	2	0	0	1.000	3.40	0	0
C Monroe	CF	229.3	63	0	0	1	.984	2.47	0	0
A Gomez	CF	11.0	2	0	0	0	1.000	1.64	0	0
B Inge	CF	1.0	0	0	0	0	0.000	0.00	0	0
M Ordonez	RF	672.3	139	5	0	1	.993	1.93	0	0
C Monroe	RF	632.3	132	4	2	2	.971	1.94	0	0
M Thames	RF	82.0	14	0	0	1	.933	1.54	0	0
B Higginson	RF	48.0	6	0	0	0	1.000	1.13	0	0
D Young	RF	1.0	0	0	0	0	0.000	0.00	0	0

Incremental Baserunning Runs		
Name	IR	IRP
Nook Logan	2.59	162
Ivan Rodriguez	1.86	134
Chris Shelton	1.25	125
Placido Polanco	0.74	116
John McDonald	0.21	116
Marcus Thames	0.20	177
Brandon Inge	0.15	102
Vance Wilson	0.15	111
Dmitri Young	0.10	102
Ramon Martinez	0.10	143
Tony Giarratano	0.02	103
Craig Monroe	0.02	100
Mike Maroth	-0.08	0
Omar Infante	-0.10	97
Jason Smith	-0.11	0
Carlos Pena	-0.18	93
Carlos Guillen	-0.36	90
Curtis Granderson	-0.81	45
Magglio Ordonez	-1.54	74
Rondell White	-1.72	64

Florida Marlins

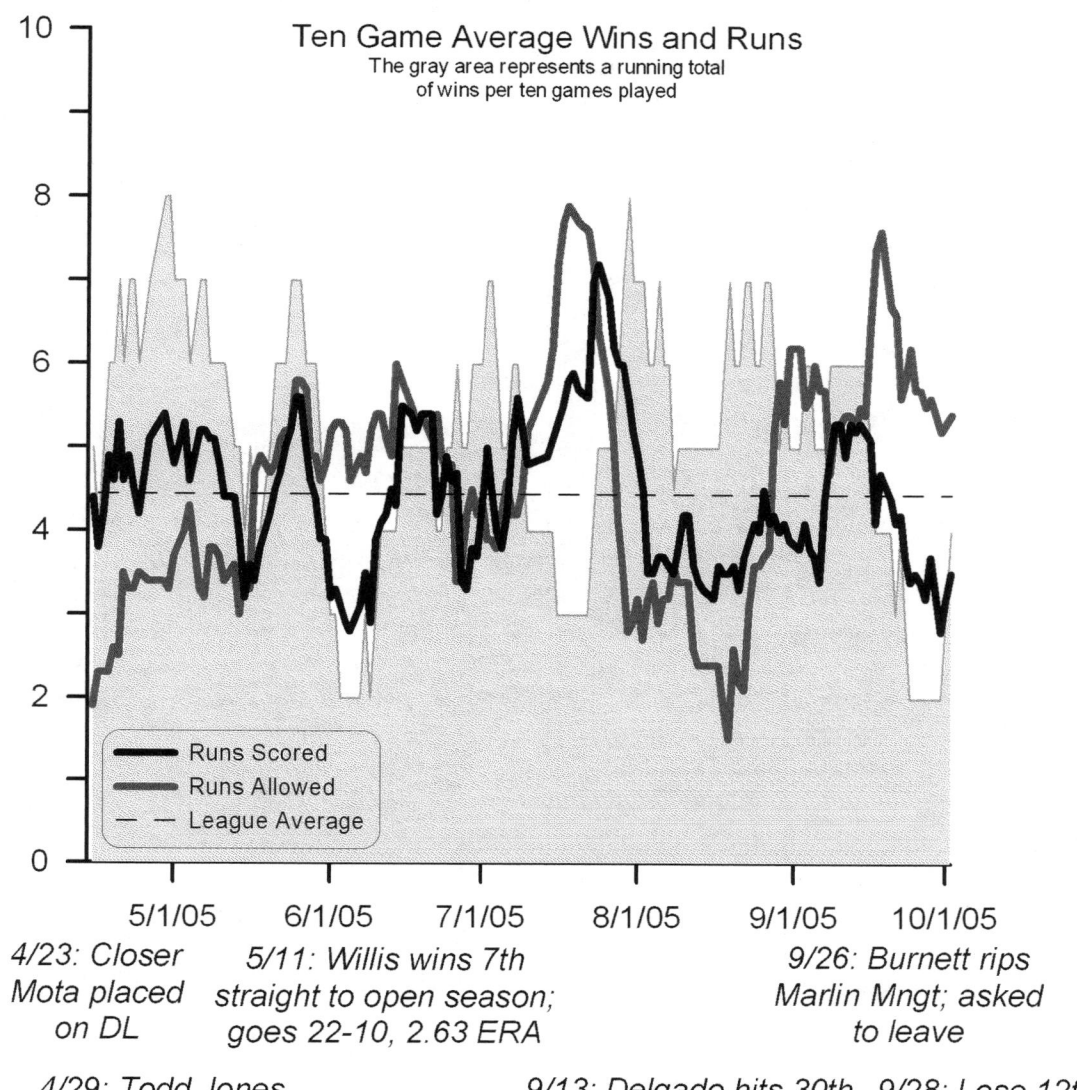

Ten Game Average Wins and Runs
The gray area represents a running total
of wins per ten games played

- —— Runs Scored
- —— Runs Allowed
- – – League Average

5/1/05 6/1/05 7/1/05 8/1/05 9/1/05 10/1/05

*4/23: Closer
Mota placed
on DL*

*5/11: Willis wins 7th
straight to open season;
goes 22-10, 2.63 ERA*

*9/26: Burnett rips
Marlin Mngt; asked
to leave*

*4/29: Todd Jones
earns first of 40
saves*

*9/13: Delgado hits 30th
HR, joining Cabrera in
30 HR club*

*9/28: Lose 12th of
last 14 to end
postseason hopes*

Team Batting and Pitching/Fielding Stats by Month						
	April	May	June	July	Aug	Spt/Oct
Wins	14	13	13	13	17	13
Losses	8	14	14	13	14	16
OBP	.339	.335	.343	.359	.308	.350
SLG	.412	.433	.397	.454	.353	.411
FIP	3.49	3.67	4.24	3.83	3.69	4.13
DER	.749	.671	.689	.678	.714	.667

Batting Stats

Player	RC	Runs	RBI	PA	Outs	P/PA	H	2B	3B	HR	TB	K	BB	IBB	HBP	SH	SF	SB	CS	GDP	BA	OBP	SLG	GPA
Delgado C.	126	81	115	616	380	3.86	157	41	3	33	303	121	72	20	17	0	6	0	0	16	.301	.399	.582	.325
Cabrera M.	123	106	116	685	435	3.84	198	43	2	33	344	125	64	12	2	0	6	1	0	20	.323	.385	.561	.314
Encarnacion	91	59	76	563	375	3.79	145	27	3	16	226	104	41	2	9	4	3	6	5	9	.287	.349	.447	.269
Pierre J.	86	96	47	719	502	3.70	181	19	13	2	232	45	41	1	9	10	2	57	17	10	.276	.326	.354	.235
Castillo L.	70	72	30	524	325	3.94	132	12	4	4	164	32	65	1	1	18	1	10	7	11	.301	.391	.374	.269
Lo Duca P.	58	45	57	496	338	3.69	126	23	1	6	169	31	34	5	4	5	8	4	3	16	.283	.334	.380	.245
Gonzalez A.	53	45	45	478	334	3.54	115	30	0	5	160	81	31	10	5	4	3	5	3	11	.264	.319	.368	.235
Lowell M.	53	56	58	558	396	3.65	118	36	1	8	180	58	46	1	2	1	9	4	0	14	.236	.298	.360	.224
Conine J.	52	42	33	384	245	3.86	102	20	2	3	135	58	38	2	3	2	6	2	0	12	.304	.374	.403	.269
Easley D.	37	37	30	304	210	3.76	64	19	1	9	112	47	26	3	4	3	4	4	1	6	.240	.312	.419	.245
Harris L.	15	5	13	78	52	3.67	22	4	0	1	29	11	7	1	1	0	0	0	1	3	.314	.385	.414	.277
Treanor M.	15	10	13	154	112	4.08	27	8	0	0	35	28	16	1	3	1	0	0	0	5	.201	.301	.261	.201
Hermida J.	12	9	11	47	30	4.19	12	2	0	4	26	12	6	1	0	0	0	2	0	1	.293	.383	.634	.331
Willis D.	10	14	11	101	70	3.36	24	4	0	1	31	13	3	0	1	4	1	0	0	2	.261	.289	.337	.214
Aguila C.	5	11	4	81	60	3.52	19	3	0	0	22	19	3	0	0	0	0	0	1	0	.244	.272	.282	.193
Beckett J.	4	5	6	71	51	3.68	9	3	0	1	15	17	7	0	0	4	1	0	0	1	.153	.239	.254	.171
Willingham J	3	3	4	28	17	4.04	7	1	0	0	8	5	2	0	2	1	0	0	0	1	.304	.407	.348	.270
Vargas J.	3	3	2	27	18	4.15	8	2	0	0	10	7	1	0	0	0	0	0	0	0	.308	.333	.385	.246
Messenger R.	1	0	0	4	2	4.25	1	0	0	0	1	1	1	0	0	0	0	0	0	0	.333	.500	.333	.308
Andino R.	1	4	1	50	39	3.74	7	4	0	0	11	8	5	1	0	1	0	1	0	2	.159	.245	.250	.173
Jones T.	1	0	0	3	2	4.67	1	0	0	0	1	2	0	0	0	0	0	0	0	0	.333	.333	.333	.233
Johnson J.	-0	1	0	4	3	4.50	1	0	0	0	1	2	0	0	0	0	0	0	0	0	.250	.250	.250	.175
Bump N.	-0	1	0	6	4	3.17	1	0	0	0	1	4	0	0	1	0	0	0	0	0	.200	.200	.200	.140
Castillo F.	-0	0	0	1	1	2.00	0	0	0	0	0	0	0	0	0	0	0	0	0	0	.000	.000	.000	.000
Villone R.	-0	0	0	1	1	3.00	0	0	0	0	0	1	0	0	0	0	0	0	0	0	.000	.000	.000	.000
Bazardo Y.	-0	0	0	1	1	5.00	0	0	0	0	0	1	0	0	0	0	0	0	0	0	.000	.000	.000	.000
Resop C.	-0	0	0	1	1	3.00	0	0	0	0	0	1	0	0	0	0	0	0	0	0	.000	.000	.000	.000
Mordecai M.	-0	0	0	2	2	3.00	0	0	0	0	0	1	0	0	0	0	0	0	0	0	.000	.000	.000	.000
Riedling J.	-0	0	0	2	2	4.50	0	0	0	0	0	1	0	0	0	0	0	0	0	0	.000	.000	.000	.000
Moehler B.	-0	1	3	47	37	3.38	3	1	0	0	4	15	1	0	1	5	0	0	0	0	.075	.119	.100	.079
Olsen S.	-0	0	0	4	3	2.75	0	0	0	0	0	1	0	0	0	1	0	0	0	0	.000	.000	.000	.000
Mota G.	-0	0	0	3	3	3.00	0	0	0	0	0	3	0	0	0	0	0	0	0	0	.000	.000	.000	.000
Valdez I.	-0	0	0	16	11	3.25	2	0	0	0	2	2	0	0	0	3	0	0	0	0	.154	.154	.154	.108
Wilson J.	-0	2	0	11	9	4.82	1	1	0	0	2	4	0	0	1	0	0	0	0	0	.100	.182	.200	.132
Jorgensen R.	-0	0	0	4	4	4.25	0	0	0	0	0	3	0	0	0	0	0	0	0	0	.000	.000	.000	.000
Burnett A.	-1	3	2	79	59	3.76	10	2	2	1	19	34	1	0	1	9	0	0	0	1	.147	.171	.279	.147
Dillon J.	-1	6	1	39	33	4.54	6	1	0	1	10	8	1	0	1	1	0	0	0	3	.167	.211	.278	.164
Leiter A.	-2	0	0	22	18	3.36	0	0	0	0	0	12	0	0	0	4	0	0	0	0	.000	.000	.000	.000

Pitching Stats

Player	PR	IP	BFP	G	GS	P/PA	K	BB	IBB	HBP	H	HR	DP	DER	SB	CS	PO	W	L	Sv	Op	Hld	RA	ERA	FIP
Willis D.	36	236.3	960	34	34	3.70	170	55	3	8	213	11	26	.718	1	5	1	22	10	0	0	0	3.01	2.63	2.95
Jones T.	17	73.0	289	68	0	3.58	62	14	2	3	61	2	8	.716	3	1	0	1	5	40	45	1	2.34	2.10	2.34
Beckett J.	11	178.7	729	29	29	3.85	166	58	2	7	153	14	21	.713	6	7	1	15	8	0	0	0	3.78	3.38	3.23
Mecir J.	4	43.3	184	52	0	3.99	34	17	2	5	39	2	6	.706	3	1	1	1	4	0	4	13	3.53	3.12	3.54
Burnett A.	4	209.0	873	32	32	3.78	198	79	1	7	184	12	28	.702	24	6	1	12	12	0	0	0	4.18	3.44	3.07
Perisho M.	3	14.0	65	24	0	3.66	10	11	0	1	12	1	1	.738	0	1	1	2	0	0	0	4	2.57	1.93	5.05
Vargas J.	1	73.7	325	17	13	3.88	59	31	4	4	71	4	4	.705	11	0	1	5	5	0	0	0	4.15	4.03	3.51
Johnson J.	1	12.3	55	4	1	4.07	10	10	0	1	11	0	3	.676	5	1	0	0	0	0	0	0	3.65	3.65	4.04
Bump N.	0	38.0	165	31	0	3.49	18	12	1	2	43	5	8	.703	2	1	1	0	3	0	1	2	4.26	4.03	4.85
Alfonseca A.	-2	27.3	117	33	0	3.82	16	14	4	2	29	2	8	.675	2	1	0	1	1	0	2	8	4.94	4.94	4.52
Smith T.	-3	10.7	52	12	0	3.62	9	5	1	2	17	1	0	.568	1	0	0	0	0	0	0	0	6.75	6.75	3.92
Castillo F.	-3	4.3	22	1	1	4.23	4	5	0	0	4	0	0	.692	2	0	0	0	1	0	0	0	10.38	10.38	4.60
Olsen S.	-3	20.3	91	5	4	3.96	21	10	0	0	21	5	1	.709	2	2	1	1	1	0	0	0	5.75	3.98	5.59
Bazardo Y.	-4	1.7	12	1	0	3.92	2	2	0	0	5	0	1	.375	1	0	0	0	0	0	0	0	27.00	21.60	4.18
Messenger R.	-4	37.0	178	29	0	3.92	29	30	7	0	39	5	3	.702	6	0	0	0	0	0	0	2	5.35	5.35	5.60
Kensing L.	-5	5.7	31	3	0	4.06	4	3	0	0	11	2	0	.591	1	0	0	0	0	0	0	1	11.12	11.12	7.75
de los Santo	-5	22.0	103	27	0	3.92	16	12	3	2	25	4	3	.696	2	0	0	1	2	0	1	1	6.14	6.14	5.80
Quantrill P.	-5	5.3	28	6	0	3.93	1	5	0	0	8	1	1	.667	0	0	0	0	1	0	0	0	11.81	8.44	7.86
Mota G.	-6	67.0	293	56	0	3.99	60	32	7	1	65	5	5	.692	10	3	0	2	2	2	4	14	5.10	4.70	3.64
Moehler B.	-6	158.3	696	37	25	3.55	95	42	9	5	198	16	20	.662	16	5	1	6	12	0	0	1	4.66	4.55	3.99
Bentz C.	-6	2.0	14	4	0	2.64	0	0	0	0	8	2	0	.500	0	0	0	0	0	0	0	2	31.50	31.50	15.98
Crowell J.	-7	3.3	22	4	0	3.36	2	0	0	2	10	1	0	.471	0	0	0	0	0	0	0	0	21.60	21.60	7.48
Valdez I.	-8	50.7	237	14	7	3.49	27	22	6	5	64	6	6	.672	5	1	0	2	2	0	0	0	5.68	5.33	5.05
Resop C.	-8	17.0	80	15	0	3.89	15	9	0	1	22	1	2	.611	1	1	0	2	0	0	0	0	8.47	8.47	3.75
Villone R.	-9	23.7	109	27	0	4.18	29	12	1	2	24	2	1	.656	0	0	0	3	2	0	3	4	7.61	6.85	3.40
Riedling J.	-10	27.7	130	29	0	3.65	16	13	1	2	34	3	2	.680	3	0	0	4	1	0	0	2	7.48	7.16	4.75
Leiter A.	-24	80.0	376	17	16	4.31	52	60	2	6	88	9	17	.683	11	2	0	3	7	0	0	0	6.86	6.64	5.62

Win Shares Stats

Player	WS	Bat	Pitch	Field	ExpWS	WSP	WSAB	CWS	NetWSValue
Delgado, C	31	30.2	0.0	1.1	17	.947	20	243	$13,351,563
Cabrera, M	29	27.4	0.0	2.2	18	.806	17	63	$13,172,528
Willis, D	26	0.7	25.1	0.0	11	1.189	19	50	$15,120,052
Encarnacio, J	19	17.8	0.0	1.6	15	.632	9	93	$4,337,129
Castillo, L	17	11.3	0.0	6.0	14	.617	7	134	$2,971,556
Beckett, J	14	-0.6	14.7	0.0	8	.829	9	42	$4,740,485
Pierre, J	14	11.6	0.0	2.9	19	.379	1	93	($2,937,053)
Jones, T	13	0.3	13.2	0.0	7	.968	9	99	$6,325,570
Gonzalez, A	13	6.9	0.0	6.2	13	.492	4	76	$1,133,111
Burnett, A	12	-2.4	14.1	0.0	10	.594	6	50	$822,426
Lo Duca, P	11	7.7	0.0	3.8	14	.425	2	104	($3,286,292)
Conine, J	10	8.9	0.0	1.1	10	.495	3	182	$666,107
Easley, D	9	5.9	0.0	3.2	8	.556	3	127	$2,407,715
Lowell, M	9	5.3	0.0	4.2	15	.310	-1	127	($5,332,984)
Moehler, B	5	-1.3	6.1	0.0	8	.308	0	54	$48,680
Mota, G	2	-0.1	2.7	0.0	4	.321	-0	37	($2,600,000)
Leiter, A	-3	-1.4	-1.8	0.0	4	-.403	-6	149	($7,000,000)

Fielding and Baserunning Stats

Name	POS	Inn	SBA/G	CS%	ERA	WP+PB/G	PO	A	TE	FE
Lo Duca	C	1033.3	0.98	21%	3.80	0.305	817	61	7	1
Treanor	C	366.7	0.81	27%	4.79	0.393	309	14	5	0
Willingham	C	31.7	0.85	0%	9.66	0.853	22	0	0	0
Jorgensen	C	10.7	1.69	0%	5.06	0.000	7	0	0	0

Name	POS	Inn	PO	A	TE	FE	FPct	RF	DPS	DPT
C Delgado	1B	1206.0	1147	83	4	10	.989	9.18	10	2
J Conine	1B	231.3	246	18	1	3	.985	10.27	4	1
L Harris	1B	3.0	3	0	0	0	1.000	9.00	0	0
J Dillon	1B	2.0	2	0	0	0	1.000	9.00	0	0
L Castillo	2B	1012.0	245	352	1	6	.988	5.31	35	49
D Easley	2B	324.0	80	98	2	2	.978	4.94	12	13
M Lowell	2B	67.0	19	13	1	0	.970	4.30	2	1
J Dillon	2B	26.0	5	7	0	1	.923	4.15	1	2
J Wilson	2B	7.0	1	1	0	0	1.000	2.57	0	0
M Mordecai	2B	6.0	2	2	0	0	1.000	6.00	0	0
A Gonzalez	SS	1087.0	221	367	7	9	.974	4.87	50	46
D Easley	SS	215.7	43	77	2	2	.968	5.01	4	10
R Andino	SS	120.0	19	25	1	1	.957	3.30	4	3
J Wilson	SS	18.0	3	6	0	0	1.000	4.50	1	1
M Mordecai	SS	1.3	0	0	0	0	0.000	0.00	0	0
M Lowell	3B	1126.0	107	243	4	2	.983	2.80	30	3
M Cabrera	3B	238.0	21	46	1	1	.971	2.53	4	0
D Easley	3B	66.3	9	16	0	1	.962	3.39	1	0
J Dillon	3B	9.0	2	1	0	0	1.000	3.00	0	0
L Harris	3B	2.3	0	0	0	0	0.000	0.00	0	0
M Cabrera	LF	1105.0	188	12	1	4	.976	1.63	6	0
J Conine	LF	257.7	54	2	0	0	1.000	1.96	0	0
C Aguila	LF	53.3	13	0	0	0	1.000	2.19	0	0
J Hermida	LF	17.0	3	0	0	0	1.000	1.59	0	0
J Dillon	LF	6.0	2	0	0	0	1.000	3.00	0	0
L Harris	LF	1.7	0	0	0	0	0.000	0.00	0	0
J Willingham	LF	1.0	0	0	0	0	0.000	0.00	0	0
J Pierre	CF	1383.0	332	7	1	3	.988	2.21	6	0
J Encarnacio	CF	52.3	10	0	0	0	1.000	1.72	0	0
C Aguila	CF	7.0	3	0	0	0	1.000	3.86	0	0
J Encarnacio	RF	1112.0	216	4	1	3	.982	1.78	0	0
J Conine	RF	186.7	51	0	0	3	.944	2.46	0	0
C Aguila	RF	84.0	24	1	0	0	1.000	2.68	0	0
J Hermida	RF	58.7	17	0	0	0	1.000	2.61	0	0
L Harris	RF	0.3	0	0	0	0	0.000	0.00	0	0

Incremental Baserunning Runs

Name	IR	IRP
Juan Pierre	2.97	155
Luis Castillo	1.68	121
Damion Easley	1.17	130
Joe Dillon	0.36	189
Jeremy Hermida	0.26	276
Lenny Harris	0.26	153
Robert Andino	0.22	449
Josh Wilson	0.17	127
Chris Aguila	0.11	108
Nate Bump	0.10	140
Miguel Cabrera	-0.02	100
AJ Burnett	-0.03	0
Jason Vargas	-0.05	0
Ismael Valdez	-0.08	0
Josh Johnson	-0.19	0
Brian Moehler	-0.21	0
Matt Treanor	-0.41	74
Dontrelle Willis	-0.54	65
Josh Willingham	-0.56	40
Paul Lo Duca	-0.66	84
Josh Beckett	-1.01	5
Mike Lowell	-1.77	70
Alex Gonzalez	-1.98	66
Jeff Conine	-2.24	51
Juan Encarnacion	-2.38	52
Carlos Delgado	-3.00	58

Houston Astros

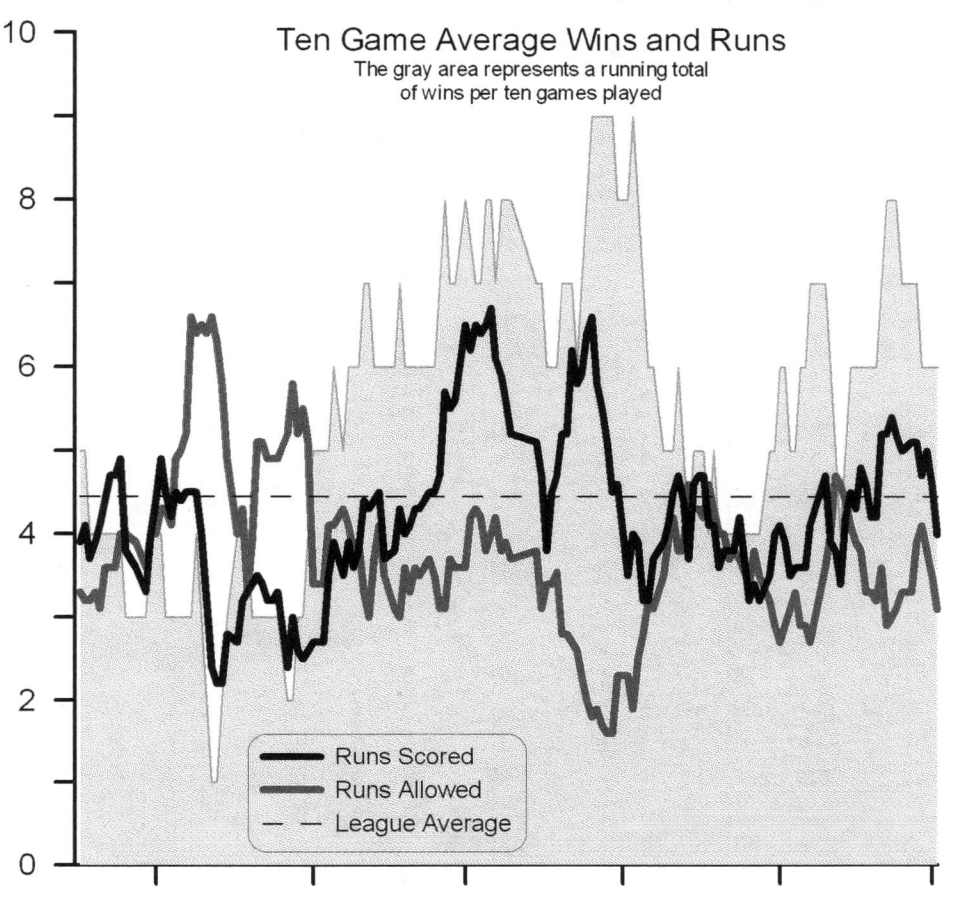

Ten Game Average Wins and Runs
The gray area represents a running total
of wins per ten games played

— Runs Scored
— Runs Allowed
– – League Average

*5/10: Bagwell placed
on DL, returns 9/9*

*5/6: Berkman
plays in first
game*

*6/1: Three rookies start
in OF (Burke, Taveras,
Self) for first time in Hou
since 10/2/82*

*6/29: Biggio plunked
by Byung-Hyun Kim
to become MLB's all-
time HBP leader with 268.*

*7/19: Win both games
of DH vs. Pirates to
move above .500
for good*

*10/2: Clinch NL
Wild Card*

Team Batting and Pitching/Fielding Stats by Month						
	April	May	June	July	Aug	Spt/Oct
Wins	9	10	16	22	13	19
Losses	13	19	9	7	14	11
OBP	.325	.290	.329	.340	.325	.324
SLG	.392	.365	.421	.459	.391	.412
FIP	3.42	4.59	3.62	3.32	4.19	4.16
DER	.716	.697	.706	.733	.737	.724

Batting Stats

Player	RC	Runs	RBI	PA	Outs	P/PA	H	2B	3B	HR	TB	K	BB	IBB	HBP	SH	SF	SB	CS	GDP	BA	OBP	SLG	GPA
Ensberg M.	110	86	101	624	396	3.95	149	30	3	36	293	119	85	9	8	0	5	6	7	12	.283	.388	.557	.314
Berkman L.	90	76	82	565	350	3.86	137	34	1	24	245	72	91	12	4	0	2	4	1	18	.293	.411	.524	.316
Biggio C.	82	94	69	651	445	3.47	156	40	1	26	276	90	37	2	17	4	3	11	1	10	.264	.325	.468	.263
Lane J.	74	65	78	561	391	3.64	138	34	4	26	258	105	32	1	7	0	5	6	2	10	.267	.316	.499	.267
Taveras W.	63	82	29	635	435	3.52	172	13	4	3	202	103	25	1	7	7	4	34	11	4	.291	.325	.341	.231
Everett A.	62	58	54	595	425	3.53	136	27	2	11	200	103	26	1	8	8	4	21	7	5	.248	.290	.364	.221
Ausmus B.	43	35	47	451	307	3.66	100	19	0	3	128	48	51	8	5	7	1	5	3	17	.258	.351	.331	.241
Lamb M.	39	41	53	349	257	3.72	76	13	5	12	135	65	22	1	1	0	4	1	1	10	.236	.284	.419	.232
Burke C.	36	49	26	359	252	3.69	79	19	2	5	117	62	23	0	6	9	3	11	6	7	.248	.309	.368	.231
Palmeiro O.	29	22	20	231	151	3.77	58	17	2	3	88	23	15	1	4	5	3	3	1	4	.284	.341	.431	.261
Vizcaino J.	22	15	23	205	143	3.59	46	10	2	1	63	40	15	4	0	1	2	2	0	2	.246	.299	.337	.219
Bagwell J.	18	11	19	123	77	3.93	25	4	0	3	38	21	18	1	1	0	4	0	0	2	.250	.358	.380	.256
Bruntlett E.	13	19	14	121	91	4.17	24	5	2	4	45	25	10	0	1	1	0	7	2	4	.220	.292	.413	.234
Backe B.	7	5	6	53	35	3.92	10	2	2	0	16	12	3	0	0	5	0	1	0	0	.222	.271	.356	.211
Scott L.	6	6	4	89	66	4.24	15	4	2	0	23	23	9	1	0	0	0	1	1	0	.188	.270	.288	.193
Self T.	5	7	4	49	38	4.55	9	2	0	1	14	9	3	0	0	1	0	0	0	2	.200	.250	.311	.190
Clemens R.	3	2	4	69	47	3.59	12	2	0	0	14	18	5	0	1	5	0	0	0	1	.207	.281	.241	.187
Oswalt R.	3	1	2	83	60	3.28	13	0	0	0	13	19	2	0	1	7	0	0	0	0	.178	.211	.178	.139
Chavez R.	2	6	6	105	87	3.73	17	3	0	2	26	18	4	0	1	0	1	1	0	5	.172	.210	.263	.160
Quintero H.	2	6	8	57	47	3.26	10	1	0	1	14	10	1	1	0	2	0	0	0	3	.185	.200	.259	.155
Duckworth B.	1	1	0	3	1	5.00	2	1	0	0	3	0	0	0	0	0	0	0	0	0	.667	.667	1.000	.550
Gipson C.	1	2	1	14	10	3.07	2	1	0	0	3	3	1	0	0	2	0	1	1	0	.182	.250	.273	.181
Rodriguez W.	1	3	1	43	34	3.65	6	0	0	0	6	16	2	0	0	1	0	0	0	0	.150	.190	.150	.123
Harville C.	-0	0	0	1	1	5.00	0	0	0	0	0	1	0	0	0	0	0	0	0	0	.000	.000	.000	.000
Qualls C.	-0	0	0	1	1	3.00	0	0	0	0	0	1	0	0	0	0	0	0	0	0	.000	.000	.000	.000
Astacio E.	-1	0	0	23	18	3.09	3	0	0	0	3	12	0	0	0	2	0	0	0	0	.143	.143	.143	.100
Pettitte A.	-1	1	3	79	57	3.54	5	0	0	0	5	19	1	0	0	15	1	0	0	0	.081	.094	.081	.062

Pitching Stats

Player	PR	IP	BFP	G	GS	P/PA	K	BB	IBB	HBP	H	HR	DP	DER	SB	CS	PO	W	L	Sv	Op	Hld	RA	ERA	FIP
Clemens R.	57	211.3	838	32	32	3.82	185	62	5	3	151	11	19	.757	8	4	2	13	8	0	0	0	2.17	1.87	2.83
Pettitte A.	48	222.3	875	33	33	3.65	171	41	0	3	188	17	26	.734	5	4	2	17	9	0	0	0	2.67	2.39	3.03
Oswalt R.	39	241.7	1002	35	35	3.59	184	48	3	8	243	18	25	.698	3	4	1	20	12	0	0	0	3.17	2.94	3.12
Wheeler D.	19	73.3	288	71	0	3.77	69	19	3	3	53	7	7	.758	6	0	0	2	3	3	5	17	2.21	2.21	3.24
Lidge B.	15	70.7	291	70	0	3.91	103	23	1	3	58	5	3	.662	5	2	1	4	4	42	46	0	2.67	2.29	2.09
Qualls C.	8	79.7	329	77	0	3.40	60	23	2	6	73	7	12	.717	4	2	0	6	4	0	0	22	3.73	3.28	3.71
Gallo M.	4	20.3	87	36	0	3.69	12	10	2	2	18	1	3	.726	3	0	0	0	1	0	2	8	2.66	2.66	4.21
Driskill T.	1	1.0	4	1	0	4.75	2	0	0	0	1	0	0	.500	0	0	0	0	0	0	0	0	0.00	0.00	-1.02
Strickland S	-1	4.0	16	5	0	4.31	2	0	0	0	4	2	0	.833	1	0	0	0	0	0	0	0	6.75	6.75	8.48
Harville C.	-1	38.3	173	37	0	3.92	33	24	1	4	36	7	6	.724	3	2	0	0	2	0	1	2	4.93	4.46	5.83
Burns Jr. M.	-2	31.0	136	27	0	3.79	20	8	1	5	29	6	1	.763	0	0	0	0	0	0	0	1	5.23	4.94	5.47
Springer R.	-4	59.0	246	62	0	4.30	54	21	3	3	49	9	4	.748	3	0	0	4	4	0	3	10	5.19	4.73	4.36
Franco J.	-5	15.0	77	31	0	3.79	16	9	2	1	23	0	1	.549	0	1	0	0	1	0	1	6	7.80	7.20	2.85
Backe B.	-5	149.3	653	26	25	3.55	97	67	1	4	151	19	14	.717	4	4	0	10	8	0	0	0	4.94	4.76	4.76
Duckworth B.	-11	16.3	82	7	2	3.61	10	7	1	5	24	4	1	.643	0	1	0	0	1	0	0	0	11.02	11.02	7.15
Astacio E.	-14	81.0	366	22	14	3.79	66	25	2	1	100	23	3	.693	3	1	1	3	6	0	0	0	6.22	5.67	6.01
Rodriguez W.	-16	128.7	560	25	22	3.71	80	53	2	8	135	19	21	.710	5	6	2	10	10	0	0	0	5.74	5.53	5.08

Win Shares Stats

Player	WS	Bat	Pitch	Field	ExpWS	WSP	WSAB	CWS	NetWSValue
Ensberg, M	29	24.6	0.0	4.6	17	.833	17	56	$13,218,179
Clemens, R	25	-0.5	25.5	0.0	10	1.211	19	423	$4,104,184
Pettitte, A	22	-2.4	24.4	0.0	11	1.015	15	154	$7,253,121
Oswalt, R	22	-1.3	23.2	0.0	12	.935	15	86	$5,456,517
Berkman, L	21	19.3	0.0	1.9	16	.679	10	151	($3,330,168)
Biggio, C	19	14.1	0.0	5.1	18	.545	7	414	$3,823,634
Lane, J	16	13.1	0.0	3.2	16	.515	5	25	$4,082,367
Ausmus, B	15	4.5	0.0	10.4	13	.569	6	142	$2,912,010
Everett, A	14	7.6	0.0	6.2	17	.408	2	37	$1,413,483
Taveras, W	13	6.3	0.0	6.6	18	.368	1	13	$508,098
Lidge, B	12	0.0	11.9	0.0	7	.873	7	38	$5,445,290
Wheeler, D	9	0.0	9.2	0.0	5	1.013	6	17	$4,695,424
Qualls, C	7	-0.0	7.1	0.0	5	.766	4	11	$3,012,522
Backe, B	7	1.2	6.1	0.0	7	.512	3	13	$2,338,745
Lamb, M	7	5.1	0.0	1.6	9	.351	0	40	($1,088,812)
Palmeiro, O	6	5.0	0.0	1.1	6	.500	2	48	$1,153,156
Burke, C	6	4.0	0.0	2.1	10	.303	-1	6	($316,000)
Vizcaino, J	4	2.7	0.0	1.2	5	.369	0	122	($400,605)
Rodriguez, W	1	-1.0	2.5	0.0	6	.120	-2	1	($316,000)
Astacio, E	0	-0.9	0.1	0.0	4	-.106	-3	0	($316,000)

Fielding and Baserunning Stats

Name	POS	Inn	SBA/G	CS%	ERA	WP+PB/G	PO	A	TE	FE
Ausmus	C	1065.7	0.44	25%	3.16	0.262	884	66	1	0
Chavez	C	253.3	0.64	61%	4.83	0.355	213	19	1	0
Quintero	C	124.0	0.58	13%	3.92	0.218	86	5	1	0

Name	POS	Inn	PO	A	TE	FE	FPct	RF	DPS	DPT
L Berkman	1B	737.7	772	49	2	3	.994	10.02	8	1
M Lamb	1B	428.0	430	28	3	2	.989	9.63	3	1
J Bagwell	1B	202.7	211	14	0	0	1.000	9.99	1	0
J Vizcaino	1B	72.7	63	4	0	2	.971	8.30	1	0
E Bruntlett	1B	1.0	1	0	0	0	1.000	9.00	0	0
H Quintero	1B	1.0	0	1	0	0	1.000	9.00	0	0
C Biggio	2B	1172.0	249	394	2	14	.976	4.94	25	55
J Vizcaino	2B	109.7	30	39	0	0	1.000	5.66	4	10
C Burke	2B	80.3	15	24	0	0	1.000	4.37	1	4
E Bruntlett	2B	79.7	10	16	0	2	.929	2.94	1	2
B Ausmus	2B	1.0	0	0	0	0	0.000	0.00	0	0
A Everett	SS	1291.0	208	420	9	5	.978	4.38	51	40
J Vizcaino	SS	101.3	9	34	0	0	1.000	3.82	1	0
E Bruntlett	SS	49.0	9	21	0	0	1.000	5.51	1	3
B Ausmus	SS	1.0	1	1	0	0	1.000	18.00	0	1
M Ensberg	3B	1286.0	100	295	8	7	.963	2.76	27	1
M Lamb	3B	103.3	16	34	0	1	.980	4.35	0	0
J Vizcaino	3B	40.3	2	9	2	1	.786	2.45	2	0
E Bruntlett	3B	13.0	1	1	0	0	1.000	1.38	0	0
C Burke	LF	634.0	120	3	0	1	.992	1.75	2	0
L Berkman	LF	284.7	50	2	1	2	.945	1.64	2	0
O Palmeiro	LF	187.3	27	0	0	0	1.000	1.30	0	0
L Scott	LF	151.3	22	2	0	1	.960	1.43	0	0
M Lamb	LF	90.0	11	0	0	0	1.000	1.10	0	0
E Bruntlett	LF	28.7	11	0	0	0	1.000	3.45	0	0
J Lane	LF	24.0	3	0	0	1	1.000	1.13	0	0
C Gipson	LF	23.0	3	0	0	0	1.000	1.17	0	0
T Self	LF	20.0	3	0	0	0	1.000	1.35	0	0
W Taveras	CF	1254.0	332	10	0	3	.991	2.45	4	0
E Bruntlett	CF	95.0	34	2	0	0	1.000	3.41	2	0
J Lane	CF	37.0	11	0	0	0	1.000	2.68	0	0
O Palmeiro	CF	30.0	6	0	0	0	1.000	1.80	0	0
C Burke	CF	13.0	1	0	0	0	1.000	0.69	0	0
C Gipson	CF	12.0	3	0	0	0	1.000	2.25	0	0
C Jimerson	CF	1.0	0	0	0	0	0.000	0.00	0	0
L Scott	CF	1.0	0	0	0	0	0.000	0.00	0	0

Name	POS	Inn	PO	A	TE	FE	FPct	RF	DPS	DPT
J Lane	RF	1115.0	225	4	3	3	.974	1.85	0	0
O Palmeiro	RF	149.3	35	2	0	1	.974	2.23	4	0
L Berkman	RF	78.0	16	0	0	0	1.000	1.85	0	0
T Self	RF	72.0	20	0	0	0	1.000	2.50	0	0
L Scott	RF	18.0	2	0	0	0	1.000	1.00	0	0
M Lamb	RF	7.0	1	0	0	0	1.000	1.29	0	0
E Bruntlett	RF	2.0	1	1	0	0	1.000	9.00	2	0
C Gipson	RF	1.0	0	0	0	0	0.000	0.00	0	0

Incremental Baserunning Runs		
Name	IR	IRP
Willy Taveras	2.28	129
Craig Biggio	1.43	121
Morgan Ensberg	1.20	121
Chris Burke	1.14	129
Adam Everett	1.09	116
Orlando Palmeiro	0.69	124
Jose Vizcaino	0.63	150
Luke Scott	0.30	131
Brandon Backe	0.28	118
Humberto Quintero	0.20	225
Eric Bruntlett	0.11	105
Todd Self	0.08	109
Brandon Duckworth	-0.02	0
Mike Lamb	-0.08	97
Roger Clemens	-0.28	0
Raul Chavez	-0.41	40
Roy Oswalt	-0.50	46
Wandy Rodriguez	-0.67	0
Jason Lane	-1.09	78
Charles Gipson	-1.22	-101
Brad Ausmus	-1.64	70
Andy Pettitte	-1.73	-41
Jeff Bagwell	-2.12	10
Lance Berkman	-4.52	1

Kansas City Royals

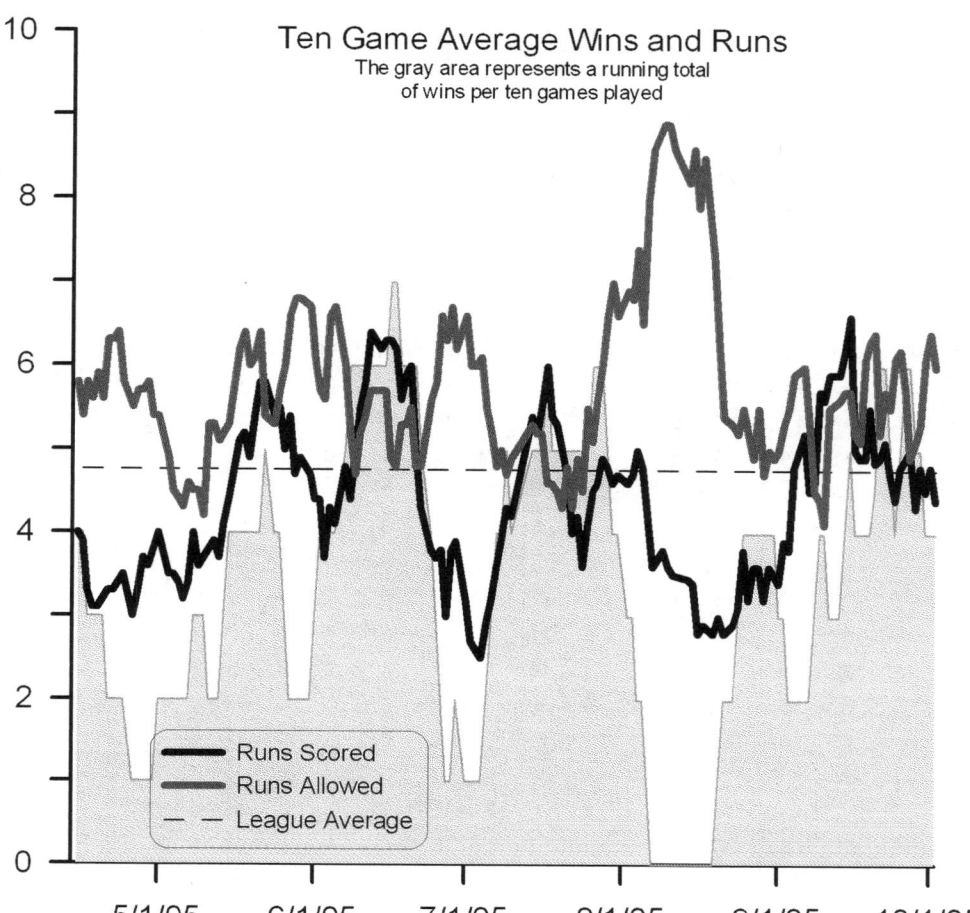

Ten Game Average Wins and Runs
The gray area represents a running total
of wins per ten games played

— Runs Scored
— Runs Allowed
– – League Average

*5/10: Pena resigns
as manager*

*5/11: Bell hired,
wins 11 of
first 15 games*

*7/28: Loss to TB
begins 19-game
losing streak;
outscored 148-64*

*8/28: DeJesus
injures shoulder;
out for season*

*9/30: Blowout loss to
TOR is franchise-worst
106th loss of season*

Team Batting and Pitching/Fielding Stats by Month						
	April	May	June	July	Aug	Spt/Oct
Wins	6	8	12	12	5	13
Losses	18	19	14	16	21	18
OBP	.298	.313	.342	.323	.299	.340
SLG	.368	.403	.418	.405	.346	.429
FIP	4.19	5.16	4.77	4.21	5.04	5.13
DER	.696	.714	.684	.650	.680	.681

251

Batting Stats

Player	RC	Runs	RBI	PA	Outs	P/PA	H	2B	3B	HR	TB	K	BB	IBB	HBP	SH	SF	SB	CS	GDP	BA	OBP	SLG	GPA
Brown E.	92	75	86	609	404	3.74	156	31	5	17	248	108	48	1	8	1	7	10	1	14	.286	.349	.455	.271
Sweeney M.	81	63	83	514	345	3.55	141	39	0	21	243	61	33	7	4	1	6	3	0	16	.300	.347	.517	.285
DeJesus D.	78	69	56	523	337	3.79	135	31	6	9	205	76	42	1	9	5	6	5	5	6	.293	.359	.445	.273
Stairs M.	71	55	66	466	298	3.94	109	26	1	13	176	69	60	4	5	0	5	1	2	9	.275	.373	.444	.279
Berroa A.	69	68	55	652	462	3.35	164	21	5	11	228	108	18	3	14	10	2	7	5	13	.270	.305	.375	.231
Long T.	58	62	53	489	346	3.47	127	21	3	6	172	56	30	0	0	0	4	3	3	15	.279	.321	.378	.239
Teahen M.	53	60	55	491	352	3.91	110	29	4	7	168	107	40	2	1	2	1	7	2	13	.246	.309	.376	.233
Buck J.	43	40	47	430	315	3.52	97	21	1	12	156	94	23	2	3	1	2	2	2	9	.242	.287	.389	.226
Graffanino T	33	29	18	217	141	3.80	57	5	2	3	75	28	22	1	2	2	0	3	1	6	.298	.377	.393	.268
Gotay R.	31	32	29	317	223	3.90	64	14	2	5	97	51	22	0	4	4	5	2	2	3	.227	.288	.344	.215
Guiel A.	14	18	7	121	80	3.86	32	5	0	4	49	21	6	1	5	0	1	1	0	3	.294	.355	.450	.272
Ambres C.	13	25	9	167	117	4.11	35	8	0	4	55	32	16	1	2	3	1	3	2	5	.241	.323	.379	.240
Castillo A.	12	13	14	114	81	3.94	21	5	1	1	31	21	12	0	0	1	1	1	0	2	.210	.292	.310	.209
Diaz M.	12	7	9	97	68	3.29	25	4	2	1	36	15	4	0	2	1	1	0	1	3	.281	.323	.404	.246
McEwing J.	11	16	6	191	146	3.87	43	7	0	1	53	35	6	0	0	5	0	4	4	5	.239	.263	.294	.192
Hocking D.	9	14	7	71	46	4.23	16	1	0	0	17	10	10	0	0	1	0	0	1	1	.267	.371	.283	.238
Phillips P.	8	6	9	67	53	3.09	18	4	1	1	27	5	0	0	0	0	0	0	0	4	.269	.269	.403	.222
Costa S.	7	13	7	88	65	3.52	19	2	0	2	27	11	5	0	1	1	0	0	0	3	.235	.287	.333	.213
Harvey K.	4	4	5	48	35	3.58	10	3	0	1	16	13	3	0	0	0	0	0	0	0	.222	.271	.356	.211
Huber J.	4	6	6	85	62	3.68	17	3	0	0	20	20	5	0	1	0	1	0	0	1	.218	.271	.256	.186
Blanco A.	3	6	5	86	66	2.84	17	0	1	0	19	5	0	0	1	4	2	0	1	3	.215	.220	.241	.159
Marrero E.	2	11	9	100	76	3.47	14	4	0	4	30	18	7	0	1	1	3	1	0	2	.159	.222	.341	.185
Murphy D.	1	4	8	88	69	4.16	12	5	0	1	20	23	9	0	0	1	1	0	1	3	.156	.241	.260	.174
Pickering C.	1	4	3	31	23	4.13	4	0	0	1	7	14	3	0	0	0	1	0	0	0	.148	.226	.259	.166
Lima J.	0	0	0	4	2	3.25	1	0	0	0	1	2	0	0	0	1	0	0	0	0	.333	.333	.333	.233
Greinke Z.	0	1	1	2	1	2.00	1	0	0	1	4	0	0	0	0	0	0	0	0	0	.500	.500	2.000	.725
Jensen R.	-0	0	0	1	1	4.00	0	0	0	0	0	1	0	0	0	0	0	0	0	0	.000	.000	.000	.000
Sisco A.	-0	0	0	1	1	5.00	0	0	0	0	0	1	0	0	0	0	0	0	0	0	.000	.000	.000	.000
Howell J.	-0	0	0	3	3	3.67	0	0	0	0	0	1	0	0	0	0	0	0	0	0	.000	.000	.000	.000
Hernandez R.	-1	0	0	5	5	4.20	0	0	0	0	0	1	0	0	0	0	0	0	0	0	.000	.000	.000	.000
Carrasco D.	-1	0	0	8	7	3.63	0	0	0	0	0	1	0	0	0	1	0	0	0	0	.000	.000	.000	.000

Pitching Stats

Player	PR	IP	BFP	G	GS	P/PA	K	BB	IBB	HBP	H	HR	DP	DER	SB	CS	PO	W	L	Sv	Op	Hld	RA	ERA	FIP
Sisco A.	12	75.3	329	67	0	4.26	76	42	4	2	68	6	10	.695	3	2	1	2	5	0	5	14	3.23	3.11	3.81
MacDougal M.	4	70.3	299	68	0	3.89	72	24	2	3	69	6	8	.675	5	2	0	5	6	21	25	0	4.09	3.33	3.26
Burgos A.	3	63.3	278	59	0	3.87	65	31	1	5	60	6	6	.684	2	3	0	3	5	2	6	11	4.12	3.98	3.93
Bayliss J.	-0	11.7	48	11	0	4.06	10	4	0	2	7	2	1	.833	1	0	0	0	0	0	0	0	4.63	4.63	5.10
Stemle S.	-1	10.7	43	6	0	3.47	9	4	0	0	10	6	2	.667	0	1	0	0	0	0	0	1	5.06	5.06	2.48
Field N.	-4	6.7	35	7	0	4.09	4	5	2	0	13	1	0	.520	0	1	0	0	0	0	0	1	9.45	9.45	6.04
Cerda J.	-4	19.0	89	20	0	4.43	18	11	2	0	21	3	0	.684	0	0	0	1	4	0	1	3	6.63	6.63	4.94
Bautista D.	-5	35.7	159	7	7	3.97	23	17	0	2	36	2	5	.704	2	0	0	2	2	0	0	0	5.80	5.80	4.08
Demaria C.	-6	9.0	44	8	0	3.95	11	5	0	0	14	3	1	.560	0	0	0	1	0	0	0	0	10.00	9.00	6.60
Gobble J.	-7	53.7	249	28	4	3.98	38	30	4	1	64	9	7	.678	5	1	0	1	1	0	0	4	5.70	5.70	5.54
Jensen R.	-7	25.3	115	9	3	3.76	18	7	1	2	31	4	1	.679	1	1	1	3	2	0	1	0	7.11	7.11	4.74
Wood M.	-8	115.0	520	47	10	3.64	60	52	5	8	129	18	22	.709	1	3	2	5	8	2	2	7	5.17	4.46	5.60
Anderson B.	-9	30.7	133	6	6	3.59	17	4	1	0	39	7	3	.695	1	1	1	1	2	0	0	0	7.04	6.75	5.29
Carrasco D.	-9	114.7	511	21	20	3.58	49	51	2	6	129	11	17	.701	2	6	0	6	8	0	0	0	5.26	4.79	4.93
Affeldt J.	-10	49.7	232	49	0	4.06	39	29	2	0	56	3	7	.671	3	0	0	0	2	0	0	12	6.34	5.26	4.01
Snyder K.	-11	36.0	169	13	3	3.56	19	10	1	1	55	3	4	.618	3	1	0	1	3	0	0	0	7.25	6.75	3.99
Camp S.	-16	49.0	228	29	0	3.52	28	13	3	4	69	4	5	.637	3	3	1	1	4	0	2	0	7.35	6.43	4.00
Nunez L.	-18	53.7	246	41	0	3.56	32	18	2	3	73	9	5	.652	2	3	1	3	2	0	1	2	7.55	7.55	5.20
Howell J.	-19	72.7	328	15	15	3.92	54	39	0	6	73	9	10	.709	6	3	1	3	5	0	0	0	6.81	6.19	5.02
Hernandez R.	-20	159.7	706	29	29	3.61	88	70	0	7	172	18	17	.706	15	6	1	8	14	0	0	0	5.69	5.52	4.85
Greinke Z.	-33	183.0	829	33	33	3.73	114	53	0	13	233	23	19	.665	5	3	1	5	17	0	0	0	6.15	5.80	4.51
Lima J.	-56	168.7	780	32	32	3.68	80	61	1	9	219	31	13	.686	10	4	1	5	16	0	0	0	7.47	6.99	5.73

Win Shares Stats

Player	WS	Bat	Pitch	Field	ExpWS	WSP	WSAB	CWS	NetWSValue
Brown, E	20	18.7	0.0	1.1	15	.641	9	24	$7,036,382
Sweeney, M	17	17.1	0.0	0.4	11	.801	10	140	$1,334,004
DeJesus, D	17	15.5	0.0	1.9	13	.660	8	26	$6,450,197
Stairs, M	15	14.5	0.0	0.6	11	.703	8	128	$5,453,282
Berroa, A	11	7.9	0.0	3.3	17	.333	-1	39	($500,000)
Teahen, M	10	7.2	0.0	2.6	13	.378	1	10	$564,664
Buck, J	9	5.2	0.0	4.1	11	.409	1	13	$1,061,745
Long, T	9	8.3	0.0	1.0	12	.378	1	71	($4,586,632)
Sisco, A	7	-0.0	6.9	0.0	5	.625	3	7	$2,380,836
Graffanino, T	7	6.2	0.0	0.6	6	.615	3	56	$3,300,968
MacDougal, M	7	0.0	7.4	0.0	7	.568	3	17	$2,220,704
Burgos, A	5	0.0	4.7	0.0	5	.493	1	5	$1,063,689
Wood, M	5	0.0	5.4	0.0	7	.365	0	7	$177,177
Gotay, R	5	3.4	0.0	1.4	8	.296	-1	7	($316,000)
Carrasco, D	4	-0.6	5.0	0.0	6	.354	1	12	$524,811
Hernandez, R	4	-0.5	4.4	0.0	9	.230	-1	15	($325,000)
Greinke, Z	2	-0.0	2.5	0.0	10	.127	-3	13	($330,500)
Ambres, C	1	0.7	0.0	0.5	4	.137	-2	1	($316,000)
Howell, J	0	-0.1	0.4	0.0	4	.042	-2	0	($316,000)
McEwing, J	0	-0.9	0.0	1.0	5	.015	-3	32	($316,000)
Lima, J	-2	-0.1	-2.7	0.0	9	-.154	-8	56	($2,500,000)

Fielding and Baserunning Stats

Name	POS	Inn	SBA/G	CS%	ERA	WP+PB/G	PO	A	TE	FE
Buck	C	976.7	0.80	31%	5.67	0.498	638	57	2	1
Castillo	C	277.0	0.39	50%	5.10	0.292	235	10	2	0
Phillips	C	159.7	0.56	60%	5.69	0.620	91	10	0	1

Name	POS	Inn	PO	A	TE	FE	FPct	RF	DPS	DPT
M Stairs	1B	509.7	501	36	1	3	.993	9.48	9	0
M Sweeney	1B	419.3	441	29	1	0	.998	10.09	4	0
J Huber	1B	142.3	123	8	0	3	.978	8.28	1	0
T Graffanino	1B	134.0	137	7	0	1	.993	9.67	0	0
J McEwing	1B	97.3	101	11	0	0	1.000	10.36	2	0
E Marrero	1B	73.7	72	3	0	1	.987	9.16	1	0
K Harvey	1B	37.0	41	0	0	0	1.000	9.97	0	0
R Gotay	2B	666.0	156	231	3	5	.980	5.23	25	26
D Murphy	2B	204.7	42	61	1	2	.972	4.53	9	6
A Blanco	2B	184.0	57	68	1	2	.977	6.11	10	14
T Graffanino	2B	163.3	31	46	1	0	.987	4.24	3	4
D Hocking	2B	119.0	33	48	2	0	.976	6.13	7	7
J McEwing	2B	76.3	15	25	0	0	1.000	4.72	2	5
A Berroa	SS	1360.0	254	441	6	19	.965	4.60	53	54
A Blanco	SS	24.0	7	7	0	0	1.000	5.25	1	0
J McEwing	SS	24.0	7	10	1	0	.944	6.38	2	2
D Murphy	SS	2.0	0	0	0	1	0.000	0.00	0	0
D Hocking	SS	2.0	1	3	0	0	1.000	18.00	1	1
T Graffanino	SS	1.0	1	0	0	0	1.000	9.00	0	0
M Teahen	3B	1068.0	113	244	9	10	.947	3.01	25	0
J McEwing	3B	208.7	19	57	3	0	.962	3.28	2	0
T Graffanino	3B	134.3	7	31	5	0	.884	2.55	3	0
D Hocking	3B	2.0	0	0	0	0	0.000	0.00	0	0
T Long	LF	794.0	166	9	0	2	.989	1.98	1	0
C Ambres	LF	170.0	36	0	0	1	.973	1.91	0	0
S Costa	LF	162.0	30	1	0	0	1.000	1.72	0	0
M Diaz	LF	136.0	34	0	0	2	.944	2.25	0	0
E Brown	LF	82.3	21	2	1	0	.958	2.51	0	0
E Marrero	LF	59.0	15	1	0	0	1.000	2.44	0	0
M Stairs	LF	6.0	1	0	0	0	1.000	1.50	0	0
J McEwing	LF	4.0	1	0	0	0	1.000	2.25	0	0
D DeJesus	CF	1005.0	306	7	1	3	.987	2.80	6	0
A Guiel	CF	185.0	54	1	0	1	.982	2.68	0	0
C Ambres	CF	157.0	47	2	0	0	1.000	2.81	0	0
T Long	CF	35.0	5	0	0	0	1.000	1.29	0	0
E Marrero	CF	30.0	5	0	0	0	1.000	1.50	0	0
J McEwing	CF	1.0	0	0	0	0	0.000	0.00	0	0

Name	POS	Inn	PO	A	TE	FE	FPct	RF	DPS	DPT
E Brown	RF	1097.0	243	7	0	11	.958	2.05	0	0
T Long	RF	128.0	32	3	0	1	.972	2.46	0	0
M Stairs	RF	94.3	17	0	0	0	1.000	1.62	0	0
A Guiel	RF	47.7	10	0	0	0	1.000	1.89	0	0
E Marrero	RF	34.0	7	1	0	1	.889	2.12	0	0
M Diaz	RF	11.0	4	0	0	0	1.000	3.27	0	0
J McEwing	RF	1.0	0	0	0	0	0.000	0.00	0	0

Incremental Baserunning Runs		
Name	IR	IRP
David DeJesus	3.03	145
Terrence Long	2.51	163
Ruben Gotay	2.44	148
Angel Berroa	2.03	131
Aaron Guiel	1.67	191
Mark Teahen	1.65	132
Denny Hocking	0.56	147
Andres Blanco	0.49	189
Chip Ambres	0.35	128
Shane Costa	0.15	162
Eli Marrero	0.13	120
Tony Graffanino	-0.02	99
John Buck	-0.10	98
Donnie Murphy	-0.23	0
Matt Diaz	-0.29	0
Justin Huber	-0.37	0
Alberto Castillo	-0.38	82
Calvin Pickering	-0.52	-416
Emil Brown	-0.53	94
Joe McEwing	-0.60	51
Mike Sweeney	-0.82	81
Paul Phillips	-0.93	28
Ken Harvey	-1.13	-110
Matt Stairs	-2.35	61

Los Angeles Angels of Anaheim

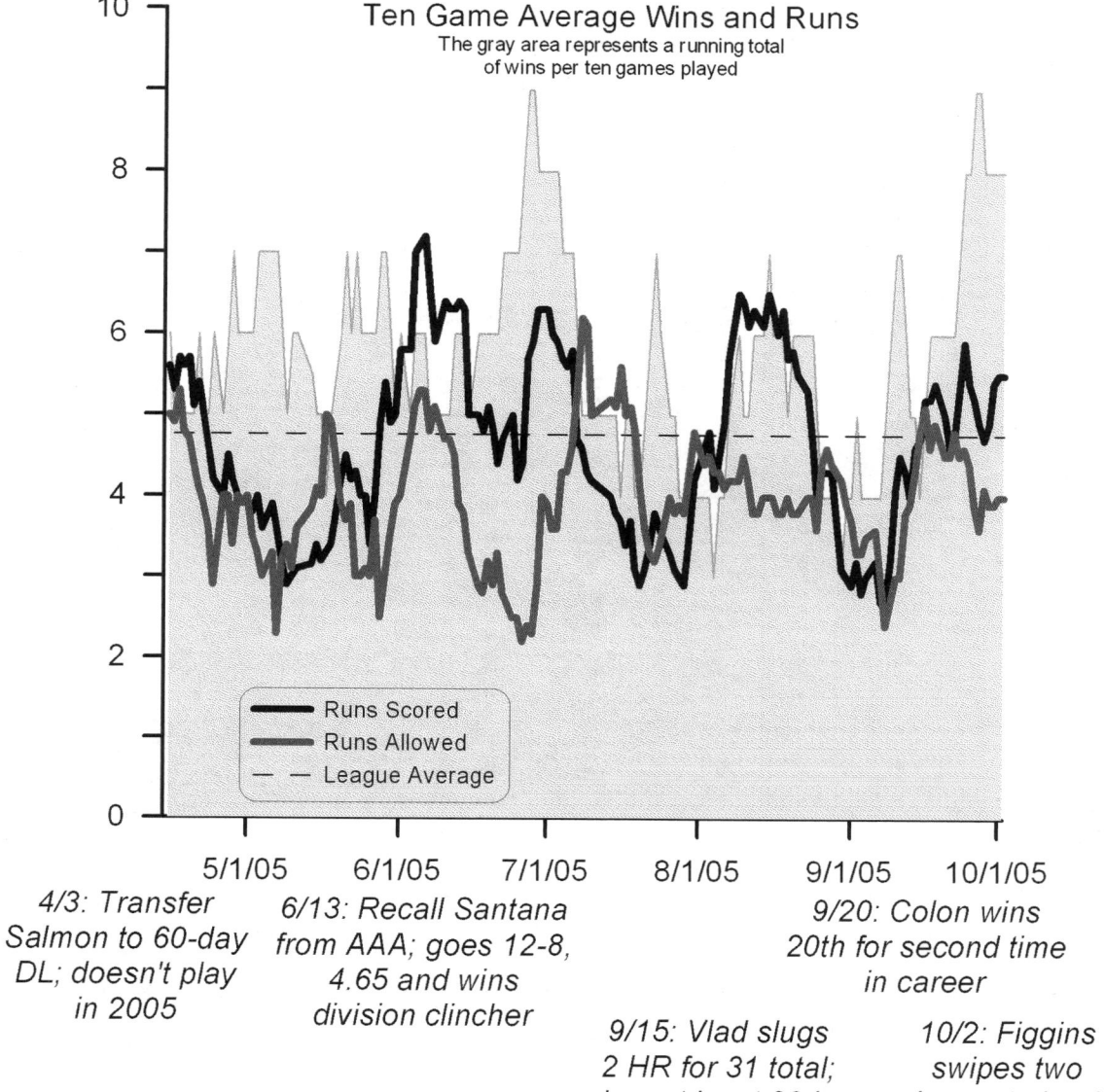

Ten Game Average Wins and Runs
The gray area represents a running total
of wins per ten games played

Runs Scored
Runs Allowed
League Average

4/3: Transfer Salmon to 60-day DL; doesn't play in 2005

6/13: Recall Santana from AAA; goes 12-8, 4.65 and wins division clincher

9/15: Vlad slugs 2 HR for 31 total; has at least 30 in 7 of last 8 years

9/20: Colon wins 20th for second time in career

10/2: Figgins swipes two bases to lead majors with 62

Team Batting and Pitching/Fielding Stats by Month						
	April	May	June	July	Aug	Spt/Oct
Wins	13	17	17	13	14	21
Losses	11	11	9	14	13	9
OBP	.306	.300	.360	.310	.344	.326
SLG	.408	.371	.466	.365	.411	.428
FIP	4.18	3.89	3.95	4.01	3.91	3.93
DER	.698	.708	.725	.720	.710	.713

Batting Stats

Player	RC	Runs	RBI	PA	Outs	P/PA	H	2B	3B	HR	TB	K	BB	IBB	HBP	SH	SF	SB	CS	GDP	BA	OBP	SLG	GPA
Guerrero V.	113	95	108	594	373	3.26	165	29	2	32	294	48	61	26	8	0	5	13	1	17	.317	.394	.565	.319
Figgins C.	99	113	57	720	482	3.91	186	25	10	8	255	101	64	1	0	9	5	62	17	9	.290	.352	.397	.258
Anderson G.	86	68	96	603	426	3.28	163	34	1	17	250	84	23	8	0	0	5	1	1	13	.283	.308	.435	.248
Erstad D.	82	86	66	667	454	3.85	166	33	3	7	226	109	47	3	1	4	2	10	3	8	.273	.325	.371	.239
Kennedy A.	65	49	37	460	300	3.73	125	23	0	2	154	64	29	1	7	5	3	19	4	5	.300	.354	.370	.252
Cabrera O.	64	70	57	587	413	3.51	139	28	3	8	197	50	38	4	3	4	2	21	2	10	.257	.309	.365	.230
Molina B.	56	45	69	449	305	3.53	121	17	0	15	183	41	27	2	1	5	6	0	2	14	.295	.336	.446	.263
Rivera J.	51	46	59	376	279	3.64	95	17	1	15	159	44	23	0	0	2	1	1	9	15	.271	.316	.454	.256
Finley S.	41	41	54	440	326	3.84	90	20	3	12	152	71	26	3	3	1	4	8	4	6	.222	.271	.374	.216
McPherson D.	29	29	26	220	163	3.83	50	14	2	8	92	64	14	0	1	0	0	3	3	5	.244	.295	.449	.245
DaVanon J.	27	42	15	271	185	4.06	52	10	1	2	70	44	39	1	2	3	2	11	6	6	.231	.347	.311	.234
Izturis M.	26	18	15	210	152	3.74	47	8	4	1	66	21	17	2	0	1	1	9	3	5	.246	.306	.346	.224
Kotchman C.	22	16	22	143	95	3.63	35	5	0	7	61	18	15	0	0	1	1	1	1	3	.278	.352	.484	.279
Molina J.	20	14	25	203	147	3.91	42	4	0	6	64	41	13	0	2	4	0	2	0	5	.228	.286	.348	.216
Quinlan R.	11	17	14	143	108	3.61	31	8	0	5	54	26	7	0	1	0	1	0	1	4	.231	.273	.403	.223
Paul J.	3	4	4	40	31	3.63	7	1	0	2	14	9	2	0	0	1	0	0	0	1	.189	.231	.378	.198
Colon B.	1	0	1	3	2	3.67	1	0	0	0	1	2	0	0	0	0	0	0	0	0	.333	.333	.333	.233
Mathis J.	0	1	0	3	2	2.33	1	0	0	0	1	1	0	0	0	0	0	0	0	0	.333	.333	.333	.233
Byrd P.	0	0	0	4	3	3.50	1	0	0	0	1	0	0	0	0	0	0	0	0	0	.250	.250	.250	.175
Sorensen Z.	-0	3	0	13	10	3.31	2	1	0	0	3	2	0	0	0	1	0	0	0	0	.167	.167	.250	.138
Escobar K.	-0	0	0	2	1	3.50	0	0	0	0	0	0	0	0	0	1	0	0	0	0	.000	.000	.000	.000
Washburn J.	-0	1	0	5	4	3.00	0	0	0	0	0	0	1	0	0	0	0	0	0	0	.000	.200	.000	.090
Donnelly B.	-0	0	0	1	1	2.00	0	0	0	0	0	0	0	0	0	0	0	0	0	0	.000	.000	.000	.000
Matranga D.	-0	0	0	1	1	5.00	0	0	0	0	0	0	0	0	0	0	0	0	0	0	.000	.000	.000	.000
Shields S.	-0	0	0	1	1	4.00	0	0	0	0	0	1	0	0	0	0	0	0	0	0	.000	.000	.000	.000
Merloni L.	-0	1	1	7	5	4.14	0	0	0	0	0	2	1	0	0	0	1	0	0	0	.000	.143	.000	.064
Prieto C.	-0	0	0	3	2	2.67	0	0	0	0	0	0	0	0	0	1	0	0	0	0	.000	.000	.000	.000
Lackey J.	-1	0	0	6	6	2.50	0	0	0	0	0	1	0	0	0	0	0	0	0	0	.000	.000	.000	.000
Pride C.	-1	2	0	11	10	3.55	1	1	0	0	2	4	0	0	0	0	0	0	0	0	.091	.091	.182	.086

Pitching Stats

Player	PR	IP	BFP	G	GS	P/PA	K	BB	IBB	HBP	H	HR	DP	DER	SB	CS	PO	W	L	Sv	Op	Hld	RA	ERA	FIP
Washburn J.	25	177.3	740	29	29	3.66	94	51	0	8	184	19	29	.710	0	6	1	8	8	0	0	0	3.35	3.20	4.37
Lackey J.	22	209.0	892	33	33	3.91	199	71	3	11	208	13	22	.674	11	8	2	14	5	0	0	0	3.66	3.44	3.12
Colon B.	21	222.7	906	33	33	3.58	157	43	0	3	215	26	25	.721	2	4	0	21	8	0	0	0	3.76	3.48	3.77
Rodriguez F.	15	67.3	279	66	0	3.97	91	32	3	0	45	7	1	.745	2	0	0	2	5	45	50	0	2.67	2.67	3.12
Shields S.	14	91.7	375	78	0	4.02	98	37	2	2	66	5	7	.738	6	2	0	10	11	7	13	33	3.24	2.75	2.89
Escobar K.	10	59.7	242	16	7	3.69	63	21	1	2	45	4	4	.730	5	3	0	3	2	1	1	2	3.17	3.02	2.96
Byrd P.	9	204.3	842	31	31	3.47	102	28	1	7	216	22	23	.716	13	6	0	12	11	0	0	0	4.18	3.74	3.96
Donnelly B.	3	65.3	271	66	0	4.07	53	19	3	2	60	9	2	.729	3	3	0	9	3	0	5	16	4.13	3.72	4.18
Peralta J.	3	34.7	145	28	0	4.17	30	14	2	0	28	6	0	.768	1	2	2	1	0	0	0	0	3.89	3.89	4.77
Bootcheck C.	3	18.7	80	5	2	3.59	8	4	1	0	19	1	1	.731	1	1	0	0	1	1	1	0	3.38	3.38	3.53
Christiansen	1	3.7	20	12	0	3.95	4	2	0	0	7	0	0	.500	0	0	0	0	0	0	0	0	2.45	2.45	2.50
Prinz B.	1	3.0	14	3	0	4.36	1	1	0	0	4	1	0	.727	1	0	0	0	1	0	0	0	3.00	3.00	7.71
Jones G.	-1	5.3	24	6	0	3.58	6	2	0	0	7	2	1	.643	0	0	0	0	0	0	0	0	6.75	6.75	6.79
Yan E.	-2	66.7	293	49	0	3.67	45	30	4	0	66	8	3	.724	5	2	0	1	1	0	0	1	4.86	4.59	4.60
Saunders J.	-3	9.3	41	2	2	3.71	4	4	0	0	10	3	1	.767	1	0	0	0	0	0	0	0	7.71	7.71	7.65
Woods J.	-4	27.7	122	28	0	4.10	20	8	0	2	30	7	3	.729	3	0	0	1	1	0	0	2	5.86	4.55	5.97
Gregg K.	-4	64.3	289	33	2	3.96	52	29	2	3	70	8	8	.685	6	0	0	1	2	0	1	1	5.18	5.04	4.54
Santana E.	-5	133.7	583	23	23	3.87	99	47	2	8	139	17	9	.704	8	5	1	12	8	0	0	0	4.92	4.65	4.45

Win Shares Stats

Player	WS	Bat	Pitch	Field	ExpWS	WSP	WSAB	CWS	NetWSValue
Guerrero, V	27	24.5	0.0	2.3	15	.893	16	222	$5,482,021
Figgins, C	22	16.2	0.0	5.5	19	.586	9	50	$6,828,139
Colon, B	19	0.3	19.2	0.0	12	.827	12	131	$3,931,541
Lackey, J	17	-0.5	17.2	0.0	11	.752	10	43	$7,811,719
Kennedy, A	17	10.9	0.0	5.7	13	.652	8	81	$3,043,743
Anderson, G	16	14.5	0.0	1.7	15	.549	6	179	($995,877)
Washburn, J	15	-0.1	14.7	0.0	9	.773	9	80	$93,380
Molina, B	15	8.1	0.0	6.9	12	.641	7	75	$2,332,770
Erstad, D	15	12.0	0.0	2.7	17	.430	3	146	($2,651,845)
Byrd, P	14	-0.1	13.7	0.0	11	.627	7	68	$2,765,836
Cabrera, O	14	8.0	0.0	6.5	16	.464	4	108	($636,107)
Shields, S	12	-0.0	12.2	0.0	8	.783	7	43	$4,631,395
Rodriguez, F	11	0.0	11.2	0.0	8	.718	6	36	$4,387,123
Rivera, J	9	7.8	0.0	1.3	9	.493	3	28	$2,003,022
Donnelly, B	7	-0.0	6.6	0.0	5	.664	3	30	$2,335,935
Molina, J	7	1.8	0.0	5.0	6	.605	3	17	$1,797,282
Santana, E	7	0.0	7.0	0.0	7	.495	3	7	$2,165,443
McPherson, D	6	4.7	0.0	1.4	6	.518	2	7	$1,569,382
Izturis, M	6	3.7	0.0	2.1	6	.504	2	7	$1,396,646
Finley, S	6	3.4	0.0	3.0	12	.277	-2	287	($4,776,882)
DaVanon, J	4	2.9	0.0	1.3	6	.327	-0	28	($922,517)
Yan, E	3	0.0	2.6	0.0	4	.322	-0	38	($592,058)
Gregg, K	2	0.0	1.8	0.0	4	.225	-1	10	($360,000)
Quinlan, R	1	0.4	0.0	0.9	4	.175	-1	9	($360,000)

Fielding and Baserunning Stats

Name	POS	Inn	SBA/G	CS%	ERA	WP+PB/G	PO	A	TE	FE
Molina, B	C	873.3	0.64	29%	3.55	0.515	641	48	3	0
Molina, J	C	480.3	0.69	49%	3.65	0.543	409	40	2	0
Paul	C	105.7	0.60	29%	5.03	0.341	84	4	1	0
Mathis	C	5.0	0.00	0%	0.00	0.000	4	0	0	0

Name	POS	Inn	PO	A	TE	FE	FPct	RF	DPS	DPT
D Erstad	1B	1279.0	1220	77	2	2	.997	9.13	19	1
C Kotchman	1B	131.0	111	7	0	0	1.000	8.11	0	0
R Quinlan	1B	42.0	38	1	0	0	1.000	8.36	0	0
J Molina	1B	10.0	10	0	0	0	1.000	9.00	0	0
L Merloni	1B	2.0	0	0	0	0	0.000	0.00	0	0
A Kennedy	2B	1107.0	212	352	4	1	.991	4.59	26	43
C Figgins	2B	322.3	67	101	3	2	.971	4.69	4	15
Z Sorensen	2B	24.3	3	5	0	0	1.000	2.96	2	0
M Izturis	2B	8.0	4	4	0	0	1.000	9.00	0	0
D Matranga	2B	2.0	2	1	0	0	1.000	13.50	2	0
O Cabrera	SS	1240.0	229	347	1	6	.988	4.18	44	26
M Izturis	SS	212.7	44	55	1	1	.980	4.19	3	6
C Figgins	SS	11.0	2	4	0	0	1.000	4.91	0	0
D McPherson	3B	483.3	32	86	5	1	.944	2.20	15	1
C Figgins	3B	437.7	34	95	1	2	.977	2.65	8	0
M Izturis	3B	275.7	20	62	3	5	.911	2.68	6	0
R Quinlan	3B	243.0	22	51	5	2	.913	2.70	5	0
L Merloni	3B	16.7	1	8	0	0	1.000	4.86	0	0
Z Sorensen	3B	8.0	2	3	0	1	.833	5.63	0	0
G Anderson	LF	920.0	201	4	1	4	.976	2.01	2	0
J Rivera	LF	297.7	72	3	0	0	1.000	2.27	0	0
C Figgins	LF	130.0	27	1	0	0	1.000	1.94	1	0
J DaVanon	LF	88.7	30	1	0	0	1.000	3.15	0	0
R Quinlan	LF	20.0	3	0	0	0	1.000	1.35	0	0
C Pride	LF	5.0	2	0	0	0	1.000	3.60	0	0
J Paul	LF	3.0	0	0	0	0	0.000	0.00	0	0
S Finley	CF	895.7	266	5	1	3	.985	2.72	4	0
C Figgins	CF	398.3	131	1	0	2	.985	2.98	1	0
J DaVanon	CF	130.7	45	0	0	1	.978	3.10	0	0
J Rivera	CF	30.0	10	0	0	0	1.000	3.00	0	0
C Prieto	CF	9.0	5	0	0	0	1.000	5.00	0	0
M Izturis	CF	0.7	1	1	0	0	1.000	27.00	0	1
V Guerrero	RF	1040.0	242	8	0	3	.988	2.16	4	0
J Rivera	RF	237.7	45	2	0	1	.979	1.78	3	0
J DaVanon	RF	133.7	30	0	0	0	1.000	2.02	0	0
C Figgins	RF	53.0	12	1	0	0	1.000	2.21	0	0

Incremental Baserunning Runs		
Name	IR	IRP
Darin Erstad	3.05	138
Chone Figgins	3.02	136
Orlando Cabrera	2.00	129
Jeff DaVanon	1.90	140
Zach Sorensen	0.89	219
Maicer Izturis	0.66	152
Steve Finley	0.43	106
Jeff Mathis	0.14	123
Casey Kotchman	0.06	116
Josh Paul	0.02	166
Vladimir Guerrero	-0.03	100
Robb Quinlan	-0.09	97
Juan Rivera	-0.10	96
Curtis Pride	-0.16	0
Jose Molina	-0.17	88
Garret Anderson	-1.13	83
Adam Kennedy	-1.94	77
Dallas McPherson	-2.19	24
Bengie Molina	-4.10	22

Los Angeles Dodgers

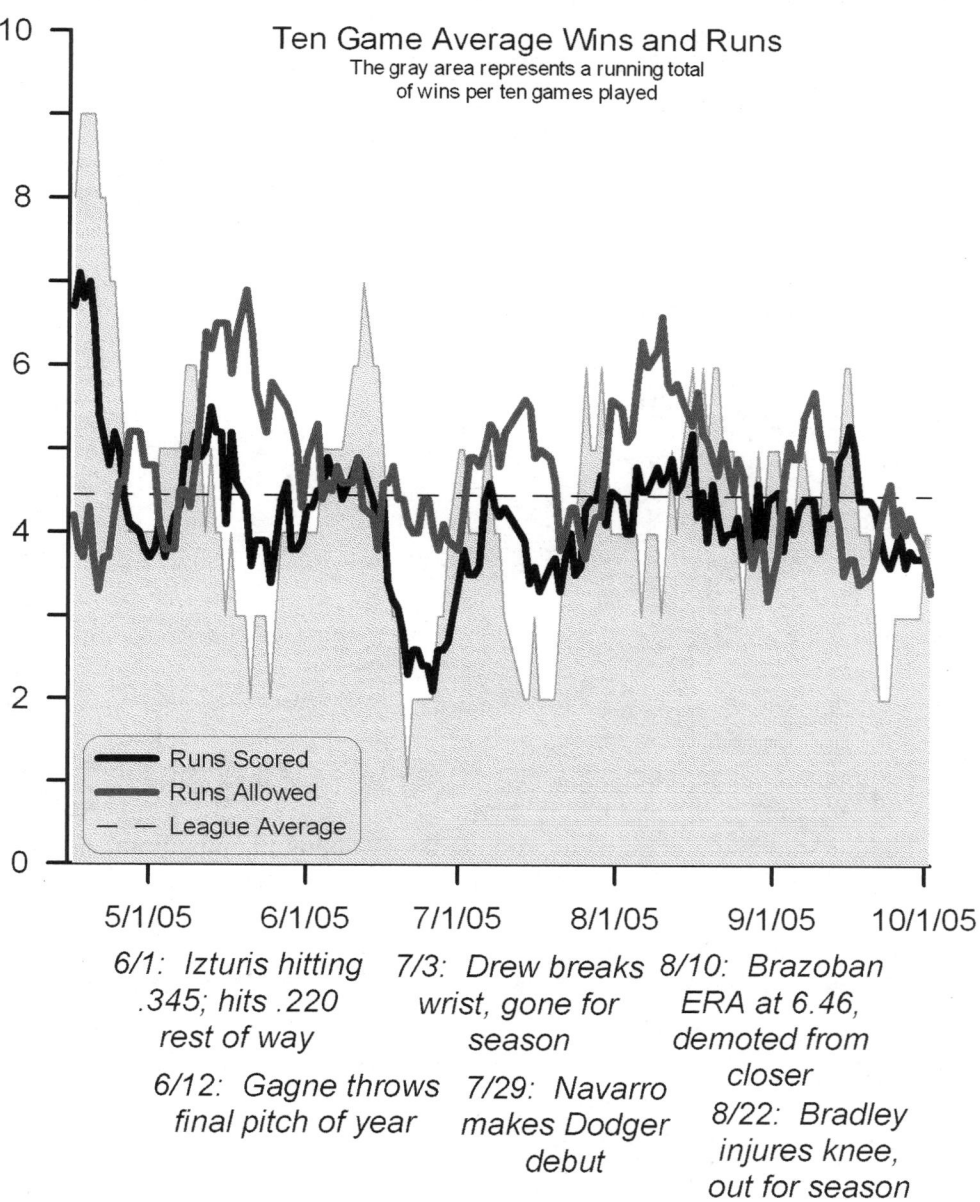

Ten Game Average Wins and Runs
The gray area represents a running total
of wins per ten games played

- Runs Scored
- Runs Allowed
- — League Average

6/1: Izturis hitting .345; hits .220 rest of way

6/12: Gagne throws final pitch of year

7/3: Drew breaks wrist, gone for season

7/29: Navarro makes Dodger debut

8/10: Brazoban ERA at 6.46, demoted from closer

8/22: Bradley injures knee, out for season

Team Batting and Pitching/Fielding Stats by Month						
	April	May	June	July	Aug	Spt/Oct
Wins	15	11	11	10	14	10
Losses	8	17	16	17	14	19
OBP	.358	.327	.311	.325	.322	.319
SLG	.451	.389	.392	.395	.383	.370
FIP	4.12	4.90	4.01	4.77	4.28	4.50
DER	.724	.688	.717	.712	.709	.740

Batting Stats

Player	RC	Runs	RBI	PA	Outs	P/PA	H	2B	3B	HR	TB	K	BB	IBB	HBP	SH	SF	SB	CS	GDP	BA	OBP	SLG	GPA
Kent J.	113	100	105	637	414	3.56	160	36	0	29	283	85	72	8	8	0	4	6	2	19	.289	.377	.512	.297
Saenz O.	54	39	63	352	248	3.87	84	24	0	15	153	63	27	1	3	0	2	0	1	12	.263	.325	.480	.266
Drew J.	52	48	36	311	184	3.88	72	12	1	15	131	50	51	3	5	0	3	1	1	3	.286	.412	.520	.315
Werth J.	47	46	43	395	270	4.62	79	22	2	7	126	114	48	2	6	1	3	11	2	10	.234	.338	.374	.245
Phillips J.	46	38	55	434	321	3.54	95	20	0	10	145	50	25	4	4	2	4	0	1	16	.238	.287	.363	.220
Robles O.	44	44	34	399	281	4.02	99	18	1	5	134	33	31	0	2	1	1	0	8	8	.272	.332	.368	.241
Bradley M.	43	49	38	316	208	3.60	82	14	1	13	137	47	25	1	2	4	1	6	1	6	.290	.350	.484	.279
Perez A.	43	28	23	287	190	4.20	77	13	2	3	103	61	21	1	5	1	1	11	4	4	.297	.360	.398	.261
Choi H.	42	40	42	368	252	4.02	81	15	2	15	145	80	34	1	8	2	4	1	3	10	.253	.336	.453	.265
Izturis C.	40	48	31	478	349	3.64	114	19	2	2	143	51	25	1	4	4	1	8	8	11	.257	.302	.322	.216
Ledee R.	36	31	39	266	176	3.71	66	16	1	7	105	55	20	1	3	0	6	0	0	5	.278	.335	.443	.261
Cruz J.	31	23	22	179	114	3.98	47	14	2	6	83	43	23	1	0	0	0	0	1	4	.301	.391	.532	.309
Repko J.	30	43	30	301	222	3.88	61	15	3	8	106	80	16	1	7	2	0	5	0	7	.221	.281	.384	.222
Aybar W.	22	12	10	105	59	3.92	28	8	0	1	39	11	18	0	1	0	0	3	1	0	.326	.448	.453	.315
Edwards M.	21	23	15	258	187	3.59	59	9	2	3	81	34	16	0	2	1	0	1	1	6	.247	.300	.339	.220
Navarro D.	20	21	14	199	131	3.95	48	9	0	3	66	21	20	1	2	1	0	0	0	3	.273	.354	.375	.253
Valentin J.	17	17	14	184	125	4.36	25	4	2	2	39	38	31	2	4	0	2	3	1	2	.170	.326	.265	.213
Weaver J.	8	6	7	78	54	3.45	16	2	0	0	18	19	2	0	0	6	0	0	0	0	.229	.250	.257	.177
Grabowski J.	8	14	12	124	98	3.68	18	0	0	4	30	29	10	1	0	0	1	1	0	4	.161	.228	.268	.169
Bako P.	7	1	4	47	30	3.81	10	2	0	0	12	12	7	1	0	0	0	0	0	0	.250	.362	.300	.238
Myrow B.	3	2	0	25	16	4.52	4	1	0	0	5	8	5	0	0	0	0	0	0	0	.200	.360	.250	.225
Penny B.	2	1	3	61	42	3.10	8	3	0	0	11	17	1	0	1	9	0	0	0	0	.160	.192	.220	.142
Lowe D.	2	3	4	76	57	3.13	10	2	0	0	12	17	2	0	0	9	0	1	0	2	.154	.179	.185	.127
Chen C.	1	1	2	8	6	5.00	2	0	0	0	2	4	0	0	0	0	0	0	0	0	.250	.250	.250	.175
Rose M.	1	2	1	46	37	3.93	9	2	0	1	14	6	3	0	0	0	0	0	0	3	.209	.261	.326	.199
Erickson S.	0	0	0	14	11	3.71	2	0	0	0	2	5	0	0	0	1	0	0	0	0	.154	.154	.154	.108
Houlton D.	0	1	1	35	27	4.14	3	1	0	0	4	18	3	0	0	2	0	0	0	0	.100	.182	.133	.115
Carrara G.	-0	0	0	2	1	4.50	0	0	0	0	0	1	0	0	0	1	0	0	0	0	.000	.000	.000	.000
Schmoll S.	-0	0	0	1	1	2.00	0	0	0	0	0	0	0	0	0	0	0	0	0	0	.000	.000	.000	.000
Wunsch K.	-0	0	0	1	1	3.00	0	0	0	0	0	1	0	0	0	0	0	0	0	0	.000	.000	.000	.000
Alvarez W.	-0	0	0	3	2	2.00	0	0	0	0	0	1	0	0	0	1	0	0	0	0	.000	.000	.000	.000
Brazoban Y.	-0	0	0	2	2	3.00	0	0	0	0	0	1	0	0	0	0	0	0	0	0	.000	.000	.000	.000
Osoria F.	-0	0	0	3	3	3.33	0	0	0	0	0	2	0	0	0	0	0	0	0	0	.000	.000	.000	.000
Ross C.	-0	1	1	26	22	4.35	4	1	0	0	5	10	1	0	0	0	0	0	0	1	.160	.192	.200	.137
Jackson E.	-0	0	1	11	8	3.27	2	0	0	0	2	2	1	0	0	0	0	0	0	0	.200	.273	.200	.173
Thompson D.	-0	0	0	5	4	2.60	0	0	0	0	0	2	0	0	0	1	0	0	0	0	.000	.000	.000	.000
Sanchez D.	-0	0	0	4	4	2.25	0	0	0	0	0	0	0	0	0	0	0	0	0	0	.000	.000	.000	.000
Dessens E.	-1	0	0	10	10	4.10	0	0	0	0	0	6	0	0	0	0	0	0	0	0	.000	.000	.000	.000
Perez O.	-1	2	0	42	29	2.31	4	0	0	0	4	10	1	0	0	8	0	0	0	0	.121	.147	.121	.096
Nakamura N.	-1	1	3	41	37	3.80	5	2	0	0	7	7	2	0	0	0	0	0	0	3	.128	.171	.179	.122

Pitching Stats

Player	PR	IP	BFP	G	GS	P/PA	K	BB	IBB	HBP	H	HR	DP	DER	SB	CS	PO	W	L	Sv	Op	Hld	RA	ERA	FIP
Penny B.	8	175.3	738	29	29	3.77	122	41	2	3	185	17	15	.697	17	5	1	7	9	0	0	0	4.00	3.90	3.60
Sanchez D.	4	82.0	353	79	0	3.58	71	36	6	3	75	8	10	.715	8	1	1	4	7	8	12	13	3.95	3.73	3.95
Gagne E.	3	13.3	53	14	0	4.09	22	3	0	0	10	2	0	.692	2	0	0	1	0	8	8	0	2.70	2.70	2.31
Dessens E.	2	65.7	277	28	7	3.81	37	19	2	1	63	6	10	.734	5	1	0	1	2	0	0	1	4.11	3.56	3.96
Carrara G.	2	75.7	326	72	0	3.85	56	38	5	6	65	6	10	.732	4	1	1	7	4	0	2	11	4.16	3.93	4.28
Thompson D.	2	18.0	74	4	3	4.20	13	10	1	0	16	0	4	.686	4	3	1	0	0	0	0	0	3.50	3.50	3.20
Osoria F.	1	29.7	122	24	0	3.08	15	8	0	3	28	3	6	.731	1	1	0	0	2	0	2	3	4.25	3.94	4.40
Wunsch K.	-0	23.7	105	46	0	3.72	22	14	2	2	20	2	2	.723	2	1	2	1	1	0	1	15	4.56	4.56	4.25
Kuo H.	-1	5.3	26	9	0	4.88	10	5	1	0	5	1	0	.600	0	0	0	0	1	0	1	3	6.75	6.75	4.48
Weaver J.	-2	224.0	930	34	34	3.63	157	43	1	18	220	35	20	.727	20	6	1	14	11	0	0	0	4.46	4.22	4.43
Alvarez W.	-3	24.0	109	21	2	3.66	16	7	0	0	31	7	1	.696	2	0	0	1	4	0	0	2	5.63	5.63	6.32
Broxton J.	-4	13.7	68	14	0	4.24	22	12	2	1	13	0	0	.606	5	0	0	1	0	0	1	1	7.24	5.93	2.62
Lowe D.	-5	222.0	934	35	35	3.56	146	55	1	5	223	28	21	.721	19	6	0	12	15	0	0	0	4.58	3.61	4.12
Perez O.	-6	108.7	453	19	19	3.62	74	28	2	0	109	13	11	.716	14	2	2	7	8	0	0	0	4.89	4.56	3.95
Carlyle B.	-6	14.0	62	10	0	3.82	13	4	0	1	16	4	1	.700	0	0	0	0	0	0	1	0	8.36	8.36	5.91
Schmoll S.	-6	46.7	205	48	0	3.83	29	22	2	3	47	4	5	.707	2	0	0	2	2	3	4	9	5.59	5.01	4.46
Jackson E.	-8	28.7	134	7	6	4.16	13	17	0	1	31	2	2	.713	2	1	0	2	2	0	0	0	6.91	6.28	4.87
Erickson S.	-10	55.3	249	19	8	3.36	15	25	0	4	62	12	8	.741	1	0	0	1	4	0	0	0	6.02	6.02	6.83
Brazoban Y.	-11	72.7	317	74	0	3.82	61	32	4	5	70	11	6	.716	8	2	0	4	10	21	27	8	5.70	5.33	4.80
Houlton D.	-17	129.0	578	35	19	3.77	90	52	3	8	145	21	9	.695	14	4	1	6	9	0	0	0	5.51	5.16	5.10

Win Shares Stats

Player	WS	Bat	Pitch	Field	ExpWS	WSP	WSAB	CWS	NetWSValue
Kent, J	30	26.0	0.0	4.3	18	.866	18	299	$9,994,216
Drew, J	13	11.9	0.0	1.5	9	.782	7	128	$312,054
Weaver, J	13	0.7	12.1	0.0	11	.598	6	73	($430,117)
Saenz, O	12	11.1	0.0	0.7	9	.640	5	37	$3,858,126
Lowe, D	11	-1.2	12.7	0.0	11	.535	5	107	($69,771)
Bradley, M	11	8.3	0.0	2.4	9	.621	5	58	$1,233,144
Perez, A	10	8.5	0.0	1.5	8	.654	5	13	$3,679,288
Penny, B	10	-0.8	10.3	0.0	8	.567	5	50	($1,819,682)
Werth, J	10	7.9	0.0	2.5	11	.477	3	24	$2,179,366
Robles, O	9	6.3	0.0	2.3	11	.401	1	9	$865,828
Cruz, J	8	7.3	0.0	1.0	5	.843	5	119	$2,050,310
Phillips, J	8	5.7	0.0	2.4	12	.335	-0	28	($311,537)
Ledee, R	7	6.7	0.0	0.7	7	.522	2	50	$1,516,333
Choi, H	7	6.6	0.0	0.8	10	.377	1	26	$381,486
Sanchez, D	6	-0.1	6.1	0.0	5	.560	2	12	$1,753,126
Repko, J	6	3.7	0.0	1.8	9	.324	-0	6	($316,000)
Izturis, C	6	2.5	0.0	3.6	13	.235	-3	50	($2,150,000)
Navarro, D	4	2.5	0.0	1.5	6	.359	0	4	$78,495
Perez, O	3	-1.4	4.5	0.0	5	.298	-0	42	($2,555,922)
Valentin, J	2	1.6	0.0	0.8	5	.240	-1	167	($2,807,639)
Houlton, D	2	-0.8	2.6	0.0	6	.135	-2	2	($316,000)
Brazoban, Y	2	-0.1	1.7	0.0	6	.137	-3	6	($319,500)
Edwards, M	2	1.3	0.0	1.0	7	.159	-3	2	($316,000)

Fielding and Baserunning Stats

Name	POS	Inn	SBA/G	CS%	ERA	WP+PB/G	PO	A	TE	FE
Phillips	C	774.0	1.08	16%	4.34	0.291	562	36	4	0
Navarro	C	435.7	0.85	20%	4.34	0.227	336	29	2	0
Rose	C	110.7	1.63	10%	3.90	0.244	83	5	1	0
Bako	C	107.0	0.25	67%	5.38	0.505	61	6	1	0

Name	POS	Inn	PO	A	TE	FE	FPct	RF	DPS	DPT
H Choi	1B	664.7	701	59	0	2	.997	10.29	7	0
O Saenz	1B	475.0	460	19	0	1	.998	9.08	6	0
J Phillips	1B	156.7	143	12	0	0	1.000	8.90	0	0
J Kent	1B	81.3	93	5	1	1	.980	10.84	0	0
B Myrow	1B	26.7	20	0	0	0	1.000	6.75	0	0
N Nakamura	1B	15.0	18	0	0	1	.947	10.80	0	0
J Grabowski	1B	8.0	11	0	0	0	1.000	12.38	0	0
J Kent	2B	1209.0	284	424	3	13	.978	5.27	24	58
A Perez	2B	184.3	40	57	0	3	.970	4.74	5	5
W Aybar	2B	23.3	2	6	0	0	1.000	3.09	0	1
O Robles	2B	8.0	0	1	0	1	.500	1.13	1	0
N Nakamura	2B	2.0	1	0	0	0	1.000	4.50	0	0
C Izturis	SS	918.0	145	325	3	8	.977	4.61	30	30
O Robles	SS	437.3	76	132	2	2	.981	4.28	15	12
A Perez	SS	65.0	10	25	0	1	.972	4.85	3	3
N Nakamura	SS	3.0	0	1	0	0	1.000	3.00	1	0
J Valentin	SS	2.0	0	2	0	0	1.000	9.00	1	0
M Edwards	SS	2.0	0	2	0	0	1.000	9.00	0	0
M Edwards	3B	294.7	22	56	2	5	.918	2.38	5	0
O Robles	3B	292.3	24	70	0	2	.979	2.89	5	0
A Perez	3B	273.0	18	70	1	4	.946	2.90	4	0
J Valentin	3B	216.3	19	54	4	3	.913	3.04	3	0
W Aybar	3B	174.0	16	35	2	0	.962	2.64	4	0
O Saenz	3B	120.0	17	22	1	1	.951	2.93	4	0
N Nakamura	3B	57.0	3	16	0	0	1.000	3.00	2	0
R Ledee	LF	390.3	57	1	1	1	.967	1.34	2	0
J Werth	LF	345.3	84	3	0	0	1.000	2.27	0	0
M Edwards	LF	223.3	51	0	0	0	1.000	2.06	0	0
J Grabowski	LF	170.0	31	1	0	1	.970	1.69	0	0
J Valentin	LF	158.3	35	0	0	1	.972	1.99	0	0
J Repko	LF	127.0	26	0	0	1	.963	1.84	0	0
C Chen	LF	11.0	2	0	0	0	1.000	1.64	0	0
J Cruz	LF	1.0	0	0	0	0	0.000	0.00	0	0
A Perez	LF	1.0	0	0	0	0	0.000	0.00	0	0
M Bradley	CF	628.0	181	6	2	0	.989	2.68	0	0
J Repko	CF	363.0	97	5	1	0	.990	2.53	2	0
J Drew	CF	241.7	64	0	0	0	1.000	2.38	0	0
J Werth	CF	194.7	63	1	0	3	.955	2.96	0	0

Name	POS	Inn	PO	A	TE	FE	FPct	RF	DPS	DPT
J Drew	RF	382.0	83	3	1	1	.977	2.03	0	0
J Cruz	RF	366.3	100	3	2	3	.954	2.53	0	0
J Werth	RF	291.0	71	3	0	0	1.000	2.29	2	0
J Repko	RF	213.7	50	2	2	2	.929	2.19	3	0
R Ledee	RF	87.7	19	1	0	0	1.000	2.05	0	0
C Ross	RF	52.3	12	2	0	1	.933	2.41	2	0
J Grabowski	RF	23.3	5	0	0	0	1.000	1.93	0	0
M Edwards	RF	11.0	2	0	0	0	1.000	1.64	0	0

Incremental Baserunning Runs		
Name	IR	IRP
Jeff Kent	1.22	118
Antonio Perez	0.97	148
Jayson Werth	0.43	124
Willy Aybar	0.22	125
Norihiro Nakamura	0.20	234
Brian Myrow	0.16	262
Derek Lowe	0.15	173
Cesar Izturis	-0.01	100
Jose Valentin	-0.02	97
Ricky Ledee	-0.02	99
Brad Penny	-0.05	0
Cody Ross	-0.07	0
Jason Repko	-0.10	97
Odalis Perez	-0.10	0
Chin-Feng Chen	-0.13	28
Scott Erickson	-0.14	0
Oscar Robles	-0.19	92
Jeff Weaver	-0.20	79
Hee-Seop Choi	-0.20	94
Mike Rose	-0.23	0
Jose Cruz	-0.50	70
Mike Edwards	-0.68	81
JD Drew	-0.78	76
Jason Grabowski	-1.01	-14
Dioner Navarro	-1.55	55
Olmedo Saenz	-2.05	34
Milton Bradley	-2.50	48
Jason Phillips	-2.68	40

Milwaukee Brewers

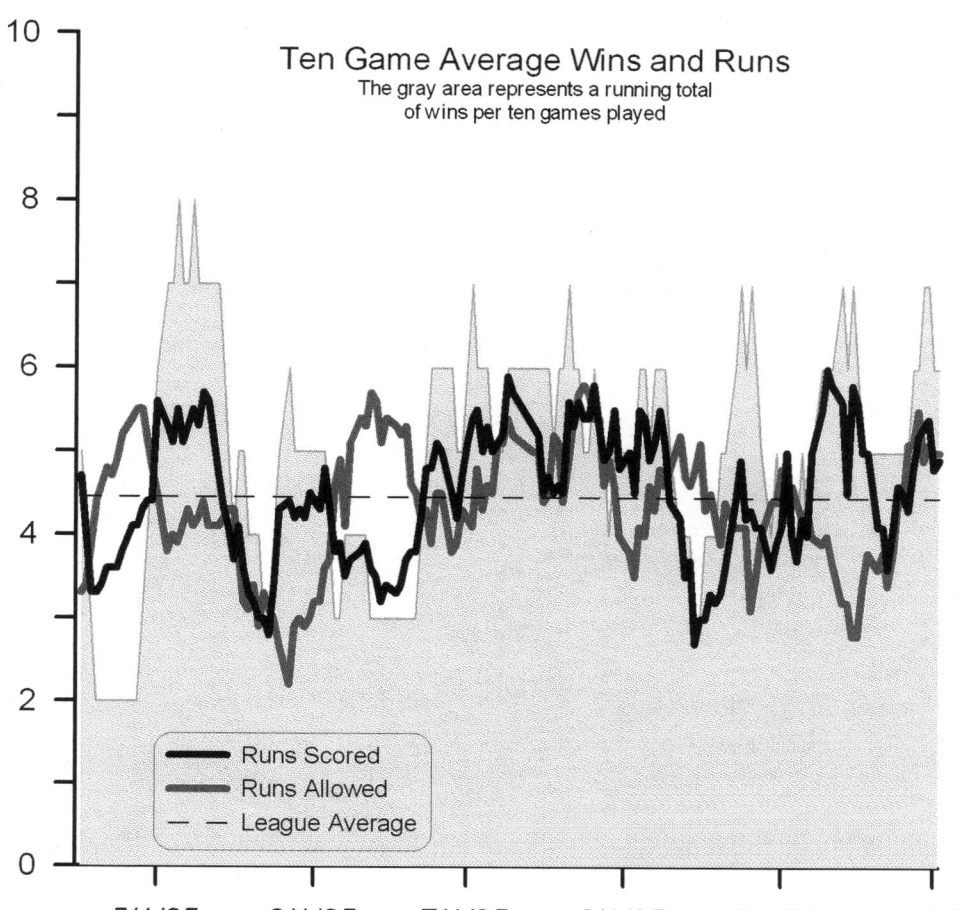

Ten Game Average Wins and Runs
The gray area represents a running total
of wins per ten games played

Legend:
— Runs Scored
— Runs Allowed
– – League Average

4/21: Sheets hospitalized with inner-ear ailment. Returns May 28th.

4/24: Turnbow records first save en route to excellent relief season

6/11 & 6/13: Weeks and Fielder called up

7/10: Hardy hits .560 OPS in first 67 games, .865 in 2nd half (57 games)

8/26:- Sheets strains lat muscle, out for season

10/2 - Finish 81-81, first non-losing season in 12 years

Team Batting and Pitching/Fielding Stats by Month						
	April	May	June	July	Aug	Spt/Oct
Wins	10	14	12	16	13	16
Losses	13	14	15	12	14	13
OBP	.319	.343	.324	.341	.298	.359
SLG	.377	.435	.437	.440	.383	.458
FIP	4.40	4.37	5.07	4.08	4.08	3.77
DER	.722	.752	.712	.715	.680	.713

Batting Stats

Player	RC	Runs	RBI	PA	Outs	P/PA	H	2B	3B	HR	TB	K	BB	IBB	HBP	SH	SF	SB	CS	GDP	BA	OBP	SLG	GPA
Lee C.	100	85	114	688	466	3.78	164	41	0	32	301	87	57	7	2	0	11	13	4	8	.265	.324	.487	.268
Clark B.	93	94	53	674	442	3.55	183	31	1	13	255	55	47	1	18	8	2	10	13	13	.306	.372	.426	.274
Jenkins G.	88	87	86	618	394	3.76	157	42	1	25	276	138	56	9	19	0	5	0	0	13	.292	.375	.513	.297
Overbay L.	85	80	72	622	406	3.97	148	34	1	19	241	98	78	8	2	1	4	1	0	17	.276	.367	.449	.277
Hall B.	73	69	62	546	372	4.17	146	39	6	17	248	103	39	2	1	2	3	18	6	11	.291	.342	.495	.278
Hardy J.	50	46	50	427	290	3.58	92	22	1	9	143	48	44	7	1	8	2	0	0	10	.247	.327	.384	.243
Weeks R.	49	56	42	414	287	4.15	86	13	2	13	142	96	40	2	11	2	1	15	2	11	.239	.333	.394	.248
Miller D.	40	50	43	431	297	3.86	105	25	1	9	159	94	37	6	4	2	3	0	1	16	.273	.340	.413	.256
Branyan R.	39	23	31	242	153	4.16	52	11	0	12	99	80	39	10	0	1	0	1	0	3	.257	.378	.490	.292
Cirillo J.	30	29	23	219	138	3.57	52	15	0	4	79	22	23	0	4	7	0	4	2	3	.281	.373	.427	.274
Helms W.	26	18	24	188	126	3.86	50	13	1	4	77	30	14	0	3	0	3	0	1	7	.298	.356	.458	.275
Spivey J.	16	22	17	202	145	4.06	43	8	1	5	68	57	18	1	1	1	0	7	3	3	.236	.308	.374	.232
Moeller C.	14	23	23	216	167	3.67	41	9	1	7	73	48	13	1	1	2	1	0	0	9	.206	.257	.367	.207
Fielder P.	10	2	10	62	42	3.85	17	4	0	2	27	17	2	0	0	0	1	0	0	0	.288	.306	.458	.252
Magruder C.	10	16	13	155	113	3.66	28	9	0	2	43	33	7	1	5	4	1	3	0	3	.203	.265	.312	.197
Hart C.	4	9	7	63	52	3.60	11	2	1	2	21	11	6	0	0	0	0	2	0	6	.193	.270	.368	.214
Durrington T	2	3	2	18	13	3.56	3	1	0	0	4	3	1	0	0	3	0	5	2	0	.214	.267	.286	.191
Capuano C.	2	5	9	79	60	3.43	12	3	0	0	15	33	2	0	0	5	1	0	0	1	.169	.189	.211	.138
Cruz N.	1	1	0	7	4	4.29	1	1	0	0	2	0	2	0	0	0	0	0	0	0	.200	.429	.400	.293
Obermueller	1	1	0	16	12	3.13	3	1	1	0	6	2	0	0	0	1	0	0	0	0	.200	.200	.400	.190
Wise M.	1	0	1	1	0	3.00	1	0	0	0	1	0	0	0	0	0	0	0	0	0	1.000	1.000	1.000	.700
Glover G.	1	3	1	26	18	3.62	2	0	0	0	2	9	2	0	1	3	0	0	0	0	.100	.217	.100	.123
Eveland D.	-0	0	0	2	1	1.50	0	0	0	0	0	0	0	0	0	1	0	0	0	0	.000	.000	.000	.000
Santana J.	-0	0	0	1	1	2.00	0	0	0	0	0	0	0	0	0	0	0	0	0	0	.000	.000	.000	.000
Mosquera J.	-0	0	0	1	1	2.00	0	0	0	0	0	0	0	0	0	0	0	0	0	0	.000	.000	.000	.000
Davis D.	-0	2	3	76	64	3.47	10	3	1	0	15	34	1	0	0	2	0	0	0	1	.137	.149	.205	.118
Lehr J.	-1	0	0	3	4	3.33	0	0	0	0	0	2	0	0	0	0	0	0	0	1	.000	.000	.000	.000
Krynzel D.	-1	0	0	7	7	4.57	0	0	0	0	0	3	0	0	0	0	0	0	0	0	.000	.000	.000	.000
Ohka T.	-2	1	3	42	36	3.71	2	0	0	0	2	20	2	0	0	2	0	0	0	0	.053	.100	.053	.058
Helling R.	-2	0	0	14	14	4.07	0	0	0	0	0	9	0	0	0	1	0	0	0	1	.000	.000	.000	.000
Santos V.	-2	1	0	43	37	3.53	3	0	0	0	3	13	0	0	0	3	0	0	0	0	.075	.075	.075	.053
Sheets B.	-4	0	0	53	44	3.25	1	0	0	0	1	17	1	0	0	7	0	0	0	0	.022	.043	.022	.025

Pitching Stats

Player	PR	IP	BFP	G	GS	P/PA	K	BB	IBB	HBP	H	HR	DP	DER	SB	CS	PO	W	L	Sv	Op	Hld	RA	ERA	FIP
Turnbow D.	19	67.3	271	69	0	3.87	64	24	2	1	49	5	8	.751	0	0	0	7	1	39	43	2	2.00	1.74	3.16
Sheets B.	14	156.7	633	22	22	3.63	141	25	1	2	142	19	9	.724	14	2	0	10	9	0	0	0	3.79	3.33	3.28
Helling R.	12	49.0	199	15	7	3.91	42	18	1	2	39	2	5	.726	6	1	0	3	1	0	0	2	2.39	2.39	3.02
Davis D.	10	222.7	946	35	35	3.94	208	93	5	4	196	26	22	.724	11	7	5	11	11	0	0	0	4.16	3.84	3.94
Wise M.	8	64.3	262	49	0	4.02	62	25	5	3	37	6	4	.813	10	0	0	4	4	1	3	10	3.50	3.36	3.57
Capuano C.	6	219.0	949	35	35	3.84	176	91	6	12	212	31	20	.717	2	9	12	18	12	0	0	0	4.32	3.99	4.63
Adams M.	3	13.3	61	13	0	4.15	14	10	1	0	12	2	1	.714	1	0	0	0	1	1	2	2	2.70	2.70	5.08
Davis K.	2	16.7	70	15	0	4.10	11	10	0	0	10	2	1	.830	1	1	0	1	1	0	2	2	3.24	2.70	5.02
Capellan J.	2	15.7	67	17	0	3.55	14	5	0	0	17	1	0	.660	2	1	0	1	1	0	0	3	3.45	2.87	2.98
Santana J.	0	42.0	177	41	0	3.86	49	19	4	0	34	6	3	.728	2	0	1	3	5	1	4	11	4.50	4.50	3.86
Phelps T.	-0	23.3	106	29	0	3.79	14	12	4	2	25	2	3	.697	1	0	0	0	2	1	2	4	4.63	4.63	4.70
Ohka T.	-1	126.3	543	22	20	3.58	81	28	4	2	145	16	15	.690	4	2	2	7	6	0	0	1	4.63	4.35	4.06
Lehr J.	-1	34.7	154	23	0	3.47	23	18	2	1	32	4	3	.741	4	1	3	1	1	0	1	3	4.93	3.89	4.80
de la Rosa J	-2	42.3	208	38	0	4.26	42	38	4	0	48	1	7	.630	4	0	0	2	2	0	2	5	4.89	4.46	4.00
Bottalico R.	-3	41.7	188	40	0	3.75	29	19	0	3	43	7	4	.723	1	2	0	2	2	2	6	9	5.18	4.54	5.36
Eveland D.	-5	31.7	146	27	0	3.66	23	18	3	1	40	2	8	.627	0	0	0	1	1	1	2	7	5.97	5.97	4.15
Obermueller	-8	65.0	305	23	8	3.66	33	36	2	5	74	7	6	.701	7	1	0	1	4	0	0	0	5.68	5.26	5.26
Glover G.	-8	64.7	284	15	11	4.02	58	20	0	2	74	10	6	.670	7	5	1	5	4	0	0	0	5.71	5.57	4.22
Santos V.	-15	141.7	639	29	24	3.77	89	60	8	5	153	20	13	.714	9	2	1	4	13	0	0	0	5.53	4.57	4.94

Win Shares Stats

Player	WS	Bat	Pitch	Field	ExpWS	WSP	WSAB	CWS	NetWSValue
Clark, B	24	16.5	0.0	7.2	18	.657	11	48	$7,788,656
Lee, C	24	19.7	0.0	4.0	19	.633	11	124	($279,230)
Jenkins, G	22	17.7	0.0	4.2	17	.652	10	111	$3,735,744
Hall, B	18	13.7	0.0	4.2	15	.603	8	31	$5,927,018
Overbay, L	18	16.0	0.0	2.3	17	.542	6	45	$5,001,556
Turnbow, D	14	0.0	13.7	0.0	6	1.054	9	19	$7,214,918
Capuano, C	12	-1.2	13.8	0.0	10	.600	6	16	$4,938,563
Davis, D	11	-1.9	13.3	0.0	11	.532	5	48	$1,972,072
Hardy, J	11	7.8	0.0	3.7	12	.485	3	11	$2,533,286
Weeks, R	10	7.7	0.0	1.9	11	.427	2	10	($1,654,613)
Miller, D	10	4.5	0.0	5.4	12	.415	2	85	($563,266)
Branyan, R	9	8.3	0.0	1.2	7	.727	5	45	$3,357,824
Sheets, B	9	-2.7	11.6	0.0	8	.572	4	53	($3,072,320)
Cirillo, J	7	5.7	0.0	1.0	6	.580	3	156	$2,077,875
Wise, M	6	0.3	5.8	0.0	4	.828	4	13	$2,772,694
Helms, W	6	4.8	0.0	0.8	5	.586	2	29	($1,020,440)
Ohka, T	4	-1.7	6.1	0.0	6	.351	1	42	($572,387)
Moeller, C	3	-0.2	0.0	3.3	6	.247	-1	19	($700,000)
Spivey, J	2	1.1	0.0	1.0	5	.193	-2	46	($2,054,098)
Santos, V	2	-1.8	3.4	0.0	7	.113	-3	11	($420,000)
Magruder, C	1	-0.1	0.0	0.7	4	.075	-2	4	($325,000)

Fielding and Baserunning Stats

Name	POS	Inn	SBA/G	CS%	ERA	WP+PB/G	PO	A	TE	FE
Miller	C	917.3	0.66	22%	4.02	0.373	723	50	2	0
Moeller	C	520.7	0.69	15%	3.91	0.622	454	32	2	0

Name	POS	Inn	PO	A	TE	FE	FPct	RF	DPS	DPT
L Overbay	1B	1265.0	1137	95	2	7	.992	8.77	9	0
W Helms	1B	114.3	103	9	0	1	.991	8.82	2	0
P Fielder	1B	34.0	26	4	0	0	1.000	7.94	0	0
R Branyan	1B	24.0	29	2	0	0	1.000	11.63	0	0
J Cirillo	1B	0.7	0	0	0	0	0.000	0.00	0	0
R Weeks	2B	837.3	178	233	10	11	.951	4.42	23	33
J Spivey	2B	404.0	93	117	2	5	.968	4.68	9	16
B Hall	2B	185.0	44	53	1	3	.960	4.72	2	3
J Cirillo	2B	11.7	4	2	0	0	1.000	4.63	0	1
J Hardy	SS	937.7	133	259	3	7	.975	3.76	33	16
B Hall	SS	500.3	87	158	4	2	.976	4.41	15	16
R Branyan	3B	456.7	40	83	4	3	.946	2.42	8	0
B Hall	3B	435.3	39	84	4	2	.953	2.54	8	0
J Cirillo	3B	365.3	28	70	2	3	.951	2.41	9	0
W Helms	3B	178.7	12	41	1	1	.964	2.67	4	0
T Durrington	3B	2.0	0	0	1	2	0.000	0.00	1	0
C Lee	LF	1404.0	307	8	2	4	.981	2.02	4	0
C Magruder	LF	19.0	3	0	0	0	1.000	1.42	0	0
R Branyan	LF	7.0	1	0	0	0	1.000	1.29	0	0
C Hart	LF	6.0	1	0	0	0	1.000	1.50	0	0
N Cruz	LF	2.0	0	0	0	0	0.000	0.00	0	0
B Clark	CF	1275.0	399	5	0	2	.995	2.85	8	0
C Hart	CF	96.0	19	0	0	0	1.000	1.78	0	0
C Magruder	CF	58.3	19	0	1	1	.905	2.93	0	0
D Krynzel	CF	8.3	2	0	0	0	1.000	2.16	0	0
G Jenkins	RF	1241.0	307	10	2	3	.984	2.30	14	0
C Magruder	RF	153.7	32	0	0	0	1.000	1.87	0	0
C Hart	RF	27.0	8	1	0	1	.900	3.00	0	0
N Cruz	RF	16.0	4	0	0	0	1.000	2.25	0	0

Incremental Baserunnings Runs		
Name	IR	IRP
Lyle Overbay	1.49	117
JJ Hardy	1.14	123
Jeff Cirillo	1.09	202
Brady Clark	1.04	116
Junior Spivey	0.85	139
Bill Hall	0.54	112
Damian Miller	0.53	108
Russell Branyan	0.36	125
Chris Capuano	0.14	122
Wes Helms	0.11	109
Tomo Ohka	0.06	109
Victor Santos	0.02	159
Trent Durrington	-0.02	0
Doug Davis	-0.06	0
Ben Sheets	-0.07	0
Prince Fielder	-0.08	0
Chad Moeller	-0.31	81
Chris Magruder	-0.59	64
Corey Hart	-0.63	63
Gary Glover	-1.16	-110
Geoff Jenkins	-1.57	71
Carlos Lee	-2.79	17
Rickie Weeks	-2.83	47

Minnesota Twins

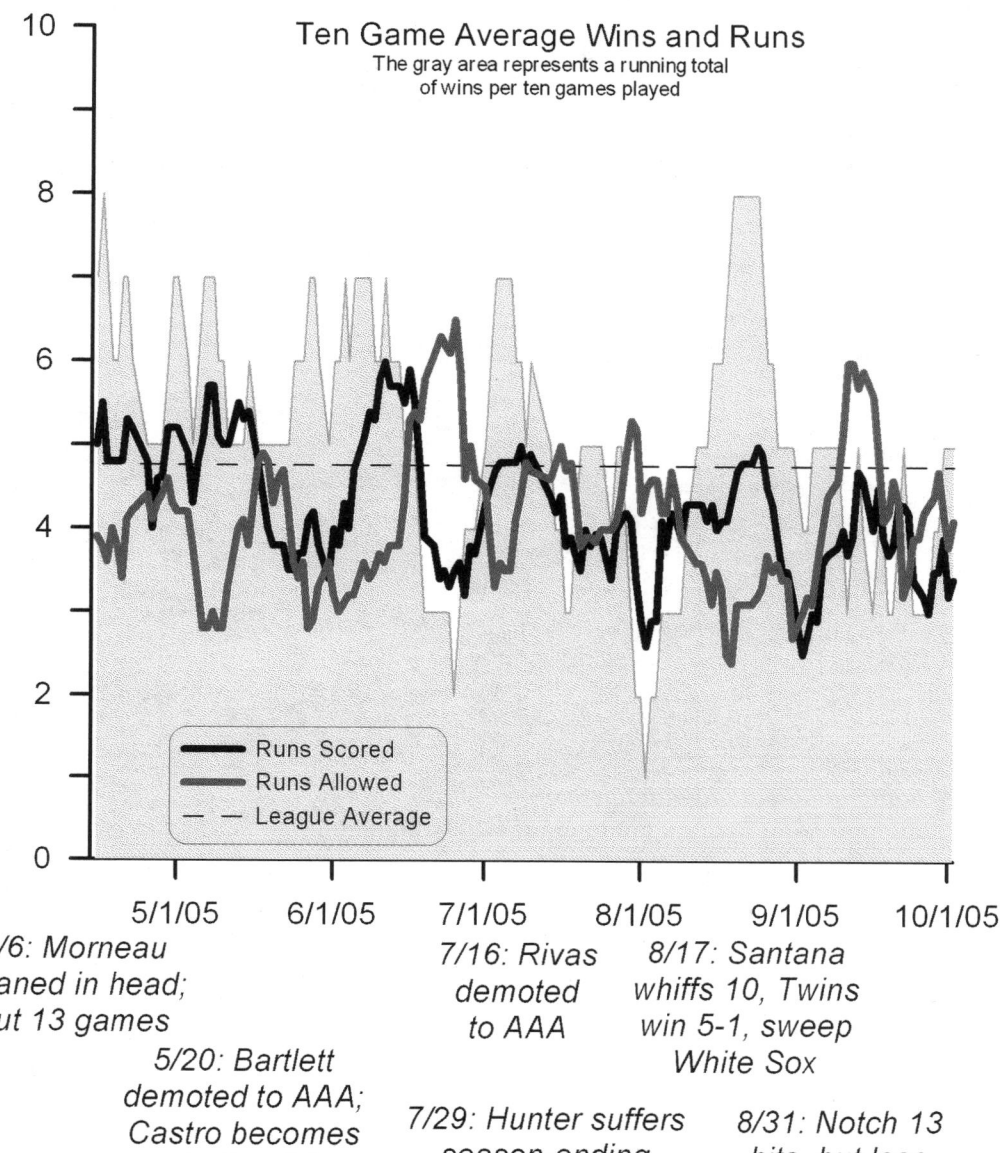

Ten Game Average Wins and Runs

The gray area represents a running total
of wins per ten games played

Runs Scored
Runs Allowed
League Average

4/6: Morneau
beaned in head;
out 13 games

5/20: Bartlett
demoted to AAA;
Castro becomes
starting SS

7/16: Rivas
demoted
to AAA

7/29: Hunter suffers
season-ending
broken ankle

8/17: Santana
whiffs 10, Twins
win 5-1, sweep
White Sox

8/31: Notch 13
hits, but lose
1-0 to Royals

Team Batting and Pitching/Fielding Stats by Month						
	April	May	June	July	Aug	Spt/Oct
Wins	15	14	13	12	16	13
Losses	8	13	13	16	13	16
OBP	.351	.319	.329	.320	.311	.311
SLG	.411	.391	.428	.377	.382	.364
FIP	4.02	4.02	4.28	4.21	3.84	4.21
DER	.720	.728	.702	.697	.738	.715

Batting Stats

Player	RC	Runs	RBI	PA	Outs	P/PA	H	2B	3B	HR	TB	K	BB	IBB	HBP	SH	SF	SB	CS	GDP	BA	OBP	SLG	GPA
Mauer J.	81	61	55	554	355	3.87	144	26	2	9	201	64	61	12	1	0	3	13	1	9	.294	.372	.411	.270
Jones J.	75	74	73	585	414	3.59	130	22	4	23	229	120	51	12	5	2	4	13	4	17	.249	.319	.438	.253
Ford L.	73	70	53	590	399	3.99	138	30	4	7	197	85	45	2	16	2	5	13	6	9	.264	.338	.377	.247
Stewart S.	71	69	56	599	416	3.57	151	27	3	10	214	73	34	2	8	1	5	7	5	11	.274	.323	.388	.242
Morneau J.	61	62	79	543	387	3.53	117	23	4	22	214	94	44	8	4	0	5	0	2	12	.239	.304	.437	.246
Hunter T.	56	63	56	416	287	3.48	100	24	1	14	168	65	34	3	6	0	4	23	7	8	.269	.337	.452	.264
LeCroy M.	50	33	50	350	232	4.21	79	5	0	17	135	85	41	2	4	0	1	0	0	7	.260	.354	.444	.270
Cuddyer M.	45	55	42	470	334	3.81	111	25	3	12	178	93	41	5	3	1	3	3	4	19	.263	.330	.422	.254
Punto N.	37	45	26	439	317	4.04	94	18	4	4	132	86	36	0	0	7	2	13	8	9	.239	.301	.335	.219
Castro J.	29	27	33	292	211	3.17	70	18	1	5	105	39	9	1	0	9	2	0	1	8	.257	.279	.386	.222
Rodriguez L.	28	21	20	203	134	3.64	47	10	2	2	67	23	18	0	1	6	3	2	2	4	.269	.335	.383	.246
Redmond M.	24	17	26	159	111	3.53	46	9	0	1	58	14	6	0	3	2	0	0	0	9	.311	.350	.392	.256
Bartlett J.	22	33	16	252	177	3.94	54	10	1	3	75	37	21	0	4	2	1	4	0	7	.241	.316	.335	.226
Rivas L.	16	21	12	148	103	3.54	35	3	1	1	43	17	9	0	2	0	1	4	0	2	.257	.311	.316	.219
Ryan M.	10	7	13	131	97	3.81	27	5	0	2	38	22	9	1	0	4	1	1	2	5	.231	.283	.325	.209
Williams G.	9	3	3	43	25	3.40	17	1	0	0	18	7	2	0	0	1	0	1	2	0	.425	.452	.450	.316
Tyner J.	9	8	5	60	40	3.53	18	1	1	0	21	4	4	0	0	0	0	2	0	2	.321	.367	.375	.259
Tiffee T.	8	9	15	159	129	3.33	31	8	1	1	44	15	8	1	0	0	1	1	0	10	.207	.245	.293	.184
Abernathy B.	6	5	6	79	53	3.90	16	1	0	1	20	9	7	0	1	3	1	2	0	2	.239	.316	.299	.217
Boone B.	2	3	3	58	47	3.91	9	0	0	0	9	13	4	0	1	0	0	0	0	3	.170	.241	.170	.151
Heintz C.	2	1	2	26	21	4.04	5	3	0	0	8	6	1	0	0	0	0	0	0	1	.200	.231	.320	.184
Mays J.	1	0	0	3	2	3.00	1	0	0	0	1	0	0	0	0	0	0	0	0	0	.333	.333	.333	.233
Guerrier M.	-0	0	0	1	1	1.00	0	0	0	0	0	0	0	0	0	0	0	0	0	0	.000	.000	.000	.000
Silva C.	-0	0	0	2	2	4.50	0	0	0	0	0	2	0	0	0	0	0	0	0	0	.000	.000	.000	.000
Radke B.	-0	0	0	7	5	3.14	0	0	0	0	0	2	0	0	0	2	0	0	0	0	.000	.000	.000	.000
Santana J.	-1	1	0	6	6	2.00	1	0	0	0	1	0	0	0	0	0	0	0	0	1	.167	.167	.167	.117
Lohse K.	-1	0	0	5	6	2.60	0	0	0	0	0	1	0	0	0	0	0	0	0	1	.000	.000	.000	.000
Miller C.	-1	0	0	12	12	3.25	0	0	0	0	0	2	0	0	0	0	0	0	0	0	.000	.000	.000	.000

Pitching Stats

Player	PR	IP	BFP	G	GS	P/PA	K	BB	IBB	HBP	H	HR	DP	DER	SB	CS	PO	W	L	Sv	Op	Hld	RA	ERA	FIP
Santana J.	45	231.7	910	33	33	3.66	238	45	1	1	180	22	11	.738	4	5	0	16	7	0	0	0	2.99	2.87	2.82
Silva C.	16	188.3	749	27	27	3.06	71	9	2	3	212	25	43	.708	7	4	0	9	8	0	0	0	3.97	3.44	4.21
Nathan J.	15	70.0	276	69	0	4.16	94	22	1	0	46	5	2	.735	2	1	0	7	4	43	48	0	2.83	2.70	2.23
Rincon J.	14	77.0	319	75	0	4.14	84	30	3	3	63	2	5	.695	2	2	2	6	6	0	5	25	3.04	2.45	2.48
Crain J.	14	79.7	326	75	0	3.33	25	29	7	5	61	6	15	.789	3	0	0	12	5	1	4	11	3.16	2.71	4.68
Lohse K.	9	178.7	769	31	30	3.74	86	44	5	9	211	22	25	.689	3	6	3	9	13	0	0	0	4.28	4.18	4.57
Guerrier M.	9	71.7	306	43	0	3.58	46	24	5	3	71	6	5	.714	2	3	1	0	3	0	0	1	3.64	3.39	3.98
Radke B.	7	200.7	831	31	31	3.53	117	23	1	7	214	33	18	.722	8	3	0	9	12	0	0	0	4.40	4.04	4.46
Baker S.	7	53.7	217	10	9	3.80	32	14	0	0	48	5	5	.741	0	3	1	3	3	0	0	1	3.52	3.35	3.84
Romero J.	4	57.0	264	68	0	3.89	48	39	8	6	50	6	7	.733	5	1	0	4	3	0	1	11	4.11	3.47	5.10
Mulholland T	1	59.0	246	49	0	3.30	18	17	4	2	61	6	10	.729	1	1	0	0	2	0	1	3	4.58	4.27	4.72
Bowyer T.	-1	9.7	42	8	0	4.40	12	3	0	1	10	3	1	.696	2	0	0	0	1	0	1	0	5.59	5.59	5.84
Liriano F.	-3	23.7	93	6	4	3.91	33	7	0	0	19	4	2	.694	3	1	1	1	2	0	0	0	5.70	5.70	3.34
Gassner D.	-3	7.7	34	2	2	3.71	2	1	0	0	9	1	0	.733	0	1	1	1	0	0	0	0	8.22	5.87	4.61
Mays J.	-27	156.0	690	31	26	3.47	59	41	1	3	203	23	22	.681	2	5	0	6	10	0	0	0	6.29	5.65	5.05

Win Shares Stats

Player	WS	Bat	Pitch	Field	ExpWS	WSP	WSAB	CWS	NetWSValue
Santana, J	23	-0.5	23.1	0.0	12	.917	15	80	$7,013,718
Mauer, J	23	13.7	0.0	9.2	14	.802	13	29	$10,176,018
Jones, J	15	10.7	0.0	4.1	15	.479	4	98	($2,127,520)
Nathan, J	14	0.0	13.9	0.0	8	.862	8	49	$4,528,599
Silva, C	14	-0.1	13.9	0.0	10	.695	8	40	$4,605,705
Ford, L	13	9.9	0.0	3.1	14	.452	3	39	$2,243,340
Radke, B	12	-0.2	11.8	0.0	11	.540	5	149	($1,204,187)
Hunter, T	12	8.5	0.0	3.8	11	.567	5	95	($4,898,804)
Stewart, S	12	8.8	0.0	3.4	16	.394	1	138	($2,368,771)
Crain, J	10	0.0	10.1	0.0	6	.915	6	14	$4,935,946
Lohse, K	10	-0.5	10.5	0.0	10	.525	4	40	$1,027,704
Rincon, J	9	0.0	9.5	0.0	6	.804	5	28	$4,099,837
LeCroy, M	8	8.1	0.0	0.2	7	.555	3	34	$1,905,174
Castro, J	8	2.5	0.0	5.1	8	.466	2	32	$1,077,929
Morneau, J	8	7.2	0.0	1.0	15	.279	-2	19	($345,000)
Redmond, M	7	3.5	0.0	3.1	4	.752	4	53	$2,444,296
Rodriguez, L	6	4.2	0.0	2.0	6	.556	2	6	$1,804,292
Bartlett, J	6	1.3	0.0	4.3	7	.405	1	6	$599,351
Punto, N	6	1.4	0.0	4.9	12	.268	-2	11	($325,000)
Cuddyer, M	6	3.8	0.0	2.6	13	.248	-3	20	($347,500)
Guerrier, M	5	-0.0	4.9	0.0	4	.550	2	5	$1,390,095
Romero, J	4	0.0	4.5	0.0	4	.583	2	31	$378,543
Rivas, L	3	1.6	0.0	1.8	4	.407	0	33	($1,095,431)
Mulholland, T	3	0.0	2.8	0.0	4	.370	0	114	$116,421
Mays, J	2	0.2	1.8	0.0	8	.124	-3	44	($7,250,000)
Tiffee, T	0	-1.3	0.0	0.4	4	-.112	-4	1	($316,000)

Fielding and Baserunning Stats

Name	POS	Inn	SBA/G	CS%	ERA	WP+PB/G	PO	A	TE	FE
Mauer	C	999.7	0.44	37%	3.69	0.288	693	45	2	3
Redmond	C	376.3	0.41	47%	3.87	0.167	230	13	0	0
Heintz	C	60.0	0.60	25%	3.90	0.000	48	1	0	0
Miller	C	27.3	0.99	67%	2.63	1.646	24	2	0	0
LeCroy	C	1.0	0.00	0%	0.00	0.000	0	0	0	0

Name	POS	Inn	PO	A	TE	FE	FPct	RF	DPS	DPT
J Morneau	1B	1166.0	1194	88	2	4	.994	9.90	13	2
M LeCroy	1B	179.0	203	8	0	3	.986	10.61	3	0
T Tiffee	1B	86.0	92	7	0	1	.990	10.36	1	0
M Cuddyer	1B	33.0	36	1	0	0	1.000	10.09	0	0
N Punto	2B	564.3	131	193	2	5	.979	5.17	20	26
L Rivas	2B	360.0	77	112	0	1	.995	4.73	5	20
L Rodriguez	2B	216.0	53	73	0	0	1.000	5.25	10	12
B Abernathy	2B	124.0	24	37	0	2	.968	4.43	3	5
B Boone	2B	122.0	39	37	1	1	.974	5.61	5	6
M Cuddyer	2B	55.0	12	18	0	0	1.000	4.91	3	4
J Castro	2B	23.0	4	9	0	0	1.000	5.09	1	2
J Bartlett	SS	585.7	95	227	2	5	.979	4.95	27	18
J Castro	SS	568.7	97	231	2	3	.985	5.19	23	25
N Punto	SS	244.0	47	76	1	1	.984	4.54	8	7
L Rodriguez	SS	44.0	8	14	0	0	1.000	4.50	3	0
L Rivas	SS	22.0	3	5	1	0	.889	3.27	0	0
M Cuddyer	3B	816.0	57	188	8	7	.942	2.70	15	0
L Rodriguez	3B	198.0	14	43	1	2	.950	2.59	4	0
T Tiffee	3B	176.3	18	34	3	2	.912	2.65	6	0
J Castro	3B	123.0	14	22	1	3	.900	2.63	1	0
G Williams	3B	81.0	7	19	0	2	.929	2.89	2	0
N Punto	3B	69.0	6	22	0	0	1.000	3.65	4	0
M Ryan	3B	1.0	0	0	0	0	0.000	0.00	0	0
S Stewart	LF	1107.0	249	7	2	2	.985	2.08	4	0
L Ford	LF	134.0	32	2	0	1	.971	2.28	0	0
M Ryan	LF	99.0	13	1	0	0	1.000	1.27	0	0
J Tyner	LF	93.0	19	0	0	0	1.000	1.84	0	0
B Abernathy	LF	31.3	5	0	0	0	1.000	1.44	0	0
T Hunter	CF	813.3	218	8	1	2	.987	2.50	7	0
L Ford	CF	548.0	140	7	2	2	.974	2.41	2	0
J Jones	CF	86.0	17	1	0	0	1.000	1.88	0	0
N Punto	CF	11.0	0	0	0	0	0.000	0.00	0	0
J Tyner	CF	6.0	3	0	0	0	1.000	4.50	0	0

Name	POS	Inn	PO	A	TE	FE	FPct	RF	DPS	DPT
J Jones	RF	1080.0	261	9	0	4	.985	2.25	3	0
M Cuddyer	RF	159.0	35	0	0	0	1.000	1.98	0	0
L Ford	RF	133.0	26	0	1	0	.963	1.76	0	0
M Ryan	RF	76.0	17	1	0	0	1.000	2.13	2	0
J Tyner	RF	14.0	8	0	0	0	1.000	5.14	0	0
N Punto	RF	2.0	1	0	0	0	1.000	4.50	0	0

Incremental Baserunning Runs

Name	IR	IRP
Lew Ford	1.82	122
Joe Mauer	1.19	127
Nick Punto	0.92	115
Justin Morneau	0.82	123
Michael Cuddyer	0.79	114
Jacque Jones	0.58	114
Luis Rivas	0.29	109
Jason Bartlett	0.26	110
Jason Tyner	0.01	101
Shannon Stewart	-0.02	100
Brent Abernathy	-0.05	84
Juan Castro	-0.10	94
Joe Mays	-0.14	0
Johan Santana	-0.14	0
Glenn Williams	-0.15	70
Luis Rodriguez	-0.31	83
Terry Tiffee	-0.40	0
Mike Redmond	-0.84	67
Michael Ryan	-1.00	-9
Bret Boone	-1.06	-135
Torii Hunter	-1.55	69
Matthew LeCroy	-2.10	0

New York Mets

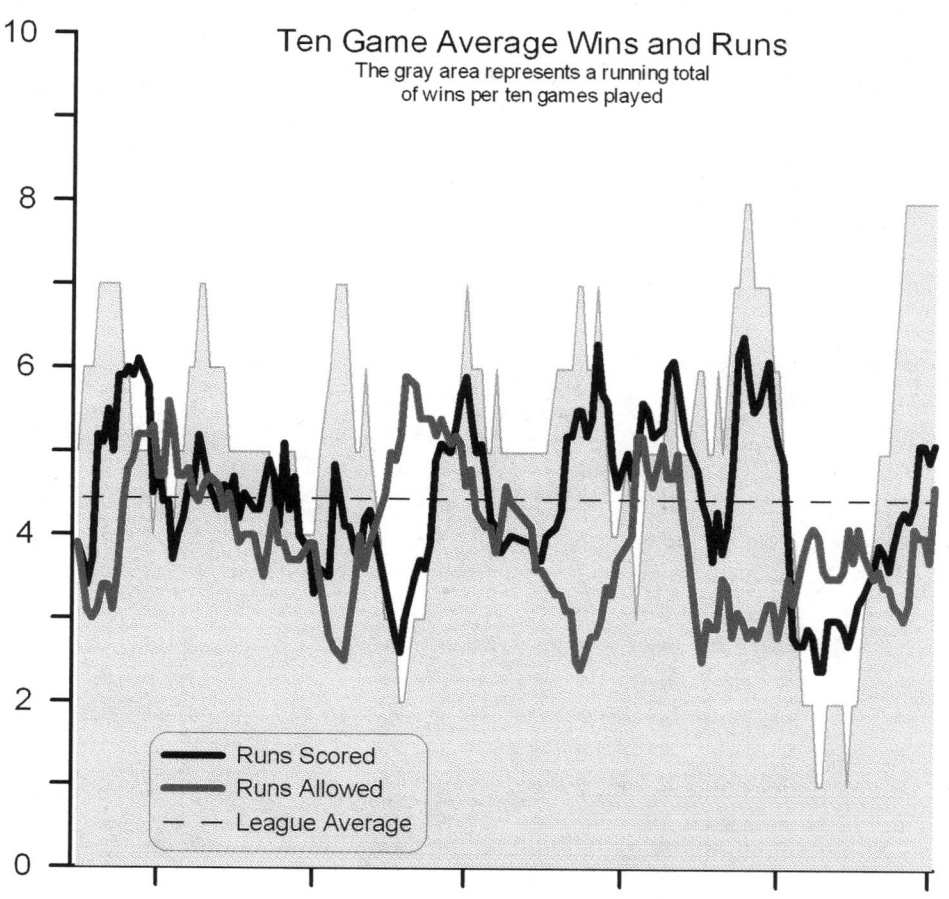

Ten Game Average Wins and Runs
The gray area represents a running total
of wins per ten games played

Legend:
- ▬▬▬ Runs Scored
- ▬▬▬ Runs Allowed
- – – – League Average

*5/3: Reyes draws
first walk of season;
finishes with
.300 OBP*

*5/5: Cameron plays
first game; bats
.372/.476/.686 in May*

*8/11: Beltran and
Cameron collide;
Cameron out for
season*

*8/30: Castro hits 3-run
homer in 8th to beat Phils;
Mets 1/2 game out of
wild card*

*9/15: Lose 12th
game in 14,
ending wild
card bid*

Team Batting and Pitching/Fielding Stats by Month						
	April	May	June	July	Aug	Spt/Oct
Wins	11	15	13	14	16	14
Losses	13	13	13	13	11	16
OBP	.335	.324	.314	.310	.334	.313
SLG	.418	.424	.403	.414	.422	.413
FIP	4.09	3.98	4.28	3.54	4.04	4.29
DER	.714	.715	.715	.718	.718	.718

Batting Stats

Player	RC	Runs	RBI	PA	Outs	P/PA	H	2B	3B	HR	TB	K	BB	IBB	HBP	SH	SF	SB	CS	GDP	BA	OBP	SLG	GPA
Wright D.	110	99	102	657	422	3.99	176	42	1	27	301	113	72	2	7	0	3	17	7	16	.306	.388	.523	.306
Floyd C.	103	85	98	626	407	3.71	150	22	2	34	278	98	63	13	11	0	2	12	2	5	.273	.358	.505	.287
Beltran C.	92	83	78	650	442	3.79	155	34	2	16	241	96	56	5	2	4	6	17	6	9	.266	.330	.414	.252
Reyes J.	88	99	58	733	528	3.63	190	24	17	7	269	78	27	0	2	4	4	60	15	7	.273	.300	.386	.232
Piazza M.	58	41	62	442	305	3.48	100	23	0	19	180	67	41	6	3	0	0	0	0	7	.251	.326	.452	.260
Cameron M.	54	47	39	343	230	4.06	84	23	2	12	147	85	29	0	4	1	1	13	1	5	.273	.342	.477	.273
Diaz V.	37	41	38	313	223	3.69	72	17	3	12	131	82	30	7	1	0	2	6	2	13	.257	.329	.468	.265
Castro R.	31	26	41	240	165	3.87	51	16	0	8	91	58	25	2	0	3	3	1	0	7	.244	.321	.435	.253
Cairo M.	30	31	19	367	253	3.50	82	18	0	2	106	31	19	2	4	12	5	13	3	5	.251	.296	.324	.214
Mientkiewicz	28	36	29	313	222	4.00	66	13	0	11	112	39	32	7	2	2	2	0	1	12	.240	.322	.407	.247
Matsui K.	28	31	24	295	202	3.70	68	9	4	3	94	43	14	1	5	5	4	6	1	2	.255	.300	.352	.223
Anderson M.	24	31	19	260	176	3.88	62	9	0	7	92	45	18	0	1	4	2	6	1	2	.264	.316	.391	.240
Jacobs M.	22	19	23	112	74	3.39	31	7	0	11	71	22	10	0	1	0	1	0	0	5	.310	.375	.710	.346
Woodward C.	21	16	18	192	126	3.93	49	10	0	3	68	46	13	0	2	2	2	0	0	2	.283	.337	.393	.250
Offerman J.	10	5	10	80	57	3.83	18	2	0	1	23	11	6	0	1	1	0	0	0	3	.250	.316	.319	.222
Benson K.	5	4	6	61	40	3.89	9	1	0	0	10	22	5	0	1	6	0	0	0	0	.184	.273	.204	.174
Williams G.	4	9	3	32	23	3.75	7	2	0	1	12	7	1	0	0	1	0	2	0	0	.233	.258	.400	.216
Valent E.	3	4	1	50	35	4.36	8	3	0	0	11	17	7	3	0	0	0	0	0	0	.186	.300	.256	.199
Ishii K.	2	1	2	30	20	3.30	5	0	0	0	5	12	1	0	0	4	0	0	0	0	.200	.231	.200	.154
Glavine T.	2	2	3	71	51	3.73	13	0	0	0	13	13	2	0	0	5	0	0	0	0	.203	.227	.203	.153
Daubach B.	2	4	3	34	24	3.79	3	2	0	1	8	5	7	1	1	0	1	0	0	2	.120	.324	.320	.226
Seo J.	1	2	4	34	26	3.56	3	1	0	0	4	11	3	0	0	2	0	0	0	0	.103	.188	.138	.119
Koo D.	1	1	0	2	1	3.50	1	1	0	0	2	1	0	0	0	0	0	0	0	0	.500	.500	1.000	.475
Padilla J.	0	0	0	2	1	3.50	1	0	0	0	1	1	0	0	0	0	0	0	0	0	.500	.500	.500	.350
DiFelice M.	-0	0	0	19	16	3.95	2	0	0	0	2	5	2	0	0	0	0	0	0	1	.118	.211	.118	.124
Bell H.	-0	0	0	3	3	4.00	0	0	0	0	0	1	0	0	0	0	0	0	0	0	.000	.000	.000	.000
Trachsel S.	-1	0	0	15	14	3.33	1	0	0	0	1	7	0	0	0	0	0	0	0	0	.067	.067	.067	.047
Heilman A.	-1	0	0	17	14	3.65	0	0	0	0	0	7	1	0	0	2	0	0	0	0	.000	.067	.000	.030
Zambrano V.	-1	2	2	58	46	3.17	7	0	1	0	9	22	0	0	0	5	0	0	0	0	.132	.132	.170	.102
Hernandez A.	-1	1	0	19	18	3.42	1	0	0	0	1	4	1	0	0	0	0	0	1	0	.056	.105	.056	.061
Martinez P.	-3	2	1	76	64	3.50	6	0	0	0	6	26	1	0	0	6	0	0	0	1	.087	.100	.087	.067

Pitching Stats

Player	PR	IP	BFP	G	GS	P/PA	K	BB	IBB	HBP	H	HR	DP	DER	SB	CS	PO	W	L	Sv	Op	Hld	RA	ERA	FIP
Martinez P.	39	217.0	843	31	31	3.61	208	47	3	4	159	19	15	.752	14	4	0	15	8	0	0	0	2.86	2.82	2.91
Seo J.	19	90.3	363	14	14	3.77	59	16	0	1	84	9	7	.730	7	1	0	8	2	0	0	0	2.59	2.59	3.54
Glavine T.	17	211.3	901	33	33	3.63	105	61	5	3	227	12	25	.701	4	5	2	13	13	0	0	0	3.75	3.53	3.64
Hernandez R.	15	69.7	291	67	0	3.86	61	28	4	2	57	5	5	.733	9	1	0	8	6	4	10	18	2.58	2.58	3.46
Heilman A.	14	108.0	439	53	7	3.97	106	37	4	6	87	6	16	.715	9	3	0	5	3	5	6	5	3.33	3.17	2.94
Padilla J.	11	36.3	149	24	0	3.55	17	13	2	2	24	0	3	.795	0	0	0	3	1	1	2	6	1.73	1.49	3.29
Takatsu S.	2	7.7	38	9	0	4.05	6	3	1	0	11	2	1	.667	0	0	0	1	0	0	2	1	2.35	2.35	5.98
Heredia F.	1	2.7	10	3	0	4.40	2	1	0	1	1	0	0	.833	0	0	0	0	0	0	0	0	0.00	0.00	3.73
Santiago J.	1	5.7	27	4	0	3.74	3	2	0	1	10	0	1	.524	0	1	0	0	0	0	0	0	3.18	3.18	3.51
Benson K.	0	174.3	737	28	28	3.72	95	49	5	4	171	24	18	.740	14	0	0	10	8	0	0	0	4.44	4.13	4.59
Koo D.	-1	23.0	106	33	0	4.13	23	13	1	2	22	2	0	.697	0	1	0	0	0	0	2	6	4.70	3.91	4.07
Ring R.	-1	10.7	51	15	0	4.18	8	10	1	0	10	0	2	.697	1	0	0	0	2	0	0	3	5.06	5.06	4.29
Looper B.	-2	59.3	271	60	0	3.94	27	22	3	5	65	7	6	.724	2	1	0	4	7	28	36	0	4.70	3.94	4.97
Trachsel S.	-2	37.0	157	6	6	3.57	24	12	0	1	37	6	4	.728	4	0	0	1	4	0	0	0	4.86	4.14	4.85
Zambrano V.	-3	166.3	748	31	27	3.73	112	77	2	15	170	12	17	.703	25	4	0	7	12	0	0	0	4.60	4.17	4.23
Matthews M.	-4	5.0	28	6	0	4.14	2	4	1	0	9	0	0	.591	1	0	0	1	0	0	0	0	10.80	10.80	4.58
Aybar M.	-5	25.3	114	22	0	3.80	27	7	1	1	31	4	0	.640	3	0	0	0	0	0	1	2	6.04	6.04	3.85
Hamulack T.	-5	2.3	14	6	0	3.57	2	1	1	0	7	3	1	.500	0	0	0	0	0	0	0	1	23.14	23.14	19.27
DeJean M.	-6	25.7	131	28	0	3.65	17	18	2	1	36	3	3	.641	2	0	0	3	1	0	0	2	6.66	6.31	5.40
Bell H.	-7	46.7	206	42	0	3.88	43	13	3	1	56	3	6	.637	4	0	0	1	3	0	0	4	5.79	5.59	2.88
Graves D.	-7	20.3	98	20	0	3.38	12	8	1	3	29	5	5	.657	0	0	0	0	0	0	0	1	7.52	5.75	6.62
Ishii K.	-14	91.0	399	19	16	3.72	53	49	3	3	87	13	11	.737	8	4	3	3	9	0	0	0	5.84	5.14	5.39

Win Shares Stats

Player	WS	Bat	Pitch	Field	ExpWS	WSP	WSAB	CWS	NetWSValue
Wright, D	28	23.1	0.0	4.8	18	.763	15	37	$11,921,775
Floyd, C	26	21.0	0.0	4.9	17	.753	14	171	$7,113,839
Beltran, C	23	16.0	0.0	7.2	18	.653	11	155	$1,655,479
Martinez, P	18	-2.9	21.1	0.0	11	.864	12	243	$3,004,628
Reyes, J	17	12.4	0.0	4.4	20	.425	3	34	$2,317,109
Glavine, T	14	-1.2	15.0	0.0	10	.675	8	290	($278,740)
Cameron, M	13	10.7	0.0	1.9	9	.678	6	161	$579,802
Piazza, M	13	9.7	0.0	3.3	12	.549	5	310	($5,828,998)
Seo, J	9	-0.4	10.0	0.0	4	1.090	7	21	$5,456,011
Hernandez, R	9	0.0	9.4	0.0	5	.984	6	137	$4,554,737
Heilman, A	9	-0.8	9.6	0.0	6	.759	5	9	$3,740,743
Benson, K	9	0.0	9.3	0.0	8	.551	4	51	$315,845
Castro, R	8	5.3	0.0	2.6	7	.576	3	18	$2,350,160
Diaz, V	8	5.4	0.0	2.2	9	.439	2	9	$1,222,114
Zambrano, V	6	-1.7	7.4	0.0	8	.356	1	35	($1,300,291)
Matsui, K	5	2.6	0.0	2.1	8	.294	-1	19	($4,775,514)
Cairo, M	5	2.0	0.0	2.9	10	.240	-2	58	($900,000)
Woodward, C	4	2.9	0.0	1.2	5	.378	0	29	$5,862
Looper, B	4	0.0	3.7	0.0	6	.319	-0	54	($572,923)
Anderson, M	4	2.4	0.0	1.3	7	.277	-1	58	($316,000)
Mientkiewi, D	3	2.5	0.0	0.9	9	.195	-3	66	($3,750,000)
Ishii, K	1	-0.0	0.8	0.0	4	.093	-2	19	($3,421,755)

Fielding and Baserunning Stats

Name	POS	Inn	SBA/G	CS%	ERA	WP+PB/G	PO	A	TE	FE
Piazza	C	809.3	1.02	11%	3.89	0.278	618	39	2	0
Castro	C	576.3	0.52	27%	3.59	0.172	402	22	3	0
DiFelice	C	50.0	0.36	50%	3.96	0.180	39	2	1	0

Name	POS	Inn	PO	A	TE	FE	FPct	RF	DPS	DPT
D Mientkiewi	1B	675.0	690	42	1	3	.995	9.76	11	0
M Jacobs	1B	236.0	237	10	0	3	.984	9.42	0	0
C Woodward	1B	199.0	206	10	1	1	.991	9.77	2	0
M Anderson	1B	155.3	173	16	0	2	.990	10.95	2	0
J Offerman	1B	76.7	81	4	0	1	.988	9.98	2	0
M Cairo	1B	50.7	48	2	0	1	.980	8.88	0	0
B Daubach	1B	43.0	39	3	1	0	.977	8.79	0	0
M Cairo	2B	657.3	151	212	3	3	.984	4.97	28	30
K Matsui	2B	560.0	107	187	3	6	.970	4.73	18	16
M Anderson	2B	141.3	35	47	0	1	.988	5.22	3	6
A Hernandez	2B	45.0	9	18	0	0	1.000	5.40	0	1
C Woodward	2B	30.0	4	7	0	2	.846	3.30	1	0
J Offerman	2B	2.0	0	0	0	0	0.000	0.00	0	0
J Reyes	SS	1398.0	237	427	7	11	.974	4.27	44	57
C Woodward	SS	33.3	5	7	0	1	.923	3.24	0	1
A Hernandez	SS	4.0	0	0	0	1	0.000	0.00	0	0
D Wright	3B	1404.0	101	337	12	10	.948	2.81	25	2
C Woodward	3B	25.3	1	11	0	0	1.000	4.26	0	0
M Cairo	3B	6.0	0	2	0	0	1.000	3.00	0	0
C Floyd	LF	1263.0	283	15	0	2	.993	2.12	0	0
C Woodward	LF	69.0	17	2	1	0	.950	2.48	1	0
M Anderson	LF	45.0	9	1	0	0	1.000	2.00	2	0
V Diaz	LF	26.0	3	1	0	0	1.000	1.38	0	0
G Williams	LF	17.0	3	0	0	0	1.000	1.59	0	0
E Valent	LF	12.0	6	0	0	0	1.000	4.50	0	0
M Cairo	LF	3.0	0	0	0	0	0.000	0.00	0	0
C Beltran	CF	1289.0	378	5	2	2	.990	2.67	2	0
M Cameron	CF	79.0	15	1	0	0	1.000	1.82	0	0
G Williams	CF	51.0	12	0	0	0	1.000	2.12	0	0
C Woodward	CF	12.3	4	0	0	0	1.000	2.92	0	0
E Valent	CF	4.0	2	0	0	0	1.000	4.50	0	0
V Diaz	RF	651.7	153	2	1	2	.981	2.14	2	0
M Cameron	RF	593.0	136	2	0	6	.958	2.09	2	0
M Anderson	RF	73.0	13	1	0	0	1.000	1.73	0	0
E Valent	RF	63.0	13	0	0	1	.929	1.86	0	0
C Woodward	RF	38.0	6	1	0	0	1.000	1.66	0	0
G Williams	RF	10.0	1	1	0	0	1.000	1.80	0	0
M Cairo	RF	7.0	1	0	0	0	1.000	1.29	0	0

Incremental Baserunning Runs		
Name	IR	IRP
Carlos Beltran	3.95	170
David Wright	3.26	144
Jose Reyes	2.11	132
Victor Diaz	1.92	160
Mike Cameron	1.17	151
Ramon Castro	0.47	119
Kazuo Matsui	0.25	108
Gerald Williams	0.17	113
Kazuhisa Ishii	0.17	258
Brian Daubach	0.06	109
Tom Glavine	0.03	104
Pedro Martinez	-0.03	93
Chris Woodward	-0.08	88
Cliff Floyd	-0.12	97
Victor Zambrano	-0.14	34
Eric Valent	-0.17	0
Kris Benson	-0.22	56
Mike Jacobs	-0.22	77
Marlon Anderson	-0.56	76
Doug Mientkiewicz	-1.00	64
Miguel Cairo	-1.08	58
Mike Piazza	-2.46	22

New York Yankees

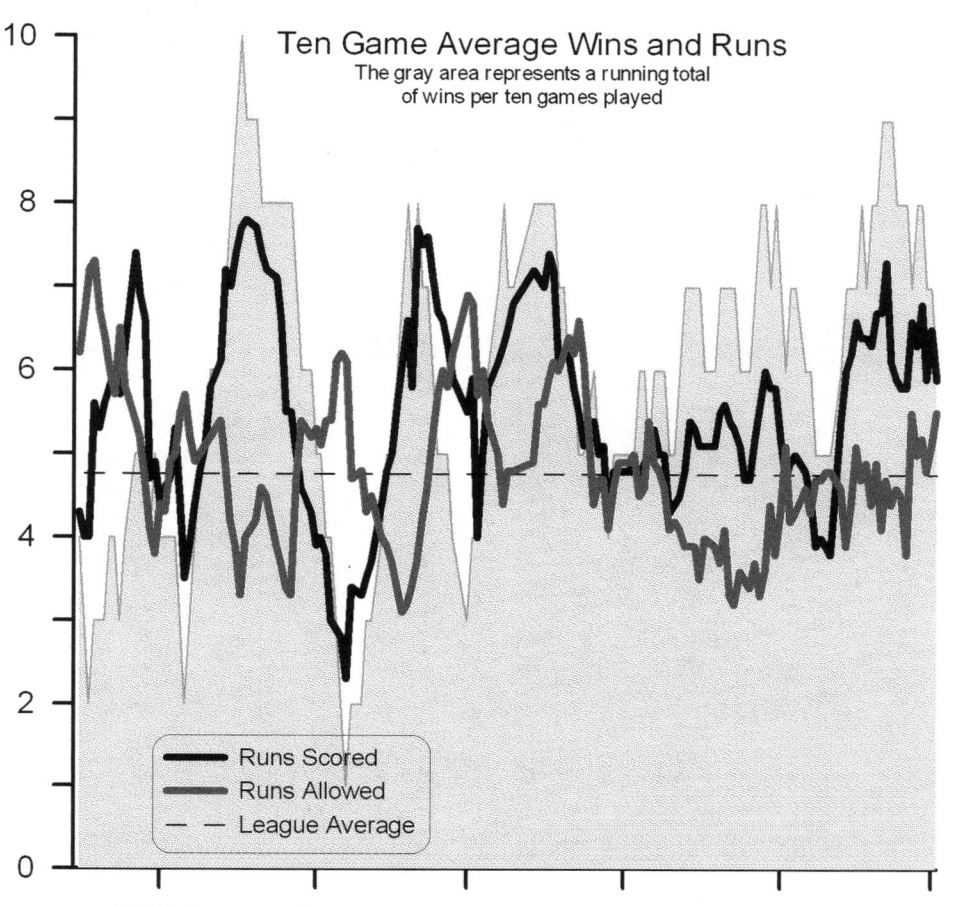

Ten Game Average Wins and Runs
The gray area represents a running total
of wins per ten games played

Runs Scored
Runs Allowed
League Average

5/6 - Lose to A's to
fall to 11-19, 9
games out of first

7/17 - Promote Small,
who goes 10-0 with
3.20 ERA

8/26 - Johnson beats
Royals to start seven-
start stretch of 5-0
with 1.64 ERA

6/15 - Giambi hits
walk-off homer,
starting 44-game
stretch of .354 with
17 HR

7/29 - Trade for Chacon,
who goes 7-3 with
2.85 ERA

9/21 - Beat Orioles
to move into first

Team Batting and Pitching/Fielding Stats by Month						
	April	May	June	July	Aug	Spt/Oct
Wins	10	17	12	17	19	20
Losses	14	10	14	9	10	10
OBP	.357	.349	.359	.357	.343	.364
SLG	.422	.452	.426	.504	.432	.462
FIP	4.26	3.74	4.58	4.61	4.17	4.37
DER	.671	.681	.718	.702	.724	.722

Batting Stats

Player	RC	Runs	RBI	PA	Outs	P/PA	H	2B	3B	HR	TB	K	BB	IBB	HBP	SH	SF	SB	CS	GDP	BA	OBP	SLG	GPA
Rodriguez A.	139	124	130	715	425	3.91	194	29	1	48	369	139	91	8	16	0	3	21	6	8	.321	.421	.610	.342
Sheffield G.	131	104	123	675	427	3.92	170	27	0	34	299	76	78	7	8	0	5	10	2	11	.291	.379	.512	.299
Matsui H.	110	108	116	704	455	3.71	192	45	3	23	312	78	63	7	3	0	8	2	2	16	.305	.367	.496	.289
Jeter D.	106	122	70	752	472	3.83	202	25	5	19	294	117	77	3	11	7	3	14	5	15	.309	.389	.450	.288
Giambi J.	103	74	87	545	311	4.21	113	14	0	32	223	109	108	5	19	0	1	0	0	7	.271	.440	.535	.332
Posada J.	72	67	71	546	358	3.82	124	23	0	19	204	94	66	5	2	0	4	1	0	8	.262	.352	.430	.266
Williams B.	63	53	64	546	382	3.58	121	19	1	12	178	75	53	1	1	1	6	1	2	16	.249	.321	.367	.236
Cano R.	60	78	62	551	386	3.05	155	34	4	14	239	68	16	1	3	7	3	1	3	16	.297	.320	.458	.258
Martinez T.	41	43	49	348	240	3.82	73	9	0	17	133	54	38	3	3	0	4	2	0	10	.241	.328	.439	.257
Womack T.	28	46	15	351	259	3.89	82	8	1	0	92	49	12	0	1	7	2	27	5	7	.249	.276	.280	.194
Sierra R.	19	14	29	181	133	3.50	39	12	0	4	63	41	9	1	0	0	2	0	0	2	.229	.265	.371	.212
Crosby B.	9	15	6	103	73	3.03	27	0	1	1	32	14	4	0	0	1	0	5	1	1	.276	.304	.327	.218
Lawton M.	3	6	4	57	42	4.00	6	0	0	2	12	8	7	0	2	0	0	1	0	0	.125	.263	.250	.181
Sanchez R.	3	7	2	48	34	2.92	12	1	0	0	13	3	2	0	1	2	0	0	1	2	.279	.326	.302	.222
Flaherty J.	2	10	11	138	110	3.51	21	5	0	2	32	26	6	0	1	2	2	0	0	4	.165	.206	.252	.156
Phillips A.	2	7	4	41	35	4.12	6	4	0	1	13	13	1	0	0	0	0	0	0	1	.150	.171	.325	.158
Johnson R.	2	5	0	20	14	3.35	4	2	0	0	6	4	1	0	1	0	0	0	0	0	.222	.300	.333	.218
Escalona F.	2	0	2	17	11	4.18	4	1	0	0	5	4	1	0	1	1	0	0	0	1	.286	.375	.357	.258
Brown K.	1	0	0	2	1	4.00	1	1	0	0	2	1	0	0	0	0	0	0	0	0	.500	.500	1.000	.475
Bellhorn M.	0	2	2	20	15	3.85	2	0	0	1	5	3	3	0	0	0	0	0	0	0	.118	.250	.294	.186
Reese K.	0	0	0	2	1	5.50	0	0	0	0	0	1	1	0	0	0	0	0	0	0	.000	.500	.000	.225
Wang C.	-0	0	0	1	1	2.00	0	0	0	0	0	0	0	0	0	0	0	0	0	0	.000	.000	.000	.000
Cabrera M.	-0	1	0	19	15	2.58	4	0	0	0	4	2	0	0	0	0	0	0	0	0	.211	.211	.211	.147
Vento M.	-0	0	0	2	2	4.00	0	0	0	0	0	1	0	0	0	0	0	0	0	0	.000	.000	.000	.000
Mussina M.	-0	0	0	3	3	2.67	0	0	0	0	0	2	0	0	0	0	0	0	0	0	.000	.000	.000	.000
Nieves W.	-0	0	0	4	4	3.50	0	0	0	0	0	1	0	0	0	0	0	0	0	0	.000	.000	.000	.000
Pavano C.	-1	0	0	7	7	2.71	0	0	0	0	0	4	0	0	0	0	0	0	0	0	.000	.000	.000	.000
Johnson R.	-1	0	0	8	8	4.13	0	0	0	0	0	2	0	0	0	0	0	0	0	0	.000	.000	.000	.000

Win Shares Stats

Player	WS	Bat	Pitch	Field	ExpWS	WSP	WSAB	CWS	NetWSValue
Rodriguez, A	37	33.3	0.0	3.3	19	.989	24	318	$3,103,945
Sheffield, G	33	30.5	0.0	2.2	17	.978	21	401	$8,903,152
Jeter, D	26	19.6	0.0	6.0	19	.672	12	245	($1,996,514)
Giambi, J	25	24.5	0.0	0.6	12	1.016	16	261	$5,036,372
Matsui, H	25	22.6	0.0	2.6	18	.711	13	73	$5,441,603
Posada, J	19	12.6	0.0	6.8	14	.684	9	173	$996,076
Rivera, M	17	0.0	17.3	0.0	9	.956	11	161	$2,478,949
Johnson, R	16	-0.6	16.4	0.0	12	.657	9	302	($2,721,203)
Cano, R	12	7.9	0.0	4.1	15	.414	2	12	$1,469,543
Williams, B	11	8.4	0.0	2.6	13	.411	2	303	($5,994,992)

Continued on the next page.

Pitching Stats

Player	PR	IP	BFP	G	GS	P/PA	K	BB	IBB	HBP	H	HR	DP	DER	SB	CS	PO	W	L	Sv	Op	Hld	RA	ERA	FIP
Rivera M.	23	78.3	306	71	0	3.88	80	18	0	4	50	2	4	.762	6	3	0	7	4	43	47	0	2.07	1.38	2.18
Gordon T.	17	80.7	324	79	0	3.83	69	29	4	0	59	8	7	.766	3	1	0	5	4	2	9	33	2.79	2.57	3.70
Johnson R.	17	225.7	920	34	34	3.72	211	47	2	12	207	32	17	.717	23	14	4	17	8	0	0	0	4.07	3.79	3.80
Chacon S.	16	79.0	330	14	12	3.97	40	30	0	6	66	7	9	.761	3	3	1	7	3	0	0	1	2.96	2.85	4.55
Small A.	13	76.0	316	15	9	3.54	37	24	0	5	71	4	9	.728	2	2	0	10	0	0	1	0	3.20	3.20	3.90
Wang C.	3	116.3	486	18	17	3.29	47	32	3	6	113	9	18	.735	9	4	0	8	5	0	0	0	4.49	4.02	4.22
Mussina M.	2	179.7	766	30	30	3.89	142	47	0	7	199	23	26	.678	15	7	0	13	8	0	0	0	4.66	4.41	4.03
Bean C.	0	2.0	9	1	0	5.00	2	2	0	0	1	0	0	.800	0	0	0	0	0	0	0	0	4.50	4.50	4.04
Groom B.	-0	25.7	116	24	0	3.71	13	7	2	3	32	3	3	.678	2	1	1	1	0	0	0	3	4.91	4.91	4.72
Rodriguez F.	-1	32.3	147	34	0	4.34	18	20	1	2	33	2	1	.705	7	2	0	0	0	0	0	3	5.01	5.01	4.78
Graman A.	-1	1.3	9	2	0	3.44	0	2	1	0	3	1	0	.667	0	0	0	0	0	0	0	0	13.50	13.50	17.29
Mendoza R.	-1	1.0	5	1	0	3.60	1	0	0	0	2	1	0	.667	0	0	0	0	0	0	0	0	18.00	18.00	14.04
Karsay S.	-2	6.0	29	6	0	3.59	5	2	1	0	10	0	0	.545	1	1	0	0	0	0	0	0	7.50	6.00	2.38
Sturtze T.	-2	78.0	332	64	1	3.68	45	27	1	6	76	10	7	.730	8	4	0	5	3	1	6	16	4.96	4.73	4.83
Anderson J.	-2	5.7	27	3	0	3.59	2	7	1	0	4	0	1	.778	0	0	0	1	0	0	0	0	7.94	7.94	6.04
DePaula J.	-2	6.7	30	3	0	3.73	3	3	0	0	8	2	2	.727	0	0	0	0	0	0	0	0	8.10	8.10	7.39
Stanton M.	-4	14.0	64	28	0	3.81	12	6	0	0	17	1	1	.644	1	0	0	1	2	0	0	4	7.07	7.07	3.54
Franklin W.	-5	12.7	57	13	0	4.63	10	8	0	1	11	1	2	.730	1	0	0	0	1	0	3	3	8.53	6.39	4.62
Redding T.	-5	1.0	11	1	1	3.73	2	4	0	0	4	0	0	.200	0	0	0	0	1	0	0	0	54.00	54.00	11.04
Embree A.	-6	14.3	68	24	0	3.74	8	3	1	1	20	2	1	.667	2	0	0	1	1	0	0	6	8.79	7.53	4.58
Quantrill P.	-7	32.0	149	22	0	3.35	11	7	2	2	48	5	2	.653	1	1	0	1	0	0	1	0	6.75	6.75	5.23
Proctor S.	-8	44.7	199	29	1	4.02	36	17	4	2	46	10	2	.731	8	0	0	1	0	0	0	0	6.45	6.04	5.62
Leiter A.	-9	62.3	293	16	10	4.18	45	38	0	6	66	4	5	.690	4	1	0	4	5	0	0	0	6.06	5.49	4.55
May D.	-9	7.0	38	2	1	4.53	3	3	0	0	14	4	0	.643	0	0	0	0	1	0	0	0	16.71	16.71	10.90
Henn S.	-10	11.3	61	3	3	4.20	3	11	0	0	18	3	2	.659	3	0	0	0	3	0	0	0	12.71	11.12	8.87
Pavano C.	-13	100.0	442	17	17	3.51	56	18	1	8	129	17	14	.673	11	4	0	4	6	0	0	0	5.94	4.77	4.91
Wright J.	-17	63.7	302	13	13	3.71	34	32	1	6	81	8	10	.671	5	1	0	5	5	0	0	0	7.21	6.08	5.40
Brown K.	-18	73.3	346	13	13	3.56	50	19	1	7	107	5	8	.615	10	1	0	4	7	0	0	0	7.00	6.50	3.63

Win Shares Stats (cont.)

Player	WS	Bat	Pitch	Field	ExpWS	WSP	WSAB	CWS	NetWSValue
Gordon, T	10	0.0	10.3	0.0	7	.769	6	163	$2,365,995
Mussina, M	10	-0.1	10.3	0.0	10	.535	4	235	($7,788,930)
Small, A	8	0.0	8.0	0.0	4	.980	6	17	$4,382,905
Chacon, S	8	0.0	7.9	0.0	4	.940	5	28	$3,988,248
Wang, C	7	-0.0	7.3	0.0	6	.595	4	7	$2,859,328
Martinez, T	7	6.2	0.0	0.8	9	.377	1	216	($1,072,175)
Sturtze, T	4	0.0	4.4	0.0	6	.385	0	33	($280,694)
Womack, T	3	0.8	0.0	2.1	9	.156	-4	117	($2,000,000)
Sierra, R	2	2.2	0.0	0.2	4	.307	-0	223	($979,951)
Pavano, C	2	-0.5	3.0	0.0	5	.228	-1	51	($5,879,313)
Brown, K	0	0.3	-0.1	0.0	4	.020	-2	241	($11,056,221)
Flaherty, J	0	-2.8	0.0	2.8	4	.001	-3	71	($800,000)

Fielding and Baserunning Stats

Name	POS	Inn	SBA/G	CS%	ERA	WP+PB/G	PO	A	TE	FE
Posada	C	1076.7	1.04	28%	4.67	0.343	718	76	1	2
Flaherty	C	345.0	1.15	20%	4.12	0.183	291	19	2	0
Nieves	C	9.0	0.00	0%	4.00	0.000	11	0	0	0

Name	POS	Inn	PO	A	TE	FE	FPct	RF	DPS	DPT
T Martinez	1B	770.7	797	49	1	6	.991	9.88	5	1
J Giambi	1B	560.0	581	19	4	2	.988	9.64	6	1
A Phillips	1B	67.0	75	2	0	1	.987	10.34	0	0
R Johnson	1B	29.0	30	0	0	0	1.000	9.31	0	0
J Flaherty	1B	3.0	1	0	0	0	1.000	3.00	0	0
F Escalona	1B	1.0	2	0	0	0	1.000	18.00	0	0
R Cano	2B	1142.0	258	391	8	9	.974	5.11	39	38
T Womack	2B	199.0	42	89	1	0	.992	5.92	13	9
R Sanchez	2B	63.0	18	24	0	1	.977	6.00	1	3
M Bellhorn	2B	16.0	4	11	0	1	.938	8.44	1	1
F Escalona	2B	9.0	1	4	0	0	1.000	5.00	1	0
R Johnson	2B	1.0	0	0	0	0	0.000	0.00	0	0
D Jeter	SS	1352.0	262	454	9	6	.979	4.77	47	45
R Sanchez	SS	38.0	7	14	1	0	.955	4.97	3	1
F Escalona	SS	29.0	8	8	0	0	1.000	4.97	1	2
A Rodriguez	SS	6.0	1	2	0	0	1.000	4.50	0	0
M Bellhorn	SS	5.0	2	2	0	0	1.000	7.20	0	0
A Rodriguez	3B	1384.0	115	288	2	10	.971	2.62	25	1
R Johnson	3B	18.0	1	2	0	0	1.000	1.50	0	0
M Bellhorn	3B	18.0	1	3	0	0	1.000	2.00	0	0
F Escalona	3B	6.0	0	1	0	0	1.000	1.50	0	0
A Phillips	3B	3.0	0	0	0	0	0.000	0.00	0	0
R Sanchez	3B	1.0	0	0	0	0	0.000	0.00	0	0
H Matsui	LF	977.3	219	7	0	3	.987	2.08	2	0
T Womack	LF	326.0	72	2	0	2	.974	2.04	0	0
R Sierra	LF	54.0	10	0	0	0	1.000	1.67	0	0
M Lawton	LF	44.3	11	0	0	0	1.000	2.23	0	0
B Crosby	LF	20.0	2	0	0	0	1.000	0.90	0	0
K Reese	LF	7.0	1	0	0	0	1.000	1.29	0	0
A Phillips	LF	2.0	0	0	0	0	0.000	0.00	0	0
B Williams	CF	862.7	226	6	0	2	.991	2.42	2	0
H Matsui	CF	222.3	54	0	0	0	1.000	2.19	0	0
T Womack	CF	150.0	36	0	0	0	1.000	2.16	0	0
B Crosby	CF	144.7	57	1	0	0	1.000	3.61	2	0
M Cabrera	CF	49.0	9	0	0	0	1.000	1.65	0	0
K Reese	CF	2.0	1	0	0	0	1.000	4.50	0	0

Name	POS	Inn	PO	A	TE	FE	FPct	RF	DPS	DPT
G Sheffield	RF	1099.0	239	5	1	2	.988	2.00	0	0
B Crosby	RF	100.0	24	1	0	0	1.000	2.25	0	0
M Lawton	RF	92.7	20	0	1	0	.952	1.94	0	0
R Sierra	RF	64.0	13	0	0	1	.929	1.83	0	0
T Womack	RF	31.7	5	0	0	0	1.000	1.42	0	0
H Matsui	RF	29.7	6	0	0	0	1.000	1.82	0	0
M Vento	RF	7.0	2	1	0	0	1.000	3.86	2	0
R Johnson	RF	6.3	1	0	0	0	1.000	1.42	0	0

Incremental Baserunning Runs		
Name	IR	IRP
Robinson Cano	3.37	149
Hideki Matsui	1.21	118
Jason Giambi	1.11	129
Derek Jeter	0.99	114
Gary Sheffield	0.90	114
Andy Phillips	0.51	224
Rey Sanchez	0.37	148
Russ Johnson	0.15	166
Mark Bellhorn	0.01	121
Ruben Sierra	-0.05	96
Alex Rodriguez	-0.15	98
Bubba Crosby	-0.16	89
Matt Lawton	-0.34	19
Bernie Williams	-0.47	92
Tony Womack	-0.55	90
Jorge Posada	-0.74	89
John Flaherty	-1.01	47
Tino Martinez	-2.69	20

Oakland Athletics

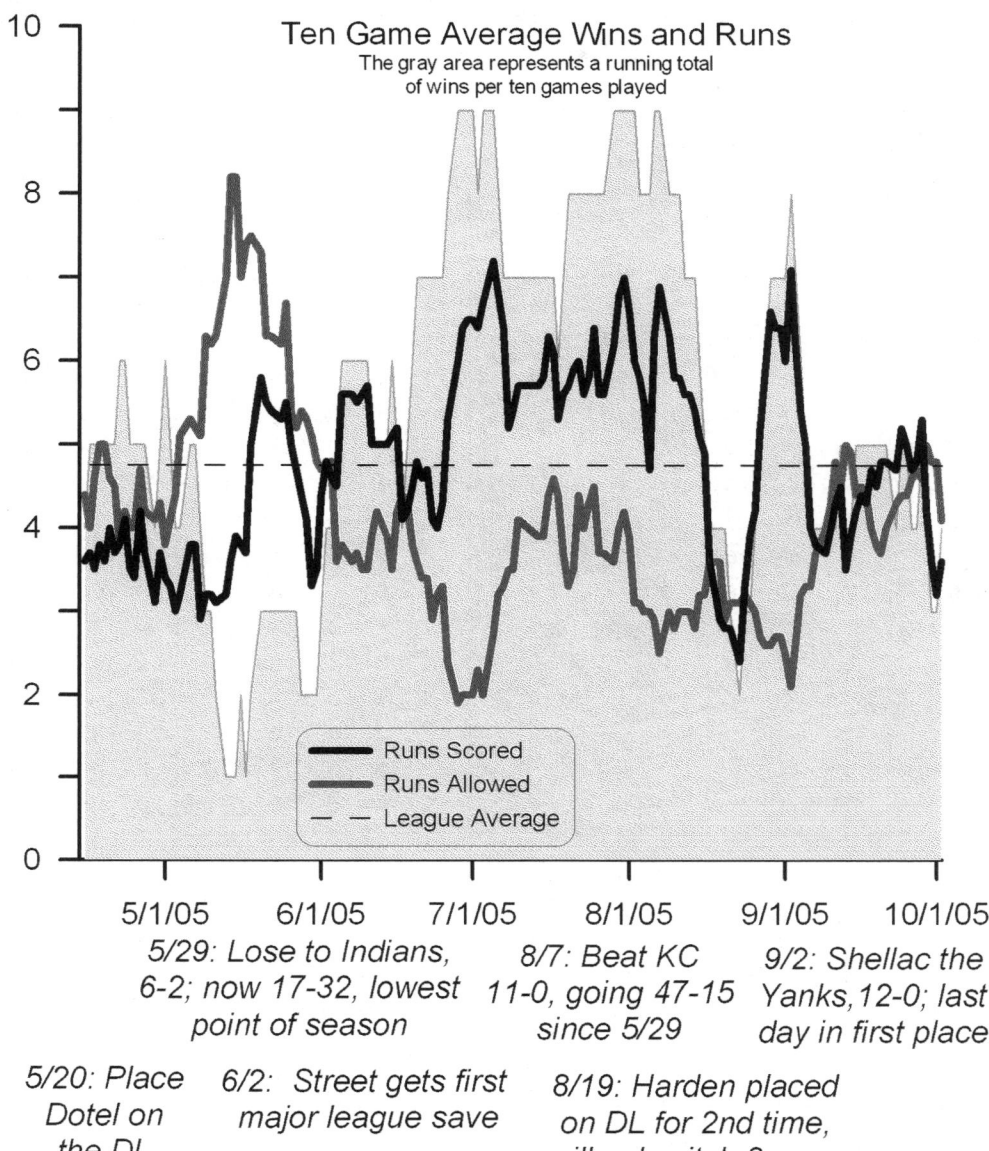

Ten Game Average Wins and Runs
The gray area represents a running total
of wins per ten games played

- Runs Scored
- Runs Allowed
- — League Average

5/29: Lose to Indians, 6-2; now 17-32, lowest point of season

8/7: Beat KC 11-0, going 47-15 since 5/29

9/2: Shellac the Yanks,12-0; last day in first place

5/20: Place Dotel on the DL

6/2: Street gets first major league save

8/19: Harden placed on DL for 2nd time, will only pitch 3 more innings

Team Batting and Pitching/Fielding Stats by Month						
	April	May	June	July	Aug	Spt/Oct
Wins	12	7	19	20	17	13
Losses	12	20	8	6	11	17
OBP	.314	.325	.356	.342	.326	.316
SLG	.343	.347	.464	.455	.419	.404
FIP	3.88	4.89	3.96	4.12	3.62	4.38
DER	.719	.714	.759	.728	.739	.716

Batting Stats

Player	RC	Runs	RBI	PA	Outs	P/PA	H	2B	3B	HR	TB	K	BB	IBB	HBP	SH	SF	SB	CS	GDP	BA	OBP	SLG	GPA
Chavez E.	96	92	101	694	466	3.94	168	40	1	27	291	129	58	4	2	0	9	6	0	9	.269	.329	.466	.264
Kotsay M.	86	75	82	629	437	3.42	163	35	1	15	245	51	40	3	1	2	4	5	5	13	.280	.325	.421	.252
Kendall J.	79	70	53	676	468	3.94	163	28	1	0	193	39	50	0	20	0	5	8	3	27	.271	.345	.321	.235
Ellis M.	78	76	52	486	310	4.00	137	21	5	13	207	51	44	1	4	4	0	1	3	10	.316	.384	.477	.292
Swisher N.	63	66	74	522	363	4.14	109	32	1	21	206	110	55	3	4	0	1	0	1	9	.236	.322	.446	.256
Hatteberg S.	61	52	59	523	368	3.85	119	19	0	7	159	54	51	4	4	2	2	0	1	22	.256	.334	.343	.236
Johnson D.	56	54	58	434	284	4.18	103	21	0	15	169	52	50	1	1	0	8	0	1	11	.275	.355	.451	.272
Kielty B.	53	55	57	433	294	3.88	99	20	0	10	149	67	50	3	2	2	2	3	2	14	.263	.350	.395	.256
Crosby B.	48	66	38	371	251	4.19	92	25	4	9	152	54	35	0	1	1	1	0	0	10	.276	.346	.456	.270
Scutaro M.	45	48	37	423	295	3.76	94	22	3	9	149	48	36	1	0	4	2	5	2	6	.247	.310	.391	.237
Payton J.	41	38	42	291	206	3.32	74	9	1	13	124	33	14	2	0	0	2	0	1	4	.269	.302	.451	.249
Byrnes E.	29	30	24	215	144	3.66	51	15	2	7	91	27	14	0	7	1	1	2	2	1	.266	.336	.474	.270
Durazo E.	16	15	16	167	122	3.42	36	6	1	4	56	24	14	0	1	0	0	1	0	6	.237	.305	.368	.230
Melhuse A.	12	11	12	102	73	3.68	24	7	0	2	37	28	5	0	0	0	0	0	0	0	.247	.284	.381	.223
Ginter K.	9	12	25	156	120	3.87	22	5	0	3	36	25	13	0	1	2	3	0	0	5	.161	.234	.263	.171
Watson M.	3	4	5	50	40	3.64	9	3	0	0	12	4	2	0	0	0	0	0	0	1	.188	.220	.250	.162
Bynum F.	1	0	1	7	5	3.86	2	1	0	0	3	3	0	0	0	0	0	0	0	0	.286	.286	.429	.236
Thomas C.	1	4	1	55	42	3.93	5	0	0	0	5	8	5	0	4	0	0	0	1	0	.109	.255	.109	.142
Haren D.	1	0	2	5	3	3.00	2	1	0	0	3	0	0	0	0	0	0	0	0	0	.400	.400	.600	.330
Clark J.	0	2	0	1	0	0.00	0	0	0	0	0	0	1	0	0	0	0	0	0	0	.000	1.000	.000	.450
Zito B.	-0	0	0	7	6	3.57	1	0	0	0	1	2	0	0	0	0	0	0	0	0	.143	.143	.143	.100
Saarloos K.	-0	0	0	1	1	1.00	0	0	0	0	0	0	0	0	0	0	0	0	0	0	.000	.000	.000	.000
Yabu K.	-0	0	0	1	1	7.00	0	0	0	0	0	0	0	0	0	0	0	0	0	0	.000	.000	.000	.000
Glynn R.	-0	0	0	1	1	6.00	0	0	0	0	0	1	0	0	0	0	0	0	0	0	.000	.000	.000	.000
Castillo A.	-0	0	0	1	1	5.00	0	0	0	0	0	1	0	0	0	0	0	0	0	0	.000	.000	.000	.000
Calero K.	-0	0	0	1	1	6.00	0	0	0	0	0	1	0	0	0	0	0	0	0	0	.000	.000	.000	.000
Bocachica H.	-0	2	0	19	17	3.84	2	0	0	0	2	7	0	0	0	0	0	0	0	0	.105	.105	.105	.074
Blanton J.	-0	0	0	4	3	2.75	1	0	0	0	1	0	0	0	0	1	0	0	0	1	.333	.333	.333	.233

Pitching Stats

Player	PR	IP	BFP	G	GS	P/PA	K	BB	IBB	HBP	H	HR	DP	DER	SB	CS	PO	W	L	Sv	Op	Hld	RA	ERA	FIP
Harden R.	24	128.0	514	22	19	3.82	121	43	0	2	93	7	12	.748	4	4	0	10	5	0	0	1	2.95	2.53	2.92
Street H.	24	78.3	306	67	0	3.88	72	26	4	2	53	3	9	.754	7	2	1	5	1	23	27	0	1.95	1.72	2.78
Duchscherer	20	85.7	338	65	0	3.95	85	19	3	2	67	7	11	.733	6	2	1	7	4	5	7	10	2.63	2.21	2.86
Blanton J.	18	201.3	835	33	33	3.68	116	67	3	5	178	23	19	.752	8	1	2	12	12	0	0	0	3.84	3.53	4.45
Zito B.	12	228.3	953	35	35	3.99	171	89	0	13	185	26	24	.757	22	4	2	14	13	0	0	0	4.18	3.86	4.37
Haren D.	11	217.0	897	34	34	3.76	163	53	5	6	212	26	30	.713	19	5	1	14	12	0	0	0	4.19	3.73	3.91
Calero K.	9	55.7	229	58	0	3.98	52	18	2	1	45	6	2	.743	7	0	0	4	1	1	2	12	3.23	3.23	3.60
Saarloos K.	7	159.7	682	29	27	3.52	53	54	8	11	170	11	28	.712	14	5	0	10	9	0	0	0	4.23	4.17	4.50
Flores R.	4	8.7	34	11	0	3.82	6	0	0	0	8	1	0	.741	0	0	0	0	0	0	0	1	1.04	1.04	3.16
Dotel O.	2	15.3	65	15	0	3.95	16	11	2	0	10	2	2	.778	4	0	0	1	2	7	11	0	3.52	3.52	4.80
Garcia J.	1	3.0	12	3	0	3.50	1	1	0	0	2	0	0	.800	0	0	0	0	0	0	0	0	3.00	3.00	3.38
Rincon R.	0	37.3	162	67	0	3.85	27	20	4	1	34	7	6	.748	0	0	0	1	1	0	2	16	4.58	4.34	5.72
Witasick J.	-1	27.7	129	28	0	4.03	33	17	2	3	26	2	1	.676	6	0	0	1	1	1	3	6	4.88	3.25	3.77
Kennedy J.	-2	60.7	262	19	8	3.79	45	20	2	1	64	8	6	.702	3	0	1	4	5	0	2	0	4.90	4.45	4.31
Harikkala T.	-3	12.7	56	8	0	3.59	7	4	0	0	16	3	2	.690	0	0	0	0	0	0	0	0	6.39	6.39	5.96
Reames B.	-3	5.7	29	2	0	3.38	4	2	0	1	10	2	1	.600	0	0	0	0	0	0	0	0	9.53	9.53	7.81
Etherton S.	-4	17.7	74	3	3	4.08	10	5	0	0	16	4	0	.782	1	0	0	1	1	0	0	0	6.62	6.62	5.70
Yabu K.	-4	58.0	262	40	0	3.50	44	26	3	8	64	6	8	.674	3	1	0	4	0	1	2	1	5.28	4.50	4.63
Glynn R.	-7	17.0	82	5	3	4.12	15	7	0	0	24	5	1	.655	1	0	0	0	4	0	0	0	8.47	6.88	6.34
Cruz J.	-17	32.7	159	28	0	3.79	34	22	4	4	38	5	4	.649	4	1	0	0	3	0	0	0	9.09	7.44	5.34

Win Shares Stats

Player	WS	Bat	Pitch	Field	ExpWS	WSP	WSAB	CWS	NetWSValue
Ellis, M	21	14.2	0.0	6.8	13	.809	12	53	$9,346,948
Chavez, E	21	16.0	0.0	5.2	18	.584	9	143	$1,759,581
Kotsay, M	19	13.3	0.0	5.5	16	.575	7	124	$2,062,779
Haren, D	15	0.2	14.3	0.0	12	.630	8	17	$6,007,205
Blanton, J	14	-0.1	14.4	0.0	11	.667	8	14	$6,185,497
Zito, B	14	-0.2	14.5	0.0	12	.591	7	94	($353,917)
Kendall, J	14	9.2	0.0	4.9	18	.399	2	178	($4,851,110)
Harden, R	13	0.0	12.9	0.0	7	.951	9	31	$6,935,099
Street, H	13	0.0	13.3	0.0	7	.920	8	13	$6,498,999
Crosby, B	12	7.3	0.0	5.0	10	.628	5	25	$4,122,129
Swisher, N	12	8.9	0.0	3.4	14	.438	2	13	$1,969,786
Duchschere, J	11	0.0	10.6	0.0	6	.863	6	22	$4,963,903
Scutaro, M	11	5.0	0.0	6.4	12	.494	3	23	$2,636,776
Kielty, B	10	7.2	0.0	2.7	11	.444	2	44	$1,025,936
Johnson, D	10	8.6	0.0	1.2	12	.423	2	10	$1,332,368
Saarloos, K	9	-0.0	9.5	0.0	8	.563	4	13	$3,500,126
Payton, J	9	6.1	0.0	2.7	8	.565	3	72	($538,086)
Hatteberg, S	8	7.2	0.0	0.6	12	.334	-0	86	($1,580,495)
Byrnes, E	7	4.9	0.0	2.5	6	.654	3	45	($2,200,000)
Calero, K	5	-0.0	5.5	0.0	4	.700	3	13	$2,164,386
Yabu, K	3	-0.0	2.8	0.0	4	.371	0	3	($307,252)
Ginter, K	1	-0.8	0.0	1.6	4	.102	-2	24	($583,333)

Fielding and Baserunning Stats

Name	POS	Inn	SBA/G	CS%	ERA	WP+PB/G	PO	A	TE	FE
Kendall	C	1286.0	0.83	15%	3.79	0.301	985	52	5	0
Melhuse	C	161.3	0.61	27%	3.01	0.167	115	7	0	0
Castillo	C	3.0	0.00	0%	0.00	0.000	2	0	0	0

Name	POS	Inn	PO	A	TE	FE	FPct	RF	DPS	DPT
D Johnson	1B	883.7	901	53	0	6	.994	9.72	12	3
S Hatteberg	1B	436.7	423	38	1	6	.985	9.50	5	0
N Swisher	1B	119.0	109	10	0	0	1.000	9.00	0	0
E Durazo	1B	8.0	8	0	0	0	1.000	9.00	0	0
M Ellis	1B	3.0	3	0	0	0	1.000	9.00	0	0
M Ellis	2B	972.0	204	333	2	4	.989	4.97	36	48
M Scutaro	2B	267.7	56	92	1	0	.993	4.98	7	13
K Ginter	2B	203.7	49	69	0	3	.975	5.21	7	10
F Bynum	2B	5.0	0	0	0	0	0.000	0.00	0	0
J Clark	2B	2.0	0	0	0	0	0.000	0.00	0	0
B Crosby	SS	743.3	117	250	5	2	.981	4.44	35	22
M Scutaro	SS	663.0	115	213	4	4	.976	4.45	21	24
M Ellis	SS	44.0	6	15	0	0	1.000	4.30	2	2
E Chavez	3B	1348.0	121	301	8	7	.966	2.82	26	1
K Ginter	3B	63.0	12	11	1	2	.885	3.29	0	0
M Scutaro	3B	21.0	4	6	0	0	1.000	4.29	1	0
H Bocachica	3B	18.0	2	3	0	0	1.000	2.50	1	0
B Kielty	LF	457.0	99	3	1	0	.990	2.01	0	0
J Payton	LF	414.3	99	0	0	0	1.000	2.15	0	0
E Byrnes	LF	388.0	109	3	0	1	.991	2.60	2	0
M Watson	LF	88.3	26	0	0	0	1.000	2.65	0	0
C Thomas	LF	77.7	17	1	0	1	.947	2.09	0	0
M Scutaro	LF	16.0	5	0	0	0	1.000	2.81	0	0
K Ginter	LF	6.0	0	0	0	0	0.000	0.00	0	0
F Bynum	LF	2.0	1	0	0	0	1.000	4.50	0	0
J Clark	LF	1.0	0	0	0	0	0.000	0.00	0	0
M Kotsay	CF	1184.0	298	7	2	2	.987	2.32	5	0
J Payton	CF	210.0	54	2	0	0	1.000	2.40	0	0
C Thomas	CF	29.0	14	0	0	0	1.000	4.34	0	0
E Byrnes	CF	15.0	3	1	0	0	1.000	2.40	2	0
F Bynum	CF	9.0	4	0	0	0	1.000	4.00	0	0
H Bocachica	CF	3.0	3	0	0	0	1.000	9.00	0	0
N Swisher	RF	1027.0	196	6	0	1	.990	1.77	3	0
B Kielty	RF	324.0	67	2	0	2	.972	1.92	2	0
C Thomas	RF	30.0	7	0	0	1	.875	2.10	0	0
E Byrnes	RF	27.0	5	0	0	1	.833	1.67	0	0
H Bocachica	RF	25.0	3	0	0	0	1.000	1.08	0	0
M Watson	RF	17.0	4	0	0	0	1.000	2.12	0	0

Incremental Baserunning Runs		
Name	IR	IRP
Eric Chavez	2.68	131
Bobby Crosby	2.25	132
Jason Kendall	1.96	129
Bobby Kielty	1.56	135
Marco Scutaro	1.50	121
Mark Kotsay	1.12	116
Jay Payton	1.11	155
Scott Hatteberg	0.84	112
Eric Byrnes	0.60	143
Dan Johnson	0.59	111
Adam Melhuse	0.59	148
Charles Thomas	0.21	157
Matt Watson	0.12	109
Keith Ginter	-0.57	70
Erubiel Durazo	-0.93	65
Nick Swisher	-0.95	80
Mark Ellis	-2.18	72

Philadelphia Phillies

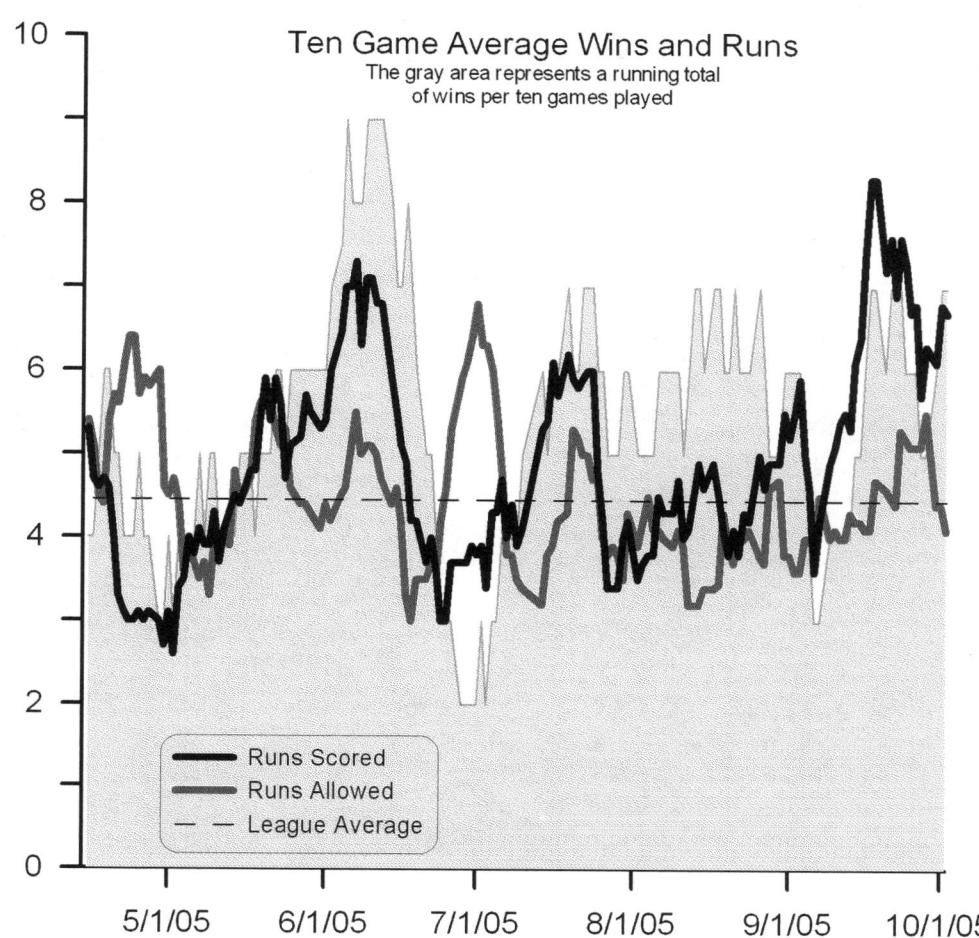

Ten Game Average Wins and Runs
The gray area represents a running total
of wins per ten games played

— Runs Scored
— Runs Allowed
– – League Average

5/3: Thome placed
on DL; Howard recalled
and hits .924 OPS
for season

6/8: Trade Polanco
for Urbina; Utley
takes over 2nd base

8/23: Rollins goes
1 for 5 vs. SF to start
36-game hit streak

9/23: Score 5 runs
in 9th to beat Reds
11-10

10/2: Win 4th straight
but end season a
game behind wild
card

Team Batting and Pitching/Fielding Stats by Month						
	April	May	June	July	Aug	Spt/Oct
Wins	10	15	15	15	16	17
Losses	14	13	12	12	11	12
OBP	.334	.369	.338	.343	.325	.375
SLG	.364	.430	.432	.421	.400	.480
FIP	4.83	4.37	4.97	3.97	3.92	3.95
DER	.706	.715	.720	.709	.747	.708

Batting Stats

Player	RC	Runs	RBI	PA	Outs	P/PA	H	2B	3B	HR	TB	K	BB	IBB	HBP	SH	SF	SB	CS	GDP	BA	OBP	SLG	GPA
Abreu B.	118	104	102	719	436	4.40	168	37	1	24	279	134	117	15	6	0	8	31	9	7	.286	.405	.474	.301
Burrell P.	111	78	117	669	416	4.27	158	27	1	32	283	160	99	6	3	0	5	0	0	12	.281	.389	.504	.301
Utley C.	104	93	105	628	398	4.03	158	39	6	28	293	109	69	5	9	0	7	16	3	10	.291	.376	.540	.304
Rollins J.	101	115	54	732	496	3.42	196	38	11	12	292	71	47	8	4	2	2	41	6	9	.290	.338	.431	.260
Lofton K.	63	67	36	406	250	3.58	123	15	5	2	154	41	32	2	2	5	0	22	3	3	.335	.392	.420	.281
Bell D.	56	53	61	617	444	3.57	138	31	1	10	201	69	47	6	5	4	4	0	1	24	.248	.310	.361	.230
Howard R.	51	52	63	348	229	3.94	90	17	2	22	177	100	33	8	1	0	2	0	1	6	.288	.356	.567	.302
Lieberthal M	50	48	47	443	295	3.44	103	25	0	12	164	35	35	14	11	0	5	0	0	6	.263	.336	.418	.256
Michaels J.	48	54	31	343	207	4.10	88	16	2	4	120	45	44	1	4	2	4	3	3	3	.304	.399	.415	.283
Polanco P.	26	26	20	173	111	3.58	50	7	0	3	66	9	12	0	3	0	0	0	0	3	.316	.376	.418	.274
Thome J.	25	26	30	242	158	3.97	40	7	0	7	68	59	45	4	2	0	2	0	0	5	.207	.360	.352	.250
Pratt T.	23	17	23	196	134	3.86	44	4	0	7	69	50	19	5	2	0	0	0	0	3	.251	.332	.394	.248
Perez T.	14	17	22	176	128	3.55	37	7	0	0	44	27	11	2	2	3	1	1	0	6	.233	.289	.277	.199
Martinez R.	7	7	9	65	41	4.08	16	2	0	1	21	7	3	0	1	2	3	0	0	1	.286	.317	.375	.237
Chavez E.	7	17	10	118	87	3.87	23	3	3	0	32	13	4	0	0	7	0	2	1	2	.215	.243	.299	.184
Victorino S.	4	5	8	19	12	3.63	5	0	0	2	11	3	0	0	0	0	2	0	0	0	.294	.263	.647	.280
Myers B.	3	1	5	80	56	3.49	10	1	0	0	11	19	4	0	0	11	0	0	0	1	.154	.203	.169	.134
Offerman J.	3	6	3	38	28	4.03	6	1	1	1	12	6	5	0	0	0	0	0	0	1	.182	.289	.364	.221
Tucker M.	3	3	3	21	15	3.67	4	0	0	0	4	4	3	0	0	0	0	0	0	1	.222	.333	.222	.206
Padilla V.	3	2	4	51	35	3.90	6	1	1	0	9	24	5	0	0	5	0	0	0	0	.146	.239	.220	.162
Byrd M.	2	0	0	15	9	3.27	4	0	0	0	4	3	1	0	1	0	0	0	0	0	.308	.400	.308	.257
Wolf R.	1	2	1	28	22	3.14	4	2	0	0	6	8	1	0	0	1	0	0	0	0	.154	.185	.231	.141
Kata M.	0	1	0	6	5	3.33	1	0	0	0	1	2	0	0	0	0	0	0	0	0	.167	.167	.167	.117
Fultz A.	0	1	0	3	2	4.00	1	0	0	0	1	2	0	0	0	0	0	0	0	0	.333	.333	.333	.233
Geary G.	0	0	0	6	5	3.83	1	0	0	0	1	4	0	0	0	0	0	0	0	0	.167	.167	.167	.117
Liriano P.	0	0	0	1	0	0.00	0	0	0	0	0	0	0	0	0	1	0	0	0	0	.000	.000	.000	.000
Cormier R.	-0	0	0	3	1	1.67	0	0	0	0	0	1	0	0	0	2	0	0	0	0	.000	.000	.000	.000
Sandoval D.	-0	1	0	2	2	3.00	0	0	0	0	0	1	0	0	0	0	0	0	0	0	.000	.000	.000	.000
Brito E.	-0	1	0	7	6	3.71	1	0	0	0	1	2	0	0	0	0	0	0	0	0	.143	.143	.143	.100
Wagner B.	-0	0	0	3	2	4.00	1	0	0	0	1	2	0	0	0	0	0	0	0	0	.333	.333	.333	.233
Floyd G.	-1	0	0	9	8	4.33	1	0	0	0	1	5	0	0	0	0	0	0	0	0	.111	.111	.111	.078
Madson R.	-1	0	0	8	7	3.75	0	0	0	0	0	0	1	0	0	1	0	0	0	1	.000	.143	.000	.064
Lidle C.	-1	2	2	67	50	3.58	8	0	0	0	8	30	1	0	0	8	0	0	0	0	.138	.153	.138	.103
Tejeda R.	-1	1	0	25	18	3.36	2	0	1	0	4	9	0	0	0	5	0	0	0	0	.100	.100	.200	.095
Lieber J.	-4	7	4	78	69	3.60	7	2	0	0	9	29	1	0	0	3	1	0	0	3	.096	.107	.123	.079

Pitching Stats

Player	PR	IP	BFP	G	GS	P/PA	K	BB	IBB	HBP	H	HR	DP	DER	SB	CS	PO	W	L	Sv	Op	Hld	RA	ERA	FIP
Wagner B.	23	77.7	297	75	0	4.02	87	20	2	3	45	6	5	.785	9	2	0	4	3	38	41	0	1.97	1.51	2.63
Myers B.	20	215.3	905	34	34	3.84	208	68	2	11	193	31	10	.724	15	4	1	13	8	0	0	0	3.93	3.72	4.02
Fultz A.	17	72.3	286	62	0	3.84	54	23	2	5	47	6	6	.793	1	2	0	4	0	0	1	2	2.61	2.24	3.73
Tejeda R.	9	85.7	371	26	13	3.97	72	51	4	8	67	5	11	.736	1	2	1	4	3	0	0	1	3.78	3.57	4.13
Lieber J.	9	218.3	912	35	35	3.43	149	41	6	5	223	33	14	.722	11	5	0	17	13	0	0	0	4.41	4.20	4.21
Urbina U.	3	52.3	214	56	0	4.21	66	25	2	0	35	8	1	.765	6	0	0	4	3	1	7	18	4.30	4.13	3.88
Lopez A.	3	12.7	57	10	0	3.98	16	7	1	0	13	2	0	.656	0	0	0	0	1	0	0	0	2.84	2.13	4.17
Brito E.	3	22.0	94	6	5	3.85	15	11	1	2	20	2	3	.719	0	0	0	1	2	0	0	0	3.68	3.68	4.57
Wolf R.	2	80.0	346	13	13	3.74	61	26	2	6	87	14	11	.695	1	1	1	6	4	0	0	0	4.50	4.39	4.93
Madson R.	2	87.0	365	78	0	3.76	79	25	6	6	84	11	12	.701	6	2	0	6	5	0	7	32	4.55	4.14	3.88
Geary G.	2	58.0	247	40	0	3.61	42	21	4	1	54	5	5	.725	5	0	0	2	1	0	1	3	4.50	3.72	3.79
Telemaco A.	1	10.7	41	7	0	3.98	8	4	0	0	5	2	2	.889	0	0	0	0	1	0	0	0	4.22	4.22	5.04
Padilla V.	-1	147.0	654	27	27	3.90	103	74	9	8	146	22	17	.723	2	1	1	9	12	0	0	0	4.84	4.71	5.20
Lidle C.	-6	184.7	792	31	31	3.53	121	40	5	6	210	18	23	.684	19	6	0	13	11	0	0	0	5.12	4.53	3.69
Liriano P.	-7	7.7	40	5	0	3.98	6	6	0	1	10	3	1	.708	1	0	0	0	0	0	0	0	12.91	10.57	9.24
Cormier R.	-7	47.3	211	57	0	3.61	34	16	1	2	56	9	8	.687	2	0	0	4	2	0	2	17	6.27	5.89	5.16
Worrell T.	-8	17.0	83	19	0	3.53	17	3	0	1	29	4	1	.569	0	1	0	0	1	1	3	3	9.00	7.41	4.75
Adams T.	-11	13.3	77	16	0	3.69	4	10	2	4	25	3	2	.607	1	0	0	0	2	0	1	2	12.83	12.83	8.46
Floyd G.	-16	26.0	127	7	4	3.68	17	16	2	3	30	5	0	.709	2	0	0	1	2	0	0	0	10.73	10.04	6.37

Win Shares Stats

Player	WS	Bat	Pitch	Field	ExpWS	WSP	WSAB	CWS	NetWSValue
Abreu, B	28	24.8	0.0	3.7	19	.733	15	230	$4,003,147
Utley, C	27	22.1	0.0	5.4	17	.801	15	40	$12,205,785
Burrell, P	26	22.9	0.0	3.2	18	.720	13	104	$2,809,066
Rollins, J	23	17.8	0.0	4.9	20	.577	9	106	$3,062,078
Wagner, B	16	-0.1	15.8	0.0	7	1.126	11	123	$3,313,275
Lofton, K	16	11.8	0.0	3.8	11	.718	8	262	$4,619,208
Myers, B	14	-1.0	15.2	0.0	10	.687	8	29	$6,205,833
Michaels, J	13	8.8	0.0	4.0	9	.700	6	32	$4,511,077
Howard, R	11	9.9	0.0	1.2	10	.580	4	12	$3,472,571
Lieberthal, M	11	7.3	0.0	4.0	13	.450	2	115	($2,383,195)
Lieber, J	10	-3.4	13.3	0.0	11	.469	4	101	($370,402)
Bell, D	9	4.5	0.0	4.7	17	.271	-3	106	($4,700,000)
Fultz, A	8	-0.1	8.0	0.0	4	1.062	5	21	$3,933,508
Polanco, P	7	4.8	0.0	1.9	5	.720	3	88	$6,281,047
Lidle, C	7	-2.0	8.5	0.0	9	.367	1	55	($678,045)
Pratt, T	6	3.2	0.0	2.6	6	.524	2	50	$1,248,998
Madson, R	6	-0.5	6.3	0.0	6	.506	2	15	$1,357,772
Padilla, V	6	-0.5	6.4	0.0	7	.413	2	46	($1,963,836)
Tejeda, R	5	-1.0	6.1	0.0	4	.608	3	5	$2,065,123
Urbina, U	5	0.0	4.7	0.0	4	.638	2	98	$515,276
Wolf, R	4	-0.3	4.6	0.0	4	.554	2	65	($5,553,869)
Thome, J	4	3.4	0.0	0.7	6	.315	-0	282	($8,142,938)
Perez, T	1	0.3	0.0	0.8	5	.129	-2	26	($650,000)

Fielding and Baserunning Stats

Name	POS	Inn	SBA/G	CS%	ERA	WP+PB/G	PO	A	TE	FE
Lieberthal	C	998.7	0.70	19%	4.52	0.270	808	44	5	1
Pratt	C	436.3	0.58	32%	3.53	0.371	377	18	0	1

Name	POS	Inn	PO	A	TE	FE	FPct	RF	DPS	DPT
R Howard	1B	706.3	707	40	0	4	.993	9.52	3	0
J Thome	1B	436.0	404	30	0	0	1.000	8.96	2	0
T Perez	1B	146.0	148	10	0	0	1.000	9.74	1	0
R Martinez	1B	76.0	75	6	0	0	1.000	9.59	0	0
C Utley	1B	54.7	45	9	0	0	.982	8.89	2	0
J Offerman	1B	16.0	15	0	1	0	.938	8.44	0	0
C Utley	2B	1195.0	296	376	7	8	.978	5.06	33	38
P Polanco	2B	229.7	57	74	0	0	1.000	5.13	14	11
M Kata	2B	5.0	0	0	0	0	0.000	0.00	0	0
R Martinez	2B	5.0	1	2	0	1	.750	5.40	0	0
J Rollins	SS	1356.0	208	411	9	3	.981	4.11	38	40
T Perez	SS	61.0	8	12	0	0	1.000	2.95	1	0
R Martinez	SS	8.0	2	0	0	0	1.000	2.25	0	0
P Polanco	SS	8.0	3	2	0	0	1.000	5.63	0	1
M Kata	SS	1.0	0	0	0	0	0.000	0.00	0	0
D Sandoval	SS	1.0	0	1	0	0	1.000	9.00	0	0
D Bell	3B	1296.0	105	304	7	14	.951	2.84	24	0
T Perez	3B	73.0	11	17	0	0	1.000	3.45	1	1
P Polanco	3B	48.3	6	17	0	0	1.000	4.28	2	0
R Martinez	3B	17.0	1	3	0	0	1.000	2.12	0	0
P Burrell	LF	1297.0	236	10	1	6	.972	1.71	3	0
E Chavez	LF	59.0	15	1	0	0	1.000	2.44	0	0
J Michaels	LF	45.3	11	1	0	0	1.000	2.38	2	0
P Polanco	LF	29.0	10	0	0	0	1.000	3.10	0	0
S Victorino	LF	4.0	0	0	0	0	0.000	0.00	0	0
K Lofton	CF	741.0	201	7	2	2	.981	2.53	2	0
J Michaels	CF	536.0	161	5	0	2	.988	2.79	2	0
E Chavez	CF	116.0	28	3	0	1	.969	2.41	2	0
M Byrd	CF	34.0	6	0	0	0	1.000	1.59	0	0
S Victorino	CF	7.0	0	0	0	0	0.000	0.00	0	0
M Tucker	CF	1.0	0	0	0	0	0.000	0.00	0	0
B Abreu	RF	1364.0	266	7	1	3	.986	1.80	0	0
J Michaels	RF	53.0	13	2	0	0	1.000	2.55	0	0
E Chavez	RF	10.0	2	0	0	0	1.000	1.80	0	0
S Victorino	RF	5.0	0	0	0	0	0.000	0.00	0	0
M Kata	RF	3.0	0	0	0	0	0.000	0.00	0	0

Incremental Baserunning Runs

Name	IR	IRP
Tomas Perez	0.62	148
Kenny Lofton	0.59	109
Chase Utley	0.49	108
Jose Offerman	0.39	192
Endy Chavez	0.34	138
Placido Polanco	0.32	113
Michael Tucker	0.12	149
Aaron Fultz	0.08	112
Robinson Tejeda	-0.01	0
Ryan Madson	-0.07	0
Brett Myers	-0.10	35
Eude Brito	-0.10	0
Jimmy Rollins	-0.25	97
Matt Kata	-0.32	0
Ryan Howard	-0.39	88
Cory Lidle	-0.43	39
David Bell	-0.49	89
Vicente Padilla	-0.50	36
Ramon Martinez	-0.59	8
Randy Wolf	-0.61	0
Jon Lieber	-0.69	53
Jason Michaels	-0.90	76
Todd Pratt	-1.17	0
Bobby Abreu	-1.76	82
Mike Lieberthal	-2.02	74
Jim Thome	-2.52	22
Pat Burrell	-5.20	25

Pittsburgh Pirates

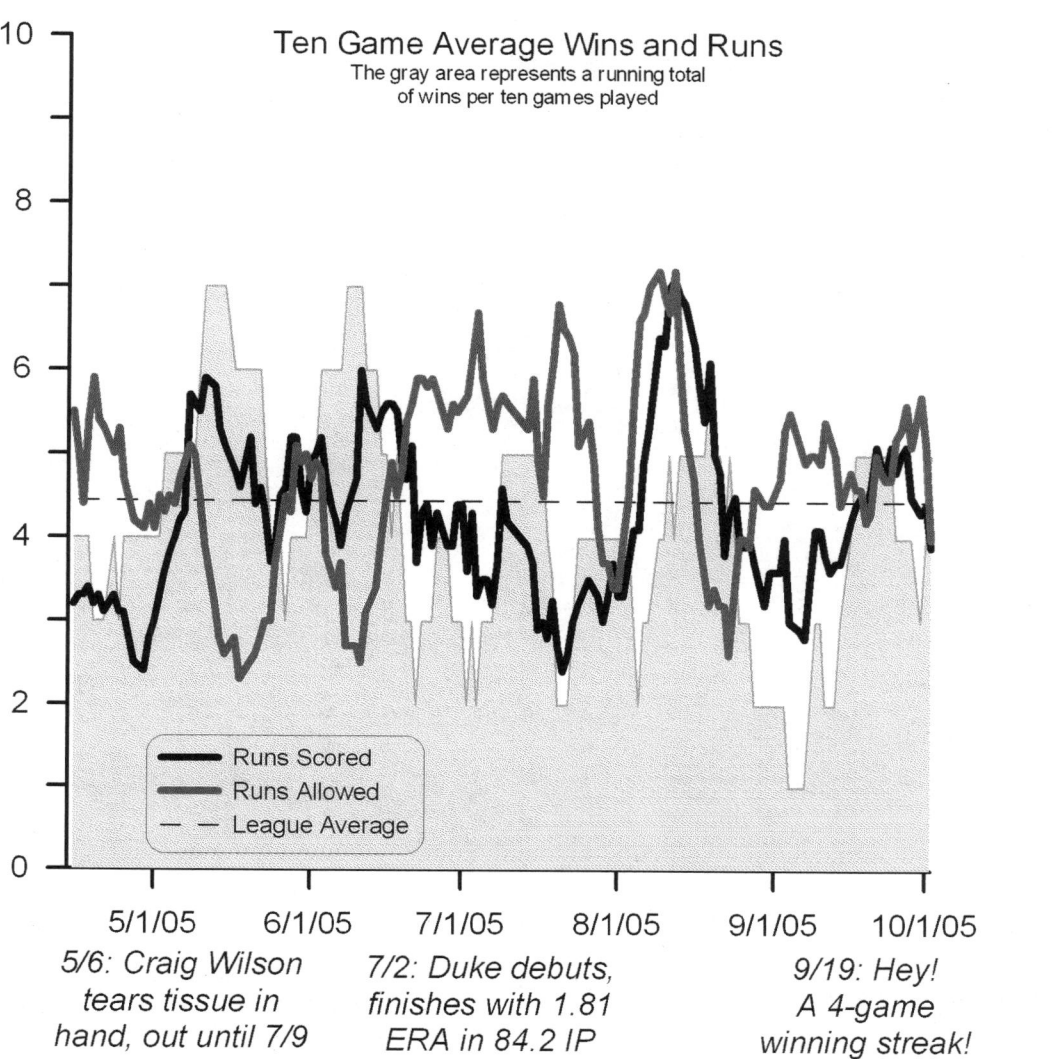

Ten Game Average Wins and Runs
The gray area represents a running total
of wins per ten games played

Runs Scored
Runs Allowed
— — League Average

5/6: Craig Wilson
tears tissue in
hand, out until 7/9

7/2: Duke debuts,
finishes with 1.81
ERA in 84.2 IP

9/19: Hey!
A 4-game
winning streak!

5/17: Jack Wilson
goes 0-4, batting
.168; will bat .283
rest of year

9/6: McClendon
fired as manager

9/24 Perez's 4th
and last quality
start, had 21 QS
in 2004

Team Batting and Pitching/Fielding Stats by Month						
	April	May	June	July	Aug	Spt/Oct
Wins	8	15	11	10	11	12
Losses	14	13	16	18	17	17
OBP	.301	.337	.325	.310	.326	.331
SLG	.349	.466	.392	.344	.422	.415
FIP	4.83	4.50	4.93	4.35	4.66	4.47
DER	.718	.739	.700	.675	.715	.718

Batting Stats

Player	RC	Runs	RBI	PA	Outs	P/PA	H	2B	3B	HR	TB	K	BB	IBB	HBP	SH	SF	SB	CS	GDP	BA	OBP	SLG	GPA
Bay J.	137	110	101	707	429	3.87	183	44	6	32	335	142	95	9	6	0	7	21	1	12	.306	.402	.559	.321
Lawton M.	65	53	44	445	288	3.83	102	28	1	10	162	61	58	0	9	0	4	16	9	7	.273	.380	.433	.279
Wilson J.	64	60	52	639	450	3.53	151	24	7	8	213	58	31	6	6	11	4	7	3	11	.257	.299	.363	.225
Mackowiak R.	63	57	58	512	348	3.67	126	21	3	9	180	100	43	4	3	2	1	8	4	7	.272	.337	.389	.249
Sanchez F.	61	54	35	492	329	3.57	132	26	4	5	181	36	27	1	5	4	3	2	2	6	.291	.336	.400	.251
Ward D.	52	46	63	453	321	3.51	106	21	1	12	165	60	37	10	1	0	8	0	2	18	.260	.318	.405	.244
Castillo J.	46	49	53	398	285	3.51	99	16	3	11	154	59	23	3	0	1	4	2	3	11	.268	.307	.416	.242
Doumit R.	34	25	35	257	178	3.32	59	13	1	6	92	48	11	1	13	1	1	2	1	5	.255	.324	.398	.245
Redman T.	32	33	26	344	248	3.52	80	12	4	2	106	27	19	0	1	2	3	4	1	8	.251	.292	.332	.215
Cota H.	32	29	43	320	233	3.60	72	20	1	7	115	80	17	2	2	1	3	0	0	8	.242	.285	.387	.225
Wilson C.	29	23	22	238	151	4.05	52	14	1	5	83	69	30	2	10	0	1	3	0	6	.264	.387	.421	.279
Wigginton T.	23	20	25	171	119	3.78	40	9	1	7	72	30	14	0	1	1	0	0	1	3	.258	.324	.465	.262
Duffy C.	23	22	9	136	86	3.45	43	4	2	1	54	22	7	0	2	1	0	2	2	1	.341	.385	.429	.280
Eldred B.	15	23	27	208	154	3.60	42	9	0	12	87	77	13	0	3	0	2	1	1	5	.221	.279	.458	.240
Hill B.	12	12	11	105	71	3.56	25	6	0	0	31	17	9	0	2	0	1	0	0	3	.269	.343	.333	.238
McLouth N.	9	20	12	120	84	3.58	28	6	0	5	49	20	3	0	5	2	1	2	0	3	.257	.305	.450	.250
Ross D.	9	9	15	119	87	3.77	24	8	0	3	41	24	6	0	1	1	3	0	0	3	.222	.263	.380	.213
Restovich M.	5	10	5	92	69	3.55	18	3	1	2	29	24	8	0	0	0	0	0	0	3	.214	.283	.345	.213
Furmaniak J.	2	3	1	30	21	4.43	5	1	1	0	8	4	4	0	0	0	0	0	0	0	.192	.300	.308	.212
Santiago B.	1	1	0	23	18	2.78	6	1	1	0	9	3	0	0	0	0	0	0	0	1	.261	.261	.391	.215
Perez O.	1	1	3	42	27	3.07	6	0	0	0	6	11	1	0	0	7	1	1	0	0	.182	.200	.182	.135
Paulino R.	1	1	0	5	2	3.40	2	0	0	0	2	0	1	0	0	0	0	0	0	0	.500	.600	.500	.395
Gerut J.	1	2	2	18	15	3.33	4	1	0	0	5	3	0	0	0	0	0	0	0	1	.222	.222	.278	.169
Sadler R.	1	1	1	8	6	4.13	2	0	0	1	5	1	0	0	0	0	0	0	0	0	.250	.250	.625	.269
Wells K.	1	4	2	61	48	3.16	9	1	0	1	13	26	0	0	1	3	0	0	0	0	.158	.172	.228	.135
Williams D.	0	2	4	50	37	3.80	5	1	0	0	6	21	1	0	0	6	1	0	0	0	.119	.136	.143	.097
Fogg J.	0	3	3	56	42	3.43	5	1	0	0	6	14	3	0	0	6	0	0	0	0	.106	.160	.128	.104
Amezaga A.	0	1	0	4	3	3.75	0	0	0	0	0	0	1	0	0	0	0	1	0	0	.000	.250	0.000	.113
Vogelsong R.	0	0	0	10	8	3.80	1	1	0	0	2	4	0	0	1	0	0	0	0	0	.111	.200	.222	.146
Torres S.	-0	0	0	4	2	4.75	2	0	0	0	2	2	0	0	0	0	0	0	0	0	.500	.500	.500	.350
Mesa J.	-0	0	0	2	1	2.50	0	0	0	0	0	1	0	0	0	1	0	0	0	0	.000	.000	.000	.000
Gorzelanny T	-0	0	0	2	1	2.00	0	0	0	0	0	1	0	0	0	1	0	0	0	0	.000	.000	.000	.000
Meadows B.	-0	0	0	1	1	1.00	0	0	0	0	0	0	0	0	0	0	0	0	0	0	.000	.000	.000	.000
White R.	-0	0	0	2	2	1.00	0	0	0	0	0	0	0	0	0	0	0	0	0	0	.000	.000	.000	.000
Maholm P.	-0	1	0	17	13	3.06	2	0	0	0	2	6	1	0	0	1	0	0	0	0	.133	.188	.133	.118
Duke Z.	-1	1	1	31	26	3.48	4	0	0	0	4	10	2	0	0	0	1	0	0	2	.143	.194	.143	.123
Snell I.	-1	0	0	8	8	3.50	0	0	0	0	0	3	0	0	0	0	0	0	0	0	.000	.000	.000	.000
Redman M.	-1	1	2	60	51	3.75	6	0	0	0	6	21	3	0	0	4	0	0	0	4	.113	.161	.113	.101
Bautista J.	-1	3	1	31	26	3.87	4	1	0	0	5	7	3	0	0	0	0	1	0	2	.143	.226	.179	.146

Pitching Stats

Player	PR	IP	BFP	G	GS	P/PA	K	BB	IBB	HBP	H	HR	DP	DER	SB	CS	PO	W	L	Sv	Op	Hld	RA	ERA	FIP
Duke Z.	23	84.7	341	14	14	3.72	58	23	2	2	79	3	16	.702	1	3	2	8	2	0	0	0	2.13	1.81	2.96
Torres S.	14	94.7	388	78	0	3.66	55	36	7	5	76	7	15	.758	2	2	0	5	5	3	3	8	3.23	2.76	4.08
Maholm P.	11	41.3	168	6	6	3.63	26	17	0	3	31	2	7	.758	2	2	0	3	1	0	0	0	2.18	2.18	3.80
Gonzalez M.	10	50.0	212	51	0	4.07	58	31	2	1	35	2	5	.725	2	1	0	1	3	3	3	15	2.70	2.70	3.10
Capps M.	0	4.0	16	4	0	4.19	3	0	0	1	5	0	1	.583	2	0	1	0	0	0	0	0	4.50	4.50	2.23
White R.	-1	75.0	338	71	0	3.54	40	29	10	4	90	3	12	.668	8	3	0	4	7	2	3	12	4.68	3.72	3.76
Mesa J.	-1	56.7	257	55	0	3.55	37	26	3	3	61	7	4	.707	4	2	0	2	8	27	34	1	4.76	4.76	4.82
Bullington B	-1	1.3	7	1	0	4.29	1	1	0	1	1	0	0	.750	0	0	0	0	0	0	0	0	13.50	13.50	5.98
Vogelsong R.	-1	81.3	369	44	0	3.79	52	40	1	8	82	5	10	.708	3	1	0	2	2	0	1	1	4.76	4.43	4.27
Williams D.	-3	138.7	600	25	25	3.71	88	58	5	8	137	20	20	.725	2	1	2	10	11	0	0	0	4.80	4.41	5.02
Johnston M.	-3	1.0	7	1	0	4.14	2	0	0	0	4	2	0	.333	0	0	0	0	0	0	0	0	36.00	36.00	24.98
Snell I.	-4	42.0	189	15	5	3.65	34	24	3	1	43	5	4	.696	1	1	0	1	2	0	0	1	5.36	5.14	4.70
Meadows B.	-4	74.7	326	65	0	3.46	44	21	7	0	84	8	9	.700	2	0	0	3	1	0	2	7	5.06	4.58	4.04
Grabow J.	-4	52.0	222	63	0	3.54	42	25	2	2	46	6	7	.728	2	1	1	2	3	0	1	14	5.37	4.85	4.42
Gorzelanny T	-5	6.0	32	3	1	3.56	3	3	0	0	10	1	0	.640	0	0	0	0	1	0	0	0	12.00	12.00	5.65
Redman M.	-9	178.3	751	30	30	3.63	101	56	3	2	188	18	31	.704	6	4	2	5	15	0	0	0	5.05	4.90	4.14
Perez O.	-15	103.0	471	20	20	3.97	97	70	1	6	102	23	13	.713	3	5	2	7	5	0	0	0	5.94	5.85	6.22
Fogg J.	-20	169.3	742	34	28	3.65	85	53	11	6	196	27	20	.704	9	7	1	6	11	0	0	0	5.63	5.05	5.10
Wells K.	-23	182.0	828	33	33	3.75	132	99	8	12	186	23	19	.710	15	3	0	8	18	0	0	0	5.74	5.09	5.00

Win Shares Stats

Player	WS	Bat	Pitch	Field	ExpWS	WSP	WSAB	CWS	NetWSValue
Bay, J	34	30.4	0.0	3.3	19	.889	20	57	$16,091,580
Lawton, M	14	11.8	0.0	2.2	12	.594	6	142	($2,153,691)
Wilson, J	14	6.0	0.0	7.9	17	.397	2	64	($2,005,442)
Sanchez, F	12	8.6	0.0	3.2	13	.453	3	12	$2,119,489
Mackowiak, R	12	9.2	0.0	3.0	14	.444	3	49	$699,305
Duke, Z	10	-1.1	11.3	0.0	4	1.241	8	10	$6,085,098
Torres, S	9	-0.1	9.4	0.0	5	.905	6	34	$3,619,404
Castillo, J	9	6.1	0.0	2.9	11	.413	1	17	$1,064,427
Ward, D	7	6.9	0.0	0.5	12	.306	-1	35	($950,000)
Duffy, C	6	4.3	0.0	1.2	4	.772	3	6	$2,385,815
Doumit, R	6	5.3	0.0	1.2	7	.488	2	6	$1,458,728
Williams, D	6	-1.2	7.1	0.0	7	.437	2	16	$1,434,214
Wilson, C	6	4.8	0.0	0.9	6	.443	1	52	($2,075,728)
Cota, H	6	3.3	0.0	2.8	9	.350	-0	8	($14,459)
Redman, T	5	2.6	0.0	2.3	9	.273	-1	28	($336,500)
White, R	4	-0.1	4.5	0.0	4	.512	1	48	$1,008,009
Wigginton, T	4	3.7	0.0	0.5	5	.461	1	33	$778,576
Meadows, B	3	-0.0	3.4	0.0	4	.417	1	29	($476,543)
Mesa, J	3	-0.1	2.6	0.0	5	.234	-1	113	($2,000,000)
Redman, M	3	-1.9	5.4	0.0	9	.200	-2	46	($4,500,000)
Fogg, J	3	-1.4	4.0	0.0	8	.157	-2	26	($2,150,000)
Wells, K	3	-1.1	3.8	0.0	9	.152	-3	49	($3,175,000)
Perez, O	1	-0.7	1.8	0.0	5	.118	-2	23	($381,000)
Eldred, B	1	0.4	0.0	0.2	6	.062	-3	1	($316,000)

Fielding and Baserunning Stats

Name	POS	Inn	SBA/G	CS%	ERA	WP+PB/G	PO	A	TE	FE
Cota	C	681.7	0.59	24%	4.36	0.396	476	38	3	1
Doumit	C	422.0	0.66	32%	4.63	0.427	285	30	5	2
Ross	C	273.0	0.40	58%	4.02	0.462	183	23	2	0
Santiago	C	48.3	0.56	0%	6.89	0.931	43	0	0	0
Paulino	C	11.0	0.82	0%	1.64	0.000	10	0	0	0

Name	POS	Inn	PO	A	TE	FE	FPct	RF	DPS	DPT
D Ward	1B	891.7	865	76	2	4	.994	9.50	10	1
B Eldred	1B	406.0	436	15	1	6	.985	10.00	1	0
C Wilson	1B	99.3	86	6	0	1	.989	8.34	0	0
T Wigginton	1B	23.0	22	2	0	0	1.000	9.39	0	0
R Mackowiak	1B	16.0	18	1	0	0	1.000	10.69	0	0
J Castillo	2B	840.3	237	279	6	6	.977	5.53	32	57
F Sanchez	2B	387.3	106	117	2	0	.991	5.18	16	26
R Mackowiak	2B	146.3	37	43	1	1	.976	4.92	9	4
J Furmaniak	2B	53.0	14	10	0	1	.960	4.08	0	1
T Wigginton	2B	8.3	3	2	0	0	1.000	5.40	0	0
B Hill	2B	0.7	0	0	0	1	0.000	0.00	0	0
J Wilson	SS	1360.0	246	521	10	4	.982	5.08	65	62
F Sanchez	SS	64.0	11	25	0	0	1.000	5.06	1	2
J Furmaniak	SS	8.0	1	4	0	0	1.000	5.63	0	0
A Amezaga	SS	4.0	1	2	0	0	1.000	6.75	0	1
F Sanchez	3B	477.7	38	130	2	2	.977	3.17	21	0
R Mackowiak	3B	447.0	38	123	4	4	.953	3.24	18	0
T Wigginton	3B	305.0	19	57	1	8	.894	2.24	4	0
B Hill	3B	147.7	10	32	0	1	.977	2.56	5	0
J Bautista	3B	58.7	6	14	1	0	.952	3.07	3	0
J Bay	LF	1185.0	265	3	0	1	.996	2.04	1	0
C Wilson	LF	138.3	27	3	0	0	1.000	1.95	2	0
M Restovich	LF	80.0	22	1	0	1	.958	2.59	0	0
R Sadler	LF	21.0	4	0	0	0	1.000	1.71	0	0
T Redman	LF	9.0	4	0	0	0	1.000	4.00	0	0
R Mackowiak	LF	2.0	0	0	0	0	0.000	0.00	0	0
T Redman	CF	523.3	158	5	1	6	.959	2.80	0	0
R Mackowiak	CF	281.7	68	2	0	1	.986	2.24	0	0
C Duffy	CF	248.0	80	1	1	0	.988	2.94	0	0
J Bay	CF	217.0	57	1	1	2	.951	2.41	0	0
N McLouth	CF	166.0	36	0	0	0	1.000	1.95	0	0
M Lawton	RF	841.7	206	4	0	1	.995	2.25	3	0
C Wilson	RF	236.0	50	0	0	1	.980	1.91	0	0
R Mackowiak	RF	127.3	34	2	1	0	.973	2.54	4	0
M Restovich	RF	83.7	17	0	0	0	1.000	1.83	0	0

Name	POS	Inn	PO	A	TE	FE	FPct	RF	DPS	DPT
N McLouth	RF	52.7	10	0	0	2	.833	1.71	0	0
T Redman	RF	37.3	8	0	0	0	1.000	1.93	0	0
J Gerut	RF	33.3	3	0	0	0	1.000	0.81	0	0
R Doumit	RF	23.0	0	0	0	0	0.000	0.00	0	0
C Duffy	RF	1.0	0	0	0	0	0.000	0.00	0	0

Incremental Baserunning Runs

Name	IR	IRP
Nate McLouth	1.76	152
Tike Redman	1.65	142
Jason Bay	1.38	115
Jose Castillo	1.25	117
Chris Duffy	0.63	114
Rob Mackowiak	0.49	108
Bobby Hill	0.45	122
Kip Wells	0.29	212
Humberto Cota	0.13	105
JJ Furmaniak	0.11	226
David Ross	0.03	105
Oliver Perez	-0.00	91
Craig Wilson	-0.01	99
Ryan Vogelsong	-0.03	0
Ryan Doumit	-0.03	99
Dave Williams	-0.16	0
Brad Eldred	-0.19	84
Zach Duke	-0.22	0
Michael Restovich	-0.24	0
Josh Fogg	-0.62	37
Freddy Sanchez	-0.68	92
Jack Wilson	-0.98	87
Mark Redman	-1.00	0
Paul Maholm	-1.16	-75
Jose Bautista	-1.35	-59
Ty Wigginton	-1.48	-19
Daryle Ward	-2.19	40
Matt Lawton	-3.51	23

St. Louis Cardinals

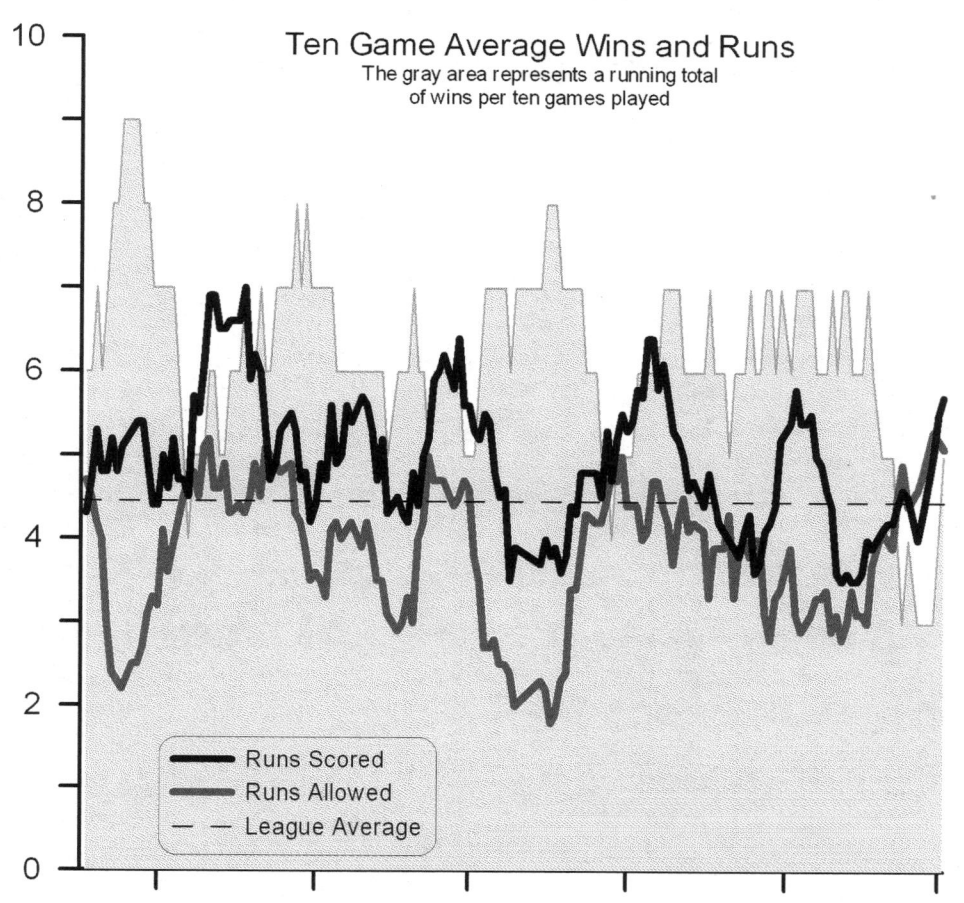

Ten Game Average Wins and Runs
The gray area represents a running total
of wins per ten games played

— Runs Scored
— Runs Allowed
– – League Average

*4/15: Eldred diagnosed
with viral infection,
returns June 12th.*

*7/15: Sanders collides
with Edmonds in OF,
fractures right fibula*

*9/17: Clinch
NL Central title*

*5/10: Rolen injures
shoulder, placed on DL.
Returns June 18th.*

*7/22: Rolen back on DL
with shoulder problems.
Has season-ending
surgery 8/29*

*10/2: last regular-
season game played
at this Busch Stadium*

Team Batting and Pitching/Fielding Stats by Month						
	April	May	June	July	Aug	Spt/Oct
Wins	15	18	16	17	19	15
Losses	7	11	11	9	11	13
OBP	.326	.348	.356	.329	.343	.329
SLG	.418	.439	.444	.428	.405	.404
FIP	3.41	4.37	4.13	4.39	4.00	4.42
DER	.700	.715	.716	.731	.730	.710

Batting Stats

Player	RC	Runs	RBI	PA	Outs	P/PA	H	2B	3B	HR	TB	K	BB	IBB	HBP	SH	SF	SB	CS	GDP	BA	OBP	SLG	GPA
Pujols A.	143	129	117	700	417	3.89	195	38	2	41	360	65	97	27	9	0	3	16	2	19	.330	.430	.609	.346
Eckstein D.	106	90	61	713	466	4.01	185	26	7	8	249	44	58	0	13	8	4	11	8	13	.294	.363	.395	.262
Edmonds J.	97	88	89	567	355	4.18	123	37	1	29	249	139	91	10	4	1	4	5	5	6	.263	.385	.533	.307
Grudzielanek	69	64	59	563	393	3.52	155	30	3	8	215	81	26	3	7	0	2	8	6	14	.294	.334	.407	.252
Taguchi S.	61	45	53	424	295	3.55	114	21	2	8	163	62	20	2	2	2	4	11	2	11	.288	.322	.412	.248
Walker L.	57	66	52	367	234	3.56	91	20	1	15	158	64	41	3	9	0	2	2	1	9	.289	.384	.502	.298
Nunez A.	55	64	44	467	308	3.55	120	13	2	5	152	63	37	4	0	9	0	0	1	6	.285	.343	.361	.245
Sanders R.	50	49	54	329	224	3.72	80	14	2	21	161	75	28	1	4	0	2	14	1	8	.271	.340	.546	.290
Molina Y.	47	36	49	421	301	3.24	97	15	1	8	138	30	23	3	2	8	3	2	3	10	.252	.295	.358	.223
Mabry J.	26	26	32	274	193	3.49	59	15	1	8	100	63	20	1	0	6	2	0	0	6	.240	.295	.407	.234
Rodriguez J.	24	15	24	176	105	3.83	44	6	0	5	65	45	19	4	3	3	2	2	0	0	.295	.382	.436	.281
Rolen S.	23	28	28	223	155	3.75	46	12	1	5	75	28	25	1	1	0	1	1	2	3	.235	.323	.383	.241
Luna H.	20	26	18	153	104	3.31	39	10	2	1	56	25	9	0	4	2	1	10	2	4	.285	.344	.409	.257
Marquis J.	13	10	10	91	60	3.46	27	8	1	1	40	11	2	0	0	2	0	0	0	0	.310	.326	.460	.262
Seabol S.	10	11	10	114	83	3.59	23	5	0	1	31	23	8	0	0	0	1	0	0	1	.219	.272	.295	.196
Diaz E.	9	14	17	139	111	3.22	27	6	0	1	36	12	5	0	2	2	0	0	0	8	.208	.248	.277	.181
Gall J.	6	5	10	39	27	3.46	10	3	0	2	19	8	1	0	0	0	1	0	0	0	.270	.282	.514	.255
Suppan J.	5	5	5	67	46	3.18	12	2	0	1	17	9	3	0	0	6	0	0	0	0	.207	.246	.293	.184
Schumaker J.	2	9	1	26	18	3.58	6	1	0	0	7	2	2	0	0	0	0	1	0	0	.250	.308	.292	.211
Mulder M.	1	3	3	67	54	3.94	9	0	0	0	9	25	3	0	0	1	1	0	0	1	.145	.182	.145	.118
Duncan C.	1	2	3	10	9	4.80	2	1	0	1	6	5	0	0	0	0	0	0	0	1	.200	.200	.600	.240
Mahoney M.	1	5	6	75	57	3.73	10	1	0	1	14	10	4	1	1	6	0	0	0	3	.156	.217	.219	.153
Reyes A.	0	0	0	3	1	5.33	0	0	0	0	0	1	1	0	0	1	0	0	0	0	.000	.500	.000	.225
Tavarez J.	0	0	0	1	0	0.00	0	0	0	0	0	0	0	0	0	1	0	0	0	0	.000	.000	.000	.000
Flores R.	-0	0	0	1	1	1.00	0	0	0	0	0	0	0	0	0	0	0	0	0	0	.000	.000	.000	.000
Cedeno R.	-0	4	8	61	52	3.66	9	1	0	0	10	6	2	0	1	0	1	0	2	2	.158	.197	.175	.132
Eldred C.	-0	0	0	2	2	4.50	0	0	0	0	0	2	0	0	0	0	0	0	0	0	.000	.000	.000	.000
Thompson B.	-0	0	0	7	5	3.71	1	0	0	0	1	2	0	0	0	1	0	0	0	0	.167	.167	.167	.117
Reyes A.	-0	0	0	4	4	2.75	0	0	0	0	0	1	0	0	0	0	0	0	0	0	.000	.000	.000	.000
Morris M.	-1	4	2	69	52	3.49	5	0	0	0	5	23	4	0	0	8	0	0	0	0	.088	.148	.088	.088
Carpenter C.	-5	7	2	93	75	3.66	5	2	0	0	7	23	5	0	0	10	1	0	1	2	.065	.120	.091	.077

Pitching Stats

Player	PR	IP	BFP	G	GS	P/PA	K	BB	IBB	HBP	H	HR	DP	DER	SB	CS	PO	W	L	Sv	Op	Hld	RA	ERA	FIP
Carpenter C.	41	241.7	953	33	33	3.56	213	51	0	3	204	18	26	.722	1	5	2	21	5	0	0	0	3.05	2.83	2.86
Reyes A.	17	62.7	244	65	0	4.29	67	20	2	5	38	5	5	.776	0	2	0	4	2	3	3	16	2.15	2.15	3.08
Isringhausen	16	59.0	245	63	0	3.76	51	27	5	1	43	4	6	.759	3	1	0	1	2	39	43	1	2.14	2.14	3.56
Mulder M.	14	205.0	868	32	32	3.47	111	70	1	9	212	19	33	.707	2	8	5	16	8	0	0	0	3.95	3.64	4.26
Eldred C.	10	37.0	160	31	1	3.97	29	18	3	2	35	3	4	.704	0	1	0	1	0	0	1	2	2.19	2.19	4.09
Thompson B.	6	55.0	225	40	0	3.44	29	15	2	4	46	5	8	.762	1	1	0	4	0	1	1	7	3.60	2.95	4.15
Suppan J.	6	194.3	834	32	32	3.64	114	63	1	7	206	24	30	.709	5	5	1	16	10	0	0	0	4.31	3.57	4.50
Tavarez J.	5	65.7	278	74	0	3.66	47	19	4	8	68	6	16	.687	2	1	0	2	3	4	6	32	3.84	3.43	3.97
King R.	3	40.0	177	77	0	3.72	23	16	0	3	46	4	6	.679	3	0	0	4	4	0	6	16	3.83	3.38	4.56
Reyes A.	3	13.3	51	4	1	3.53	12	4	1	0	6	2	0	.879	2	0	0	1	1	0	0	0	2.70	2.70	4.03
White G.	2	8.3	38	6	0	3.47	1	1	1	0	14	1	0	.629	0	1	1	0	0	0	0	0	2.16	2.16	4.66
Johnson T.	1	2.7	13	5	0	3.92	4	3	0	0	3	0	1	.500	0	0	0	0	0	0	1	1	0.00	0.00	3.36
Flores R.	-1	41.7	174	50	0	3.88	43	13	0	3	37	5	6	.709	2	1	1	3	1	1	3	11	4.75	3.46	3.63
Pulsipher B.	-1	4.0	19	5	0	2.79	1	2	1	0	5	0	0	.688	0	0	0	0	0	0	0	0	6.75	6.75	3.98
Wainwright A	-2	2.0	9	2	0	3.44	0	1	0	0	2	1	0	.857	2	0	0	0	0	0	0	0	13.50	13.50	10.98
Morris M.	-3	192.7	818	31	31	3.51	117	37	3	8	209	22	21	.705	5	1	0	14	10	0	0	0	4.72	4.11	3.95
Jarvis K.	-3	3.3	17	4	0	3.47	2	3	0	2	3	1	0	.778	1	0	0	0	1	0	1	0	13.50	13.50	10.18
Journell J.	-4	4.3	23	5	0	4.48	5	5	0	0	6	1	2	.583	0	0	0	0	1	0	0	0	12.46	10.38	7.14
Marquis J.	-5	207.0	868	33	32	3.73	100	69	2	5	206	29	31	.734	3	6	0	13	14	0	0	0	4.78	4.13	4.91
Cali C.	-5	6.0	33	6	0	4.15	5	6	1	0	10	3	1	.632	0	0	0	0	0	0	0	0	12.00	10.50	10.82

Win Shares Stats

Player	WS	Bat	Pitch	Field	ExpWS	WSP	WSAB	CWS	NetWSValue
Pujols, A	38	36.3	0.0	2.0	19	.998	25	180	$7,618,296
Edmonds, J	28	23.0	0.0	5.5	16	.907	18	269	$7,759,696
Eckstein, D	28	20.6	0.0	7.0	19	.713	14	80	$9,888,064
Carpenter, C	18	-4.2	22.7	0.0	12	.791	11	72	$8,034,976
Grudzielan, M	18	11.4	0.0	6.7	16	.578	7	149	$5,219,855
Walker, L	14	12.6	0.0	1.4	10	.709	7	311	($1,897,013)
Molina, Y	14	6.6	0.0	7.6	12	.592	6	19	$4,581,246
Taguchi, S	14	11.4	0.0	2.4	12	.587	6	24	$4,273,107
Suppan, J	13	0.2	12.5	0.0	9	.680	7	87	$3,352,431
Marquis, J	12	2.6	9.2	0.0	9	.644	6	39	$1,983,527
Mulder, M	12	-1.6	13.9	0.0	10	.611	6	85	($1,518,304)
Sanders, R	12	10.9	0.0	1.4	9	.677	6	204	$2,423,343
Nunez, A	12	8.5	0.0	3.9	13	.482	3	35	$2,704,069
Isringhaus, J	9	0.0	9.5	0.0	6	.833	5	83	$286,711
Reyes, A	8	-0.1	7.9	0.0	4	1.033	5	30	$3,926,071
Morris, M	7	-2.1	9.5	0.0	9	.393	2	86	$57,441
Luna, H	5	3.7	0.0	1.7	4	.634	2	9	$1,902,616
Rodriguez, J	5	4.7	0.0	0.9	5	.582	2	5	$1,745,385
Rolen, S	5	3.0	0.0	2.1	6	.404	1	219	($6,313,639)
Tavarez, J	4	-0.0	4.6	0.0	5	.496	1	66	($325,856)
Mabry, J	4	3.0	0.0	1.0	8	.266	-1	66	($725,000)
Diaz, E	1	-0.2	0.0	1.8	4	.203	-1	41	($600,000)

Fielding and Baserunning Stats

Name	POS	Inn	SBA/G	CS%	ERA	WP+PB/G	PO	A	TE	FE
Molina	C	959.3	0.29	55%	3.39	0.319	684	66	4	2
Diaz	C	299.0	0.51	35%	3.76	0.452	189	21	0	1
Mahoney	C	187.3	0.34	0%	3.56	0.192	110	11	1	1

Name	POS	Inn	PO	A	TE	FE	FPct	RF	DPS	DPT
A Pujols	1B	1358.0	1598	95	5	9	.992	11.22	21	1
J Mabry	1B	53.0	55	8	0	0	1.000	10.70	2	0
S Seabol	1B	23.0	33	3	0	0	1.000	14.09	0	0
E Diaz	1B	8.0	9	0	0	0	1.000	10.13	0	0
C Duncan	1B	2.0	1	0	0	0	1.000	4.50	0	0
Y Molina	1B	1.0	0	0	0	0	0.000	0.00	0	0
M Grudzielan	2B	1158.0	245	442	1	6	.990	5.34	35	69
H Luna	2B	143.0	41	52	2	0	.979	5.85	3	12
A Nunez	2B	132.0	26	38	0	2	.970	4.36	5	9
S Seabol	2B	12.3	1	5	0	0	1.000	4.38	0	0
D Eckstein	SS	1340.0	244	515	10	5	.981	5.10	68	53
A Nunez	SS	91.0	14	30	1	1	.957	4.35	6	3
H Luna	SS	14.0	3	3	0	1	.857	3.86	0	0
A Nunez	3B	720.7	54	203	3	7	.963	3.21	21	0
S Rolen	3B	486.0	22	151	1	5	.966	3.20	16	1
J Mabry	3B	106.7	12	19	0	1	.969	2.62	2	0
S Seabol	3B	103.0	9	30	1	2	.929	3.41	6	0
H Luna	3B	29.3	4	7	0	0	1.000	3.38	2	0
R Sanders	LF	636.0	108	5	0	2	.983	1.60	0	0
J Rodriguez	LF	283.3	60	2	0	1	.984	1.97	0	0
S Taguchi	LF	280.3	50	2	0	0	1.000	1.67	2	0
J Mabry	LF	117.7	19	0	0	2	.905	1.45	0	0
J Gall	LF	48.7	7	1	0	0	1.000	1.48	0	0
R Cedeno	LF	33.3	2	0	0	0	1.000	0.54	0	0
J Schumaker	LF	22.3	6	0	0	0	1.000	2.42	0	0
H Luna	LF	13.0	3	1	0	0	1.000	2.77	0	0
S Seabol	LF	11.0	5	0	0	0	1.000	4.09	0	0
J Edmonds	CF	1153.0	318	5	0	2	.994	2.52	1	0
S Taguchi	CF	274.0	58	0	0	0	1.000	1.91	0	0
J Schumaker	CF	12.3	4	0	0	0	1.000	2.92	0	0
L Walker	CF	5.0	1	0	0	0	1.000	1.80	0	0
H Luna	CF	1.0	1	0	0	0	1.000	9.00	0	0

Name	POS	Inn	PO	A	TE	FE	FPct	RF	DPS	DPT
L Walker	RF	648.7	107	5	1	1	.982	1.55	0	0
S Taguchi	RF	318.7	75	3	0	2	.975	2.20	0	0
J Mabry	RF	252.0	35	1	0	0	1.000	1.29	0	0
H Luna	RF	114.7	29	2	0	1	.939	2.43	0	0
R Cedeno	RF	42.0	7	0	1	1	.778	1.50	0	0
J Rodriguez	RF	38.3	9	1	1	0	.909	2.35	0	0
S Seabol	RF	14.0	1	0	0	0	1.000	0.64	0	0
J Schumaker	RF	10.3	3	0	0	0	1.000	2.61	0	0
R Sanders	RF	6.0	0	0	0	0	0.000	0.00	0	0
C Duncan	RF	1.0	0	0	0	0	0.000	0.00	0	0

Incremental Baserunning Runs		
Name	IR	IRP
Larry Walker	2.33	135
Mark Grudzielanek	1.52	122
Abraham Nunez	1.39	122
Jim Edmonds	1.24	127
Hector Luna	0.59	115
John Mabry	0.55	126
Jason Marquis	0.53	140
So Taguchi	0.49	122
David Eckstein	0.42	106
Jeff Suppan	0.20	115
Chris Carpenter	0.08	108
Einar Diaz	0.02	101
John Rodriguez	-0.02	99
John Gall	-0.03	92
Matt Morris	-0.08	0
Scott Rolen	-0.37	88
Scott Seabol	-0.39	79
Albert Pujols	-0.40	96
Mike Mahoney	-0.41	11
Roger Cedeno	-0.46	0
Mark Mulder	-0.56	49
Skip Schumaker	-0.87	30
Reggie Sanders	-1.20	51
Yadier Molina	-1.49	52

San Diego Padres

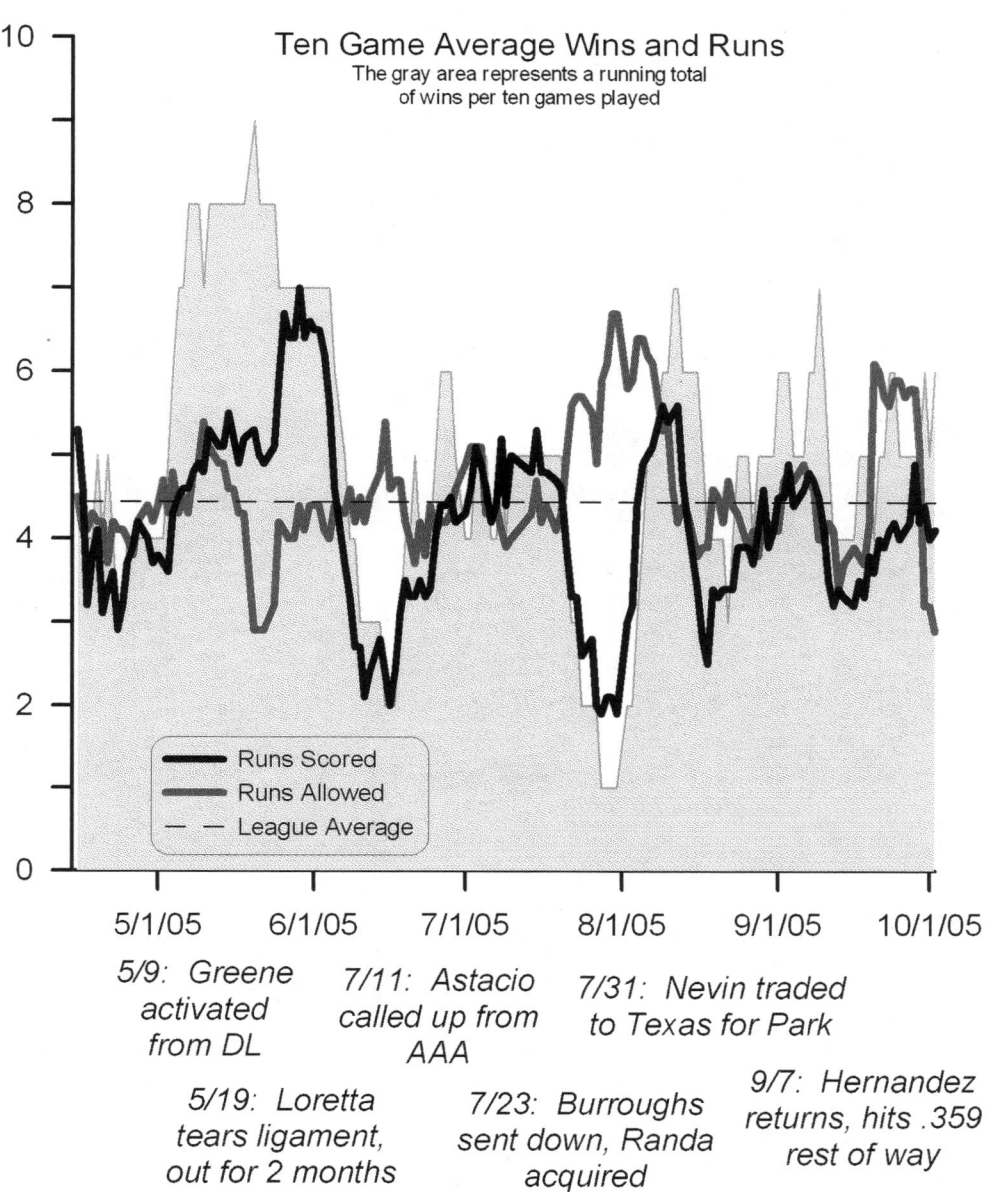

Ten Game Average Wins and Runs

The gray area represents a running total
of wins per ten games played

— Runs Scored
— Runs Allowed
– – League Average

5/9: Greene activated from DL

7/11: Astacio called up from AAA

7/31: Nevin traded to Texas for Park

5/19: Loretta tears ligament, out for 2 months

7/23: Burroughs sent down, Randa acquired

9/7: Hernandez returns, hits .359 rest of way

Team Batting and Pitching/Fielding Stats by Month						
	April	May	June	July	Aug	Spt/Oct
Wins	11	22	10	8	15	16
Losses	13	6	17	18	12	14
OBP	.331	.364	.312	.317	.342	.328
SLG	.388	.446	.379	.355	.421	.352
FIP	3.81	4.00	3.81	4.78	3.57	3.98
DER	.704	.720	.687	.691	.720	.706

Batting Stats

Player	RC	Runs	RBI	PA	Outs	P/PA	H	2B	3B	HR	TB	K	BB	IBB	HBP	SH	SF	SB	CS	GDP	BA	OBP	SLG	GPA
Giles B.	129	92	83	674	400	3.93	164	38	8	15	263	64	119	9	2	0	8	13	5	14	.301	.423	.483	.311
Klesko R.	74	61	58	520	343	3.78	110	19	1	18	185	80	75	2	1	0	1	3	4	6	.248	.358	.418	.265
Roberts D.	68	65	38	480	320	3.85	113	19	10	8	176	59	53	3	1	11	4	23	12	10	.275	.356	.428	.267
Greene K.	67	51	70	476	335	3.75	109	30	2	15	188	93	25	3	6	3	6	5	0	8	.250	.296	.431	.241
Loretta M.	62	54	38	463	306	3.95	113	16	1	3	140	34	45	4	8	2	4	8	4	11	.280	.360	.347	.249
Hernandez R.	51	36	58	392	276	3.59	107	19	2	12	166	40	18	0	1	1	3	1	0	14	.290	.322	.450	.257
Nady X.	43	40	43	356	247	3.56	85	15	2	13	143	67	22	1	7	1	0	2	1	5	.261	.321	.439	.254
Sweeney M.	43	31	40	267	162	4.09	65	12	1	8	103	58	40	3	0	1	5	4	0	6	.294	.395	.466	.294
Nevin P.	39	31	47	306	211	3.89	72	11	1	9	112	67	19	0	1	0	5	1	0	2	.256	.301	.399	.235
Jackson D.	36	44	23	313	211	3.93	70	9	0	5	94	45	30	1	4	3	1	15	2	4	.255	.335	.342	.236
Fick R.	33	25	30	260	175	3.71	61	10	2	3	84	33	26	2	1	1	2	0	2	4	.265	.340	.365	.244
Burroughs S.	27	20	17	317	220	3.69	71	7	2	1	85	41	24	4	5	3	1	4	0	7	.250	.318	.299	.218
Blum G.	26	26	22	252	177	3.88	54	13	1	5	84	28	24	0	3	0	1	3	2	5	.241	.321	.375	.238
Randa J.	24	27	20	241	172	3.70	57	17	1	4	88	29	14	1	2	0	2	0	1	5	.256	.303	.395	.235
Olivo M.	20	16	16	124	85	3.35	35	7	1	4	56	31	4	2	3	1	1	6	1	4	.304	.341	.487	.275
Young E.	19	22	12	163	113	3.79	39	9	0	2	54	12	18	0	0	3	0	7	6	4	.275	.356	.380	.255
Johnson B.	9	10	13	88	65	3.78	16	8	1	3	35	23	11	1	0	1	1	0	2	4	.213	.310	.467	.256
Ross D.	4	2	0	19	11	3.53	6	0	1	0	8	4	0	0	1	1	0	0	0	0	.353	.389	.471	.293
Valdez W.	3	0	1	15	11	3.33	3	2	0	0	5	1	2	0	0	0	0	0	0	1	.231	.333	.385	.246
Park C.	2	2	2	18	11	3.28	3	0	0	0	3	5	0	0	0	4	0	0	0	0	.214	.214	.214	.150
Peavy J.	2	5	2	63	44	3.43	10	1	0	0	11	16	4	0	1	5	0	0	0	1	.189	.259	.208	.168
Eaton A.	2	2	2	52	39	3.37	8	0	1	0	10	18	3	0	0	3	0	0	1	0	.174	.224	.217	.155
Alexander M.	1	0	0	21	16	4.33	2	1	0	0	3	5	2	1	1	0	0	0	0	0	.111	.238	.167	.149
Garcia J.	1	4	4	39	30	3.05	6	0	0	2	12	11	3	1	0	0	0	0	0	0	.167	.231	.333	.187
Hyzdu A.	1	1	4	25	18	4.00	3	1	0	0	4	4	3	0	0	1	1	1	0	1	.150	.250	.200	.163
McAnulty P.	1	4	0	29	19	3.97	5	0	0	0	5	7	3	1	1	1	0	1	0	0	.208	.321	.208	.197
Ojeda M.	1	6	6	83	66	3.83	10	3	1	0	15	21	9	2	0	1	0	1	1	2	.137	.232	.205	.156
Cassidy S.	0	0	0	2	1	5.00	0	0	0	0	0	1	1	0	0	0	0	0	0	0	.000	.500	.000	.225
Williams W.	0	3	3	55	40	3.44	7	0	0	0	7	19	0	0	0	8	1	1	0	1	.152	.149	.152	.105
Hensley C.	0	0	0	6	5	4.33	1	1	0	0	2	3	0	0	0	0	0	0	0	0	.167	.167	.333	.158
Reyes D.	-0	0	0	5	4	4.20	1	0	0	0	1	2	0	0	0	0	0	0	0	0	.200	.200	.200	.140
Linebrink S.	-0	0	0	1	1	2.00	0	0	0	0	0	0	0	0	0	0	0	0	0	0	.000	.000	.000	.000
Quantrill P.	-0	0	0	1	1	2.00	0	0	0	0	0	0	0	0	0	0	0	0	0	0	.000	.000	.000	.000
Williams R.	-0	0	0	1	1	3.00	0	0	0	0	0	0	0	0	0	0	0	0	0	0	.000	.000	.000	.000
Breslow C.	-0	0	0	1	1	5.00	0	0	0	0	0	0	0	0	0	0	0	0	0	0	.000	.000	.000	.000
Otsuka A.	-0	0	0	1	1	4.00	0	0	0	0	0	1	0	0	0	0	0	0	0	0	.000	.000	.000	.000
Oxspring C.	-0	0	0	2	2	3.50	0	0	0	0	0	0	0	0	0	0	0	0	0	0	.000	.000	.000	.000
Hammond C.	-0	0	0	3	3	3.00	0	0	0	0	0	1	0	0	0	0	0	0	0	0	.000	.000	.000	.000
May D.	-0	0	0	10	8	3.00	1	0	0	0	1	5	0	0	0	1	0	0	0	0	.111	.111	.111	.078
Stauffer T.	-1	1	1	27	21	3.33	3	1	0	0	4	10	0	0	0	3	0	0	0	0	.125	.125	.167	.098
Astacio P.	-1	1	1	22	17	2.55	1	0	0	0	1	5	1	0	0	5	0	0	0	2	.063	.118	.063	.069
Redding T.	-1	0	0	9	8	3.67	0	0	0	0	0	5	0	0	0	1	0	0	0	0	.000	.000	.000	.000
Lawrence B.	-5	2	1	69	56	3.64	5	0	0	0	5	29	2	0	0	7	1	0	0	2	.085	.113	.085	.072

Pitching Stats

Player	PR	IP	BFP	G	GS	P/PA	K	BB	IBB	HBP	H	HR	DP	DER	SB	CS	PO	W	L	Sv	Op	Hld	RA	ERA	FIP
Peavy J.	28	203.0	812	30	30	3.89	216	50	3	7	162	18	13	.724	19	5	1	13	7	0	0	0	3.10	2.88	2.85
Linebrink S.	19	73.7	288	73	0	3.95	70	23	4	0	55	4	9	.733	8	1	0	8	1	1	6	26	2.08	1.83	2.72
Hensley C.	11	47.7	189	24	1	3.63	28	17	2	0	33	0	6	.771	1	0	0	1	1	0	0	2	2.27	1.70	2.88
Seanez R.	10	60.3	248	57	0	4.00	84	22	4	2	49	4	5	.669	8	2	0	7	1	0	2	11	2.83	2.69	2.25
Astacio P.	8	59.7	252	12	10	3.78	33	26	3	1	54	4	6	.734	1	3	1	4	2	0	0	0	3.17	3.17	4.11
Hoffman T.	5	57.7	240	60	0	3.48	54	12	1	1	52	3	2	.712	1	1	0	1	6	43	46	0	3.59	2.97	2.46
Hammond C.	3	58.7	242	55	0	3.66	34	14	0	2	51	9	2	.770	1	0	0	5	1	0	3	6	3.84	3.84	4.64
Quantrill P.	2	31.7	132	22	0	3.72	24	2	1	1	37	2	3	.660	4	0	0	1	1	0	0	1	3.69	3.41	2.57
Breslow C.	2	16.3	78	14	0	4.08	14	13	0	1	15	1	2	.714	0	0	0	0	0	0	0	1	3.31	2.20	4.64
Otsuka A.	2	62.7	276	66	0	3.87	60	34	8	2	55	3	10	.706	4	0	0	2	8	1	7	22	4.02	3.59	3.41
Oxspring C.	-3	12.0	49	5	0	4.04	11	6	0	0	9	2	2	.767	0	0	0	0	0	0	0	0	6.00	3.75	4.82
Burroughs S.	-3	1.0	7	1	0	3.14	0	0	0	0	4	1	0	.500	0	0	0	0	0	0	0	0	27.00	27.00	15.98
Williams R.	-4	4.3	25	2	0	3.64	2	4	0	1	7	1	0	.647	0	0	0	1	0	0	0	0	12.46	12.46	8.52
Cassidy S.	-4	12.3	54	10	0	3.87	12	3	0	0	15	3	1	.667	0	2	0	1	1	0	0	1	7.30	6.57	4.93
Falkenborg B	-6	11.0	54	10	0	3.57	10	5	1	0	17	2	1	.595	0	0	0	0	0	0	0	0	9.00	8.18	4.89
Eaton A.	-10	128.7	568	24	22	3.93	100	44	6	5	140	14	10	.689	8	1	0	11	5	0	0	0	4.90	4.27	3.98
Reyes D.	-10	43.7	215	36	1	3.68	35	32	2	1	57	3	5	.625	7	1	1	3	2	0	1	0	6.18	5.15	4.54
May D.	-11	59.3	264	22	8	3.87	32	20	1	0	73	10	8	.688	7	3	1	1	3	0	0	0	5.76	5.61	5.11
Park C.	-12	45.7	213	10	9	3.94	33	26	0	4	50	3	5	.680	1	0	0	4	3	0	0	0	6.50	5.91	4.36
Stauffer T.	-13	81.0	355	15	14	3.80	49	29	0	2	92	10	10	.691	1	2	0	3	6	0	0	0	5.56	5.33	4.53
Lawrence B.	-15	195.7	852	33	33	3.45	109	57	7	11	211	18	22	.706	13	3	0	7	15	0	0	0	4.88	4.83	4.11
Williams W.	-18	159.7	697	28	28	3.86	106	51	1	3	174	24	11	.708	9	1	0	9	12	0	0	0	5.19	4.85	4.62
Redding T.	-23	29.7	143	9	6	3.71	17	13	1	2	40	7	4	.683	1	0	0	0	5	0	0	0	10.62	9.10	6.42

Win Shares Stats

Player	WS	Bat	Pitch	Field	ExpWS	WSP	WSAB	CWS	NetWSValue
Giles, B	35	32.3	0.0	3.1	18	.974	23	234	$13,044,900
Peavy, J	17	-0.7	18.2	0.0	10	.875	11	43	$8,626,779
Greene, K	17	12.9	0.0	4.5	13	.666	8	39	$6,486,842
Klesko, R	17	14.9	0.0	1.9	14	.619	7	226	$525,418
Roberts, D	15	12.8	0.0	2.5	13	.604	6	56	$3,937,853
Loretta, M	15	10.8	0.0	3.8	12	.586	6	148	$3,156,360
Linebrink, S	12	-0.0	11.6	0.0	5	1.198	8	29	$5,811,660
Sweeney, M	10	9.8	0.0	0.5	7	.780	6	39	$4,310,659
Hernandez, R	10	8.6	0.0	1.8	11	.489	3	83	($2,159,467)
Hoffman, T	8	0.0	7.5	0.0	6	.677	4	140	$36,795
Jackson, D	8	5.5	0.0	2.8	9	.480	2	58	$1,766,400
Nevin, P	8	6.7	0.0	0.9	8	.455	2	140	($6,397,476)
Nady, X	8	7.2	0.0	1.2	10	.436	2	16	$1,145,691
Fick, R	6	5.5	0.0	0.8	7	.465	2	52	$1,236,157
Blum, G	6	3.5	0.0	2.5	7	.448	1	49	($575,000)
Eaton, A	5	-0.9	6.4	0.0	6	.447	2	32	($2,028,113)
Randa, J	5	3.2	0.0	1.6	7	.369	0	121	$2,904,333
Otsuka, A	4	-0.0	4.2	0.0	4	.486	1	15	$617,465
Burroughs, S	4	1.7	-0.6	3.0	9	.233	-2	38	($1,675,000)
Williams, W	3	-1.5	4.2	0.0	8	.173	-2	104	($3,000,000)
Lawrence, B	1	-3.6	5.0	0.0	10	.075	-4	30	($2,375,000)

Fielding and Baserunning Stats

Name	POS	Inn	SBA/G	CS%	ERA	WP+PB/G	PO	A	TE	FE
Hernandez	C	806.0	0.78	26%	4.04	0.257	640	36	7	1
Olivo	C	287.3	0.44	21%	3.63	0.345	224	14	5	0
Fick	C	189.7	1.09	9%	4.60	0.285	167	10	3	1
Ojeda	C	124.0	0.65	0%	4.35	0.290	100	7	0	0
Ross	C	31.0	0.29	0%	5.23	0.581	28	0	0	0
Nevin	C	17.3	0.00	0%	7.79	1.038	11	1	0	0

Name	POS	Inn	PO	A	TE	FE	FPct	RF	DPS	DPT
P Nevin	1B	611.0	578	37	1	3	.994	9.06	7	0
M Sweeney	1B	337.7	314	21	2	2	.988	8.93	4	0
X Nady	1B	299.3	261	27	0	4	.986	8.66	3	2
R Fick	1B	199.3	224	13	1	1	.992	10.70	3	0
P McAnulty	1B	4.0	4	0	0	0	1.000	9.00	0	0
G Blum	1B	3.0	1	0	0	0	1.000	3.00	0	0
R Klesko	1B	1.0	2	0	0	0	1.000	18.00	0	0
M Loretta	2B	910.3	201	261	0	6	.987	4.57	20	40
D Jackson	2B	265.0	53	93	1	0	.993	4.96	8	14
G Blum	2B	162.0	28	48	0	0	1.000	4.22	2	7
E Young	2B	91.0	25	26	2	1	.944	5.04	0	8
M Alexander	2B	20.0	1	4	0	0	1.000	2.25	0	0
J Garcia	2B	7.0	2	3	0	0	1.000	6.43	0	1
K Greene	SS	1028.0	161	312	6	8	.971	4.14	36	26
D Jackson	SS	189.3	34	52	3	4	.925	4.09	10	5
J Garcia	SS	82.0	15	19	0	0	1.000	3.73	1	3
G Blum	SS	81.3	12	25	0	0	1.000	4.09	4	3
W Valdez	SS	41.0	9	8	0	1	.944	3.73	1	1
M Alexander	SS	31.0	4	10	0	1	.933	4.06	1	0
S Burroughs	SS	2.0	0	0	0	0	0.000	0.00	0	0
S Burroughs	3B	656.7	60	144	5	3	.962	2.80	16	1
J Randa	3B	493.0	50	77	3	3	.955	2.32	9	0
G Blum	3B	230.7	20	62	0	3	.965	3.20	8	0
D Jackson	3B	53.0	2	6	1	0	.889	1.36	1	0
X Nady	3B	18.0	0	6	0	0	1.000	3.00	0	0
R Fick	3B	2.0	0	0	0	0	0.000	0.00	0	0
M Loretta	3B	1.0	0	0	0	0	0.000	0.00	0	0
M Alexander	3B	1.0	0	0	0	0	0.000	0.00	0	0
R Klesko	LF	927.0	203	7	2	2	.981	2.04	2	0
E Young	LF	167.7	47	0	0	0	1.000	2.52	0	0
X Nady	LF	100.0	18	0	0	1	.947	1.62	0	0
D Jackson	LF	97.0	25	2	0	0	1.000	2.51	0	0
B Johnson	LF	56.0	10	0	0	0	1.000	1.61	0	0
A Hyzdu	LF	30.7	11	1	0	0	1.000	3.52	2	0
P McAnulty	LF	29.0	5	0	0	0	1.000	1.55	0	0
M Ojeda	LF	24.0	6	0	0	0	1.000	2.25	0	0
R Fick	LF	18.0	1	0	0	0	1.000	0.50	0	0
M Sweeney	LF	5.0	0	0	0	0	0.000	0.00	0	0
B Giles	LF	1.0	2	0	0	0	1.000	18.00	0	0

Name	POS	Inn	PO	A	TE	FE	FPct	RF	DPS	DPT
D Roberts	CF	900.7	235	4	0	2	.992	2.39	1	0
X Nady	CF	244.3	54	0	0	1	.982	1.99	0	0
B Giles	CF	133.0	32	0	0	0	1.000	2.17	0	0
D Jackson	CF	79.7	23	0	0	0	1.000	2.60	0	0
B Johnson	CF	60.0	14	0	0	1	.933	2.10	0	0
E Young	CF	20.0	6	0	0	0	1.000	2.70	0	0
A Hyzdu	CF	16.0	3	0	0	0	1.000	1.69	0	0
M Sweeney	CF	1.7	0	0	0	0	0.000	0.00	0	0
B Giles	RF	1220.0	295	6	2	2	.987	2.22	2	0
X Nady	RF	82.0	11	0	0	0	1.000	1.21	0	0
B Johnson	RF	73.3	28	0	1	0	.966	3.44	0	0
R Fick	RF	57.0	16	1	0	0	1.000	2.68	0	0
M Sweeney	RF	12.0	5	0	1	0	.833	3.75	0	0
M Ojeda	RF	10.0	4	0	0	0	1.000	3.60	0	0
D Jackson	RF	1.0	0	0	0	0	0.000	0.00	0	0

Incremental Baserunning Runs		
Name	IR	IRP
Robert Fick	1.59	215
Dave Roberts	1.50	121
Damian Jackson	1.06	116
Geoff Blum	0.71	125
Mark Sweeney	0.61	129
Miguel Ojeda	0.46	144
Woody Williams	0.21	245
Adam Hyzdu	0.18	131
Chan Ho Park	0.15	205
David Ross	0.08	129
Brian Lawrence	0.07	137
Joe Randa	0.07	102
Eric Young	0.02	101
Khalil Greene	0.01	100
Jake Peavy	0.00	100
Darrell May	-0.01	0

Incremental Baserunning Runs		
Name	IR	IRP
Ben Johnson	-0.01	83
Pedro Astacio	-0.02	0
Jesse Garcia	-0.04	0
Adam Eaton	-0.07	0
Paul McAnulty	-0.10	0
Xavier Nady	-0.20	96
Tim Stauffer	-0.32	0
Scott Cassidy	-0.32	0
Miguel Olivo	-0.42	78
Brian Giles	-0.65	92
Ryan Klesko	-0.94	79
Sean Burroughs	-0.99	53
Ramon Hernandez	-1.66	57
Phil Nevin	-2.83	43
Mark Loretta	-3.99	59

San Francisco Giants

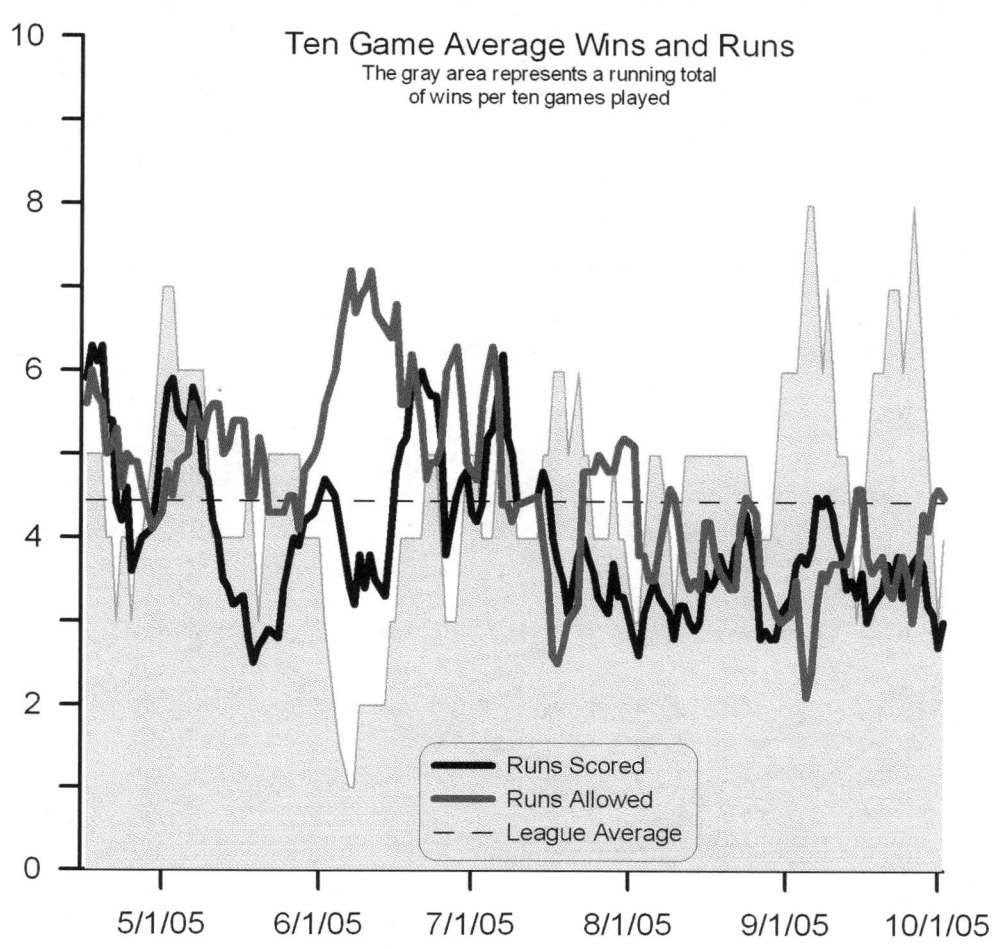

Ten Game Average Wins and Runs
The gray area represents a running total
of wins per ten games played

Legend:
- Runs Scored
- Runs Allowed
- — League Average

4/28: Benitez tears hamstring, out 4 months

6/11: Schmidt's ERA balloons to 6.12

8/28: Lowry is 5-0, 0.69 in August

5/28: Williams, Aardsma traded for Hawkins

7/31: Winn acquired from Seattle, hits .447 in Sept.

9/12: Bonds returns, hits ball off top of wall in first PA

Team Batting and Pitching/Fielding Stats by Month						
	April	May	June	July	Aug	Spt/Oct
Wins	12	11	10	12	14	16
Losses	11	16	17	15	14	14
OBP	.348	.324	.331	.305	.301	.306
SLG	.424	.402	.406	.378	.374	.395
FIP	4.52	4.97	4.80	4.32	3.97	4.15
DER	.718	.714	.676	.710	.715	.735

Batting Stats

Player	RC	Runs	RBI	PA	Outs	P/PA	H	2B	3B	HR	TB	K	BB	IBB	HBP	SH	SF	SB	CS	GDP	BA	OBP	SLG	GPA
Vizquel O.	82	66	45	651	434	3.88	154	28	4	3	199	58	56	0	5	20	2	24	10	10	.271	.341	.350	.241
Alou M.	80	67	63	490	302	3.41	137	21	3	19	221	43	56	1	3	0	4	5	1	11	.321	.400	.518	.309
Durham R.	72	67	62	560	375	3.59	144	33	0	12	213	59	48	2	7	1	7	6	3	19	.290	.356	.429	.267
Feliz P.	62	69	81	615	449	3.43	142	30	4	20	240	102	38	1	1	1	6	0	2	20	.250	.295	.422	.238
Matheny M.	56	42	59	485	349	3.56	107	34	0	13	180	91	29	10	6	3	4	0	2	11	.242	.295	.406	.234
Snow J.	52	40	40	410	272	3.68	101	17	2	4	134	61	32	1	7	2	2	1	0	6	.275	.343	.365	.246
Alfonzo E.	49	36	43	402	277	3.55	102	17	1	2	127	34	27	1	2	1	4	2	0	11	.277	.327	.345	.233
Winn R.	46	39	26	247	157	3.60	83	22	5	14	157	38	11	1	1	4	0	7	5	4	.359	.391	.680	.346
Niekro L.	38	32	46	302	221	3.44	70	16	3	12	128	53	17	0	2	0	5	0	2	11	.252	.295	.460	.248
Ellison J.	37	49	24	386	272	3.41	93	18	2	4	127	44	24	1	3	6	1	14	6	7	.264	.316	.361	.232
Tucker M.	36	32	33	286	196	3.56	60	16	1	5	93	48	28	3	2	2	4	4	0	6	.240	.317	.372	.236
Cruz D.	22	26	19	221	159	3.31	56	10	1	5	83	31	10	1	0	2	0	0	1	5	.268	.301	.397	.235
Linden T.	13	20	13	187	139	3.83	37	8	0	4	57	54	10	0	5	1	0	3	0	5	.216	.280	.333	.209
Grissom M.	10	8	15	147	118	3.52	29	4	0	2	39	18	7	0	0	2	1	1	1	9	.212	.248	.285	.183
Bonds B.	9	8	10	52	30	4.12	12	1	0	5	28	6	9	3	0	0	1	0	0	0	.286	.404	.667	.348
Lowry N.	8	6	7	75	43	3.29	16	6	0	0	22	13	3	0	0	12	1	0	0	0	.271	.302	.373	.229
Torrealba Y.	7	18	7	105	75	3.67	21	8	0	1	32	25	9	1	1	2	0	1	0	3	.226	.301	.344	.221
Hennessey B.	5	3	5	41	30	3.32	9	1	0	2	16	12	0	0	0	2	0	0	0	0	.231	.231	.410	.206
Sanchez A.	4	4	3	47	34	3.21	11	3	0	0	14	9	1	0	1	2	0	2	2	0	.256	.289	.326	.211
Tomko B.	2	3	5	67	46	3.42	9	1	0	0	10	22	2	0	0	10	0	0	0	0	.164	.193	.182	.132
Chavez A.	2	1	1	20	14	3.35	5	1	0	0	6	3	0	0	0	1	0	0	0	0	.263	.263	.316	.197
Rueter K.	1	1	1	37	26	2.65	5	1	0	0	6	2	1	0	0	6	0	0	0	1	.167	.194	.200	.137
Ortmeier D.	1	1	1	26	21	3.65	3	0	0	0	3	5	3	0	1	0	0	1	0	2	.136	.269	.136	.155
Torcato T.	1	1	0	12	10	4.08	3	0	0	0	3	2	1	0	0	0	0	0	0	2	.273	.333	.273	.218
Ramirez J.	1	3	1	4	3	3.75	1	0	0	0	1	1	0	0	0	0	0	0	0	0	.250	.250	.250	.175
Accardo J.	1	0	0	2	1	3.00	1	0	0	0	1	0	0	0	0	0	0	0	0	0	.500	.500	.500	.350
Shabala A.	0	1	4	18	13	3.67	3	0	0	0	3	5	1	0	0	1	1	0	0	1	.200	.235	.200	.156
Kinney M.	0	0	0	3	2	3.33	1	0	0	0	1	1	0	0	0	0	0	0	0	0	.333	.333	.333	.233
Eyre S.	0	0	0	3	2	4.33	0	0	0	0	0	2	1	0	0	0	0	0	0	0	.000	.333	.000	.150
Munter S.	0	0	0	1	0	0.00	0	0	0	0	0	0	0	0	0	1	0	0	0	0	.000	.000	.000	.000
Cooper B.	-0	0	0	2	1	3.00	1	0	0	0	1	0	0	0	0	0	0	0	0	0	.500	.500	.500	.350
Correia K.	-0	0	0	18	13	4.00	1	0	0	0	1	5	3	0	0	1	0	0	0	0	.071	.235	.071	.124
Walker T.	-0	0	0	1	1	7.00	0	0	0	0	0	0	0	0	0	0	0	0	0	0	.000	.000	.000	.000
Levine A.	-0	0	0	2	2	4.00	0	0	0	0	0	0	0	0	0	0	0	0	0	0	.000	.000	.000	.000
Clark D.	-0	2	0	6	5	3.00	0	0	0	0	0	2	1	0	0	0	0	0	0	0	.000	.167	.000	.075
Brower J.	-0	0	0	2	2	4.50	0	0	0	0	0	1	0	0	0	0	0	0	0	0	.000	.000	.000	.000
Williams J.	-0	0	0	4	4	2.25	0	0	0	0	0	0	0	0	0	0	0	0	0	0	.000	.000	.000	.000
Knoedler J.	-0	0	0	11	9	2.55	1	0	0	0	1	1	0	0	1	0	0	0	0	0	.100	.182	.100	.107
Dallimore B.	-1	1	0	7	7	2.29	1	1	0	0	2	0	0	0	0	0	0	0	0	1	.143	.143	.286	.136
Cain M.	-1	1	0	16	14	4.00	1	1	0	0	2	6	0	0	0	1	0	0	0	0	.067	.067	.133	.063
Fassero J.	-1	0	0	14	13	3.57	0	0	0	0	0	6	0	0	0	1	0	0	0	0	.000	.000	.000	.000
Haad Y.	-2	0	1	32	28	3.84	2	1	0	0	3	7	3	0	0	0	1	0	0	2	.071	.156	.107	.097
Schmidt J.	-2	2	2	60	48	3.78	5	0	0	1	8	32	0	0	1	6	0	0	0	0	.094	.111	.151	.088

Pitching Stats

Player	PR	IP	BFP	G	GS	P/PA	K	BB	IBB	HBP	H	HR	DP	DER	SB	CS	PO	W	L	Sv	Op	Hld	RA	ERA	FIP
Eyre S.	13	68.3	278	86	0	4.28	65	26	0	4	48	3	8	.750	1	2	1	2	2	0	2	32	2.77	2.63	2.97
Cain M.	11	46.3	181	7	7	3.96	30	19	1	0	24	4	2	.844	1	1	0	2	1	0	0	0	2.33	2.33	4.04
Lowry N.	11	204.7	874	33	33	4.06	172	76	1	7	193	21	18	.712	9	8	1	13	13	0	0	0	4.05	3.78	3.85
Taschner J.	6	22.7	95	24	0	4.13	19	13	0	0	15	0	2	.762	2	1	1	2	0	0	1	3	1.99	1.59	3.03
Munter S.	4	38.7	159	45	0	3.43	11	12	1	1	40	1	10	.709	2	3	0	2	0	0	3	12	3.49	2.56	3.76
Cooper B.	3	17.7	73	8	1	3.86	7	8	0	0	15	0	4	.741	0	0	0	0	1	0	0	0	3.06	3.06	3.55
Accardo J.	2	29.7	124	28	0	3.62	16	9	1	1	26	2	4	.750	2	0	0	1	5	0	1	4	3.94	3.94	3.79
Hawkins L.	1	37.3	167	45	0	3.99	30	17	3	0	40	3	2	.684	0	0	0	1	4	2	7	15	4.34	4.10	3.79
Walker T.	-0	61.7	279	67	0	3.75	54	27	6	3	68	9	4	.683	3	1	0	6	4	23	28	2	4.52	4.23	4.59
Herges M.	-0	21.0	90	21	0	3.37	6	7	1	0	23	2	4	.720	0	1	0	1	1	0	0	3	4.71	4.71	4.65
Correia K.	-2	58.3	264	16	11	3.80	44	31	2	4	61	12	8	.717	4	2	0	2	5	0	0	0	4.78	4.63	5.95
Foppert J.	-2	10.3	53	3	2	3.89	6	13	0	1	11	2	3	.710	3	0	0	0	0	0	0	0	6.10	5.23	8.40
Benitez A.	-2	30.0	127	30	0	4.17	23	16	0	0	25	5	4	.759	1	2	0	2	3	19	23	0	5.10	4.50	5.22
Kinney M.	-2	12.0	55	5	1	3.55	3	6	0	1	18	2	4	.628	0	1	1	2	0	0	1	0	6.00	6.00	6.40
Fassero J.	-2	91.0	384	48	6	3.68	60	31	1	0	92	7	9	.703	6	8	5	4	7	0	2	2	4.75	4.05	3.69
Tomko B.	-3	190.7	823	33	30	3.74	114	57	11	7	205	20	17	.704	5	3	0	8	15	1	1	1	4.67	4.48	4.16
Hennessey B.	-4	118.3	521	21	21	3.77	64	52	3	4	127	15	16	.710	9	4	0	5	8	0	0	0	4.79	4.64	4.97
Schmidt J.	-4	172.0	757	29	29	4.03	165	85	4	5	160	16	7	.704	24	8	0	12	7	0	0	0	4.71	4.40	3.84
Williams J.	-4	16.7	73	4	3	3.55	11	4	1	1	21	2	2	.655	1	1	1	0	2	0	0	0	6.48	6.48	4.12
Puffer B.	-5	7.0	31	3	0	3.52	1	2	0	0	9	2	1	.731	0	0	0	0	0	0	0	0	10.29	10.29	7.27
Levine A.	-6	10.3	51	9	0	3.84	4	4	1	0	16	2	0	.659	2	0	0	0	0	0	0	0	9.58	9.58	5.89
Christiansen	-6	42.0	188	56	0	3.57	17	15	2	0	48	4	3	.711	0	3	0	6	1	0	2	10	5.79	5.36	4.48
Brower J.	-7	30.3	144	32	0	3.96	25	15	0	2	40	5	2	.639	2	1	0	2	1	1	3	5	6.53	6.53	5.16
Rueter K.	-24	107.3	489	20	18	3.79	25	47	3	1	131	12	12	.705	1	4	3	2	7	0	0	0	6.54	5.95	5.31

Win Shares Stats

Player	WS	Bat	Pitch	Field	ExpWS	WSP	WSAB	CWS	NetWSValue
Alou, M	20	18.0	0.0	1.9	13	.753	11	255	$4,177,716
Matheny, M	20	8.7	0.0	11.1	14	.731	10	96	$7,129,353
Vizquel, O	20	13.3	0.0	6.3	17	.560	7	229	$4,015,920
Lowry, N	16	1.2	15.1	0.0	10	.844	11	23	$8,301,202
Durham, R	15	13.0	0.0	2.5	15	.514	5	194	($266,120)
Winn, R	14	11.5	0.0	2.2	7	1.040	9	97	$7,216,077
Snow, J	10	9.0	0.0	1.5	11	.474	3	170	$1,137,478
Feliz, P	10	7.4	0.0	2.9	17	.308	-1	30	($2,325,000)
Eyre, S	9	-0.1	8.9	0.0	4	1.009	6	28	$3,201,113
Alfonzo, E	9	7.3	0.0	1.8	11	.419	2	211	($3,164,949)
Schmidt, J	8	-2.4	10.0	0.0	8	.457	3	103	($2,707,130)
Tomko, B	8	-1.0	8.9	0.0	9	.424	2	60	$403,833
Tucker, M	7	6.2	0.0	1.2	7	.494	2	104	$590,196
Niekro, L	7	6.2	0.0	0.9	8	.453	2	7	$1,270,618
Ellison, J	7	3.8	0.0	2.8	10	.317	-1	8	($316,500)
Hennessey, B	6	0.8	5.1	0.0	6	.538	3	7	$2,079,516
Fassero, J	4	-0.8	5.0	0.0	5	.455	1	125	$646,282
Walker, T	4	-0.0	4.6	0.0	5	.429	1	8	$652,144
Cruz, D	4	2.7	0.0	1.5	6	.355	0	83	($608,944)
Linden, T	1	0.0	0.0	1.2	5	.116	-2	2	($316,000)
Grissom, M	0	-0.5	0.0	0.6	4	.013	-3	250	($2,750,000)
Rueter, K	-1	-0.6	-1.0	0.0	5	-.161	-5	83	($7,133,333)

Fielding and Baserunning Stats

Name	POS	Inn	SBA/G	CS%	ERA	WP+PB/G	PO	A	TE	FE
Matheny	C	1122.0	0.75	32%	4.47	0.257	784	77	0	1
Torrealba	C	217.3	0.70	41%	4.72	0.248	147	16	0	0
Haad	C	89.7	1.00	50%	2.51	0.502	61	6	1	1
Knoedler	C	15.3	0.00	0%	1.17	0.000	8	1	0	0

Name	POS	Inn	PO	A	TE	FE	FPct	RF	DPS	DPT
J Snow	1B	825.7	813	56	0	3	.997	9.47	0	2
L Niekro	1B	529.0	544	38	2	3	.991	9.90	4	0
P Feliz	1B	89.7	76	7	0	1	.988	8.33	2	0
R Durham	2B	1143.0	249	341	0	11	.982	4.65	24	51
D Cruz	2B	258.7	54	76	1	1	.985	4.52	14	9
A Chavez	2B	19.7	3	4	0	0	1.000	3.20	0	0
E Alfonzo	2B	12.3	4	4	0	0	1.000	5.84	0	2
B Dallimore	2B	10.7	0	6	0	0	1.000	5.06	3	0
O Vizquel	SS	1292.0	234	426	4	4	.988	4.60	42	35
D Cruz	SS	123.7	23	48	0	1	.986	5.17	7	5
A Chavez	SS	27.3	6	5	1	0	.917	3.62	2	0
B Dallimore	SS	1.0	0	0	0	0	0.000	0.00	0	0
E Alfonzo	3B	813.0	76	157	3	5	.967	2.58	9	0
P Feliz	3B	591.7	47	144	1	5	.970	2.91	17	1
D Cruz	3B	37.7	1	11	0	0	1.000	2.87	0	0
A Chavez	3B	2.0	0	0	0	0	0.000	0.00	0	0
P Feliz	LF	615.7	138	0	0	2	.979	2.02	0	0
M Alou	LF	576.0	132	1	0	4	.971	2.08	0	0
B Bonds	LF	95.0	18	0	0	0	1.000	1.71	0	0
T Linden	LF	77.0	22	0	0	1	.957	2.57	0	0
A Shabala	LF	27.3	5	0	0	1	.833	1.65	1	0
J Ellison	LF	23.3	3	0	0	1	.750	1.16	0	0
M Tucker	LF	21.0	6	0	0	0	1.000	2.57	0	0
M Grissom	LF	9.0	1	0	0	0	1.000	1.00	0	0
J Ellison	CF	591.7	196	4	2	4	.971	3.04	0	0
R Winn	CF	485.7	165	1	0	1	.994	3.08	2	0
M Grissom	CF	284.7	68	0	0	1	.986	2.15	0	0
M Tucker	CF	45.0	13	1	0	1	.933	2.80	0	0
A Sanchez	CF	31.0	9	0	1	0	.900	2.61	0	0
J Ramirez	CF	5.3	3	0	0	0	1.000	5.06	0	0
R Durham	CF	1.0	0	0	0	0	0.000	0.00	0	0
M Tucker	RF	439.7	90	5	0	1	.990	1.94	2	0
M Alou	RF	412.7	90	4	1	3	.959	2.05	5	0
T Linden	RF	318.7	92	0	0	1	.989	2.60	0	0
J Ellison	RF	166.3	36	1	0	1	.974	2.00	2	0
D Ortmeier	RF	46.7	13	0	0	0	1.000	2.51	0	0

Name	POS	Inn	PO	A	TE	FE	FPct	RF	DPS	DPT
A Sanchez	RF	41.0	10	1	0	2	.846	2.41	0	0
M Grissom	RF	8.0	0	0	0	0	0.000	0.00	0	0
J Ramirez	RF	5.3	0	0	0	0	0.000	0.00	0	0
T Torcato	RF	3.0	1	0	0	0	1.000	3.00	0	0
A Shabala	RF	3.0	2	0	0	0	1.000	6.00	0	0

Incremental Baserunning Runs		
Name	IR	IRP
Ray Durham	1.88	129
Pedro Feliz	1.62	119
Randy Winn	1.59	176
JT Snow	1.32	123
Yorvit Torrealba	0.39	127
Deivi Cruz	0.30	109
Alex Sanchez	0.25	269
Omar Vizquel	0.18	102
Doug Clark	0.18	197
Dan Ortmeier	0.11	118
Brad Hennessey	0.07	233
Barry Bonds	0.03	118
Angel Chavez	0.01	103
Adam Shabala	-0.01	0
Yamid Haad	-0.05	0
Jason Schmidt	-0.07	0
Brett Tomko	-0.10	0
Lance Niekro	-0.11	95
Todd Linden	-0.15	95
Kirk Rueter	-0.15	0
Marquis Grissom	-0.21	84
Kevin Correia	-0.24	0
Michael Tucker	-0.32	91
Mike Matheny	-0.59	82
Matt Cain	-0.64	0
Jason Ellison	-0.77	81
Moises Alou	-1.16	72
Edgardo Alfonzo	-1.55	57
Noah Lowry	-1.71	0

Seattle Mariners

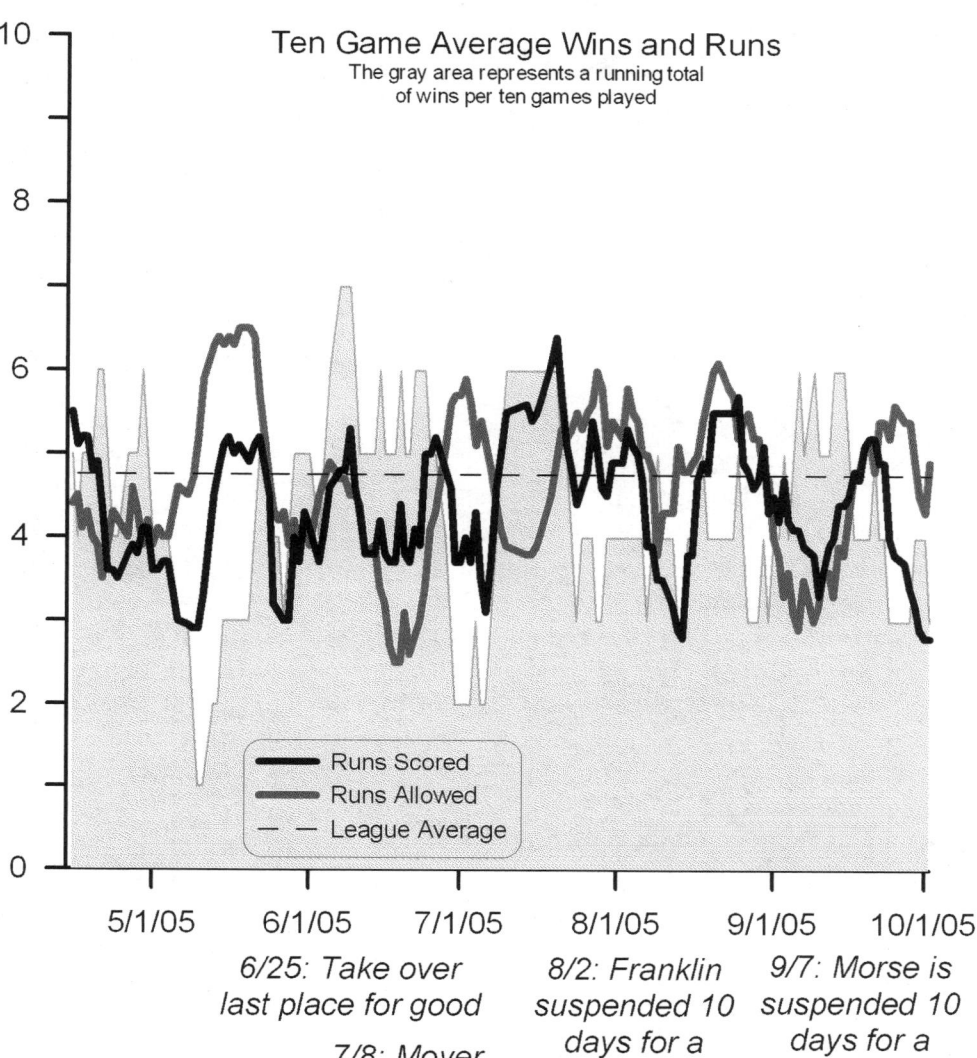

Ten Game Average Wins and Runs
The gray area represents a running total
of wins per ten games played

— Runs Scored
— Runs Allowed
– – League Average

6/25: Take over last place for good

7/8: Moyer wins 200th

8/2: Franklin suspended 10 days for a drug violation

9/7: Morse is suspended 10 days for a drug violation

8/4: Purchase contract of 19-year-old Hernandez, who goes 4-4, 2.67

9/30: Ichiro gets four hits for 5th straight 200 hit season

Team Batting and Pitching/Fielding Stats by Month						
	April	May	June	July	Aug	Spt/Oct
Wins	12	9	12	12	11	13
Losses	12	18	14	15	17	17
OBP	.323	.303	.319	.329	.306	.325
SLG	.367	.393	.396	.430	.390	.370
FIP	4.63	5.14	4.51	4.82	4.55	4.14
DER	.737	.719	.717	.688	.713	.709

Batting Stats

Player	RC	Runs	RBI	PA	Outs	P/PA	H	2B	3B	HR	TB	K	BB	IBB	HBP	SH	SF	SB	CS	GDP	BA	OBP	SLG	GPA
Sexson R.	122	99	121	656	427	3.98	147	36	1	39	302	167	89	4	6	0	3	1	1	15	.263	.369	.541	.301
Suzuki I.	114	111	68	739	486	3.58	206	21	12	15	296	66	48	23	4	2	6	33	8	5	.303	.350	.436	.267
Ibanez R.	102	92	89	690	458	3.96	172	32	2	20	268	99	71	6	2	0	3	9	4	12	.280	.355	.436	.269
Beltre A.	79	69	87	650	465	3.97	154	36	1	19	249	108	38	6	5	0	4	3	1	15	.255	.303	.413	.240
Winn R.	54	46	37	436	293	3.54	106	25	1	6	151	53	37	3	4	6	3	12	6	7	.275	.342	.391	.252
Reed J.	51	61	45	544	385	3.73	124	33	3	3	172	74	48	1	2	4	2	12	11	10	.254	.322	.352	.233
Boone B.	29	30	34	302	221	3.75	63	15	3	7	105	52	24	2	3	1	1	4	2	9	.231	.299	.385	.231
Morse M.	29	27	23	258	176	3.69	64	10	1	3	85	50	18	0	8	0	2	3	1	9	.278	.349	.370	.249
Bloomquist W	27	27	22	267	191	3.42	64	15	2	0	83	38	11	0	1	4	2	14	1	5	.257	.289	.333	.213
Lopez J.	25	18	25	203	150	3.76	47	19	0	2	72	25	6	0	4	1	2	4	2	5	.247	.282	.379	.222
Betancourt Y	22	24	15	228	162	3.19	54	11	5	1	78	24	11	0	2	2	2	1	3	2	.256	.296	.370	.226
Dobbs G.	16	8	20	154	111	3.82	35	7	1	1	47	25	9	3	0	1	2	1	0	4	.246	.288	.331	.212
Rivera R.	9	3	6	50	29	3.60	19	3	0	1	25	11	1	0	0	1	0	0	0	0	.396	.408	.521	.314
Torrealba Y.	7	14	8	119	87	3.90	26	4	0	2	36	25	7	0	1	3	0	0	0	5	.241	.293	.333	.215
Valdez W.	7	9	8	133	104	3.86	25	5	1	0	32	25	6	0	0	1	0	2	2	1	.198	.235	.254	.169
Olivo M.	6	14	18	157	133	3.92	23	4	0	5	42	49	4	0	0	0	1	1	1	3	.151	.172	.276	.146
Hansen D.	6	5	11	88	63	4.43	13	0	0	2	19	19	9	1	0	2	2	1	0	1	.173	.256	.253	.178
Borders P.	5	12	7	125	98	3.11	23	5	0	1	31	22	4	1	1	2	1	0	0	4	.197	.228	.265	.169
Gonzalez W.	5	7	2	47	34	3.02	12	5	0	0	17	3	2	0	0	0	0	0	0	1	.267	.298	.378	.228
Ojeda M.	3	2	3	37	25	3.32	5	0	0	1	8	3	6	0	2	0	0	0	1	0	.172	.314	.276	.210
Strong J.	3	6	2	24	15	3.96	5	0	1	0	7	6	2	0	1	0	1	0	0	0	.250	.333	.350	.238
Snelling C.	3	4	1	35	23	3.89	8	2	0	1	13	2	5	0	0	1	0	0	2	0	.276	.382	.448	.284
Santiago R.	1	2	0	13	7	3.69	1	0	0	0	1	2	1	0	3	1	0	0	0	0	.125	.417	.125	.219
Meche G.	1	0	1	4	3	3.25	1	0	0	0	1	1	0	0	0	0	0	0	0	0	.250	.250	.250	.175
Wilson D.	0	2	2	28	24	3.93	5	0	0	0	5	10	0	0	1	0	0	0	1	1	.185	.214	.185	.143
Choo S.	0	1	1	21	17	4.24	1	0	0	0	1	4	3	0	0	0	0	0	0	0	.056	.190	.056	.100
Moyer J.	-0	0	0	2	1	2.00	0	0	0	0	0	0	0	0	0	1	0	0	0	0	.000	.000	.000	.000
Franklin R.	-0	0	0	5	4	2.80	0	0	0	0	0	0	1	0	0	0	0	0	0	0	.000	.200	.000	.090
Sele A.	-0	1	0	4	3	2.50	0	0	0	0	0	0	0	0	0	1	0	0	0	0	.000	.000	.000	.000
Pineiro J.	-0	0	0	5	4	3.40	0	0	0	0	0	1	0	0	0	1	0	0	0	0	.000	.000	.000	.000
Bubela J.	-1	3	0	20	18	3.75	2	0	0	0	2	4	1	0	0	0	0	1	0	1	.105	.150	.105	.094
Spiezio S.	-3	2	1	51	45	4.25	3	1	0	1	7	18	4	0	0	0	0	0	0	1	.064	.137	.149	.099

Win Shares Stats

Player	WS	Bat	Pitch	Field	ExpWS	WSP	WSAB	CWS	NetWSValue
Sexson, R	27	25.4	0.0	1.6	17	.789	15	129	$8,406,559
Suzuki, I	24	19.6	0.0	4.3	19	.631	11	135	$1,042,838
Ibanez, R	19	17.5	0.0	1.3	15	.626	8	76	$4,049,857
Beltre, A	14	10.8	0.0	3.8	17	.427	3	135	($4,656,317)
Moyer, J	12	-0.1	11.9	0.0	11	.560	5	185	($318,780)
Winn, R	10	7.7	0.0	2.9	11	.468	3	93	$7,216,077
Reed, J	10	4.7	0.0	5.4	14	.348	-0	13	($44,073)
Hernandez, F	8	0.0	8.2	0.0	4	.925	6	8	$4,385,479

Continued on the next page.

Pitching Stats

Player	PR	IP	BFP	G	GS	P/PA	K	BB	IBB	HBP	H	HR	DP	DER	SB	CS	PO	W	L	Sv	Op	Hld	RA	ERA	FIP
Hernandez F.	17	84.3	328	12	12	3.71	77	23	0	2	61	5	8	.747	3	2	2	4	4	0	0	0	2.77	2.67	2.88
Mateo J.	13	88.3	364	55	1	3.49	52	17	6	7	79	12	4	.757	2	4	0	3	6	0	2	8	3.26	3.06	4.45
Villone R.	6	40.3	178	52	0	4.24	41	23	1	5	33	2	3	.710	1	1	1	2	3	1	6	17	3.12	2.45	3.74
Guardado E.	5	56.3	238	58	0	3.91	48	15	3	0	52	7	1	.732	4	1	0	2	3	36	41	0	3.67	2.72	3.75
Putz J.	3	60.0	259	64	0	3.90	45	23	2	2	58	8	7	.724	7	1	0	6	5	1	4	21	4.05	3.60	4.53
Hasegawa S.	2	66.7	279	46	0	3.61	30	16	1	3	66	4	8	.726	0	2	0	1	3	0	1	3	4.19	4.19	3.78
Soriano R.	2	7.3	30	7	0	4.93	9	1	0	1	6	0	0	.684	0	0	0	0	0	0	0	1	2.45	2.45	1.41
Nelson J.	1	36.7	166	49	0	3.81	34	22	0	4	32	3	2	.718	5	2	1	1	3	1	4	9	4.17	3.93	4.38
Campillo J.	1	2.0	9	2	1	4.33	1	1	0	0	1	0	0	.857	0	0	0	0	0	0	0	0	0.00	0.00	3.54
Moyer J.	0	200.0	868	32	32	3.76	102	52	2	8	225	23	16	.704	27	7	2	13	7	0	0	0	4.46	4.28	4.42
Kida M.	-0	2.0	8	1	0	2.88	0	0	0	0	2	1	0	.857	0	0	0	0	0	0	0	0	4.50	4.50	9.54
Harris J.	-0	53.7	227	11	8	3.80	25	20	2	3	48	9	6	.771	5	4	1	2	5	0	0	0	4.53	4.19	5.58
Madritsch B.	-1	4.3	17	1	1	3.76	1	1	0	0	4	1	0	.786	0	0	0	0	1	0	0	0	6.23	6.23	6.27
Nageotte C.	-1	4.0	19	3	0	3.47	1	1	0	1	6	0	1	.625	0	0	0	0	0	0	0	0	6.75	6.75	4.04
Atchison S.	-2	6.7	27	6	0	4.74	9	1	0	0	7	1	0	.625	1	1	0	0	0	0	0	0	6.75	6.75	2.74
Sherrill G.	-3	19.0	77	29	0	4.34	24	7	2	1	13	3	1	.762	0	0	0	4	3	0	0	9	5.68	5.21	3.83
Thornton M.	-5	57.0	262	55	0	4.23	57	42	2	0	54	13	6	.727	6	0	0	0	4	0	1	5	5.21	5.21	6.22
Franklin R.	-16	190.7	833	32	30	3.52	93	62	4	7	212	28	20	.714	7	5	2	8	15	0	0	0	5.19	5.10	5.06
Sele A.	-20	116.0	523	21	21	3.73	53	41	2	5	147	18	16	.682	6	3	1	6	12	0	0	0	5.90	5.66	5.34
Meche G.	-22	143.3	638	29	26	4.04	83	72	1	2	153	18	18	.708	8	8	2	10	8	0	0	0	5.78	5.09	5.07
Pineiro J.	-26	189.0	822	30	30	3.56	107	56	4	6	224	23	28	.681	7	2	0	7	11	0	0	0	5.62	5.62	4.48

Win Shares Stats (cont.)

Player	WS	Bat	Pitch	Field	ExpWS	WSP	WSAB	CWS	NetWSValue
Mateo, J	8	0.0	7.6	0.0	6	.659	4	19	$2,748,463
Guardado, E	8	0.0	7.9	0.0	6	.607	3	87	($808,572)
Franklin, R	6	-0.1	5.7	0.0	10	.278	-0	37	($2,600,000)
Villone, R	5	0.0	4.6	0.0	4	.658	2	46	($293,111)
Putz, J	5	0.0	5.3	0.0	5	.573	2	8	$1,637,775
Lopez, J	5	3.5	0.0	1.9	5	.493	2	8	$1,228,955
Meche, G	5	0.2	4.4	0.0	8	.306	0	30	($2,425,763)
Morse, M	5	3.4	0.0	1.2	7	.346	-0	5	($47,368)
Boone, B	5	2.8	0.0	1.9	8	.292	-1	208	($6,891,590)
Hasegawa, S	4	0.0	3.6	0.0	4	.428	1	66	($1,242,190)
Bloomquist, W	4	2.6	0.0	1.6	7	.294	-1	13	($385,000)
Betancourt, Y	3	1.9	0.0	1.6	6	.283	-1	3	($316,000)
Pineiro, J	3	-0.1	3.4	0.0	10	.164	-3	43	($4,700,000)
Olivo, M	2	-1.8	0.0	3.6	4	.205	-1	19	$995,892
Thornton, M	1	0.0	1.0	0.0	4	.141	-2	3	($323,000)
Sele, A	1	-0.1	1.6	0.0	6	.121	-2	104	($700,000)
Valdez, W	0	-1.0	0.0	1.1	4	.008	-3	0	($316,000)

Fielding and Baserunning Stats

Name	POS	Inn	SBA/G	CS%	ERA	WP+PB/G	PO	A	TE	FE
Olivo	C	402.7	0.67	30%	4.69	0.536	281	15	2	2
Torrealba	C	319.3	0.96	24%	4.42	0.085	224	18	0	0
Borders	C	313.0	0.98	26%	4.08	0.288	175	15	0	2
Gonzalez	C	115.0	0.47	50%	5.48	0.157	78	8	0	0
Rivera	C	111.0	0.41	20%	4.38	0.649	69	4	2	0
Ojeda	C	94.7	0.86	33%	4.66	0.380	69	3	1	0
Wilson	C	72.0	0.75	33%	3.75	0.000	36	3	1	0

Name	POS	Inn	PO	A	TE	FE	FPct	RF	DPS	DPT
R Sexson	1B	1303.0	1148	119	1	6	.995	8.75	11	3
G Dobbs	1B	37.0	32	8	0	0	1.000	9.73	0	0
R Ibanez	1B	34.0	26	3	0	0	1.000	7.68	0	0
D Hansen	1B	26.0	17	2	0	0	1.000	6.58	0	0
S Spiezio	1B	26.0	30	0	0	0	1.000	10.38	0	0
W Bloomquist	1B	1.7	0	1	0	0	1.000	5.40	0	0
B Boone	2B	646.7	131	192	3	4	.979	4.50	20	19
J Lopez	2B	439.0	123	159	1	4	.979	5.78	10	23
W Bloomquist	2B	254.0	60	83	2	0	.986	5.07	8	13
Y Betancourt	2B	63.0	23	21	0	0	1.000	6.29	3	2
R Santiago	2B	17.0	0	4	0	0	1.000	2.12	1	0
S Spiezio	2B	8.0	1	1	0	0	1.000	2.25	0	0
Y Betancourt	SS	454.0	82	136	1	4	.978	4.32	18	16
M Morse	SS	450.0	91	120	7	5	.946	4.22	12	18
W Valdez	SS	341.7	67	111	1	4	.973	4.69	9	13
W Bloomquist	SS	180.0	34	49	2	1	.965	4.15	4	3
R Santiago	SS	2.0	0	1	0	0	.500	4.50	0	0
A Beltre	3B	1325.0	141	271	7	7	.967	2.80	26	2
D Hansen	3B	43.0	5	7	0	0	1.000	2.51	0	0
W Bloomquist	3B	25.0	1	4	0	0	1.000	1.80	0	0
S Spiezio	3B	14.0	1	1	0	0	1.000	1.29	1	0
G Dobbs	3B	11.0	4	5	0	0	1.000	7.36	1	0
J Lopez	3B	9.0	2	2	1	0	.800	4.00	0	0
R Winn	LF	795.7	226	2	0	0	1.000	2.58	0	0
R Ibanez	LF	463.7	105	6	1	1	.982	2.15	4	0
C Snelling	LF	66.0	17	2	0	0	1.000	2.59	2	0
M Morse	LF	55.0	10	1	0	0	1.000	1.80	2	0
G Dobbs	LF	26.0	4	0	0	0	1.000	1.38	0	0
J Strong	LF	18.0	4	1	0	0	1.000	2.50	0	0
W Bloomquist	LF	2.0	0	0	0	0	0.000	0.00	0	0
J Bubela	LF	1.3	0	0	0	0	0.000	0.00	0	0
J Reed	CF	1149.0	383	7	1	2	.992	3.05	2	0
W Bloomquist	CF	117.0	25	1	0	1	.963	2.00	2	0
R Winn	CF	47.0	19	1	0	0	1.000	3.83	0	0
J Bubela	CF	45.0	17	0	0	0	1.000	3.40	0	0
S Choo	CF	39.0	16	0	0	0	1.000	3.69	0	0
J Strong	CF	30.0	8	0	0	0	1.000	2.40	0	0

Name	POS	Inn	PO	A	TE	FE	FPct	RF	DPS	DPT
I Suzuki	RF	1388.0	381	9	1	1	.995	2.53	4	0
R Ibanez	RF	24.3	0	0	0	0	0.000	0.00	0	0
C Snelling	RF	12.0	3	0	0	0	1.000	2.25	0	0
J Strong	RF	3.0	0	0	0	0	0.000	0.00	0	0

Incremental Baserunning Runs		
Name	IR	IRP
Jeremy Reed	2.06	141
Mike Morse	1.73	144
Ichiro Suzuki	1.56	120
Willie Bloomquist	1.46	188
Randy Winn	0.91	130
Yorvit Torrealba	0.66	185
Pat Borders	0.65	128
Yuniesky Betancourt	0.64	160
Adrian Beltre	0.34	107
Bret Boone	0.28	108
Dave Hansen	0.25	149
Chris Snelling	0.22	572
Wilson Valdez	0.22	116
Ramon Santiago	0.20	217
Aaron Sele	0.17	130
Jamal Strong	0.16	127
Jaime Bubela	0.12	152
Raul Ibanez	0.12	102
Shin-Soo Choo	0.03	105
Dan Wilson	-0.04	0
Miguel Olivo	-0.09	82
Greg Dobbs	-0.16	91
Miguel Ojeda	-0.16	0
Wiki Gonzalez	-0.44	15
Jamie Moyer	-0.54	0
Jose Lopez	-0.99	48
Richie Sexson	-1.26	64
Rene Rivera	-1.35	-200

Tampa Bay Devil Rays

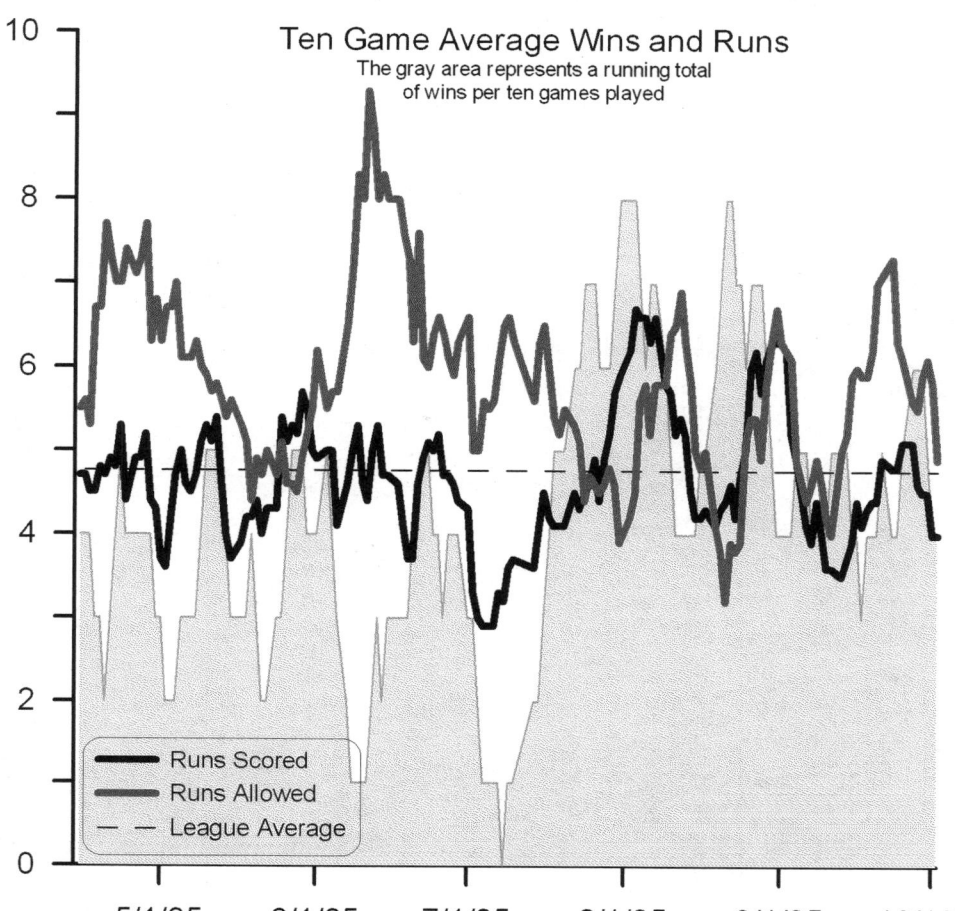

Ten Game Average Wins and Runs
The gray area represents a running total
of wins per ten games played

— Runs Scored
— Runs Allowed
- - League Average

5/1/05   6/1/05   7/1/05   8/1/05   9/1/05   10/1/05

5/7 - Take sole
possession of
last place, for
rest of season

7/14 - Beat Jays
to start a 27-15 run

9/10: Kazmir K's
11; has 1.71 ERA
in Sept

10/1: Hendrickson's
CG first of season
for TB; the longest a
team has ever gone
without one

6/14 - Promote Jonny
Gomes, who hits .280
with 19 HR

9/6 - Beat Yankees for
first winning season
against them

Team Batting and Pitching/Fielding Stats by Month						
	April	May	June	July	Aug	Spt/Oct
Wins	8	11	8	13	15	12
Losses	16	18	18	14	13	16
OBP	.341	.326	.324	.334	.335	.313
SLG	.410	.410	.403	.457	.479	.382
FIP	5.56	4.85	4.73	4.49	5.41	4.64
DER	.703	.710	.676	.699	.700	.702

Batting Stats

Player	RC	Runs	RBI	PA	Outs	P/PA	H	2B	3B	HR	TB	K	BB	IBB	HBP	SH	SF	SB	CS	GDP	BA	OBP	SLG	GPA
Crawford C.	111	101	81	687	469	3.23	194	33	15	15	302	84	27	1	5	5	6	46	8	11	.301	.331	.469	.266
Lugo J.	102	89	57	690	450	3.62	182	36	6	6	248	72	61	0	6	3	4	39	11	5	.295	.362	.403	.264
Cantu J.	95	73	117	631	451	3.30	171	40	1	28	297	83	19	1	6	0	7	1	0	24	.286	.311	.497	.264
Huff A.	84	70	92	636	444	3.63	150	26	2	22	246	88	49	13	5	0	7	8	7	12	.261	.321	.428	.251
Gomes J.	67	61	54	407	261	3.88	98	13	6	21	186	113	39	1	14	1	5	9	5	6	.282	.372	.534	.301
Lee T.	55	54	49	441	305	3.91	110	22	2	12	172	66	35	4	1	0	1	7	4	7	.272	.331	.426	.255
Hall T.	51	28	48	463	323	3.32	124	20	0	5	159	39	16	1	5	3	7	0	0	15	.287	.315	.368	.234
Hollins D.	45	44	46	369	266	3.76	85	17	1	13	143	63	23	0	1	1	2	8	1	8	.249	.296	.418	.238
Green N.	42	53	29	375	248	3.87	76	15	2	5	110	86	33	0	11	10	3	3	1	5	.239	.329	.346	.234
Gonzalez A.	40	47	38	383	269	3.77	94	20	1	9	143	74	26	1	3	2	3	2	1	13	.269	.323	.410	.248
Perez E.	33	23	28	190	128	3.81	41	6	0	11	80	30	26	0	3	0	0	0	2	6	.255	.368	.497	.290
Phelps J.	25	21	26	177	119	3.92	42	10	0	5	67	48	12	1	4	0	3	0	0	3	.266	.328	.424	.253
Gathright J.	24	29	13	218	157	3.74	56	7	3	0	69	39	10	0	2	3	0	20	5	5	.276	.316	.340	.227
Sanchez A.	21	28	13	145	93	3.18	46	8	1	2	62	25	7	1	0	3	2	6	3	3	.346	.373	.466	.284
Singleton C.	10	9	11	68	44	3.41	16	5	0	0	21	14	6	0	1	1	0	0	0	1	.271	.348	.356	.246
Johnson C.	5	5	5	55	39	4.20	9	4	0	0	13	11	9	0	0	0	0	0	0	2	.196	.327	.283	.218
LaForest P.	2	5	4	70	56	3.69	11	3	0	1	17	23	6	1	0	0	0	0	1	2	.172	.243	.266	.176
Munson E.	2	2	2	24	17	3.96	3	1	0	0	4	3	4	0	1	0	1	0	0	2	.167	.333	.222	.206
Taylor R.	1	2	1	24	18	4.13	4	2	0	0	6	7	2	0	0	0	0	2	0	0	.182	.250	.273	.181
Kazmir S.	-0	0	0	1	1	6.00	0	0	0	0	0	0	0	0	0	0	0	0	0	0	.000	.000	.000	.000
Harper T.	-0	0	0	1	1	6.00	0	0	0	0	0	1	0	0	0	0	0	0	0	0	.000	.000	.000	.000
Laker T.	-0	0	0	1	1	3.00	0	0	0	0	0	1	0	0	0	0	0	0	0	0	.000	.000	.000	.000
Fossum C.	-0	0	0	3	2	2.67	0	0	0	0	0	0	0	0	0	1	0	0	0	0	.000	.000	.000	.000
Waechter D.	-0	1	0	3	2	1.67	0	0	0	0	0	0	0	0	0	1	0	0	0	0	.000	.000	.000	.000
Hendrickson	-0	1	0	7	6	3.43	1	0	0	0	1	3	0	0	0	0	0	0	0	0	.143	.143	.143	.100
Nomo H.	-0	0	0	4	4	5.25	0	0	0	0	0	1	0	0	0	0	0	0	0	0	.000	.000	.000	.000
Cortez F.	-1	0	1	14	12	3.57	1	0	0	0	1	3	1	0	0	0	0	0	0	0	.077	.143	.077	.084
Cash K.	-1	4	2	33	29	3.85	5	1	0	2	12	13	1	0	1	0	0	0	0	3	.161	.212	.387	.192

Win Shares Stats

Player	WS	Bat	Pitch	Field	ExpWS	WSP	WSAB	CWS	NetWSValue
Lugo, J	24	18.6	0.0	5.8	17	.699	12	85	$6,296,695
Crawford, C	23	21.0	0.0	2.2	17	.672	11	63	$8,097,087
Cantu, J	18	17.1	0.0	1.1	16	.579	7	22	$5,674,040
Gomes, J	14	13.4	0.0	0.6	9	.787	8	14	$6,142,364
Huff, A	14	13.1	0.0	1.5	15	.481	4	75	($2,033,642)
Kazmir, S	13	-0.0	12.9	0.0	10	.654	7	14	$5,492,671
Hall, T	11	5.2	0.0	6.1	12	.460	3	44	$297,508
Baez, D	10	0.0	10.5	0.0	8	.627	5	44	$1,564,045
Lee, T	9	8.2	0.0	1.4	11	.421	2	77	$673,795
Hollins, D	8	6.2	0.0	1.8	10	.412	1	8	$948,622

Continued on the next page.

Pitching Stats

Player	PR	IP	BFP	G	GS	P/PA	K	BB	IBB	HBP	H	HR	DP	DER	SB	CS	PO	W	L	Sv	Op	Hld	RA	ERA	FIP
Baez D.	10	72.3	308	67	0	3.83	51	30	0	2	66	7	11	.729	4	0	0	5	4	41	49	0	3.36	2.86	4.22
Kazmir S.	5	186.0	818	32	32	4.03	174	100	3	10	172	12	18	.693	7	9	2	10	9	0	0	0	4.35	3.77	3.79
Borowski J.	3	35.3	137	32	0	3.81	16	11	1	0	26	3	3	.785	2	4	0	1	5	0	4	19	3.82	3.82	4.18
Beimel J.	2	11.0	51	7	0	3.35	3	4	1	0	15	1	1	.674	0	0	0	0	0	0	0	0	3.27	3.27	4.77
Miller T.	-0	44.3	206	61	0	3.68	35	29	6	7	45	4	7	.687	2	2	0	2	2	0	3	11	4.67	4.06	5.07
Orvella C.	-1	50.0	219	37	0	3.89	43	23	2	1	47	4	2	.709	3	0	0	3	3	1	2	14	4.68	3.60	3.80
Switzer J.	-2	4.0	25	2	0	4.40	5	7	0	0	5	0	0	.615	0	0	0	0	0	0	0	0	9.00	6.75	5.79
Carter L.	-2	57.0	239	39	0	3.64	22	15	1	1	61	9	6	.729	0	2	0	1	2	1	4	5	4.89	4.89	5.17
Nunez F.	-4	5.0	22	5	0	4.23	2	4	0	0	5	0	2	.688	0	0	0	1	0	0	0	1	10.80	10.80	4.64
Corcoran T.	-4	22.7	97	10	1	3.94	13	12	0	1	19	1	3	.743	1	0	0	0	0	0	0	0	5.96	5.96	4.19
Gardner L.	-5	7.3	37	5	0	3.57	4	2	0	0	12	2	0	.655	0	0	0	0	0	0	0	0	11.05	4.91	6.32
Colome J.	-6	45.3	212	36	0	3.53	28	18	3	2	54	7	2	.701	5	1	0	2	3	0	1	2	5.76	4.57	5.14
Webb J.	-6	4.0	23	1	1	3.65	2	4	0	1	6	1	0	.667	0	0	0	0	1	0	0	0	18.00	18.00	9.04
Bell R.	-13	25.0	129	8	3	3.51	13	12	0	2	41	7	3	.642	3	0	0	1	1	0	0	0	9.00	8.28	7.32
Fossum C.	-18	162.7	725	36	25	3.89	128	60	3	18	170	21	17	.701	10	4	1	8	12	0	1	0	5.53	4.92	4.59
Harper T.	-20	73.3	322	52	0	3.53	40	24	9	1	88	14	12	.695	1	1	0	4	6	0	3	11	7.00	6.75	5.46
Brazelton D.	-30	71.0	354	20	8	3.69	43	60	3	4	87	12	9	.681	9	5	3	1	8	0	1	1	8.24	7.61	6.73
Waechter D.	-30	157.0	692	29	25	3.37	87	38	5	3	191	29	13	.697	5	4	0	5	12	0	0	0	6.25	5.62	5.12
McClung S.	-30	109.3	501	34	17	3.97	92	62	1	7	106	20	4	.731	6	4	0	7	11	0	1	2	7.00	6.59	5.63
Nomo H.	-32	100.7	471	19	19	3.69	59	51	2	2	127	16	7	.676	7	3	0	5	8	0	0	0	7.33	7.24	5.52
Hendrickson	-36	178.3	796	31	31	3.55	89	49	1	2	227	24	20	.679	3	6	5	11	8	0	0	0	6.36	5.90	4.65

Win Shares Stats (cont.)

Player	WS	Bat	Pitch	Field	ExpWS	WSP	WSAB	CWS	NetWSValue
Perez, E	7	6.9	0.0	0.5	5	.775	4	39	$2,790,524
Fossum, C	6	-0.1	6.4	0.0	9	.361	1	16	$119,210
Gonzalez, A	6	4.2	0.0	1.7	10	.293	-1	114	($1,750,000)
Green, N	6	5.0	0.0	0.7	10	.288	-1	14	($325,000)
Sanchez, A	4	3.6	0.0	0.4	4	.564	2	30	$889,221
Orvella, C	4	0.0	3.9	0.0	4	.541	1	4	$1,098,759
Gathright, J	4	2.6	0.0	1.5	6	.353	0	4	$23,190
Hendrickso, M	4	-0.2	4.0	0.0	10	.198	-2	20	($362,500)
Carter, L	3	0.0	2.8	0.0	4	.348	-0	24	($56,210)
Waechter, D	3	-0.1	2.9	0.0	8	.167	-2	7	($316,000)
McClung, S	0	0.0	0.4	0.0	6	.033	-3	2	($320,000)
Harper, T	0	-0.0	0.2	0.0	5	.014	-3	18	($745,000)
Nomo, H	-1	-0.1	-1.0	0.0	5	-.107	-4	100	($800,000)
Brazelton, D	-2	0.0	-2.6	0.0	4	-.337	-5	5	($1,124,000)

Fielding and Baserunning Stats

Name	POS	Inn	SBA/G	CS%	ERA	WP+PB/G	PO	A	TE	FE
Hall	C	1061.7	0.63	38%	5.15	0.432	761	50	8	1
Johnson	C	136.0	0.99	13%	6.29	0.331	90	3	3	1
LaForest	C	133.0	0.54	25%	5.41	0.271	74	3	0	0
Cash	C	89.0	0.61	50%	6.98	0.607	56	8	0	0
Laker	C	2.0	0.00	0%	4.50	0.000	1	0	0	0

Name	POS	Inn	PO	A	TE	FE	FPct	RF	DPS	DPT
T Lee	1B	918.3	872	67	1	3	.996	9.20	20	0
E Perez	1B	320.0	264	17	0	2	.993	7.90	2	0
A Huff	1B	161.3	134	5	0	0	1.000	7.75	0	0
P LaForest	1B	8.0	4	0	0	0	1.000	4.50	0	0
J Phelps	1B	6.0	5	0	0	0	1.000	7.50	0	0
T Hall	1B	5.0	5	2	0	0	1.000	12.60	0	0
E Munson	1B	3.0	3	0	0	0	1.000	9.00	0	0
N Green	2B	731.0	141	195	1	2	.988	4.14	23	20
J Cantu	2B	667.7	119	181	3	6	.971	4.04	21	22
F Cortez	2B	23.0	0	3	0	0	1.000	1.17	0	0
J Lugo	SS	1338.0	311	424	12	12	.968	4.94	43	48
A Gonzalez	SS	80.0	12	18	1	1	.938	3.38	1	0
F Cortez	SS	3.0	1	2	0	0	1.000	9.00	0	0
A Gonzalez	3B	779.7	65	173	3	10	.944	2.75	10	0
J Cantu	3B	496.0	31	93	6	6	.912	2.25	9	0
N Green	3B	104.0	4	21	1	2	.893	2.16	1	0
A Huff	3B	21.0	2	2	0	0	1.000	1.71	0	0
E Munson	3B	13.0	1	1	0	0	1.000	1.38	0	0
E Perez	3B	7.0	2	0	0	0	1.000	2.57	0	0
F Cortez	3B	1.0	0	0	0	0	0.000	0.00	0	0
C Crawford	LF	1246.0	341	3	0	2	.994	2.48	2	0
J Gomes	LF	110.0	30	1	0	0	1.000	2.54	0	0
D Hollins	LF	38.0	14	1	1	1	.882	3.55	1	0
E Perez	LF	16.0	2	0	0	0	1.000	1.13	0	0
C Singleton	LF	10.0	0	1	0	0	1.000	0.90	0	0
E Munson	LF	1.0	1	0	0	0	1.000	9.00	0	0
D Hollins	CF	619.0	199	4	0	3	.985	2.95	3	0
J Gathright	CF	505.7	180	3	0	3	.984	3.26	4	0
A Sanchez	CF	144.0	50	1	0	3	.944	3.19	0	0
C Crawford	CF	65.0	20	0	0	0	1.000	2.77	0	0
R Taylor	CF	48.7	17	0	0	0	1.000	3.14	0	0
C Singleton	CF	39.3	15	0	0	0	1.000	3.43	0	0

Name	POS	Inn	PO	A	TE	FE	FPct	RF	DPS	DPT
A Huff	RF	786.7	204	6	0	3	.986	2.40	3	0
J Gomes	RF	291.0	68	6	0	4	.949	2.29	2	0
D Hollins	RF	170.0	38	3	0	1	.976	2.17	4	0
A Sanchez	RF	104.3	15	0	0	0	1.000	1.29	0	0
C Singleton	RF	62.0	20	0	0	1	.952	2.90	0	0
E Perez	RF	5.0	3	0	0	0	1.000	5.40	0	0
R Taylor	RF	1.7	0	0	0	0	0.000	0.00	0	0
N Green	RF	1.0	0	0	0	0	0.000	0.00	0	0

Incremental Baserunning Runs		
Name	**IR**	**IRP**
Julio Lugo	3.12	143
Nick Green	2.25	130
Carl Crawford	2.24	133
Travis Lee	1.18	128
Aubrey Huff	1.16	115
Jonny Gomes	1.16	132
Chris Singleton	0.73	126
Joey Gathright	0.72	146
Damon Hollins	0.66	113
Jorge Cantu	0.63	110
Kevin Cash	0.48	284
Alex Gonzalez	0.47	106
Eduardo Perez	0.42	142
Josh Phelps	0.27	125
Eric Munson	0.22	128
Alex Sanchez	0.13	111
Reggie Taylor	0.02	160
Mark Hendrickson	-0.03	0
Charles Johnson	-0.06	0
Pete LaForest	-0.41	64
Toby Hall	-2.17	48

Texas Rangers

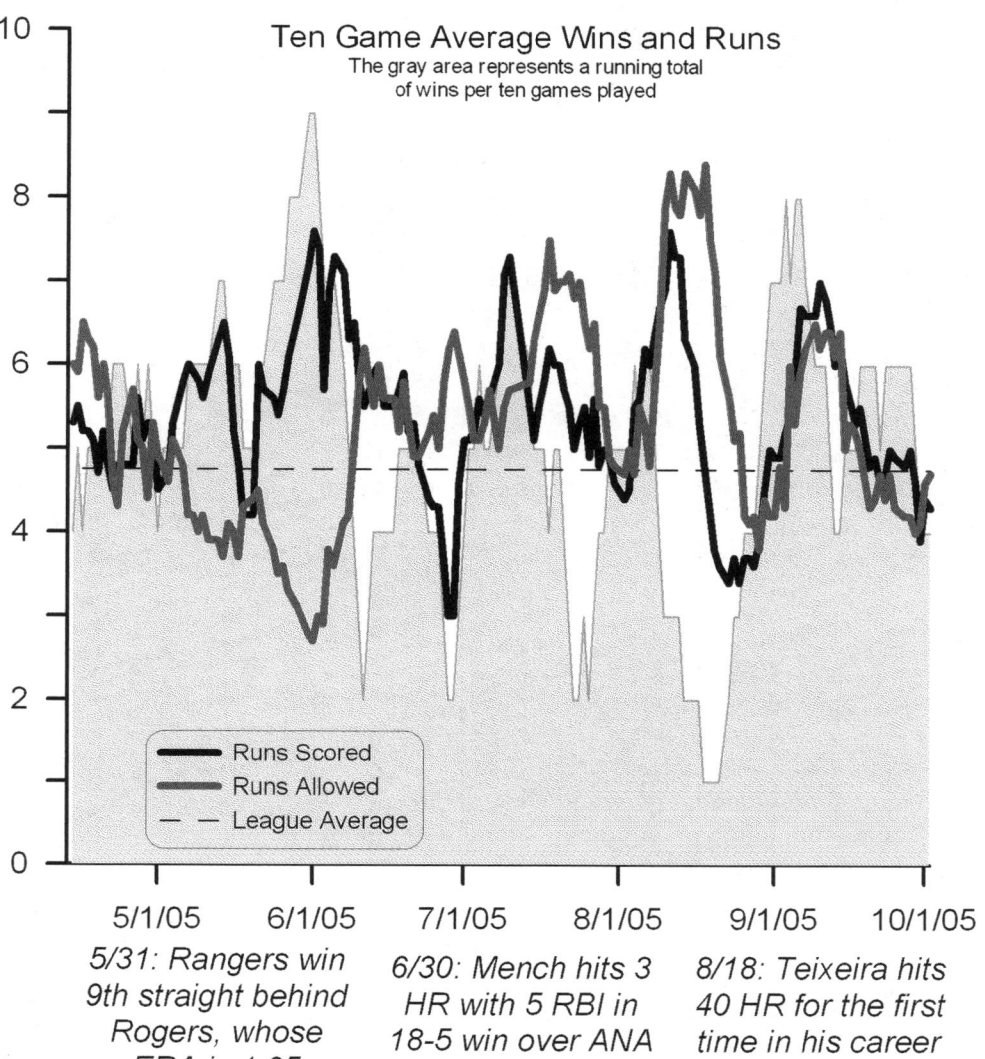

Ten Game Average Wins and Runs
The gray area represents a running total
of wins per ten games played

Runs Scored
Runs Allowed
League Average

5/1/05   6/1/05   7/1/05   8/1/05   9/1/05   10/1/05

*5/31: Rangers win
9th straight behind
Rogers, whose
ERA is 1.65*

*6/30: Mench hits 3
HR with 5 RBI in
18-5 win over ANA*

*8/18: Teixeira hits
40 HR for the first
time in his career*

*6/29: Rogers assaults
cameraman;
suspended 20 games*

*7/30: Trade Park
and cash to SD
for Nevin*

Team Batting and Pitching/Fielding Stats by Month						
	April	May	June	July	Aug	Spt/Oct
Wins	12	18	10	13	11	15
Losses	13	7	17	14	18	14
OBP	.322	.345	.327	.332	.327	.324
SLG	.430	.517	.475	.458	.477	.454
FIP	4.23	3.88	4.44	5.05	4.51	4.39
DER	.698	.709	.665	.714	.685	.705

Batting Stats

Player	RC	Runs	RBI	PA	Outs	P/PA	H	2B	3B	HR	TB	K	BB	IBB	HBP	SH	SF	SB	CS	GDP	BA	OBP	SLG	GPA
Teixeira M.	142	112	144	730	468	3.72	194	41	3	43	370	124	72	5	11	0	3	4	0	18	.301	.379	.575	.314
Young M.	125	114	91	732	469	3.73	221	40	5	24	343	91	58	0	3	0	3	5	2	20	.331	.385	.513	.302
Soriano A.	90	102	104	682	474	3.65	171	43	2	36	326	125	33	3	7	0	5	30	2	6	.268	.309	.512	.267
Blalock H.	83	80	92	705	493	3.74	170	34	0	25	279	132	51	1	3	0	4	1	0	16	.263	.318	.431	.251
Dellucci D.	78	97	65	518	336	4.22	109	17	5	29	223	121	76	0	5	0	2	5	3	7	.251	.367	.513	.293
Mench K.	72	71	73	615	419	3.82	147	33	3	25	261	68	50	4	5	0	3	4	3	6	.264	.328	.469	.265
Matthews Jr.	61	72	55	526	367	3.82	121	25	5	17	207	90	47	1	0	1	3	9	2	11	.255	.320	.436	.253
Barajas R.	53	53	60	450	312	3.80	104	24	0	21	191	70	26	0	6	4	3	0	0	6	.254	.306	.466	.254
Hidalgo R.	33	43	43	339	250	3.88	68	12	0	16	128	74	26	1	4	0	1	1	2	8	.221	.289	.416	.234
Nix L.	25	28	32	240	177	3.54	55	12	3	6	91	45	9	3	0	0	2	2	0	3	.240	.267	.397	.219
DeRosa M.	20	26	20	166	117	3.92	36	5	0	8	65	35	16	0	2	0	0	1	0	5	.243	.325	.439	.256
Alomar Jr. S	13	11	14	137	96	3.58	35	7	0	0	42	12	5	0	1	3	0	0	0	3	.273	.306	.328	.220
Gonzalez A.	13	17	17	162	119	3.66	34	7	1	6	61	37	10	2	0	0	2	0	0	3	.227	.272	.407	.224
Allen C.	6	5	5	56	41	3.84	15	1	1	0	18	13	2	0	0	1	0	0	1	2	.283	.309	.340	.224
Laird G.	4	7	4	42	32	3.36	9	2	0	1	14	7	2	0	0	0	0	0	0	1	.225	.262	.350	.205
Nevin P.	3	15	8	108	87	4.10	18	5	0	3	32	30	8	0	1	0	0	2	0	6	.182	.250	.323	.193
Botts J.	3	4	3	30	20	4.80	8	0	0	0	8	13	3	0	0	0	0	0	0	1	.296	.367	.296	.239
German E.	2	3	1	4	1	4.00	3	1	0	0	4	1	0	0	0	0	0	2	0	0	.750	.750	1.000	.588
Park C.	1	0	0	5	3	3.80	2	0	0	0	2	2	0	0	0	0	0	0	0	0	.400	.400	.400	.280
Torres A.	1	2	1	21	16	4.10	3	1	0	0	4	6	1	0	0	0	1	1	0	0	.158	.190	.211	.138
Rodriguez R.	1	0	1	3	2	2.67	1	0	0	0	1	1	0	0	0	0	0	0	0	0	.333	.333	.333	.233
Rogers K.	1	0	1	3	2	2.67	1	0	1	0	3	1	0	0	0	0	0	0	0	0	.333	.333	1.000	.400
Astacio P.	-0	0	0	1	1	2.00	0	0	0	0	0	0	0	0	0	0	0	0	0	0	.000	.000	.000	.000
Benoit J.	-0	0	0	1	1	3.00	0	0	0	0	0	0	0	0	0	0	0	0	0	0	.000	.000	.000	.000
Wasdin J.	-0	0	0	1	1	2.00	0	0	0	0	0	0	0	0	0	0	0	0	0	0	.000	.000	.000	.000
Drese R.	-0	0	0	1	1	5.00	0	0	0	0	0	1	0	0	0	0	0	0	0	0	.000	.000	.000	.000
McDougall M.	-0	3	0	18	16	4.56	3	1	0	0	4	10	0	0	0	0	0	0	0	1	.167	.167	.222	.131
Young C.	-1	0	0	5	5	4.60	0	0	0	0	0	3	0	0	0	0	0	0	0	0	.000	.000	.000	.000

Win Shares Stats

Player	WS	Bat	Pitch	Field	ExpWS	WSP	WSAB	CWS	NetWSValue
Teixeira, M	32	29.1	0.0	3.3	18	.884	20	69	$11,690,410
Young, M	27	23.0	0.0	4.5	18	.753	15	90	$9,098,605
Rogers, K	18	0.2	17.5	0.0	10	.855	11	189	$7,129,674
Soriano, A	16	14.0	0.0	2.1	17	.463	4	105	($4,983,761)
Dellucci, D	14	13.5	0.0	1.0	11	.656	7	56	$5,011,685
Blalock, H	14	10.4	0.0	4.0	18	.401	2	57	$898,227
Mench, K	13	9.7	0.0	3.3	16	.407	2	42	$1,412,070
Matthews J, G	12	7.4	0.0	4.4	14	.436	2	54	$954,401
Young, C	11	-0.4	12.0	0.0	9	.660	6	13	$4,895,942
Barajas, R	11	7.2	0.0	4.2	12	.476	3	31	$642,010
Cordero, F	10	0.0	10.5	0.0	8	.661	5	50	($98,163)
Loe, K	9	0.0	8.9	0.0	6	.733	5	9	$3,673,437

Continued on the next page.

Pitching Stats

Player	PR	IP	BFP	G	GS	P/PA	K	BB	IBB	HBP	H	HR	DP	DER	SB	CS	PO	W	L	Sv	Op	Hld	RA	ERA	FIP
Rogers K.	21	195.3	828	30	30	3.64	87	53	1	8	205	15	29	.714	3	0	0	14	8	0	0	0	3.96	3.46	4.09
Cordero F.	10	69.0	302	69	0	4.10	79	30	2	4	61	5	2	.696	4	0	0	3	1	37	45	0	3.65	3.39	3.17
Benoit J.	8	87.0	369	32	9	4.09	78	38	0	2	69	9	5	.752	5	2	0	4	4	0	0	5	4.03	3.72	3.97
Loe K.	7	92.0	392	48	8	3.60	45	31	6	2	89	7	10	.733	9	2	0	9	6	1	4	4	4.21	3.42	4.13
Young C.	6	164.7	700	31	31	4.08	137	45	2	7	162	19	8	.709	13	6	0	12	7	0	0	0	4.59	4.26	3.83
Wasdin J.	4	75.7	319	31	6	3.60	44	20	2	1	77	9	5	.722	3	0	0	3	2	4	6	4	4.40	4.28	4.26
Feldman S.	4	9.3	37	8	0	3.38	4	2	1	0	9	0	2	.710	0	1	0	0	1	0	0	1	0.96	0.96	2.83
Ramirez E.	3	23.0	96	16	0	3.28	6	3	0	2	24	3	2	.744	0	0	0	0	0	0	1	0	3.91	3.91	4.87
Dominguez J.	2	70.3	312	22	10	3.74	45	25	0	2	78	11	4	.707	7	1	0	4	6	0	1	0	4.73	4.22	4.95
Rupe J.	1	9.7	39	4	1	4.31	6	4	0	2	7	0	2	.741	1	1	0	1	0	0	0	0	3.72	2.79	3.66
Regilio N.	-0	17.7	83	18	0	4.17	14	7	1	1	22	2	1	.661	0	0	0	1	2	0	2	2	5.09	4.58	4.29
Baldwin J.	-0	17.3	76	8	0	3.75	9	7	1	1	18	3	3	.732	0	0	0	0	2	1	1	0	5.19	5.19	5.64
Standridge J	-2	2.3	16	2	0	3.69	2	1	1	0	7	0	0	.462	1	0	0	0	0	0	0	0	11.57	11.57	2.61
Tejera M.	-2	2.0	13	3	0	4.08	2	1	0	1	5	1	0	.500	0	0	0	0	0	0	0	0	13.50	13.50	10.54
Bukvich R.	-3	4.0	19	4	0	4.32	4	6	0	0	2	0	1	.778	0	0	0	0	0	0	0	1	11.25	11.25	5.54
Thompson J.	-3	1.7	9	2	0	3.00	1	0	0	0	4	2	0	.667	1	0	0	0	0	0	0	0	21.60	21.60	17.44
Almanzar C.	-5	5.0	33	6	0	3.97	3	7	0	1	10	2	0	.600	0	0	0	0	0	0	0	0	14.40	14.40	11.84
Karsay S.	-5	15.7	77	14	0	3.82	9	5	0	0	26	2	2	.607	0	0	0	0	1	0	0	2	8.04	7.47	4.51
Dickey R.	-6	29.7	134	9	4	3.70	15	17	0	2	29	4	4	.740	3	0	0	1	2	0	0	0	6.98	6.67	5.71
Riley M.	-7	12.7	62	7	0	3.84	4	10	0	1	16	2	2	.689	0	1	0	1	0	0	0	0	9.95	9.95	7.07
Rodriguez R.	-7	57.0	255	12	10	3.54	24	17	0	1	67	11	5	.723	0	0	0	2	3	0	0	0	6.16	5.53	5.66
Brocail D.	-7	73.3	344	61	0	3.84	61	34	3	4	90	2	9	.638	4	0	0	5	3	1	4	5	5.89	5.52	3.29
Shouse B.	-7	53.3	233	64	0	3.64	35	18	4	3	55	7	5	.718	2	2	1	3	2	0	2	11	6.24	5.23	4.62
Astacio P.	-8	67.0	288	12	12	3.60	45	11	1	1	79	13	4	.697	7	1	0	2	8	0	0	0	6.04	6.04	4.76
Mahay R.	-8	35.7	166	30	0	3.93	30	16	1	0	47	8	3	.652	1	1	0	0	2	1	1	6	7.07	6.81	5.62
Park C.	-9	109.7	502	20	20	4.05	80	54	1	6	130	8	19	.655	2	2	0	8	5	0	0	0	5.74	5.66	4.17
Gryboski K.	-9	9.7	55	11	0	3.82	2	8	2	1	17	1	1	.628	0	0	0	1	1	0	0	3	13.97	11.17	6.77
Wilson C.	-12	48.0	220	24	6	3.72	30	18	1	2	63	6	5	.648	1	0	0	1	7	1	1	4	7.31	6.94	4.40
Drese R.	-13	69.7	317	12	12	3.45	20	24	1	3	96	5	12	.657	1	6	1	4	6	0	0	0	6.72	6.46	4.56
Volquez E.	-14	12.7	75	6	3	3.84	11	10	0	2	25	3	1	.551	1	0	0	0	4	0	0	0	15.63	14.21	7.23

Win Shares Stats (cont.)

Player	WS	Bat	Pitch	Field	ExpWS	WSP	WSAB	CWS	NetWSValue
Benoit, J	7	-0.0	7.1	0.0	5	.651	3	19	$2,533,452
Wasdin, J	6	-0.0	5.9	0.0	5	.557	2	36	$1,726,468
Dominguez, J	5	0.0	4.6	0.0	4	.614	2	7	$1,875,756
Park, C	5	0.2	4.7	0.0	6	.419	1	87	($8,523,669)
Nix, L	5	2.3	0.0	2.3	6	.369	0	17	$185,702
Hidalgo, R	5	2.8	0.0	2.0	9	.274	-1	98	($3,889,670)
DeRosa, M	3	2.4	0.0	1.2	4	.403	0	24	$255,681
Brocail, D	3	0.0	3.4	0.0	5	.338	-0	47	($504,933)
Shouse, B	2	0.0	2.5	0.0	4	.337	-0	14	($156,713)
Alomar Jr., S	2	0.9	0.0	1.2	4	.283	-0	113	($528,686)
Astacio, P	1	-0.0	1.4	0.0	4	.194	-1	102	$909,539
Drese, R	1	-0.0	1.1	0.0	4	.152	-1	23	($550,000)

Fielding and Baserunning Stats

Name	POS	Inn	SBA/G	CS%	ERA	WP+PB/G	PO	A	TE	FE
Barajas	C	1025.3	0.57	32%	4.98	0.342	689	41	7	1
Alomar Jr.	C	315.7	0.48	0%	4.93	0.342	232	5	2	0
Laird	C	99.0	1.00	27%	5.00	0.364	61	5	2	1

Name	POS	Inn	PO	A	TE	FE	FPct	RF	DPS	DPT
M Teixeira	1B	1358.0	1379	100	0	3	.998	9.80	5	0
A Gonzalez	1B	71.0	85	6	1	1	.978	11.54	0	0
P Nevin	1B	9.0	13	1	0	0	1.000	14.00	0	0
R Barajas	1B	1.0	1	0	0	0	1.000	9.00	0	0
M DeRosa	1B	1.0	2	0	0	0	1.000	18.00	0	0
A Soriano	2B	1351.0	283	448	6	15	.972	4.87	41	57
M DeRosa	2B	78.0	13	20	0	1	.971	3.81	1	2
E German	2B	9.0	2	7	1	0	.900	9.00	0	1
McDougall	2B	2.0	0	0	0	0	0.000	0.00	0	0
M Young	SS	1356.0	240	426	9	9	.974	4.42	48	44
M DeRosa	SS	83.0	18	38	0	1	.982	6.07	4	1
McDougall	SS	1.0	1	1	0	0	1.000	18.00	1	0
H Blalock	3B	1374.0	96	304	4	6	.973	2.62	23	1
M DeRosa	3B	36.0	2	5	0	1	.875	1.75	1	0
McDougall	3B	26.0	3	4	0	0	1.000	2.42	0	0
E German	3B	3.0	0	0	0	0	0.000	0.00	0	0
P Nevin	3B	1.0	0	1	0	0	1.000	9.00	0	0
K Mench	LF	978.3	230	8	0	2	.992	2.19	6	0
D Dellucci	LF	378.7	84	4	0	2	.978	2.09	1	0
G Matthews	LF	40.0	8	0	0	0	1.000	1.80	0	0
J Botts	LF	40.0	8	1	0	1	.900	2.03	2	0
C Allen	LF	3.0	0	0	0	0	0.000	0.00	0	0
G Matthews	CF	846.0	257	5	1	4	.981	2.79	3	0
L Nix	CF	526.0	160	3	0	2	.988	2.79	2	0
A Torres	CF	30.0	11	0	0	0	1.000	3.30	0	0
D Dellucci	CF	19.0	3	0	0	0	1.000	1.42	0	0
R Hidalgo	CF	18.0	5	0	0	0	1.000	2.50	0	0
K Mench	CF	1.0	0	0	0	0	0.000	0.00	0	0

Name	POS	Inn	PO	A	TE	FE	FPct	RF	DPS	DPT
R Hidalgo	RF	699.7	174	3	1	1	.989	2.28	0	0
K Mench	RF	311.3	60	0	0	2	.968	1.73	0	0
G Matthews	RF	189.7	51	2	0	1	.981	2.51	3	0
M DeRosa	RF	185.0	46	1	0	0	1.000	2.29	0	0
D Dellucci	RF	26.0	6	0	0	1	.857	2.08	0	0
McDougall	RF	10.0	0	0	0	0	0.000	0.00	0	0
A Gonzalez	RF	8.0	3	0	0	1	.750	3.38	0	0
C Allen	RF	6.0	1	0	0	0	1.000	1.50	0	0
A Torres	RF	3.3	1	0	0	0	1.000	2.70	0	0
G Laird	RF	1.0	0	0	0	0	0.000	0.00	0	0

Incremental Baserunning Runs		
Name	IR	IRP
Michael Young	1.35	119
Mark Teixeira	1.21	113
Kevin Mench	1.18	137
Laynce Nix	1.13	126
Alfonso Soriano	0.94	113
Phil Nevin	0.59	447
David Dellucci	0.56	108
Esteban German	0.41	123
Gary Matthews	0.20	103
Andres Torres	0.17	130
Gerald Laird	0.09	114
Mark DeRosa	-0.08	95
Jason Botts	-0.10	0
Chan Ho Park	-0.10	0
Chad Allen	-0.26	58
Adrian Gonzalez	-0.37	70
Sandy Alomar	-0.52	59
Richard Hidalgo	-0.68	83
Rod Barajas	-1.77	60
Hank Blalock	-2.65	40

Toronto Blue Jays

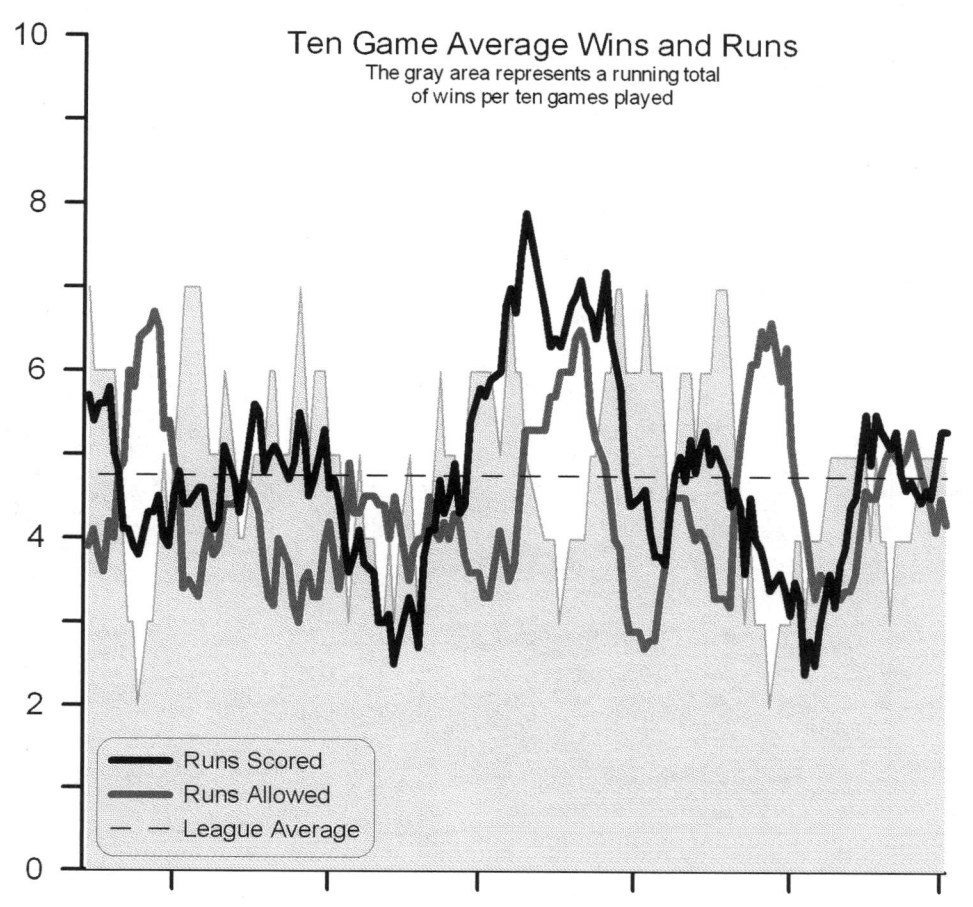

Ten Game Average Wins and Runs
The gray area represents a running total
of wins per ten games played

- Runs Scored
- Runs Allowed
- - League Average

4/16: Chacin shuts out TEX over 8 innings for third win to begin season; will go 13-9, 3.72

4/17 - Fall out of first after starting season atop division for first 13 days

7/10 - Halladay (12-4, 2.41 ERA) goes on DL with fractured leg, misses rest of season

7/28: Rally in 9th for eventual 2-1 win vs. ANA in 18 innings; longest game in franchise history

9/11 - Lose to TB; will not be above .500 again

Team Batting and Pitching/Fielding Stats by Month						
	April	May	June	July	Aug	Spt/Oct
Wins	13	15	12	13	13	14
Losses	12	12	15	12	15	16
OBP	.340	.326	.322	.354	.324	.321
SLG	.414	.436	.377	.449	.395	.376
FIP	4.37	4.27	4.48	4.51	4.79	4.32
DER	.707	.725	.724	.702	.710	.717

Batting Stats

Player	RC	Runs	RBI	PA	Outs	P/PA	H	2B	3B	HR	TB	K	BB	IBB	HBP	SH	SF	SB	CS	GDP	BA	OBP	SLG	GPA
Wells V.	93	78	97	678	469	3.38	167	30	3	28	287	86	47	3	3	0	8	8	3	13	.269	.320	.463	.260
Hillenbrand	86	91	82	645	443	3.37	173	36	2	18	267	79	26	2	22	0	3	5	1	21	.291	.343	.449	.267
Catalanotto	77	56	59	475	304	3.89	126	29	5	8	189	53	37	0	10	4	5	0	2	9	.301	.367	.451	.278
Hinske E.	69	79	68	537	364	3.89	125	31	2	15	205	121	46	4	8	0	6	8	4	8	.262	.333	.430	.257
Adams R.	64	68	63	545	365	3.74	123	27	5	8	184	57	50	1	3	3	8	11	2	5	.256	.325	.383	.242
Zaun G.	63	61	61	512	339	4.25	109	18	1	11	162	70	73	2	0	0	5	2	3	11	.251	.355	.373	.253
Hudson O.	57	62	63	501	347	3.60	125	25	5	10	190	65	30	1	3	0	7	7	1	10	.271	.315	.412	.245
Johnson R.	55	55	58	439	305	3.92	107	21	6	8	164	82	22	1	16	2	1	5	6	8	.269	.332	.412	.252
Rios A.	54	71	59	519	378	3.56	126	23	6	10	191	101	28	1	5	0	5	14	9	14	.262	.306	.397	.237
Hill A.	48	49	40	407	268	3.46	99	25	3	3	139	41	34	0	5	3	4	2	1	5	.274	.342	.385	.250
Koskie C.	39	49	36	404	277	4.15	88	20	0	11	141	90	44	3	4	0	2	4	1	10	.249	.337	.398	.251
McDonald J.	13	8	12	106	69	3.61	27	3	0	0	30	12	6	0	2	3	2	5	0	3	.290	.340	.323	.234
Menechino F.	12	22	13	180	120	3.98	32	7	0	4	51	33	25	0	6	1	0	0	1	3	.216	.352	.345	.245
Gross G.	11	11	7	102	70	4.20	23	4	1	1	32	21	10	0	0	0	0	1	1	0	.250	.324	.348	.233
Huckaby K.	4	8	6	96	72	3.46	18	4	0	0	22	19	5	0	0	4	0	0	0	3	.207	.250	.253	.176
Quiroz G.	3	3	4	39	29	3.54	7	2	0	0	9	13	2	0	1	0	0	0	0	0	.194	.256	.250	.178
Griffin J.	2	3	6	13	9	3.62	4	2	0	1	9	4	0	0	0	0	0	0	0	0	.308	.308	.692	.312
Dominique A.	0	0	0	3	2	2.67	0	0	0	0	0	0	0	0	1	0	0	0	0	0	.000	.333	.000	.150
Halladay R.	-0	0	0	2	2	5.00	0	0	0	0	0	1	0	0	0	0	0	0	0	0	.000	.000	.000	.000
Lilly T.	-0	0	0	3	3	3.67	0	0	0	0	0	2	0	0	0	0	0	0	0	0	.000	.000	.000	.000
Towers J.	-1	0	0	6	6	2.67	0	0	0	0	0	2	0	0	0	0	0	0	0	0	.000	.000	.000	.000
Chacin G.	-1	1	0	8	7	2.50	0	0	0	0	0	2	0	0	0	1	0	0	0	0	.000	.000	.000	.000
Myers G.	-1	0	1	13	13	2.69	1	0	0	0	1	1	1	0	0	0	0	0	0	2	.083	.154	.083	.090

Pitching Stats

Player	PR	IP	BFP	G	GS	P/PA	K	BB	IBB	HBP	H	HR	DP	DER	SB	CS	PO	W	L	Sv	Op	Hld	RA	ERA	FIP
Halladay R.	36	141.7	553	19	19	3.46	108	18	2	7	118	11	15	.738	16	2	0	12	4	0	0	0	2.48	2.41	3.06
Chacin G.	16	203.0	872	34	34	3.72	121	70	3	8	213	20	24	.704	8	10	5	13	9	0	0	0	4.12	3.72	4.28
Speier J.	16	66.7	264	65	0	3.96	56	15	1	3	48	10	3	.789	2	2	0	3	2	0	4	11	2.70	2.57	4.12
Walker P.	12	84.0	358	41	4	3.67	43	33	0	2	81	10	8	.737	4	2	2	6	6	2	5	4	3.54	3.54	4.82
Towers J.	11	208.7	876	33	33	3.37	112	29	2	6	237	24	22	.698	14	5	1	13	12	0	0	0	4.36	3.71	3.97
Frasor J.	9	74.7	305	67	0	4.10	62	28	2	3	67	8	17	.711	5	3	0	3	5	1	3	15	3.74	3.25	4.02
Schoeneweis	8	57.0	250	80	0	3.47	43	25	5	4	54	2	7	.705	8	1	1	3	4	1	4	21	3.63	3.32	3.52
Chulk V.	6	72.0	301	62	0	3.72	39	26	3	1	68	9	8	.739	4	0	1	0	1	0	1	13	4.13	3.88	4.71
Marcum S.	4	8.0	32	5	0	4.38	4	4	0	0	6	0	2	.750	0	0	0	0	0	0	0	0	0.00	0.00	3.54
Downs S.	2	94.0	407	26	13	3.85	75	34	0	5	93	12	11	.712	0	2	0	4	3	0	0	0	4.69	4.31	4.35
Batista M.	1	74.7	331	71	0	3.69	54	27	5	2	80	9	7	.703	2	0	0	5	8	31	39	0	4.70	4.10	4.33
Bush D.	0	136.3	575	25	24	3.72	75	29	3	13	142	20	12	.721	16	4	0	5	11	0	0	0	4.82	4.49	4.77
Miller J.	-3	2.3	12	1	0	3.42	2	0	0	0	5	3	0	.714	0	0	0	0	0	0	0	0	15.43	15.43	18.04
Whiteside M.	-6	3.7	23	2	0	4.26	5	5	0	1	6	3	0	.667	2	0	0	0	0	0	0	0	19.64	19.64	15.86
League B.	-8	35.7	162	20	0	3.53	17	20	1	2	42	8	8	.704	0	0	0	1	0	0	0	1	6.81	6.56	6.86
McGowan D.	-9	45.3	205	13	7	3.74	34	17	0	7	49	7	2	.700	7	3	1	1	3	0	0	1	6.75	6.35	5.14
Lilly T.	-11	126.3	566	25	25	3.78	96	58	1	3	135	23	8	.710	10	1	1	10	11	0	0	0	5.63	5.56	5.34
Gaudin C.	-12	13.0	74	5	3	3.92	12	6	0	1	31	6	1	.490	2	0	1	1	3	0	0	0	13.15	13.15	8.81

Win Shares Stats

Player	WS	Bat	Pitch	Field	ExpWS	WSP	WSAB	CWS	NetWSValue
Wells, V	21	14.5	0.0	6.7	18	.598	9	82	$3,857,412
Halladay, R	16	-0.1	16.1	0.0	8	1.068	12	90	($2,361,920)
Catalanott, F	16	13.9	0.0	2.6	12	.699	8	78	$5,025,871
Hudson, O	15	7.0	0.0	7.9	13	.557	6	56	$4,305,120
Zaun, G	15	8.6	0.0	5.9	14	.535	5	64	$3,589,443
Hillenbran, S	15	12.8	0.0	2.2	16	.470	4	62	($960,655)
Chacin, G	14	-0.5	14.6	0.0	11	.650	8	16	$5,994,742
Towers, J	14	-0.4	14.2	0.0	11	.618	7	31	$5,535,523
Hinske, E	12	10.4	0.0	1.2	13	.437	2	53	($1,298,952)
Johnson, R	11	7.6	0.0	2.9	12	.459	3	32	$1,962,528
Adams, R	10	8.3	0.0	2.2	14	.367	0	12	$391,724
Hill, A	9	6.6	0.0	2.8	10	.477	2	9	$1,969,529
Rios, A	9	5.4	0.0	4.0	14	.342	-0	16	($186,883)
Speier, J	8	0.0	7.6	0.0	5	.805	4	41	$1,631,439
Walker, P	7	0.0	7.2	0.0	6	.635	3	21	$2,500,055
Frasor, J	6	0.0	6.3	0.0	5	.594	3	13	$2,015,194
Bush, D	6	0.0	6.2	0.0	7	.432	2	14	$1,484,959
Batista, M	6	0.0	6.3	0.0	8	.391	1	63	($2,165,361)
Koskie, C	6	4.0	0.0	2.4	10	.317	-1	114	($2,463,027)
Schoenewei, S	5	0.0	5.4	0.0	4	.605	2	33	$471,252
Downs, S	5	0.0	5.1	0.0	5	.513	2	8	$1,667,798
Chulk, V	5	0.0	4.6	0.0	5	.472	1	9	$929,227
Lilly, T	4	-0.1	4.0	0.0	7	.291	-0	39	($3,100,000)
Menechino, F	2	0.1	0.0	1.5	4	.189	-1	39	($650,000)

Fielding and Baserunning Stats

Name	POS	Inn	SBA/G	CS%	ERA	WP+PB/G	PO	A	TE	FE
Zaun	C	1088.0	0.74	19%	3.79	0.265	761	49	5	3
Huckaby	C	243.0	0.74	40%	4.85	0.370	144	11	1	0
Quiroz	C	85.0	1.38	15%	4.98	0.318	57	4	0	0
Myers	C	25.0	1.44	25%	5.04	0.000	20	1	0	0
Dominique	C	6.0	3.00	0%	4.50	0.000	4	0	0	0

Name	POS	Inn	PO	A	TE	FE	FPct	RF	DPS	DPT
E Hinske	1B	859.7	867	69	1	5	.993	9.80	8	0
S Hillenbran	1B	587.3	627	48	1	4	.991	10.34	9	1
O Hudson	2B	1067.0	302	390	3	3	.991	5.84	35	47
F Menechino	2B	178.3	36	70	0	1	.991	5.35	8	10
A Hill	2B	177.7	33	77	0	1	.991	5.57	9	6
J McDonald	2B	23.3	9	7	0	0	1.000	6.17	2	1
R Adams	SS	1100.0	194	325	13	13	.952	4.25	31	35
J McDonald	SS	224.0	38	88	1	2	.977	5.06	10	10
A Hill	SS	121.0	18	47	0	0	1.000	4.83	2	6
F Menechino	SS	2.0	1	1	0	0	1.000	9.00	0	1
C Koskie	3B	674.3	53	157	3	4	.968	2.80	19	1
S Hillenbran	3B	451.0	31	94	1	5	.954	2.49	9	0
A Hill	3B	286.7	21	73	3	2	.949	2.95	8	0
F Menechino	3B	35.0	2	9	0	0	1.000	2.83	1	0
F Catalanott	LF	761.0	163	4	0	0	1.000	1.98	0	0
R Johnson	LF	590.7	134	4	1	0	.993	2.10	1	0
G Gross	LF	95.3	19	1	0	0	1.000	1.89	2	0
V Wells	CF	1358.0	351	12	0	0	1.000	2.41	8	0
R Johnson	CF	53.0	11	0	0	0	1.000	1.87	0	0
A Rios	CF	36.0	12	0	0	0	1.000	3.00	0	0
A Rios	RF	1056.0	245	7	1	1	.992	2.15	2	0
R Johnson	RF	247.0	51	1	1	0	.981	1.89	0	0
G Gross	RF	143.3	32	1	1	0	.971	2.07	0	0

Incremental Baserunning Runs		
Name	IR	IRP
Eric Hinske	2.14	140
Shea Hillenbrand	1.67	129
Russ Adams	0.81	114
Alex Rios	0.71	117
Orlando Hudson	0.67	111
John-Ford Griffin	0.66	886
Aaron Hill	0.29	106
Reed Johnson	0.18	104
Frank Menechino	0.16	107
Corey Koskie	0.05	102
Ken Huckaby	-0.16	74
Gabe Gross	-0.26	64
Vernon Wells	-0.39	89
John McDonald	-0.89	-11
Gregg Zaun	-1.17	77
Frank Catalanotto	-1.61	71

Washington Nationals

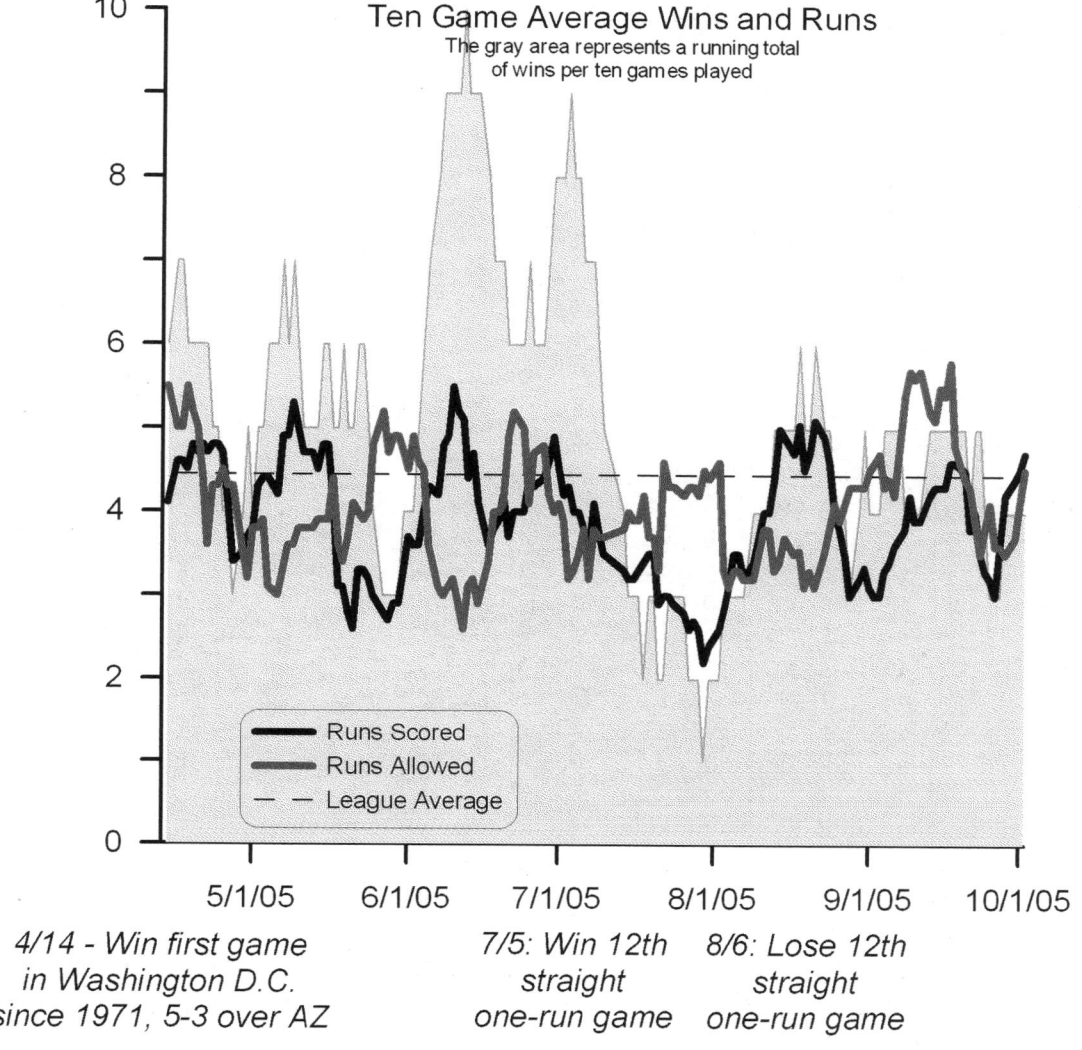

Ten Game Average Wins and Runs
The gray area represents a running total
of wins per ten games played

Runs Scored
Runs Allowed
– – League Average

4/14 - Win first game
in Washington D.C.
since 1971, 5-3 over AZ

7/5: Win 12th
straight
one-run game

8/6: Lose 12th
straight
one-run game

6/12: Finish 10
game winning
streak in first
place

7/1 - Hernandez
wins eleventh
straight game

Team Batting and Pitching/Fielding Stats by Month						
	April	May	June	July	Aug	Spt/Oct
Wins	13	14	20	9	13	12
Losses	11	14	6	18	15	17
OBP	.327	.326	.346	.296	.317	.321
SLG	.441	.362	.418	.330	.391	.383
FIP	4.12	4.41	4.20	3.67	4.19	4.52
DER	.716	.723	.699	.702	.698	.722

Batting Stats

Player	RC	Runs	RBI	PA	Outs	P/PA	H	2B	3B	HR	TB	K	BB	IBB	HBP	SH	SF	SB	CS	GDP	BA	OBP	SLG	GPA
Wilkerson B.	91	76	57	661	441	4.22	140	42	7	11	229	147	84	9	7	3	2	8	10	6	.248	.351	.405	.259
Johnson N.	90	66	74	547	345	4.11	131	35	3	15	217	87	80	8	12	0	2	3	8	15	.289	.408	.479	.303
Guillen J.	78	81	76	611	410	3.46	156	32	2	24	264	102	31	6	19	1	9	1	1	14	.283	.338	.479	.272
Castilla V.	57	53	66	549	387	3.52	125	36	1	12	199	82	43	7	7	1	4	4	2	16	.253	.319	.403	.244
Schneider B.	52	38	44	408	280	3.55	99	20	1	10	151	48	29	7	6	2	2	1	0	10	.268	.330	.409	.251
Vidro J.	45	38	32	347	233	3.52	85	21	2	7	131	30	31	3	1	2	4	0	0	9	.275	.339	.424	.259
Wilson P.	42	34	43	280	201	3.88	66	14	1	10	112	71	20	0	6	0	1	3	4	10	.261	.329	.443	.259
Carroll J.	41	44	22	358	233	4.09	76	8	1	0	86	55	34	1	5	13	3	3	4	2	.251	.333	.284	.221
Church R.	37	41	42	301	199	3.75	77	15	3	9	125	70	24	0	5	1	3	3	2	6	.287	.353	.466	.276
Byrd M.	31	20	26	244	165	4.19	57	15	2	2	82	47	18	1	1	5	4	5	1	5	.264	.318	.380	.238
Guzman C.	29	39	31	492	372	3.20	100	19	6	4	143	76	25	6	1	8	2	7	4	12	.219	.260	.314	.196
Bennett G.	19	11	21	228	163	3.93	44	7	0	1	54	37	21	3	2	3	3	0	1	7	.221	.298	.271	.202
Baerga C.	18	18	19	174	122	3.59	40	7	0	2	53	17	7	0	8	1	0	0	0	4	.253	.318	.335	.227
Spivey J.	13	15	7	91	60	4.11	17	7	0	2	30	26	11	1	2	0	1	2	0	0	.221	.330	.390	.246
Zimmerman R.	9	6	6	62	36	3.50	23	10	0	0	33	12	3	0	0	0	1	0	0	1	.397	.419	.569	.331
Blanco T.	8	7	7	65	51	3.85	11	3	0	1	17	19	2	0	1	0	0	1	0	0	.177	.215	.274	.165
Short R.	6	4	4	17	9	3.18	6	2	0	2	14	1	1	0	1	0	0	0	0	0	.400	.471	.933	.445
Sledge T.	5	7	8	46	32	4.00	9	0	1	1	14	8	7	1	0	0	2	2	1	3	.243	.348	.378	.251
Hernandez L.	4	7	7	97	66	2.81	20	2	1	2	30	8	0	0	1	14	0	0	0	4	.244	.253	.366	.205
Cruz D.	4	2	1	54	38	3.31	13	1	0	0	14	3	1	0	1	1	0	0	0	0	.255	.283	.275	.196
Watson B.	3	8	5	48	35	3.69	7	1	1	1	13	8	4	0	0	4	0	0	2	0	.175	.250	.325	.194
Harris B.	3	1	3	10	8	2.60	3	1	0	1	7	0	0	0	1	0	0	0	0	2	.333	.400	.778	.374
Davis J.	2	0	2	28	23	3.82	6	0	0	0	6	7	2	0	0	0	0	1	1	2	.231	.286	.231	.186
Hammonds J.	2	3	1	37	25	3.62	7	1	0	0	8	4	2	1	1	2	0	0	0	0	.219	.286	.250	.191
Cepicky M.	2	1	3	26	21	3.04	6	3	0	0	9	8	1	0	0	0	0	0	1	1	.240	.269	.360	.211
Chavez E.	1	2	1	12	9	3.92	2	1	0	0	3	1	3	0	0	0	0	0	1	1	.222	.417	.333	.271
Ohka T.	1	1	0	17	12	2.53	4	0	0	0	4	5	0	0	0	1	0	0	0	0	.250	.250	.250	.175
Loaiza E.	1	3	4	80	64	3.01	12	2	0	0	14	23	0	0	0	6	0	0	1	1	.162	.162	.189	.120
Bergmann J.	1	2	0	4	2	3.50	1	0	0	0	1	0	1	0	0	0	0	0	0	0	.333	.500	.333	.308
Rauch J.	1	1	1	8	6	3.25	1	0	0	0	1	5	0	0	0	1	0	0	0	0	.143	.143	.143	.100
Kelly K.	1	3	0	5	4	3.80	1	1	0	0	2	3	1	0	0	0	0	1	1	0	.250	.400	.500	.305
Ayala L.	0	0	0	4	2	2.00	1	0	0	0	1	0	0	0	0	1	0	0	0	0	.333	.333	.333	.233
Eischen J.	0	0	0	4	2	3.00	1	0	0	0	1	2	0	0	0	1	0	0	0	0	.333	.333	.333	.233
Mateo H.	0	0	0	2	1	5.50	0	0	0	0	0	0	1	0	0	0	0	0	0	0	.000	.500	.000	.225
Halama J.	0	0	0	5	4	3.60	1	0	0	0	1	1	0	0	0	0	0	0	0	0	.200	.200	.200	.140
Vargas C.	-0	0	0	2	1	4.00	1	0	0	0	1	0	0	0	0	0	0	0	0	0	.500	.500	.500	.350
Stanton M.	-0	1	0	1	1	4.00	0	0	0	0	0	0	0	0	0	0	0	0	0	0	.000	.000	.000	.000
White M.	-0	0	0	1	1	1.00	0	0	0	0	0	0	0	0	0	0	0	0	0	0	.000	.000	.000	.000
Day Z.	-0	0	0	9	7	3.67	1	0	0	0	1	3	0	0	0	1	0	0	0	0	.125	.125	.125	.088
Godwin T.	-0	0	0	3	3	2.33	0	0	0	0	0	1	0	0	0	0	0	0	0	0	.000	.000	.000	.000
Kim S.	-0	0	0	6	4	2.33	0	0	0	0	0	1	0	0	0	2	0	0	0	0	.000	.000	.000	.000
Osik K.	-0	0	0	4	4	4.00	0	0	0	0	0	2	0	0	0	0	0	0	0	0	.000	.000	.000	.000
Majewski G.	-1	0	0	7	6	2.86	0	0	0	0	0	3	0	0	0	1	0	0	0	0	.000	.000	.000	.000
Carrasco H.	-1	1	0	10	8	3.60	0	0	0	0	0	7	0	0	0	2	0	0	0	0	.000	.000	.000	.000
Drese R.	-1	0	0	19	13	3.42	1	0	0	0	1	10	0	0	0	5	0	0	0	0	.071	.071	.071	.050
Armas Jr. T.	-1	1	0	34	28	3.68	4	0	0	0	4	13	1	0	0	1	0	0	0	0	.125	.152	.125	.099
Cordero W.	-2	2	2	56	45	3.98	6	2	0	0	8	14	3	1	0	0	2	0	0	0	.118	.161	.157	.112
Patterson J.	-2	2	0	68	53	3.04	6	3	0	0	9	23	0	0	1	8	0	0	0	0	.102	.117	.153	.091

Pitching Stats

Player	PR	IP	BFP	G	GS	P/PA	K	BB	IBB	HBP	H	HR	DP	DER	SB	CS	PO	W	L	Sv	Op	Hld	RA	ERA	FIP
Patterson J.	26	198.3	817	31	31	3.89	185	65	11	5	172	19	12	.718	26	11	2	9	7	0	0	0	3.22	3.13	3.42
Carrasco H.	21	88.3	358	64	5	4.04	75	38	7	6	59	6	10	.773	4	0	2	5	4	2	4	8	2.34	2.04	3.66
Cordero C.	12	74.3	300	74	0	4.03	61	17	2	2	55	9	3	.782	1	2	0	2	4	47	54	0	2.91	1.82	3.68
Loaiza E.	12	217.0	912	34	34	3.66	173	55	3	5	227	18	30	.684	4	2	0	12	10	0	0	0	3.86	3.77	3.30
Ayala L.	12	71.0	293	68	0	3.48	40	14	4	6	75	7	14	.699	2	0	0	8	7	1	3	22	2.92	2.66	3.98
Majewski G.	10	86.0	376	79	0	3.78	50	37	6	7	80	2	8	.721	2	0	0	4	4	1	5	24	3.35	2.93	3.66
Eischen J.	4	36.3	169	57	0	3.70	30	19	7	6	34	1	2	.708	2	0	0	2	1	0	1	8	3.47	3.22	3.75
Bergmann J.	4	19.7	85	15	1	3.88	21	11	1	2	14	1	2	.740	3	1	0	2	0	0	0	1	2.75	2.75	3.49
Ohka T.	3	54.0	231	10	9	3.80	17	27	1	1	44	6	6	.789	1	3	0	4	3	0	0	0	3.83	3.33	5.35
Rauch J.	3	30.0	124	15	1	3.98	23	11	2	1	24	3	2	.756	4	0	0	2	4	0	0	0	3.60	3.60	3.95
Hernandez L.	2	246.3	1065	35	35	3.76	147	84	14	13	268	25	30	.695	14	11	2	15	10	0	0	0	4.24	3.98	4.29
Rasner D.	1	7.3	31	5	1	3.97	4	2	1	2	5	0	1	.783	0	0	0	0	1	0	0	0	3.68	3.68	3.53
Stanton M.	0	27.7	118	30	0	3.54	14	9	4	0	31	2	6	.688	2	0	1	2	1	0	1	5	4.23	3.58	3.89
Halama J.	-1	21.3	93	10	3	3.52	11	8	0	0	23	1	2	.699	1	1	1	0	3	0	0	0	4.64	4.64	3.69
Nitkowski C.	-1	3.3	17	7	0	3.24	2	2	0	0	5	0	0	.615	0	0	0	0	0	0	0	1	8.10	8.10	3.58
Hughes T.	-2	13.0	64	14	0	3.67	8	8	1	1	18	4	1	.674	0	1	0	1	1	0	1	0	5.54	5.54	7.83
White M.	-2	4.0	20	1	1	3.30	3	3	0	1	4	0	0	.692	0	0	0	0	1	0	0	0	9.00	9.00	4.48
Tucker T.	-3	12.7	58	13	0	3.93	5	2	0	0	20	4	1	.660	1	0	0	1	0	0	0	0	6.39	6.39	6.77
Kim S.	-6	29.3	135	12	2	3.60	17	8	2	2	41	3	4	.638	1	1	0	1	2	0	0	0	6.14	6.14	4.18
Armas Jr. T.	-9	101.3	451	19	19	3.97	59	54	4	5	100	16	10	.735	3	4	1	7	7	0	0	0	5.06	4.97	5.62
Vargas C.	-9	12.7	66	4	4	3.80	5	7	2	0	22	4	1	.640	0	0	0	0	3	0	0	0	10.66	9.24	7.96
Drese R.	-10	59.7	266	11	11	3.56	26	22	1	5	66	3	6	.700	3	3	1	3	6	0	0	0	5.73	4.98	4.12
Osuna A.	-10	2.3	23	4	0	3.61	0	7	1	0	9	2	0	.500	0	0	0	0	0	0	0	0	42.43	42.43	23.13
Day Z.	-12	36.0	170	12	5	3.75	16	25	3	1	41	4	5	.702	2	1	0	1	2	0	0	0	7.25	6.75	5.70
Horgan J.	-13	6.0	44	8	0	3.14	5	4	0	1	19	0	1	.441	0	0	0	0	0	0	0	0	22.50	21.00	3.82

Win Shares Stats

Player	WS	Bat	Pitch	Field	ExpWS	WSP	WSAB	CWS	NetWSValue
Wilkerson, B	23	18.4	0.0	4.3	18	.644	10	81	$5,085,883
Johnson, N	22	20.6	0.0	1.8	15	.764	12	54	$8,326,520
Guillen, J	18	14.7	0.0	3.2	16	.549	7	90	$3,203,468
Schneider, B	17	9.2	0.0	7.4	11	.732	9	59	$4,936,642
Cordero, C	12	0.0	11.8	0.0	7	.823	7	24	$5,325,048
Patterson, J	12	-2.6	14.7	0.0	10	.629	6	17	$4,987,671
Hernandez, L	12	-0.9	12.8	0.0	11	.523	5	103	($645,462)
Castilla, V	12	8.2	0.0	3.7	15	.396	1	157	($538,102)
Loaiza, E	11	-1.7	12.6	0.0	10	.527	5	95	$2,148,746
Vidro, J	11	8.3	0.0	2.5	9	.589	4	130	($569,891)
Wilson, P	10	8.7	0.0	1.7	8	.680	5	87	($3,198,906)
Carrasco, H	9	-0.7	9.8	0.0	5	.942	6	50	$4,504,217
Church, R	9	6.5	0.0	2.3	8	.544	3	9	$2,469,710
Carroll, J	9	5.8	0.0	3.4	10	.477	2	21	$1,915,584
Ayala, L	7	-0.1	7.2	0.0	4	.831	4	27	$3,220,583
Majewski, G	7	-0.6	7.2	0.0	5	.636	3	7	$2,368,788
Byrd, M	7	5.5	0.0	1.5	7	.533	2	28	$2,009,620
Bennett, G	5	1.2	0.0	3.4	6	.366	0	24	($105,055)
Guzman, C	3	-1.9	0.0	5.2	14	.121	-6	79	($4,200,000)
Armas Jr., T	1	-1.2	2.8	0.0	5	.156	-1	30	($2,260,000)

Fielding and Baserunning Stats

Name	POS	Inn	SBA/G	CS%	ERA	WP+PB/G	PO	A	TE	FE
Schneider	C	926.7	0.75	38%	3.88	0.369	654	52	3	2
Bennett	C	523.3	0.53	19%	3.87	0.310	384	25	3	3
Osik	C	8.0	3.38	0%	2.25	0.000	8	0	0	0

Name	POS	Inn	PO	A	TE	FE	FPct	RF	DPS	DPT
N Johnson	1B	1098.0	1017	95	2	2	.996	9.11	12	1
B Wilkerson	1B	185.3	172	14	0	0	.995	9.03	4	0
C Baerga	1B	86.7	65	2	0	1	.985	6.96	0	0
W Cordero	1B	68.7	66	2	0	0	1.000	8.91	2	0
T Blanco	1B	14.0	11	1	0	2	.857	7.71	0	0
R Short	1B	4.7	4	1	0	0	1.000	9.64	0	0
J Vidro	2B	665.3	134	191	1	4	.985	4.40	18	19
J Carroll	2B	427.7	96	145	3	2	.980	5.07	11	18
J Spivey	2B	190.0	34	62	0	0	1.000	4.55	7	6
D Cruz	2B	79.7	27	25	0	0	1.000	5.87	3	5
C Baerga	2B	46.0	15	19	0	3	.919	6.65	1	2
R Short	2B	30.0	7	8	0	1	.938	4.50	0	2
B Harris	2B	13.3	2	5	0	0	1.000	4.73	0	1
H Mateo	2B	6.0	1	2	0	0	1.000	4.50	0	0
C Guzman	SS	1161.0	217	327	8	7	.973	4.22	44	42
J Carroll	SS	241.0	53	65	0	0	1.000	4.41	7	10
D Cruz	SS	47.0	4	13	0	1	.944	3.26	2	0
R Zimmerman	SS	9.0	3	4	0	2	.778	7.00	0	0
V Castilla	3B	1171.0	142	209	3	8	.970	2.70	21	1
R Zimmerman	3B	111.0	6	26	0	0	1.000	2.59	4	1
C Baerga	3B	100.7	7	16	0	2	.920	2.06	1	0
J Carroll	3B	54.0	1	8	0	0	1.000	1.50	0	0
T Blanco	3B	13.0	0	3	0	0	1.000	2.08	0	0
B Harris	3B	8.0	1	4	0	0	1.000	5.63	0	0
M Byrd	LF	386.0	101	5	1	1	.981	2.47	4	0
R Church	LF	334.7	77	2	0	0	1.000	2.12	0	0
B Wilkerson	LF	288.3	67	0	1	0	.985	2.09	0	0
P Wilson	LF	94.0	20	0	0	0	1.000	1.91	0	0
T Sledge	LF	79.3	21	1	0	0	1.000	2.50	0	0
B Watson	LF	69.0	11	1	0	1	.923	1.57	0	0
J Hammonds	LF	58.0	16	0	0	0	1.000	2.48	0	0
J Davis	LF	54.0	15	1	0	0	1.000	2.67	0	0
T Blanco	LF	42.0	9	1	0	0	1.000	2.14	2	0
M Cepicky	LF	35.7	13	0	0	0	1.000	3.28	0	0
J Guillen	LF	17.0	2	0	0	0	1.000	1.06	0	0

Name	POS	Inn	PO	A	TE	FE	FPct	RF	DPS	DPT
B Wilkerson	CF	758.7	233	6	1	2	.988	2.84	2	0
P Wilson	CF	488.7	125	3	0	0	1.000	2.36	0	0
R Church	CF	125.7	49	0	0	0	1.000	3.51	0	0
M Byrd	CF	61.0	14	0	0	0	1.000	2.07	0	0
E Chavez	CF	21.0	4	0	0	0	1.000	1.71	0	0
B Watson	CF	3.0	2	0	0	0	1.000	6.00	0	0
J Guillen	RF	1189.0	299	10	3	4	.978	2.34	9	0
R Church	RF	135.7	43	0	0	0	1.000	2.85	0	0
B Wilkerson	RF	45.7	12	0	1	0	.923	2.36	0	0
M Byrd	RF	34.0	10	0	0	0	1.000	2.65	0	0
P Wilson	RF	17.0	4	0	0	0	1.000	2.12	0	0
T Blanco	RF	9.0	1	0	0	0	1.000	1.00	0	0
J Hammonds	RF	9.0	2	0	0	0	1.000	2.00	0	0
M Cepicky	RF	9.0	5	0	0	0	1.000	5.00	0	0
K Kelly	RF	4.0	0	0	0	0	0.000	0.00	0	0
J Davis	RF	3.0	1	0	0	0	1.000	3.00	0	0
T Sledge	RF	2.0	0	0	0	0	0.000	0.00	0	0

Incremental Baserunning Runs		
Name	IR	IRP
Brandon Watson	1.01	225
Junior Spivey	0.80	189
Brad Wilkerson	0.30	104
Ryan Zimmerman	0.25	128
Jamey Carroll	0.23	105
Tony Blanco	0.17	190
Deivi Cruz	0.15	127
Brian Schneider	0.14	103
Ryan Church	0.14	103
Jason Bergmann	0.14	201
Kenny Kelly	0.14	123
Vinny Castilla	0.10	102
Rick Short	0.06	122
Jeffrey Hammonds	0.00	105
Hector Carrasco	-0.01	89
Wil Cordero	-0.01	0

Incremental Baserunning Runs		
Name	IR	IRP
Carlos Baerga	-0.05	97
JJ Davis	-0.10	0
Terrmel Sledge	-0.14	0
Cristian Guzman	-0.16	93
Nick Johnson	-0.18	97
Tomo Ohka	-0.19	0
Tony Armas	-0.19	0
Gary Bennett	-0.20	78
Jose Guillen	-0.44	91
Matt Cepicky	-0.61	0
Preston Wilson	-0.64	86
John Patterson	-0.68	0
Livan Hernandez	-0.86	0
Jose Vidro	-1.16	67
Esteban Loaiza	-1.54	-41
Marlon Byrd	-2.08	32

Fielding Range Stats

Toward the end of the summer, David Gassko wrote an article on The Hardball Times website entitled "Measuring Range." David drew on the data that THT purchases from Baseball Info Solutions to estimate how many batted balls were in each fielder's "zones," how many he successfully fielded, and how his performance compared to the major league average. As a final step, David assigned run values to the number of estimated hits the fielder allowed. The result is a stat that estimates the number of runs above and below average each player contributed with the glove.

Here is a little more detail, from David's article:

...let me try to explain this system in as few paragraphs as possible. First, I split up a team's Balls In Play (BIP) based on the number of ground balls, fly balls and line drives they allowed. This allows me to estimate how many outs should have been made by infielders and how many outs should have been made by outfielders. For infielders, only grounders count, while for outfielders, I use outfield line drives and fly balls less home runs.

Next, I find a team's BIP against left-handed batters and right-handed batters. Using "Position Rates" published by Charlie Saeger, I estimate how many balls in play were hit to each fielder.

These are the two biggest advantages of my system over any other non-PBP system. Because I use batted ball data and because I know how balls were put into play by left-handed batters and how many were put into play by right-handed

batters, I can come up with an estimate of each fielder's "chances." Therefore, the greatest disadvantage a non-PBP system has in comparison to a PBP system is minimized.

The final steps are easy. Let me explain them through an example:

In 2004, Yankees pitchers allowed 2,027 ground balls. Based on the amount of balls put into play by left-handed and right-handed batters against the Yankees, I expected Yankee shortstops to make 450 assists. Derek Jeter played 93% of defensive innings played by the Yankees, so I expected him to have 419 assists. Jeter actually had 392 assists, which puts him at -27 assists above average. Converted to runs, he's -16.

This exercise is repeated for every player at positions four through nine (meaning I don't look at first basemen, pitchers or catchers). For outfielders, of course, I use putouts instead of assists.

For *The Hardball Times Annual*, David has also extended his sytem to catchers and first basemen. His results are listed on the next few pages, including all fielders with at least 600 innings played at each position, ranked by "RAA" or Runs Above Average.

Those who have purchased the *Annual* can download a spreadsheet with RAA for every fielder at every position. The web address for this spreadsheet is http://www.hardballtimes.com/THT2005Annual/. The username is "reader" and the password is "kaline".

Catchers

Name	Team	Innings	RAA	Per 150 G
Molina, Y	STL	959	7.2	5.1
Schneider, B	WAS	927	6.3	4.3
Matheny, M	SF	1122	5.9	4.9
Rodriguez, I	DET	1033	5.5	4.2
Hall, T	TB	1062	4.3	3.4
Mauer, J	MIN	1000	4.2	3.1
Barajas, R	TEX	1025	4.1	3.1
Ausmus, B	HOU	1066	3.3	2.6
Posada, J	NYA	1077	3.3	2.6
LaRue, J	CIN	915	3.2	2.2
Hernandez, R	SD	806	2.5	1.5
Lieberthal, M	PHI	999	2.3	1.7
Buck, J	KC	977	1.0	0.7
Estrada, J	ATL	826	-0.6	-0.4

Name	Team	Innings	RAA	Per 150 G
Martinez, V	CLE	1233	-0.6	-0.5
Cota, H	PIT	682	-1.1	-0.6
Zaun, G	TOR	1088	-1.1	-0.9
Varitek, J	BOS	1089	-1.7	-1.4
Lo Duca, P	FLA	1033	-1.9	-1.4
Miller, D	MIL	917	-1.9	-1.3
Barrett, M	CHN	1018	-2.8	-2.1
Molina, B	LAA	873	-3.4	-2.2
Snyder, C	ARI	916	-3.8	-2.6
Phillips, J	LAN	774	-4.2	-2.4
Lopez, J	BAL	629	-6.1	-2.8
Kendall, J	OAK	1286	-6.4	-6.1
Pierzynski, A	CHA	1118	-7.5	-6.2
Piazza, M	NYN	809	-7.6	-4.5

First Basemen

Name	Team	Innings	RAA	Per 150 G
Erstad, D	LAA	1279	22.8	21.6
Lee, T	TB	918	21.3	14.5
Johnson, N	WAS	1098	16.2	13.2
Millar, K	BOS	796	14.0	8.2
Konerko, P	CHA	1272	10.6	10.0
Pujols, A	STL	1358	9.3	9.4
Overbay, L	MIL	1265	8.9	8.4
Berkman, L	HOU	738	8.4	4.6
Helton, T	COL	1229	6.5	5.9
Broussard, B	CLE	1050	6.3	4.9
Nevin, P	SD	611	6.1	2.8
Johnson, D	OAK	884	5.4	3.6
Choi, H	LAN	665	4.9	2.4
Snow, J	SF	826	3.8	2.3
Lee, D	CHN	1386	2.7	2.8
Tracy, C	ARI	653	1.9	0.9
Mientkiewicz, D	NYN	675	1.8	0.9
Howard, R	PHI	706	1.7	0.9
Casey, S	CIN	1138	1.4	1.1
LaRoche, A	ATL	1019	-0.8	-0.6
Palmeiro, R	BAL	748	-1.8	-1.0
Teixeira, M	TEX	1358	-2.2	-2.2
Martinez, T	NYA	771	-2.7	-1.6
Shelton, C	DET	738	-3.9	-2.1
Hinske, E	TOR	860	-7.9	-5.1
Morneau, J	MIN	1166	-8.0	-6.9
Clark, T	ARI	643	-9.5	-4.5
Sexson, R	SEA	1303	-13.6	-13.1
Delgado, C	FLA	1206	-15.6	-13.9
Ward, D	PIT	892	-26.3	-17.4

Second Basemen

Name	Team	Innings	RAA	Per 150 G
Counsell, C	ARI	1244	20.4	18.8
Castillo, L	FLA	1012	17.9	13.4
Castillo, J	PIT	840	15.6	9.7
Hudson, O	TOR	1067	13.9	11.0
Ellis, M	OAK	972	13.5	9.7
Belliard, R	CLE	1243	12.4	11.4
Grudzielanek, M	STL	1158	12.3	10.6
Kennedy, A	LAA	1107	8.5	6.9
Biggio, C	HOU	1172	8.3	7.2
Bellhorn, M	BOS	712	7.9	4.1
Giles, M	ATL	1276	6.8	6.5
Miles, A	COL	602	1.7	0.7
Polanco, P	DET	716	0.5	0.3
Kent, J	LAN	1209	0.5	0.5
Cairo, M	NYN	657	0.2	0.1
Roberts, B	BAL	1208	-1.1	-1.0
Iguchi, T	CHA	1171	-2.1	-1.8
Walker, T	CHN	798	-2.3	-1.4
Gotay, R	KC	666	-2.5	-1.2
Weeks, R	MIL	837	-2.6	-1.6
Utley, C	PHI	1195	-3.5	-3.1
Vidro, J	WAS	665	-8.6	-4.2
Durham, R	SF	1143	-9.4	-8.0
Boone, B	SEA	647	-11.5	-5.5
Cantu, J	TB	668	-11.8	-5.8
Cano, R	NYA	1142	-12.7	-10.8
Green, N	TB	731	-14.7	-8.0
Loretta, M	SD	910	-17.3	-11.7
Soriano, A	TEX	1351	-27.4	-27.4

Shortstops

Name	Team	Innings	RAA	Per 150 G
Furcal, R	ATL	1306	32.2	31.1
Wilson, J	PIT	1360	27.1	27.3
Perez, N	CHN	1063	24.5	19.3
Izturis, C	LAN	918	15.2	10.3
Crosby, B	OAK	743	11.3	6.2
Uribe, J	CHA	1293	10.9	10.4
Vizquel, O	SF	1292	9.3	8.9
Barmes, C	COL	682	8.4	4.3
Gonzalez, A	FLA	1087	7.3	5.9
Tejada, M	BAL	1394	7.2	7.5
Eckstein, D	STL	1340	6.8	6.8
Lugo, J	TB	1338	4.7	4.7
Scutaro, M	OAK	663	4.2	2.1
Guillen, C	DET	625	3.4	1.6
Everett, A	HOU	1291	1.0	0.9
Clayton, R	ARI	1177	-0.5	-0.4
Guzman, C	WAS	1161	-2.0	-1.7
Greene, K	SD	1028	-2.1	-1.6
Peralta, J	CLE	1232	-2.1	-1.9
Rollins, J	PHI	1356	-5.0	-5.0
Cabrera, O	LAA	1240	-6.8	-6.2
Renteria, E	BOS	1293	-11.4	-10.9
Hardy, J	MIL	938	-14.7	-10.2
Reyes, J	NYN	1398	-15.4	-16.0
Jeter, D	NYA	1352	-15.7	-15.7
Berroa, A	KC	1360	-20.4	-20.5
Lopez, F	CIN	1175	-23.1	-20.1
Adams, R	TOR	1100	-34.1	-27.8
Young, M	TEX	1356	-34.4	-34.6

Third Basemen

Name	Team	Innings	RAA	Per 150 G
Inge, B	DET	1399	22.4	23.2
Bell, D	PHI	1296	20.3	19.5
Wright, D	NYN	1404	15.7	16.3
Chavez, E	OAK	1348	11.1	11.0
Nunez, A	STL	721	9.8	5.2
Glaus, T	ARI	1264	7.6	7.1
Ensberg, M	HOU	1286	6.7	6.4
Mora, M	BAL	1289	6.4	6.1
Burroughs, S	SD	657	5.1	2.5
Crede, J	CHA	1120	4.7	3.9
Gonzalez, A	TB	780	3.6	2.1
Boone, A	CLE	1249	2.7	2.5
Mueller, B	BOS	1209	2.0	1.8
Cuddyer, M	MIN	816	-0.2	-0.1
Koskie, C	TOR	674	-2.1	-1.0
Beltre, A	SEA	1325	-3.4	-3.4
Atkins, G	COL	1161	-5.2	-4.5
Lowell, M	FLA	1126	-5.5	-4.6
Teahen, M	KC	1068	-5.5	-4.3
Ramirez, A	CHN	1020	-5.9	-4.5
Castilla, V	WAS	1171	-6.5	-5.6
Alfonzo, E	SF	813	-11.7	-7.0
Randa, J	CIN	717	-12.7	-6.8
Jones, C	ATL	830	-13.5	-8.3
Blalock, H	TEX	1374	-16.1	-16.4
Rodriguez, A	NYA	1384	-26.6	-27.2

Left Fielders

Name	Team	Innings	RAA	Per 150 G
Crisp, C	CLE	1200	33.6	29.9
Johnson, K	ATL	648	22.1	10.6
Podsednik, S	CHA	1061	21.7	17.0
Crawford, C	TB	1246	19.7	18.2
Winn, R	SEA	796	18.9	11.1
Bay, J	PIT	1185	12.5	11.0
Mench, K	TEX	978	7.0	5.0
Stewart, S	MIN	1107	6.9	5.7
Floyd, C	NYN	1263	6.4	6.0
Matsui, H	NYA	977	3.0	2.2
Holliday, M	COL	1049	1.6	1.2
Lee, C	MIL	1404	1.5	1.6
Feliz, P	SF	616	1.4	0.6
Catalanotto, F	TOR	761	-0.9	-0.5
Klesko, R	SD	927	-1.0	-0.7
Burke, C	HOU	634	-2.5	-1.2
Gonzalez, L	ARI	1318	-5.3	-5.2
Sanders, R	STL	636	-7.4	-3.5
Anderson, G	LAA	920	-8.4	-5.7
Dunn, A	CIN	1090	-9.2	-7.4
Long, T	KC	794	-14.5	-8.5
Burrell, P	PHI	1297	-17.8	-17.1
Cabrera, M	FLA	1105	-20.2	-16.5
Ramirez, M	BOS	1225	-31.8	-28.9

Center Fielders

Name	Team	Innings	RAA	Per 150 G
Edmonds, J	STL	1153	24.6	21.0
Clark, B	MIL	1275	22.6	21.4
Logan, N	DET	874	20.5	13.3
Matos, L	BAL	990	16.8	12.3
Damon, J	BOS	1225	15.6	14.1
Reed, J	SEA	1149	10.3	8.8
Beltran, C	NYN	1289	9.9	9.5
Taveras, W	HOU	1254	9.9	9.2
Matthews Jr., G	TEX	846	7.9	5.0
Bradley, M	LAN	628	6.8	3.1
Rowand, A	CHA	1367	6.2	6.2
Lofton, K	PHI	741	5.8	3.2
Wilkerson, B	WAS	759	5.0	2.8
Sizemore, G	CLE	1370	1.6	1.6
Jones, A	ATL	1366	1.3	1.3
Finley, S	LAA	896	0.2	0.1
DeJesus, D	KC	1005	-0.6	-0.4
Hollins, D	TB	619	-3.1	-1.4
Sullivan, C	COL	618	-5.1	-2.3
Hunter, T	MIN	813	-7.4	-4.5
Patterson, C	CHN	987	-7.8	-5.7
Williams, B	NYA	863	-13.2	-8.4
Kotsay, M	OAK	1184	-13.6	-12.0
Roberts, D	SD	901	-14.1	-9.4
Pierre, J	FLA	1383	-16.4	-16.8
Wells, V	TOR	1358	-21.6	-21.7
Griffey Jr., K	CIN	1065	-36.3	-28.7

Right Fielders

Name	Team	Innings	RAA	Per 150 G
Suzuki, I	SEA	1388	17.6	18.1
Blake, C	CLE	1188	16.8	14.8
Burnitz, J	CHN	1359	15.4	15.5
Guillen, J	WAS	1189	12.5	11.0
Giles, B	SD	1220	12.4	11.2
Jenkins, G	MIL	1241	10.9	10.1
Jones, J	MIN	1080	10.7	8.6
Nixon, T	BOS	935	9.0	6.2
Hidalgo, R	TEX	700	7.6	3.9
Lawton, M	PIT	842	6.2	3.9
Rios, A	TOR	1056	3.2	2.5
Diaz, V	NYN	652	3.1	1.5
Kearns, A	CIN	890	3.0	2.0
Green, S	ARI	1031	2.2	1.7

Name	Team	Innings	RAA	Per 150 G
Lane, J	HOU	1115	-1.9	-1.6
Guerrero, V	LAA	1040	-3.0	-2.3
Huff, A	TB	787	-4.1	-2.4
Sheffield, G	NYA	1099	-8.4	-6.8
Hawpe, B	COL	693	-10.1	-5.2
Dye, J	CHA	1235	-10.6	-9.7
Encarnacion, J	FLA	1112	-11.0	-9.1
Monroe, C	DET	632	-11.0	-5.1
Abreu, B	PHI	1364	-12.6	-12.7
Ordonez, M	DET	672	-12.6	-6.3
Walker, L	STL	649	-15.1	-7.3
Swisher, N	OAK	1027	-17.4	-13.2
Brown, E	KC	1097	-18.4	-14.9

Plate Appearance Outcomes

Welcome to the back of the book. Since you've made it this far, you probably know that we do a lot of work with batted ball information. In just this *Annual*, we used Baseball Info Solutions' batted ball data to estimate the worth of a batted ball, examine how well batters and pitchers can control batted balls, calculate the best and worst fielding teams and players, and even determine batted ball park factors.

In our leaderboards we listed the best players at hitting line drives, or keeping the ball in or out of the park. But you're probably still wondering, "Hey, I wonder how many whatis who's-his-face hit last year." Maybe that's why you came to the back of the book in the first place. Good move.

On the next six pages, you'll find every batter with at least 400 plate appearances in 2005, and, in the next section, every pitcher with at least 300 batters faced. Next to their plate appearance totals, we've listed the percent of times they struck out, walked and hit what type of batted ball. If a player played with more than one team, we've broken his stats out by team.

For reference, here are the run values of each type of batted ball, along with the average major league occurrence for each:

K	BB	GB	OF	IF	LD	Bunt
-0.287	0.304	-0.101	0.035	-0.243	0.356	-0.103
16%	9%	32%	22%	3%	15%	2%

As an official purchaser of *The Hardball Times Annual*, you are also eligible to download a spreadsheet with the batted ball stats for every major league player at http://www.hardballtimes.com/THT2005Annual/. The username is "reader" and the password is "kaline".

Batters

Player	Team	PA	K	BB	GB	OF	IF	LD	Oth
Abreu B.	PHI	719	19%	17%	30%	18%	1%	15%	0%
Adams R.	TOR	545	10%	10%	36%	21%	5%	16%	2%
Alfonzo E.	SF	402	8%	7%	31%	30%	5%	18%	0%
Alou M.	SF	490	9%	12%	33%	25%	4%	16%	0%
Anderson G.	LAA	603	14%	4%	34%	27%	4%	17%	0%
Atkins G.	COL	573	13%	9%	36%	21%	2%	19%	0%
Aurilia R.	CIN	468	14%	8%	31%	25%	4%	16%	2%
Ausmus B.	HOU	451	11%	12%	40%	17%	2%	16%	3%
Barajas R.	TEX	450	16%	7%	22%	30%	9%	15%	1%
Barrett M.	CHN	477	13%	10%	33%	23%	2%	18%	1%
Bay J.	PIT	707	20%	14%	25%	24%	2%	15%	0%
Bell D.	PHI	617	11%	8%	32%	24%	5%	19%	1%
Belliard R.	CLE	587	12%	6%	36%	26%	4%	15%	2%
Beltran C.	NYN	650	15%	9%	33%	24%	4%	14%	1%
Beltre A.	SEA	650	17%	7%	35%	24%	3%	14%	0%
Berkman L.	HOU	565	13%	17%	32%	20%	2%	16%	0%
Berroa A.	KC	652	17%	5%	38%	20%	4%	15%	2%
Biggio C.	HOU	651	14%	8%	33%	24%	7%	13%	1%
Blake C.	CLE	583	20%	9%	26%	25%	5%	14%	1%
Blalock H.	TEX	705	19%	8%	29%	24%	3%	18%	0%
Boone A.	CLE	565	16%	8%	33%	22%	4%	16%	1%
Broussard B.	CLE	505	19%	7%	30%	24%	3%	16%	0%
Brown E.	KC	609	18%	9%	31%	21%	3%	18%	0%
Buck J.	KC	430	22%	6%	31%	24%	4%	12%	0%
Burnitz J.	CHN	671	16%	9%	32%	24%	5%	14%	0%
Burrell P.	PHI	669	24%	15%	19%	25%	3%	15%	0%
Cabrera M.	FLA	685	18%	10%	28%	24%	3%	18%	0%

Player	Team	PA	K	BB	GB	OF	IF	LD	Oth
Cabrera O.	LAA	587	9%	7%	34%	28%	5%	16%	1%
Cano R.	NYA	551	12%	3%	42%	22%	3%	17%	1%
Cantu J.	TB	631	13%	4%	34%	29%	2%	18%	1%
Casey S.	CIN	587	8%	9%	43%	23%	2%	16%	0%
Castilla V.	WAS	549	15%	9%	32%	25%	4%	14%	0%
Castillo L.	FLA	524	6%	13%	48%	10%	2%	17%	5%
Catalanotto	TOR	475	11%	10%	35%	24%	3%	16%	1%
Chavez E.	OAK	694	19%	9%	28%	25%	6%	13%	0%
Clark B.	MIL	674	8%	10%	30%	26%	4%	21%	2%
Clayton R.	ARI	573	18%	7%	41%	14%	1%	14%	4%
Counsell C.	ARI	670	10%	13%	37%	20%	4%	15%	2%
Crawford C.	TB	687	12%	5%	37%	25%	4%	16%	2%
Crede J.	CHA	471	14%	7%	28%	27%	9%	14%	1%
Crisp C.	CLE	656	12%	7%	36%	23%	4%	15%	4%
Cuddyer M.	MIN	470	20%	9%	37%	16%	4%	13%	1%
Damon J.	BOS	688	10%	8%	36%	22%	4%	19%	1%
DeJesus D.	KC	523	15%	10%	33%	21%	3%	16%	2%
Delgado C.	FLA	616	20%	14%	26%	22%	2%	15%	0%
Dellucci D.	TEX	518	23%	16%	25%	23%	3%	10%	0%
Dunn A.	CIN	671	25%	19%	20%	22%	4%	10%	0%
Durham R.	SF	560	11%	10%	37%	23%	3%	17%	0%
Dye J.	CHA	579	17%	8%	28%	25%	6%	15%	0%
Eckstein D.	STL	713	6%	10%	37%	21%	4%	19%	3%
Edmonds J.	STL	567	25%	17%	20%	24%	3%	11%	1%
Ellis M.	OAK	486	10%	10%	36%	22%	5%	14%	2%
Encarnacion	FLA	563	18%	9%	27%	21%	5%	17%	2%
Ensberg M.	HOU	624	19%	15%	25%	26%	4%	11%	0%

Plate Appearance Outcomes

Player	Team	PA	K	BB	GB	OF	IF	LD	Oth
Erstad D.	LAA	667	16%	7%	36%	20%	3%	16%	1%
Everett A.	HOU	595	17%	6%	29%	26%	5%	14%	3%
Everett C.	CHA	547	18%	9%	32%	25%	4%	12%	0%
Feliz P.	SF	615	17%	6%	34%	25%	5%	13%	0%
Figgins C.	LAA	720	14%	9%	30%	23%	4%	16%	4%
Finley S.	LAA	440	16%	7%	30%	25%	7%	13%	1%
Floyd C.	NYN	626	16%	12%	30%	26%	4%	13%	0%
Ford L.	MIN	590	14%	10%	40%	18%	4%	12%	1%
Freel R.	CIN	432	14%	14%	37%	14%	3%	16%	3%
Furcal R.	ATL	689	11%	9%	34%	18%	4%	18%	6%
Giambi J.	NYA	545	20%	23%	19%	23%	3%	11%	1%
Gibbons J.	BAL	518	11%	6%	31%	31%	8%	14%	0%
Giles B.	SD	674	9%	18%	27%	24%	4%	17%	0%
Giles M.	ATL	654	17%	11%	29%	27%	2%	14%	1%
Glaus T.	ARI	634	23%	14%	23%	25%	4%	11%	0%
Gomes J.	TB	407	28%	13%	17%	24%	4%	14%	0%
Gonzalez A.	FLA	478	17%	8%	27%	26%	8%	13%	2%
Gonzalez L.	ARI	672	13%	13%	28%	26%	5%	14%	0%
Gonzalez L.	COL	442	14%	6%	40%	19%	2%	17%	2%
Green S.	ARI	656	14%	10%	39%	20%	3%	13%	0%
Greene K.	SD	476	20%	7%	24%	27%	5%	16%	1%
Griffey Jr.	CIN	555	17%	10%	25%	30%	3%	16%	0%
Grudzielanek	STL	563	14%	6%	39%	20%	2%	19%	0%
Guerrero V.	LAA	594	8%	12%	35%	26%	5%	14%	0%
Guillen J.	WAS	611	17%	8%	33%	21%	5%	16%	0%
Guzman C.	WAS	492	15%	5%	42%	16%	2%	15%	3%
Hafner T.	CLE	578	21%	15%	28%	22%	1%	13%	0%
Hairston Jr.	CHN	430	11%	10%	33%	22%	4%	17%	4%
Hall B.	MIL	546	19%	7%	31%	22%	3%	17%	1%
Hall T.	TB	463	8%	5%	35%	28%	5%	17%	2%
Hardy J.	MIL	427	11%	11%	33%	22%	5%	15%	3%
Hatteberg S.	OAK	523	10%	11%	37%	21%	5%	15%	1%
Helton T.	COL	626	13%	18%	23%	26%	3%	17%	0%
Hill A.	TOR	407	10%	10%	34%	24%	4%	17%	1%
Hillenbrand	TOR	645	12%	7%	34%	23%	6%	16%	0%
Hinske E.	TOR	537	23%	10%	28%	23%	3%	13%	0%
Holliday M.	COL	526	15%	8%	37%	21%	3%	16%	0%
Hudson O.	TOR	501	13%	7%	42%	22%	1%	16%	0%
Huff A.	TB	636	14%	8%	37%	25%	3%	11%	0%
Hunter T.	MIN	416	16%	10%	37%	22%	5%	11%	1%
Ibanez R.	SEA	690	14%	11%	34%	23%	2%	16%	0%
Iguchi T.	CHA	582	20%	9%	34%	18%	2%	15%	2%
Infante O.	DET	434	17%	4%	25%	31%	8%	12%	4%
Inge B.	DET	694	20%	10%	28%	26%	3%	12%	1%
Izturis C.	LAN	478	11%	6%	42%	18%	4%	18%	3%
Jenkins G.	MIL	618	22%	12%	26%	21%	1%	17%	0%
Jeter D.	NYA	752	16%	12%	43%	14%	0%	14%	2%

Player	Team	PA	K	BB	GB	OF	IF	LD	Oth
Johnson D.	OAK	434	12%	12%	29%	24%	5%	18%	0%
Johnson N.	WAS	547	16%	17%	29%	21%	2%	14%	1%
Johnson R.	TOR	439	19%	9%	36%	16%	3%	16%	2%
Jones A.	ATL	672	17%	12%	30%	26%	4%	11%	0%
Jones C.	ATL	432	13%	17%	29%	24%	1%	16%	0%
Jones J.	MIN	585	21%	10%	41%	17%	2%	10%	1%
Kearns A.	CIN	448	24%	13%	31%	15%	3%	14%	0%
Kendall J.	OAK	676	6%	10%	44%	21%	1%	17%	1%
Kennedy A.	LAA	460	14%	8%	31%	24%	2%	18%	3%
Kent J.	LAN	637	13%	13%	23%	29%	6%	16%	0%
Kielty B.	OAK	433	15%	12%	32%	24%	2%	14%	0%
Klesko R.	SD	520	15%	15%	30%	24%	4%	12%	0%
Konerko P.	CHA	664	16%	13%	24%	26%	4%	17%	0%
Koskie C.	TOR	404	22%	12%	30%	19%	4%	12%	0%
Kotsay M.	OAK	629	8%	7%	34%	27%	3%	21%	1%
Lane J.	HOU	561	19%	7%	22%	33%	5%	14%	0%
LaRoche A.	ATL	502	17%	9%	33%	23%	2%	16%	1%
LaRue J.	CIN	422	24%	13%	26%	18%	4%	14%	1%
Lawton M.	PIT	445	14%	15%	36%	19%	3%	13%	0%
Lee C.	MIL	688	13%	9%	26%	30%	6%	16%	0%
Lee D.	CHN	691	16%	13%	27%	26%	2%	16%	0%
Lee T.	TB	441	15%	8%	34%	24%	2%	16%	0%
Lieberthal M	PHI	443	8%	10%	31%	29%	4%	17%	0%
Lo Duca P.	FLA	496	6%	8%	38%	22%	3%	21%	2%
Lofton K.	PHI	406	10%	8%	38%	18%	1%	21%	3%
Long T.	KC	489	11%	6%	39%	21%	4%	18%	0%
Lopez F.	CIN	648	17%	9%	39%	18%	1%	14%	1%
Lopez J.	BAL	423	16%	6%	36%	18%	7%	17%	0%
Loretta M.	SD	463	7%	11%	32%	22%	4%	22%	1%
Lowell M.	FLA	558	10%	9%	26%	33%	5%	17%	1%
Lugo J.	TB	690	10%	10%	38%	21%	3%	16%	3%
Mackowiak R.	PIT	512	20%	9%	36%	19%	3%	14%	1%
Martinez V.	CLE	622	13%	11%	36%	22%	2%	16%	0%
Matheny M.	SF	485	19%	7%	30%	22%	3%	18%	1%
Matos L.	BAL	433	13%	9%	32%	25%	3%	14%	3%
Matsui H.	NYA	704	11%	9%	38%	27%	2%	13%	0%
Matthews Jr.	TEX	526	17%	9%	38%	19%	5%	12%	0%
Mauer J.	MIN	554	12%	11%	40%	18%	1%	18%	1%
Mench K.	TEX	615	11%	9%	30%	29%	7%	14%	0%
Millar K.	BOS	519	14%	12%	25%	31%	4%	14%	0%
Miller D.	MIL	431	22%	10%	34%	16%	1%	17%	0%
Molina B.	LAA	449	9%	6%	35%	29%	3%	17%	1%
Molina Y.	STL	421	7%	6%	43%	23%	3%	15%	2%
Monroe C.	DET	623	15%	7%	38%	20%	4%	15%	0%
Mora M.	BAL	664	17%	9%	26%	27%	5%	13%	4%
Morneau J.	MIN	543	17%	9%	31%	26%	4%	13%	0%
Mueller B.	BOS	590	13%	11%	32%	22%	2%	19%	0%

Player	Team	PA	K	BB	GB	OF	IF	LD	Oth
Nixon T.	BOS	470	13%	12%	30%	28%	3%	15%	0%
Nunez A.	STL	467	13%	8%	41%	15%	1%	18%	3%
Ortiz D.	BOS	713	17%	14%	21%	28%	3%	15%	0%
Overbay L.	MIL	622	16%	13%	36%	18%	1%	15%	0%
Palmeiro R.	BAL	422	10%	11%	33%	27%	4%	16%	0%
Patterson C.	CHN	483	24%	5%	30%	18%	6%	11%	6%
Peralta J.	CLE	570	22%	11%	30%	22%	1%	13%	0%
Perez N.	CHN	609	8%	3%	37%	24%	3%	19%	6%
Phillips J.	LAN	434	12%	7%	37%	23%	4%	17%	0%
Piazza M.	NYN	442	15%	10%	34%	24%	2%	14%	0%
Pierre J.	FLA	719	6%	7%	42%	13%	2%	19%	10%
Pierzynski A	CHA	497	14%	7%	36%	23%	3%	17%	1%
Podsednik S.	CHA	568	13%	9%	40%	15%	2%	15%	7%
Posada J.	NYA	546	17%	12%	31%	25%	3%	12%	0%
Pujols A.	STL	700	9%	15%	32%	24%	5%	15%	0%
Punto N.	MIN	439	20%	8%	34%	16%	2%	14%	5%
Ramirez A.	CHN	506	12%	8%	31%	29%	3%	16%	0%
Ramirez M.	BOS	650	18%	14%	25%	24%	2%	16%	0%
Reed J.	SEA	544	14%	9%	36%	21%	4%	14%	3%
Renteria E.	BOS	692	14%	8%	36%	20%	2%	18%	2%
Reyes J.	NYN	733	11%	4%	38%	25%	2%	16%	4%
Rios A.	TOR	519	19%	6%	36%	21%	2%	14%	0%
Roberts B.	BAL	640	13%	11%	26%	25%	3%	20%	2%
Roberts D.	SD	480	12%	11%	35%	17%	2%	15%	7%
Rodriguez A.	NYA	715	19%	15%	29%	24%	2%	10%	0%
Rodriguez I.	DET	525	18%	2%	38%	20%	3%	18%	0%
Rollins J.	PHI	732	10%	7%	36%	23%	3%	19%	2%
Rowand A.	CHA	640	18%	8%	37%	17%	3%	15%	2%
Sanchez F.	PIT	492	7%	7%	39%	22%	4%	20%	2%
Schneider B.	WAS	408	12%	9%	37%	23%	3%	16%	1%
Scutaro M.	OAK	423	11%	9%	34%	24%	4%	16%	2%
Sexson R.	SEA	656	25%	14%	24%	22%	2%	12%	0%
Sheffield G.	NYA	675	11%	13%	32%	26%	5%	13%	-0%
Shelton C.	DET	431	20%	9%	27%	23%	3%	17%	0%

Player	Team	PA	K	BB	GB	OF	IF	LD	Oth
Sizemore G.	CLE	706	19%	8%	32%	21%	2%	17%	1%
Snow J.	SF	410	15%	10%	29%	25%	4%	17%	0%
Soriano A.	TEX	682	18%	6%	26%	33%	3%	14%	0%
Sosa S.	BAL	424	20%	10%	31%	24%	4%	11%	0%
Stairs M.	KC	466	15%	14%	28%	24%	5%	13%	0%
Stewart S.	MIN	599	12%	7%	37%	26%	2%	16%	0%
Sullivan C.	COL	424	20%	7%	29%	15%	1%	21%	7%
Suzuki I.	SEA	739	9%	7%	45%	19%	1%	18%	1%
Sweeney M.	KC	514	12%	7%	29%	31%	6%	14%	1%
Swisher N.	OAK	522	21%	11%	26%	25%	4%	13%	0%
Taguchi S.	STL	424	15%	5%	36%	21%	2%	19%	1%
Taveras W.	HOU	635	16%	5%	37%	16%	2%	13%	10%
Teahen M.	KC	491	22%	8%	37%	15%	1%	16%	0%
Teixeira M.	TEX	730	17%	11%	28%	25%	3%	15%	1%
Tejada M.	BAL	704	12%	7%	39%	23%	4%	15%	0%
Tracy C.	ARI	553	14%	8%	27%	30%	3%	19%	0%
Uribe J.	CHA	540	14%	7%	30%	26%	6%	15%	2%
Utley C.	PHI	628	17%	12%	25%	26%	3%	16%	0%
Varitek J.	BOS	539	22%	12%	30%	18%	3%	15%	1%
Vizquel O.	SF	651	9%	9%	34%	22%	3%	18%	4%
Walker T.	CHN	433	9%	7%	32%	30%	3%	18%	1%
Ward D.	PIT	453	13%	8%	31%	27%	4%	16%	0%
Weeks R.	MIL	414	23%	12%	31%	17%	3%	13%	1%
Wells V.	TOR	678	13%	7%	33%	25%	7%	15%	0%
White R.	DET	400	12%	6%	45%	19%	5%	14%	0%
Wilkerson B.	WAS	661	22%	14%	19%	26%	2%	15%	2%
Williams B.	NYA	546	14%	10%	34%	25%	4%	14%	0%
Wilson J.	PIT	639	9%	6%	39%	23%	5%	15%	4%
Winn R.	SEA	436	12%	9%	40%	19%	1%	17%	2%
Wright D.	NYN	657	17%	12%	28%	24%	1%	18%	0%
Young D.	DET	509	20%	7%	34%	21%	2%	15%	0%
Young M.	TEX	732	12%	8%	36%	21%	2%	20%	0%
Zaun G.	TOR	512	14%	14%	33%	21%	5%	14%	1%

Pitchers

Player	Team	BFP	K	BB	GB	OF	IF	LD	Oth
Armas Jr. T.	WAS	451	13%	13%	27%	27%	4%	15%	1%
Arroyo B.	BOS	878	11%	8%	30%	30%	5%	15%	1%
Astacio E.	HOU	366	18%	7%	27%	31%	2%	13%	1%
Backe B.	HOU	653	15%	11%	30%	23%	4%	14%	2%
Baez D.	TB	308	17%	10%	33%	21%	3%	14%	2%
Batista M.	TOR	331	16%	9%	35%	20%	5%	14%	1%
Beckett J.	FLA	729	23%	9%	28%	20%	3%	14%	2%
Bedard E.	BAL	606	21%	10%	27%	21%	3%	16%	2%
Belisle M.	CIN	382	15%	8%	39%	17%	2%	16%	2%
Benoit J.	TEX	369	21%	11%	22%	27%	5%	13%	1%
Benson K.	NYN	737	13%	7%	34%	26%	3%	15%	2%
Blanton J.	OAK	835	14%	9%	35%	25%	4%	13%	1%
Bonderman J.	DET	801	18%	8%	35%	22%	3%	14%	1%
Brazelton D.	TB	354	12%	18%	25%	29%	2%	12%	1%
Brazoban Y.	LAN	317	19%	12%	26%	23%	4%	14%	2%
Brocail D.	TEX	344	18%	11%	35%	16%	3%	16%	1%
Brown K.	NYA	346	14%	8%	39%	21%	2%	15%	1%
Buehrle M.	CHA	971	15%	5%	36%	23%	2%	17%	2%
Burnett A.	FLA	873	23%	10%	38%	13%	1%	13%	2%
Bush D.	TOR	575	13%	7%	36%	23%	5%	15%	1%
Byrd P.	LAA	842	12%	4%	31%	31%	4%	16%	3%
Cabrera D.	BAL	716	22%	14%	34%	18%	1%	11%	1%
Capuano C.	MIL	949	19%	11%	26%	23%	5%	14%	2%
Carpenter C.	STL	953	22%	6%	38%	17%	1%	14%	2%
Carrara G.	LAN	326	17%	13%	26%	25%	3%	11%	5%
Carrasco D.	KC	511	10%	11%	42%	17%	2%	17%	1%
Carrasco H.	WAS	358	21%	12%	27%	18%	6%	13%	2%
Chacin G.	TOR	872	14%	9%	31%	23%	5%	16%	2%
Chacon S.	NYA	330	12%	11%	34%	21%	8%	13%	1%
Chacon S.	COL	322	12%	14%	25%	26%	2%	17%	4%
Chen B.	BAL	832	16%	9%	28%	24%	5%	16%	2%
Chulk V.	TOR	301	13%	9%	32%	23%	6%	15%	3%
Claussen B.	CIN	731	17%	9%	27%	26%	6%	14%	2%
Clemens R.	HOU	838	22%	8%	34%	19%	2%	14%	2%
Clement M.	BOS	830	18%	10%	32%	22%	2%	15%	1%
Colon B.	LAA	906	17%	5%	33%	25%	5%	13%	2%
Contreras J.	CHA	857	18%	10%	32%	22%	3%	14%	1%
Cook A.	COL	357	7%	5%	54%	16%	1%	17%	1%
Cordero C.	WAS	300	20%	6%	26%	29%	6%	11%	1%
Cordero F.	TEX	302	26%	11%	26%	21%	2%	12%	2%
Cormier L.	ARI	356	18%	13%	33%	17%	1%	15%	2%
Crain J.	MIN	326	8%	10%	36%	23%	6%	13%	5%
Davies K.	ATL	403	15%	12%	24%	25%	3%	17%	2%
Davis D.	MIL	946	22%	10%	28%	20%	3%	13%	3%

Player	Team	BFP	K	BB	GB	OF	IF	LD	Oth
Dempster R.	CHN	401	22%	13%	36%	12%	1%	13%	2%
Dominguez J.	TEX	312	14%	9%	35%	20%	6%	14%	2%
Douglass S.	DET	374	15%	9%	33%	25%	3%	14%	1%
Downs S.	TOR	407	18%	10%	38%	15%	2%	16%	1%
Drese R.	TEX	317	6%	9%	48%	18%	2%	16%	1%
Duchscherer	OAK	338	25%	6%	30%	20%	4%	12%	2%
Duke Z.	PIT	341	17%	7%	35%	16%	3%	19%	2%
Eaton A.	SD	568	18%	9%	30%	23%	2%	17%	1%
Elarton S.	CLE	774	13%	7%	26%	31%	5%	17%	1%
Estes S.	ARI	535	12%	9%	39%	19%	1%	17%	3%
Fassero J.	SF	384	16%	8%	38%	17%	3%	16%	2%
Fogg J.	PIT	742	11%	8%	32%	24%	6%	16%	2%
Fossum C.	TB	725	18%	11%	28%	24%	4%	15%	1%
Francis J.	COL	828	15%	9%	29%	23%	5%	16%	2%
Franklin R.	SEA	833	11%	8%	33%	28%	5%	13%	1%
Frasor J.	TOR	305	20%	10%	34%	19%	3%	12%	1%
Fuentes B.	COL	321	28%	14%	21%	17%	2%	15%	2%
Garcia F.	CHA	943	15%	7%	37%	21%	2%	16%	1%
Garland J.	CHA	901	13%	6%	38%	21%	5%	17%	2%
Glavine T.	NYN	901	12%	7%	37%	21%	2%	18%	3%
Gordon T.	NYA	324	21%	9%	37%	22%	2%	8%	1%
Greinke Z.	KC	829	14%	8%	30%	25%	4%	18%	1%
Guerrier M.	MIN	306	15%	9%	35%	21%	4%	14%	3%
Halladay R.	TOR	553	20%	5%	46%	15%	1%	13%	1%
Halsey B.	ARI	700	12%	7%	32%	23%	5%	18%	3%
Harang A.	CIN	887	18%	7%	28%	24%	4%	16%	3%
Harden R.	OAK	514	24%	9%	29%	18%	3%	17%	1%
Haren D.	OAK	897	18%	7%	35%	20%	4%	15%	1%
Harper T.	TB	322	12%	8%	26%	29%	3%	19%	3%
Heilman A.	NYN	439	24%	10%	30%	18%	2%	15%	1%
Hendrickson	TB	796	11%	6%	37%	21%	4%	18%	2%
Hennessey B.	SF	521	12%	11%	36%	20%	3%	15%	2%
Hernandez F.	SEA	328	23%	8%	45%	11%	2%	9%	1%
Hernandez L.	WAS	1065	14%	9%	29%	23%	3%	20%	3%
Hernandez O.	CHA	568	16%	11%	29%	23%	5%	15%	1%
Hernandez R.	KC	706	12%	11%	29%	29%	4%	14%	1%
Houlton D.	LAN	578	16%	10%	24%	26%	4%	16%	3%
Howell J.	KC	328	16%	14%	40%	13%	4%	13%	2%
Hudson L.	CIN	380	14%	16%	26%	22%	6%	14%	2%
Hudson T.	ATL	817	14%	9%	44%	14%	1%	15%	2%
Ishii K.	NYN	399	13%	13%	27%	27%	3%	14%	3%
Jennings J.	COL	551	14%	12%	35%	17%	3%	18%	2%
Johnson J.	DET	888	10%	6%	42%	21%	4%	14%	2%
Johnson R.	NYA	920	23%	6%	31%	24%	3%	12%	1%

Player	Team	BFP	K	BB	GB	OF	IF	LD	Oth
Julio J.	BAL	314	18%	8%	29%	27%	3%	13%	1%
Kazmir S.	TB	818	21%	13%	27%	21%	4%	13%	1%
Kennedy J.	COL	442	12%	11%	36%	22%	1%	17%	2%
Kim B.	COL	668	17%	13%	28%	23%	3%	13%	2%
Lackey J.	LAA	892	22%	9%	30%	19%	3%	15%	1%
Lawrence B.	SD	852	13%	8%	36%	23%	2%	16%	2%
Lee C.	CLE	838	17%	6%	27%	28%	5%	16%	1%
Leiter A.	FLA	376	14%	18%	25%	22%	5%	13%	4%
Lidle C.	PHI	792	15%	6%	38%	17%	2%	19%	3%
Lieber J.	PHI	912	16%	5%	35%	21%	3%	16%	3%
Lilly T.	TOR	566	17%	11%	26%	26%	4%	16%	1%
Lima J.	KC	780	10%	9%	29%	29%	3%	18%	2%
Loaiza E.	WAS	912	19%	7%	31%	22%	3%	16%	3%
Loe K.	TEX	392	11%	8%	48%	13%	5%	13%	2%
Lohse K.	MIN	769	11%	7%	36%	24%	4%	18%	1%
Lopez R.	BAL	918	13%	8%	34%	25%	3%	16%	1%
Lowe D.	LAN	934	16%	6%	48%	14%	2%	12%	2%
Lowry N.	SF	874	20%	9%	28%	21%	5%	14%	2%
Maddux G.	CHN	936	15%	5%	40%	19%	2%	17%	3%
Madson R.	PHI	365	22%	8%	33%	16%	2%	17%	2%
Majewski G.	WAS	376	13%	12%	34%	22%	3%	15%	2%
Maroth M.	DET	889	13%	7%	38%	21%	7%	13%	1%
Marquis J.	STL	868	12%	9%	41%	21%	4%	13%	1%
Martinez P.	NYN	843	25%	6%	26%	26%	4%	12%	2%
Mateo J.	SEA	364	14%	7%	25%	34%	6%	12%	3%
Mays J.	MIN	690	9%	6%	39%	22%	3%	18%	2%
McClung S.	TB	501	18%	14%	25%	24%	5%	14%	0%
Meadows B.	PIT	326	13%	6%	35%	21%	5%	16%	3%
Meche G.	SEA	638	13%	12%	30%	27%	3%	15%	1%
Miller W.	BOS	414	15%	12%	31%	20%	3%	17%	1%
Millwood K.	CLE	799	18%	7%	34%	21%	3%	15%	2%
Milton E.	CIN	855	14%	7%	26%	31%	4%	15%	2%
Moehler B.	FLA	696	14%	7%	33%	20%	3%	19%	4%
Morris M.	STL	818	14%	6%	38%	20%	3%	17%	2%
Moyer J.	SEA	868	12%	7%	30%	28%	5%	18%	1%
Mulder M.	STL	868	13%	9%	46%	15%	1%	14%	2%
Mussina M.	NYA	766	19%	7%	33%	25%	2%	13%	1%
Myers B.	PHI	905	23%	9%	31%	18%	2%	15%	2%
Nomo H.	TB	471	13%	11%	23%	33%	3%	14%	3%
Obermueller	MIL	305	11%	13%	34%	19%	5%	16%	2%
Ohka T.	MIL	543	15%	6%	33%	23%	4%	17%	2%
Ortiz R.	CIN	755	13%	8%	34%	23%	6%	13%	2%
Ortiz R.	ARI	551	8%	13%	29%	23%	5%	20%	2%
Oswalt R.	HOU	1002	18%	6%	36%	20%	2%	16%	2%
Padilla V.	PHI	654	16%	13%	32%	20%	3%	15%	2%
Park C.	TEX	502	16%	12%	35%	19%	2%	14%	2%
Patterson J.	WAS	817	23%	9%	20%	27%	4%	16%	2%

Player	Team	BFP	K	BB	GB	OF	IF	LD	Oth
Pavano C.	NYA	442	13%	6%	40%	22%	3%	15%	1%
Peavy J.	SD	812	27%	7%	29%	20%	3%	13%	1%
Penny B.	LAN	738	17%	6%	35%	22%	4%	15%	2%
Perez O.	PIT	471	21%	16%	21%	25%	5%	11%	2%
Perez O.	LAN	453	16%	6%	33%	25%	2%	15%	4%
Pettitte A.	HOU	875	20%	5%	37%	18%	2%	17%	2%
Pineiro J.	SEA	822	13%	8%	36%	24%	2%	17%	1%
Ponson S.	BAL	595	11%	9%	42%	21%	1%	16%	1%
Prior M.	CHN	701	27%	9%	23%	23%	3%	13%	2%
Qualls C.	HOU	329	18%	9%	42%	12%	2%	15%	2%
Radke B.	MIN	831	14%	4%	34%	27%	5%	16%	1%
Ramirez H.	ATL	847	9%	8%	38%	20%	3%	18%	3%
Redman M.	PIT	751	13%	8%	37%	21%	2%	16%	3%
Reitsma C.	ATL	307	14%	5%	43%	18%	3%	17%	1%
Rincon J.	MIN	319	26%	10%	29%	17%	3%	13%	2%
Rivera M.	NYA	306	26%	7%	38%	17%	2%	9%	1%
Robertson N.	DET	846	14%	9%	37%	21%	2%	15%	1%
Rodriguez W.	HOU	560	14%	11%	34%	20%	3%	17%	1%
Rogers K.	TEX	828	11%	7%	38%	23%	3%	16%	1%
Rueter K.	SF	489	5%	10%	36%	25%	4%	17%	3%
Rusch G.	CHN	655	17%	8%	27%	22%	3%	20%	3%
Saarloos K.	OAK	682	8%	10%	46%	17%	2%	17%	1%
Sabathia C.	CLE	823	20%	8%	35%	19%	3%	14%	1%
Sanchez D.	LAN	353	20%	11%	29%	19%	4%	14%	3%
Santana E.	LAA	583	17%	9%	27%	28%	5%	14%	1%
Santana J.	MIN	910	26%	5%	27%	23%	5%	11%	2%
Santos V.	MIL	639	14%	10%	31%	25%	2%	17%	1%
Schilling C.	BOS	418	21%	6%	24%	27%	5%	17%	1%
Schmidt J.	SF	757	22%	12%	25%	21%	5%	14%	2%
Sele A.	SEA	523	10%	9%	32%	29%	2%	16%	2%
Seo J.	NYN	363	16%	5%	28%	25%	4%	17%	4%
Sheets B.	MIL	633	22%	4%	26%	27%	3%	15%	2%
Shields S.	LAA	375	26%	10%	34%	16%	1%	11%	2%
Silva C.	MIN	749	9%	2%	43%	26%	2%	17%	1%
Sisco A.	KC	329	23%	13%	26%	20%	4%	13%	1%
Small A.	NYA	316	12%	9%	34%	23%	5%	15%	1%
Smoltz J.	ATL	931	18%	6%	35%	20%	2%	16%	2%
Sosa J.	ATL	577	15%	11%	25%	27%	3%	17%	2%
Stauffer T.	SD	355	14%	9%	32%	22%	5%	17%	1%
Street H.	OAK	306	24%	9%	30%	22%	4%	11%	1%
Sturtze T.	NYA	332	14%	10%	35%	25%	4%	11%	2%
Suppan J.	STL	834	14%	8%	35%	21%	3%	16%	3%
Tejeda R.	PHI	371	19%	16%	23%	24%	4%	13%	1%
Thomson J.	ATL	427	14%	7%	35%	20%	2%	19%	2%
Timlin M.	BOS	342	17%	6%	34%	19%	3%	20%	1%
Tomko B.	SF	823	14%	8%	31%	26%	3%	17%	1%
Torres S.	PIT	388	14%	11%	37%	21%	4%	12%	1%

Player	Team	BFP	K	BB	GB	OF	IF	LD	Oth
Towers J.	TOR	876	13%	4%	36%	26%	4%	15%	2%
Vargas C.	ARI	520	17%	9%	26%	25%	4%	17%	2%
Vargas J.	FLA	325	18%	11%	22%	26%	7%	15%	2%
Vazquez J.	ARI	904	21%	6%	31%	20%	4%	16%	3%
Vizcaino L.	CHA	305	14%	10%	31%	21%	5%	15%	3%
Vogelsong R.	PIT	369	14%	13%	31%	22%	2%	15%	2%
Waechter D.	TB	692	13%	6%	31%	30%	3%	17%	1%
Wakefield T.	BOS	943	16%	8%	31%	26%	5%	13%	1%
Walker P.	TOR	358	12%	10%	37%	25%	3%	13%	0%
Wang C.	NYA	486	10%	8%	51%	16%	2%	12%	2%
Wasdin J.	TEX	319	14%	7%	29%	26%	7%	18%	1%
Washburn J.	LAA	740	13%	8%	30%	27%	3%	16%	2%
Weathers D.	CIN	331	18%	9%	35%	19%	1%	15%	2%
Weaver J.	LAN	930	17%	7%	31%	25%	4%	15%	2%
Webb B.	ARI	943	18%	6%	47%	11%	1%	14%	2%
Wells D.	BOS	780	14%	4%	39%	22%	2%	18%	1%
Wells K.	PIT	828	16%	13%	32%	20%	3%	14%	2%

Player	Team	BFP	K	BB	GB	OF	IF	LD	Oth
Westbrook J.	CLE	895	13%	7%	50%	12%	3%	14%	1%
White R.	PIT	338	12%	10%	41%	14%	3%	17%	4%
Williams D.	PIT	600	15%	11%	28%	27%	3%	14%	3%
Williams J.	CHN	459	13%	12%	33%	23%	3%	13%	3%
Williams T.	BAL	321	12%	9%	51%	12%	2%	12%	1%
Williams W.	SD	697	15%	8%	27%	28%	4%	16%	2%
Willis D.	FLA	960	18%	7%	33%	20%	3%	18%	2%
Wolf R.	PHI	346	18%	9%	25%	25%	5%	16%	3%
Wood M.	KC	520	12%	12%	40%	21%	2%	13%	2%
Wright J.	COL	782	13%	12%	38%	18%	1%	15%	2%
Wright J.	NYA	302	11%	13%	34%	21%	3%	18%	1%
Wuertz M.	CHN	319	28%	13%	25%	21%	2%	10%	2%
Young C.	TEX	700	20%	7%	23%	31%	4%	13%	1%
Zambrano C.	CHN	909	22%	10%	33%	17%	2%	13%	2%
Zambrano V.	NYN	748	15%	12%	36%	20%	1%	15%	2%
Zito B.	OAK	953	18%	11%	29%	21%	5%	14%	2%

Who's Who

Thomas Ayers is a university student and Blue Jays fan living in Etobicoke, Ontario. His writing can be found at www.battersbox.ca.

Alex Belth writes about the Yankees at BronxBanter.BaseballToaster.com. His first book, *Stepping Up: The Story of All-Star Curt Flood and His Fight for Baseball Players' Rights*, will be published in the spring of 2006. Alex lives and works in New York City.

Carolina Bolado is a Miami native (Go Marlins!) who graduated from the University of Chicago (Go White Sox!) and now lives in New Jersey, where she is a food writer by day and THT copy editor by night. When not watching baseball, she spends her time swimming, cooking, reading Jane Austen and watching an unhealthy amount of *Law & Order*.

A graduate of Michigan State University, **Brian Borawski** is a CPA and works for a Detroit-area real estate developer. A lifelong Tigers fan, Brian writes about his favorite team at www.tigerblog.net. In 2004, Brian became a member of SABR, and is currently on the Business of Baseball committee.

J.C. Bradbury teaches economics at The University of the South in Sewanee, Tennessee. He is an avid Braves fan and runs Sabernomics.com. His book on economics in baseball is forthcoming from Dutton in early 2007.

John Brattain is Canadian who has been featured across the web ranting about assorted baseball esoterica. Special thanks to Gian Trotta, Steve Hoffstetter, Brian Dunn, Lee Sinins, Neil deMause, the deviants at Baseball Think Factory, Dale Sprenkle and the assorted folks at the DTFC, his brother Robert and father Bob, and of course his wonderful wife Kelly and daughters Belinda and Kataryna who have to put up with his mutterings as he pounds away on his keyboard like a hyperactive chimpanzee.

Maury Brown is the co-chair of SABR's Business of Baseball committee and is the publisher of BusinessOfBaseball.com. He lives in Portland, Oregon with his wife Glenna, and two sons, Tyler and Travis, where they support his need to obsess on baseball daily.

Craig Burley works as an attorney in Toronto and lives in Hamilton, Ontario. Craig is a longtime Blue Jays and Expos fan, considers the Expos' loss on "Blue Monday" to be one of the most important events in his life, and is a SABR member.

David Cameron resides in Winston-Salem, North Carolina, where he spends too much time at the local minor league ballparks. He is a member of the team of writers for USSMariner.com and his other passion, photography, can be found at DaveCameron.net.

John Dewan has consistently broken new ground in the area of sports statistical analysis, first as one of the founders and former CEO of STATS, Inc. and now as the owner of Baseball Info Solutions. He is also currently the co-publisher of ACTA Publications. As a noted sports expert, he is heard weekly on WSCR, "The Score," an all-sports radio station in Chicago, where he lives with his wife and two children.

Joe Dimino is a network security analyst and runs the Hall of Merit at Baseball Think Factory in his spare time. The greatest moment of his life was when the Yankees won the 1996 World Series.

Bryan Donovan is a lifelong A's fan and baseball stats buff currently residing in Portland, Oregon. He works as a quality engineer at Sun Microsystems, Inc., where he develops web applications that report and analyze manufacturing quality data.

Dan Fox is a software developer for Compassion International by day and spends too much time sifting through baseball statistics by night. He is a lifelong Cubs fan, a SABR member, and has been writing about baseball on his blog, DanAgonistes.blogspot.com, since 2003. He lives in Colorado Springs with his lovely wife Beth, and daughters Laura and Anna.

David Gassko is a hapless Red Sox fan living in the Boston area. He has yet to realize that the Red Sox won the World Series, and is currently bemoaning the loss of Theo Epstein.

Aaron Gleeman is a freelance writer living in Minnesota. The founder and Editor-in-Chief of THT, he also writes for FoxSports.com, RotoWorld.com, InsiderBaseball.com, and his blog, AaronGleeman.com. Aaron would specifically like to thank his mom, Judi, and his dog, Samantha. And Luis Rivas.

Brian Gunn is a writer living in Los Angeles. A Cardinals fan since the days of Kenny Reitz, he is the man behind the dearly departed blog, *Redbird Nation*.

Ben Jacobs is a die-hard Red Sox fan and a sports reporter at the *Ithaca Journal*. He's found it much easier to live in Yankee country now that Boston is a more recent World Series winner than New York.

Bill James lives in Lawrence, Kansas with his lovely wife, two sons, and a daughter who is off at college. He's been doing this kind of stuff for a long time.

A lifelong Mets fan and SABR member since 2002, **John Murphy** was born in Brooklyn, New York and lived on Long Island for 25 years, but has been a resident of Raleigh, North Carolina for the last 13. When he's not busy with baseball, he helps operate both a commercial janitorial enterprise and a retail internet business.

Rob Neyer has been writing about baseball for ESPN.com since 1996. The author or co-author of many books, his *Big Book of Baseball Blunders* will be published in 2006.

Dave Studenmund lives in the greater Chicago area with his wife, who is wonderful, and three kids, who are teenagers. He's also the manager of the Baseball Graphs website (www.baseballgraphs.com), the neglected stepchild of the family.

Greg Tamer lives in the Midwest with his wife, Angela, and son, Charlie. He is a lifelong Reds fan, spends too much time playing Diamond Mind and rotisserie baseball, and somehow continues his postdoctoral research work in the field of functional imaging.

Steve Treder has presented papers to the Cooperstown Symposium on Baseball and American Culture, and had numerous articles published in *Nine: A Journal of Baseball History and Culture*. A lifelong San Francisco Giants fan, he is Vice President for Strategic Development for Western Management Group, a compensation consulting firm headquartered in Los Gatos, California.

Bryan Tsao is a third year Cognitive Science student at the University of California, San Diego. In between editing articles for THT and rooting for the Oakland A's, he works as an undergraduate researcher in the Interactive Cognition Lab and the Distributed Cognition Labs at UCSD. His writing has also been published in the *UCSD Guardian* and the *Taiwan News*.

Often proclaiming himself "the Derrel Thomas of the writing world," **Jon Weisman** has worked the trade for the *Los Angeles Times, Los Angeles Daily News*, and *Variety*, and had television scripts produced by Columbia and Disney. He is currently Senior Writer/Editor at the Los Angeles County Museum of Art and writes about the Dodgers at DodgerThoughts.com.

Matt Welch is Associate Editor for *Reason* magazine, for whom he writes a monthly column about the media. His work has appeared in the *Los Angeles Times*, ESPN. com, the *National Post*, Salon.com, *Orange County Register, Wired News*, and elsewhere. He maintains a blog at MattWelch.com.

Other New Products from ACTA Sports

(www.actasports.com)

THE BALLGAME OF LIFE
Lessons for Parents and Coaches of Young Baseball Players
DAVID ALLEN SMITH and JOSEPH AVERSA

Good coaches and good parents both try to teach kids the same things: persistence, hard work, how to handle pressure, and how to be a good winner. Baseball can help young players learn these lessons, but only if the coaches and parents stay focused on them.

112 pages, paperback, $9.95

THE LIFE OF LOU GEHRIG
Told by a Fan
SARA KADEN BRUNSVOLD

A new biography of the great Yankees' first baseman that covers his life from start to finish, while always being careful to highlight the human stories from his life that fill in the gaps between the facts, such as his cures for hitting slumps, his favorite foods, and even his attempt at comedy.

288 pages, paperback, $14.95

STRAT-O-MATIC FANATICS
The Unlikely Success Story of a Game That Became an American Passion
GLENN GUZZO

This is the true story behind the creation—and re-creation—of America's most popular sports board game ever: Strat-O-Matic. *Strat-O-Matic Fanatics* looks at the hobby from every angle: the personal demons that Hal Richman overcame to bring his dream to life, the crises that nearly engulfed the small company, and fascinating anecdotes from real players of the game.

320 pages, paperback, $14.95

DIAMOND PRESENCE
Twelve Stories of Finding God at the Old Ball Park
Edited by GREGORY F. AUGUSTINE PIERCE
Foreword by JOHN DEWAN

There are two things that one can never say often enough: one, that the game exists only to be enjoyed; and two, that there is no limit to the number of ways that it can be enjoyed. Diamond Presence shines a light upon these two truths.
– Bill James, author of the ***The Bill James Handbook***

A touching collection of twelve true, short stories in which the authors relate how they came to feel the presence of God while enjoying the great American pastime of baseball as players, coaches, parents, children or just plain fans.

176 pages, hardcover, $17.95